ADVANCED
OS/2
PROGRAMMING

ADVANCED OS/2 PROGRAMMING

RAY DUNCAN

The Microsoft® Guide to the OS/2 Kernel
for Assembly Language and C Programmers.

PUBLISHED BY

Microsoft Press
A Division of Microsoft Corporation
16011 NE 36th Way, Box 97017, Redmond, Washington 98073-9717

Library of Congress Cataloging in Publication Data

Duncan, Ray, 1952-
Advanced OS/2 programming: the Microsoft guide to the OS/2 kernel for
assembly language and C programmers / Ray Duncan
                    p.   cm.
Includes index.
1. OS/2 (Computer operating system)   2. Assembler language
(Computer program language)   I. Title.
QA76.76.063D8585   1989   88-21103
005.4'469—dc19   CIP
ISBN 1-55615-045-8
Printed and bound in the United States of America.

1 2 3 4 5 6 7 8 9   FGFG   3 2 1 0 9 8

Distributed to the book trade in the United States
by Harper & Row.

Distributed to the book trade in Canada by General
Publishing Company, Ltd.

Distributed to the book trade outside the United States
and Canada by Penguin Books Ltd.

Penguin Books Ltd., Harmondworth, Middlesex, England
Penguin Books Australia Ltd., Ringwood, Victoria, Australia
Penguin Books N.Z. Ltd., 182-190 Wairu Road, Auckland 10, New Zealand

British Cataloging in Publication Data available

Acquisitions Editor: Claudette Moore   **Project Editor:** Eric Stroo   **Technical Editor:** Mike Halvorson

For Kathleen

Contents

Road Map to Important Figures and Tables

Acknowledgments

In a book project of this size and duration, the list of people involved at every level — technical review, editing, design, word processing, typography, proofreading, and marketing — grows extremely long. Although I cannot thank each of these people individually, I hope they know how much I appreciate their fine and patient work. Special thanks to Pat Combs, Mike Halvorson, Claudette Moore, and Eric Stroo for their editorial contributions, and to David Maritz, Anthony Short, Ben Slivka, and Mark Zbikowski for technical assistance beyond the call of duty.

INTRODUCTION

Operating System/2, Microsoft's protected mode operating system for 80286-based and 80386-based microcomputers, provides programmers with a powerful new platform for application design. It also challenges them to assimilate a body of technical information whose size is unprecedented in the microcomputer world. The reference manuals for OS/2 and its extensions (such as the Presentation Manager and LAN Manager) already fill several shelves—only a year after the system was first released—and the Microsoft or IBM Programmer's Toolkit, along with the necessary development tools and libraries, can devour a sizable fixed disk.

No single book can cover everything you need to know about OS/2 programming; there are no shortcuts to mastery of such a complex system, and there are few simple answers. This particular book, *Advanced OS/2 Programming,* focuses solely on the OS/2 kernel and its facilities for character-oriented input and output, file access, virtual memory management, multitasking, interprocess communication, dynamic linking, and the like. Graphically oriented Presentation Manager applications and the Presentation Manager itself are mentioned only in passing; for further information on these topics, see Charles Petzold's excellent book, *Programming the OS/2 Presentation Manager* (also from Microsoft Press).

Advanced OS/2 Programming is essentially divided into six sections, which reflects my prejudices about how the operating system should be studied.

Section One is descriptive: It begins with an introduction to the important features of OS/2, followed by an explanation of OS/2's components and initialization, a discussion of the structure of OS/2 application programs, and an operational summary of the Microsoft programming tools.

Sections Two and Three address the fundamental concerns of every application programmer: management of the keyboard, display, pointing device, and mass storage. A chapter on the internal structure of FAT (MS-DOS–compatible) file systems is also included, although this material will become less important in subsequent versions of OS/2, for which support of installable file systems is planned.

Section Four is devoted to virtual memory management, multitasking, interprocess communication, direct hardware control, and programmable timers. For most programmers with an MS-DOS background, this section will be both the most interesting and the most relevant to exploiting fully the capabilities of OS/2.

Finally, Section Five contains information on four special classes of OS/2 programs: filters, device monitors, device drivers, and dynlink libraries. Although you will probably never need to write one of these types of programs, you might still find it useful to browse these chapters for a general sense of how such programs work and are put together.

The remainder of the book — Section Six and the Appendixes — is intended to fill all the reference needs of the typical kernel application programmer. All the OS/2 kernel services made available to application programs, the I/O control subfunctions, and the Device Driver Helper (DevHlp) functions are described with their arguments and results and with cross-references to related functions. The OS/2 error codes, executable file format, and module definition (DEF) file syntax are also covered in detail.

Each major OS/2 programming issue and concept is illustrated with complete sample programs in both C and assembly language. For linking the sample programs, OS2.LIB and DOSCALLS.LIB are interchangeable. The programs were written with Solution System's BRIEF editor and assembled or compiled with Microsoft MASM version 5.1 and Microsoft C version 5.1. They have been tested under OS/2 versions 1.0 and 1.1 on a Compaq Portable 286, a Compaq DeskPro 386, and an IBM PS/2 Model 80. As far as I know, they contain no software or hardware dependencies that prevent their running properly on any IBM PC/AT–compatible or PS/2–compatible machine running OS/2 version 1.0 or 1.1.

To make the sample programs useful to programmers using other languages or non-Microsoft programming tools, I have endeavored to make them as self-contained and "generic" as possible. The source listings do not rely on any header files found in the Microsoft or IBM Programmer's Toolkit, the special reentrant runtime libraries supplied with Microsoft C version 5.1, or the new constructs and directives that were added to Microsoft MASM in version 5.0. For the same reasons, the reference sections shun the macros, arbitrary namings, manifest constants, and customized data types (*typedefs*) which pervade the *Microsoft OS/2 Programmer's Reference*.

Please feel free to contact me with your questions, comments, and suggestions for future editions via MCI Mail (user name LMI), CompuServe (user ID 72406,1577), or BIX (user name rduncan).

Ray Duncan
Los Angeles, California
December 1988

THE OS/2 OPERATING SYSTEM

INTRODUCTION TO OS/2

OS/2 is the Microsoft multitasking, virtual memory, single-user operating system for personal computers based on the Intel 80286 and 80386 microprocessors. It is the first software product to be brought to market as a result of the Joint Development Agreement signed by IBM and Microsoft in August 1985.

OS/2 is positioned between the MS-DOS single-tasking operating system and the XENIX/UNIX multi-user multitasking operating system (Figure 1-1 on the following page). Although it is compatible with MS-DOS file systems and can run many existing MS-DOS applications, and although it has a hierarchical directory structure, I/O redirection, and some interprocess communication mechanisms similar to XENIX/UNIX, OS/2 is neither an overblown MS-DOS nor a stripped-down XENIX/UNIX. It is a completely new operating system, designed to support high performance, intensely interactive applications in a business environment.

During the next few years, the increasing dominance of 80286- and 80386-based machines, and the accompanying penetration of OS/2, will have a vast influence on the work habits and productivity of computer users. It will also force many changes on programmers and software publishers. Although porting existing MS-DOS products to OS/2 is a straightforward process, taking full advantage of OS/2's capabilities will involve a wholesale rethinking and redesign of most applications. In return, OS/2 offers programmers a ''clean slate'' and the opportunity to set new standards.

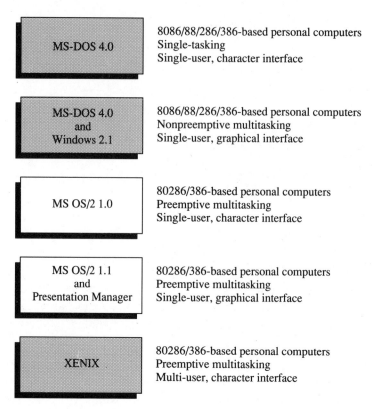

MS-DOS 4.0	8086/88/286/386-based personal computers Single-tasking Single-user, character interface
MS-DOS 4.0 and Windows 2.1	8086/88/286/386-based personal computers Nonpreemptive multitasking Single-user, graphical interface
MS OS/2 1.0	80286/386-based personal computers Preemptive multitasking Single-user, character interface
MS OS/2 1.1 and Presentation Manager	80286/386-based personal computers Preemptive multitasking Single-user, graphical interface
XENIX	80286/386-based personal computers Preemptive multitasking Multi-user, character interface

Figure 1-1. *The Microsoft family of operating systems for personal computers based on the Intel 80x86 line of microprocessors.*

Key Features of OS/2

From the programmer's point of view, the key features of software development under OS/2 are the following:

- A graphical user interface
- A new Application Program Interface (API)
- Memory protection and virtual memory
- Preemptive multitasking
- Interprocess communication facilities
- Dynamic linking
- MS-DOS compatibility

These features have many important implications for the structure of the operating system itself, and for the design and operation of application programs.

Graphical User Interface

The OS/2 graphical user interface is called the Presentation Manager. With Presentation Manager facilities, the user can view multiple applications at the same time in windows (subdivisions of the screen), whose size, shape, and position the user can control. The Presentation Manager offers the programmer a wide variety of vector and raster graphics operations and extensive font support, including multiple font styles and sizes; it allows the development of hardware-independent applications that can run on a broad range of all-points-addressable (APA) output devices.

Application programs written to run under the Presentation Manager have a common appearance and style of interaction, using pull-down menus, scroll bars, and dialog boxes. The user can select from menus with either a mouse or the keyboard, and can cut and paste data and graphic images from the domain of one program into another in a ''natural'' manner. These features help users work more efficiently, and they shorten the learning curve for new application programs.

The Application Program Interface

The OS/2 kernel—the part of the operating system that manages files, memory, multitasking, timers, and interprocess communications—provides about 250 services to application programs. The Presentation Manager supports an additional 500-odd functions related to window management and the graphical user interface. These services, known collectively as the Application Program Interface (API), are invoked by far calls to individual named entry points. Parameters for API functions are passed on the stack, and values are returned in variables (commonly structures) in the caller's memory space. Addresses are always passed or returned in the form of *far pointers* (selector and offset).

Although the OS/2 API is a considerable architectural change from the familiar INT 21H of MS-DOS, its advantages are significant. The API allows OS/2 to take full advantage of the 80286's hardware mechanisms for parameter passing and to enforce the separation between kernel and user privilege levels. It is compatible with the procedure-calling conventions of most high level languages, allowing programs written in high level languages to access operating system services directly without the need for intermediary library functions. And the API can easily be extended for future 32-bit versions of the operating system that will take greater advantage of the 80386 and its successors.

Memory Protection and Virtual Memory

The CPUs in the Intel 80x86 family generate memory addresses by combining the contents of *segment registers* (which can be thought of as base pointers) with an offset, or displacement. The offset can be specified in the machine instruction or in one or more index registers (or in both places). The way that the hardware interprets a value in a segment register depends on whether the processor is running in *real mode* or *protected mode*.

In real mode, the value in a segment register is a *paragraph* address: a 20-bit physical address divided by 16. To form a complete memory address, the processor shifts the contents of a segment register to the left four bits and adds a 16-bit offset. In real mode, the hardware provides no memory protection mechanisms; any program can read or write any memory address or access any I/O port. MS-DOS and its applications execute in real mode, regardless of the type of processor.

In protected mode, a level of addressing indirection is added. Segment registers do not point directly to the base of an area of memory; instead, they contain values called *selectors*. A selector is an index to an entry in a *descriptor table;* the entry contains the base address and length of a memory segment, its attributes (executable, read-only, or read-write), and privilege information. Each time a program references memory, the hardware uses information from the descriptor table to generate the physical address and simultaneously validates the memory access. OS/2 executes on the 80286 or 80386 in protected mode; the 8086 and 8088 processors do not support protected mode, which is the reason they cannot run OS/2.

Because only the operating system can manipulate descriptor tables, which govern the addressable memory space of all programs, a protected mode operating system can completely isolate programs from one another. If a program attempts to read or write memory that does not belong to it, or if it calls a routine to which it has not been given access, a CPU fault occurs and the operating system regains control. The presence of this memory protection makes for a very robust programming and debugging environment: An aberrant program rarely brings down the entire system.

Protected mode also provides privilege levels that can be used to constrain application programs. The four hardware-enforced privilege levels are referred to as ring 0, ring 1, ring 2, and ring 3. Applications ordinarily execute at ring 3 (the lowest privilege level); if a ring 3 program attempts to clear interrupts, read or write I/O ports, or modify CPU registers that would compromise memory protection, a CPU fault is generated and the program is terminated. The operating system kernel executes at ring 0, which provides unrestricted access to all instructions, memory addresses, and I/O ports. OS/2 does not use ring 1 at all. A limited class of applications that require direct access to adapters (such as non–Presentation Manager graphics applications) are allowed to run at ring 2 and perform I/O operations.

The flip side of the memory protection coin is virtual memory. OS/2 can manage as much as 16 MB of physical memory, but the amount of installed RAM is nearly irrelevant to the average application program running in protected mode. When the sum of the memory owned by active programs in the system exceeds the actual amount of physical memory, memory segments are rolled in and out as needed from a swap file (or simply discarded and reloaded in the case of code segments or read-only data segments). This segment swapping is accomplished by an OS/2 module known as the Memory Manager, with the aid of the processor's hardware memory protection mechanisms, and is completely invisible to application programs. The theoretical limit on the amount of memory a program can own or share is about 128 MB (in OS/2 version 1.1), but the practical limit is the amount of physical RAM plus the free space on the logical drive that contains the swap file.

Preemptive Multitasking

Preemptive multitasking (sometimes called *time-slicing*) refers to OS/2's ability to allocate processor time among multiple programs in a manner that is invisible to those programs. A hardware interrupt called the *timer tick,* generated by a programmable timer chip, allows the operating system to regain control at predetermined intervals. After updating the current date and time, the timer tick interrupt handler transfers control to the *scheduler,* which maintains a list of the active tasks and their states and decides which piece of code will run next.

For the user, the interface to OS/2's multitasking capabilities is simple and easy to understand. A user starts a program by picking its name from a menu or by entering the name at a command prompt. OS/2 programs that are compatible with the Presentation Manager can run within windows, whereas those that are not compatible occupy the full screen. In either case, when more than one program is running, the user can press hot keys or choose from a menu to select a program with which to interact.

The programmer can control OS/2 multitasking at three levels of system activity: *processes, threads,* and *sessions.* The simplest case of a process is similar to a program loaded under MS-DOS: A process is initiated when the operating system allocates some memory, loads the necessary code and data from a disk file, and gives it control at an entry point that is specified in the file. Subsequently, the process can obtain and release additional resources, such as memory segments, disk files, interprocess communication facilities, and timers.

When a process starts, it contains a single point of execution: its primary *thread*. That thread can in turn create other threads, all of which share equal access to the memory, files, and other resources owned by the process. The OS/2 scheduler deals with threads rather than with processes; for each active thread, it keeps track of the state (executing, ready to execute, or waiting for some event), priority, register contents and flags, and instruction pointer. The ability to decompose an application into multiple asynchronous threads, which can communicate rapidly through a common data space, is an extremely powerful feature of OS/2.

Each process is a member of a session (sometimes called a *screen group*), which is associated with a virtual console: a virtual screen, keyboard, and mouse. When the user chooses a session, the virtual devices are bound to the physical devices, and the user can interact with the programs in that session. OS/2 can support as many as 12 protected mode sessions and 1 real mode user session, and each session can contain one or more processes. (The Presentation Manager and all its applications, for example, run in a single session.)

Interprocess Communication

OS/2 supports all the methods of interprocess communication (IPC) that are found in other multitasking operating systems:

Semaphores are simple IPC objects that have only two states: set (or owned) and cleared (or not owned). They are used between threads or processes for signaling and for synchronization of access to any type of resource. OS/2 supports several different types of semaphores to meet a variety of speed and security needs.

Pipes, as in XENIX/UNIX, allow high performance transfer of variable length messages. A process can read and write them much as it does files, except that the data is always kept resident in memory. Unnamed (anonymous) pipes are used by closely related processes running on the same machine, whereas named pipes allow communication between unrelated processes running on the same or different machines.

Shared memory segments can be accessed by any process that can reference the segment by name. IPC by shared memory is potentially the fastest available mechanism, because its speed is limited only by the rate at which bytes can be copied from one place to another.

Queues are named, global objects and can be thought of as structured lists of shared memory segments. Queue records can be ordered by first-in-first-out (FIFO), last-in-first-out (LIFO), or by an assigned priority, and a queue's size is limited only by the number of available selectors and the disk swap space.

Signals are similar to their implementation in XENIX/UNIX; they simulate an interrupt for the receiving process in that they divert its execution immediately to a signal handler. The system provides a default handler for each signal type; the process can register its own handler for a particular type, or it can notify the system to ignore the signal.

Dynamic Linking

The 80286 and 80386 support for protected, virtual memory makes it possible to place frequently used procedures into special files known as dynamic link (dynlink) libraries. Dynlink libraries are, in essence, shareable subroutine libraries which are loaded on demand. Placing common procedures in dynlink libraries allows those routines to be altered, improved, or replaced without changing the application programs which invoke them. Their use also conserves both RAM and disk storage, because the size of each individual EXE file is reduced, and because the same copy of a dynlink library procedure in memory is shared by all the processes which use it. The dynlink library concept is so powerful and so widely useful that most OS/2 kernel and Presentation Manager functions available to application programs are distributed in this form.

Calls from a program to routines in a dynamic link library are resolved in two stages. The Linker is informed that a particular external name is a dynlink routine either by an IMPORTS statement in the program's module definition file or by the occurrence of a special dynlink reference record in an object module library. It then builds the information necessary for dynamic linking into the program's EXE file header: the names of the dynlink routines that are needed, the names of the dynlink library files in which those routines are found, and a list for each routine of all the addresses within the program at which it is called. When the application is loaded for execution, OS/2 examines the list of imported routines, fetches from disk any external routines that are not already resident in memory, and fixes up the addresses within the calling program. This technique is sometimes called *late binding*.

MS-DOS Compatibility

OS/2 provides upward compatibility and a smooth transition from MS-DOS at three levels: the user interface, the file system, and the DOS compatibility mode (sometimes called the *3.x Box*).

The command line interface of OS/2 is virtually identical to that of MS-DOS versions 2.x and 3.x, with the exception of a few new or enhanced commands, batch file directives, and CONFIG.SYS file options. Similarly, the "desktop" of the OS/2 Presentation Manager, with its overlapping windows, pull-down menus, and dialog boxes, closely resembles the visual shell of MS-DOS version 4.

The file structure for both flexible and fixed disks — that is, the layout of the partition table, directories, file allocation tables, and the files area — is exactly the same for the initial release of OS/2 as it is for MS-DOS. Developers can therefore exchange files and move back and forth between the two environments with a minimum of difficulty. A future release of OS/2 will support *installable file systems,* which will relieve users of the historical MS-DOS limitations on volume sizes and filename lengths.

DOS compatibility mode is a component of the OS/2 operating system that allows a single "old," real mode (MS-DOS) application to run alongside "new," protected mode applications. OS/2 traps MS-DOS function calls by the real mode application and translates them into API calls, switching back and forth between real mode and protected mode as necessary to perform I/O and other services. DOS compatibility mode also provides a realistic-looking milieu for more hardware-dependent MS-DOS programs by supporting certain "undocumented" MS-DOS services and internal flags, by supplying a "clock tick" interrupt at the appropriate frequency, by maintaining a ROM BIOS data area at segment 40H, and so forth.

The user can determine how much memory the system allocates to DOS compatibility mode by adding a directive in the CONFIG.SYS file, or the user can disable the mode completely. One disadvantage of supporting compatibility mode is that the entire system is left vulnerable. "Ill-behaved" MS-DOS programs can crash the system, an unfortunate trade-off for allowing the real mode programs to be used at all.

OS/2 STRUCTURE AND INITIALIZATION

The software that runs on present-day computer systems is, by convention, organized into layers with varying degrees of independence from the characteristics of the underlying hardware. The objectives of this layering are to minimize the impact on programs of differences among hardware devices or changes in the hardware, to centralize and optimize the code for common operations, and to simplify the task of moving programs and their data from one machine to another.

To give you a feel for the territory, let's divide the software in a system into three layers, as shown in Figure 2-1 on the following page. In this simplified view of a system, the top layer is the least hardware-dependent. It is composed of application programs, which perform a specific job, interact with the user, and manipulate data in units of files and records. Such programs are sometimes called *transient* because they are brought into RAM (random access memory) for execution when they are needed and then discarded from memory when their job is finished.

The middle layer is the operating system kernel, which allocates system resources such as memory and peripheral devices, implements the file system, and provides a host of hardware-independent services to application programs. The kernel is usually brought into memory from disk when you turn on or restart the system, and it remains fixed in memory until the system is turned off.

The lowest software layer is made up of specialized programs called device drivers. Device drivers are responsible for transferring data between a peripheral device (such as a disk or terminal) and RAM, where it can be used by other programs. Drivers shield the operating system kernel from the

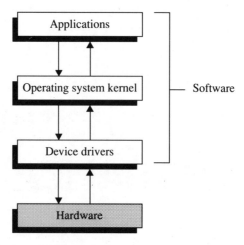

Figure 2-1. *A simplistic view of OS/2 system layers.*

need to deal with the I/O port addresses of the hardware, its operating characteristics, and the peculiarities of a particular peripheral device, just as the kernel in turn shields application programs from the details of memory and file management.

With these basic concepts in hand, let's take a look at the actual organization of OS/2 (still recognizing, however, that the real operating system is more complicated than either model).

The Structure of OS/2

The major elements of the OS/2 operating system are the following:

- Device drivers
- Kernel
- Dynlink libraries
- Command processor
- Presentation Manager

The operating system components interact in complicated ways, and a particular system capability is not always located where you might expect. Some OS/2 components execute at the kernel level (ring 0), some in user mode with I/O privilege (ring 2), and some at the lowest privilege level (ring 3), yet this distinction is generally invisible to application programs (Figure 2-2).

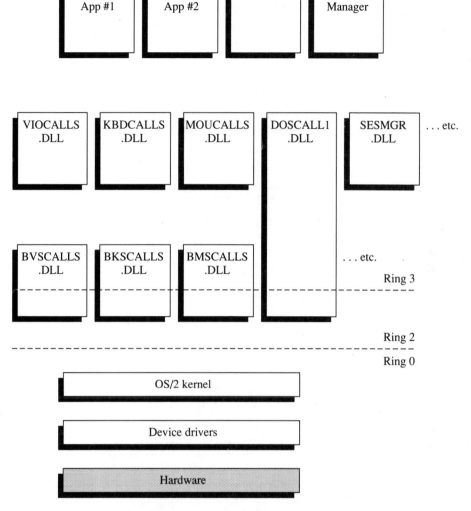

Figure 2-2. *A less simplistic view of OS/2 system layers. The OS/2 kernel and device drivers run at ring 0 and have unrestricted access to all I/O ports and memory addresses. Application programs and dynlink libraries normally run in ring 3 and cannot access the hardware; ring 3 programs are fully protected from each other. Some application programs and dynlink libraries contain I/O privilege segments and are allowed to perform I/O operations in ring 2; however, servicing of interrupts is reserved for ring 0 routines. Presentation Manager applications and dynlink libraries are not shown here.*

Device Drivers

The basic OS/2 system includes a large number of device drivers, which are supplied in individual files with the SYS extension (Figure 2-3). A "base set" of device drivers for the keyboard, display, floppy disk, fixed disk, printer, and real time clock is always loaded during system initialization. These drivers are selected automatically from the drivers on the boot disk based on the system type (PC/AT or PS/2). The other standard OS/2 drivers, such as ANSI.SYS, MOUSEA01.SYS, POINTDD.SYS, COM01.SYS, and EGA.SYS, are loaded only if the appropriate DEVICE directive is present in the CONFIG.SYS file. Drivers supplied by third party manufacturers can also be loaded during initialization with DEVICE directives.

Driver	Description
ANSI.SYS	ANSI console driver for real mode (logical device CON)
CLOCK01.SYS	Real time clock driver for PC/AT (logical device CLOCK$)
CLOCK02.SYS	Real time clock driver for PS/2 (logical device CLOCK$)
COM01.SYS	Serial communications port driver for PC/AT (logical devices COM1 and COM2)
COM02.SYS	Serial communications port driver for PS/2 (logical devices COM1, COM2, and COM3)
COUNTRY.SYS	Country-dependent information, such as collating tables and time, date, and currency formats
DISK01.SYS	Floppy disk and fixed disk driver for PC/AT
DISK02.SYS	Floppy disk and fixed disk driver for PS/2
EGA.SYS	Supplementary EGA display driver for real mode; saves and restores state for the EGA write-only control registers
EXTDSKDD.SYS	Creates a new logical drive letter for a block device; optionally configures the medium type and number of heads, tracks, and sectors for the device
KBD01.SYS	Keyboard driver (logical device KBD$) for PC/AT
KBD02.SYS	Keyboard driver (logical device KBD$) for PS/2
MOUSEA00.SYS	Serial interface Mouse Systems PC Mouse driver for PC/AT (logical device MOUSE$)
MOUSEA01.SYS	Serial interface Visi-On Mouse driver for PC/AT (logical device MOUSE$)
MOUSEA02.SYS	Serial interface Microsoft Mouse driver for PC/AT (logical device MOUSE$)
MOUSEA03.SYS	Bus interface Microsoft Mouse driver for PC/AT (logical device MOUSE$)
MOUSEA04.SYS	Driver for Inport Microsoft Mouse for PC/AT (logical device MOUSE$)

(continued)

Figure 2-3. *Device drivers provided with the OS/2 kernel. Device drivers specific to the Presentation Manager are not listed here.*

Figure 2-3. *continued*

Driver	Description
MOUSEB00.SYS	Serial interface Mouse Systems PC Mouse driver for PS/2 (logical device MOUSE$)
MOUSEB01.SYS	Serial interface Visi-On Mouse driver for PS/2 (logical device MOUSE$)
MOUSEB02.SYS	Serial interface Microsoft Mouse driver for PS/2 (logical device MOUSE$)
MOUSEB05.SYS	Driver for IBM In-board Mouse for PS/2 (logical device MOUSE$)
POINTDD.SYS	Pointing device cursor driver (called by mouse drivers, logical device POINTER$)
PRINT01.SYS	Parallel port printer driver (logical devices PRN or LPT1, LPT2, and LPT3) for PC/AT
PRINT02.SYS	Parallel port printer driver (logical devices PRN or LPT1, LPT2, and LPT3) for PS/2
SCREEN01.SYS	Video display driver (logical device SCREEN$) for PC/AT
SCREEN02.SYS	Video display driver (logical device SCREEN$) for PS/2
VDISK.SYS	Electronic or virtual disk (RAM disk) driver

The OS/2 kernel communicates with device drivers through I/O request packets; the drivers translate these requests into the proper commands for the peripheral device controllers (''adapters''). In IBM PS/2 systems, the most primitive parts of the hardware drivers are in ROM (read-only memory); these protected mode routines are referred to as the ROM ABIOS (''Advanced Basic I/O System'') to differentiate them from the more familiar real mode ROM BIOS.

Installable drivers will be discussed in more detail under ''How OS/2 Is Loaded'' later in this chapter, and in Chapter 17 (Device Drivers).

The OS/2 Kernel

The kernel implements the fundamental OS/2 services offered to application programs. These services include:

- File and record management
- Character device input and output
- Memory management
- ''Spawning'' of other programs
- Interprocess communication
- Real time clock services including date, time, and programmable timers
- MS-DOS emulation

Programs access kernel functions through the OS/2 API by pushing parameters on the stack and executing a far call to a named entry point. Use of the API is described further in Chapter 3.

The OS/2 kernel is read into memory during system initialization from the file OS2DOS.COM on the boot disk.

Dynlink Libraries

Dynamic link libraries (also called dynlink libraries, or DLLs) are shareable subroutine libraries that are loaded on demand. In contrast to the routines stored in traditional object libraries, which are bound permanently into an application's executable file, dynlink library routines are bound to an application at its load time. Much of OS/2 is distributed in the form of DLLs (see Figure 2-4). In particular, the entry points for nearly all of the documented OS/2 kernel API routines are present within eight dynlink libraries: DOSCALL1.DLL, KBDCALLS.DLL, MONCALLS.DLL, MSG.DLL,

Library	Description
ANSICALL.DLL	Supports ANSI escape sequences for keyboard redefinition and screen control in protected mode screen groups
BKSCALLS.DLL	Basic keyboard subsystem, called by KBDCALLS.DLL
BMSCALLS.DLL	Basic mouse subsystem, called by MOUCALLS.DLL
BVSCALLS.DLL	Basic video subsystem, called by VIOCALLS.DLL
DOSCALL1.DLL	Contains entry points for most of the DOS API functions, including those for file management, time and date, memory management, and interprocess communication
KBDCALLS.DLL	Keyboard subsystem router, contains entry points for KBD API functions; based on the caller's screen group, requests are passed to a keyboard subsystem DLL (such as BKSCALLS.DLL) for processing
MONCALLS.DLL	Contains entry points for the device monitor API
MOUCALLS.DLL	Contains entry points for the MOU API functions; based on the caller's screen group, requests are passed to a mouse subsystem DLL (such as BMSCALLS.DLL) for processing
MSG.DLL	Contains entry points for message management API
NLS.DLL	Contains entry points for internationalization support API
QUECALLS.DLL	Contains entry points for queue management API
SESMGR.DLL	Contains entry points for session management API
SPOOLCP.DLL	Support for print spooler
VIOCALLS.DLL	Video subsystem router, contains entry points for the VIO API functions; based on the caller's screen group, requests are passed to a video subsystem DLL (such as BVSCALLS.DLL) for processing

Figure 2-4. *Dynamic link libraries provided with the OS/2 kernel. DLLs specific to the Presentation Manager are not listed here.*

MOUCALLS.DLL, NLS.DLL, QUECALLS.DLL, and VIOCALLS.DLL. The other dynlink libraries supplied with the kernel, such as SESMGR.DLL or SPOOLCP.DLL, provide specialized functions which normal applications do not need or cannot access.

The code within a dynlink library runs within the context of the calling program and uses its local descriptor table (LDT). Thus, a library always runs in user mode (ring 3) or, in a few cases, with I/O privilege (ring 2). Code that must run at ring 0 is always located in the kernel or in device drivers and is entered by a *call gate* from a DLL or (less commonly) directly from an application. The actual location of the code that performs an API function and the mode in which it executes are invisible to applications and subject to change.

The Command Processor

The command processor provides a line-oriented user interface to the operating system. It parses and carries out user commands for common services, such as copying, renaming, and deleting files; creating and destroying directories; getting and setting the time and date; listing the contents of directories; and starting programs.

The default protected mode command processor is found in the CMD.EXE file. You can be running multiple copies of CMD.EXE simultaneously — one or more in each protected mode session. Because code (text) segments are always shared in OS/2, the actual memory overhead of each additional copy of CMD.EXE is relatively small. CMD.EXE runs as a normal process in user mode (ring 3) and calls documented API services to carry out its functions.

The default real mode command processor is implemented in the file COMMAND.COM, just as under MS-DOS. Because the memory that real mode programs can use is a relatively limited resource, COMMAND.COM is divided into three sections — *resident, initialization,* and *transient* — each of which guards its memory allocation to a different degree.

The resident section is loaded at the low end of the memory allocated for DOS compatibility mode. It contains the routines to process Ctrl-Break and Ctrl-C entries and critical runtime errors for a real mode program, as well as the routines to terminate such programs. It also contains the code to reload the transient portion of COMMAND.COM when necessary.

The initialization section of COMMAND.COM is loaded above the resident part when a real mode session starts. This section processes the AUTOEXEC.BAT file (the user's list of initialization commands for a real mode session) and is then discarded.

The transient part of COMMAND.COM is loaded at the high end of the memory allocated for compatibility mode, and real mode programs can use its memory for their own purposes. The transient section issues the user prompt, reads commands from the keyboard or batch file, and causes them to be executed. When a real mode program terminates, the resident portion of COMMAND.COM does a checksum of the transient part to determine whether it has been destroyed and fetches a fresh copy from the disk if necessary.

The user commands that CMD.EXE and COMMAND.COM accept fall into three categories:

- Internal commands

- External commands

- Batch files

Internal commands are those carried out by code that is embedded in the command processor itself. Commands in this category include COPY, REN(AME), DIR(ECTORY), and DEL(ETE). In the case of the real mode processor, COMMAND.COM, the routines for the internal commands are in the transient portion.

External commands are simply names of disk files containing executable programs. The term *external command* usually refers to a program file distributed on the OS/2 operating system disks; in reality, however, OS/2 does not distinguish between those programs and any other executable programs when it loads them.

A batch file is an ASCII text file that contains a list of internal, external, or batch commands. Batch files are processed by a special interpreter, built into the command processor, that reads the file a line at a time and carries out each of the specified operations in order. Batch files used in the protected mode session have the extension CMD. As under MS-DOS, the extension BAT identifies batch files intended for the real mode command processor, which has its batch file interpreter in the transient portion.

From a user perspective, CMD.EXE and COMMAND.COM operate almost identically, although CMD.EXE's internal commands and handling of I/O redirection are somewhat more sophisticated. When the user enters a command, the command processor first checks its list of internal commands to see if it can handle the command directly. If not, the command processor searches the current directory and then each directory named in the environment's PATH string for a file with the same name and the extension

COM, EXE, or CMD/BAT (in that order). Of course, if the command processor finds a COM or EXE file, the file must have the appropriate type of header (or none for COM files) for the current CPU mode (real or protected). If the search fails for all file types in all possible locations, the system displays an error message.

You can replace both the real and protected mode command processors with alternative, customized command processors by adding or changing a line in the CONFIG.SYS file and restarting the system. Specify the command processor for protected mode with the PROTSHELL directive; use the SHELL directive for the real mode command processor. You can also use these directives to designate locations for the command processors other than the root directory of the system boot disk or to identify a program or batch file to execute when the command processor is first loaded.

The Presentation Manager

The Presentation Manager is the graphical user interface for OS/2 version 1.1; it replaces the character mode Session Manager that was shipped with OS/2 version 1.0 and renders the command processor CMD.EXE largely superfluous. Parts of the Presentation Manager run as normal processes and interact with the user, whereas other parts are distributed among dynlink libraries and provide graphical services to application programs. The Presentation Manager is loaded with a *PROTSHELL=* statement in the CONFIG.SYS file, which also specifies the protected mode command processor.

The three main components of the Presentation Manager's user interface are called Start Programs, Task Manager, and File System. All three run in windows on the Presentation Manager desktop and can be visible simultaneously. The user controls the sizes and positions of the windows, as well as the behavior of the mouse and the colors of the desktop background, text, menus, and title and scroll bars.

Start Programs allows the user to start new processes (including command processors) by name from a menu. Well-behaved character-based applications and graphical applications that are written to Presentation Manager conventions run in additional windows, while incompatible applications are run ''full-screen'' in separate sessions. The Task Manager allows the user to switch between processes and sessions with hot keys or with the mouse. The File System component displays graphical representations of directory trees and lists of directories and files, and it allows files to be copied, moved, renamed, deleted, printed, or selected for execution.

The structure and operation of the Presentation Manager is a complex subject that is beyond the scope of this book. For further details, refer to *Programming the OS/2 Presentation Manager,* by Charles Petzold, published by Microsoft Press.

How OS/2 Is Loaded

When you power up or reset an 80286 or 80386 CPU, program execution begins in real mode at a predetermined address (FFFF0H for the 80286, FFFFFFF0H for the 80386). This is a hard-wired characteristic of the processor and has nothing to do with OS/2. Computers based on these CPUs are usually designed so that the initial execution address lies within ROM and contains a jump instruction to system test code and the ROM bootstrap routine (Figure 2-5).

The ROM bootstrap's job is to read the disk bootstrap into memory from a floppy or fixed disk. The disk bootstrap is a short program that is placed in a disk's boot sector (track 0, head 0, sector 1 for floppy disks) by the FORMAT program. If the read operation is successful, the ROM bootstrap transfers control to the disk bootstrap (Figure 2-6); otherwise, it executes Int 18H to start ROM BASIC.

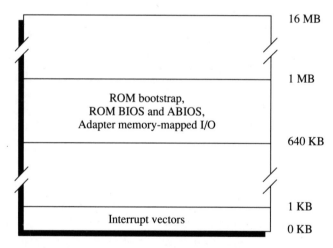

Figure 2-5. *Memory map when system is turned on or restarted. The CPU begins execution in real mode at location FFFF0H (80286 systems) or FFFFFFF0H (80386 systems); control passes from there to the ROM bootstrap routine.*

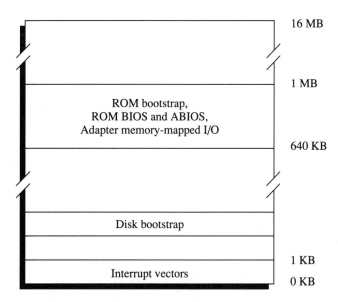

Figure 2-6. *The ROM bootstrap has read the disk bootstrap into memory from the first sector of the boot drive and given it control. The system is in real mode.*

The disk bootstrap first checks to see if the boot disk contains a copy of OS/2. It does this by inspecting a table of information (also placed in the boot sector by the FORMAT program) that describes the characteristics of the disk medium, such as the number of tracks, heads, and sectors per track. Using this table, called the BIOS parameter block (BPB), the disk bootstrap can calculate the location of the root directory and then search the directory for the file OS2LDR. If OS2LDR is found, it is read into memory and receives control (Figure 2-7 on the following page). Otherwise, the disk bootstrap displays the following message:

```
The file OS2LDR cannot be found.
Insert a system diskette and restart the system.
```

OS2LDR consists almost entirely of a full-fledged loader for segmented executable ("new EXE") files along with a primitive file system built on the ROM BIOS disk driver. OS2LDR first determines the size and location of all contiguous memory below 640 KB and above 1 MB. It then searches the root directory of the boot disk for the file OS2KRNL (which, despite its lack of an extension, is actually a file in the new EXE format) and loads it into memory segment by segment, performing all necessary relocations. Finally, OS2LDR transfers control to OS2KRNL and passes a map of system memory and some other configuration information (Figure 2-8 on page 23).

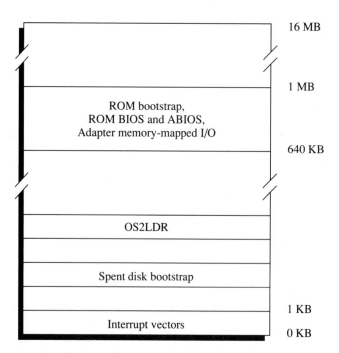

	16 MB
	1 MB
ROM bootstrap, ROM BIOS and ABIOS, Adapter memory-mapped I/O	
	640 KB
OS2LDR	
Spent disk bootstrap	
	1 KB
Interrupt vectors	0 KB

Figure 2-7. *The disk bootstrap has read the OS2LDR file into memory and given it control. The memory occupied by the disk bootstrap program will be overlaid by other OS/2 modules. The system is still in real mode.*

The OS2KRNL file is made up of many code and data segments containing the vital modules of the OS/2 kernel. The system initialization module (SysInit) receives control when OS2KRNL is first entered. SysInit's first job is to establish protected mode operation: It creates the necessary global descriptor table (GDT), interrupt descriptor table (IDT), task state segment (TSS), and so on, after which it sets the PE bit in the machine status word (CR0) to switch modes. Creation of a valid IDT permits the system to initialize the two 8259 programmable interrupt controllers (PICs), which enable and service interrupts.

SysInit then proceeds with the remaining CPU and memory initialization by moving the various kernel modules to their final locations. To provide a maximum amount of memory for real mode operations, it leaves only the most critical kernel components, such as the scheduler, in the 0–640 KB region ("System Low"); the remaining components, such as the file system and signal handlers, are placed above the 1 MB boundary ("System High"). It then initializes the physical memory manager (PMM), virtual memory manager (VMM), and the system memory arena (the area of dynamically allocatable memory).

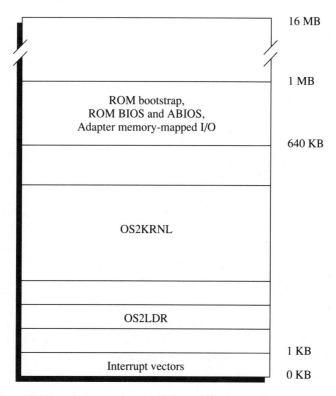

Figure 2-8. *OS2LDR, which contains a full-fledged loader for segmented executable files, has brought OS2KRNL into memory. OS2KRNL contains the critical portions of the OS/2 kernel, including the physical and virtual memory managers, the scheduler, and the file system. When control passes to OS2KRNL, the system is switched from real mode to protected mode, and the memory occupied by OS2LDR can be reused.*

Next, SysInit reads the CONFIG.SYS file into memory from the root directory of the boot disk. This file contains directives that control various aspects of the kernel's operation. Based on the detected hardware configuration, SysInit then loads the base set of device drivers: For a PC/AT or compatible, these are DISK01.SYS (fixed disk and floppy disk), KBD01.SYS (keyboard), SCREEN01.SYS (video display), CLOCK01.SYS (real time clock), and PRINT01.SYS (parallel port). The system file table and disk buffers are then allocated, and the file system is initialized. As under MS-DOS, the number of disk buffers is controlled by a *BUFFERS=* statement in CONFIG.SYS. The system file table, however, can grow dynamically; any *FILES=* statement in CONFIG.SYS is ignored.

Until this point in the loading sequence, SysInit has been running autonomously at the highest privilege level (ring 0). SysInit brings the OS/2 kernel to life by calling a special scheduler entry point, which causes the scheduler to allocate memory for its dispatch table and then initialize it. Upon return from the scheduler, SysInit finds itself running as a normal process in user mode (ring 3).

Most of the remaining SysInit tasks are carried out through documented API services. Because SysInit was not brought into memory by the system loader, which ordinarily resolves dynamic links to API entry points on behalf of processes, SysInit must use *DosLoadModule* and *DosGetProcAddr* (discussed in Chapter 19) to establish links to the API functions it requires.

SysInit also uses *DosLoadModule* to load optional device drivers specified by DEVICE directives in the CONFIG.SYS file. A special kernel entry point provided for SysInit lets it request that the kernel run the driver's Init routine after the driver is loaded. During its Init procedure, the driver allocates any additional fixed memory it needs, initializes its adapter, and captures the necessary interrupt vectors.

Similarly, SysInit uses *DosExecPgm* to launch any background, or "daemon," processes specified with RUN directives in the CONFIG.SYS file. Such processes are placed in a "black box" and must use special popup video calls if they need to interact with the user. Finally, SysInit loads and executes the Presentation Manager shell program named in the PROTSHELL directive in CONFIG.SYS and then calls *DosExit* to terminate. The memory SysInit has occupied is then reclaimed like that of any other process.

The Presentation Manager shell switches the system into graphics mode and displays the desktop with the Task Manager, DOS compatibility box, and Print Spooler icons. It then inspects the root directory of the boot disk for a batch file named STARTUP.CMD. If the file exists, a copy of CMD.EXE is started in a window to carry out the commands in the file. Finally, the Program Starter menu is displayed, and the system awaits a command from the user.

Figures 2-9 and 2-10 illustrate two possible configurations that result from the OS/2 boot process. The two configurations are basically the same except for the way they use lower memory. When DOS compatibility mode is enabled (Figure 2-9), the storage below the boundary specified by the RMSIZE directive in CONFIG.SYS (or 640 KB, if RMSIZE is absent) is reserved for COMMAND.COM and real mode applications — apart from the area occupied by OS/2 "System Low" and the device drivers, of course. Protected mode programs (Figure 2-10) can still use any memory below 640 KB that is *above* the boundary specified by the RMSIZE directive.

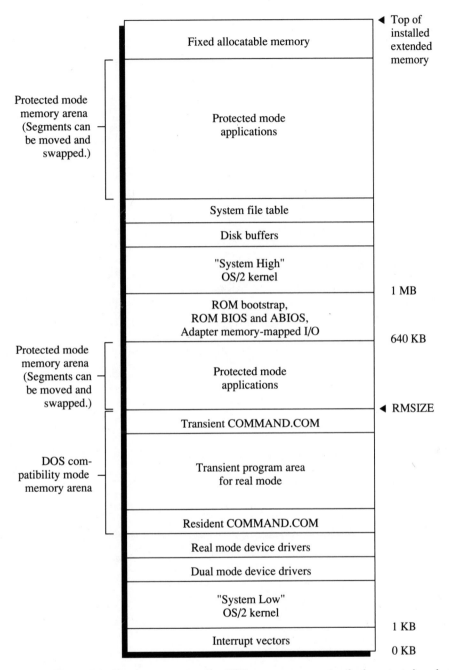

Figure 2-9. *Final memory map for OS/2 systems supporting both protected mode and real mode applications (PROTECTONLY=NO). Depending on the RMSIZE directive in CONFIG.SYS, the memory arena for DOS compatibility mode can occupy all or only part of the memory below 640 KB that is not used by OS/2 "System Low" and its device drivers.*

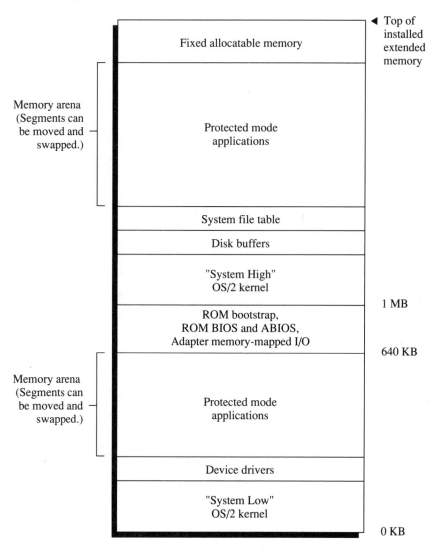

Figure 2-10. *Final memory map for OS/2 systems supporting protected mode applications only (PROTECTONLY=YES in CONFIG.SYS). Note that in a protected-mode-only system the interrupt vector table is not fixed at location 0 but can float anywhere in memory.*

OS/2 APPLICATION PROGRAMS

OS/2 is both a platform for a new generation of multitasking graphical applications and a bridge from the 640 KB real mode MS-DOS environment. Consequently, you can write new applications for OS/2 at several different levels of complexity:

- Kernel applications

- Family applications

- Presentation Manager applications

Kernel applications execute only in protected mode and use the OS/2 kernel services for keyboard, screen, and mouse I/O rather than using those offered by the Presentation Manager (PM). They have full access to OS/2's multitasking, virtual memory, interprocess communication, and asynchronous I/O capabilities. Although Kernel applications can run in a window under the Presentation Manager, they are ordinarily limited to character-oriented displays. (If a program includes its own graphics drivers, it gives up the ability to run in a window.)

Family applications are built like Kernel applications; however, they use only those OS/2 functions that have direct counterparts in MS-DOS, and they do not contain any machine instructions that are unique to the 80286 or 80386. A Family application goes through an extra linkage step which "binds" it to code that intercepts OS/2 API calls, if the program is loaded in real mode, and converts them to MS-DOS Int 21H calls. Such a "bound" program can run in either protected mode or real mode under OS/2 or MS-DOS on any 8086/88, 80286, or 80386-based machine. Many Microsoft programming tools are written as Family applications so that they can be used to cross-compile OS/2 programs under MS-DOS or vice versa.

Presentation Manager applications have a radically different internal structure and flow of control than do Family or Kernel applications. The "main" routine is a simple loop that reads a message off an input queue, optionally translates the message, and then redispatches the message to a relatively autonomous routine, known as a *window procedure*, that is associated with a specific screen region. The message might consist of a keypress, a key release, a mouse movement, a signal from the system to repaint part of a window, a notification that the application has been "iconized," and so forth. Presentation Manager applications have full access to the powerful PM library of device-independent graphics services.

The remainder of this chapter, and indeed most of the remainder of this book, concerns itself only with Kernel applications: their structure in source code, on disk, and in memory, and the way in which they are loaded, communicate with the operating system and other processes, obtain system resources such as files and additional memory, and terminate.

OS/2 Program Source Structure

An OS/2 Kernel application is built from two basic types of text files: one or more language-specific source files that can be compiled or assembled into relocatable object modules, and a module definition file that describes the program's segment characteristics. This chapter confines itself to a discussion of MASM applications, although most of the principles involved apply to high level languages as well.

An OS/2 assembly language program has a well-defined structure at two levels: the level of segments and that of procedures. Segments are physical groupings of like items within a program and an enforced separation of dissimilar items; procedures are functional subdivisions of the executable program. Figure 3-1 contains a segmentation skeleton of an OS/2 assembly language program.

In 80286 protected mode, a memory segment occupies from 1 to 65,536 bytes and carries one of three attributes: executable code (text), read/write data, or read-only (static) data. An executable selector cannot be used to write to its segment; code segments are sometimes described as "pure" because under normal circumstances they are not modifiable. (OS/2 does provide a way to obtain executable and data selectors that refer to the same physical memory segment; this method will be discussed in Chapter 11.)

```
        title   MYPROG -- Segmentation Skeleton
        page    55,132
        .286                    ; allow 80286 instructions

        .                       ; miscellaneous equates,
        .                       ; structures, and other
        .                       ; declarations go here

        extrn   DosExit:far     ; system services used by
                                ; program are declared here

DGROUP  group   _DATA           ; declare 'automatic data
                                ; group' for OS/2 loader

_DATA   segment word public 'DATA'

        .                       ; all variable and constant
        .                       ; data goes in this segment
        .

_DATA   ends

_TEXT   segment word public 'CODE'

        assume  cs:_TEXT,ds:DGROUP

main    proc    far             ; routine which initially
        .                       ; receives control can be
        .                       ; called anything...
        .
        push    1               ; main routine terminates
        push    0               ; all threads and passes a
        call    DosExit         ; return code to OS/2

main    endp

        .                       ; other routines needed by
        .                       ; the program go here
        .

_TEXT   ends

        end     main            ; declares end of module
                                ; and initial entry point
```

Figure 3-1. *Skeleton of a properly segmented assembly language application for OS/2.*

The 80286's insistence on separation of executable code and data in protected mode dictates that every program that runs under OS/2, including assembly language programs, must have a minimum of two segments: a code segment and a data segment. The "near data" segment, or the segment that the program expects to address with offsets from the DS register, should be named as a component of DGROUP with the *group* directive. DGROUP is known as the "automatic data segment" and receives special treatment by the OS/2 loader.

Programs are classified into one memory model or another by the number of their code and data segments. The most commonly used memory model for assembly language programs is the *small model,* which has one code and one data segment, but several others may also be used (Figure 3-2). For each model, Microsoft has established certain segment and class names that are used by all its high level language compilers (Figure 3-3). I recommend that you follow these conventions in assembly language programming too, because they make it easier to integrate routines from high level language (HLL) libraries into your assembly programs or to use your assembly language subroutines in HLL programs.

The program must have a primary procedure that receives control from OS/2. To specify the entry point, include the procedure name in the END statement at the end of the file. The main procedure's attribute (*near* or *far*) is not particularly important because a program terminates its execution by a *DosExit* function call rather than by a subroutine RETurn instruction. By convention, people assign the *far* attribute to the main procedure. (OS/2 function calls are discussed later in this chapter.)

Other procedures are assigned a *near* or *far* attribute depending on the memory model and depending on whether they are called only from the same segment or are the target of intersegment calls. Keep procedures reentrant whenever possible so that they can be shared between concurrent threads (subprocesses) without any special synchronization. If you are coding in C, procedures are almost naturally reentrant unless you declare variables static; if you are coding in assembly language, the 80286's *enter* and *leave* instructions allow the easy implementation of local, automatic variables for subroutines.

Model	Code Segments	Data Segments
Small	One	One
Medium	Multiple	One
Compact	One	Multiple
Large	Multiple	Multiple

Figure 3-2. *Terminology for memory models commonly used in assembly language and C programs. Two additional models exist that are not relevant to this book: the* tiny *model, which consists of intermixed code and data in a single segment (for example, a COM file under MS-DOS); and the* huge *model, which is supported by the Microsoft C Compiler and allows use of data structures larger than 64 KB.*

Memory Model	Segment Name	Align Type	Combine Class	Class Name	Group
Small	_TEXT	word	public	CODE	
	_DATA	word	public	DATA	DGROUP
	STACK	para	stack	STACK	DGROUP
Medium	*module*_TEXT	word	public	CODE	
	.				
	.				
	.				
	_DATA	word	public	DATA	DGROUP
	STACK	para	stack	STACK	DGROUP
Compact	_TEXT	word	public	CODE	
	data	para	private	FAR_DATA	
	.				
	.				
	_DATA	word	public	DATA	DGROUP
	STACK	para	stack	STACK	DGROUP
Large	*module*_TEXT	word	public	CODE	
	.				
	.				
	data	para	private	FAR_DATA	
	.				
	.				
	_DATA	word	public	DATA	DGROUP
	STACK	para	stack	STACK	DGROUP

Figure 3-3. *Segments, groups, and classes for the standard memory models as used with assembly language programs. Microsoft C programs use a superset of these segments and classes.*

Module Definition Files

A module definition file (with the extension DEF) describes the segment characteristics of an OS/2 application program or dynamic link library. The major elements of a definition file are the following:

- The executable program or dynlink library name, defined with the NAME or LIBRARY directive, respectively

- The initial size of the local heap for C programs, defined with the HEAPSIZE directive (The heap can be expanded automatically as needed at run time, as long as the total of the program's data, stack, and local heap does not exceed 65,536 bytes.)

- The stack size, defined with the STACKSIZE directive

- The characteristics of the code and data segments, defined with the CODE and DATA directives along with suitable modifiers

- The names of imported (dynamically linked) or exported routines

Other DEF file directives determine whether a code segment has I/O privilege (IOPL), place descriptive strings into a load module for documentation purposes, or specify the filename of an MS-DOS–compatible stub program which will be merged into the new executable file and receive control if it is loaded in real mode.

Module definition files are also used by the IMPLIB utility to create *import libraries* — special object module libraries that contain reference records for the entry points in dynlink libraries. When the Linker resolves an *extrn* reference in an application against a reference record, an IMPORTS statement in the module definition file is not necessary. Thus, import libraries simplify the application building process; they are discussed further in Chapter 19.

Figure 3-4 contains a summary of module definition file syntax. For more detailed information, refer to Appendix E.

NAME [*module name*]
      [WINDOWAPI | WINDOWCOMPAT | NOTWINDOWCOMPAT]
DESCRIPTION *'string'*
HEAPSIZE *bytes*
STACKSIZE *bytes*
PROTMODE | REALMODE
EXETYPE [**OS2** | WINDOWS | DOS4]

CODE [PRELOAD | **LOADONCALL**] [EXECUTEONLY | **EXECUTEREAD**]
      [IOPL | **NOIOPL**] [CONFORMING | **NONCONFORMING**]

          If no CODE statement is present, the default attributes are
          LOADONCALL EXECUTEREAD NOIOPL NONCONFORMING

DATA [PRELOAD | **LOADONCALL**] [READONLY | **READWRITE**]
      [NONE | SINGLE | **MULTIPLE**] [SHARED | **NONSHARED**]
      [IOPL | **NOIOPL**]

          If no DATA statement is present, the attributes are
          LOADONCALL READWRITE MULTIPLE NONSHARED NOIOPL

SEGMENTS
     name [CLASS ['*classname*']] [PRELOAD | **LOADONCALL**]
        [READONLY | **READWRITE**]
        [EXECUTEONLY | **EXECUTEREAD**][IOPL | **NOIOPL**]
        [CONFORMING | **NONCONFORMING**]
        [SHARED | **NONSHARED**]

                                  Number of stack parameters (words);
                                  required only for IOPL segments
EXPORTS
     exportname [*stackparams*]

IMPORTS
     [*internalname* =] *modulename.entryname* | *modulename.ordinal*

STUB '*filename.*EXE'

Figure 3-4. *Syntax summary of a module definition file for OS/2 applications.*
Defaults are in **boldface**. *Keywords must always be entered in uppercase letters. A*
similar syntax summary for drivers and dynlink libraries appears in Chapter 19.

OS/2 Program Files

Source code files are first translated to *relocatable object modules,* which contain machine code and symbolic information, by an assembler or compiler. Object modules are not suitable for execution without further processing. For easier management they are often collected together into *object module libraries.*

Object modules are converted into executable programs (with the aid of module definition files, import libraries, and object module libraries) by a utility called the Segmented Executable Linker. The executable programs then reside on the disk as load modules called "segmented executable" files, or "new EXE" files. The format of a segmented executable file is identical to that of the load modules used by Microsoft Windows and is a superset of the "old EXE" format of MS-DOS. It has the following components:

- A header describing the program's structure
- A "stub" program for real mode
- At least one code segment
- At least one data segment

The header contains, among other elements, a "signature" (identifying the type of load module), a checksum, the program entry point, information about the code and data segments in the file, and a list of external routines to be dynamically linked at load time (also called imported routines). The stub program is executed if the program is invoked in real mode (either in DOS compatibility mode or under MS-DOS). The default stub program is a short routine inserted by the Linker that displays the message *This program cannot run in DOS mode* and terminates.

Each segment in the file has an attribute (code, read-only data, or read/write data), its own relocation table, and flags indicating whether it should be preloaded or loaded on demand. Code segments are always read-only ("pure") and can be shared among multiple instances of the same program.

Theoretically, the size of an OS/2 program is limited only by the number of symbols and segments that the Linker can process. Practically speaking, program size is limited by the amount of disk space available to hold the executable file, the virtual memory manager's swap file, and the number of available LDT selectors—this still allows for some pretty large programs!

A block diagram of a segmented EXE file can be found in Figure 3-5. See Appendix D for a more detailed description of the file format.

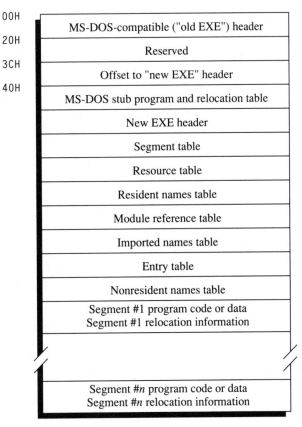

00H	MS-DOS-compatible ("old EXE") header
20H	Reserved
3CH	Offset to "new EXE" header
40H	MS-DOS stub program and relocation table
	New EXE header
	Segment table
	Resource table
	Resident names table
	Module reference table
	Imported names table
	Entry table
	Nonresident names table
	Segment #1 program code or data Segment #1 relocation information
	Segment #n program code or data Segment #n relocation information

Figure 3-5. *Block diagram of the "new EXE" format for executable program files under OS/2. In Presentation Manager applications, "resources" (such as icons, bitmaps, string tables, and menus) follow the last code or data segment.*

Program Loading

A general-purpose mechanism called the *system loader* brings programs into memory and prepares them for execution. Command processors and other programs invoke the loader by calling the OS/2 function *DosExecPgm* (described in more detail in Chapter 12).

When the loader is called upon to load a program, it inspects the EXE file header and allocates sufficient memory to hold the segments in the program that are marked "preload." These typically include at least one segment holding machine code (*text*), a segment for the program's data and stack, and a segment for the environment, program name, and command line information (Figure 3-6 on the following page).

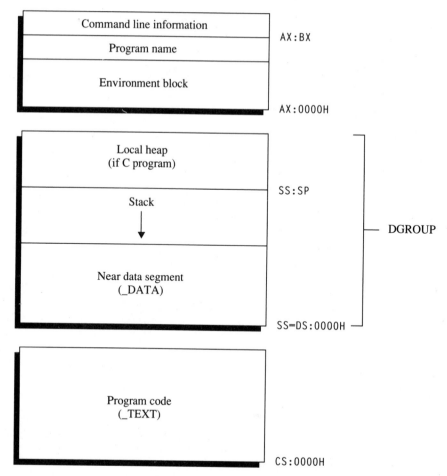

Figure 3-6. *Memory image of a typical "small model" MASM or C program immediately after loading. The program's data, stack, and local heap reside in the same physical segment, called DGROUP. The segments need not be arranged in the order shown here; in fact, the physical location is not visible to the program itself. The entry point can be anywhere in the code segment and is specified by an* end *statement in one of the source modules of the program.*

The loader also performs a *memory overcommit* calculation to make sure that enough physical memory and swap file space will be available at any point during the program's execution. The loader's attempts to allocate memory for a new program might cause the memory manager to move, swap, or discard segments belonging to other programs.

As each segment is read into memory from the EXE file, the loader performs any necessary selector fixups as specified by the segment's associated relocation table. Segments that are marked "load on demand" are assigned a selector but are not initially brought into physical memory. The loader also performs any loadtime dynamic linking that may be required, fixing up the addresses in far calls to OS/2 system services or to application-specific dynlink libraries.

Once the essential parts of a program have been loaded into memory and relocated, any dynamic links have been resolved, and the program has been added to the list of jobs maintained by the kernel's *scheduler,* the program becomes a *process.*

Program Entry Conditions

The initial values of the code segment (CS) and instruction pointer (IP) registers are calculated from the entry point information in the EXE file header. The data segment (DS) and stack segment (SS) registers are initialized with the segment selector for DGROUP, which contains the program's near data, stack, and (for C programs) local heap. The stack pointer (SP) is loaded with the offset of the base of the program's stack, while the AX and BX registers are set up with a selector and offset that provide access to the program's environment block, filename, and command line. Other registers contain less vital information, such as the stack size and heap size (Figure 3-7).

The environment block for a particular process is inherited from the process's parent. It consists of a series of null-terminated ASCII (ASCIIZ) strings, called environment variables, of the following form:

NAME=PARAMETER

Variables are placed in the environment block as a result of certain directives in the CONFIG.SYS file, and by the command processor as a result of PROMPT, PATH, and SET commands (Figure 3-8 on the following page).

Register	Contents
CS:IP	Initial entry point
SS:SP	Base of default stack
DS	Segment selector for *DGROUP*
ES	Zero
AX	Segment selector of environment
BX	Offset of command line information following environment
CX	Initial size of *DGROUP* (0 = 65,536 bytes)
DX	Initial size of default stack
SI	Initial size of local heap (C programs)
DI	Module handle for the process
BP	Zero

Figure 3-7. *Register contents at entry to a protected mode OS/2 application.*

```
COMSPEC=C:\OS2\PBIN\CMD.EXE
PROMPT=$p$_PM$g
PATH=C:\;C:\OS2\BIN;C:\OS2\PBIN;C:\OS2TOOLS
INCLUDE=c:\os2tools\include
LIB=c:\os2tools\lib
TMP=c:\temp
TEMP=c:\temp
INIT=c:\init
USER=c:\init
```

Figure 3-8. *Typical environment block for protected mode session (displayed with the command SET).*

When multiple sessions are active, the command processor in each session maintains a "master environment" for that session.

Environment variables provide information to command processors and application programs; they do not affect the operation of the OS/2 kernel. For example, the Microsoft C Compiler looks in the environment for *INCLUDE*, *LIB*, and *TMP* variables to tell it where to find header (.H) files and object module libraries and where to put temporary working files.

The last null-terminated string in the environment block is followed by an additional null byte, which signifies the end of the block. Immediately following that byte, OS/2 places the fully qualified name of the file from which the program was loaded, including the logical drive identifier and full path from the root of that drive. This ASCIIZ string corresponds to *argv[0]* in C programs; the program can use this information to create another instance of itself or to find its "home directory" in order to load overlays or configuration files.

The program filename is followed by the command line information, in the form of a set of ASCIIZ strings called the "argument strings." When a program is loaded by CMD.EXE, the first argument string is the simple name of the program and the second is the command tail (the command line excluding the program name). The argument strings are terminated by an additional null byte, in the same fashion as the environment block. Redirection or piping parameters do not appear in the argument strings passed by CMD.EXE because redirection is transparent to applications.

Figure 3-9 contains a hex and ASCII dump of a typical program's environment block, filename, and argument strings. To produce the dump in the figure, the OS/2 FIND utility was run with the following command line:

```
C>find /n "extrn" start.asm <Enter>
```

```
              0  1  2  3  4  5  6  7  8  9  A  B  C  D  E  F    0123456789ABCDEF
005F:0000    33 58 42 4F 58 3D 63 3A 5C 6F 73 32 73 79 73 5C   3XBOX=c:\os2sys\
005F:0010    63 6F 6D 6D 61 6E 64 2E 63 6F 6D 00 43 4F 4D 53   command.com.COMS
005F:0020    50 45 43 3D 43 3A 5C 4F 53 32 53 59 53 5C 43 4D   PEC=C:\OS2SYS\CM
005F:0030    44 2E 45 58 45 00 50 41 54 48 3D 43 3A 5C 3B 43   D.EXE.PATH=C:\;C
005F:0040    3A 5C 4F 53 32 53 59 53 3B 43 3A 5C 54 4F 4F 4C   :\OS2SYS;C:\TOOL
005F:0050    53 00 44 50 41 54 48 3D 43 3A 5C 3B 43 3A 5C 4F   S.DPATH=C:\;C:\O
005F:0060    53 32 53 59 53 3B 43 3A 5C 54 4F 4F 4C 53 00 49   S2SYS;C:\TOOLS.I
005F:0070    4E 43 4C 55 44 45 3D 63 3A 5C 69 6E 63 6C 75 64   NCLUDE=c:\includ
005F:0080    65 00 4C 49 42 3D 63 3A 5C 6C 69 62 00 49 4E 49   e.LIB=c:\lib.INI
005F:0090    54 3D 63 3A 5C 69 6E 69 74 00 54 4D 50 3D 63 3A   T=c:\init.TMP=c:
005F:00A0    5C 74 65 6D 70 00 54 45 4D 50 3D 63 3A 5C 74 65   \temp.TEMP=c:\te
005F:00B0    6D 70 00 50 52 4F 4D 50 54 3D 24 70 24 5F 50 4D   mp.PROMPT=$p$_PM
005F:00C0    24 67 00 00 43 3A 5C 50 4D 46 5C 46 49 4E 44 2E   $g..C:\PMF\FIND.
005F:00D0    45 58 45 00 66 69 6E 64 00 20 2F 6E 20 22 65 78   EXE.find. /n "ex
005F:00E0    74 72 6E 22 20 73 74 61 72 74 2E 61 73 6D 00 00   trn" start.asm..
```

Figure 3-9. *Sample hex dump of the information that is passed to an OS/2 program at entry. The two zero bytes at offset* 00C2H *mark the end of the environment and are followed by the program filename. The two argument strings appear at offsets* 00D4H *and* 00D9H.

Process Execution and the API

While a process is executing, it communicates with the operating system via the Application Program Interface (API). The API functions allow a program to request and release additional system resources, start and communicate with other processes, and perform input and output in a hardware-independent fashion. Some API services also allow a process to obtain additional information about its environment and about the system state and hardware capabilities (Figure 3-10 on the following page). A subset of the API functions, called the Family API (FAPI), corresponds directly to the functions supported by MS-DOS.

Each API function has a named entry point, is declared with an *extrn far* statement, and is entered by a far call. Parameters for API functions are pushed onto the stack prior to the call. A parameter can be a value, or it can be an address of a value or variable (commonly a structure). For kernel API functions, a status code is returned to the program in register AX. This code is zero if the function succeeded or an error code if the function failed. Other returned values are placed in variables whose addresses were passed on the stack in the original call. (Presentation Manager API functions use other conventions.)

Function	Description
DosDevConfig	Gets information about system configuration: number of floppy disks, type of monitor, presence/absence of 80287 or 80387, PC model type, number of printers and serial ports.
DosGetCtryInfo	Gets internationalization information such as the country code, date and time format, and currency symbol.
DosGetDateTime	Gets the current date, time, and day of the week.
DosGetEnv	Gets a pointer to process's environment block, program filename, and command line.
DosGetInfoSeg	Gets pointers to read-only global and local information segments containing the process ID, screen group number, current date, time, length of timeslice, and other useful information.
DosGetMachineMode	Returns a flag indicating whether the process is running in real mode or protected mode.
DosGetPID	Returns the current process ID, thread ID, and parent's process ID.
DosGetPrty	Gets the execution priority of a thread.
DosGetVersion	Gets the OS/2 version number.
DosMemAvail	Returns the size of the largest free block in physical memory.
DosQCurDir	Gets the pathname to the current directory.
DosQCurDisk	Gets the identifier for the current disk drive.
DosQFSInfo	Returns information about the file system on the specified device, such as volume label, bytes per sector, total number of allocation units, and number of free allocation units.
DosQSysInfo	Returns system information that does not change after the system is booted.
DosQVerify	Gets the current setting of the system verify (read after write) flag for disk operations.
DosScanEnv	Searches the environment block for an environment variable.
VioGetConfig	Returns information about the type of video display and adapter, and the amount of memory installed on the adapter.
VioGetMode	Returns information about the current video display mode, including the number of lines, columns, and displayable colors.
VioGetState	Returns information about the video controller state: palette, intensity/blink toggle, and border color.

Figure 3-10. *API functions which can be used by a program to obtain information about its execution environment and the system state and capabilities. These functions are described again in more detail at appropriate locations elsewhere in this book.*

For example, the kernel function *DosWrite* takes as its parameters the handle for a file or device, the address and length of the data to be written, and the address of a variable in which it will return the actual number of bytes written.

```
          extrn   DosWrite:far
stdout   equ     1                       ; standard output handle
wlen     dw      ?                       ; receives length written
msg      db      'Hello World!'          ; message to be written
msg_len  equ     $-msg                   ; length of message
          .
          .
          .

          push    stdout                 ; standard output handle
          push    ds                     ; address of message
          push    offset DGROUP:msg
          push    msg_len                ; length of message
          push    ds                     ; receives bytes written
          push    offset DGROUP:wlen
          call    DosWrite               ; transfer to OS/2
          or      ax,ax                  ; was write successful?
          jnz     error                  ; jump if function failed
          .
          .
          .
```

Calling the OS/2 API is equally efficient from a high level language or from assembly language, because high level languages typically use the stack for parameter passing, just as the OS/2 API does. For example, to call an OS/2 API function from a C program, you simply declare it as *far pascal* — indicating that the parameters are pushed left to right and that the called routine clears the stack — and then invoke it directly by name:

```
unsigned extern far pascal
  DosWrite(unsigned, char far *, unsigned, unsigned far *);
      .
      .
      .

      unsigned status, wlen;
      char *msg = "Hello World!";
      status = DosWrite(1, msg, strlen(msg), &wlen);
      .
      .
      .
```

The C Compiler generates the correct code for the OS/2 call automatically. It introduces no execution time or space penalty, and it requires no intermediate library functions to shift parameters around or pop them into registers before transferring to the operating system. The OS/2 API services can be called directly in a similar fashion from Pascal, FORTRAN, or even Forth programs.

Process Termination

When an application program has finished processing, it terminates itself and passes an "exit" code back to its parent with the API function *DosExit*. A process can also be terminated by an external event, such as a call to *DosKillProcess* by its parent process, a general protection (GP) fault, the user's entry of Ctrl-C or Ctrl-Break, or the user's response to an operating system pop-up that reports a critical error.

Upon termination of a process, regardless of the cause, OS/2 discontinues any pending I/O, closes any open files, and releases all memory and other system resources owned by the process. OS/2 then notifies the process's parent of the exit code and manner of termination, if the parent requested that information.

A process can intercept or disable some external events to prevent its termination or to allow an orderly cleanup before termination. For these purposes, the API includes the functions *DosError*, *DosSetSigHandler*, *DosSetVec*, and *DosExitList*. A process cannot, however, prevent termination resulting from a GP fault.

A Sample OS/2 Application

Let's look at a traditional, trivial program, written in Microsoft Macro Assembler, that displays the message *Hello World!* on the standard output device (which defaults to the video display). This sample program is created from two files: HELLO.ASM (the assembly language source file) and HELLO.DEF (the module definition file).

The Source File HELLO.ASM

The file HELLO.ASM contains the assembly language source code for our sample program (Figure 3-11). It demonstrates the fundamental structure of a small model assembly language program that is destined to become an OS/2 EXE file. Because this program is so short and simple, a relatively high proportion of the source code consists of assembler directives that do not result in any executable code.

The *title* directive, on line 1, specifies the text string (limited to 60 characters) to be printed on the upper left corner of each page. The *title* directive is optional, but it cannot be used more than once in each assembly language source file.

```
 1:          title   HELLO -- Display Message on stdout
 2:          page    55,132
 3:          .286
 4:
 5: ;
 6: ; HELLO.EXE
 7: ;
 8: ; A simple OS/2 assembly language program.
 9: ;
10: ; Copyright (C) 1986 Ray Duncan
11: ;
12:
13: stdin   equ     0               ; standard input handle
14: stdout  equ     1               ; standard output handle
15: stderr  equ     2               ; standard error handle
16:
17:         extrn   DosWrite:far
18:         extrn   DosExit:far
19:
20: DGROUP  group   _DATA
21:
22:
23: _DATA   segment word public 'DATA'
24:
25: msg     db      0dh,0ah,"Hello World!",0dh,0ah
26: msg_len equ     $-msg
27:
28: wlen    dw      ?               ; receives bytes written
29:
30: _DATA   ends
31:
32:
33: _TEXT   segment word public 'CODE'
34:
35:         assume  cs:_TEXT,ds:DGROUP
36:
37: print   proc    far
38:
39:         push    stdout      ; standard output handle
40:         push    ds          ; address of data
41:         push    offset DGROUP:msg
42:         push    msg_len     ; length of data
43:         push    ds          ; receives bytes written
44:         push    offset DGROUP:wlen
45:         call    DosWrite    ; transfer to OS/2
```

(continued)

Figure 3-11. *Source file HELLO.ASM for the sample application HELLO.EXE. Line numbers at left are for reference in the text and are not part of the actual source file.*

Figure 3-11. *continued*

```
46:          or      ax,ax       ; was write successful?
47:          jnz     error       ; jump if function failed
48:
49:          push    1           ; terminate all threads
50:          push    0           ; return success code
51:          call    DosExit     ; transfer to OS/2
52:
53: error:   push    1           ; terminate all threads
54:          push    1           ; return error code
55:          call    DosExit     ; transfer to OS/2
56:
57: print    endp
58:
59: _TEXT    ends
60:
61:          end     print
```

The *page* directive, when used with two operands as in line 2, defines the length and width of the printer page. These default to 66 lines long and 80 characters wide. If you use a *page* directive within your listing without any operands, it causes a form feed to be sent to the printer and a heading printed. In larger programs, use the *page* directive liberally to place each of your procedures on a separate sheet for easy reading.

The *.286* directive (line 3) enables the assembly of 80286 nonprivileged instructions that are not present in the 8086 instruction set. The most handy of these is the *push immediate* instruction, which saves time and space when setting up parameters for an OS/2 API call.

Lines 13–15 equate symbols to the predefined handles for the *standard input, standard output,* and *standard error* devices. Although we wouldn't expect these values ever to change, assigning them meaningful names makes the program more readable.

References to OS/2 API entry points are accomplished with *extrn* directives, which assign a *far* attribute to the external name (lines 17 and 18). The assembler, of course, does not know the nature of the procedure represented by the external name, only that it has to generate a far call to reach it and that the final address will be fixed up later.

The declaration of *DGROUP* with the *group* directive (line 20) is mandatory. *DGROUP* is a "magic" name that specifies the application's automatic data segment, which also contains the default stack. Unlike MS-DOS, OS/2 automatically initializes the DS register to point to *DGROUP* before it transfers control to the program's entry point. (The other conditions at entry to a protected mode application were discussed earlier in this chapter and are summarized in Figure 3-7 on page 37.)

Now let's examine lines 23 through 30, where we declare a data segment that contains the variables and constants used by our program. The data segment is initiated with the *segment* directive in line 23; it is given the name *_DATA* by the label field of the statement and acquires certain attributes (*word, public,* and the classname *DATA*) from the operand field. The data segment is terminated with an *ends* directive in line 30. The Linker knows, by the class name and the association of segment name *_DATA* with the group name *DGROUP*, that this segment of the program does not contain executable machine code.

Next we come to the declaration of a machine code segment that begins in line 33 with a *segment* directive and terminates line 59 with the *ends* directive. The *segment* instruction assigns the name *_TEXT* and the attributes *word, public,* and the classname *CODE* to the segment. You will find it quite helpful to read the *Microsoft Macro Assembler Programmer's Guide* for detailed explanations of each possible attribute of a segment. The *_TEXT* and *_DATA* segment names are simply conventions which are used by the Microsoft high level language compilers; these conventions are explained in great detail in the MASM and Microsoft C Compiler manuals.

Following the *segment* instruction, we encounter an *assume* directive in line 35. In this statement we assert that the CS and DS segment registers have been loaded, at this point of execution of the final program, with the selectors for the *_TEXT* segment and *DGROUP*, respectively. The *assume* directive often baffles new assembly language programmers. It doesn't appear to do anything—it generates no code—it only notifies the assembler which segment registers point to which memory segments, so that the assembler can generate segment override prefix bytes when they are needed. The responsibility for actually loading the segment registers remains with the programmer and the operating system.

Within the *_TEXT* segment, we come to another type of block declaration, begun with the *proc* directive in line 37 and closed with *endp* in line 57. These two instructions declare the beginning and end of a procedure, or block of executable code that performs a single distinct function. The procedure is given a name by the label in the leftmost field of the *proc* statement, and an attribute in the operand field—in this case, the name of the procedure is *print.* If the procedure carries the *near* attribute, it can be called only by other code in the same segment, whereas procedures with the *far* attribute can be called from program code located anywhere in the process's address space.

Calls to two different OS/2 services, *DosWrite* and *DosExit*, are demonstrated in lines 39 through 55.

DosWrite, which we encountered earlier in this chapter, performs a synchronous write to a file or device ("synchronous" in that the write request is logically completed before control returns to the requesting process); it is analogous to MS-DOS's Int 21H Function 40H. The returned status of the operation is tested in lines 46–47; the status is zero if the operation succeeded.

DosExit terminates a process, passing a return code back to its parent process; it is comparable to MS-DOS's Int 21H Function 4CH. Our program contains two calls to *DosExit*: lines 49–51, which pass a return code of zero (signifying that our program ran successfully), and lines 53–55, which pass a nonzero return code (indicating that an error condition caused the program to terminate). The latter call executes if *DosWrite* returns an error status.

The *end* directive in line 61 winds up our little sample program; it tells the Macro Assembler that it has reached the end of the source file and designates the initial entry point when the executable program is loaded by OS/2.

Note that we did not declare a segment with attribute *STACK* in this source file, as we would have done under MS-DOS. In OS/2 programs, the stack is conveniently declared in the module definition file instead. You can, however, still declare it the old-fashioned way within the ASM file with a *segment...ends* sequence or with the special MASM directive *.STACK*.

The Module Definition File HELLO.DEF

The file HELLO.DEF (Figure 3-12) is the module definition file for our program. It demonstrates only a few of the possible directives and options that can be used in such a file.

The NAME directive states that we are building an executable program rather than a dynamic link library (whose DEF file would contain LIBRARY instead). PROTMODE signifies that the program will run in protected mode.

```
NAME HELLO WINDOWCOMPAT ; module name
PROTMODE                 ; protected mode only
DATA PRELOAD READWRITE
CODE PRELOAD
STACKSIZE 4096
```

Figure 3-12. *The module definition file HELLO.DEF for the sample application program HELLO.EXE. Note that the stack size is declared here rather than in the HELLO.ASM file.*

The lines beginning with *DATA* and *CODE* declare a few of the many possible segment attributes for the segments that use the Microsoft naming conventions *_DATA* and *_TEXT*. Segments in the program that used other names would be assigned attributes with the SEGMENTS directive.

The stack size for the program's initial point of execution is defined by the STACKSIZE directive; *PUSH* and *POP* instructions will access this area of scratch memory. This stack is placed in *DGROUP* above the program's data and is referenced using the same selector (that is, DS=SS). Microsoft recommends that at least 2 KB of stack space be available at the time of any kernel API call, in addition to the stack space used by the program. Stacks for additional threads must be allocated by the program at run time (as is explained further in Chapter 12).

OS/2 PROGRAMMING TOOLS

Writing an OS/2 Kernel application is an iterative cycle with four basic steps:

1. Use a text editor to create or modify an ASCII source code file and module definition (DEF) file.

2. Use an assembler or high level language compiler to translate the source file into relocatable object code.

3. Use a linker to transform the relocatable object code into an executable OS/2 load module.

4. Use a debugger to methodically test and debug the program.

An OS/2 software developer might find the following additional utilities necessary or helpful:

- LIB, which creates and maintains object module libraries

- IMPLIB, which creates import reference libraries

- CREF, which generates a cross-reference listing

- MAKE, which compares dates of files and carries out operations based on the result of the comparison

- BIND, which converts a protected mode executable file into one that can be used in either protected mode or real mode

- MARKEXE, which marks an application's header so that it can run in a window under Presentation Manager

- RC, which compiles Presentation Manager resources such as icons, bit-maps, and menus and merges them into an application

- CodeView, Microsoft's symbolic debugger

This chapter is an operational overview of the Microsoft (and IBM) tools for programming OS/2 Kernel applications, including the Macro Assembler, C Compiler, Linker, Library Manager, MAKE, CREF, and BIND. The CodeView debugger, the MARKEXE utility, and the tools specific to the Presentation Manager (such as RC) are not discussed here, and IMPLIB is covered in Chapter 19. Even if your preferred programming language is not C or assembler, you will need at least a passing familiarity with the tools described in this chapter because all the examples in the IBM and Microsoft OS/2 reference manuals are written in either C or assembler.

The survey in this chapter, together with the sample programs and reference section elsewhere in this book, is intended to provide the experienced programmer with sufficient information to begin writing useful programs. If you lack a background in C, assembly language, or the 80286/386 architecture, refer to the tutorial and reference works listed in Appendix C.

File Types

The OS/2 programming tools can create and process files of many types. The extensions conventionally used for these files appear in Figure 4-1.

Extension	*File Type*
ASM	Assembly language source file
C	C program source file
CRF	Cross-reference information file, produced by the assembler for processing by CREF
DEF	Module definition file, which specifies the characteristics of each program segment, the size of the heap and stack, and any imported and exported functions for dynamic linking
DLL	An OS/2 dynamic link library
EXE	An OS/2 segmented executable load module; requires additional relocation and dynamic linking at run time
H	C "header" file; contains C source code for constants, macros, and functions and is merged into another C program with #include
INC	"Include" file for assembly language programs; typically contains macros and/or equates for systemwide values such as error codes
LIB	Object module library file comprising one or more OBJ files, indexed and manipulated by the LIB utility

(continued)

Figure 4-1. *Conventionally assigned extensions associated with various file types under OS/2.*

Figure 4-1. *continued*

Extension	File Type
LST	Program listing produced by the assembler; includes machine code, memory locations, original program text, and any error messages
MAP	Listing of symbols and their locations within a load module, produced by the Linker
OBJ	Relocatable object code file produced by an assembler or compiler
RC	Resource Compiler source file; specifies menus, dialog boxes, strings, icons, cursors, and bitmaps for inclusion in a PM application
REF	Cross-reference listing produced by CREF from the information in a CRF file
RES	Intermediate file produced by Resource Compiler from an RC file; merged into an EXE file to build a PM application
SYS	An OS/2 device driver

Using the Macro Assembler

The Microsoft Macro Assembler is distributed as the file MASM.EXE. When it begins a program translation, the Macro Assembler needs the following information: the name of the file containing the source program, the filename for the object program to be created, the destination of the program listing, and the filename for the information that is later processed by the cross-reference utility (CREF).

You can invoke the assembler in two ways. If you enter the name of the assembler alone, you will be prompted for the names of each of the various input and output files. The assembler supplies reasonable defaults for all responses except the source filename. For example:

```
[C:\] MASM  <Enter>
Microsoft (R) Macro Assembler Version 5.10
Copyright (C) Microsoft Corp 1981, 1988. All rights reserved.

Source filename [.ASM]: HELLO  <Enter>
Object filename [HELLO.OBJ]:  <Enter>
Source listing  [NUL.LST]:  <Enter>
Cross-reference [NUL.CRF]:  <Enter>

  48982 Bytes symbol space free

      0 Warning Errors
      0 Severe  Errors

[C:\]
```

You can use a logical device name (such as PRN or COM1) at any of the assembler prompts to send any of the outputs of the assembler to a character device rather than to a file. Note that the default destination for the listing and cross-reference files is the NUL device; that is, no file is created. If you end any response with a semicolon, the remaining responses are assumed to be the default.

A more efficient way to use the assembler is to supply all parameters on the command line:

MASM [*options*] *source*,[*object*],[*listing*],[*crossref*]

For example, the following command lines are equivalent to the interactive session above:

```
[C:\] MASM HELLO,,NUL,NUL  <Enter>
```

or

```
[C:\] MASM HELLO;  <Enter>
```

These commands use the file HELLO.ASM as source, generate the object code file HELLO.OBJ, and send the listing and cross-reference files to the bit bucket.

The Macro Assembler accepts a number of optional parameters or switches on the command line that control code generation and output files. The switches accepted by MASM versions 5.1 and later are listed in Figure 4-2. In other versions of the Microsoft Macro Assembler, additional or fewer switches might be available. For exact instructions, see the manual that corresponds to the version of the assembler you are using.

Switch	*Meaning*
/A	Arranges segments in alphabetic order
/B*n*	Sets size of source file buffer (in KB)
/C	Forces creation of a cross-reference (CRF) file
/D	Produces listing on both passes (to find phase errors)
/D*symbol*	Defines *symbol* as a null text string (*symbol* can be referenced by conditional assembly directives in file)
/E	Assembles for 80x87 numeric coprocessor emulator using IEEE real number format

(continued)

Figure 4-2. *Summary of Microsoft Macro Assembler version 5.1 switches and options.*

Figure 4-2. *continued*

Switch	Meaning
/H	Displays the MASM command line syntax and available options
/I*path*	Sets search path for include files
/L	Forces creation of a program listing file
/LA	Forces listing of all generated code
/ML	Preserves case sensitivity in all names (uppercase names are distinct from their lowercase equivalents)
/MU	Converts all lowercase names to uppercase
/MX	Preserves lowercase in external names only (names defined with *public* or *extrn* directives)
/N	Suppresses generation of tables of macros, structures, records, segments, groups, and symbols at the end of the listing
/P	Checks for impure code in 80286/386 protected mode
/S	Arranges segments in order of occurrence (default)
/T	"Terse" mode, suppresses all messages unless errors are encountered during the assembly
/V	"Verbose" mode, reports number of lines and symbols at end of assembly
/W*n*	Sets error display ("warning") level, $n = 0$, 1, or 2
/X	Forces listing of false conditionals
/Z	Displays source lines containing errors on the screen
/Zd	Includes line number information in OBJ file
/Zi	Includes line number and symbol information in OBJ file

The assembler allows you to override the default extensions on any file—a "feature" that can be rather dangerous. For example, if in the previous example you had responded to the *Object filename* prompt with HELLO.ASM, the assembler would have accepted the entry without comment and over-written your source file. You are unlikely to make this mistake in the interactive command mode, but you must be very careful with file extensions when MASM is run from a batch or "make" file.

Using the C Compiler

The Microsoft C Compiler consists of three executable files (C1.EXE, C2.EXE, and C3.EXE) that implement the C preprocessor, language translator, code generator, and code optimizer. An additional control program, CL.EXE, is provided to execute the three compiler files in order (passing each the necessary information about filenames and compilation options) and to execute the Microsoft Segmented Executable Linker (LINK.EXE).

Before you use the C Compiler and the Linker, set up four environment variables:

PATH=*path*	Used by CL.EXE to find the three executable C compiler files (C1, C2, and C3) if they are not found in the current directory
INCLUDE=*path*	Specifies the location of include files that do not reside in the current directory
LIB=*path*	Specifies the location(s) for object code libraries that do not reside in the current directory
TMP=*path*	Specifies the location for temporary working files created by the C Compiler and Linker

CL.EXE does not support an interactive mode or response files. You always invoke it with a command line of the form:

CL [*options*] *file* [*file* ...]

You can list any number of files; if a file has a C extension, it is compiled into a relocatable object (OBJ) module file. Ordinarily, if no errors are encountered during compilation, all resulting OBJ files and any additional OBJ files specified on the command line are automatically passed to the Linker along with the names of the appropriate runtime libraries.

The C Compiler has many options for controlling its memory models, output files, and code generation and optimization. These options are summarized in Figure 4-3. Unlike the options available in MASM, the options available in the C Compiler are case-sensitive. The arcane switch syntax is largely derived from UNIX, so don't expect it to make any sense.

Switch	Meaning
/A*x*	Selects memory model
	d = assume DS = SS
	C = compact model
	H = huge model
	L = large model
	M = medium model
	S = small model (default)
	u = assume DS != SS; DS reloaded on function entry
	w = assume DS != SS; DS not reloaded on function entry
/c	Compiles only, does not invoke Linker
/C	Does not strip comments
/D<*name*>[=*text*]	Defines macro or constant used in source file
/E	Sends preprocessor output to standard output
/EP	Same as /E, but no line numbers
/F <*n*>	Sets stack size (in hex bytes)

(continued)

Figure 4-3. *Summary of Microsoft C version 5.1 compiler switches and options.*

Figure 4-3. *continued*

Switch	Meaning
/Fa[*filename*]	Generates assembly listing
/Fb[*filename*]	Invokes BIND and LINK to create dual mode executable
/Fc[*filename*]	Generates mixed source/object listing
/Fe[*filename*]	Forces executable filename
/Fl[*filename*]	Generates object listing file
/Fm[*filename*]	Generates map file
/Fo[*filename*]	Forces object module filename
/FP*x*	Floating point control
	a = calls with alternate math library
	c = calls with emulator library
	c87 = calls with 8087 library
	i = inline with emulator (default)
	i87 = inline with 8087
/Fs[*filename*]	Generates source listing
/G*x*	Selects code generation
	0 = 8086 instructions (default)
	1 = 186 instructions
	2 = 286 instructions
	c = Pascal style function calls
	s = no stack checking
	t[n] = data size threshold
/H<*n*>	Specifies external name length
/HELP	Displays the C Compiler command line syntax and available options
/I<*path*>	Specifies additional *#include* path
/J	Sets default *char* type to *unsigned*
/Lc	Links for execution under MS-DOS
/link [*options*]	Passes switches and library names to Linker
/Lp	Links for execution under OS/2
/Lr	Same as /Lc
/ND *name*	Assigns *name* to data segment
/NM *name*	Assigns *name* to module
/NT *name*	Assigns *name* to code (text) segment
/O*x*	Selects optimization
	a = ignore aliasing
	d = disable optimizations
	i = enable intrinsic functions
	l = enable loop optimizations
	n = disable "unsafe" optimizations
	p = enable precision optimizations
	r = disable in-line return
	s = optimize for space
	t = optimize for speed (default)
	w = ignore aliasing except across function calls
	x = maximum optimization (/Oailt /Gs)

(continued)

Figure 4-3. *continued*

Switch	Meaning
/P	Sends preprocessor output to file
/S*x*	Source listing control
	l<columns> = set line width
	p<lines> = set page length
	s<string> = set subtitle string
	t<string> = set title string
/Tc*<file>*	Compiles file without C extension
/u	Removes all predefined macros
/U*<name>*	Removes specified predefined macro
/V*<string>*	Sets version string
/W*<n>*	Sets warning level (0–3)
/X	Ignores the *INCLUDE* environment variable when searching for include files
/Z*x*	Miscellaneous compilation control
	a = disable extensions
	c = make Pascal functions case-insensitive
	d = line number information
	e = enable extensions (default)
	g = generate declarations
	i = symbolic debugging information
	l = remove default library information
	p<n> = pack structures on n-*byte boundary*
	s = syntax check only

Using the Linker

The object module produced by an assembler or compiler from a source file is in a form that contains relocation information. It can also contain unresolved references to external locations or routines. The Linker accepts one or more object modules, resolves external references, includes any necessary routines from designated libraries, performs any offset relocations that might be necessary, and writes a file that can be loaded and executed by the OS/2 operating system.

As with the Macro Assembler, you can supply parameters to the Linker interactively or enter all the required information on a single command line. If you simply enter the utility name alone, the following dialog ensues.

```
[C:\] LINK  <Enter>

Microsoft (R) Segmented-Executable Linker  Version 5.01.21
Copyright (C) Microsoft Corp 1984-1988.  All rights reserved.

Object Modules [.OBJ]: HELLO  <Enter>
Run File [HELLO.EXE]:  <Enter>
List File [NUL.MAP]: HELLO  <Enter>
Libraries [.LIB]: OS2  <Enter>
Definitions File [NUL.DEF]: HELLO  <Enter>

[C:\]
```

The input files for this run of the Linker are the object module HELLO.OBJ,
the module definition file HELLO.DEF, and the import library OS2.LIB
(which contains dynlink reference records for the OS/2 kernel API). The
output files are HELLO.EXE (the executable program) and HELLO.MAP
(the load map produced by the Linker after all references and addresses are
resolved, Figure 4-4).

```
 HELLO

 Start      Length    Name                    Class
 0001:0000  00012H    _DATA                   DATA
 0002:0000  00027H    _TEXT                   CODE


 Origin     Group
 0001:0     DGROUP


 Program entry point at 0002:0000
```

Figure 4-4. *Map produced by Linker during the generation of the HELLO.EXE program, Figure 3-11 in Chapter 3. The program contains one CODE segment and one
DATA segment. The STACK size was set by an entry in the HELLO.DEF file and is
therefore not shown as a segment. The first instruction to be executed lies in the first
byte of the CODE segment. This simple program declares only one group: the "automatic data group" DGROUP, which must be present in all OS/2 programs.*

You can obtain the same result more quickly by entering all parameters on the command line:

LINK [*options*] *objectfiles*, [*exefile*], [*mapfile*], [*libraries*], [*deffile*]

Thus, the command line equivalent to the session above is as follows:

```
[C:\] LINK HELLO,,HELLO,OS2,HELLO  <Enter>
```

The entry of a semicolon as the last character of the command line causes the Linker to assume the default values for all further parameters. This is not normally a useful feature in OS/2 development, however, because dynamic link reference libraries and module definition files are almost always required.

A third method of commanding the Linker is to use a *response file*. A response file contains lines of text that correspond to the responses you would give the Linker interactively. The name of the response file is specified on the command line with a leading @ character:

LINK @*filename*

The name of a response file can also be entered at any prompt. If the response file is not complete, a prompt is issued for the missing information.

When entering Linker commands, you can specify multiple object files with the + operator or with spaces, as in the following:

```
[C:\] LINK HELLO+VMODE+DOSINT,MYPROG,,OS2,HELLO  <Enter>
```

which links the files HELLO.OBJ, VMODE.OBJ, and DOSINT.OBJ, using the import library OS2.LIB, and produces a file named MYPROG.EXE. LINK uses the current drive and directory if you do not explicitly specify otherwise in a filename. It does not automatically use the same drive and directory you specified for a previous file on the same command line.

If multiple library files are to be searched, enter them in the *libraries* field separated by + or space characters. You can specify a maximum of 32 libraries. The default libraries provided with each of the high level language compilers are searched during the linkage process (if the Linker can find them), unless you explicitly exclude them with the /NOD option. The Linker first looks for libraries in the current directory of the default disk drive, then along any paths that are provided in the command line, and finally along the path or paths specified by the LIB variable (if it is present in the environment).

The Linker accepts a number of optional parameters as part of the command line or at the end of any interactive prompt. These switches are listed in Figure 4-5. The number of options available varies between different versions of the Microsoft Linker. See your Linker reference manual for detailed information about your particular version.

Switch	Meaning
/A:*n*	Sets segment *sector* alignment factor. N must be a power of 2 (default = 512). Not related to logical segment alignment (byte, word, para, page, etc.). Relevant to segmented executable files (Microsoft Windows and OS/2) only.
/B	Suppresses Linker prompt if a library cannot be found in the current directory or in the locations specified by the *LIB* environment variable.
/CO	Includes symbolic debugging information in the EXE file for use by CodeView.
/CP	Sets the field in the EXE file header controlling the amount of memory allocated to the program in addition to the memory required for the program's code, stack, and initialized data. Relevant to real mode programs only.
/DO	Uses standard Microsoft segment naming and ordering conventions.
/DS	Loads data at the high end of the data segment. Relevant to real mode programs only.
/E	Packs executable file by removing sequences of repeated bytes and optimizing relocation table.
/F	Optimizes far calls to labels that are within the same physical segment for speed by replacing them with near calls and NOPs.
/HE	Displays information about available options.
/HI	Loads the program as high in memory as possible. Relevant to real mode programs only.
/I	Displays information about link progress, including pass numbers and the names of object files being linked.
/INC	Forces production of SYM and ILK files for subsequent use by ILINK (incremental Linker). Cannot be used with /EXEPACK.
/LI	Writes the address of the first instruction that corresponds to each source code line to the map file. Has no effect if compiler does not include line number information in the object module. Forces creation of a map file.

(continued)

Figure 4-5. *Switches accepted by Linker versions 5.01 and later.*

Figure 4-5. *continued*

Switch	Meaning
/M[:*n*]	Forces creation of a MAP file listing all public symbols sorted by name and by location. The optional value *n* is the maximum number of symbols which may be sorted (default = 2048); when *n* is supplied, the alphabetically sorted list is omitted.
/NOD	Skips search of any default compiler libraries that are specified in OBJ file.
/NOE	Ignores the extended library dictionary (if it is present). The extended dictionary ordinarily provides the linker with information about inter-module dependencies to speed up linking.
/NOF	Disables optimization of far calls to labels within the same segment.
/NOG	Causes the Linker to ignore group associations when assigning addresses to data and code items. Revelant for real mode programs only.
/NOI	Does not ignore case in names during LINK.
/NON	Arranges segments as for /DO but does not insert 16 null bytes at start of _TEXT segment.
/NOP	Does not pack contiguous logical code segments into a single physical segment.
/O:*n*	Controls the interrupt number used by the overlay manager supplied with some Microsoft high level languages. Relevant for real mode programs only.
/PAC[:*n*]	Packs contiguous logical code segments into a single physical code segment. *N* is the maximum size for each packed physical code segment (default = 65,536 bytes). Segments in different groups are not packed.
/PADC:*n*	Adds *n* filler bytes to the end of each code module, so that a larger module can be inserted later with ILINK (incremental Linker).
/PADD:*n*	Adds *n* filler bytes to the end of each data module, so that a larger module can be inserted later with ILINK (incremental Linker).
/PAU	Pauses during linking, allowing a change of diskettes before the EXE file is written.
/SE:*n*	Sets the maximum number of segments in the linked program (default = 128).
/ST:*n*	Sets stack size of program in bytes; ignores stack segment size declarations within object modules.
/W	Displays warning messages for offsets that are relative to a segment base that is not the same as the group base. Relevant to segmented executable files (Windows and OS/2) only.

Using the CREF Utility

The CREF cross-reference utility processes a CRF file produced by the assembler, creating an ASCII text file with the default extension REF. The file contains a cross-reference listing of all symbols declared in the program and the line numbers in which they are referenced (see Figure 4-6). The line numbers given in the cross-reference listing correspond to the line numbers that are generated by the assembler in the program listing (LST) file — *not* to any physical line count in the original source file.

```
Microsoft Cross-Reference  Version 5.10      Thu Feb 09 10:04:22 1989
HELLO -- Display Message on stdout


   Symbol Cross-Reference          (# definition, + modification)     Cref-1


@CPU . . . . . . . . . . . . .      1#      3#
@VERSION . . . . . . . . . .        1#


CODE . . . . . . . . . . . .        33


DATA . . . . . . . . . . .          23
DGROUP . . . . . . . . . . .        20      35      41      44
DOSEXIT. . . . . . . . . . .        18#     51      55
DOSWRITE . . . . . . . . . .        17#     45


ERROR. . . . . . . . . . . .        47      53#


MSG. . . . . . . . . . . . .        25#     41
MSG_LEN. . . . . . . . . . .        26#     42


PRINT. . . . . . . . . . . .        37#     57      61


STDERR . . . . . . . . . . .        15#
STDIN. . . . . . . . . . . .        13#
STDOUT . . . . . . . . . . .        14#     39


WLEN . . . . . . . . . . . .        28#     44


_DATA. . . . . . . . . . . .        20      23#     30
_TEXT. . . . . . . . . . . .        33#     35      59


17 Symbols
```

Figure 4-6. *Cross-reference listing HELLO.REF produced by the CREF utility from the file HELLO.CRF, for the HELLO.EXE program example, Figure 3-11 in Chapter 3. The symbols declared in the program are listed on the left in alphabetic order. To the right of each symbol is a list of all of the lines where that symbol is referenced. The number with a # sign after it denotes the line where the symbol is declared. Numbers followed by a + sign indicate that the symbol is modified at the specified line.*

You can supply parameters for CREF interactively or include them on a single command line. If you enter the name CREF alone, it prompts you for the input and output filenames:

```
[C:\] CREF  <Enter>
Microsoft (R) Cross-Reference Utility  Version 5.10
Copyright (C) Microsoft Corp 1981-1985, 1987.  All rights reserved.

Cross-reference [.CRF]: HELLO  <Enter>
Listing [HELLO.REF]:  <Enter>

17 Symbols

[C:\]
```

The parameters can also be entered on the command line as follows:

CREF *crossreffile*,[*listingfile*]

For example, the command line equivalent to the interactive session above is the following:

```
[C:\] CREF HELLO;  <Enter>
```

If CREF cannot find the specified CRF file, an error message is displayed. Otherwise, the cross-reference listing is left in the specified file on the disk. To direct CREF to send the cross-reference listing directly to a character device (such as the printer) as it is generated, respond with the name of the device at the *Listing* prompt.

Using the Library Manager

Although the object modules that are produced by the assembler or by high level language compilers can be linked directly into executable load modules, they can also be collected into special files called *object module libraries*. The modules in a library are indexed by name and by the public symbols they contain so that the Linker can extract them to satisfy external references in a program.

The Microsoft Library Manager (LIB) creates and maintains object module libraries — adding, updating, and deleting object modules as needed. The Librarian is also capable of checking a library file for internal consistency, or of printing a table of its contents. Figure 4-7 shows a portion of such a table for the Microsoft C library SLIBC.LIB. The first part of the listing is an alphabetic list of all public names declared in all of the modules in the library. Each name is associated with the object module to which it belongs. The second part of the listing is an alphabetic list of the module names in the library. Each name is followed by the offset of the object module within the library file and its actual size in bytes. Following the entry for each module is a summary of the public names declared within it.

LIB follows the command conventions of most other Microsoft programming tools. You must supply it with the name of a library file to work on, one or more *operations,* the name of a listing file or device, and (optionally) the name of the output library. If no name is specified for the output library, it is given the same name as the input library, and the extension of the input library is changed to BAK.

The LIB *operations* are simply names of object modules, with a prefix character that specifies the action to be taken: − to delete an object module from the library, * to extract a module and place it in a separate OBJ file, or + to add an object module or the entire contents of another library to the

```
_abort...........abort              _abs.............abs
_access..........access             _asctime.........asctime
_atof............atof               _atoi............atoi
_atol............atol               _bdos............bdos
_brk.............brk                _brkctl..........brkctl
_bsearch.........bsearch            _calloc..........calloc
_cgets...........cgets              _chdir...........dir
_chmod...........chmod              _chsize..........chsize


              .                                  .
              .                                  .
              .                                  .


_exit            Offset: 00000010H  Code and data size: 44H
   __exit


_filbuf          Offset: 00000160H  Code and data size: BBH
   __filbuf


_file            Offset: 00000300H  Code and data size: CAH
   __iob           __iob2              __lastiob


              .                                  .
              .                                  .
              .                                  .
```

Figure 4-7. *Extract from the table-of-contents listing produced by the Library Manager for the Microsoft C library SCLIBC.LIB.*

program library. The command prefixes can also be combined: −+ has the effect of replacing a module, while ∗− has the effect of extracting a module into a new file and then deleting it from the library.

When the Librarian is invoked with its name alone, it will request the other information it needs interactively. For example:

```
[C:\] LIB  <Enter>

Microsoft (R) Library Manager  Version 3.11
Copyright (C) Microsoft Corp 1983-1988. All rights reserved.

Library name:  SLIBC  <Enter>
Operations: +VIDEO  <Enter>
List file:  SLIBC.LST  <Enter>
Output library:  SLIBC2  <Enter>

[C:\]
```

In this case, the object module VIDEO.OBJ was added to the library SLIBC.LIB, a library table of contents was written into the file SLIB.LST, and the resulting new library was named SLIBC2.LIB.

The Library Manager can also be run with a command line as follows:

LIB *library* [*operations*],[*list*],[*newlibrary*]

For example, the following command line is equivalent to the preceding interactive session:

```
[C:\] LIB SLIBC +VIDEO,SLIBC.LST,SLIBC2  <Enter>
```

As with the other Microsoft utilities, a semicolon at the end of the command line causes the default responses to be used for any parameters that are omitted.

Like the Linker, the Librarian is capable of accepting its commands from a response file. The contents of the file are simply lines of text that correspond exactly to the responses you would give LIB interactively. Specify the name of the response file on the command line with a leading @ character:

LIB @*filename*

LIB has only three options: /I (/IGNORECASE), /N (/NOIGNORECASE), and /PAGESIZE. Using /NOIGNORECASE causes LIB to regard symbols that differ only in the case of their component letters as distinct. (The default is to ignore case.)

The /PAGESIZE switch is used in the following form:

/PAGESIZE:*number*

It is placed immediately after the library filename. Specify the library page size in bytes as a power of 2 between 16 and 32,768 (16, 32, 64...); the default is 16 bytes. The page size defines the size of a unit of allocation space for a given library. Because the index to a library is always a fixed number of pages, setting a larger page size allows you to store more object modules in that library; it will, on the other hand, result in more unused space within the file.

Using BIND and API.LIB

The BIND utility converts a protected mode segmented executable file into a file that can be executed in either protected mode or real mode. BIND accomplishes this somewhat magical feat by appending a real mode loader to the program, along with a real mode routine specific to each API service that it uses. When the file is used in real mode, the API-specific procedures remap the API call parameters into MS-DOS or ROM BIOS function calls. When the file is loaded in protected mode, the real mode loader and other routines appended by BIND are simply ignored.

The BIND utility can process any protected mode program. However, for the file to be *executed* successfully, it must meet the following conditions:

- The program cannot use any OS/2 kernel services that are not members of the Family API when it is running in real mode.

- The entire program and the code appended to it by BIND must fit into the available "conventional" memory space (below 640 KB).

BIND is command line driven — it does not have an interactive mode, nor can it handle response files. The BIND utility is invoked with an entry of the following form:

BIND *infile* [*file*.LIB...] [*file*.OBJ ...] [*options*]

Under normal conditions, the two libraries API.LIB and OS2.LIB must be specified in the command line. Other libraries, particularly dynlink reference libraries, might also be necessary. BIND does not search the directories named in the *LIB* environment variable, so the locations of libraries must be explicit.

The default extension for *infile* is EXE; the output of BIND will receive the same filename unless otherwise specified with an *options* switch. The BIND options are listed in Figure 4-8 on the following page.

Option	Description
/o *outfile*	Specifies the name of the output EXE file (default = same name as input EXE file)
/n *name(s)*	Specifies one or more ''protected mode only'' functions to be mapped to the *BadDynLink* function
/n @*filename*	Specifies the name of a file containing one or more ''protected mode only'' function names to be mapped to the *BadDynLink* function
/m	Produces a map file named *outfile*.BM

Figure 4-8. *Options for the BIND utility, version 1.1.*

Using the MAKE Utility

The primary function of the MAKE utility is to compare dates of files and to carry out commands based on the result of that comparison. Because of this single, rather basic capability, MAKE can be used to maintain complex programs built from many modules. The dates of source, object, and executable files are simply compared in a logical sequence, and the assembler, compiler, linker, and other programming tools are invoked as appropriate.

The MAKE utility processes a plain ASCII text file called, as you might expect, a ''make'' file. The utility is command line driven and is started with an entry of the following form:

MAKE *makefile* [*options*]

By convention, a make file has the same name as the executable file which is being maintained, but it takes no extension. The available MAKE options are listed in Figure 4-9.

Option	Description
/D	Displays last modification date of each file as it is processed
/I	Ignores exit (''return'') codes returned by commands and programs executed as a result of dependency statements
/N	Displays commands that would be executed as a result of dependency statements but does not execute those commands
/S	Does not display commands as they are executed
/X *filename*	Directs error messages from MAKE, or from any program that MAKE runs, to the specified file; if *filename* is a hyphen (-), error messages are directed to the standard output

Figure 4-9. *Options for the MAKE utility, version 4.07.*

A simple make file contains one or more *dependency statements* separated by blank lines. Each dependency statement can be followed by a list of OS/2 commands in the following form:

targetfile : *sourcefile ...*
    command
    command
    .
    .
    .

If the date and time of any *sourcefile* are later than the *targetfile*, the accompanying list of commands is carried out. Comment lines, which begin with a # character, can be used freely. MAKE can also process inference rules and macro definitions; for further details on these advanced capabilities, see the Microsoft or IBM documentation.

A Complete Example

Let's put together everything we've learned about using the OS/2 programming tools up to this point. The general process of creating an application program for OS/2, including use of the Resource Compiler (RC) to build a Presentation Manager application (not within the scope of this book), is illustrated in Figure 4-10 on the following page.

Assume that we have the source for the HELLO program discussed in Chapter 3 in the file HELLO.ASM, and assume that the definition file for the same program is named HELLO.DEF. Assume further that both files are located in the current directory. To assemble the source program into the relocatable object module HELLO.OBJ, producing a program listing in the file HELLO.LST and a cross-reference data file HELLO.CRF, we would enter the following command:

```
[C:\] MASM HELLO,,HELLO,HELLO  <Enter>
```

To convert the relocatable object file HELLO.OBJ into the executable file HELLO.EXE, using the module definition file HELLO.DEF and the import library OS2.LIB, and to create a load map in the file HELLO.MAP, we would enter the following:

```
[C:\] LINK HELLO,,HELLO,OS2,HELLO  <Enter>
```

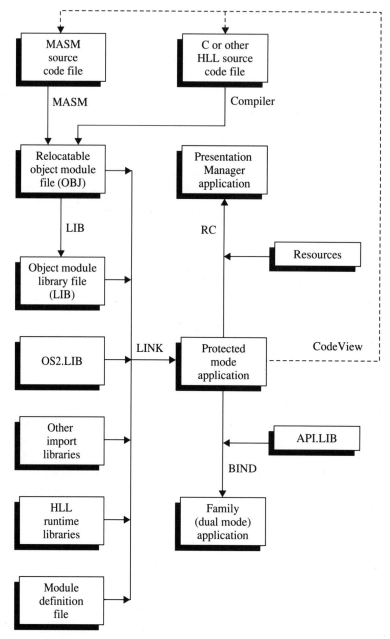

Figure 4-10. *Creation of an OS/2 application program, proceeding from source code to executable file.*

Because our HELLO program uses only the OS/2 functions *DosWrite* and *DosExit*, both of which are members of the Family API, it can be converted to a Family application that runs in either DOS compatibility mode or protected mode. This conversion is performed with the BIND utility and API.LIB by entering the following command:

```
[C:\] BIND HELLO.EXE \LIB\API.LIB \LIB\OS2.LIB <Enter>
```

OS2.LIB must also be specified because its functions are exported by ordinal numbers rather than by name. Without reference to the ordinals in the OS2.LIB file, BIND can't match the functions imported in the HELLO.EXE header to API.LIB. Note also that BIND.EXE does *not* use the LIB environment variable, so the locations of API.LIB and OS2.LIB must be explicit (including drive name if necessary).

The new HELLO.EXE file produced by BIND can execute in either real mode or protected mode on an 80286 or 80386 machine. To truly generalize this program and obtain a HELLO.EXE file that could run on any 80x86-based machine under MS-DOS or OS/2, we would have to replace all 80286-specific instructions in the source code with equivalent sequences that can run on an 8086/88. For example, we would need to replace the instruction

```
push    msg_len
```

with the instructions

```
mov     ax,msg_len
push    ax
```

To locate the 80286-specific instructions in a program, simply remove the *.286* directive from the source file and reassemble it; each instruction that does not run on an 8086/88 processor is then flagged as an error.

To automate the entire process we have described, we could create a make file named HELLO (with no extension) that contains the following:

```
HELLO.OBJ : HELLO.ASM
        MASM /T HELLO,,HELLO,HELLO

HELLO.EXE : HELLO.OBJ HELLO.DEF
        LINK HELLO,,HELLO,OS2,HELLO
        BIND HELLO.EXE \LIB\API.LIB \LIB\OS2.LIB
```

Then, whenever we change either HELLO.ASM or HELLO.DEF and want to rebuild the executable HELLO.EXE file, we need only enter the following:

```
[C:\] MAKE HELLO   <Enter>
```

Note that the /T switch in the MASM command line suppresses all messages unless errors are encountered during assembly.

PROGRAMMING THE USER INTERFACE

KEYBOARD AND MOUSE INPUT

The two primary means of user input in OS/2 are the keyboard and mouse. Keyboard support is, of course, always available; the base keyboard driver is always loaded during system initialization. In contrast, loading of the mouse driver is optional; the user must select the appropriate mouse driver by adding a DEVICE directive to the system's CONFIG.SYS file. The OS/2 retail package includes drivers for several brands of mice, including all models of the Microsoft Mouse.

Keyboard Methods and Modes

A Kernel application can obtain input from the keyboard in three ways:

- *Kbd* (keyboard subsystem) API calls

- *DosRead* with the predefined handle for the standard input (0)

- *DosRead* with a handle obtained by opening logical device CON or KBD$

The *Kbd* functions provide the most flexibility in keyboard management. Functionally, they are a superset of the ROM BIOS keyboard driver (Int 16H) calls that real mode DOS applications commonly use.

Ordinarily, the second method, calling *DosRead* with the standard input handle, is used only by applications — such as filters, compilers, and linkers — that process simple text streams and do not require rapid and flexible interaction with the user. The user can easily redirect the standard input to a file or character device other than the keyboard.

The last method, *DosRead* with a handle obtained by an explicit open of CON or KBD$, is rarely used. It is appropriate for a program that processes simple text streams but must circumvent redirection, or that needs to use *DosRead* and also perform *DosDevIOCtl* calls to the keyboard driver.

Each screen group has its own default logical keyboard, and the driver maintains a distinct state for each keyboard. (Additional logical keyboards can be created by applications, as will be discussed later in the chapter.) The keyboard state affects the behavior of all the keyboard input functions and includes the status of the shift keys and toggles, the *turnaround character* (logical end-of-line character, usually the Enter key), an echo flag, and an input mode.

The input mode is the element of the keyboard state that is most likely to concern the application programmer. A particular logical keyboard is either in *ASCII* ("*cooked*") *mode* or *binary* ("*raw*") *mode* at any given time.

In ASCII mode (the default condition), the key combinations Ctrl-C, Ctrl-Break, Ctrl-S, Ctrl-P, and Ctrl-PrtSc are detected by the operating system and receive special treatment. The echoing of characters to the display and the handling of "extended" keys and the turnaround character depend on the input function being used.

In binary mode, characters are never echoed to the display. The turnaround character, extended keys, and special key combinations Ctrl-C, Ctrl-Break, Ctrl-S, Ctrl-P, and Ctrl-PrtSc are passed through to the application unchanged.

> **NOTE:** *The special characters Ctrl-Esc, Alt-Esc, Ctrl-Alt-Del, Ctrl-Alt-NumLock, and PrtSc are always trapped by the operating system, regardless of the input mode, and an application cannot read or intercept them.*

Input with *Kbd* Functions

The *Kbd* functions provide a variety of keyboard input and control services (Figure 5-1). These range in complexity from single character input to installation of custom code pages (tables that map the keyboard to specific character codes).

The prototypal *Kbd* input operation is *KbdCharIn*, which returns an ASCII character code, a scan code, a time stamp, and a word of flags for the keyboard shift keys and toggles. The character is not echoed to the display. Extended keys return a 00H or an E0H in the ASCII character field; the application must inspect the scan code to identify the key. *KbdCharIn* has a

Function	Description
Keyboard Input	
KbdCharIn	Reads character without echo
KbdPeek	Returns next character (if any) without removing it from the input buffer
KbdStringIn	Reads a buffered line with echo and editing capability
KbdFlushBuffer	Discards all waiting characters
KbdXlate	Translates scan code and shift states to character
Logical Keyboards	
KbdOpen	Creates logical keyboard
KbdGetFocus	Binds logical keyboard to physical keyboard
KbdFreeFocus	Releases logical to physical keyboard bonding
KbdClose	Destroys logical keyboard
Keyboard Status	
KbdGetCp	Returns keyboard code page ID
KbdGetStatus	Returns keyboard state and flags
Keyboard Configuration	
KbdSetCp	Selects keyboard code page
KbdSetCustXt	Installs custom code page
KbdSetStatus	Configures keyboard state and flags
KbdSynch	Synchronizes keyboard access
Register/Deregister Keyboard Subsystem	
KbdRegister	Registers alternative keyboard subsystem
KbdDeRegister	Deregisters alternative keyboard subsystem

Figure 5-1. *The* Kbd *API at a glance.*

wait/no-wait option, which allows the caller to specify whether the function should block until a key is ready or return immediately if no key is available.

A related function, *KbdPeek*, returns the same information as *KbdCharIn* but does not remove the character from the keyboard input buffer. It allows an application to test keyboard status and to ''look ahead'' by one character. Avoid using *KbdPeek* to ''poll'' the keyboard, however; such polling can severely degrade system performance.

KbdStringIn provides buffered line input. It is called with the address of a buffer, a wait/no-wait parameter, and the address of a structure that contains the buffer length and the amount of data already in the buffer which can be used as an editing template (if any). Upon return, the function places the actual number of characters read in the same structure.

If *KbdStringIn* is called and the keyboard is in ASCII mode, the editing keys are active and all other extended keys are ignored and thrown away. Each character is echoed to the display unless the echo flag is off. Tabs are expanded to spaces using 8-column tab stops when they are echoed, although they are left as the code 09H in the buffer. Input is terminated by the Enter key (placed in the buffer as the single character 0DH) or by the buffer's reaching capacity: When one less than the requested length has been read, additional keystrokes are discarded and a warning beep is sounded until the user presses Enter. The no-wait option is not available in ASCII mode.

In binary mode, *KbdStringIn* returns when the buffer is full, keys are not echoed to the display, and the editing keys are not active. Extended keys are placed in the buffer as a 2-byte sequence: a 00H or an E0H byte followed by the scan code. If a program calls *KbdStringIn* in binary mode with the no-wait option, the function returns immediately with whatever keys are already waiting (up to the maximum requested).

Figures 5-2 and 5-3 illustrate the use of the *KbdCharIn* and *KbdStringIn* calls.

```
                                   ; this structure receives
                                   ; information from KbdCharIn
        kbdinfo db      0          ; ASCII character code
                db      0          ; scan code
                db      0          ; character status
                db      0          ; NLS shift status
                dw      0          ; keyboard shift status
                dd      0          ; time stamp

                .
                .
                .
                                   ; read a character
                push    ds         ; address of structure
                push    offset DGROUP:kbdinfo
                push    0          ; 0 = wait for character
                                   ; 1 = no wait
                push    0          ; default keyboard handle
                call    KbdCharIn  ; transfer to OS/2
                or      ax,ax      ; did read succeed?
                jnz     error      ; jump if function failed
                .
                .
                .
```

Figure 5-2. *Reading a character from the keyboard with* KbdCharIn. *If the no-wait option is used, bit 6 of the character status byte is set if a character was obtained; bit 6 is clear if no character was ready.*

```
buffer  db      80 dup (0)          ; keyboard data goes here

buflen  dw      80                  ; contains length of buffer
        dw      0                   ; contains length of data in
                                    ; buffer for editing and
                                    ; receives length of data
        .
        .
        .

                                    ; indicate nothing is in
                                    ; buffer to be edited...
        mov     word ptr buflen+2,0

        push    ds                  ; input buffer address
        push    offset DGROUP:buffer
        push    ds                  ; control structure address
        push    offset DGROUP:buflen
        push    0                   ; 0 = wait for data
                                    ; 1 = no wait
        push    0                   ; default keyboard handle
        call    KbdStringIn         ; transfer to OS/2
        or      ax,ax               ; did read succeed?
        jnz     error               ; jump if function failed
        .
        .
        .
```

Figure 5-3. *Reading a buffered line from the keyboard with* KbdStringIn. *Note that the second word of the* buflen *structure controls whether the user can edit data already in the buffer (typically from the previous call to* KbdStringIn).

Input with *DosRead*

The general-purpose function *DosRead* accepts a handle, a buffer address, a buffer length, and the address of a variable. The handle must be the system's predefined standard input handle, a handle to a file, device, or pipe inherited from the process's parent, or a handle obtained from a successful *DosOpen* operation. When *DosRead* returns, the requested data is in the buffer, and the actual number of bytes read is in the specified variable. Figure 5-4 on the following page contains an example of buffered keyboard input using *DosRead*.

When *DosRead* is called with the standard input handle (and the standard input has not been redirected) or with a handle that is opened to device KBD$, the kernel converts the *DosRead* into a call to *KbdStringIn*. However, such a *DosRead* request behaves somewhat differently from *KbdStringIn* in two respects.

```
stdin     equ     0               ; standard input handle

buflen    equ     80              ; length of input buffer


buffer    db      buflen dup (0)  ; keyboard data goes here

rdlen     dw      0               ; receives character count


          .
          .
          .
          push    stdin           ; standard input handle
          push    ds              ; input buffer address
          push    offset DGROUP:buffer
          push    buflen          ; maximum characters to read
          push    ds              ; receives actual length
          push    offset DGROUP:rdlen
          call    DosRead         ; transfer to OS/2
          or      ax,ax           ; did read succeed?
          jnz     error           ; jump if function failed
          .
          .
          .
```

Figure 5-4. *Reading a buffered line from the keyboard with* DosRead. *When* DosRead *returns,* rdlen *contains the number of characters actually transferred to the buffer.*

First, in ASCII mode, *DosRead* translates the Enter key into a 2-character sequence in the buffer: a carriage return (0DH) followed by a linefeed (0AH). In binary mode, *DosRead* leaves the Enter key in the buffer as a carriage return only.

The other difference is more subtle. Regardless of the buffer length specified in the *DosRead* call, the kernel calls *KbdStringIn* with a buffer size of 253 characters. This means that the keyboard will not begin to beep and ignore keystrokes until the user has entered 252 keys. However, the number of characters specified in the *DosRead* call is used as the maximum for the input returned to the application, and any excess characters (possibly including the carriage return and linefeed) are discarded.

Although keyboard input with *DosRead* is appropriate for filters — which need the capability of redirectable input — this method is not recommended for interactive applications. The *Kbd* calls are preferred because they are more efficient, allow closer control of the keyboard, and return more detailed information.

If you want to take full advantage of the *Kbd* interface while allowing input redirection in your application, call *DosQHandType* with the standard input handle to determine whether the standard input has been redirected. If *DosQHandType* returns the code for a character device and a device driver attribute word with bit 0 set (1), then the standard input handle has not been redirected, and the application can use the *Kbd* calls throughout its execution. Otherwise, the application should use *DosRead*.

Keyboard Status and Control

Application programs can query or control many aspects of the logical keyboard state, including the code page, the mode (ASCII or binary), the status of shift keys and toggles, the automatic echoing of keys to the display by *KbdStringIn*, and the turnaround key. *Kbd* functions are available to inspect or to alter each of these parameters. A similar set of *DosDevIOCtl* functions is available and can be used by applications that use the *DosRead* model for keyboard input (Figure 5-5).

The most common need for keyboard control in an application is undoubtedly to select ASCII or binary mode. Programs that use the *Kbd* calls can get

Function Number	Operation
50H	Set code page
51H	Set input mode
52H	Set interim character flags
53H	Set shift state
54H	Set typematic rate and delay
55H	Notify change of foreground session
56H	Select Task Manager hot key
57H	Bind logical keyboard to physical keyboard
58H	Set code page ID
5CH	Set national language support and custom code page
5DH	Create logical keyboard
5EH	Destroy logical keyboard
71H	Get input mode
72H	Get interim character flags
73H	Get shift state
74H	Read character
75H	Peek character
76H	Get Task Manager hot key
77H	Get keyboard type
78H	Get code page ID
79H	Translate scan code to ASCII

Figure 5-5. DosDevIOCtl *Category 4 functions for keyboard status and control.*

or set the mode with *KbdGetStatus* and *KbdSetStatus*. These functions use a common data structure that contains much other information, so a program should call *KbdGetStatus* first to fill the structure with valid data. The ASCII/binary mode bits can then be modified and the structure written back to the system with *KbdSetStatus* (Figure 5-6).

```
                             ; keyboard info structure
kdbinfo dw      10           ; length of structure
        dw      0            ; various mode bits
        dw      0            ; logical end-of-line character
        dw      0            ; interim character flags
        dw      0            ; keyboard shift states

oldmode dw      0            ; previous keyboard mode

        .
        .
        .
                             ; get keyboard status...
        push    ds           ; address of structure
        push    offset DGROUP:kbdinfo
        push    0            ; default keyboard handle
        call    KbdGetStatus ; transfer to OS/2
        or      ax,ax        ; did function succeed?
        jnz     error        ; jump if function failed

        mov     ax,kbdinfo+2 ; save current input mode so
        mov     oldmode,ax   ; we can restore it later...

                             ; turn off ASCII bit and
                             ; turn on binary mode bit
        and     word ptr kbdinfo+2,0fff7h
        or      word ptr kbdinfo+2,4

                             ; now set keyboard status...
        push    ds           ; address of structure
        push    offset DGROUP:kbdinfo
        push    0            ; default keyboard handle
        call    KbdSetStatus ; transfer to OS/2
        or      ax,ax        ; did function succeed?
        jnz     error        ; jump if function failed
        .
        .
        .
```

Figure 5-6. *Putting the default logical keyboard into binary mode with* KbdGetStatus *and* KbdSetStatus *so that the application can read Ctrl-C and other special characters. The original mode is saved so that it can be restored later.*

Programs that use *DosRead* for keyboard input can manipulate the mode with *DosDevIOCtl* Category 4 Functions 71H (Get Mode) and 51H (Set Mode). These functions can be used only with a handle obtained by opening KBD$ with *DosOpen*; if you use them with the handle for the standard input or with a handle from a *DosOpen* of CON, the system returns error code 22 *Bad Command* (Figure 5-7).

```
kbdname db      'KBD$',0            ; keyboard device name
khandle dw      0                   ; keyboard handle

oldmode db      0                   ; previous keyboard mode

newmode db      80h                 ; new keyboard mode
                                    ; 0 = ASCII, 80H = binary

        .
        .
        .
                                    ; get keyboard handle...
        push    ds                  ; address of device name
        push    offset DGROUP:kbdname
        push    ds                  ; receives handle
        push    offset DGROUP:khandle
        push    ds                  ; receives DosOpen action
        push    offset DGROUP:kaction
        push    0                   ; file size (not applicable)
        push    0
        push    0                   ; file attribute (ditto)
        push    1                   ; action = open, no create
        push    42h                 ; mode = r/w, deny none
        push    0                   ; reserved DWORD 0
        push    0
        call    DosOpen             ; transfer to OS/2
        or      ax,ax               ; did open succeed?
        jnz     error               ; jump if function failed
        .
        .
        .
```

(continued)

Figure 5-7. *Putting the keyboard into binary mode with* DosDevIOCtl *Category 4 Function 51H so that the application can read Ctrl-C and other special characters. The original mode is obtained first with Category 4 Function 71H so that it can be restored later. Note that* DosDevIOCtl *cannot be used with the standard input handle.*

Figure 5-7. *continued*

```
                                  ; get current input mode so
                                  ; we can restore it later...
          push    ds              ; data packet pointer
          push    offset DGROUP:oldmode
          push    0               ; parameter packet addr. (none)
          push    0
          push    71h             ; function code
          push    4               ; category code
          push    khandle         ; device handle
          call    DosDevIOCtl     ; transfer to OS/2
          or      ax,ax           ; did function succeed?
          jnz     error           ; jump if function failed

                                  ; now set binary mode...
          push    0               ; data packet pointer (none)
          push    0
          push    ds              ; parameter packet pointer
          push    offset DGROUP:newmode
          push    51h             ; function code
          push    4               ; category code
          push    khandle         ; device handle
          call    DosDevIOCtl     ; transfer to OS/2
          or      ax,ax           ; did function succeed?
          jnz     error           ; jump if function failed
          .
          .
          .
```

Using Logical Keyboards

Each screen group has a default logical keyboard that any process can access without further preliminaries using the *Kbd* calls and keyboard handle 0 or using *DosRead* with the standard input handle (0). When a user brings a screen group to the foreground, its logical keyboard is "bound" to the physical keyboard, and the processes in that group can read any keys the user presses. When a screen group is in the background, processes in the group that attempt to read from the keyboard are blocked.

Processes that use the default logical keyboard are vulnerable to interference by other processes in the same group that also use the default. For example, if a process is interacting with the user and performing key-by-key input, and another process also requests a key, the input received by both programs will be unpredictable.

To circumvent this problem, a program can create a new logical keyboard for its screen group with *KbdOpen*, bind that logical keyboard to the physical keyboard with *KbdGetFocus*, and then perform its *Kbd* input operations with the new handle obtained from *KbdOpen* (Figure 5-8). Keyboard input operations by other processes in the same screen group that use the handle for the default keyboard (0) or any other logical keyboard will be blocked while a *KbdGetFocus* is in effect.

When the process finishes obtaining input, it can use *KbdFreeFocus* to sever the bond between its logical keyboard and the physical keyboard, thereby allowing other processes to proceed with *Kbd* operations. The logical keyboard created with *KbdOpen* can be destroyed with *KbdClose*; in any event, it is destroyed when the process terminates as part of the kernel's normal cleanup.

```
khandle dw      0                       ; receives handle for
                                        ; new logical keyboard
        .
        .
        .
                                        ; create a logical keyboard
        push    ds                      ; receives keyboard handle
        push    offset DGROUP:khandle
        call    KbdOpen                 ; transfer to OS/2
        or      ax,ax                   ; did open succeed?
        jnz     error                   ; jump if function failed
        .
        .
        .
                                        ; ready for input, get
                                        ; keyboard focus...
        push    0                       ; 0 = wait if necessary
        push    khandle                 ; keyboard handle
        call    KbdGetFocus             ; transfer to OS/2
        or      ax,ax                   ; did we get focus?
        jnz     error                   ; jump if function failed
        .
        .
                                        ; perform input here...
```

Figure 5-8. *Creating and using a new logical keyboard to prevent keyboard interference by other processes in the same screen group.*

Figure 5-8. *continued*

```
                              ; done with input, release
                              ; keyboard focus...
    push    khandle           ; keyboard handle
    call    KbdFreeFocus      ; transfer to OS/2
    or      ax,ax             ; did release succeed?
    jnz     error             ; jump if function failed
     .
     .
     .

                              ; logical keyboard no longer
                              ; needed, destroy it...
    push    khandle           ; keyboard handle
    call    KbdClose          ; transfer to OS/2
     .
     .
     .
```

Keyboard Subsystems and Drivers

The OS/2 substructure for the keyboard support visible to an application is divided among several modules (Figure 5-9). The character device driver KBD$ (loaded from the file KBD01.SYS or KBD02.SYS) services keyboard interrupts, reads keyboard scan codes from the keyboard controller, and interprets those scan codes as characters according to the code page for the current screen group. KBD$ also cooperates with the kernel's monitor dispatcher to create and maintain device monitor chains for each screen group. The keyboard driver runs in kernel mode (ring 0).

The dynlink library BKSCALLS.DLL contains the Basic Keyboard Subsystem, which implements the *Kbd* services. BKSCALLS communicates with the KBD$ driver through *DosDevIOCtl* calls only; it does not issue *DosRead* or *DosWrite* calls.

The dynlink library KBDCALLS.DLL is called the "keyboard router." It contains the entry points for the *Kbd* API and passes the calls onward to the appropriate subsystem (such as BKSCALLS) on a per-screen-group basis. Both BKSCALLS and KBDCALLS run in user mode and thus access the keyboard hardware only indirectly.

Although BKSCALLS is the default keyboard subsystem for each screen group, part or all of its services can be replaced on a per-screen-group basis. To activate a new subsystem, call *KbdRegister* with a dynlink library name, an entry point name, and a set of flags that indicate which *Kbd* services the module supports; those functions that the module does not support continue to be passed to BKSCALLS. A call to *KbdDeRegister* deactivates the previously registered subsystem and causes all *Kbd* processing to revert to BKSCALLS.

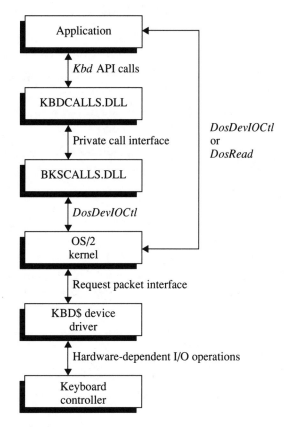

Figure 5-9. *The system modules responsible for keyboard support. The role of device monitors is not shown here.*

Keyboard Monitors

Several OS/2 character device drivers, including the keyboard driver, support a special class of applications called *device monitors*. A process that registers with the keyboard driver as a monitor can inspect and modify the raw keyboard data stream on a per-screen-group basis. Multiple applications can be registered concurrently as keyboard monitors and can even specify where they want to be located in the chain of all monitors. This facility makes it easy to write "well-behaved" keyboard enhancers, macro processors, and popup utilities.

In Chapter 18, keyboard device monitors are discussed in more detail, and a working sample program is presented. For now, simply note the following:

■ A monitor receives a data packet for each keyboard event (press or release of any key); the packet contains the original scan code, the translated ASCII code (if any), a time stamp, the keyboard shift state, and a word of flags.

■ A monitor can consume, modify, or insert keyboard data packets.

■ A monitor is responsible for passing the keyboard data through its monitor buffers promptly to avoid interfering with other processes in the screen group it is monitoring. (A dedicated thread with time-critical priority is usually created for this purpose.)

■ A process can register as a keyboard monitor for a screen group other than the one in which it is running and as a monitor for multiple screen groups.

Mouse Input

In keeping with its emphasis on graphical user interfaces and pointing devices, OS/2 provides applications with a variety of mouse support functions (Figures 5-10 and 5-11). The full list of *Mou* API services might appear intimidating, but the average application needs only a few of them.

Function	Description
Enable/Disable Mouse Support	
MouOpen	Obtains mouse handle
MouClose	Releases mouse handle
Mouse Event Messages	
MouReadEventQue	Reads mouse event record (position and button status)
MouGetNumQueEl	Returns number of waiting mouse event records
MouFlushQue	Discards any waiting event records
Mouse Pointer Control	
MouGetPtrPos	Returns mouse pointer position
MouSetPtrPos	Sets mouse pointer position
MouGetPtrShape	Returns mouse pointer shape
MouSetPtrShape	Defines mouse pointer shape
MouDrawPtr	Displays mouse pointer
MouRemovePtr	Defines mouse pointer exclusion area

Figure 5-10. *The* Mou *API at a glance.*   *(continued)*

Figure 5-10. *continued*

Function	Description
Mouse Driver Status	
MouGetDevStatus	Returns mouse driver status flags
MouGetEventMask	Returns mouse driver event mask
MouGetHotKey	Returns mouse button(s) defined as system hot key
MouGetNumButtons	Returns number of mouse buttons
MouGetNumMickeys	Returns number of mickeys per centimeter
MouGetScaleFact	Returns scaling factors for mouse coordinates
Mouse Driver Configuration	
MouInitReal	Initializes mouse driver for real mode session
MouSetDevStatus	Enables or disables pointer drawing and configures position reporting
MouSetEventMask	Sets mouse driver event mask, controls generation of mouse event queue records
MouSetHotKey	Defines mouse button(s) as system hot key
MouSetScaleFact	Sets scaling factors for mouse coordinates
MouSynch	Synchronizes access to mouse driver
Register/Deregister Mouse Subsystem	
MouRegister	Registers alternative mouse subsystem
MouDeRegister	Deregisters alternative mouse subsystem

A process first calls *MouOpen* to initialize the mouse subsystem for its screen group, if it is not already initialized, and to obtain a logical mouse handle. If the call succeeds, the mouse is "alive" and the application can obtain its state and position; however, the pointer does not appear on the screen until the process calls *MouDrawPtr*.

The process can then use *MouReadEventQue* to obtain mouse event packets from the mouse driver's FIFO queue. These packets contain flags that indicate the type of event (button press, button release, mouse movement, or a combination), a time stamp, and the mouse screen position. *MouReadEvent-Que* has a no-wait option so that the application can avoid blocking if no mouse events are waiting. Unlike other OS/2 kernel functions, the *MouReadEventQue* wait/no-wait parameter is 1 to wait for an event and 0 to return immediately; *MouReadEventQue* is also unique in passing the wait/no-wait parameter by reference rather than by value. An application can test the number of waiting events with *MouGetNumQueEl*.

As an alternative to *MouReadEventQue,* an application can simply poll the mouse position at convenient intervals with *MouGetPtrPos*. This function, however, does not return the current state of the mouse buttons, and frequent polling can (as with *KbdPeek*) degrade the performance of the entire system. Regardless of whether it uses *MouGetPtrPos* or *MouReadEventQue,* the application should create a separate thread to handle the mouse so that keyboard activity does not affect mouse tracking and vice versa.

When the application is finished with the mouse, it can call *MouClose* to release its mouse handle. Otherwise, the OS/2 kernel closes the mouse handle on behalf of the process as part of the normal cleanup at termination. When the last process using the mouse in the screen group terminates or calls *MouClose,* the mouse subsystem is disabled for the screen group, and the mouse pointer is removed from the screen.

The default size of the mouse queue is 10 events. If mouse events occur more rapidly than the application can process them, the oldest events are simply overwritten. This will not usually cause a problem because the application is typically interested in the current position of the mouse, not the history of where it has been! The user can increase the size of the mouse

Function Number	Operation
50H	Enables pointer drawing after session switch
51H	Notifies of display mode change
52H	Notifies of impending session switch
53H	Sets scaling factors
54H	Sets event mask
55H	Sets system hot key button
56H	Sets pointer shape
57H	Cancels exclusion area (equivalent to *MouDrawPtr*)
58H	Sets exclusion area (equivalent to *MouRemovePtr*)
59H	Sets pointer position
5AH	Sets address of protected mode pointer-draw routine
5BH	Sets address of real mode pointer-draw routine
5CH	Sets mouse driver status
60H	Gets number of buttons
61H	Gets number of mickeys per centimeter
62H	Gets mouse driver status
63H	Reads event queue
64H	Gets event queue status
65H	Gets event mask
66H	Gets scaling factors
67H	Gets pointer position
68H	Gets pointer shape
69H	Gets system hot key button

Figure 5-11. DosDevIOCtl *Category 7 functions for mouse status and control. The majority of these are present to provide the underpinnings for the* Mou *calls and can be used by applications, but a few are intended only for use by the Task Manager.*

event queue with an optional parameter in the *DEVICE=* statement (in the CONFIG.SYS file) that loads the mouse driver.

All processes in a screen group share the same mouse event queue and can read or change the mouse position, event mask, or pointer shape at any time. The *Mou* functions provide no analog to the *KbdGetFocus* and *KbdFreeFocus* calls that would allow a process to prevent interference by other processes in the same group.

Mouse support is restricted for programs not running in the Presentation Manager screen group: The MOUSE$ driver works properly in all "standard" text and graphics modes, but the system's mouse cursor can be used only in text modes. If a non–Presentation Manager application selects a graphics mode and intends to use the mouse, it must disable the system's pointer driver with *MouSetDevStatus* and provide the mouse cursor itself.

A small demonstration program, which monitors and displays the mouse's position and status, appears in Figure 5-12.

```
/*
        MOUDEMO.C

        A simple demo of the OS/2 mouse API.

        Compile with:  C> cl moudemo.c

        Usage is:  C> moudemo

        Copyright (C) 1988 Ray Duncan
*/

#include <stdio.h>
#define API unsigned extern far pascal

API MouReadEventQue(void far *, unsigned far *, unsigned);
API MouOpen(void far *, unsigned far *);
API MouClose(unsigned);
API MouDrawPtr(unsigned);
API VioScrollUp(unsigned, unsigned, unsigned,
                       unsigned, unsigned, char far *, unsigned);
API VioWrtCharStr(void far *, unsigned, unsigned,
                       unsigned, unsigned);
```

(continued)

Figure 5-12. *MOUDEMO.C, a simple demonstration program for the* Mou *API. This program reads mouse events and displays the mouse position; it terminates when both mouse buttons are pressed simultaneously.*

Figure 5-12. *continued*

```
struct _MouEventInfo {  unsigned Flags;
                        unsigned long Timestamp;
                        unsigned Row;
                        unsigned Col;
                     } MouEvent ;

main(int argc, char *argv[])
{
        char OutStr[40];                /* for output formatting */

        unsigned Cell = 0x0720;         /* ASCII space and
                                           normal attribute */

        unsigned MouHandle;             /* mouse logical handle */
        unsigned Status;                /* returned from API */
        int WaitOption = 1;             /* 1 = block for event,
                                           0 = do not block */

                                        /* open mouse device */
        Status = MouOpen(0L, &MouHandle);

        if(Status)                      /* exit if no mouse */
        {       printf("\nMouOpen failed.\n");
                exit(1);
        }
                                        /* clear the screen */
        VioScrollUp(0, 0, -1, -1, -1, &(char)Cell, 0);

        puts("Press Both Mouse Buttons To Exit");

        MouDrawPtr(MouHandle);          /* display mouse cursor */

        do                              /* format mouse position */
        {       sprintf(OutStr, "X=%2d Y=%2d", MouEvent.Col, MouEvent.Row);

                                        /* display mouse position */
                VioWrtCharStr(OutStr, strlen(OutStr), 0, 0, 0);

                                        /* wait for a mouse event */
                MouReadEventQue(&MouEvent, &WaitOption, MouHandle);

                                        /* exit if both buttons down */
        } while((MouEvent.Flags & 0x14) != 0x14) ;

        MouClose(MouHandle);            /* release mouse handle */

        puts("Have a Mice Day!");
}
```

Mouse Subsystems and Drivers

As with the keyboard, the OS/2 mouse support is divided among several modules (Figure 5-13). The character device driver MOUSE$, loaded from one of the MOUSE*XX*.SYS files, services mouse interrupts and keeps track of the mouse position and button states. The POINTER$ driver, loaded from POINTDD.SYS, maintains the pointer on the screen. This functional division is not visible at the API level.

The MOUSE$ driver supports device monitors in much the same manner as the keyboard driver. Each time a mouse "event" occurs, a data packet is passed through the chain of monitor buffers that contains the event type, a time stamp, and the mouse position. A process registered as a mouse monitor can consume, modify, or add data packets to the monitor chain; if it is

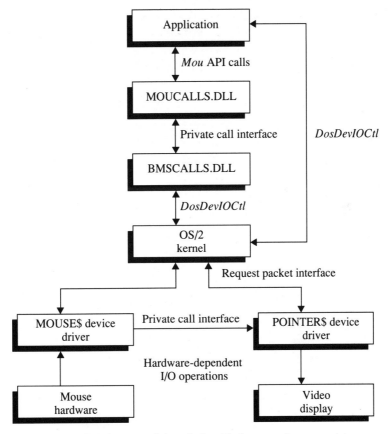

Figure 5-13. *Simplified diagram of the relationship between the mouse drivers, dynlink libraries, kernel, and applications.*

also registered as a keyboard monitor, it can conceivably translate mouse movements to keystrokes and vice versa! The format of the mouse monitor data packet is shown in Chapter 18.

At the dynlink library level, the mouse subsystem is organized much like the keyboard subsystem. The dynlink library BMSCALLS.DLL contains the Basic Mouse Subsystem, which implements the *Mou* services and communicates with the MOUSE$ driver through *DosDevIOCtl* calls. MOUCALLS.DLL is the ''mouse router''; it contains the entry points for the *Mou* API functions, and it passes incoming calls to the appropriate subsystem (such as BMSCALLS) on a per-screen-group basis. BMSCALLS and MOUCALLS both run in user mode and thus have no direct access to the hardware. Some or all of the default services provided by BMSCALLS can be replaced using *MouRegister* and *MouDeRegister*.

A particularly interesting aspect of the mouse subsystem is that the MOUSE$ and POINTER$ drivers communicate directly using a private far call interface. Although this is a wayward arrangement as far as the overall system architecture is concerned, it allows hardware dependence on mouse type and display type to be segregated into two drivers that can be maintained separately while avoiding excessive overhead for pointer tracking.

MOUCALLS.DLL establishes the linkage between the mouse and pointer drivers at the time of a *MouOpen* request. MOUCALLS first invokes *DosOpen* for POINTER$, and then it calls *DosDevIOCtl* Category 3 Function 72H to get the entry point. MOUCALLS then performs a *DosOpen* for MOUSE$, followed by a call to *DosDevIOCtl* Category 7 Function 5AH to pass it the POINTER$ entry address.

CHAPTER SIX

THE VIDEO DISPLAY

OS/2 provides application programs with a rich selection of function calls to control the video display. These functions span the complete spectrum of hardware independence:

■ Presentation Manager graphical services

■ *DosWrite* with the predefined handle for standard output (1) or standard error (2)

■ *DosWrite* with a handle obtained by opening the logical device CON or SCREEN$

■ The *Vio* (video subsystem) functions

■ Direct access to the screen group's logical video buffer

■ Direct access to the physical video buffer

The Presentation Manager provides applications with a uniform graphical user interface. It supports text fonts, windowing and clipping, pull-down menus, popup dialog boxes, pointing devices, and a broad range of high performance drawing and painting operations. To take full advantage of these capabilities, applications must have a special structure and must abide by an intricate set of conventions. The payoff is complete portability between machines and output devices that support the Presentation Manager, invisible adjustment of the program's output to compensate for the display's resolution and aspect ratio and to exploit available fonts, and a shortened learning curve for the user.

When writing character-oriented applications, you can use the general purpose function *DosWrite* to display text. You can control the video mode, foreground and background colors, and cursor position with ANSI escape sequences embedded in the output. *DosWrite* is analogous to Int 21H Function 40H (Write to File or Device) under MS-DOS and is most appropriate for filters and other utility programs in which the ability to redirect output is important and interactive performance is not an issue. Programs that use this function avoid the complexity of the Presentation Manager graphical interface but retain device independence and the ability to run in a PM window.

You can use the *Vio* functions, which offer more flexibility and speed than *DosWrite*, for interactive character-oriented applications that do not require redirectable output. The *Vio* functions provide such capabilities as scrolling the screen in all four directions, controlling cursor shape, assigning character attributes and colors, and reading strings back from the screen buffer. The *Vio* calls are a functional superset of the ROM BIOS video driver (Int 10H) calls available under MS-DOS; they are immune to redirection of the standard output and (with the exception of one function) ignore control codes and escape sequences. Applications that use a defined subset of the *Vio* calls and avoid other hardware dependence will run in a PM window.

Last, we come to the two hardware-dependent display methods. You might use them in applications that have special requirements, such as a need to present a graphics display without the aid of the Presentation Manager, or to drive the controller in a mode or resolution not supported by OS/2's built-in screen driver. The first of these techniques is to obtain a selector from OS/2 that gives the application direct access to the screen group's logical video buffer (LVB). The LVB is a "shadow" of the screen group's display; when it is not in the foreground, it receives output from programs in that group. After modifying the contents of the LVB, the program issues an additional command to refresh the physical display buffer—with no effect if the application's screen group is in the background. Use of the LVB allows very high display throughput and does not interfere with processes in other screen groups.

The second, and potentially more destructive, hardware-dependent technique is to obtain a selector for the physical video buffer from OS/2. After "locking" the screen with a function call, the application can write directly to the buffer, "unlocking" the screen with another function call when it is finished. If the application contains a segment with IOPL (I/O privilege), it can also issue commands directly to the video adapter's I/O ports. While the screen lock is in effect, the user cannot switch to another screen group, and background tasks cannot "pop up" to interact with the user.

This chapter will focus on the *DosWrite* and *Vio* calls used by Kernel applications to display text and control the screen. The programming of true Presentation Manager applications is beyond the scope of this book. At the other extreme, the hardware-dependent methods tend to be incompatible with the Presentation Manager and should therefore be avoided.

Video Display Modes

With one exception — the original Monochrome Display Adapter (MDA) — the video adapters used in OS/2-compatible personal computers support two or more display modes (Figure 6-1). The modes fall into two distinct classes: alphanumeric, or text, modes and all-points-addressable (APA), or graphics, modes. The video adapters have a hybrid interface to the CPU and are controlled by a mixture of memory-mapped and port-addressed I/O.

In text modes, each character on the screen is represented by two adjacent bytes in a buffer, called the refresh (or ''regen'') buffer, that is dedicated to use by the video controller. The first byte of such a pair contains the character code, and the second byte contains the character ''attribute.'' The attribute controls special display characteristics such as the foreground and

Resolution	Colors	Text/Graphics	MDA	CGA	EGA	VGA
40-by-25	16	Text		♦	♦	♦
80-by-25	2*	Text	♦		♦	♦
80-by-25	16	Text		♦	♦	♦
80-by-43	16	Text			♦	♦
80-by-50	16	Text				♦
320-by-200	4	Graphics		♦	♦	♦
320-by-200	16	Graphics			♦	♦
320-by-200	256	Graphics				♦
640-by-200	2	Graphics		♦	♦	♦
640-by-200	16	Graphics			♦	♦
640-by-350	2†	Graphics			♦	♦
640-by-350	4	Graphics			♦‡	
640-by-350	16	Graphics			♦§	♦
640-by-480	2	Graphics				♦
640-by-480	16	Graphics				♦

MDA = Monochrome Display Adapter
CGA = Color/Graphics Adapter
EGA = Enhanced Graphics Adapter
VGA = Video Graphics Array

* Monochrome monitor only
† Monochrome monitor only
‡ EGA with 64 KB of RAM
§ EGA with 128 KB or more of RAM

Figure 6-1. *The video modes available on various video adapters used in OS/2-compatible computers.*

background colors, blink, and underline. A hardware character generator translates the ASCII code into a pattern of pixels on the screen at a column and row corresponding to the character's position in the refresh buffer.

In graphics modes, the bits in the refresh buffer are mapped directly to the pixels on the screen. This bit mapping might differ drastically between graphics modes with different resolutions. No hardware character generator is available to translate ASCII codes to an array of pixels; instead, the software itself must turn the bits in the buffer on or off to form a character or figure on the display.

OS/2's support for graphics modes is, for the most part, exploitable only within a Presentation Manager application. Kernel or Family applications that select a graphics mode cannot run in a PM window and must contain their own software character generators and graphics drawing primitives.

Using *DosWrite* for Output

The general purpose function *DosWrite* accepts a handle for a file or device, the address of the data to be written, the length of the data (up to 65,535 bytes), and the address of a variable. *DosWrite* returns the actual number of bytes written in the specified variable (Figure 6-2).

```
stdout   equ    1                    ; standard output handle

msg      db     'HELLO'              ; message to be displayed
msg_len  equ    $-msg                ; length of message

wlen     dw     ?                    ; receives actual number
                                     ; of bytes written




         .
         .

         .
         push   stdout               ; standard output handle
         push   ds                   ; address of text
         push   offset DGROUP:msg
         push   msg_len              ; length of text
         push   ds                   ; receives bytes written
         push   offset DGROUP:wlen
         call   DosWrite             ; transfer to OS/2
         or     ax,ax                ; was write successful?
```

(continued)

Figure 6-2. *Writing text to the display using* DosWrite *and the standard output handle.*

Figure 6-2. *continued*

```
        jnz     error           ; jump if function failed
          .
          .
          .
```

When you use *DosWrite* to display text on the screen, the handle must be either one of the system's predefined handles for standard output (1) or standard error (2), or a handle obtained from a successful *DosOpen* of the logical device CON or SCREEN$. The *DosOpen* method is typically used by processes that need to circumvent any redirection of the standard devices that might be in effect (Figure 6-3).

```
sname    db     'CON',0          ; device name
shandle  dw     ?                ; receives device handle
action   dw     ?                ; receives DosOpen action
wlen     dw     ?                ; receives bytes written

msg      db     'HELLO'          ; message to be displayed
msg_len  equ    $-msg            ; length of message

           .
           .
           .

         push   ds               ; address of device name
         push   offset DGROUP:sname
         push   ds               ; variable to receive handle
         push   offset DGROUP:shandle
         push   ds               ; variable to receive action
         push   offset DGROUP:action
         push   0                ; filesize (not applicable)
         push   0
         push   0                ; attribute (not applicable)
         push   1h               ; action = open, no create
         push   42h              ; mode = rd/wt, deny-none
         push   0                ; reserved (0)
         push   0
         call   DosOpen          ; transfer to OS/2
         or     ax,ax            ; did open succeed?
         jnz    error            ; jump if function failed
           .
           .
           .
```

(continued)

Figure 6-3. *Bypassing output redirection by opening the screen driver as if it were a file and using the new handle obtained for subsequent text output.*

Figure 6-3. *continued*

```
push    shandle          ; handle for CON
push    ds               ; address of message
push    offset DGROUP:msg
push    msg_len          ; length of message
push    ds               ; address of variable
push    offset DGROUP:wlen
call    DosWrite         ; transfer to OS/2
or      ax,ax            ; did write succeed?
jnz     error            ; jump if function failed
  .
  .
  .
```

DosWrite treats the display as a "glass teletype." It provides line wrapping and screen scrolling; and carriage returns, linefeeds, tabs, bell codes, and backspaces embedded in the output have their expected effects. In general, it always writes the exact number of characters specified. The output terminates prematurely (reflected in the value returned in the variable) only if it is redirected to a disk file and the disk is full, or if the data contains a Ctrl-Z character (1AH).

Although *DosWrite* is appropriate for filters and other programs that process streams of simple text, you should avoid using it in interactive applications. The kernel translates any call to *DosWrite* that uses a handle for the display to *VioWrtTTY* anyway, so calling *DosWrite* is intrinsically less efficient than calling *Vio* functions directly.

Controlling Character Attributes with *DosWrite*

If your program uses *DosWrite* for display, you can use a subset of the ANSI 3.64–1979 standard escape sequences to select character attributes and colors, clear the screen, and position the cursor. Escape sequences are so called because they always start with the ASCII ESC character code (1BH). You can embed these sequences within other text strings or send them to the screen driver separately with *DosWrite*. Before you use escape sequences, verify that ANSI support is enabled with the functions *VioGetAnsi* and *VioSetAnsi*.

Character attributes, such as reverse, high intensity, or underline on monochrome adapters or foreground and background colors on color adapters, are controlled with the escape sequences of the following form:

<Esc>[*n*m

where *n* has the values shown in the following table.

Value of n	Attribute
0	No special attributes
1	High intensity
2	Low intensity
3	Italic
4	Underline
5	Blink
7	Reverse video
8	Concealed text (no display)

For color control, you can also replace *n* with the following values:

Foreground	Background	Color
30	40	Black
31	41	Red
32	42	Green
33	43	Yellow
34	44	Blue
35	45	Magenta
36	46	Cyan
37	47	White

To specify multiple attributes in the same escape sequence, separate them with semicolons. After you select an attribute, it is applied to all subsequent text written to the screen until another escape sequence alters it. For example, the code illustrated in Figure 6-4 causes all subsequent text to be displayed in reverse video.

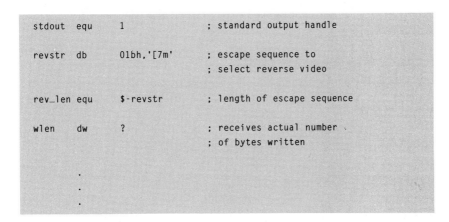

```
stdout   equ    1              ; standard output handle

revstr   db     01bh,'[7m'     ; escape sequence to
                               ; select reverse video

rev_len  equ    $-revstr       ; length of escape sequence

wlen     dw     ?              ; receives actual number
                               ; of bytes written

         .
         .
         .
```

(continued)

Figure 6-4. *Using an escape sequence to select the reverse video attribute for all text that is subsequently displayed.*

Figure 6-4. *continued*

```
push    stdout           ; standard output handle
push    ds               ; address of escape sequence
push    offset DGROUP:revstr
push    rev_len          ; length of escape sequence
push    ds               ; address of variable
push    offset DGROUP:wlen
call    DosWrite         ; transfer to OS/2
or      ax,ax            ; did write succeed?
jnz     error            ; jump if function failed
    .
    .
    .
```

Clearing the Screen and Scrolling with *DosWrite*

Two escape sequences are available to clear all or part of the screen. The first such string clears the screen and positions the cursor in the upper left corner:

<Esc>[2J

The other string clears from the cursor to the end of the current line and leaves the cursor position unchanged:

<Esc>[K

You can scroll the screen upward with *DosWrite* by positioning the cursor on the last line of the screen and then sending a linefeed (0AH) character. The entire new line receives the attribute of the last character on the preceding line. Scrolling in the other three directions is not supported for output with *DosWrite*.

Cursor Control with *DosWrite*

The cursor can be positioned with the sequence

<Esc>[*row;col*H

where *row* is the *y* coordinate and *col* is the *x* coordinate. The *row* and *col* values are one-based, decimal numbers expressed as ASCII strings and are not binary values. Position $(x,y) = (1,1)$ is the upper left corner of the screen; the maximum values for the *x* and *y* coordinates depend on the current display mode.* Escape sequences ending with *f* have the same effect as those ending with *H*. An example of cursor positioning is provided in Figure 6-5.

---

*While the ANSI screen driver uses (1,1) as the home position, nearly all other OS/2 services use (0,0) as the home coordinate. Throughout the remainder of the book, assume that screen addressing is zero-based unless explicitly noted otherwise.

```
stdout    equ     1                  ; standard output handle

movstr    db      01bh,'[25;1H'      ; escape sequence to move
                                     ; cursor to (x,y) = (1,25)

mov_len   equ     $-movstr           ; length of escape sequence

wlen      dw      ?                  ; receives actual number
                                     ; of bytes written

          .
          .
          .

          push    stdout             ; standard output handle
          push    ds                 ; address of escape sequence
          push    offset DGROUP:movstr
          push    mov_len            ; length of escape sequence
          push    ds                 ; address of variable
          push    offset DGROUP:wlen
          call    DosWrite           ; transfer to OS/2
          or      ax,ax              ; did write succeed?
          jnz     error              ; jump if function failed
          .
          .
          .
```

Figure 6-5. *Using an ANSI escape sequence to position the cursor at screen coordinates (0,24); in other words, the first column of the last line on the screen. Note that coordinates in escape sequences are one-based—expressed relative to a home position of (1,1).*

Escape sequences also exist to move the cursor relative to its current position; these sequences do not scroll the screen if the cursor reaches the edge:

<Esc>[*n*A ——— Move cursor up *n* rows
<Esc>[*n*B ——— Move cursor down *n* rows
<Esc>[*n*C ——— Move cursor right *n* columns
<Esc>[*n*D ——— Move cursor left *n* columns

To determine the current cursor position, the program can send the following sequence:

<Esc>[6n

The program can then use *DosRead* to obtain the cursor position from the standard input in the format

<Esc>[*row;col*R

where *row* and *col* are one or more ASCII digits. For example, if the cursor is positioned at the one-based coordinates $(x,y) = (25,7)$, the position is reported with the character sequence

<Esc>[25;07R

Decoding such position reports is inconvenient at best. In most cases, the need for such decoding can be avoided with the two escape sequences

<Esc>[s
<Esc>[u

Note that the driver can "remember" only one position at a time.

Mode Control with *DosWrite*

You can use the escape sequence

<Esc>[=*n*h

to select the display mode for the active video adapter, where the value of *n* has the following meanings:

Value of n	Video Display Mode
0	40-by-25 16-color text (color burst off)
1	40-by-25 16-color text
2	80-by-25 16-color text (color burst off)
3	80-by-25 16-color text
4	320-by-200 4-color graphics
5	320-by-200 4-color graphics (color burst off)
6	640-by-200 2-color graphics

The values of *n* are the same as the video display mode numbers used in the old IBM ROM BIOS. You cannot use an escape sequence to select the higher resolution graphics modes available on an EGA or VGA adapter, to obtain the current display mode, or to activate another adapter if the system contains more than one.

Using *Vio* Functions for Output

The *Vio* subsystem is a high performance, character-oriented display interface for Kernel and Family applications. The *Vio* functions are summarized by category in Figure 6-6.

You can use several different *Vio* functions to display text. The simplest and most general is *VioWrtTTY*, which is called with the address and length of a string and a *Vio* handle. The function returns a status code of zero if the write succeeded or an error code if it failed. Figure 6-7 on page 105 demonstrates a call to the function.

Function	Description
Display	
VioWrtTTY †	Writes string in "teletype" mode
VioWrtCellStr †	Writes string of alternating characters and attribute bytes
VioWrtCharStr †	Writes string without attribute control
VioWrtCharStrAtt †	Writes string applying the same attribute to each character
VioReadCellStr †	Reads characters and attributes from display
VioReadCharStr †	Reads characters from display
Replication	
VioWrtNAttr †	Replicates attribute byte
VioWrtNCell †	Replicates character and attribute byte
VioWrtNChar †	Replicates character
Cursor Size and Position	
VioGetCurPos †	Gets cursor position
VioSetCurPos †	Sets cursor position
VioGetCurType †	Gets cursor shape and size
VioSetCurType †	Sets cursor shape and size
Scroll or Clear Screen	
VioScrollDn †	Scrolls display down
VioScrollLf †	Scrolls display left
VioScrollRt †	Scrolls display right
VioScrollUp †	Scrolls display up
Display Mode Control	
VioSetAnsi †	Enables or disables ANSI support
VioSetCp †	Selects code page
VioSetFont † ‡	Downloads display font
VioSetMode ‡	Selects display mode
VioSetState ‡	Sets palette, border color, or blink/intensity toggle
Mode Information	
VioGetAnsi †	Gets ANSI support state
VioGetBuf †	Gets selector for logical video buffer
VioGetConfig	Gets video adapter information
VioGetCp †	Gets current code page
VioGetFont ‡	Gets character dimensions and font
VioGetMode	Gets current display mode
VioGetPhysBuf ‡	Gets selector for physical video buffer
VioGetState ‡	Gets palette, border color, and blink/intensity toggle

† = not supported in graphics mode in non–Presentation Manager screen groups.

‡ = restricted or not allowed in Presentation Manager screen groups. _(continued)_

Figure 6-6. Vio _functions at a glance. The advanced_ Vio _functions are present to support the OS/2 Presentation Manager and are not available in OS/2 version 1.0._

Figure 6-6. *continued*

Function	Description
Miscellaneous Functions	
VioPrtSc †	Prints screen
VioPrtScToggle †	Turns print echo on or off
VioScrLock †	Disables screen switching
VioScrUnLock ‡	Enables screen switching
VioShowBuf †	Updates physical display buffer from logical buffer
Pop-Up Support	
VioPopUp	Allocates full-screen text-mode popup display
VioEndPopUp	Deallocates popup display
Support for Non-PM Graphics Applications	
VioSavRedrawWait ‡	Returns when screen should be saved or redrawn
VioSavRedrawUndo ‡	Cancels *VioSavRedrawWait* call by another thread
VioModeWait ‡	Returns when display mode should be restored
VioModeUndo ‡	Cancels *VioModeWait* call by another thread
Advanced Vio Functions	
VioAssociate	Associates *Vio* presentation space with device context
VioCreateLogFont	Creates logical font for use with *Vio* presentation space
VioCreatePS	Allocates *Vio* presentation space
VioDeleteSetId	Releases logical font identifier
VioDestroyPS	Destroys *Vio* presentation space
VioGetDeviceCellSize	Returns character cell height and width
VioGetOrg	Returns screen coordinates for origin of *Vio* presentation space
VioQueryFonts	Returns list of available fonts for specified typeface
VioQuerySetIds	Returns list of loaded fonts
VioSetDeviceCellSize	Sets character cell height and width
VioSetOrg	Sets screen coordinates of origin for *Vio* presentation space
VioShowPS	Updates display from *Vio* presentation space
Vio *Function Replacement*	
VioRegister ‡	Replaces default *Vio* functions with new routines
VioDeRegister ‡	Deregisters alternative *Vio* routines

† = not supported in graphics mode in non–Presentation Manager screen groups.

‡ = restricted or not allowed in Presentation Manager screen groups.

```
msg       db        'Hello World'      ; message to display
msg_len   equ $-msg                    ; length of message

          .
          .
          .
          push      ds                 ; address of message
          push      offset DGROUP:msg
          push      msg_len            ; length of message
          push      0                  ; Vio handle
          call      VioWrtTTY          ; transfer to OS/2
          or        ax,ax              ; did write succeed?
          jnz       error              ; jump if function failed
          .
          .
          .
```

Figure 6-7. *Using* VioWrtTTY *to write the string* Hello World *to the screen at the current cursor position. The cursor position is updated appropriately after the write.*

VioWrtTTY handles the control characters linefeed, carriage return, backspace, and bell properly. Line wrapping and scrolling are provided (unless they are intentionally disabled), the cursor position is updated, and ANSI escape sequences described for *DosWrite* are interpreted unless ANSI support is turned off. The attribute for all characters is the one most recently selected with the appropriate ANSI escape sequence; when the screen is scrolled, the entire new line is given the attribute of the last character written to the previous line.

Ordinarily, the only error code that *VioWrtTTY* returns is 436 (*Invalid Vio Handle*). Providing the function with an invalid string address or length does not usually result in an error code but may well cause a GP fault that terminates the process.

Three other *Vio* calls, which are slightly trickier to use, are also available for displaying text: *VioWrtCharStr*, *VioWrtCharStrAtt*, and *VioWrtCellStr*. These functions are faster than *VioWrtTTY* and provide direct control over screen placement, but they do not update the cursor position. Their support for line wrapping is limited: If the text is too long for the current line, it wraps onto the next line; however, if the end of the screen is reached, any remaining characters are discarded, the screen is not scrolled, and no error is returned. All three functions ignore ANSI escape sequences or control characters; any nonalphanumeric characters embedded in the string are displayed as their graphics character equivalents.

VioWrtCharStr is the simplest of the three functions listed above. It accepts the address and length of a string, the screen position at which to begin writing the string, and a *Vio* handle. The new text assumes the attributes of the characters previously displayed at the same screen positions.

The *VioWrtCharStrAtt* call is similar to the *VioWrtCharStr* function; it has, however, one additional parameter: the address of an attribute byte which is applied to every character in the string (as demonstrated in Figure 6-8). On adapters with monochrome monitors, the attribute byte specifies normal or reverse video, intensity (highlight), blinking, and underline (Figure 6-9). On adapters with color monitors in text modes, the attribute byte contains the background color in the upper four bits and the foreground color in the lower four bits (Figure 6-10).

VioWrtCellStr displays a string that consists of alternating character and attribute bytes. *VioWrtCellStr* is designed to be used in combination with *VioReadCellStr* to restore an area of the display that was previously saved into a buffer. This function is not appropriate for routine text output for a number of reasons. Generating initialized strings with embedded attribute

```
attr      db        70h              ; reverse video attribute

msg       db        'Hello World'    ; message to display
msg_len   equ       $-msg            ; length of message



          .
          .
          .
          push      ds               ; address of string
          push      offset DGROUP:msg
          push      msg_len          ; length of string
          push      5                ; y position
          push      10               ; x position
          push      ds               ; video attribute address
          push      offset DGROUP:attr
          push      0                ; Vio handle
          call      VioWrtCharStrAtt ; transfer to OS/2
          or        ax,ax            ; did write succeed?
          jnz       error            ; jump if function failed
          .
          .
          .
```

Figure 6-8. *Using the* VioWrtCharStrAtt *function to write to the screen. This code displays the string* Hello World *in reverse video at cursor location (10,5) (column 10, row 5).*

bytes is awkward in most languages, and such strings are bulky. Furthermore, applications rarely need to display a string where each successive character has a different attribute.

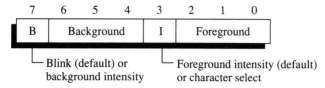

Display	Background	Foreground
No display (black)	000	000
No display (white) *	111	111
Underline	000	001
Normal video	000	111
Reverse video	111	000

* VGA only

Figure 6-9. *The mapping of attribute bytes for the monochrome display adapter (MDA) or for the EGA or VGA in monochrome text mode.*

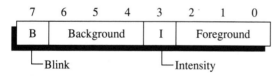

Value	Color	Value	Color
0	Black	8	Gray
1	Blue	9	Light blue
2	Green	10	Light green
3	Cyan	11	Light cyan
4	Red	12	Light red
5	Magenta	13	Light magenta
6	Brown	14	Yellow
7	White	15	Intense white

Figure 6-10. *The attribute byte for CGA, EGA, or VGA graphics adapters in color text modes is divided into two 4-bit fields that control the foreground and background colors. The color assignments shown are fixed for the CGA and are the defaults for the EGA or VGA. (Other color assignments can be obtained by programming the palette.) These assignments also assume that the B or I bit controls intensity.*

The *Vio* functions *VioWrtNChar*, *VioWrtNAttr*, and *VioWrtNCell* offer some special capabilities that supplement the other text display functions, and they require similar parameters. You can use *VioWrtNAttr* to modify the attribute bytes of a selected area of the screen without disturbing the text displayed at that position; *VioWrtNChar* and *VioWrtNCell* let you draw borders and highlighted areas efficiently in text mode.

The *Vio* functions are not affected by command line redirection parameters. An OS/2 application that wants to take full advantage of the *Vio* interface while allowing redirection can call *DosQHandType* with the standard output handle during its initialization to determine whether standard output has been redirected. If *DosQHandType* indicates that standard output is associated with a file or a pipe, the application should use *DosWrite* throughout its execution. If the standard output is a character device, and the device attribute word returned by *DosQHandType* has bit 1 set, the application can proceed to use the *Vio* calls.

Scrolling and Clearing the Screen with *Vio*

The *Vio* calls allow great flexibility in scrolling or clearing selected areas of the screen. You can use the scroll functions *VioScrollUp*, *VioScrollDn*, *VioScrollLf*, and *VioScrollRt* to clear a window of arbitrary size and position or to scroll it up, down, left, or right any number of columns or rows. You can specify any character-attribute pair to fill the newly blanked or scrolled lines. All four functions have the following parameters: the screen coordinates of the upper left corner and lower right corner of a window, the number of lines to be scrolled or blanked, the address of a character and attribute pair to fill the blanked lines, and a *Vio* handle.

You can clear the entire display in any mode without first determining the screen dimensions with a special-case call to any of the four scroll functions: Use an upper left coordinate of (0,0), a lower right coordinate of (−1,−1), and the value −1 as the number of lines to scroll. Figure 6-11 demonstrates clearing the screen to ASCII blanks with a normal video attribute. Scrolling a selected portion of the screen is also easily done, as demonstrated in Figure 6-12.

```
cell    db      20h,07h         ; ASCII blank, normal video
        .
        .
        .
        push    0               ; y upper left
        push    0               ; x upper left
        push    -1              ; y lower right
        push    -1              ; x lower right
        push    -1              ; number of blank lines
        push    ds              ; char/attrib address
        push    offset DGROUP:cell
        push    0               ; Vio handle
        call    VioScrollUp     ; transfer to OS/2
        or      ax,ax           ; did function succeed?
        jnz     error           ; jump if function failed
        .
        .
        .
```

Figure 6-11. *Clearing the screen to ASCII blanks with a normal video attribute, using one of the four* Vio *scroll functions. This special-case call with an upper left window coordinate of (0,0), lower right coordinate of (−1,−1), and −1 as the number of lines to scroll does not require you to first determine the dimensions of the active display.*

```
cell    db      20h,07h         ; ASCII blank, normal video
        .
        .
        .
        push    12              ; y upper left
        push    0               ; x upper left
        push    24              ; y lower right
        push    79              ; x lower right
        push    1               ; number of lines to scroll
        push    ds              ; address of char & attrib
        push    offset DGROUP:cell
        push    0               ; Vio handle
        call    VioScrollUp     ; transfer to OS/2
        or      ax,ax           ; did scroll succeed?
        jnz     error           ; jump if function failed
        .
        .
        .
```

Figure 6-12. *Scrolling selected portions of the screen in any direction can be accomplished very easily with the VioScrollxx functions. For example, this code scrolls the bottom half of the screen up one line, filling the newly blanked line with ASCII blanks with a normal video attribute, leaving the top half of the screen untouched.*

Cursor Control with *Vio*

The *Vio* subsystem supports a comprehensive set of functions to control cursor shape and position. The efficiency of these functions relieves you of the need to access the video hardware directly.

Use the function *VioSetCurPos* to position the cursor. In addition to being faster than the ANSI driver method, *VioSetCurPos* is also much simpler to use. The zero-based binary screen coordinates are simply pushed onto the stack, instead of being converted to one-based ASCII strings and embedded in an ANSI escape sequence. For example, the code in Figure 6-13 positions the cursor on the first column of the last line of the screen.

Use the parallel function *VioGetCurPos* to obtain the current cursor location (Figure 6-14). Both *VioSetCurPos* and *VioGetCurPos* use zero-based text coordinates and assume that the coordinates of the home position—the upper left corner of the screen—are (0,0).

The functions *VioGetCurType* and *VioSetCurType* obtain or change the cursor height, width, and hidden/visible attribute. Both use a 4-word data structure with the same format—quite convenient when the cursor must be altered or hidden temporarily (Figure 6-15). You can use *VioGetMode* to determine the vertical resolution and number of text lines in the current screen mode, from which you can calculate the size of the character cell and the valid starting and ending scan lines for the cursor.

```
        .
        .
        .
        push    24              ; y coordinate
        push    0               ; x coordinate
        push    0               ; Vio handle
        call    VioSetCurPos    ; transfer to OS/2
        or      ax,ax           ; did function succeed?
        jnz     error           ; jump if function failed
        .
        .
        .
```

Figure 6-13. *Cursor positioning with the* Vio *calls. This code places the cursor at position* (x,y) = (0,24), *that is, on the first column of the twenty-fifth row of the screen. Compare this fragment with Figure 6-5.*

```
CurY     dw      ?                       ; cursor y position
CurX     dw      ?                       ; cursor x position

         .
         .
         .

         push    ds                      ; receives y coord
         push    offset DGROUP:CurY
         push    ds                      ; receives x coord
         push    offset DGROUP:CurX
         push    0                       ; Vio handle
         call    VioGetCurPos            ; transfer to OS/2
         or      ax,ax                   ; cursor position obtained?
         jnz     error                   ; jump if function failed
         .
         .
         .
```

Figure 6-14. *Reading the cursor position with* VioGetCurPos. *The cursor location is returned in text coordinates that assume a home position of (0,0).*

```
CurData  label   word                    ; cursor data structure
CurBeg   dw      ?                       ; starting scan line
CurEnd   dw      ?                       ; ending scan line
CurWid   dw      ?                       ; width (0 = default)
CurAttr  dw      ?                       ; cursor attribute
                                         ; (0 = visible, -1 = hidden)

CurPrev  dw      ?                       ; previous cursor start line

         .
         .
         .

         push    ds                      ; receives cursor info
         push    offset DGROUP:CurData
         push    0                       ; Vio handle
         call    VioGetCurType           ; transfer to OS/2
         or      ax,ax                   ; cursor info obtained?
         jnz     error                   ; jump if function failed
         mov     ax,CurBeg               ; save cursor starting line
         mov     CurPrev,ax
```

(continued)

Figure 6-15. *Example of altering the cursor to a block and later restoring it to its original shape.*

Figure 6-15. *continued*

```
        mov      CurBeg,0          ; force starting line to
                                   ; zero to get block cursor


        push     ds                ; contains cursor info
        push     offset DGROUP:CurData
        push     0                 ; Vio handle
        call     VioSetCurType     ; transfer to OS/2
        or       ax,ax             ; did we change cursor?
        jnz      error             ; jump if function failed


        .
        .                          ; other code goes here...
        .


        mov      ax,CurPrev        ; restore cursor shape
        mov      CurBeg,ax


        push     ds                ; contains cursor info
        push     offset DGROUP:CurData
        push     0                 ; Vio handle
        call     VioSetCurType     ; transfer to OS/2
        or       ax,ax             ; did we change cursor?
        jnz      error             ; jump if function failed
        .
        .
        .
```

Mode Control with *Vio*

The functions *VioGetMode* and *VioSetMode* query or select the video mode
without resorting to the "magic numbers" inherited from the original IBM
PC ROM BIOS. Both functions use a data structure that specifies the adapter
type, text or graphics mode, color burst enable, and the number of display-
able colors, text columns and rows, and pixel columns and rows.

This approach is open-ended. It allows the application to deal with the
adapter on the basis of its capabilities and doesn't require the programmer
to remember an ever-expanding list of "mode numbers" that have less and
less relationship to the display modes they represent. For example, the code
in Figure 6-16 selects 80-by-25 16-color text mode with color burst enabled
and is exactly equivalent to the escape sequence

<Esc>[3h

used with *DosWrite* or *VioWrtTTY*.

```
                                  ; video mode data structure
    ModeInf  dw      8            ; length of structure
             db      1            ; non-MDA, text mode, color
             db      4            ; 16 colors
             dw      80           ; 80 text columns
             dw      25           ; 25 text rows


             .
             .
             .

             push    ds           ; contains mode info
             push    offset DGROUP:ModeInf
             push    0            ; Vio handle
             call    VioSetMode   ; transfer to OS/2
             or      ax,ax        ; did function succeed?
             jnz     error        ; jump if function failed
             .
             .
             .
```

Figure 6-16. *The functions* VioGetMode *and* VioSetMode *interrogate or select the display mode based on the controller's capabilities rather than magic numbers. This code selects 80-by-25 16-color text mode with color burst enabled.*

Pop-Up Support

The functions *VioPopUp* and *VioEndPopUp* let a background process temporarily assume control of the screen and interact with the user. Background processes, which are launched with the DETACH command, cannot ordinarily perform *Kbd* or *Mou* input calls, and their output to the screen is discarded. A process can determine whether it was started with DETACH by issuing a *VioGetAnsi* function call—this call returns an error code if output calls will also fail.

To gain access to the screen, the background process first calls *VioPopUp*. This function provides two options: wait or no-wait, and transparent or nontransparent. If wait is specified, the calling process is suspended until the screen is available; if no-wait is selected, the function returns immediately with an error code if the screen cannot be preempted (for example, if another background process has called *VioPopUp*).

If the *VioPopUp* call is successful, the transparent/nontransparent option comes into play. First, the current contents of the screen (belonging to the foreground process) are saved by the system. If the nontransparent option was selected, the screen is blanked and placed into an 80-by-25 text mode, and the cursor is placed in the home position ($x,y = 0,0$). Otherwise, no mode change occurs and the screen contents are left intact. In either case, all subsequent *Vio* calls by the background process are directed to the active display.

At this point, the background process can interact freely with the user. Other processes continue to run normally, their output going to the usual logical video buffer until they require input or call *VioPopUp*, at which point they are blocked. When the background process is finished with its pop-up, it must call *VioEndPopUp* to release control of the screen. The state of the display at the time of the pop-up is then restored, regardless of whether the transparent or nontransparent option was used. Figure 6-17 contains the skeleton code for a screen pop-up.

```
msg       db      'Surprise!'          ; message for popup screen
msg_len   equ     $-msg                ; length of message

option    dw      1                    ; Option flags for VioPopUp
                                       ; bit 0: 1 = wait, 0 = no-wait
                                       ; bit 1: 1 = transparent mode
                                       ;           0 = nontransparent mode

kbddata   db      10 dup (0)           ; structure for KbdCharIn

          .
          .
          .
                                       ; put up popup window...
          push    ds                   ; address of option flags
          push    offset DGROUP:option
          push    0                    ; Vio handle
          call    VioPopUp             ; transfer to OS/2
          or      ax,ax                ; did we capture display?
          jnz     error                ; jump if function failed
```

(continued)

Figure 6-17. *A background process using* VioPopUp *and* VioEndPopUp *to interact with the user. Note that after a successful call to* VioPopUp, *the program must be careful not to take any branch away from the main line of execution toward* VioEndPopUp.

Figure 6-17. *continued*

```
                                ; display popup message...
        push    ds              ; address of message
        push    offset DGROUP:msg
        push    msg_len         ; length of message
        push    12              ; y
        push    (80-msg_len)/2  ; x (center it)
        push    0               ; Vio handle
        call    VioWrtCharStr   ; transfer to OS/2

                                ; wait for any key...
        push    ds              ; receives keyboard data
        push    offset DGROUP:kbddata
        push    0               ; 0 = wait for a character
        push    0               ; default keyboard handle
        call    KbdCharIn       ; transfer to OS/2

                                ; take down popup window...
        push    0               ; Vio handle
        call    VioEndPopUp     ; transfer to OS/2
        .                       ; (should never fail)
        .
        .
```

A background process that uses *VioPopUp* may have difficulty getting access to the screen if the current foreground process is computation-intensive rather than I/O-intensive. This is because the threads of a foreground process get an artificial boost to their priority to keep the user happy, and OS/2's scheduler always chooses the thread with the highest priority that is ready to run. The background process can circumvent this problem by promoting the *VioPopUp* thread to a time-critical priority and then ensuring that this thread is blocking at all other times.

Use of *VioPopUp* should be kept to a minimum and reserved for true background processes. This is because screen group switching is disabled during a *VioPopUp...VioEndPopUp* sequence, and the abrupt transition from a normal display to the largely blank display of a nontransparent pop-up (with a possible concomitant change in display mode) can be startling and disruptive to the user. An ordinary application that uses popup windows as part of its normal interaction can achieve much more pleasing results by using the *VioReadCellStr* and *VioWrtCellStr* functions to save and restore small portions of the display.

Video Subsystems and Drivers

The OS/2 substructure for the video support available to an application is organized in an atypical fashion (Figure 6-18). The character device driver SCREEN$, loaded from the file SCREEN01.SYS or SCREEN02.SYS, plays little role in the control of the display. Its main function is to return a selector for the physical video buffer; it has no documented *DosDevIOCtl* calls.

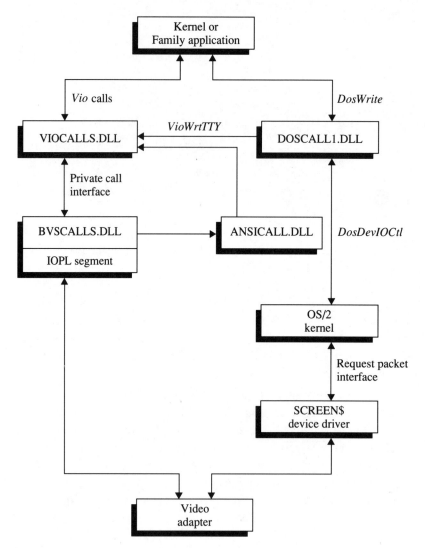

Figure 6-18. *The system modules responsible for video support.*

The dynlink library BVSCALLS.DLL is the Basic Video Subsystem that implements the *Vio* services. BVSCALLS contains the true driver for the video adapter; it manipulates the physical video buffer (using the selector obtained from SCREEN$). BVSCALLS contains an IOPL segment so that it can read and write the adapter's I/O ports to set the display mode, program the palette, and so forth.

The dynlink library VIOCALLS.DLL is a "router." It contains the entry points for the *Vio* API and passes the calls onward to the appropriate subsystem (such as BVSCALLS) on a per-screen-group basis. Interpretation of ANSI escape sequences (when ANSI support is enabled) is carried out by ANSICALL.DLL.

Although BVSCALLS is the default video subsystem for each screen group, part or all of its services can be replaced on a per-screen-group basis. To activate a new subsystem, call *VioRegister* with a module (dynlink library) name, an entry point name, and a set of flags that indicate which *Vio* services the module supports; those functions not present continue to be passed to BVSCALLS. *VioDeRegister* deactivates an alternative *Vio* subsystem and causes all *Vio* processing to rely on BVSCALLS.

PRINTER AND SERIAL PORTS

OS/2 supplies drivers for *parallel ports* and *serial ports* that let you control printers, plotters, modems, and other devices for hard copy output or communication. Parallel ports are so named because they transfer a byte — 8 bits — in parallel to the destination device over 8 separate physical paths (plus additional status and handshaking signal wires). The serial port also communicates with the CPU using bytes, but it sends data to or receives data from its destination device serially — a bit at a time — over a single physical connection in each direction (plus a ground and optional handshaking signal wires).

On personal computers, parallel ports are typically used for high-speed output devices, such as line printers, over relatively short distances (less than 50 feet). They are rarely used for devices that require two-way communication with the computer. Serial ports are used for lower-speed devices, such as modems and terminals that require two-way communication (although some printers also have serial interfaces). A serial port can drive a device reliably over much longer distances without extra hardware.

The standard version of OS/2 includes drivers for three parallel adapters and for two serial adapters on the PC/AT (three on the PS/2). The logical names for these devices are LPT1 (which also has the alias PRN), LPT2, LPT3, COM1, COM2, and COM3. The device driver for the parallel ports, PRINT01.SYS or PRINT02.SYS, is always loaded during system initialization. The serial port driver, COM01.SYS or COM02.SYS, is loaded only if the user adds the appropriate *DEVICE=* statement to the CONFIG.SYS file in the root directory on the system boot disk.

Sending Output to the Printer

To send text and control codes to the printer, you must first call *DosOpen* with the logical device name of a printer (PRN, LPT1, LPT2, or LPT3); a handle is returned if the printer is available. You can use the deny-all sharing parameter for *DosOpen* to ensure that another process will not be permitted to use the printer at the same time. (This precaution is unnecessary if the print spooler is running.) Unlike DOS, OS/2 provides no predefined *standard list device* handle.

When the printer is opened, *DosWrite* can be called as many times as necessary; a call to this function requires that you supply the handle, the address of data to be written, the length of the data (0–65,535 bytes), and the address of a variable (Figure 7-1). When *DosWrite* returns, it places the actual number of bytes written to the printer in the specified variable; this number is always the same as the number requested, barring some unexpected system error. Control characters and escape sequences are passed to the printer unfiltered and unchanged. (*DosWrite* always writes to character devices other than the standard output in binary mode.)

```
pname     db      'LPT1',0        ; device name
phandle   dw      ?               ; receives device handle

action    dw      ?               ; receives DosOpen action

msg       db      'HELLO'         ; text of message
msg_len   equ     $-msg           ; length of message

wlen      dw      ?               ; receives bytes written

          .
          .
          .

          push    ds              ; device name address
          push    offset DGROUP:pname
          push    ds              ; receives handle
          push    offset DGROUP:phandle
          push    ds              ; receives DosOpen action
          push    offset DGROUP:action
          push    0               ; filesize (N/A)
          push    0
```

(continued)

Figure 7-1. *Obtaining a handle for the first list device (LPT1) with* DosOpen, *and then sending a message to the device with* DosWrite.

Figure 7-1. *continued*

```
        push    0               ; attribute (N/A)
        push    1h              ; flag: open, no create
        push    41h             ; mode: write-only, deny-none
        push    0               ; reserved DWORD 0
        push    0
        call    DosOpen         ; transfer to OS/2
        or      ax,ax           ; did open succeed?
        jnz     error           ; jump if function failed
        .
        .
        .
        push    phandle         ; handle for LPT1
        push    ds              ; message address
        push    offset DGROUP:msg
        push    msg_len         ; message length
        push    ds              ; receives bytes written
        push    offset DGROUP:wlen
        call    DosWrite        ; transfer to OS/2
        or      ax,ax           ; did write succeed?
        jnz     error           ; jump if function failed
        .
        .
        .
```

An application can initialize and configure the printer or obtain printer status with the Category 5 *DosDevIOCtl* functions (Figure 7-2). If your program reconfigures the printer, it should first obtain and save the printer's original configuration and then restore that status before terminating.

Function Number	Action
42H	Sets frame control (chars/line, lines/inch)
44H	Sets infinite retry
46H	Initializes printer
48H	Activates font
62H	Gets frame control
64H	Gets infinite retry
66H	Gets printer status
69H	Queries active font
6AH	Verifies code page and font

Figure 7-2. *Category 5* DosDevIOCtl *functions for control of the printer.*

The Print Spooler

OS/2 includes a true print spooler that lets the user run multiple processes that generate printer output simultaneously. Using the print spooler is optional; to launch it in OS/2 1.0, issue a RUN directive in CONFIG.SYS or a START command. In OS/2 1.1, the spooler is installed as a default and can be disabled with the Control Panel. The spooler runs as a normal process in user mode and uses only documented API functions.

When the print spooler is active, data that is logically written to the printer (from the application's point of view) might be buffered within the system for an unpredictable length of time. The spooler stores the output in a file at least until a *DosClose* is issued for the printer handle or until the process terminates, and then it adds the name of the file to its spool queue.

The print spooler sends the contents of the file onward to the printer when the printer is on-line and when all previous files in the spool queue have been processed. If you are designing an application program, take a conservative approach with data that is "printed"; do not delete it from other storage unless it can be regenerated easily — in case the system crashes or is turned off before the spool queue is emptied.

For the purposes of this book, the spooler is of interest mainly as an illustration of the power of the device monitor concept (see also Chapter 18). Under normal circumstances (when the print spooler is not loaded), data written by an application to the printer follows a simple and predictable path through the system (Figure 7-3). That is, the data is passed from the application to the OS/2 kernel by *DosWrite* calls, the kernel passes the data to the printer device driver in "write request packets," and the driver issues commands to the parallel port's hard-wired I/O addresses.

When the print spooler is loaded, this simple data pathway changes. The spooler registers itself as a monitor with the printer driver and becomes an integral part of the driver's internal data stream. The driver collects the characters received from the OS/2 kernel into data packets that are passed through the buffers of all the monitors registered with the driver. The last monitor returns the packets to the driver, which then sends the data to the printer. Special packets are also sent to the monitors when the driver receives "open" and "close" commands from the kernel on behalf of an application.

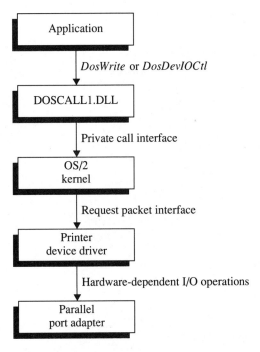

Figure 7-3. *The flow of printer data when the spooler is not loaded is straightforward. The* DosWrite *calls issued by an application are passed by DOSCALL1.DLL to the kernel. The kernel translates the* DosWrite *request into driver request packets, which are shipped to the printer driver. The driver processes the packets and transmits the data to the parallel port adapter.*

The job of the spooler is thus quite straightforward. When it sees an "open" packet, it creates a temporary spool file and consumes the subsequent data packets, writing the data to the file with ordinary *DosWrite* operations (Figure 7-4 on the following page). When the spooler sees a monitor "close" packet, it closes the spool file and adds the filename to its spool queue. When the spool file reaches the head of the queue, the spooler opens it, fetches its contents with *DosRead*, and stuffs the data back into the printer monitor chain; after traversing the buffers of any other monitors, the data arrives back at the printer driver and is written to the physical device. After the entire spool file is processed, the spooler deletes it.

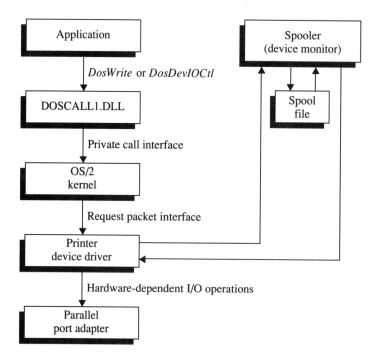

Figure 7-4. *The flow of printer data when the spooler is loaded. The spooler is a process that registers as a device monitor with the printer driver. Data sent to the printer driver by the kernel passes through the chain of monitor buffers. The spooler removes the data from the chain and writes it into a temporary file. When the printer is available, the spooler reads the file back into memory and inserts the data into the monitor chain so that the driver can transfer it to the physical device.*

Serial Port Input and Output

To use a serial port, an application must first call *DosOpen* with the logical device name of the desired port (COM1, COM2, or COM3). To claim exclusive use of a serial port and prevent interference by other processes, specify deny-all sharing mode in the *DosOpen* call. If the port is available, *DosOpen* returns a handle. As with the printer, OS/2 provides no predefined *standard auxiliary device* handle for the serial port that is equivalent to the handle supplied to applications under DOS.

The general-purpose functions *DosRead* and *DosWrite* are used for input and output. They require familiar parameters — a handle, the address and length of a data buffer, and a variable to receive the actual number of bytes read or written. Figure 7-5 offers an example. The driver services *DosRead* and *DosWrite* requests independently, in the order that they are received; transmit and receive operations can be (and frequently are) in progress simultaneously.

```
cname    db      'COM1',0          ; device name
chandle  dw      ?                 ; receives handle

action   dw      ?                 ; receives DosOpen action

msg      db      'HELLO'           ; text of message
msg_len  equ     $-msg             ; length of message

wlen     dw      ?                 ; receives bytes written

         .
         .
         .
         push    ds                ; device name address
         push    offset DGROUP:cname
         push    ds                ; receives device handle
         push    offset DGROUP:chandle
         push    ds                ; receives DosOpen action
         push    offset DGROUP:action
         push    0                 ; filesize (N/A)
         push    0
         push    0                 ; attribute (N/A)
         push    1h                ; flag: open, no create
         push    12h               ; mode: read/write, deny-all
         push    0                 ; reserved DWORD 0
         push    0
         call    DosOpen           ; transfer to OS/2
         or      ax,ax             ; did open succeed?
         jnz     error             ; jump if function failed
         .
         .
         .
         push    chandle           ; handle for COM1
         push    ds                ; message address
         push    offset DGROUP:msg
         push    msg_len           ; message length
         push    ds                ; receives bytes written
         push    offset DGROUP:wlen
         call    DosWrite          ; transfer to OS/2
         or      ax,ax             ; did write succeed?
         jnz     error             ; jump if function failed
         .
         .
         .
```

Figure 7-5. *Obtaining a handle for COM1 with* DosOpen, *and then sending a message to it with* DosWrite.

The serial port driver is fully interrupt-driven and buffers characters internally. Thus, completion of a *DosWrite* operation (from the application's point of view) does not necessarily mean that the characters have been physically transmitted. The sizes of the driver's internal buffers are subject to change from version to version and may even (in a future version) be adjusted dynamically as a function of system activity. In OS/2 version 1.1, the receive buffer is 1024 bytes and the transmit buffer is 128 bytes.

Handles for the serial port are always read and written in binary mode; ordinarily, control characters and escape sequences do not receive any special treatment and are passed through unchanged. If a process enables flow control, however, the XON and XOFF character codes are intercepted and processed by the driver.

When the driver receives an XOFF from the serial port, it stops transmitting until it receives an XON code. Similarly, when its receive buffer is nearly full, the driver sends an XOFF to the serial port; when calls to *DosRead* from an application program empty the buffer to half-full or less, the driver sends an XON to the serial port so that the remote device can resume transmission. The default XON code is 11H (Ctrl-Q) and the default XOFF code is 13H (Ctrl-S), but your program can set each to another value.

Configuring the Serial Port

OS/2 provides protected mode applications with a comprehensive array of Category 1 *DosDevIOCtl* functions to control a number of options, among them the serial port baud rate, parity, character length, stop bits, timeout delays, and flow control (XON/XOFF processing). Functions are also available to check the serial port status and the configuration, the size of the serial port driver's receive and transmit buffers, and the number of characters waiting in those buffers.

For those applications that must control modems or perform hardware handshaking, the following signals at the serial port connector can be controlled by *DosDevIOCtl* calls:

- Data Terminal Ready (DTR)
- Request to Send (RTS)

Similarly, an application can use *DosDevIOCtl* calls to query the state of the following incoming signals at the serial port connector:

- Data Set Ready (DSR)
- Clear to Send (CTS)

- Data Carrier Detect (DCD)

- Ring Indicator (RI)

The *DosDevIOCtl* functions for the serial port driver (Category 1) are summarized in Figure 7-6.

Take care when reconfiguring the serial port "on the fly." The serial port driver processes *DosDevIOCtl* requests immediately upon receipt and does not attempt to serialize them with read and write requests; thus, the results can be unpredictable if the driver receives (for example) a *DosDevIOCtl* command to change the baud rate while it is in the process of receiving or transmitting data.

The default configuration for each serial port, established during system initialization, is 1200 baud, 7-bit character length, even parity, and 1 stop bit. The DTR and RTS signals are initially off. They are turned on when the COM device is opened by an application, and they are turned off again when the COM device is closed and the transmit buffer is empty. Many other factors, however, can affect these signals during serial port communication.

Function Number	Action
41H	Sets baud rate
42H	Sets line characteristics (data bits, parity, stop bits)
44H	Transmits byte immediate
45H	Sets break off
46H	Sets modem control signals (DTR, RTS)
47H	Stops transmitting (as if XOFF received)
48H	Starts transmitting (as if XON received)
4BH	Sets break on
53H	Sets device control block
61H	Gets baud rate
62H	Gets line characteristics (data bits, parity, stop bits, break status)
64H	Gets COM status
65H	Gets transmit data status
66H	Gets modem output control signals (DTR, RTS)
67H	Gets modem input control signals (DSR, CTS, DCD, RI)
68H	Gets number of characters in receive buffer
69H	Gets number of characters in transmit buffer
6DH	Gets COM error information
72H	Gets COM event information
73H	Gets device control block

Figure 7-6. *Category 1* DosDevIOCtl *functions for control of the serial port.*

To examine a more complete example of serial port programming under OS/2, see the DUMBTERM.C or DUMBTERM.ASM program in Chapter 12. This is a simple "dumb terminal" program that takes advantage of multiple threads to avoid the need for polling. DUMBTERM configures the serial port according to #define or equ statements in the source file; then it exchanges characters between the console (keyboard and video display) and the serial port until it receives an exit command.

The Serial Port and Real Mode Applications

The job of OS/2's serial port driver is complicated by the need to support the DOS compatibility environment. Because the DOS and ROM BIOS serial port drivers do not buffer data and are not interrupt-driven, most real mode applications control the serial port adapter directly and bypass operating system services completely.

The driver uses some fairly simple strategies to arbitrate serial port usage between protected mode and real mode applications. It clears out the words in the ROM BIOS data area that normally contain the base port addresses of the serial adapters (location 0040:0000H for COM1, 0040:0002H for COM2). Consequently, real mode applications that test for the existence of the serial port by inspecting the ROM BIOS data area or by calling the ROM BIOS serial port driver will conclude that the adapter is not present. The OS/2 real mode command SETCOM40 updates the ROM BIOS data area to indicate the presence of a port.

A real mode application can acquire a COM device in a number of ways: It can perform an Int 21H read, write, or IOCtl function call using the predefined handle (3) for the first serial port device, or it can explicitly open COM1, COM2, or COM3. Yet another method is to modify the interrupt vector for a serial port. OS/2 periodically checks the interrupt vector table; if it detects that the vector for a serial port has been changed, it assumes that the serial port has been claimed by the real mode application. When a real mode program is using a serial port, OS/2 fails all *DosOpen* requests by protected mode applications for that port until the real mode application terminates, closes the device, or restores the interrupt vector.

If a protected mode program owns a COM port, and a real mode application attempts to open it or capture the interrupt vector, the user is notified by a critical error pop-up. The user can then elect to terminate the real mode application, ignore the error and continue, or (in the case of an attempted open) retry the operation.

PROGRAMMING MASS STORAGE

FILE MANAGEMENT

Although the face of an application is the dexterity with which it manipulates the display, its heart is the set of routines that fetch, manipulate, and store data on media such as magnetic disks. The data on disk is organized into files, which are identified by name; files in turn can be organized by being grouped into directories; directories and files are stored on logical volumes. Applications concern themselves only with the names and contents of files; the details of a file's physical location on the disk and its retrieval are the province of the operating system.

OS/2 provides applications with a variety of services to manipulate files, directories, and volumes in a hardware-independent manner. This chapter explains the OS/2 functions that create, open, close, rename, and delete disk files; read data from and write data to disk files; and inspect or change the information associated with filenames in disk directories (Figure 8-1 on the following page). Directories and volumes are covered in Chapter 9; the physical structure of OS/2 file systems is covered in Chapter 10.

> **NOTE:** *The discussion of disk storage in this book centers on the so-called FAT (file allocation table) file systems, which are identical to those used by MS-DOS. Although OS/2 is designed to allow installation of other file systems as it evolves, the benefits of media compatibility with the vast installed base of MS-DOS machines guarantee that FAT file systems will prevail in OS/2 for a long time to come.*

Function	Description
File Operations	
DosBufReset	Flushes file buffers to disk and updates directory
DosClose	Flushes file buffers to disk, updates directory entry, and releases handle
DosDelete	Removes a file from the directory
DosDupHandle	Returns a new handle that duplicates an existing handle, or forces one handle to track another
DosMove	Renames and/or moves a file (also renames directories)
DosNewSize	Truncates or extends an existing file
DosOpen	Opens, creates, or replaces a file, returning a handle
DosSetMaxFH	Sets maximum handles for process
I/O Operations	
DosChgFilePtr	Sets file pointer relative to start of file, current position, or end of file
DosFileLocks	Locks or unlocks file region
DosRead	Reads from file, device, or pipe (synchronous)
DosReadAsync	Reads from file, device, or pipe (asynchronous)
DosWrite	Writes to file, device, or pipe (synchronous)
DosWriteAsync	Writes to file, device, or pipe (asynchronous)
File Information	
DosQFHandState	Returns handle characteristics
DosQFileInfo	Returns file date, time, attributes, and size
DosQFileMode	Returns file attributes
DosQHandType	Returns file, pipe, or device code for a handle
DosSetFHandState	Sets handle characteristics
DosSetFileInfo	Sets file date and time
DosSetFileMode	Sets file attributes

Figure 8-1. *OS/2 file management services at a glance.*

Filenames and Handles

To manipulate a file, a program must identify it to the operating system with a null-terminated (ASCIIZ) character string called a pathname. A pathname can contain four different elements in the following form:

drive:path\filename.extension

The *drive* code takes the form of a single letter followed by a colon (:) and identifies the logical volume that holds the file. The *path* identifies the directory that contains the filename; it can be a complete specification from the root directory of the volume, or it can be a relative specification (more about this in Chapter 9). If *drive* is absent, the current drive is assumed; if *path* is absent, the current directory is assumed. For each process, the system maintains a current drive and (for each drive) a current directory.

The *filename* is the only component that *must* be present in a pathname. It contains a maximum of eight characters. The *extension*, when present, is really part of the filename; it appends a maximum of three characters, separated from the filename by a period. (These restrictions on filenames and extensions might not apply in non-FAT file systems.) Although extensions generally signify a file's "type" or contents, this is only a convention.

Functions that operate on a file as a whole, such as those that delete or rename files, require only the ASCIIZ pathname. Functions that operate on the contents of files, however, refer to files with *handles*. A handle is a 16-bit token—usually a small positive integer—that OS/2 provides to a program for its use in manipulating the associated file. (In a few moments, you'll see how a program obtains handles.) The value of a handle has no special significance, except that it is different from the values of handles for other files or devices being used at the same time by the same process.

The default limit on the number of handles that a single process can own is 20. Three handles are preassigned to the *standard input, standard output,* and *standard error* devices (mentioned earlier in Chapters 5 and 6 in connection with the keyboard and video display). A process can inherit additional handles from its parent, further infringing on the initial allotment of 20. Fortunately, you can increase the per-process handle limit at run time with the function *DosSetMaxFH*.

Creating, Opening, and Closing Files

The API function *DosOpen* is the bridge between the functions that use pathnames and the functions that use handles. It accepts the pathname of a file to be created, opened, or replaced, and it returns a handle that can be used to manipulate the contents or attributes of the file. As we saw in Chapters 5–7, you can also use *DosOpen* to open character devices for input and output as though they were files.

The *DosOpen* function is flexible; consequently, it requires many parameters and is the most complex file management function to master. Your program must supply *DosOpen* with the following information:

- The address of an ASCIIZ pathname for the file or device
- The *OpenFlag* and *OpenMode* parameters
- A file size
- A file attribute
- The addresses of two variables that will receive information from OS/2

The *OpenFlag* parameter has two fields that allow the *DosOpen* operation to be tailored to the previous existence or nonexistence of the file (Figure 8-2). For example, the combination "create if file does not exist" and "fail if file exists" amounts to a "test and lock" operation that can be used to implement semaphores in the form of files across a network.

The *OpenMode* parameter controls a number of characteristics of the open file. It governs the process's access to the file, the manner of error handling and data buffering to be used, the direct disk access option (see Chapter 10), the level at which the file can be shared with other processes, and whether access to the file is inherited by child processes (Figure 8-3). If one or more other processes have already opened the same file, the outcome of the *DosOpen* operation depends on the requested access rights and sharing mode as shown in Figure 8-4 on p. 136.

A process should ensure that its own *DosOpen* requests succeed in all appropriate conditions by specifying the minimum necessary access rights; for example, the process should not request read/write access when it only needs to read the file. Similarly, the process should avoid requesting restrictive sharing modes whenever possible.

The *DosOpen* attribute and size parameters are relevant only when a file is being created or replaced. The attribute parameter marks the file as hidden, system, read-only, or modified since last backup (archive), as shown in Figure 8-5 on p. 136. The size parameter preallocates disk space for the file; the data in the preallocated area is undefined. (Later versions of OS/2 might attempt to preallocate contiguous disk space to improve file access times.) When an existing file is opened, the attribute and size parameters are ignored.

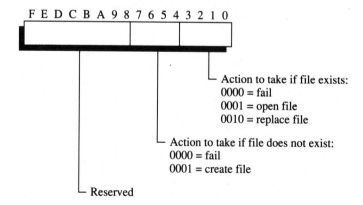

Figure 8-2. OpenFlag *parameter for the* DosOpen *function.*

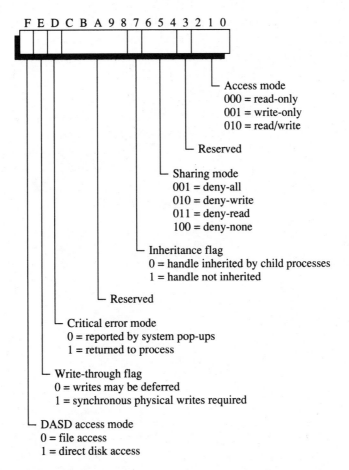

Figure 8-3. OpenMode *parameter for the* DosOpen *function. Use of* DosOpen *with the DASD bit set for direct disk access is discussed in Chapter 10.*

If the *DosOpen* operation succeeds, the function returns zero in register AX. The file handle, to be used for subsequent read, write, seek, and close operations, is returned in one of the variables. An "action" code is returned in the other variable: 0001 if the file existed and was opened, 0002 if the file was created, or 0003 if the file existed and was replaced (the previous data in the file was lost).

If the call to *DosOpen* fails, an error code is returned in AX. The function call can fail for many reasons, including bad pathnames or other parameters, sharing conflicts with another process, inadequate access rights (to a network directory, for example), and exhaustion of process or system resources (such as handles).

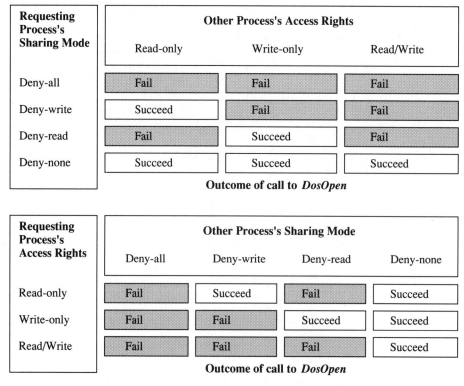

Requesting Process's Sharing Mode	Other Process's Access Rights		
	Read-only	Write-only	Read/Write
Deny-all	Fail	Fail	Fail
Deny-write	Succeed	Fail	Fail
Deny-read	Fail	Succeed	Fail
Deny-none	Succeed	Succeed	Succeed

Outcome of call to *DosOpen*

Requesting Process's Access Rights	Other Process's Sharing Mode			
	Deny-all	Deny-write	Deny-read	Deny-none
Read-only	Fail	Succeed	Fail	Succeed
Write-only	Fail	Fail	Succeed	Succeed
Read/Write	Fail	Fail	Fail	Succeed

Outcome of call to *DosOpen*

Figure 8-4. *Outcome of* DosOpen *based on sharing mode and access rights of the requesting process and those of another process that previously opened the file.*

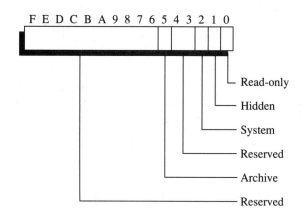

F E D C B A 9 8 7 6 5 4 3 2 1 0

Read-only
Hidden
System
Reserved
Archive
Reserved

Figure 8-5. *Attribute parameter for the* DosOpen *function when it is used to create a file. Do not use the read-only attribute bit with* DosOpen; *you can apply it to the file later with* DosSetFileMode. *Also, do not use bits 3 and 4 with* DosOpen; *these bits, which indicate directories and volume labels in FAT file systems, are discussed further in Chapter 9.*

DosOpen is a good example of an OS/2 function call that is better suited to high level languages than to assembler. The large number of parameters that must be pushed on the stack bloat the source code (Figure 8-6). You might find it useful to encapsulate *DosOpen* within a subroutine that assumes reasonable default values for most parameters. If you also write the subroutine so that it places its local variables on the stack, multiple threads can share the subroutine without any need for semaphores or other synchronization mechanisms (Figure 8-7 on the following pages).

```
fname    db      'MYFILE.DAT',0  ; ASCIIZ pathname
fhandle  dw      0               ; receives handle
faction  dw      0               ; receives DosOpen action


         .
         .
         .

         push    ds              ; ASCIIZ pathname
         push    offset DGROUP:fname
         push    ds              ; receives handle
         push    offset DGROUP:fhandle
         push    ds              ; receives DosOpen action
         push    offset DGROUP:faction
         push    0               ; file size (ignored)
         push    0
         push    0               ; file attribute (ignored)
         push    1               ; flag: fail if file
                                 ;       doesn't exist
         push    42h             ; mode: deny-none,
                                 ;       access read/write
         push    0               ; reserved DWORD 0
         push    0
         call    DosOpen         ; transfer to OS/2
         or      ax,ax           ; did open succeed?
         jnz     error           ; jump if function failed
         .
         .
         .
```

Figure 8-6. *Example of in-line code to open a file. When an existing file is opened, the attribute and size parameters are ignored. Compare with Figure 8-7.*

```
; FOPEN: reentrant routine to open a file or device
;
; Call with:    DS:DX = address of ASCIIZ pathname
;               AX    = OpenMode
; Returns:      Z     = true if successful
;               BX    = handle
;               AX    = DosOpen action
;               or
;               Z     = false if failed
;               AX    = DosOpen error code
; Uses:         DX

fhandle equ     [bp-2]
faction equ     [bp-4]


fopen   proc    near

        push    bp              ; save original BP value
        mov     bp,sp           ; set up stack frame
        sub     sp,4            ; allocate local variables

        push    ds              ; ASCIIZ pathname
        push    dx
        push    ss              ; receives handle
        lea     dx,fhandle
        push    dx
        push    ss              ; receives DosOpen action
        lea     dx,faction
        push    dx
        push    0               ; file size (ignored)
        push    0
        push    0               ; file attribute (ignored)
        push    1               ; flag: fail if file
                                ;       doesn't exist
        push    ax              ; mode: from caller
        push    0               ; reserved DWORD 0
        push    0

        call    DosOpen         ; transfer to OS/2

        or      ax,ax           ; set Z flag to indicate
        jnz     fopen1          ; success or failure
```

(continued)

Figure 8-7. *Example of a reentrant procedure to encapsulate the job of opening a file. Local variables are created on the stack to receive the results of the* DosOpen *operation. Compare with Figure 8-6.*

Figure 8-7. *continued*

```
        mov     bx,fhandle      ; get handle
        mov     ax,faction      ; get DosOpen action

fopen1: mov     sp,bp           ; discard local variables
        pop     bp              ; restore original BP
        ret                     ; back to caller

fopen   endp
```

Once a file has been opened or created, a process can use several auxiliary functions to obtain or modify information associated with the file. *DosQHandType* returns information indicating whether a handle is associated with a file, a pipe, or a character device; *DosQFileMode* returns a file's attributes; *DosQFileInfo* returns a file's size, attributes, and date and time stamps; and *DosQFHandState* returns the write-through, inheritance, sharing, and access rights associated with a file handle. These functions are especially useful to a child process that has inherited a handle and needs to know how that handle may be used. A similar set of functions permits a process to change attributes, access rights, and the like "on the fly."

When a process finishes using a file, it calls *DosClose* to release the handle, flush to disk any unwritten data that is buffered within OS/2, and update the size, date, and time in the directory entry for the file if it has been modified. Under normal circumstances, a *DosClose* operation fails only if the file was on a floppy disk, the file was modified, and the user removed the disk while the file was open.

Reading and Writing Files

After a process opens or creates a file, it is ready to do useful work: fetching and displaying information from the file, modifying the data already stored in the file, or adding new data to the file. Let's review some key terms related to file access:

- *Reading* and *writing*
- The *file pointer*
- *Sequential* and *random* access
- *Synchronous* and *asynchronous* access

Reading is copying data from disk into RAM; the data on the disk is unchanged, and the previous contents of the area of RAM are lost. *Writing* is copying data from RAM onto disk; the contents of RAM are unchanged, and the previous contents of the disk area are lost. Data is not necessarily physically transferred between the disk and RAM when an application's read or write request is "logically" complete; OS/2 often buffers disk data internally for extended periods to improve performance.

OS/2 maintains a *file pointer* for each handle in the system file table (SFT). When an application issues a read or write request, the current value of the file pointer for that handle determines the byte offset (from the start of the file) at which the transfer will begin. When the transfer is complete, OS/2 updates the file pointer so that it points one byte past the last byte that was read or written. An application can also set the file pointer to an arbitrary value — this is often referred to as a *seek* operation (not to be confused with the physical seek performed by a disk drive, which involves moving the read/write heads to a specific cylinder).

Sequential access is reading or writing consecutive data in a file. This type of processing is typically used for accessing files with variable-length records; a text file, in which each line can be considered a record delimited by a newline character, is an example of such a file. A program that processes files sequentially need not concern itself with the file pointer because OS/2 maintains it.

Random access is reading and writing nonsequential records — the physical ordering of the records in the file does not determine the order in which they are processed. (The term is not particularly apt, of course, because the processing is not at all random.) In simple applications, random access is typically used for files that contain fixed-length records. A program can calculate the location of a record (by multiplying a record number times the record size), set the file pointer to that offset, and then request a read or write. The indexed file access methods used by more sophisticated applications are much more versatile.

In the classic definition of *synchronous* access, the process requesting the read or write operation is suspended until the transfer is complete. On the other hand, when *asynchronous* access is requested, the operating system starts the transfer and then returns control to the process, notifying the process by some other means when the read or write operation is finished.

With this terminology in hand, let's take a look at OS/2's five fundamental services for reading and writing files: *DosRead*, *DosReadAsync*, *DosWrite*, *DosWriteAsync*, and *DosChgFilePtr*. Figure 8-8 contains a sample code skeleton for file access by an OS/2 application.

```
recsize   equ    1024              ; file record size

fname1    db     'OLDFILE.DAT',0 ; input filename
fname2    db     'NEWFILE.DAT',0 ; output filename

fhandl1 dw       0                 ; input file handle
fhandl2 dw       0                 ; output file handle

faction dw       0                 ; receives DosOpen action

rlen     dw      0                 ; length from DosRead
wlen     dw      0                 ; length from DosWrite

buffer   db      recsize dup (?) ; buffer for file I/O

                .
                .
                .
                          ; open input file...
          push   ds                ; input filename
          push   offset DGROUP:fname1
          push   ds                ; receives handle
          push   offset DGROUP:fhandl1
          push   ds                ; receives DosOpen action
          push   offset DGROUP:faction
          push   0                 ; file size (ignored)
          push   0
          push   0                 ; file attribute (ignored)
          push   1                 ; flag: fail if file
                          ;         doesn't exist
          push   40h               ; mode: deny-none,
                          ;         access read-only
          push   0                 ; reserved DWORD 0
          push   0
          call   DosOpen           ; transfer to OS/2

          or     ax,ax             ; was open successful?
          jnz    error             ; jump if function failed
                .
                .
                .
                          ; create output file...
```

(continued)

Figure 8-8. *Skeleton code for an OS/2 assembly language program that performs synchronous, sequential file access. In this simple example, partial records at end of file do not receive any special treatment, and the error status returned by* DosClose *is ignored.*

Figure 8-8. *continued*

```
        push    ds                    ; output filename
        push    offset DGROUP:fname2
        push    ds                    ; receives handle
        push    offset DGROUP:fhandl2
        push    ds                    ; receives DosOpen action
        push    offset DGROUP:faction
        push    0                     ; initial file size = 0
        push    0
        push    0                     ; attribute = normal
        push    12                    ; flag: create or replace
        push    41h                   ; mode: deny-none,
                                      ;       access write-only
        push    0                     ; reserved DWORD 0
        push    0
        call    DosOpen               ; transfer to OS/2

        or      ax,ax                 ; was create successful?
        jnz     error                 ; jump if function failed

next:                                 ; read next record from
                                      ; input file...

        push    fhandl1               ; input file handle
        push    ds                    ; buffer address
        push    offset DGROUP:buffer
        push    recsize               ; length to read
        push    ds                    ; receives actual length
        push    offset DGROUP:rlen
        call    DosRead               ; transfer to OS/2

        or      ax,ax                 ; was read successful?
        jnz     error                 ; jump if function failed

        cmp     rlen,0                ; read length = 0?
        je      done                  ; jump if end of file

        .                             ; other processing of record
        .                             ; performed here...
        .
                                      ; write processed record
                                      ; to output file...

        push    fhandl2               ; output file handle
        push    ds                    ; buffer address
```

(continued)

Figure 8-8. *continued*

```
        push    offset DGROUP:buffer
        push    rlen            ; write length = read length
        push    ds              ; receives actual length
        push    offset DGROUP:wlen
        call    DosWrite        ; transfer to OS/2

        or      ax,ax           ; was write successful?
        jnz     error           ; jump if function failed

        mov     ax,rlen         ; was write complete?
        cmp     ax,wlen
        jne     error           ; jump if disk full

        jmp     next            ; process another record

done:                           ; end of file reached...

        push    fhandl1         ; close input file
        call    DosClose        ; transfer to OS/2

        push    fhandl2         ; close output file
        call    DosClose        ; transfer to OS/2

                                ; now terminate process...
        push    1               ; terminate all threads
        push    0               ; return code = 0 (success)
        call    DosExit         ; transfer to OS/2
```

DosRead and *DosWrite* perform synchronous reads and writes. Both functions require a handle, the address of the data to be written or the buffer to receive the data to be read, a length, and the address of a variable. When the functions return, the variable contains the number of bytes actually transferred. In the case of files, the number of bytes transferred might be less than the number requested for two reasons: The data was being written to disk, and the disk was full; or the data was being read from disk, and the end of the file was reached. Neither of these events is considered to be an error; that is, zero is returned in AX for both.

The functions *DosReadAsync* and *DosWriteAsync* provide asynchronous reads and writes. These functions require the same parameters as *DosRead* and *DosWrite*; in addition, they require addresses for a RAM semaphore and a variable to receive an error code. The program sets the semaphore before calling *DosReadAsync* or *DosWriteAsync*; when the requested operation is complete, the semaphore is cleared, and an error code and number of bytes transferred are returned in variables. (Chapter 13 provides more information about semaphores.)

OS/2's support for threads provided a simple means of implementing *DosReadAsync* and *DosWriteAsync*. These functions merely create a new thread on behalf of the calling process that executes—carrying out the I/O, clearing the semaphore, and then destroying itself—while the original thread continues its execution. You can generally get better performance in your application by using multiple threads explicitly, rather than letting them be created and destroyed in this hidden manner.

DosChgFilePtr allows a process to set the file pointer associated with a handle to an arbitrary offset. The program supplies a code that indicates the "method" in which the offset is specified: relative to the start of file (method 0), to the current file pointer (method 1), or to the end of file (method 2). When methods 1 and 2 are used, the offset can be either positive or negative. In any case, the function returns the resulting absolute offset from the start of file.

There is little distinction between sequential and random access under OS/2. When a file is opened or created, its file pointer is initially set to zero. If a process simply issues reads or writes without ever calling *DosChgFilePtr*, then its access to the file is sequential. If a process requires random access, it need only call *DosChgFilePtr* before each read or write to position the file pointer appropriately. Naturally, these techniques can be used together; a process can seek to a specific record and then process sequential records by consecutive read or write operations.

Note the following special uses of *DosChgFilePtr*: To obtain the current position of the file pointer without modifying it, call the function with method 1 and an offset of zero; to find the file size, call *DosChgFilePtr* with method 2 and an offset of zero.

> **WARNING:** *When multiple threads use the same file handle, they must do so cooperatively because OS/2 does not attempt to serialize requests from different threads or protect one thread from another. For example, if a thread calls* DosChgFilePtr *followed by* DosRead *to read a specific record—and another thread's request using the same handle gets serviced in between—the file pointer will be changed, and the first thread will get the wrong data. The order in which requests from different threads are completed depends on the priorities of the threads and on the physical location of the data on the disk as well as on the order of the requests themselves.*

Forcing Disk Updates

OS/2's ability to buffer data internally to eliminate unnecessary reads or defer writes improves system throughput. However, some programs must be able to bring a file—on demand—to a consistent state on the physical disk, in case power fails, the system crashes, or the process terminates unexpectedly. Imagine, for example, the potential problems if the index to a database was updated but the corresponding record was never written, or vice versa.

The function *DosBufReset* writes the system's internal buffers associated with a specific file handle to the disk and updates the corresponding entry in the disk directory; the original handle remains open for further use. If *DosBufReset* is called with a handle of −1, the buffers are flushed and the directory entries updated for *all* of the process's open files. If any files are on removable media and those media were changed, OS/2 prompts the user to mount the necessary disks.

The methods used in MS-DOS programming to force a disk update—closing and reopening a handle or duplicating and closing a handle—are inefficient and unnecessary in OS/2.

File and Record Locking

In a multitasking, network-oriented environment such as OS/2, it is to be expected that the user will (intentionally or unintentionally) attempt to use the same file with several programs at once, or open a file on a network server that is also in use by a program running in another network node. If programs do not defend themselves against the user by proper use of OS/2's sharing and locking facilities, deadlocks or race conditions can occur, and data can be lost or corrupted.[†]

You can restrict access by other processes to an entire file by using the proper sharing mode in a *DosOpen* call. After a process successfully opens a file with a sharing mode of deny-all or deny-write, it can modify the file with impunity. Such a process is not regarded as "friendly" in a multitasking environment, however, because it interferes with other processes' access to the file for a prolonged period.

---

† A deadlock occurs when two processes are each waiting for the other. (For example, Process A has opened file X with deny-all sharing mode and needs file Y, and Process B has opened file Y with deny-all and needs file X.) A race condition occurs when two process are modifying shared data without cooperating; the final state of the data depends on which process runs when.

A better approach is to open the file with a sharing mode of deny-none and then to exclude other processes from access to specific file regions only during updates of those regions. The function *DosFileLocks* allows a process to lock, or request exclusive access to, a file region of arbitrary position and size. Another locked region can be unlocked during the same function call. While a lock is in effect, calls issued by other processes to read, write, or lock the same file region will fail. If a process cannot lock a file region, it can delay and retry the lock operation, or it can display a message so that the user can resolve the contention.

The system recognizes locks on file regions on a per-process basis. Thus, child processes do not inherit region locks, although they *do* inherit overall sharing modes and access rights for a file. Also, a *DosFileLocks* call does not protect one thread against interference by another using the same handle; such protection must be obtained by other means.

Renaming and Deleting Files

Use *DosMove* to rename a file or move it to another directory of the same drive (or to do both at once). The function requires two ASCIIZ pathnames for the old and new locations and names of the file; it returns an error if the file is currently opened by the same or another process, if some element of the old or new directory path does not exist, or if a file by the new name already exists in the destination directory. In contrast to the user-level RENAME command, *DosMove* works on one file at a time and does not accept wildcard characters in filenames.

The function *DosDelete* removes a file from the disk directory. It fails if the file is read-only or is currently opened by the same or another process. Unlike the DEL and ERASE user commands supported by CMD.EXE and COMMAND.COM, *DosDelete* does not tolerate pathnames that contain wildcards and only deletes one file at a time.

When you delete a file in FAT file systems, its directory entry is marked as available by a change in the first byte of the entry (to a reserved value). The disk sectors previously allocated to the file are released. The remainder of the directory entry and the actual contents of the disk sectors are not altered, making it possible for "un-erase" programs to reclaim the file under some circumstances. A program that requires a higher degree of security should overwrite the entire file with zeros or other data before it deletes the file.

Sample Programs: DUMP.ASM and DUMP.C

The listings DUMP.C (Figure 8-9) and DUMP.ASM (Figure 8-10) are the source code for DUMP.EXE, a utility program that displays the binary contents of a file in hex and ASCII. These listings illustrate many of the basic file management techniques you will need in your own application programs. The two programs are symmetric and produce identical output (an example of which is shown in Figure 8-14 on p. 163).

```
/*
        DUMP.C

        Displays the binary contents of a file in hex and ASCII
        on the standard output device. Demonstrates direct
        calls to OS/2 API from a C program.

        Compile with:  C> cl dump.c

        Usage is:  C> dump pathname.ext [>destination]

        Copyright (C) 1987 Ray Duncan
*/

#include <stdio.h>

#define RECSIZE 16                  /* size of file records */

#define API unsigned extern far pascal

API DosClose(unsigned);            /* function prototypes */

API DosOpen(char far *, unsigned far *, unsigned far *, unsigned long,
        unsigned, unsigned, unsigned, unsigned long);

API DosRead(unsigned, void far *, unsigned, unsigned far *);

main(int argc, char *argv[])
{
    char file_buf[RECSIZE];        /* data block from file */
    unsigned long foffset = 0L;    /* file offset in bytes */
```

(continued)

Figure 8-9. *DUMP.C, the C source code for DUMP.EXE.*

Figure 8-9. *continued*

```
    unsigned handle;                /* DosOpen variable */
    unsigned action, length;        /* DosRead variables */
    unsigned flag = 0x01;           /* fail if file not found */
    unsigned mode = 0x40;           /* read-only, deny-none */

    if(argc < 2)                    /* check command tail */
    {
        fprintf(stderr, "\ndump: missing filename\n");
        exit(1);
    }
                                    /* open file or exit */
    if(DosOpen(argv[1], &handle, &action, 0L, 0, flag, mode, 0L))
    {
        fprintf(stderr, "\ndump: can't find file %s\n", argv[1]);
        exit(1);
    }
                                    /* read and dump records */
    while((DosRead(handle, file_buf, RECSIZE, &length) == 0)
          && (length != 0))
    {
        dump_rec(file_buf, foffset, length);
        foffset += RECSIZE;
    }
    printf("\n");                   /* extra blank line */
    DosClose(handle);               /* close the input file */
    exit(0);                        /* return success code */
}


/*
    Display record (16 bytes) in hex and ASCII on standard output.
*/
dump_rec(char *buffer, long foffset, int length)
{
    int i;                          /* index to current record */

    if(foffset % 128 == 0)          /* maybe print heading */
        printf("\n\n        0 1 2 3 4 5 6 7 8 9 A B C D E F");

    printf("\n%04lX ", foffset);    /* file offset */

    for(i = 0; i < length; i++)     /* print hex equivalent of each byte */
        printf(" %02X", (unsigned char) buffer[i]);

    if(length != 16)                /* space over if last record */
        for(i=0; i<(16-length); i++) printf("   ");
```

(continued)

Figure 8-9. *continued*

```
    printf("  ");
    for(i = 0; i < length; i++)        /* print ASCII equiv. of bytes */
    {
        if(buffer[i] < 32 || buffer[i] > 126) putchar('.');
        else putchar(buffer[i]);
    }
}
```

```
        title   DUMP -- Display File Contents
        page    55,132
        .286


;
; DUMP.ASM
;
; Displays the binary contents of a file in hex and ASCII on the
; standard output device.
;
; Assemble with:  C> masm dump.asm;
; Link with:  C> link dump,,,os2,dump
;
; Usage is:  C> dump pathname.ext [>destination]
;
; Copyright (C) 1988 Ray Duncan
;

cr      equ     0dh                    ; ASCII carriage return
lf      equ     0ah                    ; ASCII line feed
blank   equ     20h                    ; ASCII space code

blksize equ     16                     ; size of input file records

stdout  equ     1                      ; standard output handle
stderr  equ     2                      ; standard error handle

        extrn   DosOpen:far
        extrn   DosRead:far
        extrn   DosWrite:far
        extrn   DosClose:far
        extrn   DosExit:far
```

(continued)

Figure 8-10. *DUMP.ASM, the MASM source code for DUMP.EXE. Figures 8-11 and 8-12 provide the source code for the subroutines ARGV and ARGC.*

Figure 8-10. *continued*

```
          extrn    argc:near              ; returns argument count
          extrn    argv:near              ; returns argument pointer

DGROUP  group    _DATA


_DATA   segment word public 'DATA'

fname   db       64 dup (0)               ; name of input file

fhandle dw       0                        ; input file handle

faction dw       0                        ; action from DosOpen

fptr    dw       0                        ; relative file address

rlen    dw       0                        ; actual number of bytes
                                          ; read by DosRead

wlen    dw       0                        ; actual number of bytes
                                          ; written by DosWrite

output  db       'nnnn',blank,blank       ; output format area
outputa db       16 dup ('nn',blank)
        db       blank
outputb db       16 dup (blank),cr,lf
output_len equ $-output

hdg     db       cr,lf
        db       7 dup (blank)
        db       '0 1 2 3 4 5 6 7 '
        db       '8 9 A B C D E F',cr,lf
hdg_len equ $-hdg

fbuff   db       blksize dup (?)          ; data from file

msg1    db       cr,lf
        db       'dump: file not found'
        db       cr,lf
msg1_len equ $-msg1

msg2    db       cr,lf
        db       'dump: missing filename'
        db       cr,lf
msg2_len equ $-msg2
```

(continued)

Figure 8-10. *continued*

```
msg3        db        cr,lf
            db        'dump: empty file'
            db        cr,lf
msg3_len equ $-msg3


_DATA     ends

_TEXT     segment word public 'CODE'

          assume  cs:_TEXT,ds:DGROUP

dump      proc    far                         ; entry point from OS/2

          push    ds                          ; make DGROUP addressable
          pop     es                          ; via ES

          call    argc                        ; is filename present
          cmp     ax,2                        ; in command tail?
          je      dump1                       ; yes, proceed

          mov     dx,offset msg2              ; missing or illegal filespec,
          mov     cx,msg2_len
          jmp     dump9                       ; display error message and exit

dump1:                                        ; copy filename from command
                                              ; tail to local buffer

          mov     ax,1                        ; get pointer to command tail
          call    argv                        ; argument in ES:BX
          mov     cx,ax                       ; CX = filename length
          mov     di,offset fname             ; DS:DI = local buffer

dump2:    mov     al,es:[bx]                  ; copy filename byte by byte
          mov     [di],al
          inc     bx
          inc     di
          loop    dump2

          push    ds                          ; restore ES = DGROUP
          pop     es

dump4:                                        ; try to open file...
          push    ds                          ; address of filename
          push    offset fname
          push    ds                          ; receives file handle
```

(continued)

Figure 8-10. *continued*

```
          push    offset fhandle
          push    ds
          push    offset faction          ; receives DosOpen action
          push    0                       ; file size (ignored)
          push    0
          push    0                       ; file attribute (ignored)
          push    1                       ; OpenFlag:
                                          ; fail if file doesn't exist
          push    40h                     ; OpenMode:
                                          ; deny-none, access = read-only
          push    0                       ; reserved DWORD 0
          push    0
          call    DosOpen                 ; transfer to OS/2
          or      ax,ax                   ; was open successful?
          jz      dump5                   ; yes, proceed

          mov     dx,offset msg1          ; open failed, display
          mov     cx,msg1_len             ; error message and exit
          jmp     dump9

dump5:    call    rdblk                   ; initialize file buffer
          cmp     rlen,0                  ; anything read?
          jne     dump6                   ; jump, got some data
          cmp     fptr,0                  ; no data, was this first read?
          jne     dump8                   ; no, end of file reached

          mov     dx,offset msg3          ; empty file, print error
          mov     cx,msg3_len             ; message and exit
          jmp     dump9

dump6:    test    fptr,07fh               ; time for a heading?
          jnz     dump7                   ; no, jump

                                          ; write heading...
          push    stdout                  ; standard output handle
          push    ds                      ; address of heading
          push    offset hdg
          push    hdg_len                 ; length of heading
          push    ds                      ; receives bytes written
          push    offset wlen
          call    DosWrite

dump7:    call    cnvblk                  ; convert one block of
                                          ; binary data to ASCII
```

(continued)

Figure 8-10. *continued*

```
                                            ; write formatted output...
          push    stdout                    ; standard output handle
          push    ds                        ; address of output
          push    offset output
          push    output_len                ; length of output
          push    ds                        ; receives bytes written
          push    offset wlen
          call    DosWrite

          jmp     dump5                     ; get more data

dump8:                                      ; end of file reached...
          push    fhandle                   ; close input file
          call    DosClose                  ; transfer to OS/2

                                            ; final exit to OS/2...
          push    1                         ; terminate all threads
          push    0                         ; return code = 0 (success)
          call    DosExit                   ; transfer to OS/2

dump9:                                      ; print error message on
                                            ; standard error device

          push    stderr
          push    ds                        ; address of message
          push    dx
          push    cx                        ; length of message
          push    ds                        ; receives bytes written
          push    offset wlen
          call    DosWrite                  ; transfer to OS/2

                                            ; final exit to OS/2...
          push    1                         ; terminate all threads
          push    1                         ; return code = 1 (error)
          call    DosExit                   ; transfer to OS/2

dump      endp

; RDBLK:    Read block of data from input file
;
; Call with:    nothing
; Returns:      AX = error code (0 = no error)
; Uses:         nothing

rdblk     proc    near
```

(continued)

Figure 8-10. *continued*

```
          push    fhandle                  ; input file handle
          push    ds                       ; buffer address
          push    offset fbuff
          push    blksize                  ; buffer length
          push    ds                       ; receives bytes read
          push    offset rlen
          call    DosRead                  ; transfer to OS/2
          ret                              ; back to caller

rdblk     endp

; CNVBLK:       Format one binary record for output
;
; Call with:    nothing
; Returns:      nothing
; Uses:         AX, BX, CX, DX, DI

cnvblk    proc    near

          mov     di,offset output         ; clear output format
          mov     cx,output_len-2          ; area to blanks
          mov     al,blank
          rep stosb

          mov     di,offset output         ; convert current file
          mov     ax,fptr                  ; offset to ASCII
          call    wtoa

          xor     bx,bx                    ; point to start of data

cb1:      mov     al,[fbuff+bx]            ; get next byte of data
                                           ; from input file

          lea     di,[bx+outputb]         ; calculate output address
                                           ; for ASCII equivalent
          mov     byte ptr [di],'.'        ; if control character,
          cmp     al,blank                 ; substitute a period
          jb      cb2                      ; jump, not alphanumeric
          cmp     al,7eh
          ja      cb2                      ; jump, not alphanumeric
          mov     [di],al                  ; store ASCII character
```

(continued)

Figure 8-10. *continued*

```
cb2:                                    ; now convert byte to hex
        mov     di,bx                   ; calculate output address
        imul    di,di,3                 ; (position*3) + base address
        add     di,offset outputa
        call    btoa                    ; convert data byte to hex

        inc     bx                      ; advance through record
        cmp     bx,rlen                 ; entire buffer converted?
        jne     cb1                     ; no, get another byte

        add     fptr,blksize            ; update file offset

        ret                             ; back to caller

cnvblk  endp



; WTOA:         Convert word to hex ASCII
;
; Call with:    AX    = data to convert
;               ES:DI = storage address
; Returns:      nothing
; Uses:         AX, CL, DI

wtoa    proc    near

        push    ax                      ; save original value
        mov     al,ah
        call    btoa                    ; convert upper byte

        pop     ax                      ; restore original value
        call    btoa                    ; convert lower byte

        ret                             ; back to caller

wtoa    endp



; BTOA:         Convert byte to hex ASCII
;
; Call with:    AL    = data to convert
;               ES:DI = storage address
; Returns:      nothing
; Uses:         AX, CL, DI

btoa    proc    near
```

(continued)

Figure 8-10. *continued*

```
            sub     ah,ah                       ; clear upper byte

            mov     cl,16                       ; divide by 16
            div     cl

            call    ascii                       ; convert quotient
            stosb                               ; store ASCII character

            mov     al,ah
            call    ascii                       ; convert remainder
            stosb                               ; store ASCII character

            ret                                 ; back to caller

btoa    endp

; ASCII:          Convert nibble to hex ASCII
;
; Call with:      AL   = data to convert in low 4 bits
; Returns:        AL   = ASCII character
; Uses:           nothing

ascii   proc    near

            add     al,'0'                      ; add base ASCII value
            cmp     al,'9'                      ; is it in range 0-9?
            jle     ascii2                      ; jump if it is

            add     al,'A'-'9'-1                ; no, adjust for range A-F

ascii2: ret                                     ; return ASCII character in AL

ascii   endp

_TEXT   ends

            end     dump
```

DUMP parses the pathname for the file to be displayed from the command tail at the end of the environment. It sends the formatted dump to the standard output device; you can redirect the output to a file, another character device, or another process through a pipe. Error messages are sent to the standard error device so that they will not be affected by redirection of the standard output.

The C version of DUMP demonstrates calls to the OS/2 API from a high level language. Calling OS/2 functions directly for file management, instead of using the C runtime library, makes the program smaller and faster (but less portable).

The MASM version of DUMP works in much the same way as the C version but yields an EXE file that is only one-fifth as large. DUMP.ASM uses two external subroutines, ARGC.ASM (Figure 8-11) and ARGV.ASM (Figure 8-12), which you will find helpful in just about any MASM program and which will be used again several times in this book. ARGC returns the number of command line arguments, and ARGV returns the address and length of a particular command line argument.

```
            title   ARGC -- Return Argument Count
            page    55,132
            .286


;
; ARGC.ASM
;
; Return count of command line arguments. Treats blanks and
; tabs as whitespace.
;
; Assemble with:  C> masm argc.asm;
;
; Call with:      N/A
;
; Returns:        AX    = argument count (always >= 1)
;
; Uses:           nothing (other registers preserved)
;
; Copyright (C) 1987 Ray Duncan
;

tab         equ     09h             ; ASCII tab
blank       equ     20h             ; ASCII space character

            extrn   DosGetEnv:far

_TEXT       segment word public 'CODE'

            assume  cs:_TEXT
```

(continued)

Figure 8-11. *ARGC.ASM, the MASM source code for the ARGC routine called by the DUMP utility. This procedure returns the number of command line arguments.*

Figure 8-11. *continued*

```
        public  argc             ; make ARGC available to Linker

                                 ; local variables
envseg  equ     [bp-2]           ; environment segment
cmdoffs equ     [bp-4]           ; command line offset

argc    proc    near

        enter   4,0              ; make room for local variables

        push    es               ; save original ES, BX, and CX
        push    bx
        push    cx

        push    ss               ; get selector for environment
        lea     ax,envseg        ; and offset of command line
        push    ax
        push    ss
        lea     ax,cmdoffs
        push    ax
        call    DosGetEnv        ; transfer to OS/2
        or      ax,ax            ; check operation status
        mov     ax,1             ; force argc >= 1
        jnz     argc3            ; inexplicable failure

        mov     es,envseg        ; set ES:BX = command line
        mov     bx,cmdoffs

argc0:  inc     bx               ; ignore useless first field
        cmp     byte ptr es:[bx],0
        jne     argc0

argc1:  mov     cx,-1            ; set flag = outside argument

argc2:  inc     bx               ; point to next character
        cmp     byte ptr es:[bx],0
        je      argc3            ; exit if null byte
        cmp     byte ptr es:[bx],blank
        je      argc1            ; outside argument if ASCII blank
        cmp     byte ptr es:[bx],tab
        je      argc1            ; outside argument if ASCII tab

                                 ; otherwise not blank or tab,
        jcxz    argc2            ; jump if already inside argument

        inc     ax               ; else found argument, count it
        not     cx               ; set flag = inside argument
        jmp     argc2            ; and look at next character
```

(continued)

Figure 8-11. *continued*

```
argc3:  pop     cx              ; restore original BX, CX, ES
        pop     bx
        pop     es
        leave                   ; discard local variables
        ret                     ; return AX = argument count

argc    endp

_TEXT   ends

        end
```

```
        title   ARGV -- Return Argument Pointer
        page    55,132
        .286


;
; ARGV.ASM
;
; Return address and length of specified command line argument
; or fully qualified program name. Treats blanks and tabs as
; whitespace.
;
; Assemble with:  C> masm argv.asm;
;
; Call with:      AX    = argument number (0 based)
;
; Returns:        ES:BX = argument address
;                 AX    = argument length (0 = no argument)
;
; Uses:           nothing (other registers preserved)
;
; Note: if called with AX = 0 (argv[0]), returns ES:BX
; pointing to fully qualified program name in environment
; block and AX = length.
;
; Copyright (C) 1987 Ray Duncan
;
```

(continued)

Figure 8-12. *ARGV.ASM, the MASM source code for the ARGV routine called by the DUMP utility. This procedure returns the address and length of a specific command line argument.*

Figure 8-12. *continued*

```
tab       equ     09h              ; ASCII tab
blank     equ     20h              ; ASCII space character

          extrn   DosGetEnv:far

_TEXT     segment word public 'CODE'

          assume  cs:_TEXT

          public  argv             ; make ARGV available to Linker

                                   ; local variables...
envseg    equ     [bp-2]           ; environment segment
cmdoffs   equ     [bp-4]           ; command line offset

argv      proc    near

          enter   4,0              ; make room for local variables
          push    cx               ; save original CX and DI
          push    di

          push    ax               ; save argument number

          push    ss               ; get selector for environment
          lea     ax,envseg        ; and offset of command line
          push    ax
          push    ss
          lea     ax,cmdoffs
          push    ax
          call    DosGetEnv        ; transfer to OS/2
          or      ax,ax            ; test operation status
          pop     ax               ; restore argument number
          jnz     argv7            ; jump if DosGetEnv failed

          mov     es,envseg        ; set ES:BX = command line
          mov     bx,cmdoffs

          or      ax,ax            ; is requested argument = 0?
          jz      argv8            ; yes, jump to get program name

argv0:    inc     bx               ; scan off first field
          cmp     byte ptr es:[bx],0
          jne     argv0

          xor     ah,ah            ; initialize argument counter

argv1:    mov     cx,-1            ; set flag = outside argument
```

(continued)

Figure 8-12. *continued*

```
argv2:  inc     bx                      ; point to next character
        cmp     byte ptr es:[bx],0
        je      argv7                   ; exit if null byte
        cmp     byte ptr es:[bx],blank
        je      argv1                   ; outside argument if ASCII blank
        cmp     byte ptr es:[bx],tab
        je      argv1                   ; outside argument if ASCII tab

                                        ; if not blank or tab...
        jcxz    argv2                   ; jump if already inside argument

        inc     ah                      ; else count arguments found
        cmp     ah,al                   ; is this the one we're looking for?
        je      argv4                   ; yes, go find its length
        not     cx                      ; no, set flag = inside argument
        jmp     argv2                   ; and look at next character

argv4:                                  ; found desired argument, now
                                        ; determine its length...
        mov     ax,bx                   ; save parameter starting address

argv5:  inc     bx                      ; point to next character
        cmp     byte ptr es:[bx],0
        je      argv6                   ; found end if null byte
        cmp     byte ptr es:[bx],blank
        je      argv6                   ; found end if ASCII blank
        cmp     byte ptr es:[bx],tab
        jne     argv5                   ; found end if ASCII tab

argv6:  xchg    bx,ax                   ; set ES:BX = argument address
        sub     ax,bx                   ; and AX = argument length
        jmp     argvx                   ; return to caller

argv7:  xor     ax,ax                   ; set AX = 0, argument not found
        jmp     argvx                   ; return to caller

argv8:                                  ; special handling for argv = 0
        xor     di,di                   ; find the program name by
        xor     al,al                   ; first skipping over all the
        mov     cx,-1                   ; environment variables...
        cld
```

(continued)

Figure 8-12. *continued*

```
argv9:  repne scasb                 ; scan for double null (can't use
        scasb                       ; SCASW since might be odd address)
        jne     argv9               ; loop if it was a single null
        mov     bx,di               ; save program name address
        mov     cx,-1               ; now find its length...
        repne scasb                 ; scan for another null byte
        not     cx                  ; convert CX to length
        dec     cx
        mov     ax,cx               ; return length in AX

argvx:                              ; common exit point
        pop     di                  ; restore original CX and DI
        pop     cx
        leave                       ; discard stack frame
        ret                         ; return to caller

argv    endp

_TEXT   ends

        end
```

To compile DUMP.C into the relocatable object module DUMP.OBJ and then link DUMP.OBJ and the DUMP.DEF file (Figure 8-13) into the executable module DUMP.EXE, use the following command:

```
[C:\] CL DUMP.C  <Enter>
```

To assemble and link the components of the MASM version of DUMP, collect the source files DUMP.ASM, ARGC.ASM, and ARGV.ASM and the module definition file DUMP.DEF (Figure 8-13). Then enter the following sequence of commands:

```
[C:\] MASM DUMP.ASM;  <Enter>
[C:\] MASM ARGC.ASM;  <Enter>
[C:\] MASM ARGV.ASM;  <Enter>
[C:\] LINK DUMP+ARGC+ARGV,,,OS2,DUMP  <Enter>
```

```
NAME DUMP WINDOWCOMPAT
PROTMODE
STACKSIZE 4096
```

Figure 8-13. *DUMP.DEF, the module definition file for DUMP.EXE.*

The DUMP program uses only those API functions which have counterparts in MS-DOS, so DUMP is eligible to be converted to a Family application that can run in both real mode and protected mode. To make this conversion, remove the PROTMODE statement from the DUMP.DEF file, rebuild DUMP.EXE, and then bind the program with the following command:

```
[C:\] BIND DUMP.EXE OS2.LIB API.LIB <Enter>
```

The resulting DUMP.EXE file can be executed in either real mode or protected mode on an 80286- or 80386-based machine. Because the program uses 80286-specific instructions (such as PUSH ''immediate,'' ENTER, and LEAVE), you cannot use it on an 8086/88-based machine without modifying the source code.

```
       0  1  2  3  4  5  6  7  8  9  A  B  C  D  E  F
0000  80 06 00 04 44 55 4D 50 40 96 1F 00 00 04 43 4F   ....DUMP@.....CO
0010  44 45 04 44 41 54 41 06 44 47 52 4F 55 50 05 5F   DE.DATA.DGROUP._
0020  44 41 54 41 05 5F 54 45 58 54 10 98 07 00 68 86   DATA._TEXT....h.
0030  01 06 02 01 69 98 07 00 48 1F 01 05 03 01 F0 9A   ....i...H.......
0040  04 00 04 FF 02 5D 8C 30 00 08 44 4F 53 43 4C 4F   .....].O..DOSCLO
0050  53 45 00 07 44 4F 53 45 58 49 54 00 07 44 4F 53   SE..DOSEXIT..DOS
0060  4F 50 45 4E 00 07 44 4F 53 52 45 41 44 00 08 44   OPEN..DOSREAD..D
0070  4F 53 57 52 49 54 45 00 18 A0 8A 01 01 00 00 1E   OSWRITE.........
```

Figure 8-14. *Example output from DUMP.EXE.*

CHAPTER NINE

VOLUMES AND DIRECTORIES

Each file in an OS/2 system is uniquely identified by name and location. The location, in turn, has two components: a path, which identifies the directory where the filename may be found, and the logical drive on which the directory (and hence the file) resides. The drive and directory may be implicit or explicit; during a process's execution, it has a "current drive" and a "current directory" for each drive, all of which are directly controlled by the process.

Logical drives are specified by a single letter (A–Z or a–z) followed by a colon. Drive letters are always assigned starting with A; the highest drive identifier in the system depends on its configuration (number of floppy disk drives, fixed drives, RAM disks, CD-ROMs, and so forth). The number of logical drives in a system may well not be the same as the number of physical drives; for example, large fixed disk drives are commonly broken up into two or more logical drives to make them easier to manage and back up.

The key aspect of a logical drive is that it contains a self-consistent — and self-sufficient — *file system*. That is, it contains one or more directories, zero or more complete files, and all the information needed to locate the files and directories *and* to determine which disk space is free and which is already in use.

A drive's directories are simply little lists or catalogs. Each entry in a directory consists of the name, size, starting location, and attributes of a file or another directory that the drive contains as well as the date and time at which the file or directory was last modified. The detailed information about the location of every block of data assigned to a file or directory is kept in a separate control area on the disk (see Chapter 10).

Each logical drive has a *root directory,* which is distinct from all the directories created within it. The root directory is always present and has a maximum number of entries; its size is determined when you format the disk and cannot be changed. Subdirectories of the root directory, which may or may not be present on a given disk, can be nested to any level and can grow to any size (until the space on the disk is exhausted). This organizational scheme is known as a *hierarchical,* or *tree,* directory structure (Figure 9-1).

The user can interactively examine, select, create, or delete directories with the DIR, CHDIR (CD), MKDIR (MD), or RMDIR (RD) commands. Application programs can carry out similar operations using API calls (summarized in Figure 9-2) to do the following:

- Search for file or directory entries within directories

- Obtain or change the current drive or directory for a process

- Create or delete directories

- Rename directories (other than the root directory)

- Obtain, add, or change a volume label

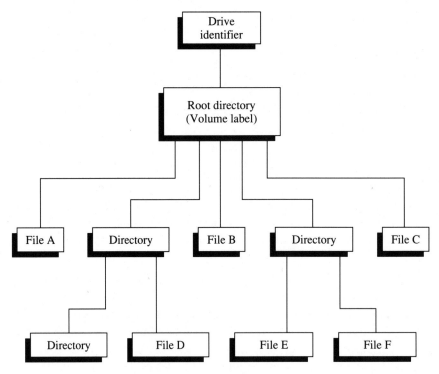

Figure 9-1. *The structure of an OS/2 FAT (MS-DOS–compatible) file system.*

Function	Description
Directory Search Operations	
DosFindFirst	Finds first matching file; returns a search handle
DosFindNext	Finds next matching file using search handle
DosFindClose	Closes a search handle
DosSearchPath	Searches list of directories for file
Directory Operations	
DosChDir	Selects current directory
DosMkDir	Creates a directory
DosRmDir	Removes a directory
DosMove	Renames a directory (also renames or moves files)
DosQCurDir	Returns current directory
DosQSysInfo	Returns maximum path length
Drive Operations	
DosQCurDisk	Returns current disk drive
DosSelectDisk	Selects current disk drive
Volume Label Operations	
DosQFSInfo	Returns volume label, date and time of volume creation
DosSetFSInfo	Adds or changes volume label

Figure 9-2. *API functions for manipulation of drives, directories, and volume labels.*

Searching Disk Directories

When you request a *DosOpen* operation on a file, you are performing an implicit search of a directory. OS/2 examines each entry of the directory to match the provided filename; if the file is found, OS/2 copies certain information from the directory into the system file table and returns a handle to the calling program. (The handle is really an indirect pointer to the SFT.) Thus, to test for the existence of a specific file, you can issue a call to *DosOpen* with the appropriate *OpenMode* and *OpenFlag* parameters and check for an error. (To avoid expending handles needlessly, follow with *DosClose* if the call to *DosOpen* succeeds.) Of course, this simplistic approach can give misleading results if the process is out of handles or if another process has opened the file with deny-all sharing mode.

Most programs need to perform more elaborate (and more reliable) directory searches than the all-or-nothing capability provided by *DosOpen*. For example, a word processor might need to find and display all files with a DOC (document) extension so that the user can choose one from a menu. To satisfy such needs, OS/2 provides three functions that let you examine disk directories in an efficient hardware-independent fashion: *DosFindFirst*, *DosFindNext*, and *DosFindClose*.

DosFindFirst accepts a file specification (which can include a drive, path, and wildcard characters) an attribute, the address and length of a buffer, and a maximum match count. It searches for the first matching file or files in the current or specified directory. If it finds no files with matching names and attributes, *DosFindFirst* returns an error. If it finds at least one match, it returns a *search handle* and a match count (1 through the specified maximum) and fills the designated buffer with one or more entries in the format shown in Figure 9-3.

In the FAT-based (MS-DOS–compatible) file system used in OS/2 versions 1.0 and 1.1, some of the information listed in Figure 9-3 is not available in the disk directory. The dates and times of creation and last access are always returned as zero, and the file allocation is returned as the file size rounded up to agree with the size of the disk's allocation units.

Note that when multiple matches are returned, the buffer entries do not have a constant length; the length of each record depends on the length of the filename. The number of matches returned is the minimum of the number available, the number requested, and the number that will fit into the buffer.

A successful *DosFindFirst* must precede a call to *DosFindNext*. If the file specification that was previously passed to *DosFindFirst* included wildcard characters and if at least one matching file exists, *DosFindNext* can be called as many times as necessary with the search handle returned by *DosFindFirst* to locate all additional matching files. Like *DosFindFirst*, *DosFindNext* returns the file information in the calling program's buffer and uses the same format (Figure 9-3). When all matching files have been located, *DosFindNext* returns an error flag.

Byte(s)	Contents		Bit(s)	Significance (if set)
00H–01H	File date of creation			
02H–03H	File time of creation		0	Read-only
04H–05H	File date of last access		1	Hidden
06H–07H	File time of last access			
08H–09H	File date of last write		2	System
0AH–0BH	File time of last write		3	Reserved
0CH–0FH	File size		4	Directory
10H–13H	File allocation		5	Archive
14H–15H	File attribute		6–15	Reserved
16H	Length of filename			
17H+	Filename followed by null byte			

Figure 9-3. *Format of file information returned in designated buffer by* DosFindFirst *and* DosFindNext.

Both *DosFindFirst* and *DosFindNext* regard the attribute specified in the *DosFindFirst* call as inclusive rather than exclusive. If the read-only, hidden, system, archive, or directory attribute bits are set in the request, all normal files are returned in addition to the files or directories with the specified attribute. (The volume label attribute bit receives special treatment, as described later in this chapter.)

After *DosFindFirst* or *DosFindNext* returns an error indicating that no more files match the specifications, the process should call *DosFindClose* to release the search handle. Although a large number of search handles (1000) are available for a single process, each active search handle has a system memory overhead and should therefore not be left active any longer than necessary. Figure 9-4 provides an example of searching a directory for all files with the ASM extension and displaying their names.

```
stdout   equ    1                ; standard output handle
cr       equ    0dh              ; ASCII carriage return
lf       equ    0ah              ; ASCII linefeed

_srec    struc                   ; search result structure...
cdate    dw     ?                ; date of creation
ctime    dw     ?                ; time of creation
adate    dw     ?                ; date of last access
atime    dw     ?                ; time of last access
wdate    dw     ?                ; date of last write
wtime    dw     ?                ; time of last write
fsize    dd     ?                ; file size
falloc   dd     ?                ; file allocation
fattr    dw     ?                ; file attribute
fcount   db     ?                ; filename count byte
fname    db     13 dup (?)       ; ASCIIZ filename
_srec    ends


wlen     dw     ?                ; receives bytes written

sname    db     '*.ASM',0        ; target name for search

sbuf     _srec  <>               ; instantiate structure to
                                 ; receive search results
sbuf_len equ    $-sbuf           ; length of result buffer
```

(continued)

Figure 9-4. *Using* DosFindFirst *and* DosFindNext *to find and display all files with the extension ASM. This simple example does not take advantage of OS/2's ability to return multiple matches on one function call.*

Figure 9-4. *continued*

```
dirhan   dw      ?                  ; receives search handle

schcnt   dw      ?                  ; receives match count

nl       db      cr,lf              ; newline (CR-LF pair)
nl_len   equ     $-nl

             .
             .
             .

         mov    dirhan,-1           ; request search handle

         mov    schcnt,1            ; set max match count

                                    ; look for first match...
         push   ds                  ; target name for search
         push   offset DGROUP:sname
         push   ds                  ; receives search handle
         push   offset DGROUP:dirhan
         push   0                   ; normal attribute
         push   ds                  ; result buffer address
         push   offset DGROUP:sbuf
         push   sbuf_len            ; result buffer length
         push   ds                  ; receives match count
         push   offset DGROUP:schcnt
         push   0                   ; reserved DWORD 0
         push   0
         call   DosFindFirst        ; transfer to OS/2
         or     ax,ax               ; any files found?
         jnz    done                ; jump if no match

display:                           ; output one filename...
         push   stdout              ; standard output handle
         push   ds                  ; filename address
         push   offset DGROUP:sbuf.fname
         mov    al,sbuf.fcount
         xor    ah,ah
         push   ax                  ; filename length
         push   ds                  ; receives bytes written
         push   offset DGROUP:wlen
         call   DosWrite            ; transfer to OS/2
```

(continued)

Figure 9-4. *continued*

```
                                ; send new line ...
        push    stdout          ; standard output handle
        push    ds              ; address of data
        push    offset DGROUP:nl
        push    nl_len          ; length of data
        push    ds              ; receives bytes written
        push    offset DGROUP:wlen
        call    DosWrite        ; transfer to OS/2


                                ; search for next file...
        push    dirhan          ; search handle
        push    ds              ; result buffer address
        push    offset DGROUP:sbuf
        push    sbuf_len        ; result buffer length
        push    ds              ; receives match count
        push    offset schcnt
        call    DosFindNext     ; transfer to OS/2
        or      ax,ax           ; any more files?
        jz      display         ; jump if match found

done:   push    dirhan          ; release search handle...
        call    DosFindClose    ; transfer to OS/2
        .
        .
        .
```

Note that OS/2 maintains the search context for each search handle in a table outside the process's memory space. Multiple interleaved searches, using different file specifications, can be in progress simultaneously, and OS/2 takes care of all the housekeeping details. The search handles are distinct from file and device handles and do not consume entries in the SFT.

Before we move on from the topic of directory searches, we need to mention one more special-purpose OS/2 function. *DosSearchPath* accepts as parameters a filename and a list of directories (or the name of an environment variable whose value is a list of directories), and searches each directory in order. It returns the fully qualified pathname of the first match found. Although this function allows wildcard characters in the filename, it does not provide any way to continue the search and identify a set of files. It is therefore best suited to locating a particular file — such as a dynamic link library or a configuration file — that is vital to the execution of an application.

Directory and Disk Control

OS/2 provides three functions for selecting the current directory or for modifying the hierarchical directory structure: *DosChDir* (select the current directory), *DosMkDir* (create a directory), and *DosRmDir* (delete a directory).

The directory functions require the address of an ASCIIZ pathname, which can include a drive code and which can be specified completely from the drive's root directory or relative to its current directory. All three directory functions return the usual status in register AX; all can fail for a variety of reasons.

The most common cause for returning an error is that some element of the indicated path does not exist. *DosRmDir* requires special attention because it can return an error for reasons that are difficult to foresee or prevent in the requesting program. For example, the function fails if the directory being deleted contains any files or directories, or if it is the current directory for the command processor of some other screen group.

Note that *DosChDir* selects the current directory for the requesting process only; it does not affect the current directory for other active processes (as you will quickly notice when your program terminates and the CMD.EXE prompt is redisplayed). The current directory is, however, inherited by child processes.

An additional function, *DosQCurDir*, obtains the ASCIIZ pathname of the current directory for the specified or default disk drive. It is commonly used to build up fully qualified path and file specifications that can be displayed, saved across invocations of a program, or passed to other processes. *DosQCurDir* is called with a drive identifier (0 = default, 1 = A, and so forth), the address of a buffer to receive the pathname, and the address of a variable that contains the length of the buffer.

The pathname returned by *DosQCurDir* does not contain a drive identifier or a leading backslash (\) character; if the current directory is the root directory, then a single null byte is returned. Also note that the function does not return the actual length of the pathname (as you might expect from the behavior of some other calls); your program must scan the string to determine its length.

You can rename directories other than the root directory with the function *DosMove*, although this use is uncommon. The parameters for *DosMove* are the old and new ASCIIZ pathnames for the directories. The function fails if any element of the path for the old or new directory does not exist, or if the new pathname is the same as an existing file or directory. Directories cannot (unlike files) be moved from one location to another with *DosMove*.

The functions *DosQCurDisk* and *DosSelectDisk* obtain or change the current drive. *DosQCurDisk* also returns a bitmap that indicates which logical drives exist in the system. *DosSelectDisk* affects only the requesting process; it does not affect the current disk for the current process's parent or any other processes active in the system. Like the current directory, the current drive is inherited by child processes.

Volume Labels

In FAT (MS-DOS–compatible) file systems, a volume label is an optional name, from 1 through 11 characters long, that the user assigns to a disk during a FORMAT operation or later with the LABEL command. You can display the volume label with the DIR, TREE, CHKDSK, LABEL, or VOL command, or you can change it with the LABEL command. The FORMAT program also assigns a semirandom 32-bit binary ID to each disk it formats, but this value is normally invisible to the user and cannot be altered.

The distinction between volumes and drives in OS/2 might seem hazy, but it is important. A volume label is associated with a specific storage medium. A drive identifier (such as A:) is associated with a physical device on which a storage medium can be mounted. In the case of fixed disk drives, the medium associated with a drive identifier does not change (hence the name). In the case of floppy disks or other removable media, however, the disk accessed with a given drive identifier might have any volume label or none at all.

As a consequence of this distinction, volume labels do not take the place of the single character drive identifier and cannot be used as part of a pathname to identify a file. In current versions of OS/2, their only real use is to identify (inconclusively) removable disks for users and application programs and to help the floppy disk driver detect that a disk has been changed with a file open.

In FAT file systems, a volume label is stored as a special type of entry in the root directory with an attribute of 08H. Volume labels cannot, however, be created with *DosOpen* or located with *DosFindFirst*—an attribute of 08H is rejected by these functions. You must use the functions *DosQFSInfo* and *DosSetFSInfo* to add, change, or inspect a volume label (Figure 9-5 on the following page).

```
stdout    equ      1                    ; standard output handle

_vlinf    struc                         ; volume label structure
vdate     dw       ?                    ; date of creation
vtime     dw       ?                    ; time of creation
vcount    db       ?                    ; length of volume name
vname     db       13 dup (?)           ; ASCIIZ volume name
_vlinf    ends


wlen      dw       ?                    ; receives bytes written

vlinf     _vlinf   <>                   ; instantiate structure to
                                        ; receive volume info
vlinf_len equ      $-vlinf              ; length of buffer


          .
          .
          .
                                        ; get volume label...
          push     0                    ; drive = default
          push     2                    ; file info level 2
          push     ds                   ; buffer receives label
          push     offset DGROUP:vlinf
          push     vlinf_len            ; size of buffer
          call     DosQFSInfo           ; transfer to OS/2
          or       ax,ax                ; call successful?
          jnz      done                 ; jump if no volume label

                                        ; display volume label...
          push     stdout               ; standard output handle
          push     ds                   ; volume label address
          push     offset DGROUP:vlinf.vname
          mov      al,vlinf.vcount      ; volume label length
          xor      ah,ah
          push     ax
          push     ds                   ; receives bytes written
          push     offset DGROUP:wlen
          call     DosWrite             ; transfer to OS/2

done:     .
          .
          .
```

Figure 9-5. *Using* DosQFSInfo *to obtain and display a volume label.*

Sample Program: WHEREIS

The listings WHEREIS.C (Figure 9-6) and WHEREIS.ASM (Figure 9-7 on p. 179) contain the source code for an OS/2 "file finder" utility. WHEREIS uses *DosFindFirst*, *DosFindNext*, and *DosFindClose* to perform a recursive search of the directory structure for a pathname (which may include wildcard characters). It displays the names of any matching files on the standard output, which can be directed to a file or to another character device.

```
/*
        WHEREIS.C

        A file finder utility that searches the current drive, starting
        with the root directory (\), for the specified pathname.
        Wildcard characters can be included.

        Compile with:  C> cl whereis.c

        Usage is:  C> whereis pathname

        Copyright (C) 1988 Ray Duncan
*/



#include <stdio.h>
#include <string.h>

#define API unsigned extern far pascal

API DosChDir(char far *, unsigned long);
API DosFindClose(unsigned);
API DosFindFirst(char far *, unsigned far *, unsigned, void far *,
                int, int far *, unsigned long);
API DosFindNext(unsigned, void far *, int, int far *);
API DosQCurDisk(int far *, unsigned long far *);
API DosQCurDir(int, void far *, int far *);
API DosSelectDisk(int);
API DosWrite(unsigned, void far *, unsigned, unsigned far *);

#define NORM       0x00              /* file attribute bits */
#define RD_ONLY    0x01
#define HIDDEN     0x02
#define SYSTEM     0x04
```

(continued)

Figure 9-6. *WHEREIS.C, the C language source code for the WHEREIS.EXE utility.*

Figure 9-6. *continued*

```
#define DIR        0x10
#define ARCHIVE    0x20

struct _srec {                          /* used by DosFindFirst */
                unsigned cdate;         /* and DosFindNext */
                unsigned ctime;
                unsigned adate;
                unsigned atime;
                unsigned wdate;
                unsigned wtime;
                long fsize;
                long falloc;
                unsigned fattr;
                char fcount;
                char fname[13];
        }
            sbuf;                       /* receives search results */

int drvno;                              /* current drive */
int count = 0;                          /* total files matched */
char sname[80];                         /* target pathname */


main(int argc, char *argv[])
{
    unsigned long drvmap;               /* logical drive map */

    if(argc < 2)                        /* exit if no parameters */
    {
        printf("\nwhereis: missing filename\n");
        exit(1);
    }

    DosQCurDisk(&drvno, &drvmap);       /* get current drive */

                                        /* any drive specified? */
    if(((strlen(argv[1])) >= 2) && ((argv[1])[1] == ':'))
    {
                                        /* get binary drive code */
        drvno = ((argv[1]) [0] | 0x20) - ('a'-1);

        if(DosSelectDisk(drvno))        /* select drive or exit */
        {
            printf("\nwhereis: bad drive\n");
            exit(1);
        }
```

(continued)

Figure 9-6. *continued*

```
        argv[1] += 2;                   /* advance past drive */
    }

    strcpy(sname,argv[1]);              /* save search target */

    schdir("\\");                       /* start search with root */

                                        /* advise if no matches */
    if(count == 0) printf("\nwhereis: no files\n");
}



/*
    SCHDIR: search directory for matching files and
            any other directories
*/

schdir(char *dirname)
{
    unsigned shan = -1;                 /* search handle */
    int scnt = 1;                       /* max search matches */

    DosChDir(dirname, 0L);              /* select new directory */

    schfile();                          /* find and list files */

                                        /* search for directories */
    if(!DosFindFirst("*.*", &shan, NORM|DIR, &sbuf, sizeof(sbuf), &scnt, 0L))
    {
        do                              /* if found directory other */
        {                               /* than . and .. aliases */
            if((sbuf.fattr & DIR) && (sbuf.fname[0] != '.'))
            {
                schdir(sbuf.fname);     /* search the directory */
                DosChDir("..", 0L);     /* restore old directory */
            }
                                        /* look for more directories */
        } while(DosFindNext(shan, &sbuf, sizeof(sbuf), &scnt) == 0);
    }

    DosFindClose(shan);                 /* close search handle */
}
```

(continued)

Figure 9-6. *continued*

```
/*
    SCHFILE: search current directory for files
             matching string in 'sname'
*/

schfile()
{
    unsigned shan = -1;                  /* search handle */
    int scnt = 1;                        /* max search matches */

    if(!DosFindFirst(sname, &shan, NORM, &sbuf, sizeof(sbuf), &scnt, 0L))
    {
        do pfile();                      /* list matching files */
        while(DosFindNext(shan, &sbuf, sizeof(sbuf), &scnt) == 0);
    }

    DosFindClose(shan);                  /* close search handle */
}


/*
    PFILE: display current drive and directory,
           followed by filename from 'sbuf.fname'
*/

pfile()
{
    count++;                             /* count matched files */
    pdir();                              /* list drive and path */
    printf("%s\n", strlwr(sbuf.fname));  /* list filename */
}


/*
    PDIR: display current drive and directory
*/

pdir()
{
    char dbuf[80];                       /* receives current dir */
    int dlen = sizeof(dbuf);             /* length of buffer */

    DosQCurDir(0, dbuf, &dlen);          /* get current directory */
```

(continued)

Figure 9-6. *continued*

```
    if(strlen(dbuf) != 0)                /* add backslash to */
        strcat(dbuf,"\\");               /* directory if not root */

                                         /* display drive and path */
    printf("%c:\\%s", drvno+'a'-1, strlwr(dbuf));
}
```

```
        title   WHEREIS -- File Finder Utility
        page    55,132
        .286


;
; WHEREIS.ASM
;
; A file finder utility that searches the current drive, starting
; with the root directory (\), for the specified pathname.
; Wildcard characters can be included.
;
; This program requires the modules ARGV.ASM and ARGC.ASM.
;
; Assemble with:  C> masm whereis.asm;
; Link with:  C> link whereis+argv+argc,,,os2,whereis
;
; Usage is:  C> whereis pathname
;
; Copyright (C) 1988 Ray Duncan
;

stdin   equ     0                       ; standard input handle
stdout  equ     1                       ; standard output handle
stderr  equ     2                       ; standard error handle

cr      equ     0dh                     ; ASCII carriage return
lf      equ     0ah                     ; ASCII linefeed


        extrn   DosChDir:far
        extrn   DosExit:far
        extrn   DosFindClose:far
        extrn   DosFindFirst:far
        extrn   DosFindNext:far
        extrn   DosQCurDir:far
```

(continued)

Figure 9-7. *WHEREIS.ASM, the MASM source code for the WHEREIS.EXE utility. The source code for the subroutines ARGV.ASM and ARGC.ASM can be found in Chapter 8.*

Figure 9-7. *continued*

```
        extrn   DosQCurDisk:far
        extrn   DosSelectDisk:far
        extrn   DosWrite:far

_srec   struc                           ; search result structure...
cdate   dw      ?                        ; date of creation
ctime   dw      ?                        ; time of creation
adate   dw      ?                        ; date of last access
atime   dw      ?                        ; time of last access
wdate   dw      ?                        ; date of last write
wtime   dw      ?                        ; time of last write
fsize   dd      ?                        ; file size
falloc  dd      ?                        ; file allocation
fattr   dw      ?                        ; file attribute
fcount  db      ?                        ; filename count byte
fname   db      13 dup (?)               ; ASCIIZ filename
_srec   ends


DGROUP  group   _DATA

_DATA   segment word public 'DATA'

root    db      '\',0                    ; name of root directory

parent  db      '..',0                   ; alias for parent directory

wild    db      '*.*',0                  ; matches all files

sname   db      64 dup (0)               ; filename for search

drvno   dw      0                        ; current drive
drvmap  dd      0                        ; logical drive bitmap

dname   db      'X:\'                    ; current drive ID
dbuf    db      80 dup (?)               ; current directory
dbuf_len dw     ?                        ; length of buffer

sbuf    _srec   <>                       ; receives search results
sbuf_len equ $-sbuf

count   dw      0                        ; total files matched
wlen    dw      ?                        ; receives bytes written
shandle dw      -1                       ; directory search handle
scount  dw      1                        ; number of files to return
```

(continued)

Figure 9-7. *continued*

```
msg1     db      cr,lf
         db      'whereis: no files found'
         db      cr,lf
msg1_len equ $-msg1


msg2     db      cr,lf
msg2_len equ $-msg2


msg3     db      cr,lf
         db      'whereis: missing filename'
         db      cr,lf
msg3_len equ $-msg3


msg4     db      cr,lf
         db      'whereis: bad drive'
         db      cr,lf
msg4_len equ $-msg4


_DATA    ends


_TEXT    segment word public 'CODE'

         assume  cs:_TEXT,ds:DGROUP


         extrn   argv:near
         extrn   argc:near

whereis proc    far

         call    argc                    ; filename present in
         cmp     ax,2                    ; command tail?
         jae     where1                  ; jump, filename present

                                         ; no filename, exit...
         mov     dx,offset DGROUP:msg3   ; error message address
         mov     cx,msg3_len             ; message length
         jmp     where6                  ; go terminate

where1:                                  ; get current drive...
         push    ds                      ; receives drive code
         push    offset DGROUP:drvno
         push    ds                      ; receives drive bitmap
         push    offset DGROUP:drvmap
         call    DosQCurDisk             ; transfer to OS/2
```

(continued)

Figure 9-7. *continued*

```
        mov     ax,1                      ; get address and length
        call    argv                      ; of filename parameter
                                          ; returns ES:BX = address
                                          ;        AX   = length
        mov     cx,ax                     ; save length in CX

        cmp     ax,2                      ; parameter length > 2?
        jle     where3                    ; no, jump
        cmp     byte ptr es:[bx+1],':'    ; drive delimiter present?
        jne     where3                    ; no, jump

        mov     al,es:[bx]                ; get ASCII drive code
        or      al,20h                    ; fold to lowercase
        xor     ah,ah
        sub     ax,'a'-1                  ; convert drive code to
        mov     drvno,ax                  ; binary and save it
        cmp     ax,1                      ; make sure drive valid
        jb      where2                    ; jump, bad drive
        cmp     ax,26
        ja      where2                    ; jump, bad drive

        add     bx,2                      ; advance command tail
        sub     cx,2                      ; pointer past drive code

                                          ; set drive for search...
        push    ax                        ; drive code
        call    DosSelectDisk             ; transfer to OS/2
        or      ax,ax                     ; drive OK?
        jz      where3                    ; jump, drive was valid

                                          ; bad drive, exit...
where2: mov     dx,offset DGROUP:msg4     ; error message address
        mov     cx,msg4_len               ; message length
        jmp     where6

where3: mov     di,offset DGROUP:sname    ; DS:DI = local buffer

where4: mov     al,es:[bx]                ; copy filename to local
        mov     [di],al                   ; buffer byte by byte...
        inc     di
        inc     bx
        loop    where4

        mov     byte ptr [di],0           ; append null byte
```

(continued)

Figure 9-7. *continued*

```
        push    ds                      ; make DGROUP addressable
        pop     es                      ; with ES
        assume  es:DGROUP
        mov     dx,offset DGROUP:root   ; start searching with
        call    schdir                  ; the root directory

        cmp     count,0                 ; any matching files found?
        jne     where5                  ; yes, exit silently

                                        ; no, display 'no files'...
        push    stdout                  ; standard output handle
        push    ds                      ; message address
        push    offset DGROUP:msg1
        push    msg1_len                ; message length
        push    ds                      ; receives bytes written
        push    offset DGROUP:wlen
        call    DosWrite                ; transfer to OS/2

where5:                                 ; final exit to OS/2...
        push    1                       ; terminate all threads
        push    0                       ; return code = 0 (success)
        call    DosExit                 ; transfer to OS/2

where6:                                 ; common error exit...
                                        ; DS:DX = msg, CX = length
        push    stderr                  ; standard output handle
        push    ds                      ; address of message
        push    dx
        push    cx                      ; length of message
        push    ds                      ; receives bytes written
        push    offset DGROUP:wlen
        call    DosWrite                ; transfer to OS/2

                                        ; final exit to OS/2...
        push    1                       ; terminate all threads
        push    1                       ; exit code = 1 (error)
        call    DosExit                 ; transfer to OS/2

whereis endp


; SCHDIR:       search a directory for matching
;               files and any other directories
;
; Call with:    DS:DX = ASCIIZ directory name
; Returns:      nothing
; Uses:         all registers
```

(continued)

Figure 9-7. *continued*

```
schdir  proc    near

        push    shandle                    ; save old search handle
        mov     shandle,-1                 ; initialize search handle

                                           ; set search directory...
        push    ds                         ; directory name address
        push    dx
        push    0                          ; reserved DWORD 0
        push    0
        call    DosChDir                   ; transfer to OS/2

        call    schfile                    ; search current directory
                                           ; for matching files

                                           ; search for directories...
        mov     scount,1                   ; max matches to return
        push    ds                         ; target name address
        push    offset DGROUP:wild
        push    ds                         ; receives search handle
        push    offset DGROUP:shandle
        push    10h                        ; normal and dir attribute
        push    ds                         ; result buffer address
        push    offset DGROUP:sbuf
        push    sbuf_len                   ; result buffer length
        push    ds                         ; receives match count
        push    offset DGROUP:scount
        push    0                          ; reserved DWORD 0
        push    0
        call    DosFindFirst               ; transfer to OS/2

        or      ax,ax                      ; find anything?
        jnz     schdir3                    ; no, jump

schdir1:                                   ; found some match...
        test    sbuf.fattr,10h             ; is it a directory?
        jz      schdir2                    ; no, skip it

        cmp     sbuf.fname,'.'             ; is it . or .. entry?
        je      schdir2                    ; yes, skip it
                                           ; no, new directory found
        mov     dx,offset DGROUP:sbuf.fname
        call    schdir                     ; call self to search it
```

(continued)

Figure 9-7. *continued*

```
                                        ; restore old directory...
        push    ds                      ; address of '..' alias
        push    offset DGROUP:parent
        push    0                       ; reserved DWORD 0
        push    0
        call    DosChDir                ; transfer to OS/2

schdir2:                                ; found at least one match,
                                        ; look for next match...
        mov     scount,1                ; max matches to return
        push    shandle                 ; handle from DosFindFirst
        push    ds                      ; result buffer address
        push    offset DGROUP:sbuf
        push    sbuf_len                ; result buffer length
        push    ds                      ; receives match count
        push    offset DGROUP:scount
        call    DosFindNext             ; transfer to OS/2

        or      ax,ax                   ; any matches found?
        jz      schdir1                 ; yes, go process it

schdir3:                                ; end of search...
        push    shandle                 ; close search handle
        call    DosFindClose            ; transfer to OS/2

        pop     shandle                 ; restore previous handle

        ret                             ; back to caller

schdir  endp


; SCHFILE:        search current directory for
;                 files matching string in 'sname'
;
; Call with:      nothing
; Returns:        nothing
; Uses:           all registers

schfile proc    near

        push    shandle                 ; save previous handle
        mov     shandle,-1              ; initialize search handle
        mov     scount,1                ; max matches to return
        push    ds                      ; name to match
```

(continued)

Figure 9-7. *continued*

```
            push    offset DGROUP:sname
            push    ds                          ; receives search handle
            push    offset DGROUP:shandle
            push    0h                          ; attribute = normal files
            push    ds                          ; result buffer address
            push    offset DGROUP:sbuf
            push    sbuf_len                    ; result buffer length
            push    ds                          ; receives match count
            push    offset DGROUP:scount
            push    0                           ; reserved DWORD 0
            push    0
            call    DosFindFirst                ; transfer to OS/2

            or      ax,ax                       ; any matches found?
            jnz     schfile3                    ; no, terminate search

schfile1:                                       ; found matching file...
            call    pfile                       ; display its name

                                                ; look for next match...
            push    shandle                     ; handle from DosFindFirst
            push    ds                          ; result buffer address
            push    offset DGROUP:sbuf
            push    sbuf_len                    ; result buffer length
            push    ds                          ; receives match count
            push    offset DGROUP:scount
            call    DosFindNext                 ; transfer to OS/2

            or      ax,ax                       ; any more matches?
            jz      schfile1                    ; yes, go display filename

schfile3:                                       ; end of search...
            push    shandle                     ; close search handle
            call    DosFindClose                ; transfer to OS/2

            pop     shandle                     ; restore previous handle
            ret                                 ; return to caller

schfile endp

; PFILE:        display current drive and directory,
;               followed by filename from 'sbuf.fname'
;
; Call with:    nothing
; Returns:      nothing
; Uses:         all registers
```

(continued)

Figure 9-7. *continued*

```
pfile   proc    near

        inc     count                   ; count matched files

        call    pdir                    ; display drive:path

                                        ; fold name to lower case
        mov     bx,offset DGROUP:sbuf.fname
        call    makelc

                                        ; display filename...
        push    stdout                  ; standard output handle
        push    ds                      ; filename address
        push    offset DGROUP:sbuf.fname
        mov     al,sbuf.fcount          ; filename length
        xor     ah,ah
        push    ax
        push    ds                      ; receives bytes written
        push    offset DGROUP:wlen
        call    DosWrite                ; transfer to OS/2

                                        ; send newline sequence...
        push    stdout                  ; standard output handle
        push    ds                      ; address of newline
        push    offset DGROUP:msg2
        push    msg2_len                ; length of newline
        push    ds                      ; receives bytes written
        push    offset DGROUP:wlen
        call    DosWrite                ; transfer to OS/2

        ret                             ; return to caller

pfile   endp

; PDIR:          display current drive and directory
;
; Call with:     nothing
; Returns:       nothing
; Uses:          AX, BX, CX, DI, ES

pdir    proc    near
        mov     ax,drvno                ; convert binary drive
        add     al,'A'-1                ; code to ASCII drive
        mov     dname,al                ; and store it for output
```

(continued)

Figure 9-7. *continued*

```
            mov      dbuf_len,dbuf_len-dbuf    ; initialize length of
                                               ; directory buffer

                                               ; get current directory...
            push     0                         ; drive 0 = default
            push     ds                        ; receives ASCIIZ path
            push     offset DGROUP:dbuf
            push     ds                        ; contains buffer length
            push     offset DGROUP:dbuf_len
            call     DosQCurDir                ; transfer to OS/2

            mov      di,offset DGROUP:dbuf     ; address of path

            cmp      byte ptr [di],0           ; is path = root?
            je       pdir1                     ; yes, jump

            mov      cx,dbuf_len-dbuf          ; no, scan for null
            xor      al,al                     ; byte at end of path...
            repne scasb

            mov      byte ptr [di-1],'\'       ; append a backslash

pdir1:      mov      bx,offset DGROUP:dname    ; fold everything to
            call     makelc                    ; lowercase

                                               ; now display drive:path...
            push     stdout                    ; standard output handle
            push     ds                        ; address of pathname
            push     offset DGROUP:dname
            sub      di,offset DGROUP:dname    ; length of drive and path
            push     di
            push     ds                        ; receives bytes written
            push     offset DGROUP:wlen
            call     DosWrite                  ; transfer to OS/2

            ret                                ; back to caller

pdir        endp

; MAKELC:     convert ASCIIZ string to lowercase
;
; Call with:  DS:BX = string address
; Returns:    nothing
; Uses:       BX
```

(continued)

Figure 9-7. *continued*

```
makelc   proc    near

make1:   cmp     byte ptr [bx],0        ; end of string?
         je      make3                  ; jump if end

         cmp     byte ptr [bx],'A'      ; check next character
         jb      make2                  ; jump, not uppercase
         cmp     byte ptr [bx],'Z'
         ja      make2                  ; jump, not uppercase

         or      byte ptr [bx],20h      ; fold to lowercase

make2:   inc     bx                     ; advance through string
         jmp     make1

make3:   ret                            ; back to caller

makelc   endp

_TEXT    ends

         end     whereis
```

WHEREIS has four major subroutines. A search begins when the program's *main* routine calls the first subroutine, *schdir*, with a plain ASCIIZ backslash (\) signifying the root directory for the current or specified drive. The *schdir* subroutine makes that directory current using *DosChDir* and calls *schfile* to find and display any matching files. The subroutine *pfile*, which is called by *schfile*, works together with *pdir* to display a fully qualified pathname. It obtains the current drive and directory with *DosQCurDisk* and *DosQCurDrive*, and then formats and displays them along with the filename that was discovered by *schfile*. The *schdir* subroutine then searches the current directory for other directories and calls itself recursively with the name of each directory found.

To compile and link the source file WHEREIS.C into the executable file WHEREIS.EXE, enter the command:

```
[C:\] CL WHEREIS.C  <Enter>
```

To assemble and link the files WHEREIS.ASM and WHEREIS.DEF (Figure 9-8) into the executable file WHEREIS.EXE, you also need the modules ARGC.ASM and ARGV.ASM from Chapter 8. Gather the four files together in the same directory and enter the commands:

```
[C:\] MASM WHEREIS.ASM;  <Enter>
[C:\] MASM ARGC.ASM;  <Enter>
[C:\] MASM ARGV.ASM;  <Enter>
[C:\] LINK WHEREIS+ARGC+ARGV,,,OS2,WHEREIS  <Enter>
```

To run either version of the utility, enter a command of the following form:

```
[C:\] WHEREIS pathname.ext  <Enter>
```

If no matching files are found, or if the command line argument is missing, an appropriate error message is displayed.

The recursive use of *DosFindFirst*, *DosFindNext*, and *DosFindClose* in the WHEREIS program is not compatible with the Family API restrictions. Thus, WHEREIS cannot be bound for use in real mode. WHEREIS could be made considerably more efficient by eliminating the calls to *DosChDir* and by requesting more than one match per call to *DosFindFirst* and *DosFindNext*; these enhancements have been left, so the saying goes, as exercises for the reader.

```
NAME WHEREIS WINDOWCOMPAT
PROTMODE
STACKSIZE 4096
```

Figure 9-8. *WHEREIS.DEF, the module definition file for the WHEREIS.EXE utility.*

DISK INTERNALS

Block storage devices for OS/2 versions 1.0 and 1.1 are organized as FAT (file allocation table) file systems, compatible with MS-DOS versions 2.0 and later. This is convenient for software developers because they can more easily transport data between MS-DOS and OS/2 systems and develop programs for MS-DOS under OS/2 (and vice versa).

FAT file systems are organized according to a rigid scheme that is easily understood and manipulated. Although most programmers never need to access the special control areas of such a device directly, an understanding of their structure leads to a better understanding of constraints on file size and file system behavior.

Distinct Volume Areas

OS/2 views each logical volume—whether it corresponds to an entire physical medium (such as a diskette) or only a part of a larger fixed disk—as a continuous sequence of *logical sectors,* starting with sector 0. (You can also implement a "logical disk volume" on other types of storage; for example, RAM disks map a disk structure onto a block of memory.) The available sectors are divided among several areas of fixed size as shown in Figure 10-1 on the following page:

- The boot sector

- An optional reserved area

- One or more FATs

- The root directory

- The files area

OS/2 translates file management requests from application programs into requests to the disk driver for transfers of logical sectors; in doing so, it uses the information in the volume's boot sector, FAT, and root directory. The sizes of these OEM areas can vary from disk to disk, but all the information needed to interpret the structure of a particular disk is on the disk itself.

The disk driver maps logical sectors onto actual physical addresses (head, cylinder, and sector). It is the operating system module that controls the disk by reading and writing the I/O ports assigned to its adapter. Any *inter-leaving* (the mapping of consecutive physical sector addresses onto non-contiguous physical sectors to improve performance) is done at the adapter level.

OS/2 disk drivers are typically written in assembly language. They must be capable of functioning in both real and protected mode and are carefully tuned for optimum performance. OS/2 always installs the "base" driver for IBM-compatible disk devices (DISK01.SYS or DISK02.SYS) during system initialization. To load disk drivers supplied by manufacturers of non-IBM-compatible disk drives, include a *DEVICE=* statement in the CONFIG.SYS file on the boot disk.

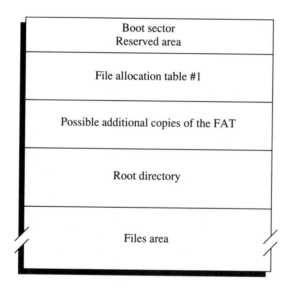

Figure 10-1. *Map of a typical OS/2 logical volume. The boot sector (logical sector 0) contains the OEM identification, BIOS parameter block (BPB), and disk bootstrap. An optional reserved area of variable size is followed by one or more copies of the file allocation table, the root directory, and the files area.*

Boot Sector

Logical sector zero is known as the *boot sector* and contains all the critical information about a volume's characteristics (Figures 10-2, 10-3, and 10-4 on the following pages). The first byte in the sector is always an 80x86 jump instruction — either a normal intrasegment JMP (opcode 0E9H) followed by a 16-bit displacement or a "short jump" (opcode 0EBH) followed by an 8-bit

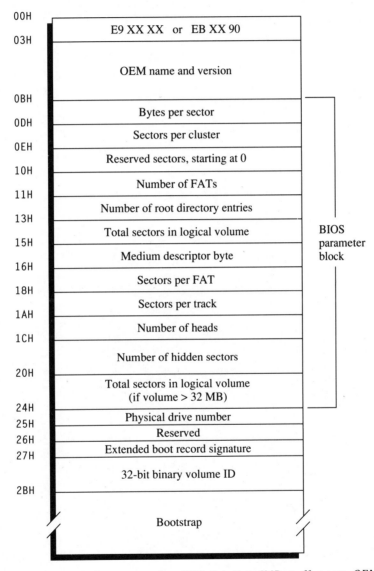

Figure 10-2. *Map of the boot sector of an OS/2 disk. Note JMP at offset zero, OEM identification field, BIOS parameter block, 32-bit binary volume ID, and disk bootstrap code.*

displacement and an NOP instruction (opcode 90H). If one of these two JMP opcodes is not present, the disk has not been formatted or was not formatted for use with OS/2 or MS-DOS. Of course, the presence of the JMP opcode is not in itself an assurance that the disk contains an OS/2-compatible file system.

```
        0  1  2  3  4  5  6  7  8  9  A  B  C  D  E  F
0000   EB 29 90 49 42 4D 20 31 30 2E 31 00 02 04 01 00   k).IBM 10.1.....
0010   02 00 02 EE FF F8 40 00 11 00 05 00 11 00 00 00   ...n.x@.........
0020   00 00 00 00 80 00 28 15 E4 A5 23 33 C0 8E D0 BC   ......(.d%#3@.P<
0030   00 7C BB C0 07 8E DB A0 10 00 F7 26 16 00 03 06   .!;@..[ ..w&....
        .
        .
        .
01C0   72 65 73 74 61 72 74 0D 0A 74 68 65 20 73 79 73   restart..the sys
01D0   74 65 6D 2E 0D 0A 00 4F 53 32 4C 44 52 20 20 20   tem....OS2LDR
01E0   20 20 00 00 00 00 00 00 00 00 00 00 00 00 00 00   .............
01F0   00 00 00 00 00 00 00 00 00 00 00 00 00 00 55 AA   ..............U*
```

Figure 10-3. *Partial dump of an OS/2 version 1.1 fixed disk boot sector. See Figures 10-2 and 10-4.*

```
        jmp     $+39            ; jump to bootstrap
        nop

        db      'IBM 10.1'      ; OEM identification

                                ; BIOS parameter block...
        dw      512             ; bytes per sector
        db      4               ; sectors per cluster
        dw      1               ; reserved sectors
        db      2               ; number of FATs
        dw      512             ; root directory entries
        dw      65518           ; total sectors
        db      0f8h            ; medium descriptor byte
        dw      64              ; sectors per FAT
        dw      17              ; sectors per track
        dw      5               ; number of heads
        dd      17              ; hidden sectors
        dd      0               ; large number of sectors
        .
        .
        .
```

Figure 10-4. *Partial disassembly of the boot sector shown in Figure 10-3.*

Following the initial JMP instruction, eight bytes are reserved for the OEM identification field. This field contains the name of the OS/2 OEM (the computer manufacturer who adapted the OS/2 system for a particular hardware configuration) and an OEM internal version number as an ASCII string.

The third component of the boot sector is the BIOS parameter block (BPB). This structure describes the physical characteristics of the disk and allows the device driver to calculate the proper physical disk address for a given logical sector number; it also contains information that OS/2 and various system utilities use to calculate the size and location of the FAT, the root directory, and the files area. The BPB is followed by a 32-bit binary volume ID, generated by the FORMAT utility, which is different for each volume.

The remainder of the boot sector contains the disk bootstrap program, which is the destination of the JMP instruction at the beginning of the sector. The ROM bootstrap reads the disk bootstrap into memory when the system is turned on or restarted; the disk bootstrap in turn reads the file OS2LDR into memory and transfers control to it. The system initialization process is described in detail in Chapter 2.

Reserved Area

The boot sector is actually part of a reserved area that comprises one or more sectors. The size of the reserved area is described by the reserved sectors field of the BIOS parameter block, at offset 0EH in the boot sector. Remember that the number in the BPB field includes the boot sector itself; so if it contains the value 1 (as it does on most floppy disk types), the length of the reserved area, as shown in Figure 10-1 on p. 196, is actually 0 sectors.

File Allocation Table

When a file is created or extended, disk sectors are assigned to it from the files area in powers of 2 known as *allocation units* or *clusters*. The number of sectors per cluster for a given medium is defined in the BIOS parameter block and can be found at offset 0DH in the disk's boot sector. For example, the following table shows the cluster sizes for some common media:

Disk Type	Power of 2	Sec/Cluster
180 KB floppy	0	1
360 KB floppy	1	2
1.2 MB floppy	2	4
Fixed disk	2, 3 ...	4, 8 ...

The FAT is divided into fields that correspond directly to the assignable clusters on the disk. These fields are either 12 bits or 16 bits, depending on the size of the medium (12 bits if the disk contains fewer than 4087 clusters, 16 bits otherwise).

The first two entries in a FAT are always reserved. On IBM-compatible media, the first eight bits of the first FAT entry contain a copy of the *medium descriptor byte* (Figure 10-5), which is also found in the boot sector's BPB.

The second, third, and (if applicable) fourth bytes, which constitute the remainder of the first two reserved FAT fields, always contain 0FFH. The currently defined IBM-format medium descriptor bytes are as follows:

Descriptor Byte	Medium Characteristics		
Value	*Size*	*Sides*	*Sectors*
0F0H	3.5"	2	18
0F8H	Fixed disk		
0F9H	5.25"	2	15
	or 3.5"	2	9
0FCH	5.25"	1	9
0FDH	5.25"	2	9
0FEH	5.25"	1	8
0FFH	5.25"	2	8

Aside from the first two reserved entries of the FAT, the remainder of the entries describe the usage of their corresponding disk clusters. The contents of the FAT fields are interpreted as follows:

Value	Meaning
(0)000H	The cluster is available
(F)FF0H–(F)FF6H	Reserved cluster
(F)FF7H	Bad cluster if not part of chain
(F)FF8H–(F)FFFH	Last cluster of a file
(X)XXXH	Next cluster in the file

```
        0  1  2  3  4  5  6  7  8  9  A  B  C  D  E  F
0000   F9 FF FF 03 F0 FF FF 6F 00 07 80 00 09 A0 00 0B
0010   C0 00 FF EF 00 0F 00 01 11 20 01 13 40 01 15 60
0020   01 17 80 01 19 A0 01 1B F0 FF 1D E0 01 1F 00 02
         .
         .
         .
```

Figure 10-5. *Dump of the first block of the file allocation table for an OS/2 version 1.1 floppy disk. Notice that the first byte of the FAT contains the medium descriptor byte for a 5.25-inch, double-sided, 15-sector (1.2 MB) floppy disk.*

Each file's entry in a disk directory contains the number of the first cluster assigned to that file, which is used as an entry point into the FAT. From the entry point on, each FAT slot contains the cluster number of the next cluster in the file, until a last cluster mark is encountered.

At the computer manufacturer's option, a volume can contain two or more identical copies of the FAT. OS/2 simultaneously updates all copies whenever space in the files area is allocated or released. If a FAT sector becomes unreadable, the other copies are tried until a successful read is obtained or until all copies are exhausted. As part of its procedure for checking the integrity of a disk, the CHKDSK program compares the multiple copies (usually two) of the FAT to verify that they are both readable and consistent.

Root Directory

A volume's root directory immediately follows the FAT(s). It contains 32-byte entries that describe files, other directories, and the optional volume label (Figures 10-6 and 10-7). An entry beginning with the byte E5H is available for reuse; it represents a file or directory that has been erased. An entry beginning with a null (zero) byte indicates the logical end of directory; that entry and all subsequent entries are unused.

The root directory has a number of special properties. Its size and position are fixed; they are determined by the FORMAT program when a disk is initialized. The number of entries in the root directory and its location on the disk can be obtained from the BPB in the boot sector.

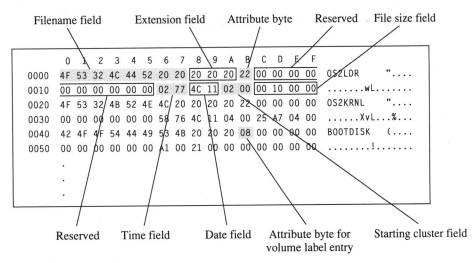

Figure 10-6. *Partial hex dump of the first sector of the root directory for an OS/2 version 1.1 disk. The directory entries for the two system files (OS2LDR and OS2KRNL) and a volume label (BOOTDISK) are shown.*

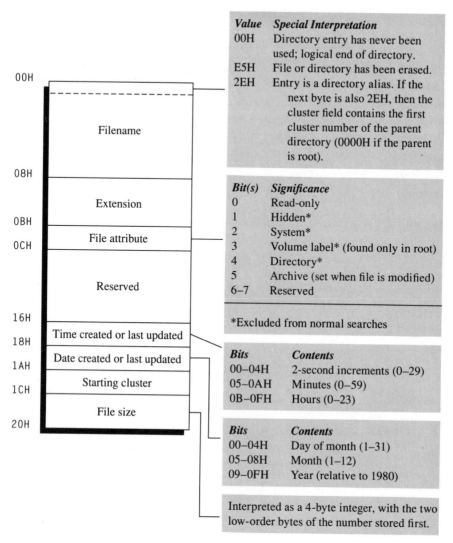

Figure 10-7. *Format of a single entry in a disk directory. Total length 32 bytes (20H bytes). The values that are explained in the filename field refer only to the first character in that field.*

Files Area

The remainder of the volume after the root directory is known as the files area, or data area. The disk sectors in this area are viewed as a pool of clusters, each containing one or more logical sectors, depending on the disk format. Each cluster has a corresponding entry in the FAT that describes its current usage: available, reserved, assigned to a file, or unusable (due to medium defects). Because the first two fields of the FAT are reserved, the first cluster in the files area is assigned the number 2.

When a file is extended, the FAT is searched from the most recently allocated cluster until a free cluster (designated by a zero FAT field) is found, and that FAT field is changed to a last cluster mark. If the file was previously empty—had no clusters assigned to it—the number of the newly assigned cluster is inserted into the directory entry for the file. Otherwise, the FAT entry of the previous last cluster for the file is updated to point to the new last cluster.

Directories other than the root directory are simply a special type of file. Their storage is allocated from the files area, and their contents are 32-byte entries—in the same format as those used in the root directory—that describe files or other directories. Directory entries that describe other directories contain an attribute byte with bit 4 set, zero in the file length field, and the date and time that the directory was created (Figure 10-8 on the following page). The first cluster field, of course, points to the first cluster in the files area that belongs to the directory. (The directory's other clusters can be found only by tracing through the FAT.)

All directories except for the root directory contain two special entries with the names . and .. that are put in place when a directory is created. These entries cannot be deleted. The . entry refers to the current directory; its cluster field points to the cluster in which it is found. The .. entry refers to the directory's "parent" (the directory immediately above it in the tree structure), and its cluster field points to the first cluster of the parent. If the parent is the root directory, the cluster field of the .. entry contains zero (Figure 10-9 on the following page).

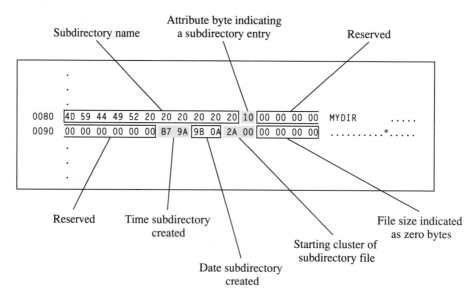

Figure 10-8. *Extract from the root directory of an OS/2 disk, showing the entry for a subdirectory named MYDIR. The entry has bit 4 in the attribute byte set, and the cluster field points to the first cluster of the subdirectory file. The date and time stamps are valid, but the file length is zero.*

```
           0  1  2  3  4  5  6  7  8  9  A  B  C  D  E  F
0000      2E 20 20 20 20 20 20 20 20 20 20 10 00 00 00 00    .           .....
0010      00 00 00 00 00 00 87 9A 9B 0A 2A 00 00 00 00 00    ..........*.....
0020      2E 2E 20 20 20 20 20 20 20 20 20 10 00 00 00 00    ..          .....
0030      00 00 00 00 00 00 87 9A 9B 0A 00 00 00 00 00 00    ...............
0040      4D 59 46 49 4C 45 20 20 44 41 54 20 00 00 00 00    MYFILE  DAT ....
0050      00 00 00 00 00 00 98 9A 9B 0A 2B 00 15 00 00 00    ..........+.....
0060      00 00 00 00 00 00 00 00 00 00 00 00 00 00 00 00    ...............
0070      00 00 00 00 00 00 00 00 00 00 00 00 00 00 00 00    ...............
```

Figure 10-9. *Dump of the first block of the directory MYDIR. Note the . and .. entries. This directory contains exactly one file, named MYFILE.DAT.*

Fixed Disk PartitionsFixed disks have another layer of organization beyond the logical volume structure we discussed earlier. The FDISK utility organizes a fixed disk into one or more *partitions* consisting of an integral number of cylinders. Each partition can contain an independent file system and, for that matter, a different operating system.

The first physical sector on a fixed disk contains the master boot record, which is laid out as follows:

Bytes	Contents
000H–1BDH	Reserved
1BEH–1CDH	Partition #1 descriptor
1CEH–1DDH	Partition #2 descriptor
1DEH–1EDH	Partition #3 descriptor
1EEH–1FDH	Partition #4 descriptor
1FEH–1FFH	Signature word (AA55H)

The partition descriptors in the master boot record define the size, location, and type of each partition:

Byte(s)	Contents
00H	Active flag (0 = not bootable, 80H = bootable)
01H	Starting head
02H–03H	Starting sector/cylinder
04H	Partition type
	0 = not used
	1 = FAT file system, 12-bit FAT entries
	4 = FAT file system, 16-bit FAT entries
	5 = extended OS/2 or MS-DOS partition
	6 = huge (>32 MB) FAT file system
05H	Ending head
06H–07H	Ending sector/cylinder
08H–0BH	Starting sector for partition, relative to beginning of disk
0CH–0FH	Partition length in sectors

The active flag, which indicates that the partition is bootable, can be set on only one partition at a time. A hex dump of a typical master boot record is shown in Figure 10-10 on the following page.

OS/2 treats partition types 1, 4, and 6 as normal logical volumes and assigns them their own drive identifiers during the system boot process. Partition type 5 can contain multiple logical volumes and has a special extended boot record that describes each volume. All OS/2 or MS-DOS partitions are initialized with the FORMAT utility, which creates the file system within the partition (boot record, file allocation table(s), root directory, and files area) and optionally places a bootable copy of the operating system in the file system.

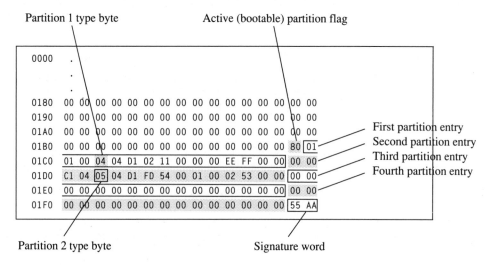

Figure 10-10. *A partial hex dump of a master block from a fixed disk. This disk contains two partitions. The first partition entry (starting at offset 01BEH) has a 16-bit FAT and is marked "active" to indicate that it contains a bootable copy of OS/2. The second partition entry (starting at offset 01CEH) is an "extended" partition. The third and fourth partition entries are not used in this example.*

Direct Disk Access

OS/2 provides mechanisms for application programs to bypass the file system and to read and write block devices at the logical sector level. These mechanisms let you write low level disk utilities (such as file recovery and repair programs) in a hardware-independent fashion.

The API functions that a program uses for direct disk access are the already familiar ones: *DosOpen, DosChgFilePtr, DosRead, DosWrite, DosClose,* and *DosDevIOCtl.* Instead of a filename, *DosOpen* is provided with an ASCIIZ drive identifier, and the "DASD" flag (bit 15) in the *OpenMode* parameter is set. If the drive exists, *DosOpen* returns a handle (as usual), but this handle refers to the entire logical volume — represented as though it were a single file.

After you obtain a handle, use it with *DosDevIOCtl* Category 8 Function 00H to "lock" the logical volume so that no other processes can use it during the direct disk access operations. The lock operation fails if any files on the volume are currently open. (This means that you cannot lock the boot drive because several dynlink libraries on that drive are always open.) After the lock succeeds, any subsequent requests to open a file on that volume will return an error.

Once the volume is locked, you can use *DosChgFilePtr*, *DosRead*, and *DosWrite* to move to any location and read or write data. It is most convenient to seek, read, and write in multiples of 512 bytes because the physical disk sector size on IBM-compatible media is always 512 bytes, but OS/2 does not constrain you to use this sector size.

When direct disk access operations are completed, unlock the logical volume with *DosDevIOCtl* Category 8 Function 01H; then release the logical volume handle in the usual fashion with *DosClose*.

Figure 10-11 contains sample code that opens and locks logical drive E for direct access, reads the drive's boot sector into a buffer, and then unlocks the drive and releases the handle.

```
secsize equ      512                ; physical sector size

dname   db      'E:',0             ; logical drive identifier
dhandle dw      ?                  ; receives drive handle
daction dw      ?                  ; receives DosOpen action

rlen    dw      ?                  ; actual bytes read

bootsec db      secsize dup (?)    ; boot sector read here

parblk  db      0                  ; DosDevIOCtl dummy
                                   ; parameter block
        .
        .
        .
```

(continued)

Figure 10-11. *Sample code for direct disk access. This sequence of calls opens and locks logical drive E for direct access, reads the drive's boot sector into a buffer, and then unlocks the drive and releases the handle.*

Figure 10-11. *continued*

```
                                  ; open drive E for direct access...
        push    ds                ; address of drive name
        push    offset DGROUP:dname
        push    ds                ; receives drive handle
        push    offset DGROUP:dhandle
        push    ds                ; receives DosOpen action
        push    offset DGROUP:daction
        push    0                 ; file allocation (N/A)
        push    0
        push    0                 ; file attribute (N/A)
        push    01h               ; action: open if exists,
                                  ;         fail if doesn't
        push    8012h             ; mode: DASD, read/write,
                                  ;       deny-all
        push    0                 ; reserved DWORD 0
        push    0
        call    DosOpen           ; transfer to OS/2
        or      ax,ax             ; was open successful?
        jnz     error             ; jump if function failed


                                  ; lock logical drive...
        push    0                 ; data buffer address
        push    0                 ; (not needed)
        push    ds                ; parameter buffer address
        push    offset DGROUP:parblk
        push    0                 ; function
        push    8                 ; category
        push    dhandle           ; drive handle
        call    DosDevIOCtl       ; transfer to OS/2
        or      ax,ax             ; was lock successful?
        jnz     error             ; jump if function failed


                                  ; now read boot sector...
        push    dhandle           ; drive handle
        push    ds                ; buffer address
        push    offset DGROUP:bootsec
        push    secsize           ; buffer length
        push    ds                ; receives actual length
        push    offset DGROUP:rlen
        call    DosRead           ; transfer to OS/2
        or      ax,ax             ; was read successful?
        jnz     error             ; jump if function failed
        cmp     rlen,secsize      ; actual = expected size?
        jnz     error             ; jump if not enough data
```

(continued)

Figure 10-11. *continued*

```
                            ; unlock logical drive...
    push    0               ; data buffer address
    push    0               ; (not needed)
    push    ds              ; parameter buffer address
    push    offset DGROUP:parblk
    push    1               ; function
    push    8               ; category
    push    dhandle         ; drive handle
    call    DosDevIOCtl     ; transfer to OS/2
    or      ax,ax           ; was unlock successful?
    jnz     error           ; jump if function failed

                            ; close logical drive...
    push    dhandle         ; drive handle
    call    DosClose        ; transfer to OS/2
    or      ax,ax           ; did close succeed?
    jnz     error           ; jump if function failed
    .
    .
    .
```

ADVANCED OS/2 TECHNIQUES

MEMORY MANAGEMENT

RAM is the fundamental resource in an OS/2 system and also the most precious. Part of the RAM is statically allocated for use by vital OS/2 modules and data structures and by the DOS compatibility environment (if it is enabled). The remainder is administered by the OS/2 memory manager and can be thought of as a large pool (sometimes called the *global heap*) from which segments can be allocated and released as necessary.

The OS/2 kernel dynamically allocates memory for the following:

- Swappable operating system modules and data structures

- The code, data, and stacks of transient processes

- Objects created by processes but controlled by the operating system, such as system semaphores and pipes

OS/2 exports the memory manager services to applications through a number of API calls (Figure 11-1 on the following page). Application programs can use these services to dynamically create and destroy memory segments for buffers, arrays, tables, and other work areas. The memory management functions fall into three categories:

- Allocation and release of global memory segments

- Local memory pool management

- Allocation and release of named, shareable memory segments

The first two categories are discussed in this chapter; the last is deferred to Chapter 13 because it falls naturally into the realm of interprocess communication. But first, a brief review of the 80286 hardware support for *memory protection* and *virtual memory* is in order. (The 80386, when running OS/2 version 1.0 or 1.1, acts exactly like an 80286.)

OS/2 Function	Description
Global Memory Management	
DosAllocSeg	Allocates memory block with maximum size 64 KB
DosCreateCSAlias	Returns executable selector for previously allocated block
DosFreeSeg	Releases memory block
DosLockSeg	Locks discardable segment
DosMemAvail	Returns size of largest contiguous block of physical memory
DosReallocSeg	Changes size of previously allocated block
DosSizeSeg	Returns size of previously allocated memory block
DosUnlockSeg	Unlocks discardable segment
Huge Block Management	
DosAllocHuge	Allocates huge memory block (larger than 64 KB)
DosGetHugeShift	Returns incrementing value for selectors of huge block
DosReallocHuge	Changes size of previously allocated huge block
Shared Memory Management (see Chapter 13)	
DosAllocShrSeg	Creates named shareable memory block
DosGetSeg	Makes selector from another process addressable
DosGetShrSeg	Obtains selector for existing named shared memory block
DosGiveSeg	Creates selector for use by another process
Local Memory Management	
DosSubAlloc	Allocates memory block from local pool
DosSubFree	Releases block to local pool
DosSubSet	Initializes or resizes local memory pool

Figure 11-1. *OS/2 memory management functions at a glance.*

Memory Protection

The Intel 80286 microprocessor starts operating in *real mode,* which is essentially an 8086 emulation mode. In real mode, segment registers contain paragraph addresses, which you can manipulate directly; you can address a maximum of 1 MB of memory. To form a 20-bit physical memory address, the hardware multiplies the value in a segment register by 16 and combines it with a 16-bit offset (Figure 11-2). Operating systems (such as MS-DOS) that run in real mode cannot intervene when a program does not use memory properly, nor can they prevent one program from writing into another's memory space.

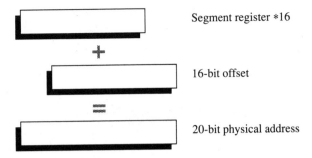

Figure 11-2. *Generation of physical addresses in real mode.*

OS/2 runs the 80286 processor in *protected mode,* which presents the programmer with hardware architecture that is quite different from that of the 8086. In protected mode, the contents of segment registers are logical *selectors* that contain several bitfields (Figure 11-3), the largest of which is an index into a *descriptor table.* Each descriptor represents a memory segment and contains the physical base address, length, and segment attributes (executable, read-only, or read/write). The descriptor also specifies the ring, or privilege level, at which a program must be running to access the segment (Figure 11-4 on the following page).

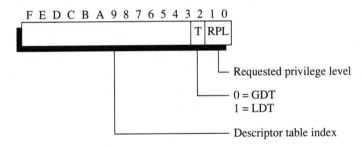

Figure 11-3. *Structure of a protected mode selector. The actual privilege level is the numeric maximum of the RPL (requested privilege level) of the selector and the CPL (current privilege level) of the process.*

When an instruction references memory in protected mode, a segment register provides a selector and indicates a specific descriptor. The base address in the descriptor is combined with a 16-bit offset to form a 24-bit physical memory address (Figure 11-5 on p. 213). Consequently, you must treat a protected mode selector much like a file handle: It is simply a token for a piece of memory. You cannot assume that a selector is unique across processes, and your program should not (with one exception) manipulate selectors arithmetically.

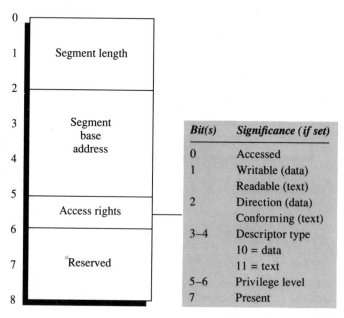

Figure 11-4. *Structure of protected mode data and text (executable) descriptors on the Intel 80286. The descriptors for system segments and call gates have a somewhat different format and are beyond the scope of this book.*

An OS/2 system contains many descriptor tables: a single global descriptor table (GDT) and, for each process, a local descriptor table (LDT). The GDT contains descriptors for all the LDTs as well as for all segments owned or occupied by the operating system; each process's LDT contains descriptors for the segments that are owned or shared by that process. Only the operating system is entrusted with both the privilege level and the knowledge of physical memory layout that are necessary to create and destroy memory segments through manipulation of descriptor tables.

The CPU hardware, using the descriptor tables, enforces memory protection between processes. If a process tries to load a segment register with a selector that is not valid for its LDT or for an entry in the GDT that requires a higher privilege level, a hardware trap occurs. (A trap is like a hardware interrupt but is internally generated.) OS/2 receives control, terminates the offending process, and displays a message to the user.

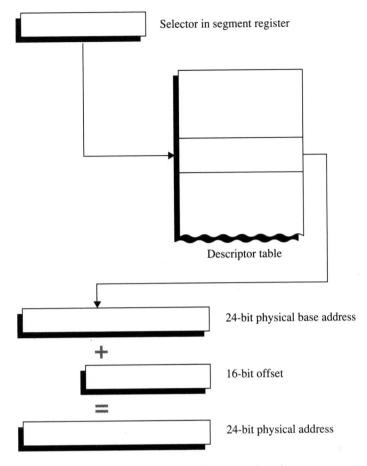

Selector in segment register

Descriptor table

24-bit physical base address

+

16-bit offset

=

24-bit physical address

Figure 11-5. *Generation of physical addresses in protected mode.*

Virtual Memory

Virtual memory allows a process to request and own more bytes of RAM than physically exist in the system. Hardware support for memory protection combines with the operation of two OS/2 modules — the virtual memory manager (VMM) and the *swapper* — to present the illusion to the task that all its segments are simultaneously present and accessible.

When a process attempts to allocate additional memory, the VMM tries to satisfy the request by moving segments to coalesce free blocks of physical memory, by throwing away read-only data segments or text segments which were loaded from an executable file on fixed disk,* or by tossing out

---

*Segments loaded from a floppy disk EXE or DLL file are swapped rather than discarded because the user might complicate matters by changing disks before the segment is needed again.

unlocked, discardable data segments. These strategies failing, the VMM invokes the swapper to move one or more segments to a swap file on disk, choosing the segments with an LRU algorithm. The physical memory occupied by each discarded or swapped segment is then freed, and the *present* bit in the segment's descriptor is cleared to indicate that the memory segment is not resident.

When a selector for a discarded or swapped-out segment is used in a memory access, a hardware trap occurs. The VMM gains control and reads the needed segment from the disk into physical memory from the swap file or from the program's original EXE or DLL file, possibly moving segments or writing another segment out to the disk to make room. It then updates the descriptor to point to the new physical address of the reloaded segment, sets the present bit in the descriptor, and restarts the process's instruction that was trying to access the segment.

Because the system implements virtual memory, the presence or absence in physical memory of any particular segment is completely transparent to the process that owns it. If a memory address is accessed that is not currently mapped to some piece of physical RAM, its segment is loaded before the access is allowed to complete. Correspondingly, the amount of memory that can be committed by all the processes in the system combined is usually limited only by the amount of physical memory plus the swap space on the disk. (Although other system-wide limits do exist, they would not be encountered during the execution of a normal application.)

Global Memory

An application program allocates a global memory segment by calling *DosAllocSeg* with three parameters: a segment size in bytes (0–65,535), the address of a variable to receive a selector, and a word of flags. A segment size of 0 is treated as a special case and results in a 65,536-byte segment. The flags word controls whether the allocated segment can be discarded in low memory situations or shared with other processes (Figure 11-6). Discardable segments are discussed further below, and shared memory segments are covered in Chapter 13; for the moment, note that a flags word of zero is appropriate for most circumstances.

If segment motion or segment swapping (or both) has not been disabled with the MEMMAN directive in the CONFIG.SYS file, segments can be written to disk or shuffled in memory (or both) to satisfy the allocation request. In such situations, the execution time of a *DosAllocSeg* call can vary

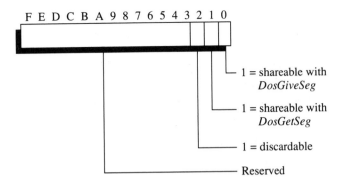

F E D C B A 9 8 7 6 5 4 3 2 1 0

1 = shareable with
DosGiveSeg

1 = shareable with
DosGetSeg

1 = discardable

Reserved

Figure 11-6. *Flags word for* DosAllocSeg *and* DosAllocHuge.

widely because the delay involved in segment swapping or movement depends on many factors (such as the location of the disk read/write head and the size of the segment).

A *DosAllocSeg* call fails if an invalid value is supplied for the flags word, if all physical memory is committed and swapping is disabled, or if all physical memory is committed and swapping is enabled but the disk holding the swap file is full. *DosAllocSeg* can also fail if the VMM's or swapper's table space is exhausted or if the per-process limit on the number of shared or unshared segments is reached;* none of these should be limiting factors for typical applications.

After the system allocates a segment, the owning process can resize it with the function *DosReallocSeg*. The function is called with the selector and the new desired size in bytes (0–65,535, with 0 interpreted as 65,536). As in the case of *DosAllocSeg*, if other segments must be moved or swapped to satisfy the request, the time required for the call is unpredictable. A *DosReallocSeg* call fails if the selector is not valid or if the program that invokes it is attempting to enlarge a segment while the physical memory and disk swap space are exhausted.

A process can release a memory segment allocated with *DosAllocSeg* by passing its selector to *DosFreeSeg* or by terminating. *DosFreeSeg* removes the descriptor for the segment from the process's LDT, so any subsequent accesses with the selector result in a GP fault. If the segment is unshared, the physical memory that it occupies is returned to the global pool; if the segment is shared, it is not destroyed until all processes that have access to it have released it or terminated.

---

*The OS/2 version 1.0 per-process limits are: (1/3) * 8192 unshared segments, (2/3) * 8192 shared segments. The OS/2 version 1.1 limits are: (1/4) * 8192 unshared segments, (3/4) * 8192 shared segments.

Figure 11-7 contains an example of allocating, resizing, and releasing a global memory block.

```
sel     dw      ?                       ; receives selector
        .
        .
        .
                                ; allocate global segment...
        push    4000h           ; initially get 16 KB
        push    ds              ; receives selector
        push    offset DGROUP:sel
        push    0               ; 0 = not shareable
                                ;     or discardable
        call    DosAllocSeg     ; transfer to OS/2
        or      ax,ax           ; was allocation successful?
        jnz     error           ; jump if function failed
        .
        .
        .
                                ; now resize segment
                                ; to 65,536 bytes...
        push    0               ; 0 indicates 64 KB
        push    sel             ; segment selector
        call    DosReallocSeg   ; transfer to OS/2
        or      ax,ax           ; was resize successful?
        jnz     error           ; jump if function failed
        .
        .
        .
                                ; fill block with -1s...
        mov     cx,8000h        ; words to initialize
        mov     es,sel          ; load segment selector
        xor     di,di           ; start at offset zero
        mov     ax,-1           ; load initializing value
        cld                     ; safety first
        rep stosw               ; fill the block
        .
        .
        .
                                ; now release the block...
        push    sel             ; segment selector
        call    DosFreeSeg      ; transfer to OS/2
        or      ax,ax           ; was release successful?
        jnz     error           ; jump if function failed
        .
        .
        .
```

Figure 11-7. *Allocating a 16 KB memory block with* DosAllocSeg, *resizing it to 64 KB with* DosReallocSeg, *filling it with* −1s, *and then releasing it with* DosFreeSeg.

Huge Memory Blocks

As we saw earlier, protected mode memory addresses are generated by combining a selector with a 16-bit offset. This means that the largest continuously addressable, *physically contiguous* chunk of memory a process can own is 65,536 bytes. For applications that need larger data structures, OS/2 offers a set of "huge memory block" functions to manage areas of *logically contiguous* storage spanning multiple segments.

A huge block is initially allocated with the function *DosAllocHuge*. Two of the parameters for this function are the same as those for *DosAllocSeg*: the flags word controlling discardability and sharing, and the address of a variable to receive a selector. The other parameters are the number of full 64 KB segments to allocate, the length in bytes (which may be zero) of an additional partial segment, and the maximum size (in 64 KB segments) to which the process can resize the block at some later time.

If the *DosAllocHuge* call succeeds, the component segments of the huge block are assigned predictable, sequential selectors. The memory within the block can therefore be smoothly addressed by incrementing the offset until a segment is exhausted and then performing special arithmetic on the selector, using an incrementing value supplied by the operating system to move to the next segment. The incrementing value is obtained with the function *DosGetHugeShift*, which returns a shift count to be applied to the value 1.

For example, if *DosGetHugeShift* returns 4, shifting the value 1 left by four bit positions yields the increment 10H (16). If *DosAllocHuge* was called to allocate 224 KB of memory and returned the base selector 017FH for the huge memory block, the entire area would be addressed as follows:

Block Range	Selector	Offsets
0–63 KB	017FH	0–FFFFH
64–127 KB	018FH	0–FFFFH
128–191 KB	019FH	0–FFFFH
192–223 KB	01AFH	0–7FFFH

DosGetHugeShift need be called only once and can be called at any time during the execution of the application. The value it returns does not change while the application is running. The shift count can also be obtained from the global information segment (see *DosGetInfoSeg*) or from a special loadtime dynlink fixup for the symbol *Huge_Shift*. Addressing of huge blocks must be performed with care to avoid generating invalid selectors, wrapping a segment, or overrunning a partial last segment; such errors cause a GP fault that terminates the application. Figure 11-8 contains a simple example of the address arithmetic that would be necessary in an actual program.

```
nsegs    equ    3               ; number of complete
                                 ; segments in huge block

nbytes   equ    8000h           ; number of bytes in
                                 ; partial last segment

nmax     equ    4               ; maximum size of huge
                                 ; block in segments

sel      dw     ?               ; receives base selector
                                 ; for huge block

shift    dw     ?               ; receives shift count
                                 ; for selector increment

         .
         .
         .
                                 ; get selector increment...
         push   ds              ; receives shift count
         push   offset DGROUP:shift
         call   DosGetHugeShift  ; transfer to OS/2
         or     ax,ax           ; did we get shift count?
         jnz    error           ; jump if function failed
         .
         .
         .
                                 ; now allocate huge block...
         push   nsegs           ; number of complete segments
         push   nbytes          ; bytes in last segment
         push   ds              ; receives base selector
         push   offset DGROUP:sel
         push   nmax            ; potential max segments
         push   0               ; 0 = segment not shared
         call   DosAllocHuge    ; transfer to OS/2
         or     ax,ax           ; was allocation successful?
         jnz    error           ; jump if function failed
         .
         .
         .
```

(continued)

Figure 11-8. *Allocating a 224 KB huge memory block with* DosAllocHuge, *filling it with −1s, and then releasing it.*

Figure 11-8. *continued*

```
                                    ; convert shift count to
                                    ; actual increment...
            mov     bx,1            ; 1 will be shifted left
            mov     cx,shift        ; count from DosGetHugeShift
            shl     bx,cl           ; BX <- selector increment

            mov     es,sel          ; load base selector
            mov     dx,nsegs        ; total segment count
            mov     ax,-1           ; load initializing value
            cld                     ; safety first

label1:                             ; initialize a segment...
            mov     cx,8000h        ; words per segment
            xor     di,di           ; start at offset zero
            rep stosw               ; fill the segment

            mov     cx,es           ; increment selector
            add     cx,bx           ; for next segment
            mov     es,cx
            dec     dx              ; another segment?
            jnz     label1          ; yes, loop

                                    ; fill partial segment...
            mov     cx,nbytes       ; length of partial segment
            xor     di,di           ; start at offset zero
            rep stosb               ; fill the segment

            .
            .                       ; other processing here
            .

                                    ; release the huge block...
            push    sel             ; base selector for block
            call    DosFreeSeg      ; transfer to OS/2
            or      ax,ax           ; was release successful?
            jnz     error           ; jump if function failed
            .
            .
            .
```

To change the size of a huge memory block after it is allocated, use
DosReallocHuge. This function is called with the base selector obtained
from *DosAllocHuge*, the new number of 64 KB segments, and the length in
bytes of any partial last segment. You can always reduce the size of a huge
block, but you cannot increase its size beyond the maximum specified when
the block was created. Such an attempt fails because OS/2 was not warned

to reserve a sufficient number of consecutive selectors. Of course, a "grow" operation might also fail for the various other reasons described above for *DosReallocSeg*.

A process can release a huge memory block by terminating or by calling *DosFreeSeg* with the base selector. All segments of a huge block are deallocated at the same time.

Discardable Segments

A *discardable segment* is created by setting bit 2 of the flags parameter for a call to *DosAllocSeg* or *DosAllocHuge*. Discardable segments are useful for tables and other data that can be regenerated quickly on demand. Such a segment might also be employed for infrequently used static data that is loaded from a file — the overhead of writing the data to a swap file and finding swap space (to duplicate data that already exists in the original file) is thereby avoided.

When a segment is allocated with the discardable bit set in the flags word, OS/2 initially considers the segment to be swappable and movable, but not discardable. The program notifies OS/2 that the segment is discardable by calling *DosUnlockSeg* with the selector for the segment. Subsequently, when a low memory situation arises, OS/2 throws away any unlocked, discardable segments on an LRU basis before it resorts to swapping nondiscardable segments. In the case of a huge memory block, all the segments that comprise the block are discarded together.

When a program needs to access an unlocked, discardable segment, it first calls *DosLockSeg* with the segment's selector (or the base selector, in the case of a huge block). If the contents of the segment are still valid, the *DosLockSeg* call is successful (AX = 0); if the segment has been discarded, an error code is returned. In the latter case, the process must reallocate the segment to its original size with *DosReallocSeg* or *DosReallocHuge* (which also perform an implicit *DosLockSeg*) and then rebuild or reload the contents of the segment. Figure 11-9 contains an example of this process.

DosLockSeg and *DosUnlockSeg* calls can be nested. If *DosLockSeg* is called multiple times to lock a segment, *DosUnlockSeg* must be called the same number of times before the segment becomes discardable again. OS/2 maintains only an 8-bit lock counter for each segment; if the count reaches 255 for a segment, the segment becomes permanently locked and subsequent calls to *DosLockSeg* or *DosUnlockSeg* have no effect.

```
sel      dw        ?                       ; receives selector


         .
         .
         .
                              ; allocate discardable global segment...
         push      8000h      ; segment is 32 KB long
         push      ds         ; variable receives selector
         push      offset DGROUP:sel
         push      4          ; 4 = discardable,
                              ;    not shareable
         call      DosAllocSeg ; transfer to OS/2
         or        ax,ax      ; was allocation successful?
         jnz       error      ; jump if function failed


         call      rtable     ; read the data table into the segment


                              ; now unlock segment...
         push      sel        ; selector from DosAllocSeg
         call      DosUnlockSeg ; transfer to OS/2
         or        ax,ax      ; was unlock successful?
         jnz       error      ; jump if function failed


         .
         .
                              ; other processing here...
         .


                              ; now lock segment so we can use data table...
         push      sel        ; selector from DosAllocSeg
         call      DosLockSeg ; transfer to OS/2
         or        ax,ax      ; was lock successful?
         jz        label1     ; jump if segment locked


                              ; segment was discarded, must reallocate it...
         push      8000h      ; size is 32 KB
         push      sel        ; selector for segment
         call      DosReallocSeg ; transfer to OS/2
         or        ax,ax      ; was resize successful?
         jnz       error      ; jump if function failed


         call      rtable     ; refresh segment by rereading data table
```

(continued)

Figure 11-9. *Allocating a discardable segment to hold a table of data, unlocking the segment so that it can be discarded in low memory situations, locking the segment when its contents are needed, and reallocating and refreshing the segment if it was discarded. Assume that the subroutine* rtable *(not shown) reads the table of data from a disk file into the memory block whose selector is in the variable* sel.

Figure 11-9. *continued*

```
label1:                          ; segment is now locked...

     .
     .                           ; use contents of segment...
     .

                                 ; unlock segment again...
     push    sel                 ; selector from DosAllocSeg
     call    DosUnlockSeg        ; transfer to OS/2
     or      ax,ax               ; was unlock successful?
     jnz     error               ; jump if function failed
     .
     .
     .
```

Writable Code Segments

On occasion, a program might want to load or dynamically create executable code in a read/write data segment and then branch to that code. Unfortunately, because a particular selector can refer to either executable code or data but not both, loading a selector for a data segment into the CS register by execution of a far JMP or CALL results in a GP fault and process termination.

The solution is to allocate two selectors for the same piece of physical memory: a read/write data selector and an executable (text) selector. The function *DosCreateCSAlias* exists specifically for this purpose: It returns an executable "alias" for a data segment currently owned by a process. This function makes it easy to write incremental compilers and other self-extending systems for OS/2.

A basic strategy to use for incremental compilers is as follows:

1. Allocate a nonshared, nondiscardable data segment that is large enough to hold the program's original machine code and any additional machine code that will be compiled during program execution.

2. Copy the current contents of the text segment to the new data segment.

3. Obtain a CS alias for the new data segment and transfer control to the new segment.

4. Release the original text segment and continue execution from the new segment, which has both text and read/write data selectors.

Figure 11-10 contains skeleton code for these four steps.

Programs which need to execute the generated code only once can use other approaches. For example, some Presentation Manager graphics modules build machine code on the stack, obtain a CS alias for the stack segment, call the new code, and then discard the code immediately.

```
dsel    dw      ?                       ; receives data selector

xoffs   dw      offset label1           ; offset of jump target
xsel    dw      ?                       ; executable selector

tsel    dw      seg _TEXT               ; selector for original
                                        ; executable (text) segment

        .
        .
        .
                                        ; allocate global segment...
        push    0                       ; segment size = 64 KB
        push    ds                      ; variable receives selector
        push    offset DGROUP:dsel
        push    0                       ; 0 = not shareable
                                        ;     or discardable
        call    DosAllocSeg             ; transfer to OS/2
        or      ax,ax                   ; was allocation successful?
        jnz     error                   ; jump if function failed

                                        ; get executable alias...
        push    dsel                    ; selector from DosAllocSeg
        push    ds                      ; receives executable alias
        push    offset DGROUP:xsel
        call    DosCreateCSAlias        ; transfer to OS/2
        or      ax,ax                   ; was function successful?
        jnz     error                   ; jump if no alias available

                                        ; copy old text segment
                                        ; to new segment...
        mov     es,dsel                 ; read/write selector
        mov     cx,pgmlen               ; length of program
        xor     si,si                   ; initialize 'from' offset
        xor     di,di                   ; initialize 'to' offset
```

(continued)

Figure 11-10. *Allocating a new data segment, obtaining a CS alias for that segment, and continuing execution from the new segment.*

Figure 11-10. *continued*

```
                                    ; move the program code
                rep movs byte ptr es:[di],byte ptr cs:[si]

                jmp     dword ptr xoffs ; transfer control to
                                    ; the new text segment

        label1:                     ; now we are executing from
                                    ; the new text segment...
                                    ; release old text segment
                push    tsel        ; segment selector
                call    DosFreeSeg  ; transfer to OS/2
                or      ax,ax       ; was release successful?
                jnz     error       ; jump if function failed
                .
                .
                .

        pgmlen  equ     $           ; get length of text segment
                                    ; at end of program
```

Local Storage

Dynamic allocation of local storage is a standard feature of C function libraries; the portion of a program's private memory set aside for this purpose is called the *local heap*. C application programs can dynamically allocate, resize, and release small blocks from the local heap for arrays and buffers with the library functions *malloc()*, *realloc()*, and *free()*, respectively. This technique allows much more efficient use of memory than statically preallocating all the data structures that a program might require only transiently during its execution.

OS/2 supports three functions that manage local memory pools (analogous to the routines provided by the C runtime library) on behalf of programs written in assembler or any high level language. You can use these functions with any read/write data segment *except for DGROUP* to which the program has access — shared or unshared.

The function *DosSubSet* initializes the OS/2 control structures for a local memory pool. The calling parameters are a segment selector obtained from *DosAllocSeg* or *DosAllocShrSeg*, a flag (1 to initialize the pool), and the heap size in bytes (not necessarily the entire segment). The heap size is always a multiple of 4 bytes, with a minimum of 12 bytes; if the size is not evenly divisible by 4, the system rounds it up. Note that *DosSubSet* considers a size of zero to be an error, although it is treated as a special case (equivalent to 65,536 bytes) by most other memory functions.

The function *DosSubAlloc* obtains a block of storage from a local memory pool. It is called with the selector of the memory segment that holds the local pool, the desired size in bytes, and the address of a variable to receive the offset of the block. The maximum size block you can allocate is the size of the pool itself less 8 bytes (the length of the OS/2 control structure at the head of the segment). The call to *DosSubAlloc* fails if the local pool contains insufficient free memory to satisfy the request; in this event, the actual size of the largest available block is returned instead.

To release a block back to a local pool, call *DosSubFree* with the selector of the segment holding the pool, and the offset and size of the block. The function fails if the offset and size parameters do not match those of a block previously allocated with *DosSubAlloc*.

OS/2 does not provide a function analogous to *DosReallocSeg* that you can use to resize a block of storage obtained with *DosSubAlloc*. A program can simulate such a function by calling *DosSubAlloc* to obtain a new block of the desired size, copying the data from the old block into the new block, and releasing the original block. To enlarge the local pool as a whole, make an additional call to *DosSubSet* and pass it the same selector as in the original call, the new size in bytes, and a flag value of 0. If the local pool already occupies the entire segment, the segment itself must first be expanded with *DosReallocSeg*. Of course, if the segment size is already 65,536 bytes, neither it nor the size of the local pool can increase further.

WARNING: *To improve their execution speed,* DosSubAlloc *and* DosSubFree *perform minimal error checking. Invalid parameters are not always detected and can produce unpredictable program behavior or a GP fault that terminates the process.*

CHAPTER TWELVE

MULTITASKING

Multitasking is the technique of dividing CPU time among programs in such a way that they appear to be running simultaneously. Of course, the processor is executing only one sequence of machine instructions within one task at any given time, but the process of switching from one task to another is invisible to both the user and the programs themselves. (Please accept the imprecise word *task* for a few paragraphs; specifics will follow.) The operating system allocates memory resources to the various tasks and resolves contending requests for peripheral devices such as video displays and disk drives.

The part of the operating system that allocates CPU time among tasks is called the *scheduler,* and the rotation from one task to another is called a *context switch.* When a context switch occurs, the scheduler must save the current state of the active task, restore the registers and program counter to their state when the imminent task was last suspended, and then transfer control to that task.

Multitasking operating systems use two basic types of schedulers: *event-driven* and *preemptive.* Event-driven schedulers rely on each task to be well-behaved—to yield control of the processor at frequent enough intervals so that every program has acceptable throughput, and none is starved for CPU cycles. This yielding of control can be explicit (calling a specific operating system function to give up control) or implicit (suspending the program when it requests the operating system to perform I/O on its behalf and regaining control only after the I/O is completed and other tasks have in turn yielded control). The event-driven strategy is efficient in transaction-oriented systems, which perform a great deal of I/O and not much computation, but such a system can be brought to its knees by a single compute-bound task such as an in-memory sort.

A preemptive scheduler relies on an external signal generated at regular intervals, typically a hardware interrupt triggered by a programmable timer or clock device. When the interrupt occurs, the operating system gains control from whatever task was executing, saves its context, evaluates the list of programs that are ready to run, and gives control to ("dispatches") the next program. This approach to multitasking is often called "time-slicing," a term based on the mental image of dividing the sweep of a second hand around a clock face into little wedges and doling them out to the eligible programs.

The central processors of mainframes and minicomputers — and of microcomputers based on the more powerful microprocessors such as the Intel 80286/386 and the Motorola 68020/30 — include features that make multitasking operating systems more efficient and robust. The two most important of these features are *privilege levels* and *memory protection.*

In the simplest use of privilege levels, the CPU is in either *kernel mode* or *user mode* at any given time. In kernel mode, which is reserved for the operating system, any machine instruction can be executed. As part of the mechanism for transferring control from the operating system to an application program, the CPU is switched into user mode. In this CPU state, execution of certain reserved instructions (such as those that disable interrupts or write to an I/O port) causes a CPU fault and returns control to the operating system.

Memory protection, as described in Chapter 11, is the hardware's ability to detect any attempt by an application program to access memory that does not belong to it. Such an access generates a CPU fault, allowing the operating system to regain control and put the wayward task to sleep forever.

Multitasking in OS/2

OS/2 is built around a preemptive, priority-based scheduler. To understand multitasking under OS/2, you need to grasp three distinct but related operating system concepts: *processes, sessions,* and *threads* (Figure 12-1). The simplest kind of OS/2 *process* is very similar to an application program loaded for execution under MS-DOS. OS/2 creates a process by allocating memory segments to hold the code, data, and stack for the process and by initializing the memory segments from the contents of the program's EXE disk file.

Once it is running, a process can access additional system resources, such as files, pipes, semaphores, queues, and additional memory, with various OS/2 function calls (Figure 12-2 on p. 230). It can start child processes, influence their fate, find out when and why they terminate, and retrieve their exit codes.

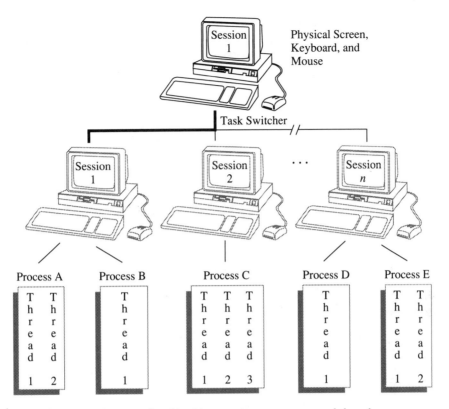

Figure 12-1. *The elements of multitasking: sessions, processes, and threads.*

Processes in turn are members of *sessions* (sometimes called *screen groups*), which are the average user's perception of OS/2 multitasking. By pressing Ctrl-Esc, the user can exit from the current session to a window displayed by the Task Manager and then select an application already executing in another session or establish a new session with the Program Starter. The user can also cycle directly between sessions by pressing Alt-Esc.

OS/2 maintains a separate virtual screen, mouse, and keyboard for each session. The virtual screen receives the output of all processes in the session and is mapped to the physical display whenever the user selects that session using the Task Manager. New processes are added to an existing session when they are launched by a process already executing within the group. The Task Manager can juggle as many as 16 sessions; however, several are dedicated to special processes, such as the swapper and critical error handler, leaving 12 protected mode sessions and 1 real mode session available for applications.

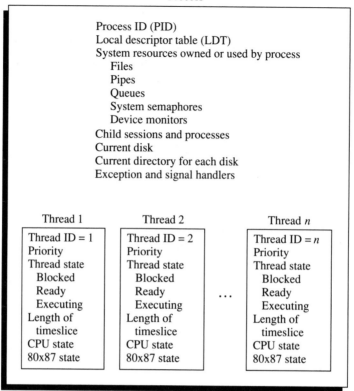

Process

```
Process ID (PID)
Local descriptor table (LDT)
System resources owned or used by process
    Files
    Pipes
    Queues
    System semaphores
    Device monitors
Child sessions and processes
Current disk
Current directory for each disk
Exception and signal handlers
```

Thread 1	Thread 2		Thread *n*

Thread ID = 1
Priority
Thread state
  Blocked
  Ready
  Executing
Length of
  timeslice
CPU state
80x87 state
	Thread ID = 2
	Priority
	Thread state
	  Blocked
	  Ready
	  Executing
	Length of
	  timeslice
	CPU state
	80x87 state
		...	Thread ID = *n*
			Priority
			Thread state
			  Blocked
			  Ready
			  Executing
			Length of
			  timeslice
			CPU state
			80x87 state

Figure 12-2. *Process-specific and thread-specific information maintained by OS/2.*

The OS/2 scheduler, however, knows nothing about processes or sessions; it distributes the CPU cycles among dispatchable entities known as *threads*. Each thread has its own priority, stack, point of execution, CPU state, and (optionally) numeric coprocessor state (Figure 12-2 again). The state includes the CPU's flags and the contents of all registers. At any given time, a thread is either blocked (waiting for I/O or some other event), ready to execute, or actually executing. The scheduler can handle a maximum of 255 threads, although the default system-wide limit (controlled by the THREADS directive in CONFIG.SYS) is 64 in OS/2 version 1.0 and 128 in OS/2 version 1.1.

Each process starts life with a *primary thread* (also called *thread 1*), whose execution begins at the entry point designated in the EXE file header. However, that first thread can start additional threads within the same process, all of which share ownership of the process's resources. Multiple threads within a process execute asynchronously to one another, can have different priorities, and can manipulate one another's priorities.

Although the threads within a process have separate stacks, they share the same near data segment (DGROUP) and thus the same local heap. Careful design of your code to use the stack for local variables makes procedures inherently shareable among threads. (This occurs naturally in C programs.) Access to static variables or other data structures must be coordinated between threads through use of semaphores or other synchronization mechanisms (see Chapter 13).

How does control of the CPU pass from one thread to another? A clock tick or other hardware interrupt causes a transition to kernel mode, whereupon OS/2 saves the current thread's state and calls the appropriate driver to handle the interrupt. Certain API calls by a thread also result in a switch to kernel mode.

When OS/2 is ready to exit kernel mode, the scheduler examines its list of active threads. The thread with the highest priority that is ready to execute gains control of the machine. If the thread that was most recently active is one of multiple eligible threads with the same priority, and if it has not used up its timeslice, it receives preference. If a thread becomes starved for CPU cycles because other threads with higher priorities are getting all the attention, OS/2 temporarily bumps that thread's priority to a higher value (see below: "Configuring the OS/2 Multitasker"). A thread that is currently reading the keyboard also receives a supplemental boost to its priority.

The Multitasking API

The OS/2 multitasking services available to application programs are summarized in Figure 12-3 on the following page. These services include:

- Starting and stopping child processes
- Obtaining the termination type and exit code of a child process
- Starting, suspending, and destroying threads
- Altering the priorities of threads
- Starting, stopping, and selecting new sessions

This range of services allows tremendous flexibility in application design. An application can be factored into asynchronously executing components in many different ways: as multiple threads in a single process sharing the same files and memory; as multiple processes sharing the same virtual screen, keyboard, and pointing device; as multiple processes with distinct virtual screens, keyboard, and pointing devices — or any combination!

OS/2 Function	Description
Thread Management	
DosCreateThread	Creates new thread of execution within same process
DosEnterCritSec	Freezes other threads in same process
DosExit	Terminates current thread
DosExitCritSec	Unfreezes other threads in same process
DosGetPrty	Gets thread priority
DosResumeThread	Reactivates specific thread
DosSetPrty	Sets thread priority
DosSuspendThread	Suspends specific thread
Process Management	
DosCwait	Checks child process status
DosExecPgm	Runs child process
DosExit	Terminates current process
DosExitList	Registers routines to be executed at process termination
DosGetPID	Returns PID of current process and its parent
DosGetPPID	Returns PID of specified process's parent
DosKillProcess	Terminates another process
DosPTrace	Inspects/modifies/traces child process
Session Management	
DosSelectSession	Brings session to foreground
DosSetSession	Sets session status
DosStartSession	Creates new session
DosStopSession	Terminates session

Figure 12-3. *OS/2 multitasking services at a glance.*

Managing Processes

The API function *DosExecPgm* is used by one process, called the *parent,* to load and execute another process, called the *child*. This function is analogous to, but considerably more powerful than, the EXEC function (Int 21H Function 4BH) in MS-DOS versions 2.0 and later. A child process can, in turn, load other processes until some essential system resource is exhausted.

The child process inherits access to some of the parent process's resources: the handles for any open files (unless the parent process explicitly opened the files with the no-inheritance flag), handles to any open pipes, the current disk and current directories of the parent, and a copy of the parent's environment (unless the parent goes to the trouble of creating a new block and passes a pointer to it).

DosExecPgm is called with the following:

- The address of the ASCIIZ program pathname

- A parameter selecting synchronous, asynchronous, or detached execution for the child process

- Addresses or NULL pointers for an argument string block and environment to be passed to the child process

- Addresses of buffers to receive the process ID of the child and certain other information

The program pathname must include the extension (typically EXE), but the OS/2 loader looks at the file header to determine whether the file is executable and does not deduce that fact from the extension. If a fully qualified pathname (including a drive, path, and filename) is supplied for the child, the loader looks only for the specified file. If only a filename and extension are supplied, the loader looks in each directory named in the process's environment PATH string for a matching file.

When a child process executes synchronously, execution of the thread (in the parent process) that made the *DosExecPgm* call is suspended until the child process terminates (either intentionally or as the result of an error condition). When the thread in the parent resumes execution, it receives the return code of the child and a termination code that indicates whether the child terminated normally or was terminated by a fault, Ctrl-C, Ctrl-Break, and so forth.

If the child process is asynchronous, OS/2 returns the child's process ID (PID), and the thread that issued the *DosExecPgm* call continues to execute while the child is running. A thread in the parent process can later use *DosCwait* to find out whether the child is still running or to resynchronize with the child process (by suspending itself until the child terminates and then obtaining the child's return code). Alternatively, the parent can use the child's PID with *DosKillProcess* to terminate unilaterally the execution of the child process (and, optionally, all grandchild processes) at any time.

When a child process is started with the detach option, the process is "orphaned" from the parent: *DosKillProcess* and *DosCwait* functions issued by the parent or its ancestors do not take notice of or affect detached child processes. The child cannot interact with the user without using *VioPopUp*. (The interactive DETACH command is implemented with this variation of *DosExecPgm*.) The system also provides *DosExecPgm* options for session managers and debuggers; however, their use is beyond the scope of this book (although they are described briefly in the reference section).

The environment block, which consists of a series of ASCIIZ strings terminated by an extra zero byte, was discussed in detail in Chapter 3. The parent process can construct a new environment for the child, or it can pass a NULL pointer, in which case the child receives an exact copy of the parent's environment.

The block of argument strings supplied to *DosExecPgm* is similar in form to the environment block. For compatibility with CMD.EXE, the parent should pass the ASCIIZ simple filename of the child (without extension), then the ASCIIZ command tail, followed by another zero byte. In the case of closely coupled child processes that the user would never run directly, the parent typically passes a NULL pointer and communicates its needs to the child by other methods.

A *DosExecPgm* call can fail for many reasons. The two most common are that the specified file cannot be found or that the drive or file containing the program was locked by another process. In a heavily loaded system, a program might not load because the system limits on threads have been reached or because the disk does not hold sufficient swap space. Another, more obscure reason is that the program references a dynlink library or entry point that the system loader can't find; in that case, the name of the missing library and procedure is returned to the parent.

Figures 12-4 and 12-5 contain simple examples of the use of *DosExecPgm* for synchronous and asynchronous execution of CHKDSK as a child process. The options for asynchronous execution provided by *DosExecPgm*, coupled with the several options available with *DosCwait* and *DosKillProcess*, allow for very flexible execution-time relationships between parent and child processes.

```
pname    db      'chkdsk.com',0  ; pathname of child

                                 ; argument strings...
args     db      'chkdsk',0      ; simple filename of child
         db      ' *.*',0        ; simulated command tail
         db      0               ; extra null ends block

                                 ; receives return codes
retcode  dw      0               ; child's termination type
         dw      0               ; child's DosExit code
```

(continued)

Figure 12-4. *Using* DosExecPgm *to run CHKDSK as a synchronous child process.*

Figure 12-4. *continued*

```
objname   db        64 dup (0)            ; receives name of dynlink
objname_len equ $-objname                 ; causing DosExecPgm failure

                .
                .
                .

                                          ; run CHKDSK as synchronous
                                          ; child process...
          push    ds                      ; receives module/entry
                                          ; point if dynlink fails
          push    offset DGROUP:objname
          push    objname_len             ; length of buffer
          push    0                       ; 0 = execute synchronously
          push    ds                      ; address of argument block
          push    offset DGROUP:args
          push    0                       ; address of environment
          push    0                       ; (0 = inherit parent's)
          push    ds                      ; receives child's exit
                                          ; and termination codes
          push    offset DGROUP:retcode
          push    ds                      ; pathname of child
          push    offset DGROUP:pname
          call    DosExecPgm              ; transfer to OS/2
          or      ax,ax                   ; did child process run?
          jnz     error                   ; jump if function failed
                .
                .
                .
```

```
pname   db      'chkdsk.com',0   ; pathname of child

                                 ; argument strings for child
args    db      'chkdsk',0       ; simple filename of child
        db      ' *.*',0         ; simulated command tail
        db      0                ; extra null ends block

                                 ; receives DosExecPgm info
cpid    dw      0                ; PID of child process
        dw      0                ; (word not used)
```

(continued)

Figure 12-5. *Using* DosExecPgm *to run CHKDSK as an asynchronous child process, then calling* DosCwait *to resynchronize with CHKDSK and retrieve its exit code and termination type.*

Figure 12-5. *continued*

```
scratch dw       0                ; PID scratch for DosCwait

                                  ; receives DosCwait info
retcode dw       0                ; child termination type
        dw       0                ; child exit code

objname db       64 dup (0)       ; receives name of dynlink
objname_len equ $-objname         ; causing DosExecPgm failure

        .
        .
        .
                                  ; run CHKDSK as asynchronous
                                  ; child process...
        push     ds               ; receives module/entry
                                  ; point if dynlink fails
        push     offset DGROUP:objname
        push     objname_len      ; length of buffer
        push     2                ; 2 = execute asynchronously
        push     ds               ; address of argument block
        push     offset DGROUP:args
        push     0                ; address of environment
        push     0                ; (0 = inherit parent's)
        push     ds               ; receives child's PID
        push     offset DGROUP:cpid
        push     ds               ; name of child program
        push     offset DGROUP:pname
        call     DosExecPgm       ; transfer to OS/2
        or       ax,ax            ; was child process started?
        jnz      error            ; jump if function failed

        .
        .                         ; other processing here...
        .

                                  ; now resynchronize with
                                  ; child process...
        push     0                ; 0 = immediate child only
        push     0                ; 0 = wait till child ends
        push     ds               ; receives termination info
        push     offset DGROUP:retcode
        push     ds               ; receives PID (N/A here)
        push     offset DGROUP:scratch
        push     cpid             ; PID to wait for
        call     DosCwait         ; transfer to OS/2
        .
        .
        .
```

Managing Threads

Multiple threads within a process share the memory space and system resources owned by the process and can communicate rapidly using shared data structures. Threads can start, suspend, or die quickly and have low system overhead; they are not visible outside the process and do not require the extensive initialization and cleanup associated with starting or terminating a process. Use of multiple threads is particularly appropriate when a process must manage devices with vastly different I/O rates and remain responsive to the needs of each.

A thread starts another thread by calling *DosCreateThread* and supplying it with the addresses of the initial execution point and stack base of the new thread. (Because the stack grows downward, you must supply the address of the last byte plus 1 in the area allocated for the stack.) If the call to *DosCreateThread* succeeds, OS/2 returns a *thread ID* and adds the thread to the scheduler's list. The thread ID is local to the process and, unlike a PID, is not unique within the system.

Each thread is initially entered through a far call from OS/2 and can terminate with a far return or by calling *DosExit*. In the latter case, the thread supplies a parameter that indicates whether the entire process or the thread alone is being terminated. In OS/2 version 1.1, a *DosExit* call by thread 1 receives special treatment and always terminates the process,* whereas in OS/2 1.0 the sole remaining thread in a process need not be thread 1.

When a thread has nothing to do, it should block on a semaphore to await reactivation by another thread or process that clears the same semaphore (see Chapter 13). An alternative (and, in most cases, less desirable) approach is for the thread to use *DosSleep* to block itself for a programmed period of time or simply to give up the remainder of its timeslice. While a thread is blocking, its cost to the system in CPU cycles is nearly zero.

Aside from using semaphores, which require cooperation, the threads in a given process can influence one another's execution in several ways. A thread can call *DosSuspendThread* or *DosResumeThread*, with the thread ID returned by *DosCreateThread*, to suspend or reactivate another thread without that thread's knowledge; a thread can protect itself from such interference with *DosEnterCritSec* and *DosExitCritSec*. Similarly, a thread can use a thread ID with *DosGetPrty* or *DosSetPrty* to inspect or modify its execution priority or that of other threads.

Thread priorities fall into three categories — idle-time, regular, and time-critical — with 32 levels within each category. The idle-time category is

---

* This is to ensure that signals can be sent to the process and that Exitlist routines can be executed when the process terminates.

intended for threads that should execute only when the system has nothing else to do; it should never be used for a thread that interacts with the user. The time-critical category is intended for threads that must respond rapidly to some event (usually timer related or I/O related) to preserve system performance; you will see a use of this category in the SNAP program (Chapter 18). The normal priority category applies to routine execution of threads in application programs, and the primary thread of a process is placed into this category by default; additional threads within a process inherit the priority of the thread that created them.

Figure 12-6 contains the source code for a simple multithreaded program. The first thread starts up another thread which emits 10 beeps at 1-second intervals, while the first thread waits for a keystroke and terminates the process when one is received. Although this is a trivial use of threading, it gives an inkling of the enormous power of the thread concept and exhibits the ease with which you can incorporate asynchronous processing into an OS/2 application.

```
stksiz    equ       2048              ; size of stack for
                                      ; new thread
             .
             .
             .
cdata     db        10 dup (0)        ; receives character data
                                      ; from KbdCharIn

sel       dw        ?                 ; receives selector
                                      ; from DosAllocSeg

tid       dw        ?                 ; receives thread ID
             .
             .
             .
                                      ; allocate stack segment
                                      ; for new thread...
          push      stksiz            ; size of new segment
          push      ds                ; receives selector
          push      offset DGROUP:sel
          push      0                 ; 0 = segment not shareable
```

(continued)

Figure 12-6. *A simple demonstration of multithreading. The first thread starts a second thread and then waits for any key to be pressed. When a key is detected, the process is terminated regardless of the state of the second thread. The second thread emits 10 beeps at 1-second intervals and then destroys itself, possibly still leaving the first thread waiting for the keyboard.*

Figure 12-6. *continued*

```
        call    DosAllocSeg     ; transfer to OS/2
        or      ax,ax           ; was allocation successful?
        jnz     error           ; jump if function failed

                                ; start new thread...
        push    cs              ; thread entry point
        push    offset _TEXT:beeper
        push    ds              ; receives thread ID
        push    offset DGROUP:tid
        push    sel             ; stack for new thread
        push    stksiz
        call    DosCreateThread ; transfer to OS/2
        or      ax,ax           ; was new thread created?
        jnz     error           ; jump if function failed

                                ; now wait for key...
        push    ds              ; receives data packet
        push    offset DGROUP:cdata
        push    0               ; 0 = wait for character
        push    0               ; keyboard handle
        call    KbdCharIn       ; transfer to OS/2

                                ; final exit to OS/2...
        push    1               ; terminate all threads
        push    0               ; exit code = 0 (success)
        call    DosExit         ; transfer to OS/2
        .
        .
        .

beeper  proc    far             ; thread entry point

        mov     cx,10           ; max of 10 beeps

beep1:                          ; sound a tone...
        push    440             ; 440 Hz
        push    100             ; 100 milliseconds
        call    DosBeep         ; transfer to OS/2

        push    0               ; now suspend thread
        push    1000            ; for 1 second...
        call    DosSleep        ; transfer to OS/2

        loop    beep1           ; loop 10 times

        ret                     ; terminate this
                                ; thread only
beeper  endp
```

Managing Sessions

The API functions for session control are present mainly to support the Task Manager, but they can also be useful at the application level in special situations. The most important of these functions, *DosStartSession*, is a sort of big brother to *DosExecPgm*: It starts a new process and at the same time creates a child session to hold that process. *DosStartSession* requires the following parameters:

- The ASCIIZ pathname for the child process to be placed in the new session

- An ASCIIZ argument string (command tail) for the child process

- An ASCIIZ session title for the Task Manager menu

- Parameters that control the behavior and visibility of the child session and process

- An optional queue name

The pathname must be fully qualified (drive, path, filename, and extension of the process to be loaded in the child session); the use of the session title is obvious. The argument string is a single ASCIIZ string, rather than the block of argument strings used by *DosExecPgm*, and it is not accompanied by a pointer to an environment for the new session and process. The initial process in a session receives an environment that is empty except for a PATH string; it is expected to synthesize an appropriate environment for its children. The new session also starts with the current drive and directory set to the root directory of the system's boot device, rather than inheriting current settings from the process that calls *DosStartSession*.

If a queue name is supplied, OS/2 places a message in the queue when the child session (actually, the initial process in the child session) terminates. (Queues will be explained in Chapter 13.) The message contains the child session's ID and the child process's return code. *DosCwait* cannot be used with *DosStartSession* to synchronize with a process in the new session.

The other parameters to *DosStartSession* determine whether the new session starts in the foreground (visible, replacing the parent session) or in the background (not visible, but available on the Task Manager switch list); whether the initial process in the session is traceable (for use by debuggers); and whether it is *related* to the parent session. When the child session is not related, it runs free, and the parent cannot further affect it. (Incidentally, the START command of CMD.EXE is implemented as a call to *DosStartSession* with parameters specifying that the new session is in the background and not related.)

When the child session *is* related, the parent can terminate the session and its member processes (and any grandchild sessions and processes) with *DosStopSession*. Related child sessions and their descendants are also exposed to a hidden danger: They are unilaterally terminated by OS/2 if the parent exits or is terminated unexpectedly. This relationship between parent and child sessions is much different than the relationship that exists between parent and child *processes* created by *DosExecPgm*.

A parent can also use two other API functions to control related child sessions. If the parent is executing in the foreground, it can make one of its child sessions visible instead with *DosSelectSession* (and later return itself to visibility in the same manner). Finally, the parent can use *DosSetSession* to determine whether a related child session is selectable via the Task Manager or to bind itself to a child session. When a parent and child session are bound together, the child session comes to the foreground whenever the child *or* parent session is selected.

Figure 12-7 contains a simple example of a *DosStartSession* call. The code launches a related child session that contains a copy of CMD.EXE. The argument string for CMD.EXE causes it to display a directory listing and then a prompt. The child session terminates when the user types *EXIT* or when the parent session terminates or issues a *DosStopSession* call.

```
                              ; child session parameters
        sesdata dw      24    ; length of structure
                dw      1     ; 0 = unrelated, 1 = related
                dw      1     ; 0 = foreground, 1 = background
                dw      0     ; 0 = not traceable, 1 = traceable
                dd      title ; pointer to session title
                dd      pname ; pointer to process name
                dd      args  ; pointer to argument string
                dd      0     ; pointer to queue name

                              ; pathname for child
        pname   db      'c:\os2\pbin\cmd.exe',0

        args    db      ' /k dir/w',0 ; argument string for child
```

(continued)

Figure 12-7. *Using* DosStartSession *to load CMD.EXE in a new screen group. The command tail passed to CMD.EXE causes it to display a directory listing followed by a prompt. Because the new session is placed in the background, you must switch to it with the Task Manager hot key in order to view the directory.*

Figure 12-7. *continued*

```
                                 ; session title
    title    db        'Child Command Processor',0

    cid      dw        0                ; receives process ID

    sid      dw        0                ; receives session ID


             .
             .
             .

                                        ; run CMD.EXE as child
                                        ; in a new session...
             push      ds               ; address of session data
             push      offset DGROUP:sesdata
             push      ds               ; receives session ID
             push      offset DGROUP:sid
             push      ds               ; receives process ID
             push      offset DGROUP:cid
             call      DosStartSession  ; transfer to OS/2
             or        ax,ax            ; was session started?
             jnz       error            ; jump if function failed
             .
             .
             .
```

Configuring the OS/2 Multitasker

Four optional CONFIG.SYS directives influence OS/2 multitasking:

THREADS=*n*
MAXWAIT=*seconds*
PRIORITY= [ABSOLUTE ¦ DYNAMIC]
TIMESLICE=*x*[,*y*]

The THREADS directive controls the number of threads that can be created simultaneously in the system. The parameter *n* must fall in the range 16 through 255, with a default of 64 in OS/2 version 1.0 and 128 in version 1.1. The upper limit of 255 cannot be expanded.

When a thread is denied the CPU for the number of seconds specified by MAXWAIT (because other higher priority threads are monopolizing the timeslices), the "starved" thread receives a temporary increase in priority for one timeslice. This provision ensures that all processes make some progress and eventually recognize events that concern them. The *seconds* parameter for MAXWAIT must be in the range 1 through 255, with a default value of 3.

The PRIORITY directive enables or disables mechanisms that OS/2 uses to alter the priority of each thread dynamically — based on the activity of other threads within the system. If PRIORITY = DYNAMIC (the default keyword), the priority of threads can be adjusted within a class as a function of their execution history and the visibility of their session. When PRIORITY =ABSOLUTE, thread priorities are not adjusted, and the MAXWAIT directive has no effect.

The TIMESLICE directive controls the length of the timeslices that the OS/2 scheduler uses. The x parameter represents the normal length of a thread's timeslice in milliseconds, and y is the maximum length; if TIMESLICE is not present in CONFIG.SYS, both default to 31. If the y parameter is absent, its value defaults to x. If a thread uses up its entire timeslice and must be preempted, its next timeslice is one tick longer, up to the limit set by the y parameter. In this way, OS/2 lets you minimize context-switching overhead when several compute-bound threads are running at the same priority.

A Simple Command Interpreter

The listings TINYCMD.C (Figure 12-8 on the following page) and TINYCMD.ASM (Figure 12-9 on p. 247) contain the source code for a simple self-contained OS/2 command interpreter. TINYCMD is table-driven so that it can be extended easily.

After the user types a command and presses the Enter key, TINYCMD tries to match the first token in the line against its table of internal (intrinsic) commands. This version of TINYCMD has only three intrinsic commands:

Command	Action
CLS	Clears the screen
EXIT	Terminates TINYCMD
VER	Displays OS/2 version number

If a command is not intrinsic, TINYCMD appends *.EXE* to the first token and attempts to load a program by that name using *DosExecPgm*. If no program file is found, TINYCMD displays the message *Bad command or filename*.

To add new intrinsic commands to TINYCMD, simply code a routine with the appropriate action, and then add the command text and the name of the associated routine to the table named COMMANDS. You can also prevent the user from running specific extrinsic programs by adding their names to the COMMANDS table and associating them with a routine that displays an error message.

To compile TINYCMD.C into the executable file TINYCMD.EXE, type the following command:

```
[C:\] CL TINYCMD.C  <Enter>
```

To assemble TINYCMD.ASM into the file TINYCMD.OBJ, type the following command:

```
[C:\] MASM TINYCMD.ASM;  <Enter>
```

Then use the following command to link TINYCMD.OBJ with the module definition file TINYCMD.DEF (Figure 12-10 on p. 254) and the import library OS2.LIB to produce TINYCMD.EXE:

```
[C:\] LINK TINYCMD,,,OS2,TINYCMD  <Enter>
```

TINYCMD is intended only as a demonstration and would require considerable additional work to approach the functionality of CMD.EXE. You would need to add code to process SET commands and maintain the environment, to interpret batch files, and to search for EXE, COM, and BAT files in that order. You would also need to add a signal handler for Ctrl-C and Ctrl-Break to enable TINYCMD to recover control when the user enters one of these key sequences to terminate a child process. (Signal handlers are discussed in Chapter 13.)

```
/*
        TINYCMD.C

        A simple command interpreter for OS/2.

        Compile with:  C> cl tinycmd.c
        Usage is:  C> tinycmd

        Copyright (C) 1988 Ray Duncan
*/

#include <stdio.h>
#include <string.h>
#include <memory.h>
                                /* macro to return number of
                                   elements in a structure */
#define DIM(x) (sizeof(x) / sizeof(x[0]))
```

(continued)

Figure 12-8. *TINYCMD.C, the source code for TINYCMD.EXE, a simple command interpreter for OS/2.*

Figure 12-8. *continued*

```
#define INPSIZE 80                         /* maximum input length */

#define API unsigned extern far pascal  /* OS/2 API prototypes */

API DosExecPgm(char far *, int, int, char far *, char far *,
               int far *, char far *);
API DosGetVersion(char far *);

unsigned intrinsic(char *);                /* local function prototypes */
void extrinsic(char *);
void cls_cmd(void);
void ver_cmd(void);
void exit_cmd(void);

struct _commands {                         /* intrinsic commands table */
    char *name;                            /* command name */
    int  (*fxn)();                         /* command function */
    }
       commands[] = { "CLS",   cls_cmd,  /* built-in commands */
                      "VER",   ver_cmd,
                      "EXIT",  exit_cmd, };

main(int argc, char *argv[])
{
    char input[INPSIZE];                   /* keyboard input buffer */

    while(1)                               /* main interpreter loop */
    {
        printf("\n>> ");                   /* display prompt */
        memset(input, 0, INPSIZE);         /* initialize input buffer */
        gets(input);                       /* get keyboard entry */
        strtok(input, " ;,=\t");           /* break out first token */
        strupr(input);                     /* and fold to uppercase */

        if(! intrinsic(input))             /* if intrinsic command,
                                              run its function */
            extrinsic(input);              /* else assume EXE file */
    }
}

/*
    Try to match first token of command line with intrinsic
    command table. If a match is found, run the associated
    routine and return true; otherwise, return false.
*/
```

(continued)

Figure 12-8. *continued*

```
unsigned intrinsic(char *input)
{
    int i;                              /* scratch variable */

    for(i=0; i < DIM(commands); i++)    /* search command table */
    {
        if(! strcmp(commands[i].name, input))
        {
            (*commands[i].fxn)();       /* if match, run routine */
            return(1);                  /* and return true */
        }
    }
    return(0);                          /* no match, return false */
}

/*
    Append .EXE to first token and attempt to execute program,
    passing address of argument strings block and null pointer
    for environment (child process inherits TINYCMD's environment).
*/
void extrinsic(char *input)
{
    char pbuff[INPSIZE];                /* buffer for program name */
    unsigned status;                    /* value from DosExecPgm */
    int cinfo[2];                       /* child process info */

    strcpy(pbuff, input);               /* copy first command token
                                           to local buffer */
    strcat(pbuff, ".EXE");              /* append .EXE to token */

                                        /* try to execute program */
    if(DosExecPgm(NULL,                 /* object name buffer pointer */
                  0,                    /* object name buffer length */
                  0,                    /* synchronous execution mode */
                  input,                /* argument strings */
                  NULL,                 /* use parent's environment */
                  cinfo,                /* receives termination info */
                  pbuff))               /* program name pointer */

        printf("\nBad command or filename\n");
}

/*
    These are the subroutines for the intrinsic commands.
*/
```

(continued)

Figure 12-8. *continued*

```
void cls_cmd(void)                       /* CLS command */
{
    printf("\033[2J");                   /* ANSI escape sequence */
}                                        /* to clear screen */

void ver_cmd(void)                       /* VER command */
{
    char verinfo[2];                     /* receives version info */

    DosGetVersion(verinfo);              /* get and display version */
    printf("\nOS/2 version %d.%02d\n", verinfo[0], verinfo[1]);
}

void exit_cmd(void)                      /* EXIT command */
{
    exit(0);                             /* terminate TINYCMD */
}
```

```
        title   TINYCMD -- Simple Command Interpreter
        page    55,132
        .286


;
; TINYCMD.ASM
;
; A simple command interpreter for OS/2.
;
; Assemble with:  C> masm tinycmd.asm;
; Link with:  C> link tinycmd,,,os2,tinycmd
;
; Usage is:  C> tinycmd
;
; Copyright (C) 1988 Ray Duncan
;

cr      equ     0dh                     ; ASCII carriage return
lf      equ     0ah                     ; ASCII linefeed
tab     equ     09h                     ; ASCII tab
blank   equ     20h                     ; ASCII blank code
escape  equ     01bh                    ; ASCII escape code

inpsize equ     80                      ; maximum input length
```

(continued)

Figure 12-9. *TINYCMD.ASM, the source code for TINYCMD.EXE, a simple command interpreter for OS/2.*

Figure 12-9. *continued*

```
        extrn   DosExecPgm:far          : OS/2 API functions
        extrn   DosExit:far
        extrn   DosGetVersion:far
        extrn   KbdStringIn:far
        extrn   VioWrtTTY:far


DGROUP  group   _DATA


_DATA   segment word public 'DATA'


; Intrinsic commands table: Each entry is an ASCIIZ string
; followed by the offset of the corresponding procedure.


commands label   byte
        db      'CLS',0                 : clear screen command
        dw      cls_cmd
        db      'VER',0                 : display OS/2 version
        dw      ver_cmd
        db      'EXIT',0                : exit from TINYCMD
        dw      exit_cmd
        db      0                       : end of table


input   db      (inpsize+2) dup (0)     : keyboard input buffer
ibinfo  dw      inpsize,0               : input buffer info


pbuff   db      (inpsize+2) dup (0)     : program name moved here


cinfo   dw      0                       : child termination type
        dw      0                       : child return code


prompt  db      cr,lf,'>> '             : TINYCMD's user prompt
pr_len  equ     $-prompt


delims  db      0,blank,tab,';,='       : delimiters for first
de_len  equ     $-delims                : command line token


pext    db      '.EXE',0                : program file extension
pe_len  equ     $-pext


wlen    dw      0                       : receives bytes written
verinfo db      0,0                     : receives OS/2 version


msg1    db      cr,lf,lf                : error message
        db      'Bad command or filename'
        db      cr,lf
msg1_len equ    $-msg1
```

(continued)

Figure 12-9. *continued*

```
msg2      db      escape,'[2J'              ; ANSI escape sequence
msg2_len equ     $-msg2                     ; to clear the screen

msg3      db      cr,lf,lf                   ; version number message
          db      'OS/2 version '
msg3a     db      'nn.'
msg3b     db      'nn'
          db      cr,lf
msg3_len equ     $-msg3

_DATA    ends


_TEXT    segment word public 'CODE'

         assume  cs:_TEXT,ds:DGROUP,es:DGROUP

main     proc    far                        ; entry point from OS/2

         push    ds                         ; make DGROUP addressable
         pop     es                         ; with ES too
         cld                                ; clear direction flag

main1:                                      ; main interpreter loop
         call    gcmd                       ; get command from user

         call    intrinsic                  ; check if intrinsic function
         jnc     main1                      ; yes, it was processed

         call    extrinsic                  ; no, run EXE file, then
         jmp     main1                      ; get another command

main     endp

; Try to match first command token against COMMANDS table.
; If match, run the routine, return Carry = False.
; If no match, return Carry = True.

intrinsic proc  near

                                            ; point to command table
         mov     si,offset DGROUP:commands

intr1:                                      ; try next table entry...
         cmp     byte ptr [si],0            ; end of entire table?
         je      intr6                      ; jump if table exhausted
```

(continued)

Figure 12-9. *continued*

```
        mov     di,offset DGROUP:input   ; point to user's command

intr2:  mov     al,[si]                  ; next character from table

        or      al,al                    ; end of table entry?
        jz      intr3                    ; yes, jump

        cmp     al,[di]                  ; compare to input character
        jnz     intr4                    ; jump, found mismatch

        inc     si                       ; advance string pointers
        inc     di
        jmp     intr2

intr3:  cmp     byte ptr [di],0          ; user's entry same length?
        jne     intr5                    ; no, not a match

        call    word ptr [si+1]          ; run the command routine

        clc                              ; return Carry = False
        ret                              ; as success signal

intr4:  lodsb                            ; look for end of this
        or      al,al                    ; command string (null byte)
        jnz     intr4                    ; not end yet, loop

intr5:  add     si,2                     ; skip over routine address
        jmp     intr1                    ; try to match next command

intr6:  stc                             ; command not matched, exit
        ret                              ; with Carry = True

intrinsic endp


; Append .EXE to first token and attempt to execute program,
; passing address of argument strings block and null pointer
; for environment. (Child process inherits TINYCMD's environment.)

extrinsic proc  near

        mov     si,offset DGROUP:input   ; copy first token of
        mov     di,offset DGROUP:pbuff   ; user command to pbuff
```

(continued)

Figure 12-9. *continued*

```
extr1:   lodsb                          ; get next character
         or      al,al                  ; found null?
         jz      extr2                  ; yes, end of token
         stosb                          ; no, copy character
         jmp     extr1                  ; and get next character


extr2:   mov     si,offset DGROUP:pext  ; append .EXE extension
         mov     cx,pe_len              ; to token, forming
         rep movsb                      ; program filename


                                        ; try to run program...
         push    0                      ; object name buffer
         push    0
         push    0                      ; object name buffer length
         push    0                      ; synchronous execution mode
         push    ds                     ; address of argument strings
         push    offset DGROUP:input
         push    0                      ; environment pointer
         push    0
         push    ds                     ; receives termination info
         push    offset DGROUP:cinfo
         push    ds                     ; address of program name
         push    offset DGROUP:pbuff
         call    DosExecPgm             ; transfer to OS/2
         or      ax,ax                  ; was function successful?
         jz      extr3                  ; yes, jump


                                        ; no, display error message...
         push    ds                     ; message address
         push    offset DGROUP:msg1
         push    msg1_len               ; message length
         push    0                      ; default video handle
         call    VioWrtTTY              ; transfer to OS/2


extr3:   ret                            ; back to caller


extrinsic endp


; Get input from user, convert it to argument strings block
; by breaking out first token with null and appending double
; null to entire line, and convert first token to uppercase.


gcmd     proc    near                   ; prompt user, get command
```

(continued)

Figure 12-9. *continued*

```
                                         ; display TINYCMD prompt...
        push    ds                       ; address of prompt
        push    offset DGROUP:prompt
        push    pr_len                   ; length of prompt
        push    0                        ; default video handle
        call    VioWrtTTY

        mov     ibinfo+2,0               ; disable buffer editing

                                         ; get entry from user...
        push    ds                       ; address of input buffer
        push    offset DGROUP:input
        push    ds                       ; input buffer info
        push    offset DGROUP:ibinfo
        push    0                        ; 0 = wait for input
        push    0                        ; default keyboard handle
        call    KbdStringIn

        mov     cx,inpsize               ; look for carriage return
        mov     al,cr                    ; if any...
        mov     di,offset DGROUP:input
        repnz scasb
        jnz     gcmd1
        dec     di
gcmd1:  mov     word ptr [di],0          ; and replace with 2 nulls
        mov     si,offset DGROUP:input   ; break out first token...

gcmd2:  lodsb                            ; compare next character
        mov     di,offset DGROUP:delims  ; to delimiter table
        mov     cx,de_len
        repnz scasb
        jnz     gcmd2                    ; jump, no match
        mov     byte ptr [si-1],0        ; replace delimiter with 0

        mov     si,offset DGROUP:input   ; fold token to uppercase

gcmd3:  cmp     byte ptr [si],0          ; end of token?
        jz      gcmd5                    ; found end, jump
        cmp     byte ptr [si],'a'
        jb      gcmd4                    ; jump if not 'a-z'
        cmp     byte ptr [si],'z'
        ja      gcmd4                    ; jump if not 'a-z'
        sub     byte ptr [si],'a'-'A'    ; convert to uppercase
```

(continued)

Figure 12-9. *continued*

```
gcmd4:  inc     si                          ; go to next character
        jmp     gcmd3

gcmd5:  ret                                 ; back to caller

gcmd    endp


cls_cmd proc    near                        ; intrinsic CLS command

                                            ; send ANSI escape sequence
                                            ; to clear the screen...
        push    ds                          ; escape sequence address
        push    offset DGROUP:msg2
        push    msg2_len                    ; escape sequence length
        push    0                           ; default video handle
        call    VioWrtTTY                   ; transfer to OS/2
        ret                                 ; back to caller

cls_cmd endp


ver_cmd proc    near                        ; intrinsic VER command

                                            ; get OS/2 version number...
        push    ds                          ; receives version info
        push    offset DGROUP:verinfo
        call    DosGetVersion               ; transfer to OS/2

                                            ; format the version...
        mov     al,verinfo                  ; convert minor version
        aam                                 ; number to ASCII
        add     ax,'00'
        xchg    al,ah
        mov     word ptr msg3b,ax           ; store ASCII characters

        mov     al,verinfo+1                ; convert major version
        aam                                 ; number to ASCII
        add     ax,'00'
        xchg    al,ah
        mov     word ptr msg3a,ax           ; store ASCII characters

                                            ; display version number...
        push    ds                          ; message address
        push    offset DGROUP:msg3
```

(continued)

Figure 12-9. *continued*

```
        push    msg3_len                ; message length
        push    0                       ; default video handle
        call    VioWrtTTY               ; transfer to OS/2

        ret                             ; back to caller

ver_cmd endp


exit_cmd proc   near                    ; intrinsic EXIT Command

                                        ; final exit to OS/2...
        push    1                       ; terminate all threads
        push    0                       ; return code = 0
        call    DosExit                 ; transfer to OS/2

exit_cmd endp

_TEXT   ends

        end     main                    ; defines entry point
```

```
NAME TINYCMD WINDOWCOMPAT
PROTMODE
STACKSIZE 4096
```

Figure 12-10. *TINYCMD.DEF, the module definition file for TINYCMD.ASM.*

A Simple Multithreaded Application

The listings DUMBTERM.C (Figure 12-11) and DUMBTERM.ASM (Figure 12-12, which begins on p. 260) contain the source code for a simple multithreaded application. DUMBTERM is a primitive terminal emulator that exchanges characters between the console (keyboard and video display) and the serial port. The user enters *Alt-X* to terminate the program.

DUMBTERM demonstrates the benefits of using multiple threads when a process must perform I/O to two or more devices. It creates one thread to read the serial port and write the resulting characters to the display, and it creates another thread to read the keyboard and write the resulting characters to the serial port. The threads run independently and block when no input is available, thus conserving CPU cycles and eliminating the need for polling.

For simplicity, DUMBTERM does not include any logic for selecting or configuring the serial port based on command line switches or menus. DUMBTERM always opens COM1 and configures it to 2400 baud, 8 bits, no parity, and 1 stop bit. To modify the settings, you must edit the *#define* or *EQU* statements at the beginning of the source code.

To compile DUMBTERM.C into the executable file DUMBTERM.EXE, type the following command:

```
[C:\] CL /F 2000 DUMBTERM.C  <Enter>
```

The /F option creates a large stack for DUMBTERM's primary thread so that the stacks for the two additional I/O threads can be allocated as automatic arrays within the main stack. You can also allocate new segments for the thread stacks, but you are then more likely to run into problems with the stack-checking routine in the C runtime library.

To assemble DUMBTERM.ASM into the file DUMBTERM.OBJ, type the following command:

```
[C:\] MASM DUMBTERM.ASM;  <Enter>
```

Then, to produce DUMBTERM.EXE, link DUMBTERM.OBJ, the import library OS2.LIB, and DUMBTERM.DEF (Figure 12-13 on p. 269), with the following command:

```
[C:\] LINK DUMBTERM,,,OS2,DUMBTERM  <Enter>
```

```
/*
        DUMBTERM.C

        A simple multithreaded OS/2 terminal program that exchanges
        characters between the console and the serial port.

        Communication parameters for COM1 are set at 2400 baud,
        8 data bits, no parity, and 1 stop bit.

        Compile with:  C> cl /F 2000 dumbterm.c

        Usage is:  C> dumbterm
```

(continued)

Figure 12-11. *DUMBTERM.C, the source code for DUMBTERM.EXE, a simple terminal emulator that illustrates use of multiple threads.*

Figure 12-11. *continued*

```
            Press Alt-X to terminate the program.

            Copyright (C) 1988 Ray Duncan

*/


#define WAIT    0                       /* parameters for KbdCharIn */
#define NOWAIT  1


#define EXITKEY   0x2d                  /* Exit key = Alt-X */


#define STKSIZE 2048                    /* stack size for threads */


#define COMPORT "COM1"                  /* COM port configuration */
#define BAUD     2400                   /* 110, 150 ... 19200 */
#define PARITY   0                      /* 0=N, 1=O, 2=E, 3=M, 4=S */
#define DATABIT 8                       /* 5-8 allowed */
#define STOPBIT 0                       /* 0=1, 1=1.5, 2=2 */


#define API unsigned extern far pascal /* OS/2 API prototypes */

API DosClose(unsigned);
API DosCreateThread(void (far *)(), unsigned far *, void far *);
API DosDevIOCtl(void far *, void far *, unsigned, unsigned, unsigned);
API DosExit(unsigned, unsigned);
API DosOpen(char far *, unsigned far *, unsigned far *, unsigned long,
            unsigned, unsigned, unsigned, unsigned long);
API DosRead(unsigned, void far *, int, unsigned far *);
API DosSemClear(unsigned long far *);
API DosSemSet(unsigned long far *);
API DosSemWait(unsigned long far *, unsigned long);
API DosSuspendThread(unsigned);
API DosWrite(unsigned, void far *, int, unsigned far *);
API KbdCharIn(void far *, unsigned, unsigned);
API KbdGetStatus(void far *, unsigned);
API KbdSetStatus(void far *, unsigned);
API VioWrtTTY(char far *, int, unsigned);


void far comin(void);                   /* local function prototypes */
void far comout(void);
void errexit(char *);


struct _F41Info {                       /* DosDevIOCtl info structure */
    int BaudRate;                       /* 110, 150 ... 19200 */
    } F41Info;
```

(continued)

Figure 12-11. *continued*

```
struct _F42Info {                /* DosDevIOCtl info structure */
    char DataBits;               /* character length 5-8 bits */
    char Parity;                 /* 0=N, 1=O, 2=E, 3=Mark, 4=Space */
    char StopBits;               /* 0=1, 1=1.5, 2=2 stop bits */
    } F42Info;

struct _KbdInfo {                /* KbdCharIn info structure */
    char CharCode;               /* ASCII character code */
    char ScanCode;               /* keyboard scan code */
    char Status;                 /* miscellaneous status flags */
    char Reserved1;              /* reserved byte */
    unsigned ShiftState;         /* keyboard shift state */
    long TimeStamp;              /* character timestamp */
    } KbdInfo;

struct _KbdStatus {              /* KbdGetStatus info structure */
    int Length;                  /* length of structure */
    unsigned Mask;               /* keyboard state flags */
    char TurnAround[2];          /* logical end-of-line */
    unsigned Interim;            /* interim character flags */
    unsigned ShiftState;         /* keyboard shift state */
    } KbdStatus;

unsigned chandle;                /* handle for COM port */
unsigned long exitsem;           /* Alt-X exit semaphore */

main()
{
    unsigned action;             /* result of DosOpen */
    unsigned openflag = 0x01;    /* fail if device not found */
    unsigned openmode = 0x12;    /* read/write, deny all */
    unsigned cominID;            /* COM input thread ID */
    unsigned comoutID;           /* COM output thread ID */
    char cominstk[STKSIZE];      /* COM input thread stack */
    char comoutstk[STKSIZE];     /* COM output thread stack */

                                 /* open COM port */
    if(DosOpen(COMPORT, &chandle, &action, 0L, 0, openflag, openmode, 0L))
        errexit("\nCan't open COM device.\n");

    F41Info.BaudRate = BAUD;     /* configure COM port */
    F42Info.DataBits = DATABIT;  /* using DosDevIOCtl */
    F42Info.Parity = PARITY;     /* Category 1 functions */
    F42Info.StopBits = STOPBIT;
```

(continued)

Figure 12-11. *continued*

```
        if(DosDevIOCtl(NULL, &F41Info, 0x41, 1, chandle))
            errexit("\nCan't set baud rate.\n");
        if(DosDevIOCtl(NULL, &F42Info, 0x42, 1, chandle))
            errexit("\nCan't configure COM port.\n");

        KbdStatus.Length = 10;                /* force keyboard */
        KbdGetStatus(&KbdStatus, 0);          /* into binary mode */
        KbdStatus.Mask &= 0xfff0;             /* with echo off */
        KbdStatus.Mask |= 0x06;
        KbdSetStatus(&KbdStatus, 0);

        exitsem = 0L;                         /* initialize and */
        DosSemSet(&exitsem);                  /* set exit semaphore */

                                              /* create COM input thread */
        if(DosCreateThread(comin, &cominID, cominstk+STKSIZE))
            errexit("\nCan't create COM input thread.\n");

                                              /* create COM output thread */
        if(DosCreateThread(comout, &comoutID, comoutstk+STKSIZE))
            errexit("\nCan't create COM output thread.\n");

        puts("\nCommunicating...");           /* sign-on message */

        DosSemWait(&exitsem, -1L);            /* wait for exit signal */

        DosSuspendThread(cominID);            /* freeze COM input and */
        DosSuspendThread(comoutID);           /* output threads */

        puts("\nTerminating...");             /* sign-off message */

        DosExit(1, 0);                        /* terminate all threads */
                                              /* return code = 0 */
}


/*
    The 'comin' thread reads characters one at a time from the
    COM port and sends them to the display.
*/
void far comin(void)
{
    unsigned rlen;                           /* scratch variable */
    char inchar;                             /* character input buffer */
```

(continued)

Figure 12-11. *continued*

```
    while(1)
    {                                      /* read character from COM */
        DosRead(chandle, &inchar, 1, &rlen);
        VioWrtTTY(&inchar, 1, 0);          /* send character to display */
    }
}


/*
    The 'comout' thread reads characters one at a time from the
    keyboard and sends them to the COM port.  If the exit key is
    detected, the main thread is signaled to clean up and exit.
*/
void far comout(void)
{
    unsigned wlen;                         /* scratch variable */

    while(1)
    {
        KbdCharIn(&KbdInfo, WAIT, 0);      /* read keyboard */
        wlen = 1;                          /* assume 1-byte character */

                                           /* extended character? */
        if((KbdInfo.CharCode == 0) || (KbdInfo.CharCode == 0xe0))
        {
            wlen = 2;                      /* yes, set length = 2 */

            if(KbdInfo.ScanCode == EXITKEY)
            {                              /* if exit key detected */
                DosSemClear(&exitsem);     /* signal thread 1 to exit */
                wlen = 0;                  /* and discard character */
            }
        }
                                           /* write COM port */
        DosWrite(chandle, &KbdInfo.CharCode, wlen, &wlen);
    }
}


/*
    Common error exit routine; displays error message
    and terminates process.
*/
void errexit(char *msg)
{
    VioWrtTTY(msg, strlen(msg), 0);        /* display error message */
    DosExit(1, 1);                         /* terminate, exit code = 1 */
}
```

```
                    title    DUMBTERM -- OS/2 Terminal Program
                    page     55,132
                    .286


        ;
        ; DUMBTERM.ASM
        ;
        ; A simple multithreaded OS/2 terminal program that exchanges
        ; characters between the console and the serial port.
        ;
        ; Communication parameters for COM1 are set at 2400 baud,
        ; 8 data bits, no parity, and 1 stop bit.
        ;
        ; Assemble with:  C> masm dumbterm.asm;
        ; Link with:  C> link dumbterm,,,os2,dumbterm
        ;
        ; Usage is:  C> dumbterm
        ;
        ; Press Alt-X to terminate the program.
        ;
        ; Copyright (C) 1988 Ray Duncan
        ;


        cr       equ     0dh             ; ASCII carriage return
        lf       equ     0ah             ; ASCII linefeed

        kwait    equ     0               ; KbdCharIn parameters
        knowait  equ     1

        stksize  equ     2048            ; stack size for threads

        exitkey  equ     2dh             ; Alt-X key is exit signal

                                         ; COM port configuration
        com1     equ     1               ; nonzero if using COM1
        com2     equ     0               ; nonzero if using COM2
        com3     equ     0               ; nonzero if using COM3
        baud     equ     2400            ; baud rate for COM port
        parity   equ     0               ; 0=N, 1=O, 2=E, 3=M, 4=S
        databit  equ     8               ; 5-8
        stopbit  equ     0               ; 0=1, 1=1.5, 2=2

                 extrn   DosAllocSeg:far ; OS/2 API functions
                 extrn   DosClose:far
                 extrn   DosCreateThread:far
                 extrn   DosDevIOCtl:far
```

(continued)

Figure 12-12. *DUMBTERM.ASM, the source code for DUMBTERM.EXE, a simple terminal application that illustrates use of multiple threads.*

Figure 12-12. *continued*

```
        extrn   DosExit:far
        extrn   DosOpen:far
        extrn   DosRead:far
        extrn   DosSemClear:far
        extrn   DosSemSet:far
        extrn   DosSemWait:far
        extrn   DosSuspendThread:far
        extrn   DosWrite:far
        extrn   KbdCharIn:far
        extrn   KbdGetStatus:far
        extrn   KbdSetStatus:far
        extrn   VioWrtTTY:far


DGROUP  group   _DATA


_DATA   segment word public 'DATA'


cname   label   byte            ; COM port logical name
        if      com1
        db      'COM1',0        ; COM1 device
        endif
        if      com2
        db      'COM2',0        ; COM2 device
        endif
        if      com3
        db      'COM3',0        ; COM3 device
        endif


f41info dw      baud            ; baud rate


f42info db      databit         ; data bits
        db      parity          ; parity
        db      stopbit         ; stop bits


kbdinfo db      0               ; character code
        db      0               ; scan code
        db      0               ; status flags
        db      0               ; reserved
        dw      0               ; shift state
        dd      0               ; timestamp


kbdstat dw      10              ; length of structure
        dw      0               ; keyboard state flags
        db      0,0             ; logical end-of-line
        dw      0               ; interim character flags
        dw      0               ; shift state
```

(continued)

Figure 12-12. *continued*

```
exitsem  dd      0                       ; exit semaphore

chandle  dw      0                       ; receives COM device handle
action   dw      0                       ; receives DosOpen action
sel      dw      0                       ; receives selector
rlen     dw      0                       ; receives bytes read count
wlen     dw      0                       ; receives bytes written count
cinID    dw      0                       ; COM input thread ID
coutID   dw      0                       ; COM output thread ID
inchar   db      0                       ; input character from COM port

msg1     db      cr,lf
         db      "Can't open COM device."
         db      cr,lf
msg1_len equ     $-msg1

msg2     db      cr,lf
         db      "Can't set baud rate."
         db      cr,lf
msg2_len equ     $-msg2

msg3     db      cr,lf
         db      "Can't configure COM port."
         db      cr,lf
msg3_len equ     $-msg3

msg4     db      cr,lf
         db      "Memory allocation failure."
         db      cr,lf
msg4_len equ     $-msg4

msg5     db      cr,lf
         db      "Can't create COM input thread."
         db      cr,lf
msg5_len equ     $-msg5

msg6     db      cr,lf
         db      "Can't create COM output thread."
         db      cr,lf
msg6_len equ     $-msg6

msg7     db      cr,lf
         db      "Communicating..."
         db      cr,lf
msg7_len equ     $-msg7
```

(continued)

Figure 12-12. *continued*

```
msg8       db      cr,lf
           db      "Terminating..."
           db      cr,lf
msg8_len equ      $-msg8


_DATA    ends



_TEXT    segment word public 'CODE'

         assume  cs:_TEXT,ds:DGROUP

main     proc    far                 ; entry point from OS/2

                                     ; open COM port...
         push    ds                  ; device name address
         push    offset DGROUP:cname
         push    ds                  ; receives device handle
         push    offset DGROUP:chandle
         push    ds                  ; receives action
         push    offset DGROUP:action
         push    0                   ; initial allocation (N/A)
         push    0
         push    0                   ; attribute (N/A)
         push    1                   ; open flag: fail if device
                                     ;             does not exist
         push    12h                 ; open mode: read/write,
                                     ;             deny-all
         push    0                   ; DWORD reserved
         push    0
         call    DosOpen             ; transfer to OS/2
         or      ax,ax               ; was function successful?
         jz      main1               ; yes, jump

         mov     cx,msg1_len         ; no, display error message
         mov     dx,offset DGROUP:msg1
         jmp     main9               ; and exit

main1:                               ; set baud rate...
         push    0                   ; data buffer address
         push    0
         push    ds                  ; parameter buffer address
         push    offset DGROUP:f41info
         push    41h                 ; function number
```

(continued)

Figure 12-12. *continued*

```
         push    1                      ; category number
         push    chandle                ; COM device handle
         call    DosDevIOCtl            ; transfer to OS/2
         or      ax,ax                  ; was function successful?
         jz      main2                  ; yes, jump

         mov     cx,msg2_len            ; no, display error message
         mov     dx,offset DGROUP:msg2
         jmp     main9                  ; and exit

main2:                                  ; configure parity, stop bits,
                                        ; and character length...
         push    0                      ; data buffer address
         push    0
         push    ds                     ; parameter buffer address
         push    offset DGROUP:f42info
         push    42h                    ; function number
         push    1                      ; category number
         push    chandle                ; COM device handle
         call    DosDevIOCtl            ; transfer to OS/2
         or      ax,ax                  ; was function successful?
         jz      main3                  ; yes, jump

         mov     cx,msg3_len            ; no, display error message
         mov     dx,offset DGROUP:msg3
         jmp     main9                  ; and exit

main3:                                  ; put keyboard in binary mode
                                        ; with echo off...

                                        ; get keyboard state
         push    ds                     ; address of info structure
         push    offset DGROUP:kbdstat
         push    0                      ; default keyboard handle
         call    KbdGetStatus           ; transfer to OS/2

                                        ; set binary mode, no echo
         and     word ptr kbdstat+2,0fff0h
         or      word ptr kbdstat+2,6

                                        ; set keyboard state
         push    ds                     ; address of info structure
         push    offset DGROUP:kbdstat
         push    0                      ; default keyboard handle
         call    KbdSetStatus           ; transfer to OS/2
```

(continued)

Figure 12-12. *continued*

```
            push    ds                  ; set exit semaphore
            push    offset DGROUP:exitsem
            call    DosSemSet           ; transfer to OS/2


                                        ; allocate thread stack
            push    stksize             ; stack size in bytes
            push    ds                  ; receives new selector
            push    offset DGROUP:sel
            push    0                   ; not shareable/discardable
            call    DosAllocSeg         ; transfer to OS/2
            or      ax,ax               ; was function successful?
            jz      main4               ; yes, jump

            mov     cx,msg4_len         ; no, display error message
            mov     dx,offset DGROUP:msg4
            jmp     main9               ; and exit

main4:                                  ; create COM input thread
            push    cs                  ; thread entry point
            push    offset _TEXT:comin
            push    ds                  ; receives thread ID
            push    offset DGROUP:cinID
            push    sel                 ; address of stack base
            push    stksize
            call    DosCreateThread     ; transfer to OS/2
            or      ax,ax               ; was function successful?
            jz      main5               ; yes, jump

            mov     cx,msg5_len         ; no, display error message
            mov     dx,offset DGROUP:msg5
            jmp     main9               ; and exit

main5:                                  ; allocate thread stack
            push    stksize             ; stack size in bytes
            push    ds                  ; receives new selector
            push    offset DGROUP:sel
            push    0                   ; not shareable/discardable
            call    DosAllocSeg         ; transfer to OS/2
            or      ax,ax               ; was function successful?
            jz      main6               ; yes, jump

            mov     cx,msg4_len         ; no, display error message
            mov     dx,offset DGROUP:msg4
            jmp     main9               ; and exit
```

(continued)

Figure 12-12. *continued*

```
main6:                            ; create COM output thread...
        push    cs                ; thread entry point
        push    offset _TEXT:comout
        push    ds                ; receives thread ID
        push    offset DGROUP:coutID
        push    sel               ; address of stack base
        push    stksize
        call    DosCreateThread   ; transfer to OS/2
        or      ax,ax             ; was function successful?
        jz      main7             ; yes, jump

        mov     cx,msg6_len       ; no, display error message
        mov     dx,offset DGROUP:msg6
        jmp     main9             ; and exit

main7:                            ; display "Communicating..."
        push    ds                ; message address
        push    offset DGROUP:msg7
        push    msg7_len          ; message length
        push    0                 ; default video handle
        call    VioWrtTTY         ; transfer to OS/2

                                  ; wait for exit signal
        push    ds                ; semaphore handle
        push    offset DGROUP:exitsem
        push    -1                ; wait indefinitely
        push    -1
        call    DosSemWait        ; transfer to OS/2

                                  ; suspend COM input thread
        push    cinID             ; thread ID
        call    DosSuspendThread  ; transfer to OS/2

                                  ; suspend COM output thread
        push    coutID            ; thread ID
        call    DosSuspendThread  ; transfer to OS/2

                                  ; display "Terminating"...
        push    ds                ; message address
        push    offset DGROUP:msg8
        push    msg8_len          ; message length
        push    0                 ; default video handle
        call    VioWrtTTY         ; transfer to OS/2

                                  ; final exit to OS/2...
        push    1                 ; terminate all threads
        push    0                 ; return code = 0 (success)
        call    DosExit           ; transfer to OS/2
```

(continued)

Figure 12-12. *continued*

```
main9:                          ; display error message...
                                ; DS:DX = msg, CX = length
        push    ds              ; address of message
        push    dx
        push    cx              ; length of message
        push    0               ; default video handle
        call    VioWrtTTY       ; transfer to OS/2

                                ; final exit to OS/2...
        push    1               ; terminate all threads
        push    1               ; return code = 1 (error)
        call    DosExit         ; transfer to OS/2

main    endp



; COM input thread: Reads characters one at a time
; from the COM port and writes them to the display.

comin   proc    far

                                ; read character from COM...
        push    chandle         ; COM device handle
        push    ds              ; receives COM data
        push    offset DGROUP:inchar
        push    1               ; length to read
        push    ds              ; receives read count
        push    offset DGROUP:rlen
        call    DosRead         ; transfer to OS/2

                                ; send character to display...
        push    ds              ; address of character
        push    offset DGROUP:inchar
        push    1               ; length to write
        push    0               ; default video handle
        call    VioWrtTTY       ; transfer to OS/2

        jmp     comin           ; wait for next character

comin   endp



; COM output thread: Reads characters from the keyboard
; in raw mode and sends them to the COM port.  If the
; exit key is detected, the main thread is signaled to
; clean up and terminate the process.
```

(continued)

Figure 12-12. *continued*

```
comout    proc    far


                                  ; read keyboard character...
          push    ds              ; receives keyboard data
          push    offset DGROUP:kbdinfo
          push    kwait           ; wait if necessary
          push    0               ; default keyboard handle
          call    KbdCharIn       ; transfer to OS/2

          mov     cx,1            ; assume writing one byte

          cmp     kbdinfo,0       ; check for extended key
          jz      comout1         ; jump, extended key
          cmp     kbdinfo,0e0h
          jnz     comout2         ; jump, not extended key

comout1:                          ; extended key detected
          mov     cx,2            ; must write 2 bytes

                                  ; check for exit key
          cmp     kbdinfo+1,exitkey
          jnz     comout2         ; not exit key, jump

                                  ; clear exit semaphore...
          push    ds              ; semaphore address
          push    offset DGROUP:exitsem
          call    DosSemClear     ; transfer to OS/2
          jmp     comout          ; discard exit key

comout2:                          ; send character to COM port...
          push    chandle         ; COM device handle
          push    ds              ; address of character
          push    offset DGROUP:kbdinfo
          push    cx              ; length to write
          push    ds              ; receives write count
          push    offset DGROUP:wlen
          call    DosWrite        ; transfer to OS/2

          jmp     comout          ; wait for next key

comout    endp

_TEXT     ends

          end     main
```

```
NAME DUMBTERM NOTWINDOWCOMPAT
PROTMODE
STACKSIZE 4096
```

Figure 12-13. *DUMBTERM.DEF, the module definition file for DUMBTERM.ASM.*

INTERPROCESS COMMUNICATION

The preceding chapter discussed the OS/2 multitasking services that applications use to create multiple threads within a process or to create child processes. However, as we have seen, the multitasking functions provide threads and processes with only limited control over one another. A thread can suspend or change the priority of another thread; it can also prevent other threads from interfering with its execution. A parent process can pass information to a child at load time, obtain the child's exit code and termination type, or unilaterally kill a child process.

OS/2's Interprocess Communication (IPC) functions supplement the multitasking functions with mechanisms for the exchange of all kinds of information between threads and processes. The IPC functions fall into five categories:*

- Semaphores

- Pipes

- Shared memory

- Queues

- Signals

When the OS/2 LAN Manager is running, an additional IPC mechanism called *mailslots* is also available (not discussed in this book).

---

*For a cogent, highly readable survey of the state of the IPC art, see Chapter 2 of *Operating Systems: Design and Implementation* by Andrew S. Tanenbaum, published by Prentice-Hall Inc., Englewood Cliffs, New Jersey, 1987.

While reading about IPC functions, bear in mind the distinctions between processes and threads that were explained in Chapter 12. When a process opens or creates a semaphore, pipe, queue, or shared memory segment, the system returns a handle or selector that any thread within that process can use. But when a thread issues an OS/2 function call that blocks on (waits for) an event (such as the clearing or release of a semaphore) or performs a synchronous read or write to a pipe or queue, only the calling thread is suspended — other threads in the process continue to run as before.

Semaphores

Think of a semaphore as a simple object with two states: set (owned) or cleared (not owned). Semaphores are a high performance IPC mechanism because they are always resident in memory and because the OS/2 routines that manipulate them are extremely fast. Figure 13-1 provides a summary of the OS/2 semaphore-related API.

The classic use of semaphores, which OS/2 fully supports, is to control access to a serially reusable resource (SRR). An SRR is a procedure, a device, or a data object that will be damaged or will produce unpredictable results

Function	Description
Access to System Semaphores	
DosCloseSem	Closes system semaphore
DosCreateSem	Creates system semaphore
DosOpenSem	Opens existing system semaphore
Semaphore Functions for Mutual Exclusion	
DosSemClear	Releases ownership of semaphore
DosSemRequest	Obtains ownership of semaphore
Semaphore Functions for Signaling	
DosMuxSemWait	Waits for any of several semaphores to be clear
DosSemClear	Unconditionally clears semaphore
DosSemSet	Unconditionally sets semaphore
DosSemSetWait	Unconditionally sets semaphore and waits until it is clear
DosSemWait	Waits until semaphore is clear
Fast-Safe RAM Semaphore Functions	
DosFSRamSemClear	Releases fast-safe RAM semaphore
DosFSRamSemRequest	Obtains ownership of fast-safe RAM semaphore

Figure 13-1. *Semaphore-related API at a glance. Semaphores can be used to coordinate use of a nonreentrant resource or for signaling between threads or processes.*

if it is used by more than one thread or process at a time. Arranging mutual exclusion among cooperating processes is easy with semaphores. A semaphore is established that represents the resource, and a thread or process refrains from accessing the resource unless it "owns" the corresponding semaphore.

For example, suppose that a process has opened an indexed database and that several threads within the process want to read or write the database using the same file handle. Each access to the file requires at least two distinct API requests — a *DosChgFilePtr* followed by a *DosRead* or *DosWrite* — so each thread must prevent its sequence of API calls from being jumbled with similar sequences by other threads.

An easy way for a thread to protect its file operations is to make them a critical section of code:

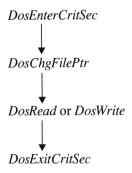

DosEnterCritSec

DosChgFilePtr

DosRead or *DosWrite*

DosExitCritSec

But this cavalier approach shuts down all other threads in the same process during the file operation, whether they are trying to use the file or not. It specifically throws away a major benefit of multitasking: the ability to continue execution during an I/O operation. A far better approach is to set up a semaphore and then abide by the convention that only the thread that owns the semaphore can use the file handle:

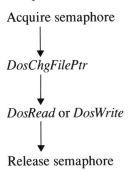

Acquire semaphore

DosChgFilePtr

DosRead or *DosWrite*

Release semaphore

When you use this method, other threads that do not need simultaneous access to the file can execute unhindered.

OS/2 semaphores can also be used for synchronization or for signaling between threads or processes. In this usage, one or more threads can suspend themselves by calling an API function to block on a semaphore. When the semaphore is cleared, threads that were blocking on that semaphore will wake up and run (subject to their priority, the type of wait operation, the semaphore's not being set again before a particular thread receives a time-slice, and so forth). When a semaphore is used for signaling and no resource that can be corrupted is involved, any thread that knows about the semaphore can set, clear, or test it at any time.

Using semaphores for signaling is appropriate when only one thread is in a position to detect an event but other threads may want to take action based on this event. For example, a screen dump utility might decouple its keyboard monitoring from the unpredictable delays involved in a screen pop-up or disk write by establishing a separate thread for each of these tasks. When the keyboard thread detects the hot key, it can simply clear a semaphore to release the screen and disk I/O threads to do their work (see SNAP.ASM in Chapter 18). Coded in this manner, the process never compromises the ability of the keyboard thread to respond rapidly to keystrokes.

OS/2 Semaphore Types

To provide for the somewhat different requirements of interthread communication, interprocess communication, and dynlink libraries, OS/2 supports three types of semaphores: *RAM semaphores, system semaphores,* and *fast-safe RAM semaphores.*

RAM semaphores let you send signals or control resources among multiple threads in the same process or between multiple processes that share memory. Each RAM semaphore requires the allocation of a doubleword of storage, which should be initialized to zero before the semaphore is used. The handle for a RAM semaphore is simply its 32-bit address (selector and offset); consequently, the number of RAM semaphores that a process can manipulate is limited only by the amount of memory it can allocate.

System semaphores are named objects that you can use for signaling or synchronization between processes; the name always takes the form:

\SEM*path**name.ext*

where the path and the extension (*.ext*) are optional. OS/2 allocates the storage for a system semaphore outside the creating process's memory space, and the pool of available system semaphores is relatively small (128 in OS/2 version 1.0 and 256 in version 1.1).

A system semaphore is created with the function *DosCreateSem*, whose parameters are the address of an ASCIIZ semaphore name, the address of a doubleword variable that receives a semaphore handle, and a flag that indicates whether ownership of the semaphore is exclusive or nonexclusive. (Only the process that owns an exclusive semaphore can change its state, although other processes can open the semaphore and *test* its state or block on it.) If the create operation is successful, the system returns a semaphore handle; the initial state of the semaphore is "not owned" (clear).

To gain access to an existing system semaphore, call *DosOpenSem*. This function requires the addresses of an ASCIIZ semaphore name and a doubleword of storage to receive a semaphore handle. Opening a semaphore does not establish ownership of, test, or change the value of the semaphore. Figure 13-2 illustrates the procedure for creating or opening a system semaphore.

```
ERROR_ALREADY_EXISTS equ 183      ; error code

sname    db       '\SEM\MYSEM',0  ; semaphore name

shandle dd       0                ; receives semaphore handle

         .
         .
         .

                                  ; create semaphore...
         push     1               ; 1 = not exclusive
         push     ds              ; receives semaphore handle
         push     offset DGROUP:shandle
         push     ds              ; address of semaphore name
         push     offset DGROUP:sname
         call     DosCreateSem    ; transfer to OS/2
         or       ax,ax           ; semaphore created?
         jz       label1          ; yes, proceed

                                  ; no, does it exist?
         cmp      ax,ERROR_ALREADY_EXISTS
         jne      error           ; jump if other error

                                  ; semaphore exists, open it...
         push     ds              ; receives semaphore handle
```

(continued)

Figure 13-2. *Creating or opening a system semaphore.*

Figure 13-2. *continued*

```
        push    offset DGROUP:shandle
        push    ds              ; address of semaphore name
        push    offset DGROUP:sname
        call    DosOpenSem      ; transfer to OS/2
        or      ax,ax           ; did open succeed?
        jnz     error           ; jump if function failed

label1:                         ; semaphore is now created
                                ; or opened...
        .
        .
        .
```

After you obtain a handle to a system semaphore, you can use it with the functions to test, set, and wait on semaphores exactly as you would use a RAM semaphore handle (which is an ordinary selector and offset). Knowing this, you might correctly predict that system semaphore handles, unlike file and pipe handles, cannot be inherited by child processes. A system semaphore handle is not, however, simply a special selector and offset combination; it is a ''magic'' value and cannot be used to inspect the contents of the semaphore.

Fast-safe RAM semaphores are designed for use by dynlink libraries with multiple client processes; they have characteristics of both RAM and system semaphores. You can use only two special-purpose functions to manipulate them, and you cannot interchange them with normal RAM and system semaphores.

Mutual Exclusion with Semaphores

A thread uses *DosSemRequest* to establish ownership of a semaphore and, by extension, ownership of the resource associated with the semaphore. *DosSemRequest* is called with the handle of a system or RAM semaphore and a timeout parameter. If the semaphore is currently unowned, the function marks it as owned and returns a success code. If the semaphore is already owned, the system either suspends the calling thread indefinitely until the semaphore becomes available, waits for a specified interval and then returns (if the semaphore does not clear) with an error code, or returns immediately with an error code—depending on the timeout parameter.

The function *DosSemClear* is called with a semaphore handle; it releases the thread's ownership of that semaphore, which implicitly releases the associated resource. If the semaphore is currently unowned, no error is returned.

If another thread has been waiting for the semaphore with a blocked *DosSemRequest* call, its request then succeeds and the suspended thread is reawakened.

When multiple threads are waiting for the semaphore and the semaphore becomes available, the *DosSemRequest* of the thread with the highest priority succeeds. The threads with lower priorities might sleep through many requests and releases of the semaphore until no requests are pending from higher priority threads. If all of the waiting threads have the same priority, you cannot predict which thread will acquire the semaphore when it is released by the current owner.

Recursive requests for a system semaphore are supported only if the semaphore was created with the exclusive option. OS/2 maintains a use count which is incremented by *DosSemRequest* and decremented by *DosSemClear*; the semaphore is not actually released until the use count becomes zero. Recursive use of RAM semaphores is not supported.

Signaling with Semaphores

A semaphore is set unconditionally by calling *DosSemSet* with the semaphore handle (Figures 13-3 and 13-4 on the following page). Similarly, you can unconditionally clear a semaphore by calling *DosSemClear* with the semaphore handle. If any threads are blocked on the semaphore, they are released and will run at the next opportunity, provided that the semaphore is not set again in the meantime. (The sole exception is explained below.)

OS/2 contains several functions that allow a thread to suspend itself until one or more semaphores are cleared. The prototypal function is *DosSemWait*, which is called with a semaphore handle and a timeout option. If the semaphore is clear, the thread regains control immediately with no error; otherwise, the thread blocks as determined by the timeout option: wait for the semaphore indefinitely, return with an error if it fails to clear within the specified interval, or return immediately with an error if the semaphore is set. *DosSemWait* also returns an error if the semaphore handle is invalid.

The function *DosSemSetWait* works like *DosSemWait*, except that it sets the semaphore if it was not already set, and then suspends the requesting thread until the semaphore is cleared by another thread or the indicated timeout expires. An important aspect of *DosSemWait* and *DosSemSetWait* is that they are level-triggered, not edge-triggered. A thread that is blocking on a semaphore with either of these functions could miss a quick clearing and resetting of the semaphore, depending on the thread's priority and scheduled position and on the activity of other threads in the system.

```
sname    db        '\SEM\MYSEM',0  ; semaphore name

shandle dd        0               ; receives semaphore handle
          .
          .
          .
                            ; open system semaphore...
        push    ds              ; receives semaphore handle
        push    offset DGROUP:shandle
        push    ds              ; address of semaphore name
        push    offset DGROUP:sname
        call    DosOpenSem      ; transfer to OS/2
        or      ax,ax           ; did open succeed?
        jnz     error           ; jump if function failed
          .
          .
          .
                            ; set system semaphore...
        push    word ptr shandle+2 ; handle from DosOpenSem
        push    word ptr shandle
        call    DosSemSet       ; transfer to OS/2
        or      ax,ax           ; did set succeed?
        jnz     error           ; jump if function failed
          .
          .
          .
```

Figure 13-3. *Opening and setting a system semaphore.*

```
mysem   dd        0               ; storage for RAM semaphore
                            ; (the address of mysem is
                            ; the semaphore handle)
          .
          .
          .
                            ; set RAM semaphore...
        push    ds              ; semaphore handle = address
        push    offset DGROUP:mysem
        call    DosSemSet       ; transfer to OS/2
        or      ax,ax           ; did set succeed?
        jnz     error           ; jump if function failed
          .
          .
          .
```

Figure 13-4. *Setting a RAM semaphore. Note that a RAM semaphore should be initialized to zero before it is used for the first time.*

The function *DosMuxSemWait* is called with a list of as many as 16 semaphores and a timeout option. The calling thread is suspended until any of the indicated semaphores is cleared or the function has timed out. Unlike *DosSemWait* and *DosSemSetWait*, *DosMuxSemWait* is edge-triggered: The waiting thread will always be awakened (at some point) if a semaphore in the list changes state from set to cleared — even if the semaphore gets set again before the waiting thread has an opportunity to run.

Closing System Semaphores

To end a process's access to a system semaphore, call *DosCloseSem* with the semaphore handle. Any subsequent use of the semaphore handle results in a GP fault. If a process terminates with open system semaphores, the system closes them on behalf of the process. A system semaphore ceases to exist when all processes that use the semaphore have issued *DosCloseSem* or terminated.

An interesting situation occurs when a process terminates while it owns a system semaphore that is still being used by other processes. Any threads in other processes that are waiting for the semaphore to clear or that subsequently attempt to acquire the semaphore receive an error code indicating that the owning process may have terminated abnormally. One of those threads must then clean up the resource represented by the semaphore and then release the semaphore for further use with *DosSemClear*.

A superior way of handling this cleanup problem takes advantage of the fact that the system always runs a process's ExitList procedures before it closes the process's remaining system semaphores. Any process that uses such semaphores should therefore use *DosExitList* to register an ExitList procedure that releases all semaphores and restores the associated system resources to a known state. This approach puts the burden of cleanup where it belongs so that other processes, which did not cause the error, do not have to figure out how to recover from it.

Using Fast-Safe RAM Semaphores

Fast-safe RAM semaphores were introduced in OS/2 version 1.1 to meet the needs of dynlink libraries with multiple clients. They combine the high speed of RAM semaphores with the system semaphore capabilities of "counting" and ownership tracking.

Fast-safe RAM semaphores are manipulated with the *DosFSRamSemRequest* and *DosFSRamSemClear* functions. The fast-safe RAM semaphore itself is a

14-byte structure in the memory space belonging to the process or dynlink library. The system supports nested calls to *DosFSRamSemRequest* by requiring that an equivalent number of calls to *DosFSRamSemClear* be issued by the semaphore's owner before it clears the semaphore and releases any blocked threads.

What's special about fast-safe RAM semaphores? Just this: If an ExitList routine (registered with *DosExitList*) calls *DosFSRamSemRequest* for a fast-safe RAM semaphore that is owned by any thread in the same process, the *DosFSRamSemRequest* succeeds and the owner thread ID and reference count fields of the semaphore are forced to 1. The ExitList routine can then take any necessary measures to clean up the resource symbolized by the semaphore and call *DosFSRamSemClear* to release the semaphore.

Fast-safe RAM semaphores are therefore ideal for representing a resource controlled by a dynlink library and accessed by multiple client processes of that library. When the dynlink library is called for the first time by a particular process, it can register an ExitList routine on behalf of that process that will clean up the resource and release the fast-safe RAM semaphore for the resource if the process terminates abnormally. Using fast-safe RAM semaphores, the dynlink library gets the advantages of a system semaphore—"counting" and cross-process usability—but avoids the speed penalty for a system semaphore.

Anonymous Pipes

Anonymous pipes are so called because (unlike system semaphores, named pipes, and queues) they do not have names and are accessed only by handles. They are an IPC mechanism midway in power between semaphores and queues. Like semaphores, pipes provide relatively high performance because the information they convey is always resident in memory; like queues, pipes can be used to pass a chunk of data of any size (up to 64 KB) between processes. Physically, an anonymous pipe is simply an area of memory owned by the operating system that is used as a ring buffer, with "in" and "out" pointers that are also maintained by the system. From a process's point of view, a pipe is manipulated somewhat like a file, but it acts more like a FIFO queue and is much faster.

To create an anonymous pipe, call the function *DosMakePipe*, supplying a maximum pipe size (as large as 64 KB less 32 bytes for a control header) and the addresses of two variables that receive read and write handles for the pipe. The size parameter is advisory—the actual size of the pipe buffer can be smaller depending on available memory; in any event, the size affects only the pipe's performance, not its behavior. *DosMakePipe* fails if memory is insufficient to create the pipe or if the process has exhausted its supply of handles.

The two handles returned by *DosMakePipe* are assigned from the same sequence as those returned by *DosOpen* for files and character devices. Any child processes started after the pipe is created inherit the handles and have access to the pipe. A common application of pipes, illustrated below, is to redirect a child process's standard input and standard output handles to pipe handles; thereafter, the child process unknowingly communicates with the parent process for its input and output instead of with the keyboard and screen. A simplified example of this technique is shown in Figure 13-5 on the following page.

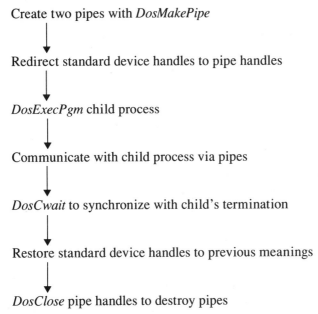

Create two pipes with *DosMakePipe*

↓

Redirect standard device handles to pipe handles

↓

DosExecPgm child process

↓

Communicate with child process via pipes

↓

DosCwait to synchronize with child's termination

↓

Restore standard device handles to previous meanings

↓

DosClose pipe handles to destroy pipes

Processes that are not direct descendants of an anonymous pipe's creator cannot inherit the handles for the pipe and thus have no way to access it. The two major restrictions on the use of anonymous pipes are thus their limitation to use for communication between closely related processes, and the 64 KB limit on the amount of data that a pipe can contain "in transit."

To read from or write to a pipe synchronously, call *DosRead* or *DosWrite* with the appropriate pipe handle, buffer address, and record length. You can read and write a pipe asynchronously with *DosReadAsync* and *DosWrite-Async*, which return control to the requesting thread immediately and clear a semaphore when the operation is complete. Because anonymous pipes must be used within a closely related group of processes, they have no associated permission mechanisms.

Don't be misled by the superficial similarities between pipe handles and file handles—they behave in subtly different ways. If a synchronous write is directed to a file and the disk is full, *DosWrite* does not return an error—it simply returns a count of bytes transferred that is smaller than the length requested. But if a synchronous write is performed to a pipe handle and the pipe is full, the requesting thread is blocked until another thread removes enough data from the pipe so that the write can be completed.

Similarly, if a synchronous read is performed with a file handle and the file pointer is at or near the end of file, *DosRead* returns anyway, indicating that a partial record or no bytes were transferred. But if *DosRead* is called with a pipe handle and the pipe is empty, the thread is suspended until some other thread writes enough data into the pipe to satisfy the request.

This un-filelike behavior can change when pipe handles are closed by participating processes. If all read handles to a pipe are closed, a *DosWrite* to the pipe returns an error. If all write handles to a pipe are closed, a *DosRead* of the pipe returns an error.

```
stdin      equ    0                ; standard input handle

preadh     dw     ?                ; handle to read pipe
pwriteh    dw     ?                ; handle to write pipe
stdinh     dw     stdin            ; stdin handle to redirect
wlen       dw     ?                ; receives bytes written

msg        db     'Hello kid!'     ; message for child process
msg_len    equ    $-msg
             .
             .
             .
```

(continued)

Figure 13-5. *Simplified example of IPC using anonymous pipes. A pipe is created, the standard input handle is redirected to the pipe's read handle, and a child process is started. A message written into the pipe by the parent is received by the child when it issues a* DosRead *to its inherited standard input handle.*

Figure 13-5. *continued*

```
                              ; first create pipe...
        push    ds            ; receives read handle
        push    offset DGROUP:preadh
        push    ds            ; receives write handle
        push    offset DGROUP:pwriteh
        push    0             ; max pipe size = default
        call    DosMakePipe   ; transfer to OS/2
        or      ax,ax         ; was pipe created?
        jnz     error         ; jump if function failed

                              ; redirect standard input
                              ; to read from pipe...
        push    preadh        ; pipe read handle
        push    ds            ; standard input handle
        push    offset DGROUP:stdinh
        call    DosDupHandle  ; transfer to OS/2
        or      ax,ax         ; redirection successful?
        jnz     error         ; jump if function failed

        .                     ; start child process
        .                     ; with DosExecPgm here...
        .                     ; (code not shown)

                              ; send message to child
                              ; through pipe...
        push    pwriteh       ; pipe write handle
        push    ds            ; address of message
        push    offset DGROUP:msg
        push    msg_len       ; length of message
        push    ds            ; receives bytes written
        push    offset DGROUP:wlen
        call    DosWrite      ; transfer to OS/2
        or      ax,ax         ; did write succeed?
        jnz     error         ; jump if function failed
        .
        .
```

Named Pipes

Named pipes were originally designed for use in the OS/2 LAN Manager, but as their general usefulness became apparent, they were subsumed into the OS/2 kernel with version 1.1. Named pipes can be used for communication between unrelated processes running on the same system or between processes running on different machines on a local area network; they always have names of the following form:

\PIPE\path\name.ext

where the path and the extension (.ext) are optional. Figure 13-6 summarizes the OS/2 API for both anonymous and named pipes.

Function	Description
Anonymous Pipes	
DosMakePipe	Creates anonymous pipe, returns read and write handles
Named Pipes	
DosCallNmPipe	Opens, writes, reads, then closes named pipe (C)
DosConnectNmPipe	Waits for client to open pipe (S)
DosDisConnectNmPipe	Unilaterally closes named pipe (S)
DosMakeNmPipe	Creates named pipe and returns handle (S)
DosPeekNmPipe	Looks ahead for data in named pipe (B)
DosQNmPHandState	Returns state information for named pipe (B)
DosQNmPipeInfo	Returns information about named pipe (B)
DosQNmPipeSemState	Returns information for pipe associated with semaphore (B)
DosSetNmPHandState	Sets state information for named pipe (B)
DosSetNmPipeSem	Associates a semaphore with a named pipe (B)
DosTransactNmPipe	Writes, then reads, named pipe (B)
DosWaitNmPipe	Conditionally waits to open named pipe (C)

Figure 13-6. *Pipe-related IPC functions at a glance. S = usable by named pipe servers (creators) only; C = usable by named pipe clients only; B = usable both by named pipe servers and by clients.*

A typical application will use only a few of the functions that the API provides for manipulating named pipes. The pipe's creator, or *server*, calls *DosMakeNmPipe* to create a named pipe. The parameters for this function include various pipe characteristics, the maximum number of instances of the pipe that can exist, and advisory sizes for the pipe's input and output buffers.

The server process can use *DosConnectNmPipe* to wait until another process has opened a pipe by name; *DosRead, DosReadAsync, DosWrite,* or *DosWriteAsync* to obtain data from or put data into the pipe; and *DosPeekNmPipe* to inspect data in the pipe without removing it. A server can also unilaterally break a pipe connection with another process with *DosDisConnectNmPipe.*

A client process, that is, a process which did not create the pipe but wants to use it, can obtain a handle for the pipe with *DosOpen* and then access the pipe with *DosRead, DosReadAsync, DosWrite,* and *DosWriteAsync.* A client process can also take advantage of the special functions *DosCallNmPipe* or

DosTransactNmPipe to exchange data with the pipe's creator in one operation. A client releases a handle for a named pipe explicitly with *DosClose* or implicitly at process termination.

Both server and client processes can use the functions *DosDupHandle*, *DosQHandType*, *DosQFHandState*, *DosSetFHandState*, and *DosBufReset* with a handle for a named pipe as though it were a file handle. Among other things, this similarity allows a child process that inherits handles for a named pipe to determine its nature.

When all the client handles for a named pipe have been closed, the pipe cannot be reopened until the server issues *DosDisConnectNmPipe* followed by *DosConnectNmPipe*. When all client and server handles for a named pipe have been closed, the pipe is destroyed. Figure 13-7 depicts the various possible states for a named pipe.

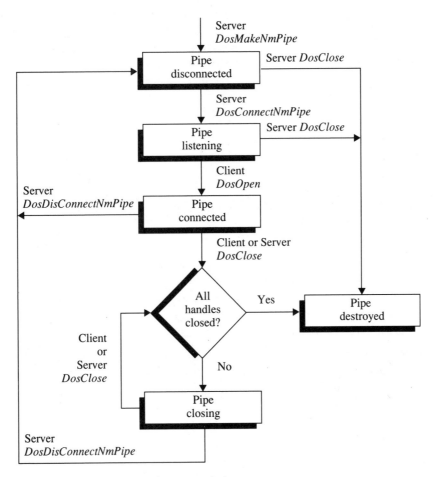

Figure 13-7. *State transitions for a named pipe.*

An important feature of named pipes—as compared to anonymous pipes—is the fact that you can create them as either byte stream pipes or message pipes. A byte stream pipe works like an anonymous pipe and is subject to the same special considerations for *DosRead* and *DosWrite*. A message pipe behaves somewhat like a FIFO queue; the length of each message written into the pipe is encoded in the pipe, and *DosRead* returns *at most* one message at a time regardless of the number of bytes requested. If you call *DosRead* with a buffer that is too small for the message, it returns a partial message along with an error code; you can recover the remainder of the message with additional calls to *DosRead*.

Shared Memory

Shared memory segments are potentially the fastest IPC mechanism. If two or more processes have a selector to the same segment, they can pass data back and forth at speeds limited only by the CPU's ability to copy bytes from one place to another—the mechanism requires no additional calls to the operating system. The threads and processes sharing the segment are responsible for using semaphores or other interlocks to synchronize any changes in its content.

OS/2 supports two distinct methods by which processes can share memory: creation of *named segments,* and *giving* and *getting* of selectors. Each method offers specific advantages for data protection and speed of access.

A named shareable segment is created by calling *DosAllocShrSeg* with the segment size, the address of a variable to receive a selector, and the address of an ASCIIZ segment name in the following form:

\SHAREMEM*path\name.ext*

where the path and the extension (*.ext*) are optional (example in Figure 13-8). The segment is always movable and swappable. *DosAllocShrSeg* fails if the system's virtual memory (physical memory plus swap space) is exhausted, if all shareable selectors are in use, or if a segment by the same name already exists.

After you create a segment with *DosAllocShrSeg*, any process that knows the segment's name can obtain a valid selector for it with *DosGetShrSeg*. The selector for a particular named segment is identical across all processes, although a descriptor is not actually built in a process's LDT until the process invokes *DosGetShrSeg*.

Sharing a memory segment by *getting* and *giving* selectors is somewhat more complicated because the selectors must be passed between the processes by another means of IPC (such as a pipe, a queue, or a named

```
                                  ; name of shared segment
    segname  db       '\SHAREMEM\MYSEG',0

    sel      dw       ?                   ; receives selector

             .
             .
             .

                                          ; create named shareable
                                          ; segment...
             push     32768               ; segment size
             push     ds                  ; address of name
             push     offset DGROUP:segname
             push     ds                  ; receives selector
             push     offset DGROUP:sel
             call     DosAllocShrSeg      ; transfer to OS/2
             or       ax,ax               ; segment created?
             jnz      error               ; jump if function failed
             .
             .
             .
```

Figure 13-8. *Creating a 32 KB named shared memory segment.*

segment). To allocate a givable or gettable shared segment, call *DosAllocSeg* or *DosAllocHuge* in the usual manner, with the proper bits in the function's shareable/discardable parameter set to indicate whether new selectors and descriptors will be needed later and how they will be obtained.

When a process *gives away* a selector to another process, it calls *DosGiveSeg* with its own selector for the segment and the PID of the receiving process. *DosGiveSeg* builds a descriptor in the receiving process's LDT that maps to the same physical memory. It returns the corresponding selector to the calling process, which must then communicate the new selector to the receiving process by some IPC method. Segment giving is best suited to IPC between closely related processes because the receiving process's PID is usually known only to its parent. Segment giving is demonstrated as part of the queue write example in Figure 13-10 on p. 290.

When a gettable segment is allocated, on the other hand, the memory manager reserves the corresponding selector position in the LDT of every process in the system. Initially, however, a descriptor is built only in the allocating process's LDT. Any other process can, once it knows the selector value, make that selector valid for its own access by calling *DosGetSeg* to build a corresponding LDT descriptor. Segment getting allows far pointers to be passed around freely, without the need for one process to know another's PID, but it is a correspondingly less secure technique than the use of givable selectors.

A process can give up its right of access to a named, gettable, or givable shared memory segment by calling *DosFreeSeg* with the segment's selector. Subsequent use of that selector by the process results in a GP fault. OS/2 maintains a reference count for each shared segment. When all processes using a segment have released their selectors for the segment or have terminated, OS/2 destroys the segment and returns its memory to the global pool.

Queues

Queues are the most powerful IPC mechanisms in OS/2 and the most complex to use. Queues are slower than pipes (and much slower than communication by semaphores or shared memory segments), but they are also far more flexible, as suggested by the following list of characteristics:

- Queues are named objects which any process can open and write.

- The amount of data in a queue is limited only by available virtual memory.

- Each record in a queue is a separately allocated block of memory storage and can be as large as 64 KB.

- The records in a queue can be ordered by first-in-first-out (FIFO), last-in-first-out (LIFO), or priority.

- The queue owner can examine records in the queue and remove them selectively, in any order.

- Data in the queue is not copied from place to place by the operating system; instead, pointers are passed to shared memory segments.

In essence, an OS/2 queue is an ordered list of shared memory segments; the operating system maintains and searches the list on behalf of the communicating processes. Figure 13-9 summarizes the queue-related functions in the OS/2 API.

To create a queue, call *DosCreateQueue* with an ASCIIZ queue name, a parameter that specifies ordering method for the queue (FIFO, LIFO, or priority), and the address of a variable to receive a queue handle. The name of a queue always takes the following form:

\QUEUES*path**name.ext*

where the path and the extension (*.ext*) are optional. An error is returned if a queue with the same name already exists, if the name or queue ordering is invalid, or if there is not enough free memory to establish the queue's supporting data structure. The creator of a queue is called the *queue owner*. After a queue is created, any process can open it by calling *DosOpenQueue* with an ASCIIZ queue name and pointers to two variables that receive a queue handle and the PID of the queue owner.

Function	Description
Queue Access	
DosCloseQueue	Closes queue, destroys queue if owner (A)
DosCreateQueue	Creates a queue and returns handle (O)
DosOpenQueue	Opens existing queue and returns handle (A)
Queue Reads and Writes	
DosPeekQueue	Nondestructively reads queue message (O)
DosReadQueue	Reads message from queue (O)
DosWriteQueue	Writes message into queue (A)
Queue Information	
DosPurgeQueue	Discards all messages in queue (O)
DosQueryQueue	Returns number of messages in queue (A)

Figure 13-9. *OS/2 queue management API at a glance. O = usable only by queue owner; A = usable by any process.*

Any thread in any process that has a queue handle can write to the queue, but adding records to a queue is much more involved than writing a record to a pipe. The procedure can be summarized as follows:

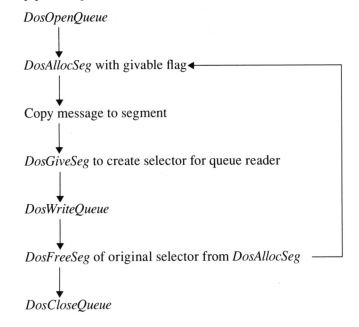

In this sequence, the writer allocates a memory segment of appropriate size with *DosAllocSeg*, specifying that the segment is givable, and copies the data for the queue record into it. Then the writer uses *DosGiveSeg*, together with the PID returned by *DosOpenQueue*, to obtain a giveaway selector that can be passed to the queue owner.

Next, the writer calls *DosWriteQueue* with a queue handle, a priority, the selector (obtained from *DosGiveSeg*) and offset for the queue message, and the message length. *DosWriteQueue* fails if the queue handle is invalid or if system memory is insufficient to expand the supporting structure of the queue; obviously, the whole sequence can also fail at an earlier point (in either *DosAllocSeg* or *DosGiveSeg*) if the system runs out of virtual memory or selectors. Last, if the writer is using segments as individual queue messages (the usual case), it should release its original selector for the shareable segment with *DosFreeSeg*. Figure 13-10 demonstrates the writing of a message to a queue.

```
qhandle dw      ?                    ; receives queue handle

qowner  dw      ?                    ; receives queue owner PID

qname   db      '\QUEUES\MYQ',0 ; queue name

qselw   dw      ?                    ; queue writer's selector

qselr   dw      ?                    ; queue reader's selector

qmsg        db      'This is my queue message'
qmsg_len equ    $-qmsg

                .
                .
                .

                                     ; first open the queue...
        push    ds                   ; receives owner's PID
        push    offset DGROUP:qowner
        push    ds                   ; receives queue handle
        push    offset DGROUP:qhandle
        push    ds                   ; address of queue name
        push    offset DGROUP:qname
```

(continued)

Figure 13-10. *Opening an existing queue, writing a message into it, and then closing it.*

Figure 13-10. *continued*

```
        call    DosOpenQueue        ; transfer to OS/2
        or      ax,ax               ; did open succeed?
        jnz     error               ; jump if function failed


                                    ; allocate givable segment
        push    qmsg_len            ; length of segment
        push    ds                  ; receives segment selector
        push    offset DGROUP:qselw
        push    1                   ; 1 = segment givable
        call    DosAllocSeg         ; transfer to OS/2
        or      ax,ax               ; did allocation succeed?
        jnz     error               ; jump if function failed

        mov     es,qselw            ; copy queue message to
        xor     di,di               ; giveaway segment
        mov     si,offset DGROUP:qmsg
        mov     cx,qmsg_len
        cld
        rep movsb

        push    ds                  ; restore ES = DGROUP
        pop     es


                                    ; get giveaway selector...
        push    qselw               ; original selector
        push    qowner              ; PID of queue reader
        push    ds                  ; receives new selector
        push    offset DGROUP:qselr
        call    DosGiveSeg          ; transfer to OS/2
        or      ax,ax               ; new selector obtained?
        jnz     error               ; no, can't send message


                                    ; write message to queue...
        push    qhandle             ; handle from DosOpenQueue
        push    0                   ; private data
        push    qmsg_len            ; queue message length
        push    qselr               ; queue message address
        push    0                   ; (using givable selector)
        push    0                   ; queue element priority
        call    DosWriteQueue       ; transfer to OS/2
        or      ax,ax               ; did queue write succeed?
        jnz     error               ; jump if function failed
```

(continued)

Figure 13-10. *continued*

```
                                    ; release original selector
                                    ; for shared segment...
            push    qselw           ; original selector
            call    DosFreeSeg      ; transfer to OS/2
            or      ax,ax           ; did release succeed?
            jnz     error           ; jump if function failed
              .
              .
              .

                                    ; now close the queue...
            push    qhandle         ; handle from DosOpenQueue
            call    DosCloseQueue   ; transfer to OS/2
            or      ax,ax           ; did close succeed?
            jnz     error           ; jump if function failed
              .
              .
              .
```

Only the queue owner can inspect or remove messages in a queue. The procedure can be summarized as follows:

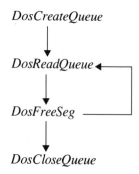

The principal queue-reading function, *DosReadQueue*, is called with a queue handle and several other selection parameters; it returns a pointer and length for a queue element. The owner can choose a message from the queue based on its position or priority or simply take the next message in line. Reading a queue can be a synchronous operation (with the calling thread suspended until a record is available) or an asynchronous operation (with the calling thread regaining control immediately and a semaphore cleared when a message becomes available). If messages are being passed one per segment, the queue reader should release the selector as soon as it has processed the message so that the amount of virtual memory tied up in the queue will not grow out of control. Figure 13-11 offers an example of reading a message from a queue.

```
qhandle  dw       ?                      ; receives queue handle

qname    db       '\QUEUES\MYQ',0 ; queue name

qident   dw       0,0                    ; writer's PID, event code

qmsglen  dw       ?                      ; length of queue message

qmsgptr  dd       0                      ; address of queue message

qmsgpri  dw       ?                      ; priority of queue message

               .
               .
               .
                                         ; first create queue...
         push    ds                      ; receives queue handle
         push    offset DGROUP:qhandle
         push    0                       ; 0 = FIFO queue ordering
         push    ds                      ; address of queue name
         push    offset DGROUP:qname
         call    DosCreateQueue ; transfer to OS/2
         or      ax,ax                   ; was create successful?
         jnz     error                   ; jump if function failed

                                         ; read message from queue...
         push    qhandle                 ; queue handle
         push    ds                      ; receives PID, event code
         push    offset DGROUP:qident
         push    ds                      ; receives message length
         push    offset DGROUP:qmsglen
         push    ds                      ; receives message pointer
         push    offset DGROUP:qmsgptr
         push    0                       ; 0 = read first element
         push    0                       ; 0 = synchronous read
         push    ds                      ; receives message priority
         push    offset DGROUP:qmsgpri
         push    0                       ; semaphore handle (unused
         push    0                       ; by synchronous read)
         call    DosReadQueue   ; transfer to OS/2
         or      ax,ax                   ; did read succeed?
         jnz     error                   ; jump if function failed
```

(continued)

Figure 13-11. *Creating a queue, waiting for a message to be written into it, retrieving the message, and then closing the queue (also destroying it because the owner is closing it).*

Figure 13-11. *continued*

```
        les     bx,qmsgptr          ; now let ES:BX point
                                    ; to queue message


        .                           ; process the queue
        .                           ; message here...
        .
                                    ; release selector for
                                    ; queue message...
        push    ds                  ; restore ES = DGROUP
        pop     es
        push    word ptr qmsgptr+2 ; selector for message
        call    DosFreeSeg          ; transfer to OS/2
        or      ax,ax               ; did release succeed?
        jnz     error               ; jump if function failed


                                    ; close the queue,
                                    ; also destroying it...
        push    qhandle             ; handle from DosCreateQueue
        call    DosCloseQueue       ; transfer to OS/2
        or      ax,ax               ; did close succeed?
        jnz     error               ; jump if function failed
        .
        .
        .
```

DosPeekQueue is similar to *DosReadQueue*, but the record is not removed from the queue when it is retrieved. Thus, the queue owner can scan the data waiting in the queue and decide on a processing strategy without disturbing the ordering of the records or copying the records to its own memory for inspection. Other, less frequently used queue functions include *DosQueryQueue*, which allows any process that can supply the handle to a queue to obtain the number of elements currently in the queue, and *DosPurgeQueue*, which discards all records in a queue. *DosPurgeQueue* can be invoked only by the queue owner.

A process relinquishes its right of access to a queue by calling *DosCloseQueue* with the queue handle. When the queue owner closes the queue or terminates, the queue is purged, its supporting data structure is destroyed, and any further attempts by other processes to write to the queue return an error. However, the memory segments that contained the queue messages are not destroyed until all processes with valid selectors for the segments release them with *DosFreeSeg* or terminate.

Signals

Signals are a unique IPC mechanism: They essentially simulate a hardware interrupt of the receiving process. If a signal occurs and the process has previously indicated its ability to handle that signal type, control transfers immediately to the routine designated as the signal handler. After the handler completes its processing and returns, control returns to the point of interruption.

OS/2 has two basic classes of signals. The first class of signals includes those listed in Figure 13-12. The SIGTERM signal results from a call to *DosKillProcess* by another process; it terminates the receiving process if that process has not registered a handler for it. SIGINTR and SIGBREAK signals go to the last process in a process subtree to register a handler for them. If an application doesn't register its own handler for SIGINTR and SIGBREAK, they are ordinarily fielded by the ancestor command process, which translates them to a SIGTERM signal for all its descendants. A process ignores SIGBROKENPIPE unless a handler has been registered for it.

Signals in the second class are known as event flags, and three are available: Flags A, B, and C. A process can send an event flag only to itself or its descendants, and it can send a single word of private data along with the flag. The meaning of the private data is known only to the signaler and signalee; it is ignored by OS/2. If an event flag signal is directed to a process which has not registered a handler for it, the signal is discarded.

A process registers a signal handler by calling *DosSetSigHandler* with the address of the handler, a code selecting one of the seven signals just described, and a code indicating the action to be taken when the signal occurs: ignore the signal, give control to the system's default handler, give control to the process's own handler, reset the current signal without affecting its disposition, or return an error to the process that sent the signal. To register handlers for more than one signal type, a process must make an individual *DosSetSigHandler* call for each.

Signal	Description
SIGINTR	Ctrl-C was detected
SIGBREAK	Ctrl-Break was detected
SIGTERM	Process is being terminated
SIGBROKENPIPE	Pipe read or write failed

Figure 13-12. *OS/2 signals in the first class.*

A process calls *DosFlagProcess* to send an event flag signal (A, B, or C) and an arbitrary word of data to itself or to a descendant process, and optionally to the entire subtree of the receiving process. An error is returned if the receiving process has previously registered its refusal to accept the incoming signal type (with a call to *DosSetSigHandler*). If no error is returned, the destination process either accepted the signal or has not registered a handler for it.

On the receiving end, when a signal occurs for which a handler has been registered, the process's primary thread (the thread which received control at the original entry point) is interrupted and control is transferred with a forced far call to the signal handler. If the primary thread is in the middle of an OS/2 call that will not complete quickly (primarily character device I/O calls), that function is aborted and returns with an error. Otherwise, the signal occurs immediately upon the thread's return from the executing function.

Because the primary thread can thus be interrupted at any time for an unknown interval, an application that expects to receive signals should reserve the primary thread for that purpose. When the process is started, it can register its signal handlers, create a new thread that becomes the main line of execution for the process, and then block the primary thread on a semaphore.

When a signal handler receives control, OS/2 has set up the stack (which is the primary thread's usual stack) with the following contents:

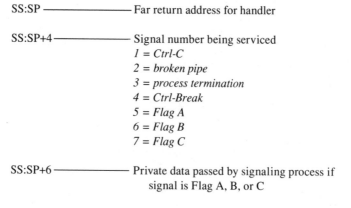

```
SS:SP ———————————— Far return address for handler

SS:SP+4 ——————————— Signal number being serviced
                    1 = Ctrl-C
                    2 = broken pipe
                    3 = process termination
                    4 = Ctrl-Break
                    5 = Flag A
                    6 = Flag B
                    7 = Flag C

SS:SP+6 ——————————— Private data passed by signaling process if
                    signal is Flag A, B, or C
```

All registers other than SS, SP, IP, CS, and the CPU flags contain the values they held at the point of the signal's arrival.

During signal processing, the handler must call *DosSetSigHandler* again with action code 4 (reset current signal); if it does not do so, further signals of that type will not be serviced. The handler exits with a far return, clearing the stack of the additional two words containing the signal number and the signal argument. OS/2 then restores all register contents and returns control to the point of interruption. Alternatively, the handler can reset the stack frame to some desired state and branch directly to another point in the program; that is, no harm is done if the handler never returns. Skeleton code for MASM and C signal handlers appears in Figures 13-13 and 13-14.

You can suppress signal handling temporarily with *DosHoldSignal* so that critical sections of code or ''slow'' OS/2 calls are not interrupted. The signals that occur while a *DosHoldSignal* is in effect are postponed and not lost. Naturally, you should postpone signals for as short a period as possible — treat them as though they were hardware interrupts being disabled.

```
SIGINTR equ     1                    ; Ctrl-C signal number

prvact  dw      ?                    ; receives previous action

prvhdlr dd      ?                    ; receives address of
                                     ; previous signal handler
    .

dummy   dd      ?                    ; dummy storage for type 4
                                     ; DosSetSigHandler call



    .
    .
    .
                                     ; register signal handler...
        push    cs                   ; address of new handler
        push    offset _TEXT:handler
        push    ds                   ; receives address of
                                     ; previous handler
        push    offset DGROUP:prvhdlr
        push    ds                   ; receives previous action
        push    offset DGROUP:prvact
        push    2                    ; action = 2: call handler
        push    SIGINTR              ; signal of interest = Ctrl-C
        call    DosSetSigHandler ; transfer to OS/2
        or      ax,ax                ; was handler registered?
        jnz     error                ; jump if function failed
    .
    .
    .
```

(continued)

Figure 13-13. *Registration of a MASM handler for Ctrl-C signals, along with a skeleton for the handler itself.*

Figure 13-13. *continued*

```
handler proc    far                 ; handler for Ctrl-C signal

                .                   ; application-specific
                .                   ; signal processing here...
                .
                                    ; reset signal so another
                                    ; can be processed...
        push    cs                  ; address of handler
        push    offset _TEXT:handler
        push    ds                  ; previous handler
        push    offset DGROUP:dummy
        push    ds                  ; previous action
        push    offset DGROUP:dummy
        push    4                   ; action 4 = reset signal
        push    SIGINTR             ; signal of interest = Ctrl-C
        call    DosSetSigHandler ; transfer to OS/2

        ret     4                   ; return from handler
                                    ; and clear stack
handler endp
```

```
#define SIGINTR 1               /* Ctrl-C signal number */

                                /* function prototypes */
void far pascal handler(unsigned, int);

unsigned extern far pascal DosSetSigHandler(void (pascal far *)
(unsigned, int) unsigned long far *, unsigned far *, int, int);

unsigned extern far pascal DosSleep(unsigned long);

main()
{
    unsigned long prevh;        /* prev. handler address */
    unsigned preva;             /* prev. handler action */
    .
    .
    .
```

(continued)

Figure 13-14. *Registration of a C handler for Ctrl-C signals, along with a skeleton for the handler itself.*

Figure 13-14. *continued*

```
                              /* register handler */
    DosSetSigHandler(handler, &prevh, &preva, 2, SIGINTR);
    .
    .
    .
}



/*
    This is the actual signal handler for Ctrl-C.
*/

void far pascal handler(unsigned sigarg, int signum)
{
    unsigned long dummy1;        /* scratch variables */
    unsigned dummy2;

                              /* reset signal */
    DosSetSigHandler(handler, &dummy1, &dummy2, 4, SIGINTR);

                              /* announce signal */
    fprintf(stderr,"\nCtrl-C Signal Received!\n");
}
```

CHAPTER FOURTEEN

IOPL SEGMENTS

As a single-user multitasking operating system, OS/2 adheres to a philosophy of protection that is vastly different than that of its multi-user cousins. Because users assume responsibility both for the programs they install on their systems and (if necessary) for securing physical access to the system, OS/2 allows applications a degree of freedom that would be unthinkable in a multi-user environment such as UNIX/XENIX. For example, programs can generate machine code dynamically in a data segment and then execute it with the aid of *DosCreateCSAlias*, and they can filter the raw data stream of the keyboard, mouse, and printer drivers with the device monitor API. They can even read or write I/O ports without relying on a device driver.

The ability to bypass OS/2 and access the I/O ports of an adapter directly is particularly important for developers of graphics applications that are not written to run in a Presentation Manager window or that rely on video modes or capabilities that are not supported by OS/2's built-in display functions. OS/2 places only three constraints on such programs:

- They may not service interrupts. (Control of the interrupt system is reserved for the kernel and true device drivers.)

- The hardware-dependent code must be segregated into special segments called IOPL segments.

- The code running in an IOPL (I/O Privilege Level) segment can call only a restricted set of API functions.

An application that manipulates the video adapter directly must also, of course, cooperate with OS/2 to save and restore the screen and adapter state across session switches.

Dynlink libraries can contain IOPL segments, which execute on behalf of the calling process. A dynlink library can therefore act much like a device driver from an application's perspective, concealing hardware characteristics inside a set of routines with a formalized parameter-passing scheme and named entry points. The OS/2 video subsystem, for example, is implemented primarily as dynlink libraries.

What Is IOPL?

Whereas segment selectors and their associated descriptors govern memory addressability for a protected mode process, as discussed in Chapter 11, the behavior of the process is also constrained by the 80286's support for four privilege levels—rings 0, 1, 2, and 3. Programs running at ring 0 have unrestricted access to the hardware, including the ability to execute any instruction, to read or write any I/O port, and to manipulate the special registers and tables that control memory protection and virtual memory.

Rings 1 through 3 are intended for the execution of progressively "less trusted" programs. Transitions from one ring to another are strictly controlled by means of *call gates,* which can be set up only by a program that is running at ring 0. Programs in ring 1, 2, or 3 cannot execute certain instructions that would compromise memory protection, nor can they touch memory segments for which they have inadequate access rights. (Included in the descriptor for each memory segment is an indication of the privilege level required for using that segment's selector.)

Nevertheless, programs in ring 1, 2, or 3 can gain restricted access to the hardware depending on the value of the IOPL field in the CPU flags register. Whenever a program is running in a ring whose number is less than or equal to the contents of the IOPL field, it can use the six instructions IN, OUT, INS, OUTS, STI, and CLI without causing a protection fault. Needless to say, the IOPL field itself can be modified only by a program running at ring 0.

Under OS/2, ring 0 is reserved for the operating system kernel and its device drivers. Ring 1 is not used at all, and normal application code runs at ring 3. After system initialization, OS/2 sets the IOPL level to 2 and uses ring 2 only for the execution of code within application IOPL segments (Figure 14-1). A program must declare at link time the names of its IOPL segments, along with the names of the routines within them which will be accessible to the rest of the application.

When an application containing an IOPL segment is loaded, OS/2 sets up call gates for each "exported" routine in that segment, and it resolves the references to those routines throughout the program so that they point to the

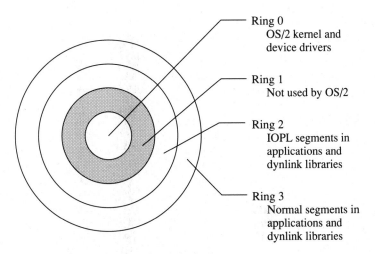

Ring 0
OS/2 kernel and
device drivers

Ring 1
Not used by OS/2

Ring 2
IOPL segments in
applications and
dynlink libraries

Ring 3
Normal segments in
applications and
dynlink libraries

Figure 14-1. *Use of the four 80286 privilege levels under OS/2.*

call gate. When the program's mainline code, which is running at ring 3, calls a routine in an IOPL segment, the hardware traps the reference to the call gate. The CPU then changes the privilege level to ring 2, switches to a new stack, copies parameters from the old stack to the new one, and enters the IOPL routine. When the IOPL routine exits with a far return, the system restores the original privilege level and stack, clears the parameters from the caller's stack, and continues execution.

Application programs with IOPL, like MS-DOS programs running in DOS compatibility mode, are clearly a weak point in system security. One can easily imagine, for example, an OS/2 protected mode Trojan horse program that would masquerade as a public domain utility but would use an IOPL segment to take over the disk controller and destroy the disk directories and file allocation table. To prevent such disasters, OS/2 can be configured so that it will not allow execution of MS-DOS programs or protected mode programs requiring IOPL. If the CONFIG.SYS file contains the statement *PROTECTONLY=YES*, MS-DOS applications are not supported; if the statement *IOPL=NO* is present, applications with IOPL segments are not loaded.

API Functions and IOPL

In OS/2 version 1.0, code running in an IOPL segment cannot call kernel API functions; all API calls must be made from ring 3 code. This restriction is loosened somewhat in OS/2 version 1.1, which permits code executing at ring 2 to call a limited number of API functions directly. These are known as "conforming" functions because they have a special call gate that lets them take on the privilege level of the caller. The conforming functions are listed in Figure 14-2 and are marked with an [IOPL] icon in the reference section.

Conforming Functions under OS/2 Version 1.1

DosAllocHuge	*DosGetHugeShift*	*DosRead*
DosAllocSeg	*DosGetInfoSeg*	*DosReadAsync*
DosAllocShrSeg	*DosGetMachineMode*	*DosReallocHuge*
DosBeep	*DosGetModHandle*	*DosReallocSeg*
DosBufReset	*DosGetModName*	*DosResumeThread*
DosCallback	*DosGetPID*	*DosRmDir*
DosChDir	*DosGetPPID*	*DosScanEnv*
DosChgFilePtr	*DosGetProcAddr*	*DosSearchPath*
DosCLIAccess	*DosGetPrty*	*DosSelectDisk*
DosClose	*DosGetResource*	*DosSemClear*
DosCloseSem	*DosGetSeg*	*DosSemRequest*
DosCreateCSAlias	*DosGetShrSeg*	*DosSemSet*
DosCreateSem	*DosGetVersion*	*DosSemSetWait*
DosCreateThread	*DosGiveSeg*	*DosSemWait*
DosCwait	*DosHoldSignal*	*DosSendSignal*
DosDelete	*DosKillProcess*	*DosSetCp*
DosDevConfig	*DosLoadModule*	*DosSetDateTime*
DosDevIOCtl	*DosLockSeg*	*DosSetFHandState*
DosDupHandle	*DosMakePipe*	*DosSetFileInfo*
DosEnterCritSec	*DosMemAvail*	*DosSetFileMode*
DosErrClass	*DosMkDir*	*DosSetFSInfo*
DosError	*DosMove*	*DosSetMaxFH*
DosExecPgm	*DosMuxSemWait*	*DosSetPrty*
DosExit	*DosNewSize*	*DosSetSigHandler*
DosExitCritSec	*DosOpen*	*DosSetVec*
DosExitList	*DosOpenSem*	*DosSetVerify*
DosFileLocks	*DosPhysicalDisk*	*DosSizeSeg*
DosFindClose	*DosPortAccess*	*DosSleep*
DosFindFirst	*DosPTrace*	*DosSubAlloc*
DosFindNext	*DosQAppType*	*DosSubFree*
DosFlagProcess	*DosQCurDir*	*DosSubSet*
DosFreeModule	*DosQCurDisk*	*DosSuspendThread*
DosFreeSeg	*DosQFHandState*	*DosTimerAsync*
DosFSRamSemClear	*DosQFileInfo*	*DosTimerStart*
DosFSRamSemRequest	*DosQFileMode*	*DosTimerStop*
DosGetCp	*DosQFSInfo*	*DosUnlockSeg*
DosGetDateTime	*DosQHandType*	*DosWrite*
DosGetEnv	*DosQVerify*	*DosWriteAsync*

Figure 14-2. *Kernel API functions that can be called by code executing within an IOPL segment.*

Four API functions are present specifically for the needs of IOPL applications: *DosCLIAccess*, *DosPortAccess*, *DosR2StackRealloc*, and *DosCallback*. *DosCLIAccess* informs the operating system that the application needs to execute the CLI and STI instructions to disable and enable interrupts, or that it no longer needs to use those instructions. Similarly, *DosPortAccess* notifies the operating system that the application requires (or no longer requires) access to a range of I/O ports. A call to *DosPortAccess* also implicitly requests the use of CLI and STI, so an additional call to *DosCLIAccess* is not required.

In the current versions of OS/2, neither *DosPortAccess* nor *DosCLIAccess* does anything; an application with I/O privilege can read or write I/O ports and execute CLI or STI whether it calls these functions or not. *DosPortAccess* and *DosCLIAccess* are present for upward compatibility with future, 80386-specific versions of the operating system. The 80386 allows access to individual I/O ports to be controlled on a per-process basis by means of an I/O permissions bitmap associated with each task state segment (TSS).

DosCallback and *DosR2StackRealloc* became available in OS/2 version 1.1. *DosR2StackRealloc* allows a thread to increase (but not to decrease) the size of its ring 2 stack, that is, the stack that it uses while executing within an IOPL segment. The default size of the stack allocated by OS/2 is 512 bytes, which is not large enough for routines that are heavily recursive or that call the kernel API (in which case Microsoft recommends a minimum stack size of 2 KB).

The function *DosCallback* is, in effect, a call gate implemented with software that allows a ring 2 routine to call ring 3 procedures in the same application. Because a stack switch is involved—and *DosCallback* does not provide for the copying of any stack items—your program must use registers to pass any parameters for the ring 3 code. If the ring 2 and ring 3 routines communicate through variables, those variables must not lie in a ring 2 data segment (that is, a data segment that has been marked IOPL in the module definition file).

Using IOPL in OS/2 Applications

If you follow a few simple rules, you will find that designing and coding an OS/2 application that uses IOPL segments is a straightforward process.

First, you must segregate from the rest of the application code all code that needs to enable or disable interrupts or to access I/O ports. This distinct segment becomes the IOPL segment. For compatibility with Microsoft C, give the segment the WORD and PUBLIC attributes and assign it to class

'CODE'. Be sure to choose a segment name that won't conflict with the standard Microsoft segment and group names (_TEXT, _DATA, DGROUP, and so forth).

Second, for the procedures in the IOPL segment to be usable from a high level language, they should follow the OS/2 API conventions of accepting their parameters on the stack and returning their results in register AX or in variables whose addresses were passed in the original call. You must declare the procedures that contain the hardware-dependent code *public* and give them the *far* attribute because they will be entered through a call gate and must exit with a far return. The parameter to the RET instruction must be the number of bytes (*not* words) to be cleared from the caller's stack.

If you are writing the body of your application in C, supply *extern far pascal* prototypes for the external IOPL routines, just as with API functions. This tells the C compiler that parameters are pushed left to right, that the called routine clears the stack, that a leading underscore should not be added to the external name, and that case in the external name can be ignored. If you are writing a MASM application, simply declare the IOPL routines as *extrn far* in the usual manner.

Third, the initialization and termination portions of your application should include a call to the kernel API function *DosPortAccess* or *DosCLIAccess*. Use of these functions in the documented manner ensures that your application will still work as expected when the 80386-specific versions of OS/2 appear.

Last, when you build the executable application, you must provide the Linker with a module definition (DEF) file which contains a SEGMENTS directive for the IOPL segment and an EXPORTS directive that declares the name and number of stack parameters for each routine in the IOPL segment that will be called from outside the segment. If you are writing your program in C, you need to compile and link in separate operations because the C compiler does not know how to pass the name of a module definition file through to the Linker.

Take special care that the EXPORTS directive matches the actual code in the corresponding IOPL routine. If too few parameters are specified in the EXPORTS directive, the parameters are not all copied to the ring 2 stack, and the IOPL routine will generate a protect fault when it tries to access one of the missing items. If too many parameters are specified in the EXPORTS directive, no harm is done unless the operand for the IOPL routine's RET instruction is also incorrect. If that operand is also too large, the system clears too many items from the caller's stack when the IOPL routine exits, and a protect fault is likely to occur at a later point in the program's execution.

A Sample IOPL Application

The program PORTS.EXE provides a simple and practical demonstration of an OS/2 application that uses direct hardware access to read and display the first 256 I/O ports. PORTS.EXE is built from three modules: PORTS.C or PORTS.ASM, PORTIO.ASM, and PORTS.DEF.

PORTIO.ASM (Figure 14-3) is the program's IOPL segment. It contains only two routines: *rport* and *wport*. The *rport* routine accepts a port address, reads the port, and returns the port data register in AX with the upper eight bits zeroed. The *wport* routine accepts a port address and a word of data, writes the lower eight bits of the data to the port, and returns nothing. Both routines use the OS/2 API conventions and can be called from either MASM or C. Notice that the code segment in this file is called IO_TEXT to differentiate it from the code segment produced by the C compiler (which has the default name _TEXT).

PORTS.C (Figure 14-4 on p. 309) is the C version of the body of the application. It invokes *DosPortAccess* to request access to a range of I/O ports; then it calls *rport* to read each port and formats the data for display with *printf()*. Before terminating, the program again calls *DosPortAccess* to release the I/O ports requested earlier. PORTS.ASM (Figure 14-5 on p. 311) is the MASM equivalent of PORTS.C.

```
        title    PORTIO -- Read/Write I/O Ports
        page     55,132
        .286


;
; PORTIO.ASM
;
; General-purpose port read/write routines for C or MASM programs.
;
; Assemble with: C> masm portio.asm;
;
; When this module is linked into a program, the following lines
; must be present in the program's module definition (DEF) file:
;
```

(continued)

Figure 14-3. *PORTIO.ASM, the source code for the IOPL segment which contains the routines to read and write I/O ports.*

Figure 14-3. *continued*

```
; SEGMENTS
;   IO_TEXT IOPL
;
; EXPORTS
;   RPORT 1
;   WPORT 2
;
; The SEGMENTS and EXPORTS directives are recognized by the Linker
; and cause information to be built into the EXE file header for
; the OS/2 program loader. The loader is signaled to give I/O
; privilege to code executing in the segment IO_TEXT and to build
; call gates for the routines 'rport' and 'wport'.
;
; Copyright (C) 1988 Ray Duncan
;


IO_TEXT segment word public 'CODE'

        assume  cs:IO_TEXT



; RPORT: Read 8-bit data from I/O port. Port address
; is passed on stack; data is returned in register AX
; with AH zeroed. Other registers are unchanged.
;
; C syntax:      unsigned port, data;
;                data = rport(port);

        public  rport
rport   proc    far

        push    bp              ; save registers and
        mov     bp,sp           ; set up stack frame
        push    dx

        mov     dx,[bp+6]       ; get port number
        in      al,dx           ; read the port
        xor     ah,ah           ; clear upper 8 bits

        pop     dx              ; restore registers
        pop     bp

        ret     2               ; discard parameters,
                                ; return port data in AX
rport   endp
```

(continued)

Figure 14-3. *continued*

```
; WPORT: Write 8-bit data to I/O port. Port address and
; data are passed on stack. All registers are unchanged.
;
; C syntax:      unsigned port, data;
;                wport(port, data);

        public  wport
wport   proc    far

        push    bp                  ; save registers and
        mov     bp,sp               ; set up stack frame
        push    ax
        push    dx

        mov     ax,[bp+6]           ; get data to write
        mov     dx,[bp+8]           ; get port number
        out     dx,al               ; write the port

        pop     dx                  ; restore registers
        pop     ax
        pop     bp

        ret     4                   ; discard parameters,
                                    ; return nothing
wport   endp

IO_TEXT ends

        end
```

```
/*
        PORTS.C

        An OS/2 IOPL demonstration program that reads and displays the
        first 256 I/O ports. Requires the separate module PORTIO.ASM.

        Compile with:  C> cl /c ports.c
        Link with:  C> link ports+portio,ports,,os2,ports
```

(continued)

Figure 14-4. *PORTS.C, the C source code for the body of the PORTS.EXE example program.*

Figure 14-4. *continued*

```
        Usage is:  C> ports

        Copyright (C) 1988 Ray Duncan
*/


#include <stdio.h>


#define API extern far pascal

unsigned API rport(unsigned);              /* function prototypes */
void     API wport(unsigned, unsigned);
void     API DosSleep(unsigned long);
unsigned API DosPortAccess(unsigned, unsigned, unsigned, unsigned);


                              /* parameters for DosPortAccess */
#define REQUEST 0                    /* request port */
#define RELEASE 1                    /* release port */
#define BPORT   0                    /* beginning port */
#define EPORT   255                  /* ending port */

main(int argc, char *argv[])
{
    int i;                           /* scratch variable */

                                     /* request port access */
    if(DosPortAccess(0, REQUEST, BPORT, EPORT))
    {
        printf("\nDosPortAccess failed.\n");
        exit(1);
    }

    printf("\n      ");              /* print title line */
    for(i=0; i<16; i++) printf(" %2X", i);

    for(i=BPORT; i<=EPORT; i++)      /* loop through all ports */
    {
        if((i & 0x0f)==0)
        {
            printf("\n%04X  ", i);   /* new line needed */
        }

        printf(" %02X", rport(i));   /* read and display port */
    }

    DosPortAccess(0, RELEASE, BPORT, EPORT);  /* release port access */
}
```

```
        title   PORTS -- IOPL Demo Program
        page    55,132
        .286


;
; PORTS.ASM
;
; An OS/2 IOPL demonstration program that reads and displays the
; first 256 I/O ports. Requires the separate module PORTIO.ASM.
;
; Assemble with:  C> masm ports.asm;
; Link with:  C> link ports+portio,ports,,os2,ports
;
; Usage is:  C> ports
;
; Copyright (C) 1988 Ray Duncan
;

cr       equ     0dh                     ; ASCII carriage return
lf       equ     0ah                     ; ASCII linefeed
blank    equ     20h                     ; ASCII space code

stdout   equ     1                       ; standard output handle
stderr   equ     2                       ; standard error handle

bport    equ     0                       ; first port to display
eport    equ     255                     ; last port to display
request  equ     0                       ; request port access
release  equ     1                       ; release port access

         extrn   DosPortAccess:far       ; kernel API functions
         extrn   DosWrite:far
         extrn   DosExit:far

         extrn   rport:far               ; PORTIO.ASM functions
         extrn   wport:far

DGROUP   group   _DATA

_DATA    segment word public 'DATA'

wlen     dw      0                       ; actual number of bytes
                                         ; written by DosWrite
```

(continued)

Figure 14-5. *PORTS.ASM, the MASM source code for the body of the PORTS.EXE example program.*

Figure 14-5. *continued*

```
msg1      db       cr,lf                          ; error message
          db       'DosPortAccess failed.'
          db       cr,lf
msg1_len equ      $-msg1

msg2      db       cr,lf                          ; heading
          db       '      0  1  2  3  4  5  6'
          db       '  7  8  9  A  B  C  D  E  F'
msg2_len equ      $-msg2

msg3      db       cr,lf                          ; display port number
msg3a     db       'NNNN '
msg3_len equ      $-msg3

msg4      db       ' '                            ; display port data
msg4a     db       'NN'
msg4_len equ      $-msg4


_DATA    ends


_TEXT    segment word public 'CODE'

         assume  cs:_TEXT,ds:DGROUP

main     proc    far                             ; entry point from OS/2

         push    ds                              ; make DGROUP addressable
         pop     es                              ; with ES too

                                                 ; request port access...
         push    0                               ; reserved
         push    request                         ; request/release
         push    bport                           ; first port number
         push    eport                           ; last port number
         call    DosPortAccess                   ; transfer to OS/2
         or      ax,ax                           ; call successful?
         jz      main1                           ; yes, jump

                                                 ; display error message...
         push    stderr                          ; standard error handle
         push    ds                              ; message address
         push    offset DGROUP:msg1
         push    msg1_len                        ; message length
         push    ds                              ; receives bytes written
         push    offset DGROUP:wlen
         call    DosWrite                        ; transfer to OS/2
```

(continued)

Figure 14-5. *continued*

```
                                   ; now terminate process...
        push    1                  ; terminate all threads
        push    1                  ; return code = 1 (error)
        call    DosExit            ; transfer to OS/2

main1:                             ; print heading...
        push    stdout             ; standard output handle
        push    ds                 ; address of heading
        push    offset DGROUP:msg2
        push    msg2_len           ; length of heading
        push    ds                 ; receives bytes written
        push    offset DGROUP:wlen
        call    DosWrite           ; transfer to OS/2

        mov     dx,bport           ; initialize port number

main2:  test    dx,0fh             ; new line needed?
        jnz     main3              ; no, jump

        mov     ax,dx              ; convert port number
        mov     di,offset DGROUP:msg3a  ; to ASCII for display
        call    wtoa

                                   ; display port number...
        push    stdout             ; standard output handle
        push    ds                 ; message address
        push    offset DGROUP:msg3
        push    msg3_len           ; message length
        push    ds                 ; receives bytes written
        push    offset DGROUP:wlen
        call    DosWrite           ; transfer to OS/2

main3:  push    dx                 ; call 'rport' to read port
        call    rport              ; returns AX = data

        mov     di,offset msg4a    ; convert port data
        call    btoa               ; to ASCII for display

                                   ; display port data...
        push    stdout             ; standard output handle
        push    ds                 ; message address
        push    offset DGROUP:msg4
        push    msg4_len           ; message length
        push    ds                 ; receives bytes written
        push    offset DGROUP:wlen
        call    DosWrite           ; transfer to OS/2
```

(continued)

Figure 14-5. *continued*

```
          inc     dx                      ; increment port number
          cmp     dx,eport                ; done with all ports?
          jbe     main2                   ; not yet, read another

                                          ; release port access...
          push    0                       ; reserved
          push    release                 ; request/release
          push    bport                   ; first port number
          push    eport                   ; last port number
          call    DosPortAccess           ; transfer to OS/2

                                          ; final exit to OS/2...
          push    1                       ; terminate all threads
          push    0                       ; return code = 0 (success)
          call    DosExit                 ; transfer to OS/2

main      endp

; WTOA:         Convert word to hex ASCII
;
; Call with:    AX    = data to convert
;               ES:DI = storage address
; Returns:      nothing
; Uses:         AX, CL, DI

wtoa      proc    near

          push    ax                      ; save original value
          mov     al,ah
          call    btoa                    ; convert upper byte

          pop     ax                      ; restore original value
          call    btoa                    ; convert lower byte

          ret                             ; back to caller

wtoa      endp


; BTOA:         Convert byte to hex ASCII
;
; Call with:    AL    = data to convert
;               ES:DI = storage address
; Returns:      nothing
; Uses:         AX, CL, DI
```

(continued)

Figure 14-5. *continued*

```
btoa    proc    near

        sub     ah,ah                       ; clear upper byte

        mov     cl,16                       ; divide by 16
        div     cl

        call    ascii                       ; convert quotient
        stosb                               ; store ASCII character

        mov     al,ah
        call    ascii                       ; convert remainder
        stosb                               ; store ASCII character

        ret                                 ; back to caller

btoa    endp


; ASCII:          Convert nibble to hex ASCII
;
; Call with:      AL     = data to convert in low 4 bits
; Returns:        AL     = ASCII character
; Uses:           nothing

ascii   proc    near

        add     al,'0'                      ; add base ASCII value
        cmp     al,'9'                      ; is it in range 0 through 9?
        jle     ascii2                      ; jump if it is

        add     al,'A'-'9'-1                ; no, adjust for range A-F

ascii2: ret                                 ; return ASCII character in AL

ascii   endp

_TEXT   ends

        end     main                        ; defines entry point
```

PORTS.DEF (Figure 14-6 on the following page) is the module definition file. The SEGMENTS directive marks IO_TEXT as an IOPL segment. The EXPORTS directive defines the number of stack parameters for RPORT and WPORT and identifies the two routines as callable from outside the IOPL segment.

```
NAME PORTS WINDOWCOMPAT
PROTMODE
STACKSIZE 4096
SEGMENTS
  IO_TEXT IOPL
EXPORTS
  RPORT 1
  WPORT 2
```

Figure 14-6. *PORTS.DEF, the module definition file for the PORTS.EXE demonstration program. Omit the STACKSIZE directive if you are linking the C version.*

To build the executable program file PORTS.EXE from the source files PORTS.C, PORTIO.ASM, and PORTS.DEF, enter the following commands:

```
[C:\] CL /c PORTS.C  <Enter>
[C:\] MASM PORTIO.ASM;  <Enter>
[C:\] LINK PORTS+PORTIO,PORTS,,OS2,PORTS  <Enter>
```

To build PORTS.EXE from the source files PORTS.ASM, PORTIO.ASM, and PORTS.DEF, enter the commands:

```
[C:\] MASM PORTS.ASM;  <Enter>
[C:\] MASM PORTIO.ASM;  <Enter>
[C:\] LINK PORTS+PORTIO,PORTS,,OS2,PORTS  <Enter>
```

Figure 14-7 shows a sample of the output for PORTS.EXE. If you get the error message *OS/2 is not presently configured to run this application*, add the statement *IOPL=YES* to your CONFIG.SYS file and reboot the system.

```
[C:\] PORTS  <Enter>

        0  1  2  3  4  5  6  7  8  9  A  B  C  D  E  F
0000   00 00 00 00 AC FF 00 00 00 FF FF FF FF 00 FF FF
0010   00 00 00 00 AC FF 00 00 00 FF FF FF FF 00 FF FF
        .
        .
        .
00E0   FF FF FF FF FF FF FF FF FF FF FF FF FF FF FF FF
00F0   FF FF FF FF FF FF FF FF FF FF FF FF FF FF FF FF

[C:\]
```

Figure 14-7. *Sample output of PORTS.EXE.*

TIME, DATE, AND TIMERS

Because OS/2 is a preemptive multitasking system, it is both time-driven and time-sensitive. Its time-related responsibilities include:

- Dividing the available CPU cycles (time-slicing) among the active threads according to their priority

- Detecting I/O timeouts

- Providing user-programmable timer events

- Maintaining the current date and current time of day

- Stamping the directory entries for files with the date and time they were created or last modified

On PC/AT and PS/2 compatible machines, OS/2 relies on two hardware components to carry out these duties: a battery-powered clock/calendar chip and a programmable counter/timer chip.

The battery-powered clock/calendar chip runs autonomously, separate from the rest of the computer system. Whenever the system is turned on or restarted, OS/2 initializes its internal time and date by reading the I/O ports that provide access to this chip. You can update the clock/calendar chip with the TIME and DATE commands or with the SETUP program.

The clock/calendar chip is also programmed during system initialization to generate a hardware interrupt (called the "timer tick") at intervals of 31 milliseconds (approximately 32 Hz).* Each time a timer tick occurs, the currently executing thread is interrupted, and control is transferred to the clock driver's interrupt handler. The handler updates the system's internal

---

*This is the interval used by Microsoft and IBM OS/2 versions 1.0 and 1.1. The interval might be different in other OEM versions.

time, date, and millisecond counters and then notifies the other kernel and driver modules of the timer tick by means of a special kernel dispatcher. Finally, the clock driver transfers control to the scheduler, which examines its list of eligible threads and selects one for execution.

The programmable counter/timer chip (an Intel 8253 or equivalent) is set up during system initialization to provide interrupts at 55-millisecond intervals (18.2 Hz). This interrupt is masked off when any protected mode session is in the foreground. When the real mode session is in the foreground, the counter/timer chip's interrupt is enabled, serviced on Int 08H (IRQ0), and distributed to real mode applications via Int 1CH for compatibility with MS-DOS.

In addition to maintaining the date and the time and servicing periodic timer interrupts for its own purposes, OS/2 exports API functions that allow application programs to do the following:

- Obtain or set the system time and date

- Suspend execution for a predetermined interval

- Be notified by means of a semaphore when a specified interval elapses

These API functions are summarized in Figure 15-1. The functions to suspend execution or to report elapsed time with semaphores accept their time parameters in milliseconds (msec.). These values are always rounded up to a multiple of the timer tick interval and are accurate only to within one or two timer ticks. The length of a timer tick interval is available in the global information segment (see p. 524). Because this value is OEM-dependent, programs should obtain it at run time rather than having it hard-coded.

Function	Description
DosGetInfoSeg	Obtains selectors for global and local information segments; global information segment includes current date, time, time zone, and day of the week
DosGetDateTime	Returns current date, time, time zone, and day of the week
DosSetDateTime	Sets system date and time
DosSleep	Suspends execution of a thread for a programmed interval
DosTimerAsync	Starts one-shot asynchronous timer that clears system semaphore
DosTimerStart	Starts periodic asynchronous timer that clears system semaphore
DosTimerStop	Disables timer previously activated with *DosTimerAsync* or *DosTimerStart*

Figure 15-1. *The OS/2 API function calls for time, date, and programmable timers.*

Reading and Setting Date and Time

Your application program can determine the current system time and date in two ways. The method you use depends on the characteristics of your program.

For the average applications program, the preferred method is to use *DosGetInfoSeg* to get a selector for the global information segment. Information related to the current date and time is located at specific offsets within the segment, as shown in Figure 15-2. An actual memory dump of the global information segment is in Figure 15-3.

When the selector for the global information segment is in hand, your program can inspect the date or time as often as necessary without the overhead of additional calls to OS/2 (Figure 15-4 on the following page). Be careful, however, not to be misled by the occurrence of a rollover in one of the fields while your program is preempted by an interrupt handler or another thread. To protect against this, read the fields of interest repeatedly

Offset	Length	Contents
00H	4	Elapsed time from 1-1-1970 in seconds
04H	4	Milliseconds since system boot
08H	1	Hours (0–23)
09H	1	Minutes (0–59)
0AH	1	Seconds (0–59)
0BH	1	Hundredths of a second (0–99)
0CH	2	Time zone (minutes ± GMT) (−1 = undefined)
0EH	2	Timer interval (units = 0.0001 seconds)
10H	1	Day (1–31)
11H	1	Month (1–12)
12H	2	Year (1980+)
14H	1	Day of the week (0 = Sunday, 1 = Monday, etc.)

Figure 15-2. *Format of current date and time in global information segment.*

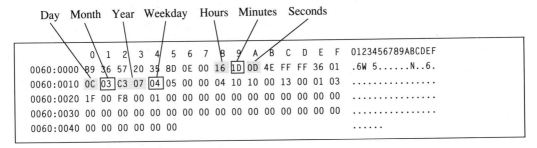

Figure 15-3. *A hex and ASCII dump of a global information segment.*

until you get two sets that are the same. An alternative (but strongly discouraged) technique is to use an IOPL routine that disables interrupts, reads the global information segment values, and then reenables interrupts.

```
                                 ; fields in global info segment...
hour    equ     08h              ; hours
min     equ     09h              ; minutes
sec     equ     0ah              ; seconds
cseg    equ     0bh              ; hundredths of a second


gseg    dw      ?                ; receives selector for
                                 ; global information segment

lseg    dw      ?                ; receives selector for
                                 ; local information segment


        .
        .
        .
                                 ; get info seg selectors...
        push    ds               ; receives global selector
        push    offset DGROUP:gseg
        push    ds               ; receives local selector
        push    offset DGROUP:lseg
        call    DosGetInfoSeg    ; transfer to OS/2
        or      ax,ax            ; were selectors attained?
        jnz     error            ; jump if function failed

                                 ; else get current time...
        mov     es,gseg          ; load selector for global
                                 ; information segment

                                 ; let AL = hours, AH = minutes
label1: mov     ax,word ptr es:hour
                                 ; let BL = seconds, BH = centiseconds
        mov     bx,word ptr es:sec
```

(continued)

Figure 15-4. *Obtaining the selector for the global information segment with DosGetInfoSeg and then using that selector to obtain the current time.*

Figure 15-4. *continued*

```
                                 ; read time again...
          mov      cx,word ptr es:hour
          mov      dx,word ptr es:sec

          cmp      ax,cx          ; check for rollover...
          jne      label1         ; rollover occurred, start over
          cmp      bx,dx
          jne      label1         ; rollover occurred, start over
          .
          .
          .
```

The second method for getting the date and time is ordinarily used only by programs that need to obtain these values infrequently or that need to *alter* the date or time. It involves use of the function *DosGetDateTime*, which is called with the address of an 11-byte structure. OS/2 fills in the structure with the current date, time, time zone, and day of the week in the format shown in Figure 15-5.

Because this method requires an operating system call each time the date or time is inspected, it is considerably slower than using the global information segment. It is useful mainly because the organization of the structure is exactly the same as for *DosSetDateTime*. When a program needs to modify some part of the time or date, it can first call *DosGetDateTime* to fill the structure with valid information, make any necessary changes, and then write the updated information back to the operating system with *DosSetDateTime* (Figure 15-6 on the following page).

Offset	Length	Contents
00H	1	Hours (0–23)
01H	1	Minutes (0–59)
02H	1	Seconds (0–59)
03H	1	Hundredths of a second (0–99)
04H	1	Day (1–31)
05H	1	Month (1–12)
06H	2	Year (1980+)
08H	2	Time zone (minutes ± GMT) (−1 = undefined)
0AH	1	Day of week (0 = Sunday, 1 = Monday, etc.)

Figure 15-5. *Format of an 11-byte structure used by both* DosGetDateTime *and* DosSetDateTime *to hold date and time information.*

```
dtinfo   label   byte              ; date/time information
hour     db      0                 ; 0
min      db      0                 ; 1
sec      db      0                 ; 2
csec     db      0                 ; 3
day      db      0                 ; 4
mon      db      0                 ; 5
year     dw      0                 ; 6
zone     dw      0                 ; 8 minutes +/- GMT
dow      db      0                 ; 10 day of week


                 .
                 .
                 .

                                   ; first read date/time...
         push    ds                ; receives date/time info
         push    offset DGROUP:dtinfo
         call    DosGetDateTime    ; transfer to OS/2
         or      ax,ax             ; did read succeed?
         jnz     error             ; jump if function failed

         mov     hour,12           ; set time to 12:00
         mov     min,0             ; clear minutes
         mov     sec,0             ; and seconds
         mov     csec,0            ; and hundredths of a second

                                   ; now set date/time...
         push    ds                ; address of structure
         push    offset DGROUP:dtinfo
         call    DosSetDateTime    ; transfer to OS/2
         or      ax,ax             ; was time/date set?
         jnz     error             ; jump if function failed
                 .
                 .
                 .
```

Figure 15-6. *Example of altering the system time with* DosSetDateTime, *using* DosGetDateTime *first to obtain all the other current information. In this example the system time is set to 12:00:00:00 (noon).*

Programmed Delays

The function *DosSleep* allows a thread to suspend itself for a programmed interval. Using *DosSleep*, a thread can make itself dormant so that it doesn't tie up CPU resources, yet wake up periodically and check for an event, poll a device, or find out if a previously unavailable resource (a file, for example, that was locked by another process) has been freed up so that the thread can continue. Only the thread that calls *DosSleep* is suspended; other threads in the same process are not affected.

DosSleep is one of the simplest functions to use in the entire OS/2 API. Its only argument is an unsigned double precision number of milliseconds, allowing an upper limit on the delay time of about $4.29 * 10^6$ seconds (1193 hours). Under normal circumstances this function cannot return an error. Figure 15-7 illustrates the use of *DosSleep* by a thread that displays the system time at approximately 1-second intervals.

A program should not rely on the *DosSleep* function if it needs to resume execution at an exact time. The delay produced by a *DosSleep* call is accurate only to the granularity of the timer tick interval; its duration will always be *at least* the requested interval, rounded up to the next clock tick. In addition, the requested interval determines only the time at which the thread is again marked runnable; it does not guarantee that the thread will run at that time. The revived execution of the thread can be delayed unpredictably by other events in the system, such as servicing of hardware interrupts or the activity of other, higher-priority threads. In general, using *DosSleep* to obtain clocklike behavior is inevitably unsatisfactory because of the cumulative effect of delays and rounding errors.

An interesting special use of *DosSleep* is to yield processor time explicitly. If the *DosSleep* parameter is zero, the thread gives up the remainder of its current timeslice but is rescheduled normally for its next timeslice.

```
        .
        .
        .
showit: call    display         ; update clock display

                                ; suspend for 1 second...
        push    0               ; push double precision
        push    1000            ; value of 1000 msec.
        call    DosSleep         ; transfer to OS/2
        or      ax,ax           ; unexpected error?
        jnz     error           ; jump if function failed

        jmp     showit          ; now display time again...
        .
        .
        .
```

Figure 15-7. *A simple clock utility, which uses the* DosSleep *function to suspend itself for 1 second and then displays the current time. Because* DosSleep *is subject to rounding errors, and because reactivation of the thread can be delayed by other activity in the system, the display does not occur at precise 1-second intervals.*

Using Timers

Two OS/2 functions, *DosTimerAsync* and *DosTimerStart*, provide for an asynchronous signal to a process after a programmed delay. The timers communicate with the process by clearing a system semaphore. *DosTimer-Async* sets up a "one-shot" timer; *DosTimerStart* establishes a "periodic" timer that continues to clear the semaphore at the requested interval until the timer is disabled.

A process that uses timers must first create a system semaphore and initialize it to a "set" state (see Chapter 13). The process then calls *DosTimer-Async* or *DosTimerStart* to create and start the timer. Both functions require the same three parameters: a system semaphore handle, an unsigned double precision timer interval, and the address of a variable. If the timer is successfully created, the system returns a timer handle to the variable; this handle can be used later with *DosTimerStop* to disable the timer.

Once the timer is armed, the process can go on to other work. A thread within the process can synchronize with the timer by calling *DosMux-SemWait* (preferred) or *DosSemWait* with a timeout value of −1 to block on the semaphore. Alternatively, it can test for the expiration of the timer at suitable intervals by calling *DosSemWait* with a timeout value of 0 — causing *DosSemWait* to return immediately with an error code if the semaphore is set. To synchronize with a periodic timer, the process must reset the semaphore immediately after the timer clears it so that it will not miss subsequent firings of the timer.

It is, of course, quite practical to control multiple threads with the same timer — all threads in a process have equal access to any system semaphores created or opened by that process. When a process is using a periodic timer, one thread should block on the semaphore with *DosSemWait* and be responsible for resetting the semaphore; by promoting this thread to a "time-critical" priority, you can ensure that its execution will never be suppressed by other activity in the system. The other threads should run at normal priority and block on the semaphore with *DosMuxSemWait* (which is the only semaphore function that is edge-triggered rather than level-triggered).

Figure 15-8 demonstrates the use of a periodic timer to display the system time at 1-second intervals. This approach is superior to the use of *DosSleep* shown in Figure 15-7 because the overhead of the time display procedure is "hidden" inside the interval controlled by the timer. However, the timer is still subject to rounding errors and to delays caused by hardware interrupt processing or the activity of other, higher-priority threads.

```
sname    db      '\SEM\TIMER.SEM',0

shandle  dd      0                ; semaphore handle

thandle  dw      0                ; timer handle

           .
           .
           .
                                ; create system semaphore...
         push    1               ; 1 = not exclusive ownership
         push    ds              ; receives semaphore handle
         push    offset DGROUP:shandle
         push    ds              ; address of semaphore name
         push    offset DGROUP:sname
         call    DosCreateSem    ; transfer to OS/2
         or      ax,ax           ; semaphore created?
         jnz     error           ; jump if function failed...

                                ; create periodic timer...
         push    0               ; interval = 1000 msec.
         push    1000
         push    word ptr shandle+2 ; semaphore handle
         push    word ptr shandle
         push    ds              ; receives timer handle
         push    offset DGROUP:thandle
         call    DosTimerStart   ; transfer to OS/2
         or      ax,ax           ; timer created?
         jnz     error           ; jump if function failed

showit:                          ; set the semaphore...
         push    word ptr shandle+2 ; semaphore handle
         push    word ptr shandle
         call    DosSemSet       ; transfer to OS/2
         or      ax,ax           ; did set succeed?
         jnz     error           ; jump if function failed

         call    display         ; update clock display

                                ; now block on semaphore...
         push    word ptr shandle+2 ; semaphore handle
         push    word ptr shandle
```

(continued)

Figure 15-8. *Another simple clock timer, similar to that in Figure 15-7, but which uses a periodic timer and system semaphore (rather than* DosSleep) *to trigger display of the clock.*

Figure 15-8. *continued*

```
        push    -1              ; timeout = -1
        push    -1              ; (wait indefinitely)
        call    DosSemWait      ; transfer to OS/2
        or      ax,ax           ; unexpected error?
        jnz     error           ; jump if wait failed

        jmp     showit          ; now display time again...
        .
        .
        .
```

The Clock Device

The system's device driver for the real time clock masquerades as a character device driver and has the logical name CLOCK$. The kernel identifies
the clock driver by a special bit in the attribute word of its header, so the
device name has no special significance to the system itself.

If you use *DosOpen* to obtain a handle for the CLOCK$ device, you can use
ordinary *DosRead* and *DosWrite* calls to read from it and write data to it.
This data must be in a special 6-byte format:

Offset	Length	Contents
00H	2	Days since January 1, 1980
02H	1	Minutes (0–59)
03H	1	Hours (0–23)
04H	1	Hundredths of a second (0–99)
05H	1	Seconds (0–59)

This is the same data format used by the real time clock driver in MS-DOS
and PC-DOS systems. There is no particular reason to use this CLOCK$
driver capability instead of *DosGetDateTime* or inspection of the global information segment; it is mentioned here only for completeness.

CUSTOMIZING OS/2

FILTERS

A filter is, essentially, a program that operates on a stream of characters. The source and the destination of the character stream can be files, another program (by means of a pipe), or almost any character device. The transformation applied by the filter to the character stream can be as simple as character substitution or as complex as fitting a curve to a set of coordinates.

The standard OS/2 package includes three simple filters: SORT, which alphabetically sorts text line by line; FIND, which searches a text stream to match a specified string; and MORE, which displays text one screenful at a time.

System Support for Filters

The operation of a filter program relies on two OS/2 features that are modeled after UNIX/XENIX: *standard devices* and *redirectable I/O*.

The *standard devices* are represented by three handles that are established by the command interpreter (CMD.EXE) and inherited by each newly created process from its immediate parent. Thus, the standard device handles are already opened when a process begins its execution, and the process can use them for read and write operations without further preliminaries. The default assignments of the standard device handles are as follows:

Handle	Name	Default Device
0	*stdin* (standard input)	KBD$
1	*stdout* (standard output)	SCREEN$
2	*stderr* (standard error)	SCREEN$

When the user executes a program by entering its name at the system (CMD.EXE) prompt or in a batch file, any or all of the three standard device handles can be redirected from its default device to another file, to a character device, or to a process. This redirection is accomplished by including one of the six special directives <, >, >>, 2>, 2>>, or ¦ on the command line, as illustrated in Figure 16-1.

The following command, for example, causes the SORT filter to read its input from the file MYFILE.TXT, sort the lines alphabetically, and write resulting text to the character device PRN (the logical name for the system's list device):

```
[C:\] SORT <MYFILE.TXT >PRN  <Enter>
```

The actions requested by the redirection parameters take place at the level of CMD.EXE and are invisible to the programs they affect. As shown at the end of this chapter, any other process can also institute such redirection.

A program that uses *Kbd* or *Vio* calls for higher performance is unaffected by redirection directives on the command line. The same is true of a program that calls *DosOpen* for KBD$, SCREEN$, or CON and uses the resulting handle for I/O. This independence can frustrate a user who is trying to drive a program with a script or capture its output into a file — the program doesn't behave "as expected." A well-behaved program should call *DosQHandType* to determine if one or more of its standard devices have been redirected, then use *DosRead* and *DosWrite* with the standard handles (rather than the *Kbd* and *Vio* subsystems) if redirection is in effect.

Syntax	Resulting Redirection
< *file*	The program takes its standard input from the specified file or device instead of from the keyboard.
> *file*	The program sends its standard output to the specified file or device instead of to the display (also 1> *file*).
>> *file*	The program appends its standard output to the current contents of the specified file instead of sending it to the display (also 1>> *file*).
2> *file*	The program sends its standard error output to the specified file or device instead of to the display.
2>> *file*	The program appends its standard error output to the current contents of the specified file instead of sending it to the display.
p1 ¦ *p2*	The standard output of process *p1* is routed to become the standard input of process *p2*. (The output of *p1* is said to be *piped*.)

Figure 16-1. *Command syntax for redirecting standard device handles.*

How Filters Work

By convention, a filter program reads its text from the standard input device and writes the results of its operations to the standard output device. When the end of the input stream is reached, the filter simply terminates. As a result, filters are both flexible and simple.

The flexibility of filter programs derives from their indifference to the source of the data they process or the destination of their output. Any character device that has a logical name within the system (CON, COM1, COM2, PRN, LPT1, LPT2, LPT3, and so on), any file on any block device (local or network) known to the system, or any other program can supply input to a filter or accept its output.

Although flexible, filters remain simple because they rely on their parent processes to supply standard input and standard output handles that have already been appropriately redirected. The parent is responsible for opening or creating any necessary files, checking the validity of logical character device names, and loading and executing the preceding or following process in a pipe. The filter can concern itself strictly with operating on the data; it can leave the I/O details to the operating system and to its parent.

Building a Filter

Creating a new filter for OS/2 is straightforward. In its simplest form, a filter need use only *DosRead* and *DosWrite* to get characters from standard input and to send them to standard output; it operates on the text stream on a character-by-character or line-by-line basis.

Figures 16-2 and 16-3 contain template filters in both assembly language (PROTO.ASM) and C (PROTO.C). The C and assembler versions run at roughly the same speed, although the C version is several times larger. Both can be assembled or compiled, linked, and run exactly as shown. Of course, in this form they simply function like a slow COPY command.

```
        title    PROTO.ASM -- Filter Template
        page     55,132
        .286
;
; PROTO.ASM
;
; MASM filter template for OS/2.
```

(continued)

Figure 16-2. *Assembly language source code for PROTO.ASM, a template for a filter.*

Figure 16-2. *continued*

```
;
; Assemble with:  C> masm proto.asm;
; Link with:  C> link proto,,,os2;
;
; Usage is:  C> proto <source >destination
;
; Copyright (C) 1988 Ray Duncan
;

stdin    equ    0              ; standard input device
stdout   equ    1              ; standard output device
stderr   equ    2              ; standard error device

cr       equ    0dh            ; ASCII carriage return
lf       equ    0ah            ; ASCII linefeed

bufsize equ     256            ; I/O buffer size

         extrn  DosRead:far
         extrn  DosWrite:far
         extrn  DosExit:far


DGROUP  group   _DATA          ; 'automatic data group'

_DATA    segment word public 'DATA'

input    db     bufsize dup (?) ; storage for input line
output   db     bufsize dup (?) ; storage for output line

rlen     dw     ?              ; receives bytes read
wlen     dw     ?              ; receives bytes written

_DATA    ends


_TEXT    segment word public 'CODE'

         assume cs:_TEXT,ds:DGROUP

main     proc   far            ; entry point from OS/2

         push   ds             ; make DGROUP addressable
         pop    es             ; via ES register too
         assume es:DGROUP
```

(continued)

Figure 16-2. *continued*

```
        cld                          ; safety first

main1:                               ; read line from standard input...
        push    stdin                ; standard input handle
        push    ds                   ; buffer address
        push    offset DGROUP:input
        push    bufsize              ; buffer length
        push    ds                   ; receives bytes read
        push    offset DGROUP:rlen
        call    DosRead              ; transfer to OS/2
        or      ax,ax                ; was read successful?
        jnz     main3                ; exit if any error

        mov     ax,rlen              ; get length of input
        or      ax,ax                ; any characters read?
        jz      main2                ; jump if end of stream

        call    translate            ; translate line if necessary

        or      ax,ax                ; anything to output?
        jz      main1                ; no, go read another line

                                     ; write line to standard output...
        push    stdout               ; standard output handle
        push    ds                   ; buffer address
        push    offset DGROUP:output
        push    ax                   ; buffer length
        push    ds                   ; receives bytes written
        push    offset DGROUP:wlen
        call    DosWrite             ; transfer to OS/2
        or      ax,ax                ; write successful?
        jnz     main3                ; exit if any error

        jmp     main1                ; go read another line

main2:                               ; end of stream reached
        push    1                    ; 1 = end all threads
        push    0                    ; 0 = exit code
        call    DosExit              ; final exit to OS/2

main3:                               ; error encountered
        push    1                    ; 1 = end all threads
        push    1                    ; 1 = exit code
        call    DosExit              ; final exit to OS/2

main    endp                         ; end of main procedure
```

(continued)

Figure 16-2. *continued*

```
; Perform any necessary translation on line stored in
; 'input' buffer, leaving result in 'output' buffer.
;
; Call with:     AX = length of data in 'input' buffer
;
; Return:        AX = length to write to standard output
;
; Action of template routine is simply to copy the line.

translate proc  near


                               ; copy input to output...
        mov     si,offset DGROUP:input
        mov     di,offset DGROUP:output
        mov     cx,ax
        rep movsb
        ret                    ; return AX = length unchanged

translate endp


_TEXT   ends

        end     main           ; program entry point
```

```
/*
        PROTO.C

        A filter template for OS/2.

        Compile with:  C> cl proto.c

        Usage is:  C> proto <source >destination

        Copyright (C) 1988 Ray Duncan
*/

#include <stdio.h>

#define STDIN   0               /* standard input handle */
#define STDOUT  1               /* standard output handle */
#define BUFSIZE 256             /* I/O buffer size */
```

(continued)

Figure 16-3. *C language source code for PROTO.C, a template for a filter.*

Figure 16-3. *continued*

```
#define API unsigned extern far pascal
API DosRead(unsigned, void far *, unsigned, unsigned far *);
API DosWrite(unsigned, void far *, unsigned, unsigned far *);

static char input[BUFSIZE];            /* buffer for input line */
static char output[BUFSIZE];           /* buffer for output line */


main(int argc,char *argv[])
{
    int rlen, wlen;                    /* scratch variables */

    while(1)                           /* do until end of file */
    {
                                       /* get line from standard
                                          input stream */
        if(DosRead(STDIN, input, BUFSIZE, &rlen))
            exit(1);                   /* exit if read error */

        if(rlen == 0) exit(0);         /* exit if end of stream */

                                       /* write translated line to
                                          standard output stream */
        if(DosWrite(STDOUT, output, translate(rlen), &wlen))
            exit(1);                   /* exit if write error */
    }
}

/*
    Perform any necessary translation on input line,
    leaving the resulting text in output buffer.
    Returns length of translated line (may be zero).
*/

int translate(int length)
{
    memcpy(output,input,length);       /* template action is */
                                       /* to copy input line */
    return(length);                    /* and return its length */
}
```

To obtain a filter that does something useful, you must insert between the reads and writes a routine that performs some modification of the text stream that is flowing by. For example, Figures 16-4 and 16-5 contain the source code for a new *translate* function that you can substitute for the original *translate* in PROTO.ASM and PROTO.C. After this alteration, the filter converts all uppercase input characters (A–Z) to lowercase (a–z) output, leaving other characters unchanged.

```
;
; Copy input buffer to output buffer, translating
; all uppercase characters to lowercase.
;
; Call with:     AX = length of data in 'input' buffer
;
; Return:        AX = length to write to standard output
;

translate proc  near

        push    ax              ; save original length

                                ; address of original line
        mov     si,offset DGROUP:input

                                ; address for converted line
        mov     di,offset DGROUP:output

        mov     cx,ax           ; length to convert
        jcxz    trans3          ; exit if empty line

trans1:                         ; convert character by character

        lodsb                   ; get input character

        cmp     al,'A'          ; if not A-Z, leave it alone
        jb      trans2
        cmp     al,'Z'
        ja      trans2

        add     al,'a'-'A'      ; it's A-Z, convert it

trans2: stosb                   ; put into output buffer

        loop    trans1          ; loop until all characters
                                ; have been transferred

trans3: pop     ax              ; get back line length
        ret                     ; and return it in AX

translate endp
```

Figure 16-4. *A substitute assembly language translation routine to create a lowercasing filter.*

```
/*

    Translate uppercase characters to lowercase
    characters, leaving resulting text in output
    buffer and returning its length.
*/

int translate(int length)
{
    int i;                         /* scratch index */

    memcpy(output,input,length);   /* copy input to output */

    for(i = 0; i < length; i++)    /* lowercase the output */
    {
        if(output[i] >= 'A' && output[i] <= 'Z')

            output[i] += 'a'-'A';
    }
    return(length);                /* return its length */
}
```

Figure 16-5. *A substitute C language translation routine to create a lowercasing filter.*

As another example, Figure 16-6 contains the C source code for a line-oriented filter called FIND. This filter (which is similar to the FIND filter supplied with OS/2 but much simpler) is invoked with a command line in the following form:

FIND "*pattern*" [<*source*] [>*destination*]

FIND searches the input stream for lines containing the pattern specified on the command line. The line number and text of any line containing a match is sent to standard output, with any tabs expanded to 8-column stops.

Unlike PROTO.C, which performed direct OS/2 function calls with *DosRead* and *DosWrite*, the FIND filter uses the C runtime library's *gets()* and *printf()* functions. This makes formatting of the output easier but drastically enlarges the size of the executable file.

The FIND program in Figure 16-6 differs from the FIND filter in the OS/2 retail package in several respects. First, it is not case-sensitive, so the pattern "foobar" will match "FOOBAR," "FooBar," and so forth. Second, this filter supports no switches; these are left as entertainment for the reader. Third, this program always reads from the standard input—it cannot open its own files.

```
/*
        FIND.C

        Searches text stream for a string.

        Compile with:  C> cl find.c

        Usage is:  C> find "pattern" [<source] [>destination]

        Copyright (C) 1988 Ray Duncan
*/

#include <stdio.h>

#define TAB       '\x09'              /* ASCII tab (^I) */
#define BLANK     '\x20'              /* ASCII space */
#define TAB_WIDTH 8                   /* columns per tab stop */
#define BUF_SIZE  256

static char input[BUF_SIZE];          /* input line buffer */
static char output[BUF_SIZE];         /* output line buffer */
static char pattern[BUF_SIZE];        /* search pattern buffer */

void writeline(int, char *);          /* function prototype */

main(int argc, char *argv[])
{
    int line = 0;                     /* initialize line variable */

    if(argc < 2)                      /* search pattern supplied? */
    {
        puts("find: missing pattern"); /* exit if no search pattern */
        exit(1);
    }

    strcpy(pattern,argv[1]);          /* save copy of search pattern */
    strupr(pattern);                  /* fold it to uppercase */

    while(gets(input) != NULL)        /* read a line from input */
    {
        line++;                       /* count lines */

        strcpy(output, input);        /* save copy of input string */
        strupr(input);                /* fold input to uppercase */
```

(continued)

Figure 16-6. *C source code for FIND.C, a FIND filter. This simple filter searches each line of a text stream for a pattern and sends the matching lines to the standard output.*

Figure 16-6. *continued*

```
        if(strstr(input, pattern))        /* if line contains pattern */
            writeline(line, output);      /* write it to standard output */
    }
    exit(0);                               /* terminate at end of file */
}


/*
    WRITELINE: Write line number and text to standard output,
    expanding any tab characters to stops defined by TAB_WIDTH.
*/

void writeline(int line, char *p)
{
    int i = 0;                            /* index to input line */
    int col = 0;                          /* output column counter */

    printf("\n%4d: ", line);              /* write line number */

    while(p[i] != NULL)                   /* while not end of line */
    {
        if(p[i] == TAB)                   /* if tab, expand it */
        {
            do putchar(BLANK);
            while((++col % TAB_WIDTH) != 0);
        }
        else                              /* otherwise leave it alone */
        {
            putchar(p[i]);                /* send character */
            col++;                        /* count columns */
        }
        i++;                              /* advance through input */
    }
}
```

Using a Filter as a Child Process

An application program can load and execute a filter as a child process to carry out a specific task instead of incorporating all the code necessary to do the same job itself. Before the child filter is loaded, the parent must arrange for the redirection of the standard input and the standard output handles (which the child inherits) to the files or to the character devices that will supply the filter's input and receive its output. This redirection is accomplished in the steps that follow.

1. The parent process uses *DosDupHandle* to create duplicates of its own standard input and standard output handles and saves the duplicates.

2. The parent uses *DosOpen* to open or create the files or devices that the child process will use for input and output.

3. The parent uses *DosDupHandle* to force its standard device handles to track the new file or device handles acquired in step 2.

4. The parent uses *DosExecPgm* with the *synchronous* option to load and execute the child process. The child inherits the redirected standard input and standard output handles and uses them to do its work. The parent regains control after the filter terminates.*

5. The parent uses the duplicate handles created in step 1, together with *DosDupHandle*, to restore its own standard input and standard output handles to their original meanings.

6. The parent closes (with *DosClose*) the duplicate handles created in step 1 because they are no longer needed.

It might seem as though the parent process could just as easily close its own standard input and standard output (handles 0 and 1), open the input and output files needed by the child, run the child process, close the files upon regaining control, and then reopen the CON device twice. Because the open operation always assigns the first free handle, this approach would have the desired effect as far as the child process is concerned. However, it would throw away any redirection that had been established for the parent process by *its* parent. Thus, the need to preserve any preexisting redirection of the parent's standard input and standard output, along with the desire to preserve the parent's usual output channel for messages right up to the actual point of the *DosExecPgm* call, is the reason for the elaborate procedure outlined above.

The program EXECSORT.ASM in Figure 16-7 demonstrates this redirection of input and output for a filter run as a child process. EXECSORT makes duplicates of its standard input and standard output handles with *DosDupHandle*; then it redirects the standard input to the file MYFILE.DAT (which it opens) and the standard output to the file MYFILE.SRT (which it creates). EXECSORT then calls *DosExecPgm* to run the SORT.EXE filter that is supplied with OS/2.

---

* If the parent uses one of *DosExecPgm*'s asynchronous options, it can proceed with other work while the child process is running and then resynchronize with the child by calling *DosCwait*.

The SORT program reads the file MYFILE.DAT via its standard input handle, sorts the file alphabetically by line, and writes the sorted data to MYFILE.SRT via its standard output handle. When SORT terminates, OS/2 closes SORT's inherited handles for the standard input and standard output, which forces an update of the directory entry for the file MYFILE.SRT. EXECSORT then resumes execution, restores its standard input and standard output handles (which are still open) to their original meanings with *DosDupHandle*, displays a success message on the standard output, and exits to OS/2.

```
        title      EXECSORT -- Run SORT.EXE as Child
        page       55,132
        .286
        .sall


;
; EXECSORT.ASM
;
; Demonstration of use of DosExecPgm to run the OS/2 filter SORT.EXE
; as a child process, redirecting its input to MYFILE.DAT and its
; output to MYFILE.SRT.
;
; Assemble with:  C> masm execsort.asm;
; Link with:  C> link execsort,,,os2,execsort
;
; Usage is:  C> execsort
;
; Copyright (C) 1988 Ray Duncan
;

stdin    equ    0              ; standard input device
stdout   equ    1              ; standard output device
stderr   equ    2              ; standard error device

cr       equ    0dh            ; ASCII carriage return
lf       equ    0ah            ; ASCII linefeed

         extrn   DosClose:far
         extrn   DosDupHandle:far
         extrn   DosExecPgm:far
         extrn   DosExit:far
         extrn   DosOpen:far
```

(continued)

Figure 16-7. *Assembly language source code for EXECSORT.ASM, which demonstrates use of a filter as a child process. This program redirects the standard input and standard output handles to files, invokes* DosExecPgm *to run SORT.EXE as a child process, and then restores the original meaning of the standard input and standard output handles.*

Figure 16-7. *continued*

```
        extrn    DosWrite:far

jerr    macro    target          ;; Macro to test AX
        local    zero            ;; and jump if AX nonzero
        or       ax,ax
        jz       zero            ;; Uses JMP DISP16 to avoid
        jmp      target          ;; branch out of range errors
zero:
        endm



DGROUP  group    _DATA
_DATA   segment  word public 'DATA'

iname   db       'MYFILE.DAT',0  ; name of input file
oname   db       'MYFILE.SRT',0  ; name of output file

ihandle dw       ?               ; handle for input file
ohandle dw       ?               ; handle for output file

action  dw       ?               ; receives DosOpen action

oldin   dw       -1              ; dup of old stdin handle
oldout  dw       -1              ; dup of old stdout handle

newin   dw       stdin           ; forced to track ihandle
newout  dw       stdout          ; forced to track ohandle

pname   db       'SORT.EXE',0    ; pathname of SORT filter

objbuff db       64              ; receives failing dynlink
objbuff_len equ $-objbuff

pcodes  dw       0,0             ; PID, exit code of child

msg     db       cr,lf,'SORT was executed as child.',cr,lf
msg_len equ $-msg

_DATA   ends


_TEXT   segment  word public 'CODE'

        assume   cs:_TEXT,ds:DGROUP
```

(continued)

Figure 16-7. *continued*

```
main    proc    far                 ; entry point from OS/2

                                    ; prepare stdin and stdout
                                    ; handles for child SORT...

                                    ; dup handle for stdin...
        push    stdin               ; standard input handle
        push    ds                  ; receives new handle
        push    offset DGROUP:oldin
        call    DosDupHandle        ; transfer to OS/2
        jerr    main1               ; exit if error

                                    ; dup handle for stdout...
        push    stdout              ; standard output handle
        push    ds                  ; receives new handle
        push    offset DGROUP:oldout
        call    DosDupHandle        ; transfer to OS/2
        jerr    main1               ; exit if error

                                    ; open input file...
        push    ds                  ; address of filename
        push    offset DGROUP:iname
        push    ds                  ; receives file handle
        push    offset DGROUP:ihandle
        push    ds                  ; receives DosOpen action
        push    offset DGROUP:action
        push    0                   ; file size (not used)
        push    0
        push    0                   ; attribute (not used)
        push    1                   ; action: open if exists
                                    ;         fail if doesn't
        push    40h                 ; access: read-only
        push    0                   ; reserved DWORD 0
        push    0
        call    DosOpen             ; transfer to OS/2
        jerr    main1               ; exit if error

                                    ; create output file...
        push    ds                  ; address of filename
        push    offset DGROUP:oname
        push    ds                  ; receives file handle
        push    offset DGROUP:ohandle
        push    ds                  ; receives DOSOPEN action
        push    offset DGROUP:action
        push    0                   ; initial file size
        push    0
```

(continued)

Figure 16-7. *continued*

```
        push    0                   ; attribute = normal
        push    12h                 ; action: create/replace
        push    41h                 ; access: write-only
        push    0                   ; reserved DWORD 0
        push    0
        call    DosOpen             ; transfer to OS/2
        jerr    main1               ; exit if error

                                    ; make stdin track
                                    ; input file handle...
        push    ihandle             ; handle from DOSOPEN
        push    ds                  ; standard input handle
        push    offset DGROUP:newin
        call    DosDupHandle        ; transfer to OS/2
        jerr    main1               ; exit if error

                                    ; make stdout track
                                    ; output file handle...
        push    ohandle             ; handle from DOSOPEN
        push    ds                  ; standard output handle
        push    offset DGROUP:newout
        call    DosDupHandle        ; transfer to OS/2
        jerr    main1               ; exit if error

                                    ; run SORT.EXE as child...
        push    ds                  ; receives failing dynlink
        push    offset DGROUP:objbuff
        push    objbuff_len         ; length of buffer
        push    0                   ; 0 = synchronous execution
        push    0                   ; argument strings pointer
        push    0
        push    0                   ; environment pointer
        push    0
        push    ds                  ; receives PID, exit code
        push    offset DGROUP:pcodes
        push    ds                  ; child program pathname
        push    offset DGROUP:pname
        call    DosExecPgm          ; transfer to OS/2
        jerr    main1               ; exit if error

                                    ; restore stdin handle
                                    ; to original meaning...
        push    oldin               ; dup of original stdin
        push    ds                  ; standard input handle
        push    offset DGROUP:newin
        call    DosDupHandle        ; transfer to OS/2
        jerr    main1               ; exit if error
```

(continued)

Figure 16-7. *continued*

```
                          ; restore stdout handle
                          ; to original meaning...
        push    oldout    ; dup of original stdout
        push    ds        ; standard output handle
        push    offset DGROUP:newout
        call    DosDupHandle ; transfer to OS/2
        jerr    main1     ; exit if error
        push    oldin     ; close dup of stdin
        call    DosClose  ; transfer to OS/2
        jerr    main1     ; exit if error

        push    oldout    ; close dup of stdout
        call    DosClose  ; transfer to OS/2
        jerr    main1     ; exit if error

        push    ihandle   ; close input file
        call    DosClose  ; transfer to OS/2
        jerr    main1     ; exit if error

        push    ohandle   ; close output file
        call    DosClose  ; transfer to OS/2
        jerr    main1     ; exit if error

                          ; display success message...
        push    stdout    ; standard output handle
        push    ds        ; address of message
        push    offset DGROUP:msg
        push    msg_len   ; length of message
        push    ds        ; receives bytes written
        push    offset DGROUP:action
        call    DosWrite  ; transfer to OS/2
        jerr    main1     ; exit if error

                          ; exit point if no errors
        push    1         ; terminate all threads
        push    0         ; exit code = 0 (success)
        call    DosExit   ; transfer to OS/2

main1:                    ; exit point if error
        push    1         ; terminate all threads
        push    1         ; exit code = 1 (error)
        call    DosExit

main    endp

_TEXT   ends

        end     main      ; defines entry point
```

To assemble the file EXECSORT.ASM into the file EXECSORT.OBJ, enter the following command:

```
[C:\] MASM EXECSORT.ASM;  <Enter>
```

To build the executable file EXECSORT.EXE from the files EXECSORT.OBJ, EXECSORT.DEF (Figure 16-8), and the import library OS2.LIB, enter the following command:

```
[C:\] LINK EXECSORT,,,OS2,EXECSORT  <Enter>
```

```
NAME EXECSORT NOTWINDOWCOMPAT
PROTMODE
STACKSIZE 4096
```

Figure 16-8. *EXECSORT.DEF, the module definition for EXECSORT.EXE.*

DEVICE DRIVERS

Device drivers are OS/2 modules that issue commands directly to peripheral devices and cause data to be transferred between those devices and RAM. They are thus the most hardware-dependent layer of OS/2. Drivers shield the operating system kernel from the need to deal with hardware I/O port addresses and variable characteristics (such as number of tracks per disk or sectors per track) of peripheral devices, in the same way that the kernel in turn shields application programs from the details of file and memory management.

By convention, OS/2 device drivers reside in individual disk files that have the extension SYS. The essential or *base* drivers—the keyboard, display, disk, printer, and clock drivers—are always loaded during the boot process. Other, optional device drivers can be loaded by *DEVICE* directives in the CONFIG.SYS file and are referred to as *installable* drivers. In reality, however, all OS/2 drivers have the same physical and logical structure and the same interface to the OS/2 kernel, and they must all be incorporated into the system at boot time.

OS/2 device drivers are similar in many ways to both MS-DOS and XENIX/UNIX device drivers, but they have a number of unique capabilities and requirements. The experienced MS-DOS programmer, in particular, must be wary of terminology that sounds familiar—the associated driver function might be vastly different. A full-fledged OS/2 driver for any device is invariably more complex than its MS-DOS equivalent.

Unique Aspects of OS/2 Drivers

Six features of OS/2 device drivers have no counterpart under MS-DOS:

- The ability to handle more than one request at a time
- The availability of OS/2 kernel services and inter-driver communication

- Bimodal operation

- Support for IBM ROM BIOS–equivalent services to real mode applications

- Support for device monitors

- The ability to "deinstall" on demand

MS-DOS is a single-tasking operating system, and under normal circumstances, a maximum of one I/O operation can be in progress. Consequently, MS-DOS drivers are easy to write because the code need not be reentrant and polled I/O can be used whenever it is convenient. In OS/2, however, multiple processes can be active simultaneously, and each process can contain multiple threads that are issuing I/O requests independently. A device driver *must,* therefore, be reentrant and must be able to manage overlapping I/O requests for the same device. And to keep the cost in CPU cycles to a minimum, the driver must take full advantage of the interrupt and DMA capabilities of its device.

OS/2's multitasking character does, however, yield some benefits for drivers. Under MS-DOS, device drivers must be self-contained. If, at the same time that it is carrying out an I/O request from the kernel, an MS-DOS driver requests a different operation from the kernel, the context of the original request is destroyed, and the system crashes. In contrast, most OS/2 kernel services are fully reentrant, and OS/2 can provide a battery of services to device drivers much as it does to application programs (although the nature of the services is, of course, much different). These services are called Device Driver Helpers, or DevHlp functions. In OS/2 version 1.1 drivers can also call each other directly through *inter-driver communication* (IDC) entry points.

The term *bimodal operation* stems from OS/2's requirement that its device drivers be capable of servicing both I/O requests and hardware interrupts in either real mode or protected mode. Bimodality improves performance by reducing the number of mode switches — for example, if the CPU is in real mode at the completion of an operation that was started in protected mode, the driver need not switch back to protected mode to service an interrupt. OS/2 assists the driver to achieve bimodal operation by providing it with special bimodal pointers and other services, which will be discussed later in the chapter.

OS/2 drivers must contain ROM BIOS support because many MS-DOS applications call the ROM BIOS directly rather than performing all their I/O through documented MS-DOS services—either to obtain increased performance or to gain functionality that MS-DOS does not offer (EGA/VGA palette programming, for example). To support such applications in DOS compatibility mode, an OS/2 driver must capture the software interrupt vectors that are used to invoke ROM BIOS services for its device. It can then either interlock the ROM BIOS routines to prevent interference with the execution of protected mode applications, or substitute a new set of routines that provide equivalent services.

Device monitors are an OS/2 innovation that allow you to write and install keyboard enhancers, macro-expanders, print spoolers, and similar utilities in a hardware-independent manner. An application program that wants to filter the data stream of a particular character device driver can register as a monitor for that device. Acting as the intermediary, the OS/2 kernel asks the driver whether it wants to accept the monitor registration. If the driver consents, it cooperates with the kernel to pass each character that it reads from or writes to the device through a buffer belonging to the monitor program, which can add, delete, or substitute characters at its discretion. Device monitors are discussed in detail in Chapter 18.

Last, OS/2 driver support for deinstallation allows efficient use of memory and a more controlled environment than MS-DOS. Under MS-DOS, you can supersede a character device driver simply by installing another driver with the same logical device name; the first driver loaded has no way to prevent being superseded, and the memory it occupied is simply lost. Under OS/2, if a driver is loaded that has the same logical name as a previously loaded driver, the kernel asks the previous driver whether it is willing to be replaced. The first driver can agree to the request and release any interrupts and other system resources that it owns, after which its memory is reclaimed and the new driver is allowed to initialize itself. Alternatively, the first driver can refuse to deinstall, and the kernel then terminates installation of the new driver.

Device Driver Types

OS/2 device drivers are categorized into two groups: *block device drivers* and *character device drivers*. A driver's membership in one of these groups determines the way OS/2 views the associated device and the particular functions the driver itself must support.

Character device drivers control peripheral devices, such as terminals or printers, that perform input and output operations one character (or byte) at a time. A particular character device driver ordinarily supports a single hardware unit, although a given SYS file can contain more than one character device driver. Each character device has a 1- to 8-character logical name; an application program can "open" the device by name for input or output (or both) as though it were a file. The logical name is strictly a means of identifying the driver to OS/2 and has no physical equivalent on the device.

Block device drivers control peripheral devices that transfer data in chunks rather than byte by byte. Block devices are usually randomly addressable devices, such as disk drives, but they can also be sequential in nature, such as magnetic tape drives. A block driver can support more than one physical unit and can also map two or more logical units onto a single physical unit (such as a partitioned fixed disk).

OS/2 assigns single-letter drive identifiers (A, B, and so forth) to block devices, instead of logical names. The letter assigned to a given block device is determined solely by the order in which the block drivers are loaded. The total number of letters assigned to a driver is determined by the number of logical units that the driver supports.

Device Driver Modes

Whenever an OS/2 device driver has control of the CPU, it is said to be executing in one of four different *modes*: *kernel mode, interrupt mode, user mode,* or *init mode*. Understanding these modes and their implications is vital to writing an OS/2 device driver because the current mode determines the kernel services (DevHlps) available to a driver and the actions that the driver can take.

A driver is in kernel mode when the kernel calls the driver's *strategy* entry point (explained later) to obtain information or to start an I/O operation, usually as the immediate result of an API call by an application. In kernel mode, the driver executes in ring 0 with nearly every DevHlp service available to it.

A driver executes in interrupt mode as the result of a hardware interrupt. The interrupt is initially fielded by the kernel, which saves all registers, sets DS to point to the driver's data segment, and then transfers control to the driver's interrupt handler. In interrupt mode, the driver also executes in ring 0 but has only a subset of DevHlp services available.

The driver executes in user mode when it is entered as a result of a software interrupt by an application executing in the DOS compatibility environment. The only drivers that must concern themselves with this mode are those that must provide IBM ROM BIOS–equivalent services in a manner consistent with the multitasking and memory protection requirements of OS/2. Because a driver runs in user mode only when the CPU is in real mode, the concept of privilege levels is irrelevant, but you can think of the driver as executing in ring 0 because no protection mechanisms prevail. Relatively few DevHlp services are available to the driver in user mode.

A driver runs in init mode only once—when the kernel calls the driver to initialize itself immediately after the driver is loaded during the boot process. In init mode, the driver runs as though it were an application program with I/O privilege (IOPL). A limited set of dynlink API calls, as well as a subset of the DevHlp services, are available to a driver in init mode.

Two additional terms that pertain to a driver's execution mode are *task time* and *interrupt time*. A driver is executing at task time when it is called *synchronously*—as the direct result of an application API request or a real mode software interrupt; this context would include both the user mode and kernel mode, as described above. Interrupt time refers to the *asynchronous* invocation of a driver routine—as the result of an external hardware event. At interrupt time, the current CPU mode, process, and LDT are unpredictable.

Device Driver Structure

An OS/2 device driver has three major components: the *device driver header*, the *strategy routine*, and the *interrupt routine*.

The Device Driver Header

The device driver header always appears at the start of the device driver's near data segment. The header contains information about the driver that the OS/2 kernel can inspect when it needs to satisfy an application program's I/O request (Figure 17-1 on the following page).

The first element of the header is a pointer to the next driver in the system's chain of all device drivers. This pointer is initialized to –1, –1; the system fills in the true value when the driver is loaded. If you include multiple drivers and headers in a single file, link the headers together and initialize only the last header's link field to –1, –1.

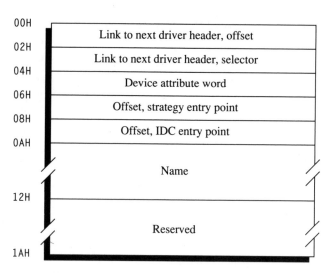

00H	Link to next driver header, offset
02H	Link to next driver header, selector
04H	Device attribute word
06H	Offset, strategy entry point
08H	Offset, IDC entry point
0AH	
	Name
12H	
	Reserved
1AH	

Figure 17-1. *OS/2 device driver header. In character device drivers, the* Name *field contains the logical name of the device padded with spaces if necessary to a length of 8 bytes. In block device drivers, the first byte of the* Name *field contains the number of logical units supported by the driver (filled in by OS/2); the remaining 7 bytes of the name field are not used.*

The other important components of the header are a word (16 bits) of device driver attribute flags, the offsets of the driver's strategy routine and IDC entry point, and the logical device name (for a character device such as PRN or COM1) or the number of logical units (for a block device). When present, the device name must be left-justified, all uppercase, and padded with spaces to a length of eight characters.

The device attribute word in the header (Figure 17-2) defines the driver's function level and indicates whether it controls a character or a block device, supports certain optional driver functions, and reads or writes IBM-compatible disk media. The least significant four bits determine whether OS/2 should use that driver as the standard input, standard output, clock, or NUL device; as you might expect, each of these four bits should be set on only one driver at a time.

Examples of source code for device driver headers appear in Figures 17-3, 17-4, and 17-5, which are all on p. 354.

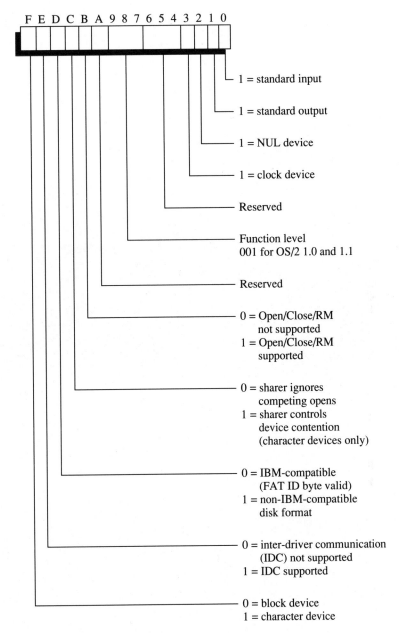

Figure 17-2. *The device attribute word in the device driver header, which describes the characteristics and capabilities of the associated driver.*

```
header   dd      -1              ; link to next driver
         dw      8880h           ; device attribute word
                                 ; bit 15 = 1 character device
                                 ; bit 11 = 1 Open/Close/RM
                                 ; bits 7-9 = 001 driver level
         dw      Strat           ; strategy entry point
         dw      0               ; IDC entry point
         db      'COM1    '      ; logical device name
         db      8 dup (0)       ; (reserved)
```

Figure 17-3. *Source code for an OS/2 character device driver header.*

```
header   dd      -1              ; link to next driver
         dw      0880h           ; device attribute word
                                 ; bit 15 = 0 block device
                                 ; bit 11 = 1 Open/Close/RM
                                 ; bits 7-9 = 001 driver level
         dw      Strat           ; strategy entry point
         dw      0               ; (reserved)
         db      0               ; units (filled in by OS/2)
         db      15 dup (0)      ; (reserved)
```

Figure 17-4. *Source code for an OS/2 block device driver header.*

```
                                 ; header for first device...
head1    dd      head2           ; link to next driver
         dw      8880h           ; device attribute word
         dw      Strat1          ; strategy entry point
         dw      0               ; IDC entry point
         db      'COM1    '      ; logical device name
         db      8 dup (0)       ; (reserved)

                                 ; header for second device...
head2    dd      -1              ; link to next driver
         dw      8880h           ; device attribute word
         dw      Strat2          ; strategy entry point
         dw      0               ; IDC entry point
         db      'COM2    '      ; logical device name
         db      8 dup (0)       ; (reserved)
```

Figure 17-5. *Source code demonstrating the linkage of two device headers in the same driver file.*

The Strategy Routine

The OS/2 kernel initiates an I/O operation by calling the driver's strategy routine (whose offset is in the device driver header) with the address of a data structure called a *request packet* in registers ES:BX. The first 13 bytes of the request packet have a fixed format and are known as the *static* portion; they are followed by data that varies according to the operation being requested (Figure 17-6). To support multiple concurrent I/O requests, the driver maintains a private queue of request packets for its pending operations with the aid of the kernel DevHlp functions.

Note that the system passes the request packet address in the form of a bimodal pointer. In a bimodal pointer, the protected mode selector is identical to the corresponding real mode segment so the same address is valid in either real mode or protected mode. As a general rule, OS/2 can generate bimodal pointers only for data structures that it creates or owns (such as request packets) because the data must be located in the first 640 KB of memory.

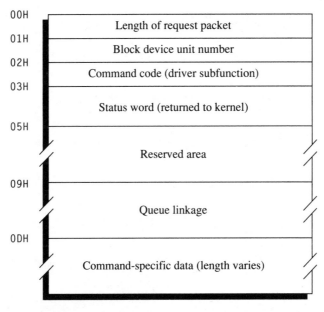

Figure 17-6. *A prototypal OS/2 device driver request packet. The OS/2 kernel requests a driver operation by passing the bimodal address of a request packet containing operation-specific parameters, and the driver communicates the results of the operation to the kernel by placing the status and other information in the same packet.*

The crucial fields of the request packet (in the static portion) are the *command code,* which selects a particular driver function, and the *status word* (Figure 17-7), which is the primary means by which the driver returns information to the kernel. The driver can carry out many functions immediately—at the time of the strategy call; in such cases, it simply places any necessary information into the request packet, sets the Done bit in the status word, and returns to the kernel. If it encounters an error, the driver also sets the Error bit in the status word, along with the appropriate code for the error type (Figure 17-8).

However, some driver functions, such as *Read* and *Write,* involve an unpredictable amount of delay and cannot be carried out during the strategy call without interfering with multitasking; they must be completed with the aid of the interrupt routine (discussed below). If the device is idle, the strategy routine starts the I/O operation and then returns control to the kernel so that other work in the system can proceed. If the device is busy, the new request packet is instead chained onto the driver's *request queue* or *work list.* Incidentally, a block device driver is expected to sort its work list in such a way that the average transfer time is minimized. (A kernel DevHlp is available to perform this sorting.)

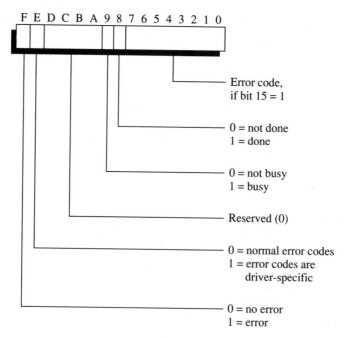

Figure 17-7. *The request packet status word returned to the kernel by the driver after an operation is completed.*

Error Code	Description
00H	Write-protect violation
01H	Unknown unit
02H	Device not ready
03H	Unknown command
04H	CRC error
05H	Bad drive request structure length
06H	Seek error
07H	Unknown medium
08H	Sector not found
09H	Printer out of paper
0AH	Write fault
0BH	Read fault
0CH	General failure
0DH	Change disk
0EH	Reserved
0FH	Reserved
10H	Uncertain medium
11H	Character I/O call interrupted
12H	Monitors not supported
13H	Invalid parameter

Figure 17-8. *The error codes used in the request packet status word. Error 0DH can be returned by drivers that map more than one logical unit onto the same physical drive. It causes the kernel to prompt the user to switch disks.*

*A driver should return error 10H (*Uncertain medium*) when a drive-not-ready condition is detected, when accessing removable media without change-line support and a delay of more than two seconds occurs between accesses, or when accessing a drive with change-line support and the change-line indicates that the disk might have been replaced. The driver should continue to return error 10H for all requests until it receives a* Reset Media *request packet (command code 17).*

The Interrupt Routine

The interrupt routine is entered from the kernel as a result of a hardware interrupt from the physical device, when an I/O operation either has been completed or has been aborted because of a hardware error. Because hardware interrupts are by nature asynchronous and unpredictable, an OS/2 device driver must be capable of servicing an interrupt properly in either protected mode or real mode. The interrupt routine queries the peripheral controller to determine the outcome of the I/O operation, sets the appropriate status and error information in the request packet, calls the DevHlp routine *DevDone* to signal the kernel that the I/O is complete, and removes the request packet from its request queue.

The interrupt routine then examines the request queue to determine whether additional requests are pending for the device. If the request queue is not empty, the interrupt routine removes the request packet from the head of the queue and starts the next I/O operation. It then clears the Carry flag and exits to the kernel with a far return.

If multiple devices (and their drivers) share the same interrupt level, the kernel calls each driver's interrupt routine in turn until one indicates its acceptance of the interrupt by clearing the Carry flag. The other interrupt routines must return with the Carry flag set.

The Command Code Functions

A total of 27 command codes are defined for OS/2 device drivers, some of which are reserved for future expansion or for backward compatibility with MS-DOS drivers. The command codes and the names of their associated functions are shown in Figure 17-9.

Some command codes are relevant only for character drivers and some only for block device drivers; a few are used in both. Whichever type of driver you are writing, you need to supply an executable routine for each command code, even if the routine does nothing but set the Done bit in the request packet status word. The following pages describe each of the command codes in detail.

Command Code	Hex Value	Function Name	Character Devices	Block Devices
0	00H	Init (Initialization)	C	B
1	01H	Media Check		B
2	02H	Build BPB		B
3	03H	Reserved		
4	04H	Read (Input)	C	B
5	05H	Nondestructive Read	C	
6	06H	Input Status	C	
7	07H	Flush Input Buffers	C	
8	08H	Write (Output)	C	B
9	09H	Write with Verify	C	B
10	0AH	Output Status	C	
11	0BH	Flush Output Buffers	C	
12	0CH	Reserved		
13	0DH	Device Open	C	B

(continued)

Figure 17-9. *The strategy routine functions selected by the command code field of the request packet.*

Figure 17-9. *continued*

Command Code	Hex Value	Function Name	Character Devices	Block Devices
14	0EH	Device Close	C	B
15	0FH	Removable Media		B
16	10H	Generic IOCtl	C	B
17	11H	Reset Media		B
18	12H	Get Logical Drive Map		B
19	13H	Set Logical Drive Map		B
20	14H	DeInstall Driver	C	
21	15H	Reserved		
22	16H	Partitionable Fixed Disk		B
23	17H	Get Fixed Disk Map		B
24	18H	Reserved		
25	19H	Reserved		
26	1AH	Reserved		

The *Init* Function

The *Init* (Initialization) routine (command code 0) for a driver is called only once — when the driver is loaded. It must ensure that the peripheral device controlled by the driver is present and functional, perform any necessary hardware initialization (such as a reset on a printer), register with the system for any interrupts that the driver will need later, and initialize driver data structures (such as semaphores or the request queue). The parameters and results for this command code are summarized in Figure 17-10 on the following page.

The kernel passes two addresses to the driver in the *Init* request packet: a bimodal pointer to the DevHlp common entry point (discussed in detail later) and a pointer to the variable part of the *DEVICE=* line (from the CONFIG.SYS file) that caused the driver to be loaded. The line is read-only and is terminated by a null (zero) byte; the driver can scan it for switches or other parameters that may influence its operation. For example, if the driver TINYDISK.SYS is loaded with the following line in the CONFIG.SYS file:

```
DEVICE=tinydisk.sys 1024K
```

the request packet contains a pointer to the following sequence of bytes:

```
74 69 6E 79 64 69 73 6B 2E 73 79 73 20 31 30 32 34 4B 00
```

Block drivers are also passed the drive code that will be assigned to their first logical unit (0 = A, 1 = B, and so forth).

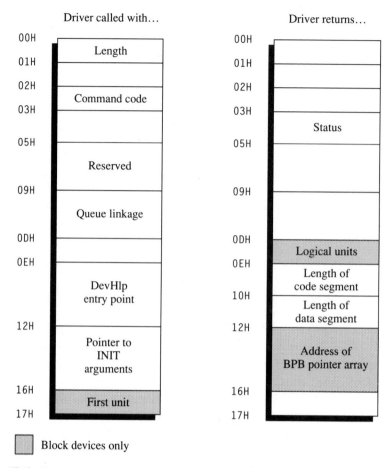

Driver called with...

00H	Length
01H	
02H	Command code
03H	
05H	Reserved
09H	Queue linkage
0DH	
0EH	DevHlp entry point
12H	Pointer to INIT arguments
16H	First unit
17H	

Driver returns...

00H	
01H	
02H	
03H	Status
05H	
09H	
0DH	Logical units
0EH	Length of code segment
10H	Length of data segment
12H	Address of BPB pointer array
16H	
17H	

☐ Block devices only

Figure 17-10. *Request packet format for the* Init *function (command code 0).*

The *Init* function must return the status and the amount of memory that it wants to reserve for the driver's code and data segments. This allocation allows the driver to discard initialization code and data (thus minimizing its memory requirements) by positioning these items at the end of their respective segments. A block device driver must also return the number of logical units it supports and the address of a *BPB pointer array*.

The number of units returned by a block driver is used to assign device identifiers. Suppose, for example, drivers are already present for four block devices (drive codes 0 through 3, corresponding to drive identifiers A through D). If a new driver is initialized that supports four units, it will be assigned the drive numbers 4 through 7 (corresponding to the drive names E through H). Although the device driver header also contains a field for the number of units, OS/2 does not inspect that field during initialization; instead, the system *sets* that header field using information returned by the *Init* function.

The BPB pointer array is an array of word offsets to BIOS parameter blocks (Figure 17-11). The array must contain one entry for each logical unit that the driver supports, although all entries can point to the same BPB to conserve memory. During the boot sequence, OS/2 scans the BPBs of every block device to determine the largest sector size used in the system; it then uses this information to set the size of the buffers in the system's disk cache.

If the *Init* routine finds that the driver's hardware device is missing or defective, it can cancel driver installation by returning the following values in the request packet: zero for the number of units, zero for the code and data segment lengths, and a status of 810CH (Error flag, Done flag, and the error code for a general failure).

If the driver's data segment (which has a maximum size of 64 KB) is not large enough, the *Init* routine can call the DevHlp function *AllocPhys* to reserve additional memory. This additional memory can be either above or below the 1 MB boundary and is not movable or swappable. The driver itself is always loaded in the first 640 KB of memory. When the driver is called in real mode, it has faster access to memory allocated below 1 MB than to memory above that boundary, but allocating low memory decreases the

Offset	Length	Contents
00H	2	Bytes per sector
02H	1	Sectors per allocation unit (cluster), always a power of two
03H	2	Reserved sectors (starting at logical sector 0)
05H	1	Number of file allocation tables
06H	2	Number of root directory entries
08H	2	Number of sectors in logical volume (including boot sector, FAT, etc.)
0AH	1	Medium descriptor byte
0BH	2	Number of sectors per FAT
0DH	2	Sectors per track
0FH	2	Number of heads
11H	4	Number of hidden sectors before reserved sectors
15H	4	Total sectors in logical volume (if word at offset 08H = 0)
19H	6	Reserved

Figure 17-11. *Structure of BIOS parameter block (BPB).*

amount of space available for a program running in DOS compatibility mode. In general, a driver should keep data items to which it needs frequent and rapid access in its near data segment or in additional memory allocated below 1 MB, and it should put large or infrequently used data structures and buffers above 1 MB.

Unlike the other command code routines, which run in kernel mode, the *Init* routine runs as though it were an application with I/O privilege (IOPL). Consequently (and also unlike all other command code routines) the *Init* routine can invoke certain file access and internationalization API functions, which are listed in Figure 17-12. These assist the driver in finding and loading font files or other device-dependent information and in displaying error or status messages. When running on an IBM PS/2 or compatible, the *Init* routine can also call ABIOS services.

Function	Description
DosBeep	Generates tone
DosCaseMap	Translates ASCII string in place
DosChgFilePtr	Moves file read/write pointer
DosClose	Closes file or device
DosDelete	Deletes file
DosDevConfig	Returns system hardware configuration
DosDevIOCtl	Device-specific commands and information
DosFindClose	Releases directory search handle
DosFindFirst	Searches for first matching file
DosFindNext	Searches for next matching file
DosGetCtryInfo	Returns internationalization information
DosGetDBCSEv	Returns DBCS environment vector
DosGetEnv	Returns pointer to environment
DosGetMessage	Returns text for system message
DosOpen	Opens file or device
DosPutMessage	Sends message to file or device
DosQCurDir	Returns current directory
DosQCurDisk	Returns current disk drive
DosQFileInfo	Returns file information
DosQFileMode	Returns file attributes
DosRead	Reads from file or device
DosWrite	Writes to file or device

Figure 17-12. *API calls that can be called during driver initialization (command code 0).*

The *Media Check* Function

The *Media Check* function (command code 1) is used in block device drivers only. The parameters with which the driver is called and the results that the function returns are summarized in Figure 17-13.

The OS/2 kernel calls the *Media Check* function before it services a drive access call other than a simple file read or write—such as a file open, close, rename, or delete. It passes the medium ID byte (Figure 17-14 on the following page) for the disk that OS/2 assumes is in the drive. The driver returns a code indicating whether the medium has been changed since the last read or write. This change code has one of the following values:

Code	Meaning
−1	Medium has been changed
0	Don't know if medium has been changed
1	Medium has not been changed

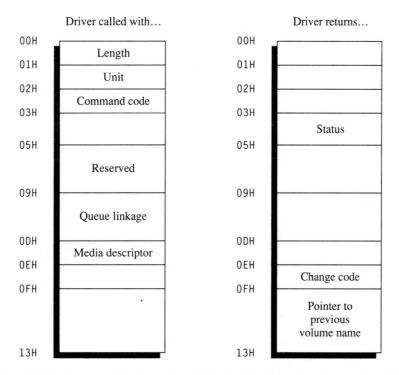

Figure 17-13. *Request packet format for the* Media Check *function (command code 1).*

If the disk has not been changed, OS/2 accesses the disk without first reread-ing its FAT. Otherwise, OS/2 calls the driver's *Build BPB* function (see below) and then reads the disk's FAT and directory.

If the Open/Close/RM flag (bit 11) is set in the attribute word of the device driver header, the *Media Check* function must also return a pointer to the ASCIIZ volume label for the previous disk in the drive (regardless of the change code). If the driver does not have the volume label, it can return a pointer to the ASCIIZ string *NO NAME*. This allows OS/2 to prompt the user to insert the correct disk if the disk has been changed and the system's buffers hold data that has not been written out.

Value	Disk Type(s)
0F0H	3.5", 2-sided, 18 sectors
0F8H	Fixed disk
0F9H	3.5", 2-sided, 9 sectors
	5.25", 2-sided, 15 sectors
0FCH	5.25", 1-sided, 9 sectors
0FDH	5.25", 2-sided, 9 sectors
	8", 1-sided, single-density
0FEH	5.25", 1-sided, 8 sectors
	8", 1-sided, single-density
	8", 2-sided, double-density
0FFH	5.25", 2-sided, 8 sectors

Figure 17-14. *Medium descriptor bytes for IBM-compatible disks. (The table includes 8-inch disk format codes for historical reasons only.)*

The *Build BPB* Function

The *Build BPB* function (command code 2) is defined for block devices only. OS/2 calls this function after a *Media Check* request returns the *Medium changed* or *Don't know* codes. The parameters with which the driver is called and the results it returns are summarized in Figure 17-15.

The *Build BPB* routine receives a pointer in the request packet to a 1-sector buffer. If bit 13 (the Non-IBM-Format bit) in the attribute word of the device driver header is clear, the buffer contains the first sector of the disk's FAT, with the medium ID byte in the first byte of the buffer. If bit 13 is set, the buffer contains the boot sector from the disk (logical sector 0). The driver should not modify the buffer contents.

The *Build BPB* function must return a status and a pointer to a BIOS parame-ter block (Figure 17-11 on p. 361) for the disk format indicated by the medium ID byte. The kernel uses the information in the BPB to interpret the disk structure, and the driver itself uses the BPB to translate logical sector addresses into physical track, sector, and head addresses. The *Build BPB* function should also read the volume label off the disk and save it.

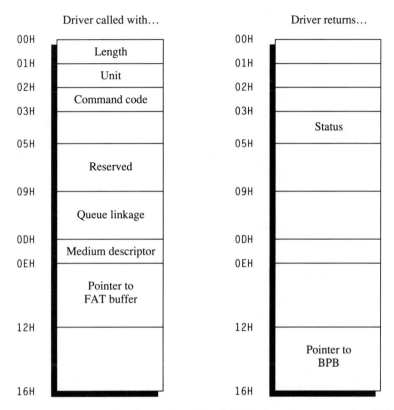

Figure 17-15. *Request packet format for the* Build BPB *function (command code 2).*

The *Read*, *Write*, and *Write with Verify* Functions

The *Read* function (command code 4) transfers data from the device to the specified memory address. The *Write* function (command code 8) transfers data from the specified memory address to the device. The *Write with Verify* function (command code 9) transfers data from the specified memory address to the device and then verifies that the data was transferred correctly (preferably by reading the data back and comparing it to the original data). The OS/2 kernel calls *Write with Verify*, instead of *Write*, whenever the system's global Verify flag is enabled with the VERIFY command or with the API function *DosSetVerify*. The parameters and results for these command codes are summarized in Figure 17-16 on the following page.

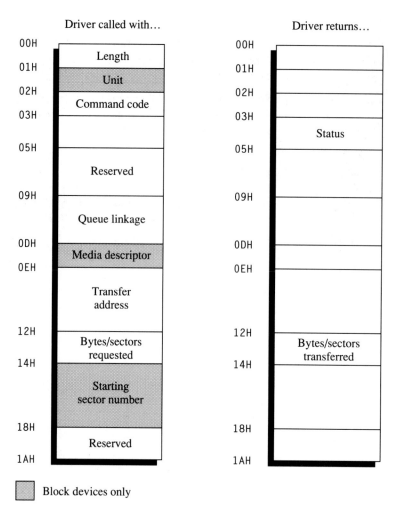

Driver called with...

00H	Length
01H	Unit
02H	Command code
03H	
05H	Reserved
09H	Queue linkage
0DH	Media descriptor
0EH	Transfer address
12H	Bytes/sectors requested
14H	Starting sector number
18H	Reserved
1AH	

Driver returns...

00H	
01H	
02H	
03H	Status
05H	
09H	
0DH	
0EH	
12H	Bytes/sectors transferred
14H	
18H	
1AH	

▨ Block devices only

Figure 17-16. *Request packet format for the* Read, Write, *and* Write with Verify *functions (command codes 4, 8, and 9). Transfer address is locked and converted to a 32-bit physical address by kernel.*

The OS/2 kernel calls all three of these driver functions with the memory address and length of the data to be transferred. The memory address is a locked 32-bit *physical address*; that is, the memory is not swappable or movable, and the segment:offset or selector:offset pair has been converted to a number in the range 00000000H through 00FFFFFFH. (Physical addresses treat the 16 MB of physical RAM as a linear array of bytes.) The driver can use DevHlp functions, which are described later, to convert the physical address into a far pointer appropriate for the current CPU mode. In the case of block device drivers, the kernel also passes the drive unit code, the starting logical sector number, and the medium ID byte for the disk. The driver uses the drive's BPB to translate the logical sector number into a physical track, head, and sector.

When the *Read, Write,* or *Write with Verify* operation is complete, the functions must return (or the interrupt routine must return on their behalf) a status and the number of bytes or sectors actually transferred. If an I/O error occurs, the Done flag, Error flag, error type, and the number of bytes or sectors successfully transferred prior to the error must be returned to the kernel. The kernel then unlocks the memory.

The *Nondestructive Read* Function

The *Nondestructive Read* function (command code 5) is meaningful in DOS compatibility mode and for character devices only. It returns the next character in the driver's internal buffer, without removing that waiting character from the buffer. Its principal use is to let OS/2 check for a Ctrl-C entered at the keyboard. The parameters and results for this command code are summarized in Figure 17-17.

The function returns its result in the Busy bit of the status word. If the driver's input buffer is empty, the function should set the Busy bit. If at least one character is waiting in the input buffer, the function should clear the Busy bit and return the character that would be obtained by a call to the driver's *Read* function, without removing that character from the buffer.

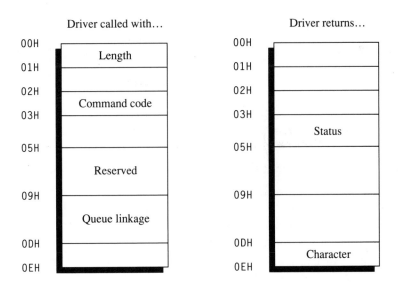

Figure 17-17. *Request packet format for* Nondestructive Read *(command code 5).*

The *Input Status* and *Output Status* Functions

The *Input Status* and *Output Status* (command codes 6 and 10) functions are defined only for character devices. Both return their results in the Busy bit of the status word. The parameters and results for these command codes are summarized in Figure 17-18.

OS/2 calls the *Input Status* function to determine whether characters are waiting, buffered within the driver. The function clears the Busy bit if at least one character is already in the driver's input buffer. It sets the Busy bit if no characters are in the buffer, in which event a *Read* request for one character would not complete immediately. If the driver does not buffer characters internally, the *Input Status* function should always clear the Busy bit so that OS/2 will not wait for a character arrive in the buffer before issuing a *Read* request.

OS/2 uses the *Output Status* function to determine whether a write operation is already in progress for the device. The function clears the Busy bit if the device is idle and if a *Write* request would start immediately, or it sets the Busy bit if a write is already in progress.

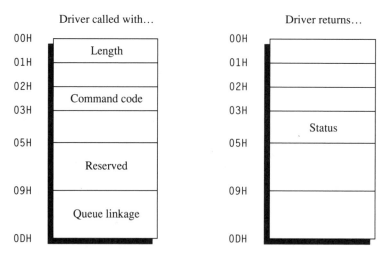

Figure 17-18. *Request packet format for the* Input Status *(command code 6),* Flush Input Buffers *(command code 7),* Output Status *(command code 10), and* Flush Output Buffers *(command code 11) functions.*

The *Flush Input Buffer* and *Flush Output Buffer* Functions

The *Flush Input Buffer* (command code 7) and *Flush Output Buffer* (command code 11) functions are supported only for character device drivers. They simply terminate any read (for *Flush Input*) or write (for *Flush Output*) operations that are in progress, discard any requests that are pending on the driver's work list, and empty the associated buffer. The parameters and results for these command codes are summarized in Figure 17-18.

These functions constitute the driver level support for *DosDevIOCtl* Category 11 Functions 01H (Flush Input Buffer) and 02H (Flush Output Buffer).

The *Device Open* and *Device Close* Functions

The *Device Open* and *Device Close* (command codes 13 and 14) functions are called only if the Open/Close/Removable Media flag (bit 11) is set in the attribute word of the device driver header. If a *Device Open* or *Device Close* request is directed to a block device driver, the request packet includes a unit code. The parameters and results for these command codes are summarized in Figure 17-19.

Each application call to *DosOpen* to open or create a file or to open a character device for input or output results in a *Device Open* request from the kernel to the corresponding device driver. Similarly, each *DosClose* call by an application to close a file or device results in a *Device Close* call by the kernel to the appropriate driver.

On block devices, you can use the *Device Open* and *Device Close* functions to manage local buffering and to maintain a reference count of the number of open files on a device. Whenever this reference count is decremented to

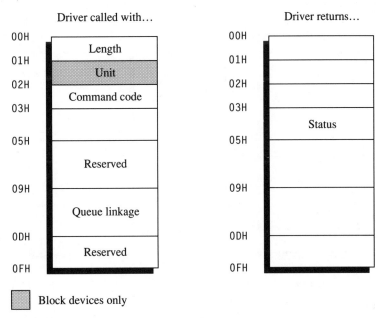

Figure 17-19. *Request packet format for the* Device Open *(command code 13) and* Device Close *(command code 14) functions.*

zero, indicating that all files on the disk have been closed, the driver should flush any internal buffers so that no data is lost if the user proceeds to change disks.

Character device drivers can respond to the *Device Open* and *Device Close* by sending hardware-dependent initialization and post-I/O strings to the associated device (for example, a reset sequence or formfeed character to precede new output, and a formfeed to follow it). If the driver is appropriately designed, an application can inspect or change the strings with *DosDevIOCtl* calls.

When an application issues a call to *DosMonOpen* or *DosMonClose*, the driver receives a special *Device Open* or *Device Close* request packet with bit 3 of the status word set. These functions assist the driver in maintaining its device monitor chain, as described in more detail in Chapter 18.

The *Removable Media* Function

The *Removable Media* function (command code 15) is defined for block devices only. OS/2 does not call this function unless the Open/Close/ Removable Media flag (bit 11) is set in the attribute word of the device driver header. This function constitutes the driver level support for the service that OS/2 provides to application programs with *DosDevIOCtl* Category 8 Function 20H (Check if Block Device Removable). The parameters and results for this command code are summarized in Figure 17-20.

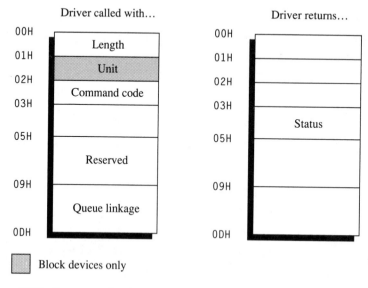

Figure 17-20. *Request packet format for the* Removable Media *(command code 15),* Reset Media *(command code 17), and* DeInstall Driver *(command code 20) functions.*

The only parameter for the *Removable Media* function is the unit code. The function returns its result in the Busy bit of the status word. The Busy bit is set if the disk is fixed; it is cleared if the disk is removable.

The *Generic IOCtl* Function

The *Generic IOCtl* function (command code 16) corresponds to the OS/2 API function *DosDevIOCtl*; it provides a general-purpose high performance channel of direct communication between applications and device drivers. The parameters and results for this command code are summarized in Figure 17-21 on the following page.

In addition to the usual information in the static portion of the request packet, the *Generic IOCtl* function is passed a category (major) code, a function (minor) code, and pointers to a parameter block and a data buffer. The pointers are virtual addresses; the driver is responsible for ensuring that the application is actually authorized to use those virtual addresses. If the request cannot be completed at task time, your driver must ensure later addressability of the parameter block and data buffer by accomplishing the following sequence of steps:

1. Lock the virtual addresses so that the corresponding memory segments will not be moved or swapped by the system's memory manager.

2. Replace the virtual addresses in the request packet with the corresponding physical addresses.

3. When the driver is able to service the request, translate the physical addresses back to virtual addresses that are appropriate for the current mode.

4. When the request has been serviced, unlock the segments.

The driver must interpret the category and function codes in the request packet and the contents of the parameter block or data buffer (or both) to determine which operation it will carry out; subsequently, it sets the status word appropriately and returns any other pertinent information in the application's data buffer.

Services that can be invoked by the *Generic IOCtl* function, if the driver supports them, include configuring a serial port, selecting nonstandard disk formats, reading and writing entire tracks, and formatting and verifying tracks. The *Generic IOCtl* function is designed to allow easy communication between closely coupled applications and custom device drivers, and is open-ended so that it can be used to extend the device driver definition in future versions of OS/2.

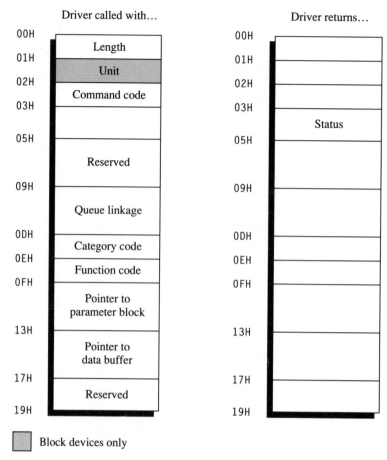

Driver called with...

00H	
	Length
01H	
	Unit
02H	
	Command code
03H	
05H	
	Reserved
09H	
	Queue linkage
0DH	
	Category code
0EH	
	Function code
0FH	
	Pointer to parameter block
13H	
	Pointer to data buffer
17H	
	Reserved
19H	

Driver returns...

00H	
01H	
02H	
03H	Status
05H	
09H	
0DH	
0EH	
0FH	
13H	
17H	
19H	

☐ Block devices only

Figure 17-21. *Request packet format for the* Generic IOCtl *function (command code 16). Both pointers are virtual addresses, with selectors from the current process's LDT. The process's right to use the addresses must be confirmed with the DevHlp function* VerifyAccess, *and the virtual addresses must be locked and converted to physical addresses if request cannot be disposed of at task time.*

The *Reset Media* Function

The *Reset Media* function (command code 17) is defined only for block devices. The function is called with no parameters in the request packet other than the command and unit codes, and it returns only a status to the kernel. The parameters and results for this command code are summarized in Figure 17-20 on p. 370.

When the driver returns an *Uncertain medium* error to a service request, the kernel calls *Reset Media* to inform the driver that it no longer needs to return that error for the drive.

The *Get Logical Drive* and *Set Logical Drive* Functions

The *Get Logical Drive* and *Set Logical Drive* functions (command codes 18 and 19) are defined for block devices only. They correspond to the API services supplied by OS/2 to application programs via *DosDevIOCtl* Category 8, Functions 03H (Set Logical Map) and 21H (Get Logical Map). Both functions are called with a logical unit code in the request packet and must return a status and a logical unit. The parameters and results for these command codes are summarized in Figure 17-22.

The *Get Logical Drive* function is called to determine whether more than one logical unit code is assigned to the same physical device. It returns a code for the last drive letter used to reference the device (1 = A, 2 = B, and so on); if only one drive letter is assigned to the device, the returned unit code should be zero.

The *Set Logical Device* function is called to inform the driver of the next logical drive code that will be used to reference the device. The unit code passed by the OS/2 kernel is zero-based relative to the logical drives supported by this particular driver. The driver performs the requested mapping and returns the logical unit unchanged.

For example, if the driver supports two logical floppy disk units (A and B), and only one physical floppy disk drive exists in the system, then a call to *Set Logical Device* with a unit number of 1 informs the driver that the next read or write request from OS/2 will be directed to logical drive B.

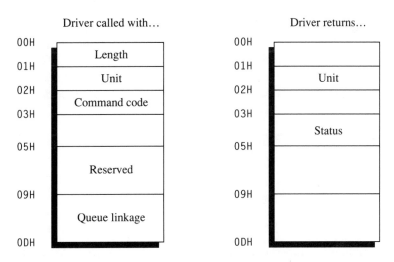

Figure 17-22. *Request packet format for the* Get Logical Drive *and* Set Logical Drive *functions (command codes 18 and 19).*

The *DeInstall Driver* Function

The *DeInstall Driver* function (command code 20) is valid for character devices only. It is called when the OS/2 kernel loads another character device driver with the same logical name as the driver that receives the *DeInstall Driver* request packet. The parameters and results for this command code are summarized in Figure 17-20 on p. 370.

If the current driver refuses the *DeInstall Driver* command, it should return to the kernel with the status word set to 8103H (Error bit, Done bit, and error code *unknown command*). In this event, the system does not load the replacement driver.

If the current driver accepts the *DeInstall Driver* command, allowing itself to be superseded, it must perform the following actions:

- Call the DevHlp function *FreePhys* to release any memory it has previously allocated with *AllocPhys*

- Call the DevHlp function *UnSetIRQ* to release any interrupts it has previously registered with *SetIRQ*

- Relinquish any device logical IDs it has previously acquired by calling the DevHlp function *FreeLIDEntry* (if the driver runs on an IBM PS/2 and uses the ABIOS)

- Perform any other necessary cleanup of system resources, such as semaphores

- Set the Done flag in the status word of the request packet

After the driver accepting the *DeInstall Driver* command returns to the kernel, its code and memory segments are released. If the physical device supported by the driver cannot be told to stop generating interrupts, then the driver must refuse the *DeInstall Driver* operation rather than risk leaving the system without an interrupt handler.

The *Partitionable Fixed Disks* Function

The *Partitionable Fixed Disks* function (command code 22) is defined for block device drivers only. The function returns a status along with the number of physical, partitionable fixed disks that the driver supports. The parameters and results for this command code are shown in Figure 17-23.

The information returned by this function allows the kernel to route the *DosDevIOCtl* Category 9 (Physical Disk Control) requests to the appropriate block device driver.

Driver called with...   Driver returns...

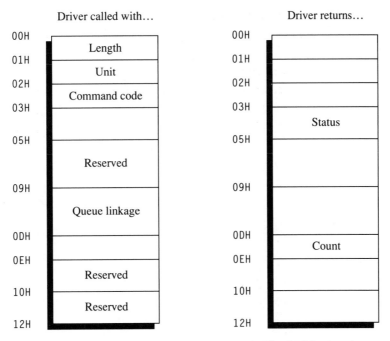

Figure 17-23. *Request packet format for the* Partitionable Fixed Disks *function (command code 22).*

The *Get Fixed Disk/Logical Unit Map* Function

The *Get Fixed Disk/Logical Unit Map* function (command code 23) is defined for block device drivers only. The function is called with the unit number for a physical fixed disk in the request header; this number is calculated on the basis of previous calls to *Partitionable Fixed Disks* (command code 22). The parameters and results for this command code are summarized in Figure 17-24 on the following page.

The device driver is responsible for returning a status and a 4-byte "units-supported bit mask" that describes which of *its own* logical units, numbered from zero, exist on the specified physical drive. The bits in the mask are assigned sequentially from the least significant bit of the first byte (the byte at the lowest address) to the most significant bit of the last byte (the byte at the highest address).

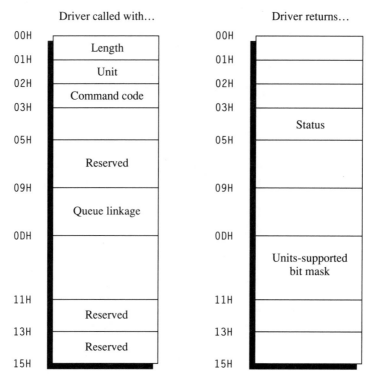

Figure 17-24. *Request packet format for the* Get Fixed Disk/Logical Unit Map *function (command code 23).*

A Skeleton Device Driver

The listing TEMPLATE.ASM (Figure 17-25) provides the source code for a skeleton character device driver called TEMPLATE.SYS. Its module definition file is TEMPLATE.DEF (Figure 17-26 on p. 383). This driver contains all the essential elements of an OS/2 device driver in rudimentary form: the device header, strategy routine, interrupt routine, and all the command code functions. It also demonstrates the preferred segment ordering and naming conventions, the use of API calls at initialization time, and the method by which initialization code and data can be discarded to minimize a driver's memory requirements.

TEMPLATE.SYS performs no useful function in its present form; it simply returns a success code for all request packets it receives from the kernel. It is intended only to serve as a starting point for your own device drivers.

```
            title    TEMPLATE -- Sample Device Driver
            page     55,132
            .286


;
; TEMPLATE.ASM
;
; A sample OS/2 character device driver. The driver command code
; routines are stubs only and have no effect but to return a
; nonerror "done" status.
;
; Assemble with:  C> masm template.asm;
; Link with:  C> link template,template.sys,,os2,template
;
; To install the driver, add "DEVICE=TEMPLATE.SYS" to CONFIG.SYS
; and reboot.
;
; Copyright (C) 1988 Ray Duncan
;

maxcmd  equ     26              ; maximum allowed command code

stdin   equ     0               ; standard device handles
stdout  equ     1
stderr  equ     2

cr      equ     0dh             ; ASCII carriage return
lf      equ     0ah             ; ASCII linefeed

        extrn   DosWrite:far


DGROUP  group   _DATA

_DATA   segment word public 'DATA'

                                ; device driver header...
header  dd      -1              ; link to next device driver
        dw      8880h           ; device attribute word
        dw      Strat           ; Strategy entry point
        dw      0               ; IDC entry point
        db      'TEMPLATE'      ; logical device name
        db      8 dup (0)       ; reserved

devhlp  dd      ?               ; DevHlp entry point
```

(continued)

Figure 17-25. *TEMPLATE.ASM, the source code for a skeleton OS/2 character device driver.*

Figure 17-25. *continued*

```
wlen     dw     ?              ; receives DosWrite length

                               ; Strategy routine dispatch table
                               ; for request packet command code...
dispch   dw     Init           ; 0  = initialize driver
         dw     MediaChk       ; 1  = media check
         dw     BuildBPB       ; 2  = build BIOS parameter block
         dw     Error          ; 3  = not used
         dw     Read           ; 4  = read from device
         dw     NdRead         ; 5  = nondestructive read
         dw     InpStat        ; 6  = return input status
         dw     InpFlush       ; 7  = flush device input buffers
         dw     Write          ; 8  = write to device
         dw     WriteVfy       ; 9  = write with verify
         dw     OutStat        ; 10 = return output status
         dw     OutFlush       ; 11 = flush output buffers
         dw     Error          ; 12 = not used
         dw     DevOpen        ; 13 = device open
         dw     DevClose       ; 14 = device close
         dw     RemMedia       ; 15 = removable media
         dw     GenIOCTL       ; 16 = generic IOCTL
         dw     ResetMed       ; 17 = reset media
         dw     GetLogDrv      ; 18 = get logical drive
         dw     SetLogDrv      ; 19 = set logical drive
         dw     DeInstall      ; 20 = deinstall
         dw     Error          ; 21 = not used
         dw     PartFD         ; 22 = partitionable fixed disks
         dw     FDMap          ; 23 = get fixed disk unit map
         dw     Error          ; 24 = not used
         dw     Error          ; 25 = not used
         dw     Error          ; 26 = not used

ident    db     cr,lf,lf
         db     'TEMPLATE Sample OS/2 Device Driver'
         db     cr,lf
ident_len equ $-ident


_DATA    ends



_TEXT    segment word public 'CODE'


         assume  cs:_TEXT,ds:DGROUP,es:NOTHING


Strat    proc    far            ; Strategy entry point
                                ; ES:BX = request packet address
```

(continued)

Figure 17-25. *continued*

```
          mov      di,es:[bx+2]      ; get command code from packet
          and      di,0ffh
          cmp      di,maxcmd         ; supported by this driver?
          jle      Strat1            ; jump if command code OK

          call     Error             ; bad command code
          jmp      Strat2

Strat1:   add      di,di             ; branch to command code routine
          call     word ptr [di+dispch]

Strat2:   mov      es:[bx+3],ax      ; status into request packet
          ret                        ; back to OS/2 kernel

Strat     endp


Intr      proc far                   ; driver Interrupt handler

          clc                        ; signal we owned interrupt
          ret                        ; return from interrupt

Intr      endp


; Command code routines are called by the Strategy routine
; via the Dispatch table with ES:BX pointing to the request
; header.  Each routine should return ES:BX unchanged
; and AX = status to be placed in request packet:
; 0100H if 'done' and no error
; 0000H if thread should block pending interrupt
; 81xxH if 'done' and error detected (xx=error code)

MediaChk proc   near                 ; function 1 = media check

          mov    ax,0100h            ; return 'done' status
          ret

MediaChk endp


BuildBPB proc   near                 ; function 2 = build BPB

          mov    ax,0100h            ; return 'done' status
          ret

BuildBPB endp
```

(continued)

Figure 17-25. *continued*

```
Read      proc    near              ; function 4 = read

          mov     ax,0100h          ; return 'done' status
          ret

Read      endp


NdRead    proc    near              ; function 5 = nondestructive read

          mov     ax,0100h          ; return 'done' status
          ret

NdRead    endp


InpStat   proc    near              ; function 6 = input status

          mov     ax,0100h          ; return 'done' status
          ret

InpStat   endp


InpFlush  proc    near              ; function 7 = flush input buffers

          mov     ax,0100h          ; return 'done' status
          ret

InpFlush  endp


Write     proc    near              ; function 8 = write

          mov     ax,0100h          ; return 'done' status
          ret

Write     endp


WriteVfy  proc    near              ; function 9 = write with verify

          mov     ax,0100h          ; return 'done' status
          ret

WriteVfy  endp
```

(continued)

Figure 17-25. *continued*

```
OutStat proc     near               ; function 10 = output status

        mov      ax,0100h           ; return 'done' status
        ret

OutStat endp


OutFlush proc    near               ; function 11 = flush output buffers

        mov      ax,0100h           ; return 'done' status
        ret

OutFlush endp


DevOpen proc     near               ; function 13 = device open

        mov      ax,0100h           ; return 'done' status
        ret

DevOpen endp


DevClose proc    near               ; function 14 = device close

        mov      ax,0100h           ; return 'done' status
        ret

DevClose endp


RemMedia proc    near               ; function 15 = removable media

        mov      ax,0100h           ; return 'done' status
        ret

RemMedia endp


GenIOCTL proc    near               ; function 16 = generic IOCTL

        mov      ax,0100h           ; return 'done' status
        ret

GenIOCTL endp
```

(continued)

Figure 17-25. *continued*

```
ResetMed proc    near              ; function 17 = reset media

         mov     ax,0100h          ; return 'done' status
         ret

ResetMed endp


GetLogDrv proc   near              ; function 18 = get logical drive

         mov     ax,0100h          ; return 'done' status
         ret

GetLogDrv endp


SetLogDrv proc   near              ; function 19 = set logical drive

         mov     ax,0100h          ; return 'done' status
         ret

SetLogDrv endp


DeInstall proc   near              ; function 20 = deinstall driver

         mov     ax,0100h          ; return 'done' status
         ret

DeInstall endp


PartFD   proc    near              ; function 22 = partitionable
                                   ;               fixed disk
         mov     ax,0100h          ; return 'done' status
         ret

PartFD   endp


FDMap    proc    near              ; function 23 = get fixed disk
                                   ;               logical unit map
         mov     ax,0100h          ; return 'done' status
         ret

FDMap    endp
```

(continued)

Figure 17-25. *continued*

```
Error    proc    near              ; bad command code

         mov     ax,8103h          ; error bit and 'done' status
                                   ; + "Unknown Command" code
         ret

Error    endp


Init     proc    near              ; function 0 = initialize

         mov     ax,es:[bx+14]     ; get DevHlp entry point
         mov     word ptr devhlp,ax
         mov     ax,es:[bx+16]
         mov     word ptr devhlp+2,ax

                                   ; set offsets to end of code
                                   ; and data segments
         mov     word ptr es:[bx+14],offset _TEXT:Init
         mov     word ptr es:[bx+16],offset DGROUP:ident

                                   ; display sign-on message...
         push    stdout            ; standard output handle
         push    ds                ; address of message
         push    offset DGROUP:ident
         push    ident_len         ; length of message
         push    ds                ; receives bytes written
         push    offset DGROUP:wlen
         call    DosWrite          ; transfer to OS/2

         mov     ax,0100h          ; return 'done' status
         ret

Init     endp

_TEXT    ends

         end
```

```
LIBRARY TEMPLATE
PROTMODE
```

Figure 17-26. *TEMPLATE.DEF, the module definition file used during linking of TEMPLATE.SYS.*

To assemble TEMPLATE.ASM, type the following command:

```
[C:\] MASM TEMPLATE.ASM;  <Enter>
```

Then link TEMPLATE.OBJ with TEMPLATE.DEF and OS2.LIB using the command:

```
[C:\] LINK TEMPLATE,TEMPLATE.SYS,,OS2,TEMPLATE  <Enter>
```

If the assembly and link are successful, you can then copy the new file TEMPLATE.SYS to the root directory of your boot disk, add the line *DE-VICE=TEMPLATE.SYS* to the CONFIG.SYS file, and restart the system to see the sign-on message for the TEMPLATE driver:

```
TEMPLATE Sample OS/2 Device Driver
```

The Device Driver Helper Functions

The Device Driver Helper functions, or DevHlps, are kernel services that assist device drivers in carrying out certain critical or complex tasks. Moving functionality that all drivers need into the kernel ensures that these activities are carried out in a uniform and efficient way. It also allows each driver to be smaller, simpler, and easier to debug.

Unlike the kernel Application Program Interface (API), for which parameters are passed on the stack and for which each function has a distinct named entry point, the DevHlp interface uses a register-based parameter-passing convention and a common entry point. The driver is provided with a bimodal pointer to the DevHlp entry point in the request packet it receives from the kernel during its initialization.

When a driver calls the DevHlp entry point, it selects a particular DevHlp function by the value it places in register DL. It passes additional parameters and addresses in other general registers as demanded by the requested function. The status of a DevHlp function is usually returned to the driver in the Zero flag or Carry flag, error codes in register AX, and addresses in registers DS:SI or ES:DI. Figure 17-27 shows a typical DevHlp call.

The fifty-odd DevHlp functions can be grouped conceptually into a few major categories (Figure 17-28 on pp. 386–89):

- Process management

- Hardware management

- Memory management

- Monitor management
- Semaphore management
- Request packet management
- Character queue management
- Timer management
- Miscellaneous device helpers
- ABIOS-related device helpers (IBM PS/2 only)

```
AllocPhys   equ   18h                    ; DevHlp function number


devhlp      dd    ?                      ; bimodal pointer to
                                         ; DevHlp common entry point
                                         ; (from Init routine)


bufptr      dd    ?                      ; receives 32-bit physical
                                         ; address of allocated block



                    .
                    .
                    .

                                         ; allocate 64 KB of
                                         ; memory above 1 MB...
            mov     ax,1                 ; AX = high word of size
            mov     bx,0                 ; BX = low word of size
            mov     dh,0                 ; 0 = above 1 MB boundary
            mov     dl,AllocPhys         ; DevHlp 18H = AllocPhys

            call    devhlp               ; indirect call to DevHlp
                                         ; common entry point

            jc      error                ; jump if allocation failed

                                         ; save 32-bit physical
                                         ; address of memory block
            mov     word ptr bufptr,bx
            mov     word ptr bufptr+2,ax
                    .
                    .
                    .
```

Figure 17-27. *Example of DevHlp call. This code allocates 64 KB of physical memory above the 1 MB boundary for use by driver. When the driver wishes to access the memory block, it must use* PhysToVirt *or* PhysToUVirt *to convert the physical address stored in* bufptr *into an appropriate virtual address for the current CPU mode.*

DevHlp Name	DevHlp Code	Modes				DevHlp Action
Process Management						
Block	04H	K		U		Blocks the calling thread until a timeout occurs or thread is unblocked by *Run*.
DevDone	01H	K	Int			Signals that the specified operation has completed. Kernel unblocks any threads waiting for the operation.
Run	05H	K	Int	U		Activates a thread which was previously suspended by a call to *Block*.
TCYield	03H	K				Similar to *Yield*, but allows other threads to execute only if they have a time-critical priority.
Yield	02H	K				Surrenders the CPU to any other threads of the same or higher priority which are ready to execute.
Hardware Management						
EOI	31H		Int		Init	Issues an End-of-Interrupt to the appropriate 8259 PIC for the specified IRQ level.
RegisterStackUsage	38H				Init	Declares stack requirements for driver's interrupt handler.
SetIRQ	1BH	K			Init	Sets the interrupt vector for the indicated interrupt request (IRQ) level to point to the driver's interrupt handler.
UnSetIRQ	1CH	K	Int		Init	Releases the interrupt vector for the specified IRQ level.
Memory Management						
AllocateGDTSelector	2DH				Init	Allocates one or more GDT selectors for use by the driver.
AllocPhys	18H	K			Init	Allocates a block of fixed (not swappable or movable) memory. Caller can specify whether the block should be above or below the 1 MB boundary.
FreePhys	19H	K			Init	Releases a block of memory previously allocated with *AllocPhys*.

(continued)

Figure 17-28. *DevHlp functions by category, their function numbers, and the driver contexts in which they may be used (K = kernel mode, Int = interrupt mode, U = user mode, Init = initialization mode).*

Figure 17-28. *continued*

DevHlp Name	DevHlp Code	Modes				DevHlp Action
Memory Management *continued*						
Lock	13H	K			Init	Locks a memory segment, that is, flags the segment as nonmovable and nonswappable.
PhysToGDTSelector	2EH	K	Int	U	Init	Maps a physical address and length onto a GDT selector.
PhysToUVirt	17H	K			Init	Converts a 32-bit physical address to a virtual address accessed through the current Local Descriptor Table (LDT).
PhysToVirt	15H	K	Int		Init	Converts a 32-bit physical (linear) address to a virtual address.
Unlock	14H	K			Init	Unlocks a memory segment.
UnPhysToVirt	32H	K	Int		Init	Signals that the virtual addresses previously obtained with *PhysToVirt* can be reused.
VerifyAccess	27H	K				Verifies that a user process has access to a segment.
VirtToPhys	16H	K			Init	Converts a virtual address (segment:offset or selector:offset) to a 32-bit physical address.
Monitor Management						
DeRegister	21H	K				Removes a process from a monitor chain.
MonFlush	23H	K				Removes all data from a monitor chain.
MonitorCreate	1FH	K			Init	Creates or removes an empty monitor chain.
MonWrite	22H	K	Int	U		Passes a data record to a monitor chain for filtering.
Register	20H	K				Adds a process to a monitor chain.
Semaphore Management						
SemClear	07H	K	Int	U		Clears a semaphore, restarting any threads that were blocking on the semaphore.
SemHandle	08H	K	Int			Converts a process's handle for a system semaphore to a virtual address that the driver can use at interrupt time.
SemRequest	06H	K		U		Claims (sets) a semaphore. If the semaphore is already set, blocks the thread until the semaphore is available.

(continued)

Figure 17-28. *continued*

DevHlp Name	DevHlp Code	Modes	DevHlp Action
Request Packet Management			
AllocReqPacket	0DH	K	Allocates a block of memory large enough to hold the largest possible request packet and returns a bimodal pointer.
FreeReqPacket	0EH	K	Releases a request packet previously allocated with *AllocReqPacket*.
PullParticular	0BH	K Int	Removes a selected request packet from the driver's linked list.
PullReqPacket	0AH	K Int	Removes the oldest request packet from the driver's linked list.
PushReqPacket	09H	K	Adds a request packet to the driver's linked list of packets.
SortReqPacket	0CH	K	Inserts a request packet into the driver's linked list of packets, sorted by sector number.
Character Queue Management			
QueueFlush	10H	K Int U	Resets the pointers to the specified buffer.
QueueInit	0FH	K Int U Init	Establishes a ring buffer for storage of characters and initializes its pointers.
QueueRead	12H	K Int U	Returns and removes a character from the specified buffer.
QueueWrite	11H	K Int U	Puts a character into the specified buffer.
Timer Management			
ResetTimer	1EH	K Int Init	Removes a timer tick handler from the system's list of such handlers.
SchedClockAddr	00H	K Init	Obtains the address of the kernel's routine to be called on each clock tick. Used only by clock driver.
SetTimer	1DH	K Init	Adds a timer tick handler, to be called on every timer tick, to the system's list of such handlers.
TickCount	33H	K Int U Init	Adds a timer tick handler, to be called at specified intervals, to the system's list of such handlers, or modifies the interval at which an existing handler is called.

(continued)

Figure 17-28. *continued*

DevHlp Name	*DevHlp Code*	*Modes*				*DevHlp Action*
Miscellaneous Device Helpers						
AttachDD	2AH	K			Init	Obtains inter-driver communication (IDC) entry point for another driver.
GetDOSVar	24H	K			Init	Returns addresses of kernel variables and entry points.
ProtToReal	30H	K	Int			Switches the CPU into real mode.
RealToProt	2FH	K	Int			Switches the CPU into protected mode.
ROMCritSection	26H			U		Protects ROM BIOS code from interrupts that might cause a context switch.
SendEvent	25H	K	Int			Signals the kernel that a key requiring special handling has been detected. Used only by keyboard driver.
SetROMVector	1AH	K			Init	Captures an interrupt vector normally used in real mode to invoke a ROM BIOS function, returning the previous contents of the vector for chaining.
ABIOS-related Device Helpers (IBM PS/2 only)						
ABIOSCall	36H	K	Int	U	Init	Invokes an Advanced BIOS (ABIOS) service on behalf of the driver.
ABIOSCommonEntry	37H	K	Int	U	Init	Transfers to an ABIOS Common Entry point on behalf of the driver.
FreeLIDEntry	35H	K		U	Init	Releases a logical ID (LID) for a physical device.
GetLIDEntry	34H	K		U	Init	Obtains a logical ID (LID) for a physical device, for use with subsequent ABIOS calls.

Some service categories are used by every OS/2 device driver because they allow the driver to perform overlapped, interrupt-driven I/O operations in a "well-behaved" manner, or because they provide access to memory addresses that the driver could not reach otherwise. The remainder are present only for convenience or to assist in the construction of unusual or highly complex drivers.

The programming reference for the DevHlp services is in Section VI, beginning on p. 657.

Process Management

The basic technique by which a driver performs overlapped or asynchronous I/O is a simple one. When the strategy routine of the driver is called, it sets up the I/O operation (or adds it to the list of pending operations if one is already in progress) and simply returns to the OS/2 kernel with the Done bit cleared in the request packet status word. The kernel then suspends the thread that initiated the I/O request.

When the I/O operation is eventually completed, the driver's interrupt routine updates the request packet that initiated the operation and then calls the DevHlp routine *DevDone*. This signals the kernel to awaken the thread that owns the I/O request, which can then perform any necessary post-I/O processing (such as translating the driver's status information into appropriate values to be returned to an application program).

The driver can also use the DevHlp functions *Block* and *Run* to suspend a thread explicitly while an I/O operation is in progress, particularly if the driver must execute a lengthy amount of code after the operation is complete. Putting such code in the strategy routine is preferable to putting it in the interrupt routine because other lower-priority interrupts are locked out by the hardware while the interrupt routine is executing.

The strategy routine sets up the I/O operation and then calls *Block* with a 32-bit identifier of its own choosing. When the interrupt routine notes that the I/O operation is complete, it calls *Run* with the same 32-bit identifier. This causes the kernel to wake up the original thread within the strategy routine, which can proceed with post-I/O processing and then exit to the kernel with the request packet's Done bit set. The biggest problem with this method is ensuring the uniqueness of the 32-bit value that the driver uses to associate a pair of *Block* and *Run* calls; the call to *Run* wakes up *all* threads that have blocked with that particular 32-bit identifier.

The additional DevHlp functions *Yield* and *TCYield* are provided for drivers that need to transfer long strings of data from one memory location to another at task time (such as a RAM disk) or whose devices do not support interrupts. A call to *Yield* simply tells the kernel's scheduler to give all other threads with the same or higher priority a chance to run before returning control to the currently executing thread, whereas *TCYield* allows only those other threads which have a "time-critical priority" to take a turn.

A driver can check the value of *YieldFlag* or *TCYieldFlag*—two variables whose addresses are returned by another DevHlp, *GetDOSVar*—to determine whether any other threads are waiting for the CPU, and it can then bypass the call to *Yield* or *TCYield* if no other thread is eligible to execute. To avoid interference with the proper operation of other drivers, make such a check (and possible *Yield*) at least every 3 milliseconds.

Hardware Management

Because the strategy and interrupt routines of device drivers execute at the highest privilege level, they have a free hand with the machine if they want it; two different drivers that access the same hardware addresses can theoretically come into conflict. However, OS/2 provides DevHlps to arbitrate interrupt vector and 8259 programmable interrupt controller (PIC) usage for cooperating drivers. Drivers that do *not* use these DevHlps to gain access to the hardware resources they need might not work properly on future 80386-specific versions of OS/2.

The DevHlp functions *SetIRQ* and *UnSetIRQ* assist drivers in the capture or release of interrupt vectors. When a driver calls *SetIRQ*, it also specifies whether it is willing to share the level with another driver. If it specifies that it wants to own the interrupt exclusively, subsequent requests for the same IRQ level by other drivers will fail; if another driver has already signed up for the interrupt, the request by the current driver will fail. In OS/2 version 1.1 a driver that uses interrupts must also declare the stack requirements of its interrupt handler during initialization by calling the DevHlp *Register-StackUsage*.

When a hardware interrupt occurs, a dispatcher in the OS/2 kernel initially receives control, saves all registers, sets the DS register to point to the driver's near data segment, and then transfers control to the driver's interrupt handler. The handler services its device, starts another I/O operation if any are waiting, calls the DevHlp function *EOI* to dismiss the interrupt at the 8259 PIC, and then returns to the kernel. Although a driver can access its own device's ports directly, you should reserve manipulation of the PIC for the kernel to isolate a driver from the interrupt architecture.

Memory Management

A driver specifies the amount of storage to reserve for its code and data segments in the information it returns to the kernel at *Init* time. If the driver needs additional memory for tables, buffers, or other data structures, it can use the DevHlp functions *AllocPhys* and *FreePhys* to dynamically allocate and release such memory. The memory assigned to the driver by *AllocPhys* is not movable or swappable, and the driver can specify whether it wants the memory to be located above or below the 1 MB boundary.

Memory addressing is one of the trickiest aspects of an OS/2 driver's operation. To execute and handle interrupts in either protected mode or real mode, a driver must be prepared to encounter three types of addresses — protected mode selector:offset pairs, real mode segment:offset pairs, and the *physical* 32-bit addresses used by DMA channels and by some devices. Further complicating the situation are the activities of the operating system's virtual memory manager, which shuffles segments around to collect unused fragments and swaps out segments to disk.

The OS/2 kernel takes several measures to shield drivers from most of the potential problems with memory addressing. First, whenever the kernel requests an explicit transfer operation from a driver using a request packet that contains the *Read* or *Write* command codes, it passes the driver a 32-bit physical address which has already been "locked" (meaning that the virtual memory manager has been notified that the memory in question should not be moved or swapped). In addition, the kernel uses bimodal pointers when it passes the driver an address of a structure (such as a request packet) or procedure (such as the DevHlp entry point) that the driver needs to access directly.

The kernel also provides six DevHlp functions that help a driver make address conversions: *AllocateGDTSelector*, *PhysToGDTSelector*, *PhysToUVirt*, *PhysToVirt*, *UnPhysToVirt*, and *VirtToPhys*. These functions assist a driver by converting physical 32-bit addresses to virtual addresses (segment:offset or selector:offset pairs) and back again. The first three are used to access static structures (such as memory allocated by *AllocPhys* or an adapter's memory-mapped I/O locations). *PhysToVirt* and *UnPhysToVirt* are used when a driver needs temporary access to data that is transient or owned by a process, allowing the driver to translate the physical address in a *Read* or *Write* request into a virtual address appropriate to the current CPU mode.

Finally, to provide for cases in which a memory address is passed to a driver in an IOCTL data packet or by some other channel of communication, the OS/2 kernel also provides the DevHlp functions *Lock*, *Unlock*, and *VerifyAccess*. The driver first calls *VerifyAccess* with the selector, offset, and length of the memory involved in the requested operation to confirm that the application is entitled to access that memory. If *VerifyAccess* succeeds, the driver calls the *Lock* function to immobilize the segment and *VirtToPhys* to obtain the physical address if necessary; then it proceeds with the I/O operation, calling *Unlock* afterwards to put the segment back under the control of the system's memory manager. Drivers must avoid blocking between the *VerifyAccess* and *Lock* calls so that no context switch can occur that might make the *VerifyAccess* result invalid.

The use of *PhysToVirt* is most interesting when the driver is entered in real mode while the memory address to be accessed lies above the 1 MB boundary. On an IBM AT–type machine, *PhysToVirt* uses an undocumented 80286 instruction (LOADALL) to set the CPU's "shadow" descriptor registers with values that allow the memory access to take place without a mode switch.* The addressability of the memory location is valid only as long as the associated segment register (which does not contain any physically meaningful value) is not reloaded; thus, interrupts must remain masked, the segment register should not be pushed and popped, and no DevHlp calls other than another *PhysToVirt* can be made until the driver completes the memory access.

On an 80386-based or IBM PS/2–type machine, which supports faster mode switching, *PhysToVirt* switches the CPU into protected mode and returns a normal selector for the memory location of interest. At first glance, this method of obtaining addressability for the data may appear more attractive, but it actually imposes a much greater burden on the driver because it invalidates any pointers previously obtained from *PhysToVirt* that did *not* cause a mode switch. The driver must be constantly on the lookout for an unexpected change in modes and must be prepared to backtrack and recalculate any saved virtual addresses.

In either hardware environment, the pool of selectors available to *PhysToVirt* is limited. When a program finishes with virtual addresses it obtained from *PhysToVirt*, it should notify the system that the selectors can be reused by calling *UnPhysToVirt*. If an earlier call to *PhysToVirt* resulted in a mode switch, *UnPhysToVirt* also restores the original CPU mode.

Monitor Management

The five monitor-related DevHlps—*MonitorCreate*, *Register*, *DeRegister*, *MonWrite*, and *MonFlush*—help the driver carry out its role in OS/2's support for device monitors. *MonitorCreate* establishes or destroys a chain of monitor buffers; *Register* and *DeRegister* add or remove a specific application's buffers from the monitor buffer chain.

The driver passes characters through the monitor buffer chain by calling *MonWrite*. The kernel calls a notification routine within the driver when

---

* When you POP or MOV a selector into a segment register, the CPU loads the segment base, length, and so forth from the corresponding descriptor into "shadow" registers. In effect, the CPU uses these otherwise inaccessible registers to cache the descriptor information on-chip. This allows most protected mode memory accesses to be as fast as they are in real mode.

data emerges from the end of the buffer chain. The driver can notify all device monitor applications to reinitialize their pointers and buffers by calling *MonFlush*.

Chapter 18 covers device monitors, as well as device driver support for monitors, in more detail.

Semaphore Management

The DevHlp functions *SemRequest* and *SemClear*, which can be called by the driver to obtain or release ownership of a semaphore, are the equivalent of the API functions *DosSemRequest* and *DosSemClear* described in Chapter 13. These operate on either RAM semaphores or system semaphores.

RAM semaphores can be located in the data segment of either a driver or an application program. (When an application RAM semaphore is used, its address would typically be passed to the driver in a *DosDevIOCtl* call.) RAM semaphores are useful for signaling between different components of a driver or between a closely coupled driver and application, or for synchronizing access to driver resources that are nonreentrant.

System semaphores can be created or opened only by an application, not by a driver. To use system semaphores for communication between a driver and an application, the application must first obtain a handle for the semaphore with *DosOpenSem* or *DosCreateSem* and pass it to the driver with a *DosDevIOCtl* call. The driver then uses the DevHlp function *SemHandle* at task time to obtain a new semaphore handle that can be used at interrupt time. Once both the driver and application have a usable handle for the semaphore, either can use the semaphore to signal or block the other.

Request Packet Management

Another set of DevHlps assists the driver in maintaining and sorting a linked list of request packets for pending I/O operations. The driver must provide a doubleword of storage (initialized to zero) that the DevHlp routines can use as a pointer to the head of the request packet queue. A reserved doubleword field within the packets is used to chain one to another.

Request packets are added to the queue by *PushReqPacket* (which adds to the queue end) or by *SortReqPacket* (which inserts a *Read* or *Write* packet into the queue based on its logical sector number). A driver can remove packets from the queue with *PullReqPacket* (which returns the oldest request) or with *PullParticular* (usually employed only when a process has terminated with I/O still pending).

The DevHlp functions *AllocReqPacket* and *FreeReqPacket* let a driver dynamically obtain and release storage for additional request packets. A driver might use these routines in cases where it needs to decompose an I/O request into two or more requests that it can queue independently—for example, it might convert a *Read* request packet into a seek followed by a transfer to avoid issuing redundant seek commands if multiple *Read* requests are pending for the same track. *AllocReqPacket* returns a bimodal pointer to a block of memory that is exactly large enough for the largest possible request packet (in contrast to *AllocPhys*, which returns a 32-bit physical address and can be used to allocate blocks of any size).

Request packets are a relatively scarce resource. A driver that uses *AllocReqPacket* should be prepared for the function to fail and should have a recovery strategy that will not degrade system performance or cause I/O requests to fail.

Character Queue Management

The kernel also supplies a group of DevHlps for managing character queues; these routines provide simple support for a *ring buffer* of characters which are received or transmitted from a device.

A character queue is declared in the following form:

```
QSize   dw      n               ; size of queue in bytes
QChrOut dw      0               ; index of next character out
QCount  dw      0               ; count of characters in buffer
Qbuff   db      n dup (?)       ; storage starts here
```

Each character queue has, in effect, two pointers: an "out" pointer, which points to the oldest character in the buffer, and an "in" pointer, which points to the buffer position for the next character to be added to the buffer. When both pointers are equal, the buffer is empty. These two pointers do not exist in storage but are formed as needed by combining the values in *QChrOut* and *QCount* with the base address *Qbuff*.

A character queue is initialized by a call to the DevHlp function *QueueInit*. You can add characters to the ring buffer with *QueueWrite* and remove them with the DevHlp function *QueueRead*. The *QueueFlush* routine resets the pointers to the specified character queue, effectively discarding its contents.

A typical character device driver has two character queues: one for received characters and one for transmitted characters. The driver's interrupt routine adds characters to the receive queue, and its strategy routine removes them with a call to the *Read* (command code 4) function. Characters are added to the write queue by the strategy routine's *Write* (command code 8) function if the device is busy or if characters are already waiting in the queue, and they are removed from the queue by the interrupt routine.

Timer Management

The timer-related DevHlps assist a driver in performing polled I/O on devices that do not support interrupts, or in setting up a "watchdog" timer to detect lost interrupts or I/O operations that never complete.

The function *SetTimer* is called with the address of a routine within the driver that must execute on each timer tick; this is the equivalent of chaining onto Int 1CH (the ROM BIOS timer tick vector) under MS-DOS. The DevHlp function *TickCount* is a more general version of *SetTimer*; rather than entering the driver's timer tick handler on every tick, it lets you specify the number of ticks between entries. The driver can call *ResetTimer* to remove its timer tick handler from the system's list of all such handlers.

The function *SchedClockAddr* is used only by the system's clock driver during its initialization. It supplies a pointer to the routine in the kernel that should be called on each clock tick. The kernel's routine then distributes the clock ticks through the system wherever they are needed—to the scheduler, for example, and to the timer tick handlers of other device drivers that have been registered with *SetTimer* or *TickCount*.

Miscellaneous Device Helpers

The remaining DevHlps—*RealToProt*, *ProtToReal*, *SendEvent*, *GetDOSVar*, *SysTrace*, *SetROMVector*, *ROMCritSection*, *AttachDD*, and the ABIOS-related services—do not fall into any convenient category.

As their names imply, *RealToProt* and *ProtToReal* allow the driver to request a CPU mode switch. Placing the mode-switching logic inside the kernel ensures that the mode switching is done properly and that it takes advantage of any special external hardware support (such as exists on the PS/2) or CPU support (such as that provided by the 80386) that can speed up the operation.

SendEvent is normally used only by the system's keyboard driver (KBD$). It allows the driver to signal the kernel when certain special keys are detected (such as Ctrl-Break or the Task Manager hot keys), so that the kernel can take immediate action rather than waiting for the keycode to percolate through the driver's character input buffer.

GetDOSVar returns bimodal addresses for several significant system variables and tables, including the Global Information Segment, the Local Information Segment, the "reboot" routine, and the system's *Yield* and *TCYield* flags (set when at least one thread is ready to execute). The driver can call *GetDOSVar* to obtain the pointers at its initialization time and store them for later use.

AttachDD allows a driver to obtain the inter-driver communication (IDC) entry point for a previously loaded character device driver. It can then invoke the other driver directly at any time with a far call. Parameter passing for IDC can take any form and is not standardized because the OS/2 kernel is not involved. *AttachDD* identifies drivers by the 8-character device name in their headers, so a block driver that wants to make an IDC entry point available needs two headers: one for the usual purposes and a second that has the character device attribute bit set and that contains a logical device name and the IDC entry point.

SetROMVector and *ROMCritSection* assist drivers — such as the keyboard, video, serial port, and printer drivers — which must support ROM BIOS calls by real mode applications; that is, drivers that can be entered in user mode. At initialization time, the driver must use *SetROMVector* to take over the software interrupt vector for the ROM BIOS services that use its device. When a real mode program makes a ROM BIOS call, the driver receives control, at which point it can use *ROMCritSection* to disable session switching, and then chain to the original ROM BIOS code or provide the same functionality within its own code.

The Processing of a Typical I/O Request

An application program requests an I/O operation from OS/2 by pushing appropriate values and addresses onto the stack and executing a far call to a named API entry point. OS/2 inspects its internal tables, searches the chain of device driver headers if necessary, and determines which device driver should receive the I/O request.

OS/2 then creates a request packet in a reserved area of memory. The system transforms disk I/O requests from file and record information into logical sector requests based on its interpretation of the disk's directory and file allocation table. (OS/2 can locate these disk structures using the information that is returned by the driver from a previous *Build BPB* call, and it issues additional driver read requests if necessary to bring their sectors into memory.)

After the request packet is prepared, OS/2 calls the device driver's strategy entry point, passing the address of the packet in registers ES:BX. If the strategy routine can dispose of the request immediately (as it typically can with a status request or a request for data which is already in the driver's own buffers), it places the appropriate information into the request packet or other buffer, sets the Done bit to indicate that the request is complete, and returns control to the kernel.

Otherwise, the strategy routine can suspend execution of the requesting thread by two different methods. It can return to the kernel with the Done bit in the request header cleared and rely on the interrupt routine to call *DevDone* later. This method has the side effect of unblocking the thread that issued the I/O request. Alternatively, it can call the DevHlp *Block* and wait for the interrupt routine to wake it up by calling the DevHlp *Run*. In this case, the strategy routine sets the Done bit in the request packet status word before it exits, and no call to *DevDone* is needed.

When the I/O is finished, the kernel transforms the request status to an application level error code if necessary and updates the application's saved AX register with the appropriate status code. It places any other necessary information (such as the number of bytes actually transferred on a *DosRead* call) into the variables whose addresses were passed on the stack in the original API call. At this point the thread which made the I/O request exits the kernel and resumes execution within the application. Figure 17-29 provides a sketch of this entire flow of control and data.

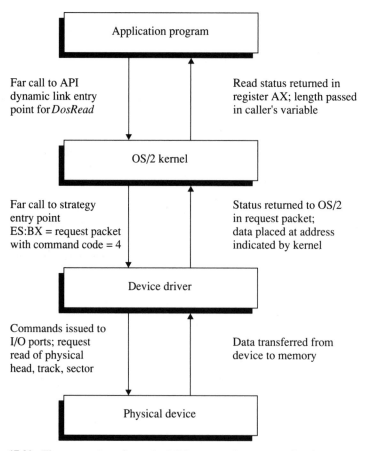

Figure 17-29. *The processing of a typical I/O request from an application program.*

Note that a single API call by an application program can result in many requests from the kernel to the device driver. For example, if an application invokes *DosOpen* to open or create a file, OS/2 might have to issue multiple sector *Read* requests to the driver while searching the directory for the filename. Similarly, a *DosRead* request on an open file might obligate OS/2 to load several FAT sectors while locating the correct cluster, before the actual file data can be transferred into memory.

Building a Device Driver

The creation of a full-fledged OS/2 device driver, particularly a driver for a high speed mass storage device with multiple units, is a large and complex project. Because a driver can contain multiple threads of execution at any given time, you must guard against the subtle bugs that result from improper handling of interrupts, incorrect synchronization of driver resources, race conditions, and routines that are not completely reentrant. In accordance with Murphy's Law, such bugs often go undiscovered until the driver is subjected to the end user's typical job mix, which stresses the driver in ways you never imagined.

You can minimize the unpleasant surprises in your OS/2 device driver by adopting an approach that stresses defensive, conservative, structured coding techniques and stepwise refinement. These techniques are valuable in any software development project, of course, but they can make the difference between success and failure in driver development.

Segments and Subroutines

OS/2 device drivers are usually written as "small model" Microsoft MASM programs with one code segment and one data segment. The data segment, with the device driver header at its beginning, should be declared before the code segment. The structure of the resulting executable file built by the Linker is shown in Figure 17-30 on the following page. The driver should not contain a stack segment — a stack is provided by the system.

The two primary components of a driver are its strategy and interrupt routines. They, in turn, call other routines which implement the various driver functions (read, write, status, and so forth), allocate or release memory, translate addresses, and manage the driver's request queue. You should design each procedure to be reentrant, if possible, even if you see no obvious need for reentrancy; it is much easier to code a routine properly that uses local variables from the outset than to graft them on later. Any action on global data items by a procedure should be clearly documented and synchronized (if necessary) by semaphores.

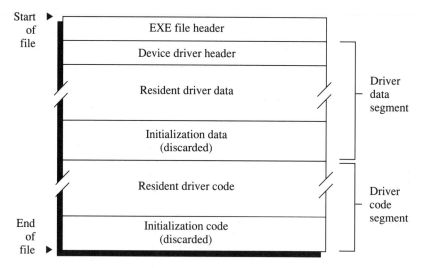

```
Start ▶  ┌─────────────────────────────────────┐
of       │            EXE file header           │
file     ├─────────────────────────────────────┤
         │         Device driver header         │        ┐
         ├─────────────────────────────────────┤        │ Driver
         │                                      │        │ data
         │         Resident driver data         │        │ segment
         │                                      │        │
         ├─────────────────────────────────────┤        │
         │         Initialization data          │        │
         │             (discarded)              │        ┘
         ├─────────────────────────────────────┤        ┐
         │                                      │        │ Driver
         │         Resident driver code         │        │ code
         │                                      │        │ segment
End      ├─────────────────────────────────────┤        │
of       │         Initialization code          │        │
file ▶   │             (discarded)              │        ┘
         └─────────────────────────────────────┘
```

Figure 17-30. *Structure of an OS/2 installable device driver file. OS/2 drivers are linked as "small model" EXE files, containing one code segment and one data segment. By convention, driver files always have the extension SYS. Note that code and data used only by the driver's initialization routine can be positioned at the end of the two segments. To minimize the driver's memory overhead, they can then be discarded after driver initialization is completed.*

Stepwise Refinement #1

The first version of a new device driver should perform all its operations by polled I/O within the strategy routine, that is, at task time. By starting out with a polled I/O version, you can validate the elements of the driver which are purely related to control of the hardware — issuing the right commands to the correct I/O ports in the proper order — without worrying about CPU mode changes, reentrancy, and interrupts.

The strategy routine runs with kernel privilege and with interrupts enabled; it has full access to all I/O ports and memory addresses and is never preempted. It is entered from the kernel with a valid stack, register DS pointing to the driver's data segment, and registers ES:BX containing a bimodal address of a request packet. The strategy routine exits to the kernel with a far return; no registers need be preserved.

To simplify initial debugging of a new driver, you can implement a minimum set of functions — sufficient to read and write the physical device — and provide stubs for the less vital services. Depending on the service it represents, a stub can return a "reasonable" result, do nothing and return a Done status, or return an Error plus Done status.

Character device drivers must support, at minimum, the device driver command code functions *Init*, *Read*, and *Write*. *Write with Verify* can be aliased to *Write*, and *DeInstall* can return an error. If your driver performs internal buffering of data, you should also fully implement *Input Status*, *Output Status*, *Nondestructive Read*, *Flush Input Buffers*, and *Flush Output Buffers*. If your driver does not provide internal buffering, these five functions can simply return with the status word set to 0100H (Busy bit clear, Done bit set). You need not provide support for the *Device Open* and *Device Close* functions unless bit 11 is set in the device header attribute word. The *Generic IOCtl* function should be stubbed out to return an error; leave the actual implementation for later.

In a rudimentary block device driver, you must implement functions *Init*, *Media Check*, *Build BPB*, *Read*, and *Write* to support file storage by OS/2. As with the character drivers, you can temporarily alias *Write with Verify* to *Write*. *Reset Media* can simply return Done status, *Get Logical Device* and *Set Logical Device* should clear the unit field of the request packet to zero and return Done status, and the *Partitionable Fixed Disk* and *Get Fixed Disk/ Logical Unit Map* functions can be stubbed out to return an error. The *Device Open*, *Device Close*, and *Removable Media* functions need not be implemented unless bit 11 is set in the header attribute word.

Stepwise Refinement #2

Once you establish that the basic device control works properly in a polled I/O environment, add interrupt handling to the driver. This change enlarges and complicates the driver considerably. Multiple requests might be pending at one time, and both the strategy and interrupt routines must be capable of manipulating the request list and initiating I/O. In addition, the CPU mode at strategy time for a given request might well be different than the mode at interrupt time.

Like the strategy routine, the interrupt routine runs with kernel privilege and has full access to all I/O ports and memory addresses. It is entered by a far call from the kernel with a valid stack and with register DS pointing to the driver's data segment. If the driver owns the interrupt level exclusively, the interrupt routine is entered with interrupts masked; otherwise, it is entered with interrupts enabled.

The interrupt routine may itself be interrupted only by other devices with higher priority, or by devices with the same priority (including its own device) once an EOI has been signaled to the 8259 PIC. The interrupt routine must test its device to verify that it generated the interrupt. If it owns the interrupt, it must service the device, start another I/O operation if any are waiting, call the DevHlp function *EOI* to dismiss the interrupt at the 8259 PIC, and return to the kernel with the Carry flag clear (0). If it does not own the interrupt, it should exit to the kernel with the Carry flag set (1).

Your first priority when adding interrupt handling to your driver is to decide which command code functions can be completed entirely at task time by the strategy routine and which functions must be deferred to be completed by the interrupt routine. In most cases, for both character and block device drivers, only *Read* and *Write* requests need to be carried out in overlapped fashion; the request packets for all other driver operations can be processed when they are received.

If the device is idle when the strategy routine is called with a *Read* or *Write* request, it should initiate the I/O immediately and then suspend the requesting thread so that the scheduler can dispatch other threads that are ready to execute while the I/O is in progress. If the device is busy, the strategy routine should simply add the request packet to the driver's request packet queue and then suspend the thread. To optimize access time, block device *Read* and *Write* requests can be queued and executed in any order, but character device *Read* and *Write* operations must be completed in the order they are received to avoid mixed output.

As we have noted, the strategy routine can suspend execution of a requesting thread either by exiting to the kernel with the Done bit in the status word cleared or by explicitly putting the thread to sleep with a call to the DevHlp function *Block*. If the strategy routine blocks within itself, it must be fully reentrant because it might be reentered by the kernel as a result of new I/O requests from other threads. Any functions called by the strategy routine must be reentrant anyway if they can also be called by interrupt routines. The strategy routine should mask interrupts while it is manipulating its work list and while it is checking the device status so that it does not get into a race condition with its own interrupt handler.

Stepwise Refinement #3

In the final development step, tune the driver to optimize scheduling of multiple pending I/O requests, to minimize both the periods of interrupt masking and total time to service an interrupt, and to yield the CPU at suitable intervals (at least every 3 milliseconds) when large amounts of data must be shifted in memory. You can also add enhancements such as watchdog timers for lost interrupts and *DosDevIOCtl* support once the driver has proven fundamentally sound.

Custom replacements for the system's keyboard, printer, and serial port drivers must support all the *DosDevIOCtl* functions documented in the OS/2 manuals, so that applications which rely on these functions will not fail unexpectedly. IOCTL support for other custom drivers is generally optional, except that block device drivers should always support *DosDevIOCtl* Category 8, Function 63H (Get Device Parameters), which is used by CHKDSK. If this function is absent, CHKDSK terminates with the error message *The System Cannot Accept the Command* after displaying the logical drive's volume label and date.

Drivers for Noninterrupting Devices

Drivers whose devices are not capable of generating interrupts can perform polled I/O by two methods. If the peripheral is a DMA-capable block device or a relatively low speed character device, the driver can use the DevHlp functions *TickCount* or *SetTimer* to register a handler that receives control on each system timer tick (or multiple thereof), and it can have that handler poll the device. (The length of the timer tick in milliseconds can be obtained from the global information segment.) This relatively benign technique does not appreciably degrade system performance.

If the device requires programmed I/O and transfers data in bursts which cannot be interrupted or deferred, or if it is a high speed character device, the driver must perform the I/O in a status-bound loop in the strategy routine. Such a driver almost inevitably degrades overall system performance because it interferes with the prompt initiation of I/O operations and the servicing of interrupts for other devices. The driver can keep the damage to a minimum by calling *Yield* or *TCYield* at intervals not greater than 3 milliseconds, even if this forces it to abort and restart some of its own I/O operations.

A Sample Block Device Driver

The listing TINYDISK.ASM (Figure 17-31 on the following page) contains the source code for a simple installable RAM disk called TINYDISK.SYS. Its module definition file, TINYDISK.DEF, is shown in Figure 17-32 on p. 417. This driver demonstrates the essential features of an OS/2 block device driver, and it illustrates the use of some crucial DevHlp functions such as *AllocPhys* and *PhysToVirt*.

```
                title    TINYDISK -- RAM Disk Device Driver
                page     55,132
                .286


        ;
        ; TINYDISK.ASM
        ;
        ; A sample OS/2 block driver that installs a 64 KB RAM disk.
        ;
        ; Assemble with:  C> masm tinydisk.asm;
        ; Link with:  C> link tinydisk,tinydisk.sys,,os2,tinydisk
        ;
        ; To install the driver, add "DEVICE=TINYDISK.SYS" to CONFIG.SYS
        ; and reboot.
        ;
        ; Copyright (C) 1988 Ray Duncan
        ;


        maxcmd  equ      26              ; maximum allowed command code

        secsize equ      512             ; bytes/sector, IBM compatible media

        stdin   equ      0               ; standard device handles
        stdout  equ      1
        stderr  equ      2

        cr      equ      0dh             ; ASCII carriage return
        lf      equ      0ah             ; ASCII linefeed

        PhysToVirt   equ 15h             ; DevHlp services
        UnPhysToVirt equ 32h
        VerifyAccess equ 27h
        AllocPhys    equ 18h

                extrn    DosWrite:far



        DGROUP  group    _DATA


        _DATA   segment word public 'DATA'
```

(continued)

Figure 17-31. *TINYDISK.ASM, the source code for TINYDISK.SYS, an installable OS/2 RAM disk driver.*

Figure 17-31. *continued*

```
                               ; device driver header...
header  dd      -1             ; link to next device driver
        dw      0080h          ; device attribute word
                               ; bits 7-9 = driver level
        dw      Strat          ; Strategy entry point
        dw      0              ; reserved
        db      0              ; units (set by OS/2)
        db      15 dup (0)     ; reserved


devhlp  dd      ?              ; DevHlp entry point


wlen    dw      ?              ; receives DosWrite length


dbase   dd      ?              ; 32-bit physical address,
                               ; base of RAM disk storage


xfrsec  dw      0              ; current sector for transfer
xfrcnt  dw      0              ; sectors successfully transferred
xfrreq  dw      0              ; number of sectors requested
xfraddr dd      0              ; working address for transfer


array   dw      bpb            ; array of pointers to BPB
                               ; for each supported unit


bootrec equ     $              ; logical sector 0 boot record
        jmp     $              ; JMP at start of boot sector,
        nop                    ; this field must be 3 bytes
        db      'IBM 10.1'     ; OEM identity field
                               ; ---BIOS Parameter Block-----
bpb     dw      secsize        ; 00H bytes per sector
        db      1              ; 02H sectors per cluster
        dw      1              ; 03H reserved sectors
        db      1              ; 05H number of FATs
        dw      64             ; 06H root directory entries
        dw      128            ; 08H total sectors
        db      0f8h           ; 0AH media descriptor
        dw      1              ; 0BH sectors per FAT
        dw      1              ; 0DH sectors per track
        dw      1              ; 0FH number of heads
        dd      0              ; 11H hidden sectors
        dd      0              ; 15H large total sectors (if
                               ;     word at offset 08H = 0)
        db      6 dup (0)      ; 19H reserved
                               ; ---End of BPB, 31 bytes-----
```

(continued)

Figure 17-31. *continued*

```
bootrec_len equ $-bootrec        ; length of boot sector data
                                 ; additional words needed by
                                 ; Generic IOCTL Cat 8 Function 63H
                                 ; Get Device Parameters call
            dw      0            ; number of cylinders
            db      7            ; device type = unknown
            dw      1            ; device attribute word
gdprec_len equ $-bpb             ; length of Generic IOCTL buffer

                                 ; Strategy routine dispatch table
                                 ; for request packet command code...
dispch  dw      Init             ; 0  = initialize driver
        dw      MediaChk         ; 1  = media check on block device
        dw      BuildBPB         ; 2  = build BIOS parameter block
        dw      Error            ; 3  = reserved
        dw      Read             ; 4  = read (input) from device
        dw      Error            ; 5  = nondestructive read
        dw      Error            ; 6  = return input status
        dw      Error            ; 7  = flush device input buffers
        dw      Write            ; 8  = write (output) to device
        dw      Write            ; 9  = write with verify
        dw      Error            ; 10 = return output status
        dw      Error            ; 11 = flush output buffers
        dw      Error            ; 12 = reserved
        dw      Error            ; 13 = device open
        dw      Error            ; 14 = device close
        dw      Error            ; 15 = removable media
        dw      GenIOCTL         ; 16 = generic IOCTL
        dw      Error            ; 17 = reset media
        dw      GSLogDrv         ; 18 = get logical drive
        dw      GSLogDrv         ; 19 = set logical drive
        dw      Error            ; 20 = deinstall
        dw      Error            ; 21 = reserved
        dw      Error            ; 22 = partitionable fixed disks
        dw      Error            ; 23 = get fixed disk unit map
        dw      Error            ; 24 = reserved
        dw      Error            ; 25 = reserved
        dw      Error            ; 26 = reserved

                                 ; start of data discarded
                                 ; after initialization

ident   db      cr,lf,lf         ; successful installation message
        db      'TINYDISK 64 KB RAM disk for OS/2'
        db      cr,lf
        db      'RAM disk will be drive '
```

(continued)

Figure 17-31. *continued*

```
drive    db      'X:'
         db      cr,lf
ident_len equ $-ident

abort    db      cr,lf               ; aborted installation message
         db      'TINYDISK installation aborted'
         db      cr,lf
abort_len equ $-abort

volname  db      'TINYDISK  '        ; volume label for RAM disk
         db      08h                 ; attribute byte
         db      10 dup (0)          ; reserved area
         dw      0                   ; time = 00:00
         dw      1021h               ; date = January 1, 1988
         db      6 dup (0)           ; reserved area
volname_len equ $-volname


_DATA    ends


_TEXT    segment word public 'CODE'

         assume  cs:_TEXT,ds:DGROUP,es:NOTHING


Strat    proc    far                 ; Strategy entry point
                                     ; ES:BX = request packet

         mov     di,es:[bx+2]        ; get command code from packet
         and     di,0ffh
         cmp     di,maxcmd           ; supported by this driver?
         jle     Strat1              ; jump if command code OK

         call    Error               ; bad command code
         jmp     Strat2

Strat1: add     di,di               ; go to command code routine
         call    word ptr [di+dispch]

Strat2:                              ; return with AX = status
         mov     es:[bx+3],ax        ; put status in request packet
         ret                         ; return to OS/2 kernel

Strat    endp
```

(continued)

Figure 17-31. *continued*

```
; Command code routines are called by the Strategy routine
; via the Dispatch table with ES:BX pointing to the request
; header.  Each routine should return ES:BX unchanged
; and AX = status to be placed in request packet:
; 0100H if 'done' and no error
; 0000H if thread should block pending interrupt
; 81xxH if 'done' and error detected (xx = error code)


MediaChk proc    near                   ; function 1 = media check

                                        ; return 'not changed' code
         mov     byte ptr es:[bx+0eh],1

         mov     ax,0100h               ; return 'done' status
         ret

MediaChk endp


BuildBPB proc    near                   ; function 2 = build BPB

                                        ; put BPB address into
                                        ; request packet
         mov     word ptr es:[bx+12h],offset DGROUP:bpb
         mov     word ptr es:[bx+14h],ds

         mov     ax,0100h               ; return 'done' status
         ret

BuildBPB endp


Read     proc    near                   ; function 4 = read

         push    es                     ; save request packet address
         push    bx

         call    setup                  ; set up transfer variables

Read1:   mov     ax,xfrcnt              ; done with all sectors yet?
         cmp     ax,xfrreq
         je      read2                  ; jump if transfer completed

         mov     ax,ds                  ; set ES = DGROUP
         mov     es,ax
```

(continued)

Figure 17-31. *continued*

```
        mov     ax,xfrsec           ; get sector number
        call    MapDS               ; and map it to DS:SI
                                    ; (may force mode switch)

        push    es                  ; save DGROUP selector

                                    ; convert destination physical
                                    ; address to virtual address...
        mov     bx,word ptr es:xfraddr
        mov     ax,word ptr es:xfraddr+2
        mov     cx,secsize          ; segment length
        mov     dh,1                ; leave result in ES:DI
        mov     dl,PhysToVirt       ; function number
        call    es:devhlp           ; transfer to kernel

        mov     cx,secsize          ; transfer logical sector from
        cld                         ; RAM disk to requestor
        rep movsb

        pop     ds                  ; restore DGROUP addressing

        sti                         ; PhysToVirt may mask interrupt

        inc     xfrsec              ; advance sector number

                                    ; advance transfer address
        add     word ptr xfraddr,secsize
        adc     word ptr xfraddr+2,0

        inc     xfrcnt              ; count sectors transferred
        jmp     read1

Read2:                              ; all sectors transferred

        mov     dl,UnPhysToVirt ; function number
        call    devhlp          ; transfer to kernel

        pop     bx                  ; restore request packet address
        pop     es

        mov     ax,xfrcnt           ; put actual transfer count
        mov     es:[bx+12h],ax  ; into request packet

        mov     ax,0100h            ; return 'done' status
        ret

Read    endp
```

(continued)

Figure 17-31. *continued*

```
Write     proc     near                  ; functions 8,9 = write

          push     es                    ; save request packet address
          push     bx

          call     setup                 ; set up transfer variables

Write1:   mov      ax,xfrcnt             ; done with all sectors yet?
          cmp      ax,xfrreq
          je       write2                ; jump if transfer completed

          mov      ax,xfrsec             ; get sector number
          call     MapES                 ; map it to ES:DI
                                         ; (may force mode switch)

          push     ds                    ; save DGROUP selector

                                         ; convert source physical
                                         ; address to virtual address...
          mov      bx,word ptr xfraddr
          mov      ax,word ptr xfraddr+2
          mov      cx,secsize            ; segment length
          mov      dh,0                  ; leave result in DS:SI
          mov      dl,PhysToVirt         ; function number
          call     devhlp                ; transfer to kernel

          mov      cx,secsize            ; transfer logical sector from
          cld                            ; requestor to RAM disk
          rep movsb         .

          pop      ds                    ; restore DGROUP addressing
          sti                            ; PhysToVirt might have masked
          inc      xfrsec                ; advance sector number

                                         ; advance transfer address
          add      word ptr xfraddr,secsize
          adc      word ptr xfraddr+2,0

          inc      xfrcnt                ; count sectors transferred
          jmp      write1

Write2:                                  ; all sectors transferred

          mov      dl,UnPhysToVirt ; function number
          call     devhlp                ; transfer to kernel
```

(continued)

Figure 17-31. *continued*

```
        pop     bx              ; restore request packet address
        pop     es

        mov     ax,xfrcnt       ; put actual transfer count
        mov     es:[bx+12h],ax  ; into request packet

        mov     ax,0100h        ; return 'done' status
        ret

Write   endp


GenIOCTL proc   near            ; function 16 = Generic IOCtl

        push    es              ; save request packet address
        push    bx

        mov     ax,8103h        ; assume unknown command

                                ; Get Device Parameters call?
        cmp     byte ptr es:[bx+0dh],8
        jne     Gen9            ; no, set 'done' and 'error'
        cmp     byte ptr es:[bx+0eh],63h
        jne     Gen9            ; no, set 'done' and 'error'

                                ; verify user's access
        mov     ax,es:[bx+15h]  ; selector
        mov     di,es:[bx+13h]  ; offset
        mov     cx,gdprec_len   ; length to be written
        mov     dh,1            ; need read/write access
        mov     dl,VerifyAccess ; function number
        call    devhlp          ; transfer to kernel

        mov     ax,810ch        ; if no access, exit with
        jc      Gen9            ; 'done' and general failure

                                ; get destination address
        les     di,dword ptr es:[bx+13h]
                                ; copy device info to caller
        mov     si,offset DGROUP:bpb
        mov     cx,gdprec_len   ; length of parameter block
        cld
        rep movsb

        mov     ax,0100h        ; set 'done' status
```

(continued)

Figure 17-31. *continued*

```
Gen9:     pop     bx                      ; restore request packet address
          pop     es
          ret                             ; and return with status

GenIOCTL endp


GSLogDrv proc    near                     ; function 18, 19 - get
                                          ; or set logical drive

                                          ; return code indicating there
                                          ; are no logical drive aliases
          mov     byte ptr es:[bx+1],0

          mov     ax,0100h                ; return 'done' status
          ret

GSLogDrv endp


Error    proc    near            ·        ; bad command code

          mov     ax,8103h                ; error bit and 'done' status
          ret                             ; and "Unknown Command" code

Error    endp


MapES    proc    near                     ; map sector number to
                                          ; virtual memory address
                                          ; call with AX = logical sector
                                          ; return ES:DI = memory address
                                          :          and Carry clear
                                          ; or      Carry set if error

          mov     di,secsize              ; bytes per sector
          mul     di                      ; * logical sector number
          xchg    ax,dx                   ; AX:BX := 32-bit physical
          mov     bx,dx                   ; sector address
          add     bx,word ptr dbase
          adc     ax,word ptr dbase+2

          mov     cx,secsize
          mov     dh,1                     ; result to ES:DI
          mov     dl,PhysToVirt            ; function number
          call    devhlp                   ; transfer to kernel
```

(continued)

Figure 17-31. *continued*

```
        ret                             ; return ES:DI = sector address


MapES   endp


MapDS   proc    near                    ; map sector number to
                                        ; virtual memory address
                                        ; call with AX = logical sector
                                        ; return DS:SI = memory address
                                        ;          and Carry clear
                                        ; or     Carry set if error

        mov     si,secsize              ; bytes per sector
        mul     si                      ; * logical sector number
        xchg    ax,dx                   ; AX:BX := 32-bit physical
        mov     bx,dx                   ; sector address
        add     bx,word ptr dbase
        adc     ax,word ptr dbase+2

        mov     cx,secsize
        mov     dh,0                    ; result to DS:SI
        mov     dl,PhysToVirt           ; function number
        call    devhlp                  ; transfer to kernel

        ret                             ; return DS:SI = sector address

MapDS   endp


Setup   proc    near                    ; set up for read/write
                                        ; ES:BX = request packet
                                        ; extracts address, start, count

        mov     ax,es:[bx+14h]  ; starting sector number
        mov     xfrsec,ax

        mov     ax,es:[bx+12h]  ; sectors requested
        mov     xfrreq,ax

        mov     ax,es:[bx+0eh]  ; requestor's buffer address
        mov     word ptr xfraddr,ax
        mov     ax,es:[bx+10h]
        mov     word ptr xfraddr+2,ax

        mov     xfrcnt,0                ; initialize sectors
                                        ; transferred counter
```

(continued)

Figure 17-31. *continued*

```
        ret

Setup   endp

                                ; start of code discarded
                                ; after initialization

Init    proc    near            ; function 0 = initialize

        mov     ax,es:[bx+0eh]  ; get DevHlp entry point
        mov     word ptr devhlp,ax
        mov     ax,es:[bx+10h]
        mov     word ptr devhlp+2,ax

        mov     al,es:[bx+16h]  ; unit code for this drive
        add     al,'A'          ; convert to ASCII and place
        mov     drive,al        ; in output string

                                ; display sign-on message...
        push    stdout          ; handle for standard output
        push    ds              ; address of message
        push    offset DGROUP:ident
        push    ident_len       ; length of message
        push    ds              ; receives bytes written
        push    offset DGROUP:wlen
        call    DosWrite

                                ; set offsets to end of code
                                ; and data segments
        mov     word ptr es:[bx+0eh],offset _TEXT:Init
        mov     word ptr es:[bx+10h],offset DGROUP:ident

                                ; logical units supported
        mov     byte ptr es:[bx+0dh],1

                                ; pointer to BPB array
        mov     word ptr es:[bx+12h],offset DGROUP:array
        mov     word ptr es:[bx+14h],ds

        push    es              ; save request packet address
        push    bx

                                ; allocate RAM disk storage
        mov     bx,0            ; AX:BX = size of allocated
        mov     ax,1            ; block in bytes
        mov     dh,0            ; request block above 1 MB
        mov     dl,AllocPhys    ; function number
```

(continued)

Figure 17-31. *continued*

```
                call    devhlp            ; transfer to kernel
                jc      Init9             ; jump if allocation failed

                                          ; save physical address
                                          ; of allocated block
        mov     word ptr dbase,bx
        mov     word ptr dbase+2,ax

        call    format            ; format the RAM disk
        jc      Init9             ; jump if format failed

        pop     bx                ; restore request packet address
        pop     es

        mov     ax,0100h          ; return 'done' status
        ret

Init9:                            ; abort driver installation

        pop     bx                ; restore request packet address
        pop     es

                                  ; display installation aborted...
        push    stdout            ; handle for standard output
        push    ds                ; address of message
        push    offset DGROUP:abort
        push    abort_len         ; length of message
        push    ds                ; receives bytes written
        push    offset DGROUP:wlen
        call    DosWrite          ; transfer to OS/2

                                  ; set zero units
        mov     byte ptr es:[bx+0dh],0

                                  ; set lengths of code and
                                  ; data segments
        mov     word ptr es:[bx+0eh],0
        mov     word ptr es:[bx+10h],0

        mov     ax,810ch          ; return error and done and
                                  ; general failure

        ret

Init    endp
```

(continued)

Figure 17-31. *continued*

```
Format   proc    near                  ; format the RAM disk area


                                       ; calculate length of
                                       ; RAM disk control areas
         mov     al,byte ptr bpb+5
         cbw                           ; number of FATs
         mov     cx,bpb+0bh            ; * sectors per FAT
         mul     cx
         mov     cx,bpb+6             ; entries in root directory
         shr     cx,4                  ; divide by 16 for sectors
         add     ax,cx                 ; (FAT + dir sectors
         add     ax,bpb+3             ; + reserved sectors)
         mov     cx,secsize           ; * bytes/sector
         mul     cx                    ; = total length
         mov     cx,ax


                                       ; convert RAM disk base to
                                       ; virtual address
         mov     bx,word ptr dbase
         mov     ax,word ptr dbase+2
         mov     dh,1                  ; leave result in ES:DI
         mov     dl,PhysToVirt        ; function number
         call    devhlp               ; transfer to kernel
         jc      Format9              ; jump if error


         xor     ax,ax                 ; now zero control areas
         cld                           ; (assume CX still = length)
         rep stosb


         mov     ax,0                  ; get address of logical
         call    MapES                ; sector zero
         jc      Format9              ; jump if error
         mov     si,offset DGROUP:bootrec
         mov     cx,bootrec_len       ; copy boot record
         rep movsb                     ; to logical sector zero


         mov     ax,word ptr bpb+3
         call    MapES                ; get address of FAT sector
         jc      Format9              ; jump if error
         mov     al,byte ptr bpb+0ah
         mov     es:[di],al           ; medium ID byte into FAT
         mov     word ptr es:[di+1],-1
```

(continued)

Figure 17-31. *continued*

```
        mov     ax,word ptr bpb+3
        add     ax,word ptr bpb+0bh
        call    MapES           ; get address of directory
        jc      Format9         ; jump if error
        mov     si,offset DGROUP:volname
        mov     cx,volname_len
        rep movsb               ; copy volume label to it

        mov     dl,UnPhysToVirt ; function number
        call    devhlp          ; transfer to kernel

        clc                     ; signal format successful

Format9:                        ; return with Carry = 0
        ret                     ; if success, 1 if error

Format  endp

_TEXT   ends

        end
```

```
LIBRARY TINYDISK
PROTMODE
```

Figure 17-32. *TINYDISK.DEF, the module definition file used during linking of TINYDISK.SYS.*

At initialization time, TINYDISK allocates itself 64 KB of fixed memory above the 1 MB boundary for use as RAM disk storage. It then initializes the RAM disk's control areas by clearing the FAT and directory, copying a simulated boot block to the RAM disk's "logical sector 0," placing the fixed disk medium ID byte at the beginning of the FAT, and copying a simulated volume label to the start of the directory. TINYDISK then displays a sign-on message that includes its drive code.

When TINYDISK receives a *Read* or *Write* request packet from the kernel, it simply translates the sector number into an offset within the RAM disk storage area, calls *PhysToVirt* to obtain virtual addresses appropriate for the current mode, and copies data directly between the application's buffer and the RAM disk memory. To keep the sample source code to a tolerable length, other request packets (such as *Build BPB*, *Media Check*, and *Generic IOCtl*) are handled in an adequate but simplistic fashion.

Note especially the sequence of events in the TINYDISK *Read* and *Write* routines. Both routines convert the address of the RAM disk storage buffer first because it always lies above the 1 MB boundary and is guaranteed to cause a switch from real mode to protected mode if a switch is going to occur at all. The segment register that points to DGROUP is not saved on the stack until after the first call to *PhysToVirt* because the value in the register might change as a side effect of a mode switch. The code in these routines illustrates on a small scale the extreme care with which addressability must be handled in a full-fledged driver.

TINYDISK.SYS is built from the source file TINYDISK.ASM and the module definition file TINYDISK.DEF with the following commands:

```
[C:\] MASM TINYDISK.ASM;  <Enter>
```

```
[C:\] LINK TINYDISK,TINYDISK.SYS,,OS2,TINYDISK  <Enter>
```

After assembling and linking the driver, copy the file TINYDISK.SYS to the root directory of your boot disk, add the line *DEVICE=TINYDISK.SYS* to your CONFIG.SYS file, and restart the system. During system initialization you will see a line such as the following:

```
TINYDISK 64 KB RAM disk for OS/2
RAM disk will be drive F:
```

You can then copy files to and from the TINYDISK drive as though it were a small but very fast fixed disk. If TINYDISK cannot install itself because memory proves insufficient or because another system error occurs, it issues the following error message:

```
TINYDISK installation aborted
```

DEVICE MONITORS

Ordinarily, the flow of data between a physical character device and an application program follows a well-defined path through the system (Figure 18-1). By the time a character reaches an application program, it has been filtered, buffered, and possibly translated in two or more layers of system software. The unprocessed data that arrives from the device is hidden from normal applications by the privilege levels and protection mechanisms of the 80286 protected mode.

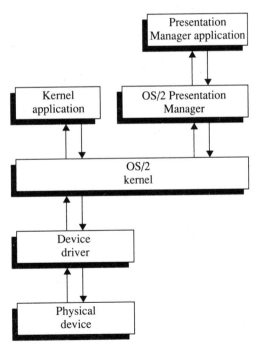

Figure 18-1. *Normal flow of data between a character device and an application.*

To let normal programs intercept characters at a low level without running afoul of protected mode restrictions, OS/2 recognizes a class of applications called *device monitors,* for which it exports a special set of API support functions (Figure 18-2). In effect, these API functions allow an application to insert a probe into a device driver's raw data stream. A device monitor can add, consume, or remap characters or "events" before they pass from the driver to the physical device or from the driver to the kernel or its subsystems for distribution to applications.

Function	*Description*
DosMonOpen	Creates connection between device monitor and character device driver
DosMonReg	Inserts application buffers into monitor buffer chain
DosMonRead	Obtains data packet from monitor chain
DosMonWrite	Propels data packet into monitor chain
DosMonClose	Terminates connection between device monitor and character device driver

Figure 18-2. *OS/2 device monitor functions at a glance.*

Print spoolers, keyboard enhancers, and similar utilities can easily be written as device monitors, eliminating the need for custom device drivers in many cases. Furthermore, multiple applications can register as monitors for the same device and can even specify where they want to be in the chain of all monitors. Similarly, a single monitor can register with multiple device drivers or register multiple times with the same driver. Because monitors (like other applications) run at the lowest privilege level, and because the usual memory protection mechanisms are always in effect, the chances of harmful or unexpected interactions between monitors are minimal.

As you might expect, OS/2's support for monitors involves an elaborate dialogue between the application, kernel, and device driver and requires a high degree of cooperation among the three to preserve the system's performance. A special kernel module, called the *monitor dispatcher,* arbitrates among the three components and moves data from the driver through the buffers of one or more monitors and back to the driver (Figure 18-3).

OS/2's default KBD$, MOUSE$, and PRN drivers all contain the necessary logic to support device monitors; its COM*x* and SCREEN$ drivers do not. Monitor support in other character drivers is optional. If you are using a custom device driver from a software or hardware vendor other than Microsoft, refer to the documentation for that driver to determine whether it supports monitors and, if so, what format its monitor data packets assume.

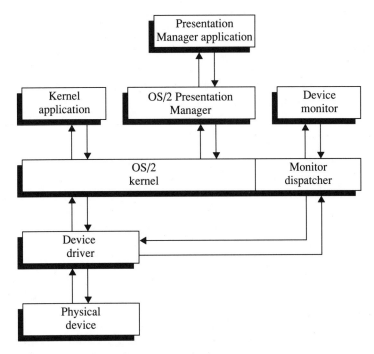

Figure 18-3. *Flow of data between a character device and an application when a device monitor is registered. A monitor runs as a normal "user" process and has access to all the usual OS/2 API services. The characters are passed in packets from the driver to the device monitor, which can translate, delete, or add characters. The characters are then passed back to the driver, and from there they flow through the operating system to application programs or from the driver to the device.*

An application can determine at run time whether a particular driver supports monitors by calling *DosDevIOCtl* Category 11 Function 60H (Query Monitor Support).

Device Monitor Organization

Device monitoring is restricted to protected mode applications; it is not available to Family or real mode programs. To register as a device monitor, an application first calls the *DosMonOpen* function with the logical name of the character device you want it to tap. If the driver for that device supports monitors, *DosMonOpen* returns a monitor handle.

The application then calls *DosMonReg* with the monitor handle and the addresses of two data buffers that will be used for input and output of device driver data packets. A suitable buffer must be at least 20 bytes longer than the monitor data packet used by the character device driver of interest. Additional parameters to the *DosMonReg* call are an *index* (which identifies the screen group for keyboard and mouse monitors) and a code that specifies the location you prefer for this program in the chain of all monitors attached to this particular driver: first, last, or no preference. If additional programs later request the first (or last) position, the first program to make the request retains first (or last) position in the chain, the second program comes next, and so on.

If the *DosMonReg* call succeeds, the program has successfully registered as a device monitor and becomes responsible for passing the driver's data through its monitor buffers without impeding the performance of the driver. To do so, it calls *DosMonRead* to obtain a data packet from the monitor chain and then *DosMonWrite* to return a packet to the chain. Typically, the program dedicates a thread with time-critical priority to a tight loop that performs no API calls except for *DosSemSet*, *DosSemClear*, and successive invocations of *DosMonRead* and *DosMonWrite*, so that other I/O operations or lengthy calculations by the monitor do not interfere with the driver's throughput.

Between each *DosMonRead* and *DosMonWrite*, the monitor can inspect the character data. It can translate characters by modifying the packets, consume characters by simply not calling *DosMonWrite*, or add characters to the data stream by constructing additional packets in the existing format and calling *DosMonWrite* to shove them into the monitor chain.

When the program wants to unhook from the character stream it is monitoring, it calls *DosMonClose* with the monitor handle it received from the original *DosMonOpen*. The program can then release its other resources and terminate without any untoward effects. Figure 18-4 shows a skeleton of the code you would use in a monitor.

The format of a monitor data packet is unique to the character device driver. The packet usually contains a date and time stamp, a byte of monitor flags, and one or more characters. Figures 18-5 through 18-8 on pp. 425–27 show the structure of the data packets used by OS/2's KBD$, MOUSE$, and PRN drivers.

```
KbdName  db       'KBD$',0           ; Kbd logical device name
KbdHan   dw       ?                  ; handle from DosMonOpen

                                     ; buffers for Kbd monitor
KbdIn    dw       128,64 dup (0)     ; monitor input buffer
KbdOut   dw       128,64 dup (0)     ; monitor output buffer

KbdPkt   db       128 dup (0)        ; receives Kbd data packet
KbdPLen  dw       ?                  ; length of data in KbdPkt

ScrGrp   dw       ?                  ; current screen group

         .
         .
         .

                                     ; open monitor connection...
         push     ds                 ; address of device name
         push     offset DGROUP:KbdName
         push     ds                 ; receives monitor handle
         push     offset DGROUP:KbdHan
         call     DosMonOpen         ; transfer to OS/2
         or       ax,ax              ; was open successful?
         jnz      error              ; jump if function failed

                                     ; register Kbd monitor...
         push     KbdHan             ; handle from DosMonOpen
         push     ds                 ; input buffer address
         push     offset DGROUP:KbdIn
         push     ds                 ; output buffer address
         push     offset DGROUP:KbdOut
         push     1                  ; request front of list
         push     ScrGrp             ; push screen group number
         call     DosMonReg          ; transfer to OS/2
         or       ax,ax              ; registration successful?
         jnz      error              ; jump if function failed
         .
         .
         .

next:                                ; this loop is the actual
                                     ; keyboard monitor...

                                     ; set max length for read
         mov      KbdPLen,KbdPLen-KbdPkt
```

(continued)

Figure 18-4. *Skeleton of application code related to function as a keyboard device monitor.*

Figure 18-4. *continued*

```
                             ; get next Kbd packet...
        push    ds           ; address of input buffer
        push    offset DGROUP:KbdIn
        push    0            ; wait until data available
        push    ds           ; receives data packet
        push    offset DGROUP:KbdPkt
        push    ds           ; receives packet length
        push    offset DGROUP:KbdPLen
        call    DosMonRead   ; transfer to OS/2
        or      ax,ax        ; was read successful?
        jnz     error        ; jump if function failed

                             ; is the key our hot key?
        cmp     byte ptr KbdPkt+3,HotKey
        jz      keyact       ; jump if it is

                             ; not hot key, pass it on...
        push    ds           ; output buffer address
        push    offset DGROUP:KbdOut
        push    ds           ; contains data packet
        push    offset DGROUP:KbdPkt
        push    KbdPLen      ; contains packet length
        call    DosMonWrite  ; transfer to OS/2
        or      ax,ax        ; was write successful?
        jnz     error        ; jump if function failed

        jmp     next         ; wait for another key
        .
        .
        .
done:                        ; cease monitoring...
        push    KbdHan       ; monitor handle
        call    DosMonClose  ; transfer to OS/2
        or      ax,ax        ; was close successful?
        jnz     error        ; jump if function failed
        .
        .
        .
```

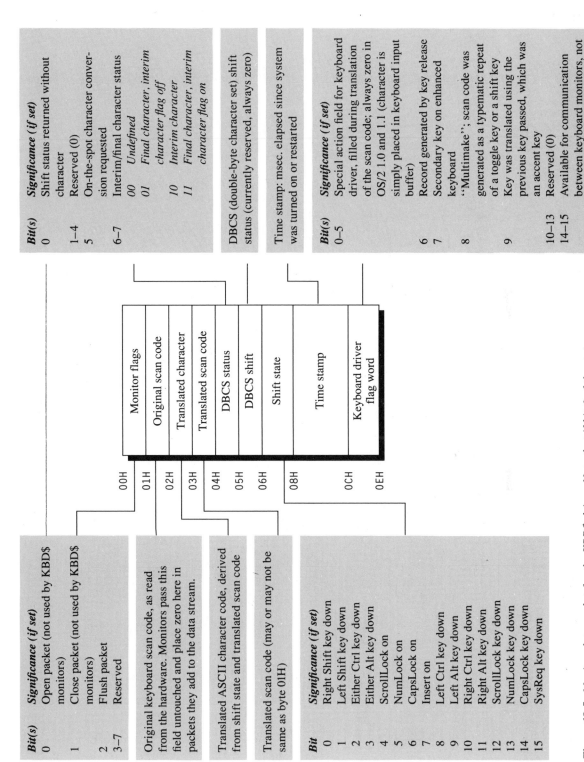

Figure 18-5. *Monitor data packet for the KBD$ driver. Note that if bit 6 of the status byte is clear, no character was returned, and the record may reflect changed shift state.*

Monitor flags (00H):

Bit(s)	Significance (if set)
0	Open packet (not used by KBD$ monitors)
1	Close packet (not used by KBD$ monitors)
2	Flush packet
3–7	Reserved

Original scan code (01H): Original keyboard scan code, as read from the hardware. Monitors pass this field untouched and place zero here in packets they add to the data stream.

Translated character (02H): Translated ASCII character code, derived from shift state and translated scan code

Translated scan code (03H): Translated scan code (may or may not be same as byte 01H)

DBCS status (04H):

Bit(s)	Significance (if set)
0	Shift status returned without character
1–4	Reserved (0)
5	On-the-spot character conversion requested
6–7	Interim/final character status
	00 Undefined
	01 Final character, interim character flag off
	10 Interim character
	11 Final character, interim character flag on

DBCS shift (05H): DBCS (double-byte character set) shift status (currently reserved, always zero)

Shift state (06H):

Bit	Significance (if set)
0	Right Shift key down
1	Left Shift key down
2	Either Ctrl key down
3	Either Alt key down
4	ScrollLock on
5	NumLock on
6	CapsLock on
7	Insert on
8	Left Ctrl key down
9	Left Alt key down
10	Right Ctrl key down
11	Right Alt key down
12	ScrollLock key down
13	NumLock key down
14	CapsLock key down
15	SysReq key down

Time stamp (08H): Time stamp: msec. elapsed since system was turned on or restarted

Keyboard driver flag word (0CH–0EH):

Bit(s)	Significance (if set)
0–5	Special action field for keyboard driver, filled during translation of the scan code; always zero in OS/2 1.0 and 1.1 (character is simply placed in keyboard input buffer)
6	Record generated by key release
7	Secondary key on enhanced keyboard
8	"Multimake"; scan code was generated as a typematic repeat of a toggle key or a shift key
9	Key was translated using the previous key passed, which was an accent key
10–13	Reserved (0)
14–15	Available for communication between keyboard monitors, not used by keyboard driver

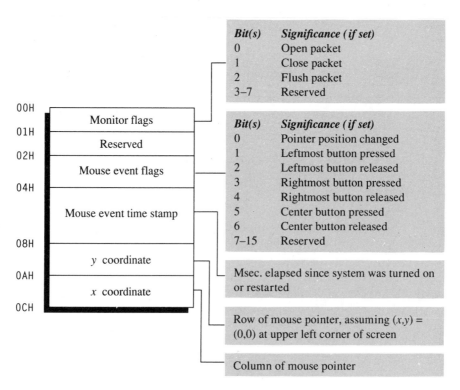

Figure 18-6. *Monitor data packet for the MOUSE$ driver.*

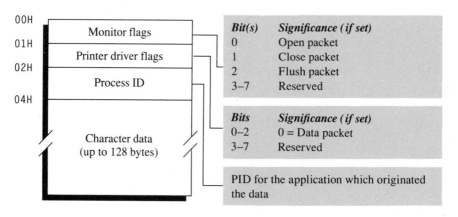

Figure 18-7. *Monitor character data packet for the PRN driver (maximum length 132 bytes). The application determines the length of the packet from the value returned by DosMonRead.*

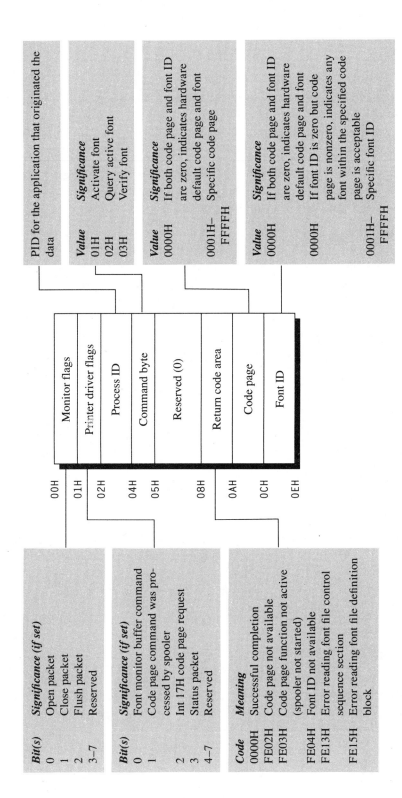

Packet offsets:

00H	Monitor flags
01H	Printer driver flags
02H	Process ID
04H	Command byte
05H	Reserved (0)
08H	Return code area
0AH	Code page
0CH	Code page
0EH	Font ID

Process ID

PID for the application that originated the data

Command byte

Value	Significance
01H	Activate font
02H	Query active font
03H	Verify font

Code page

Value	Significance
0000H	If both code page and font ID are zero, indicates hardware default code page and font
0001H–FFFFH	Specific code page

Font ID

Value	Significance
0000H	If both code page and font ID are zero, indicates hardware default code page and font
0000H	If font ID is zero but code page is nonzero, indicates any font within the specified code page is acceptable
0001H–FFFFH	Specific font ID

Monitor flags

Bit(s)	Significance (if set)
0	Open packet
1	Close packet
2	Flush packet
3–7	Reserved

Printer driver flags

Bit(s)	Significance (if set)
0	Font monitor buffer command
1	Code page command was processed by spooler
2	Int 17H code page request
3	Status packet
4–7	Reserved

Return code area

Code	Meaning
0000H	Successful completion
FE02H	Code page not available
FE03H	Code page function not active (spooler not started)
FE04H	Font ID not available
FE13H	Error reading font file control sequence section
FE15H	Error reading font file definition block

Figure 18-8. *Monitor code page packet for the PRN driver.*

Device Driver Support for Monitors

A driver informs the kernel that it is prepared to support monitors by issuing the DevHlp call *MonitorCreate*, which establishes an initial "empty chain" of device monitors and assigns a monitor handle to it. The driver can create the monitor chain during its initialization, or it can wait until the chain is needed.

When an application executes *DosMonOpen*, the driver receives a special *Device Open* request packet that has bit 3 of the status word set. At this point, the driver must create the empty monitor chain if it hasn't already done so.

The driver is informed that an application has issued *DosMonReg* by the receipt of a *Generic IOCtl* Category 10 Function 40H request packet; it then calls the DevHlp service *Register*, which causes the kernel's monitor dispatcher to insert the application's buffers into the monitor chain at the appropriate point. The driver can identify the requesting process by getting the selector for the local information segment with the DevHlp *GetDOSVar* and then extracting the PID from that segment.

After it creates the monitor chain (whether any monitors have registered or not), the driver must pass each character it receives from the device through the chain by calling the DevHlp service *MonWrite*. The kernel's monitor dispatcher calls a notification routine within the driver when data emerges from the end of the monitor chain. For the mouse and keyboard drivers, the data is then passed onward to the *Kbd* or *Mou* subsystems in the usual fashion. In the case of the printer driver, the data is then sent to the parallel port.

When an application issues *DosMonClose*, the driver receives a special *Device Close* request packet with bit 3 of the status word set. The driver can obtain the PID of the current process by the procedure previously described and then call the DevHlp service *DeRegister* to remove the application's buffers from the monitor chain. When the driver notes that all monitor connections have been closed, it can call the DevHlp *MonitorCreate* again with a parameter that causes the monitor chain to be destroyed.

Sample Device Monitor: SNAP

The listings SNAP.ASM (Figure 18-9) and SNAP.C (Figure 18-10 on page 445) contain the source code for SNAP.EXE, a sample OS/2 device monitor. After you launch SNAP from the command prompt, it registers itself as a monitor with the keyboard driver (KBD$) for the current screen group. It then watches the keyboard data stream and captures the current screen display into a disk file whenever it detects a particular hot key. The file is named SNAP*xx*.IMG (where *xx* is the current number of the current screen group) and is always located in the root directory of the drive that was current when SNAP was loaded. The user can capture multiple screen dumps into the same file; SNAP separates them with divider lines. If a file with the same name exists when SNAP is loaded, it will be overwritten with new dump data.

Although the SNAP program is relatively short, it is fairly complex and illustrates many of the OS/2 programming topics that have been discussed in this book:

- Reading and writing the video display with the *Vio* subsystem calls

- Creating, opening, and updating disk files

- Generating tones with *DosBeep*

- Creating and using RAM and system semaphores for intraprocess and interprocess signaling

- Creating multiple threads within a process and controlling one thread with another

- Spawning a child process

- Registering and deregistering a keyboard monitor and filtering the keyboard data stream for hot keys

```
        title   SNAP -- Sample OS/2 Device Monitor
        page    55,132
        .286


;
; SNAP.ASM
;
; A sample OS/2 device monitor that captures the current display into
; the file SNAPxx.IMG, where xx is the session number.  SNAP works in
; character mode only and may not be used in a PM window.  The
; following keys are defined as defaults:
;
; Alt-F10   hot key to capture a screen
; Ctrl-F10  hot key to deinstall SNAP.EXE
;
; Assemble with:  C> masm snap.asm;
; Link with:  C> link snap,,,os2,snap
;
```

(continued)

Figure 18-9. *SNAP.ASM, source code for SNAP.EXE sample device monitor.*

Figure 18-9. *continued*

```
; Usage is:  C> snap
;
; Copyright (C) 1988 Ray Duncan
;

cr      equ     0dh                     ; ASCII character codes
lf      equ     0ah


                                        ; hot key definitions:
snapkey equ     71h                     ; snapshot   Alt-F10
exitkey equ     67h                     ; exit       Ctrl-F10


stksize equ     2048                    ; stack size for threads

        extrn   DosAllocSeg:far
        extrn   DosBeep:far
        extrn   DosBufReset:far
        extrn   DosClose:far
        extrn   DosCloseSem:far
        extrn   DosCreateSem:far
        extrn   DosCreateThread:far
        extrn   DosExecPgm:far
        extrn   DosExit:far
        extrn   DosGetInfoSeg:far
        extrn   DosOpenSem:far
        extrn   DosMonClose:far
        extrn   DosMonOpen:far
        extrn   DosMonRead:far
        extrn   DosMonReg:far
        extrn   DosMonWrite:far
        extrn   DosOpen:far
        extrn   DosSemClear:far
        extrn   DosSemSet:far
        extrn   DosSemWait:far
        extrn   DosSetPrty:far
        extrn   DosSleep:far
        extrn   DosSuspendThread:far
        extrn   DosWrite:far
        extrn   VioEndPopUp:far
        extrn   VioGetMode:far
        extrn   VioPopUp:far
        extrn   VioReadCharStr:far
        extrn   VioWrtCharStr:far
```

(continued)

Figure 18-9. *continued*

```
jerr    macro   p1,p2,p3                ;; Macro to test return code
        local   zero                    ;; in AX and jump if nonzero
        or      ax,ax                   ;; Uses JMP DISP16 to avoid
        jz      zero                    ;; branch out of range errors
        mov     dx,offset DGROUP:p2     ;; p2 = message address
        mov     cx,p3                   ;; p3 = message length
        jmp     p1                      ;; routine p1 displays message
zero:
        endm


DGROUP  group   _DATA


_DATA   segment word public 'DATA'

exitsem dd      0                       ; semaphore for final exit
snapsem dd      0                       ; semaphore for 'snap' thread

sname   db      '\SEM\SNAP'             ; system semaphore name
sname1  db      'nn.LCK',0
shandle dd      0                       ; system semaphore handle

pflags  dw      0                       ; VioPopUp flags

wlen    dw      ?                       ; receives length written
action  dw      ?                       ; receives DosOpen action

watchID dw      ?                       ; keyboard thread ID
snapID  dw      ?                       ; snapshot thread ID

sel     dw      ?                       ; selector from DosAllocSeg

kname   db      'KBD$',0                ; keyboard device name
khandle dw      0                       ; keyboard monitor handle

fname   db      '\SNAP'                 ; name of snapshot file
fname1  db      'nn.IMG',0
fhandle dw      0                       ; handle for snapshot file

scrbuf  db      80 dup (0)              ; receives screen data
slen    dw      $-scrbuf                ; length of screen buffer

newline db      cr,lf                   ; carriage return-linefeed
nl_len  equ     $-newline
```

(continued)

Figure 18-9. *continued*

```
gseg        dw          ?                           ; global info seg. selector
lseg        dw          ?                           ; local info seg. selector

obuff       db          64 dup (0)                  ; receives name of dynlink
obuff_len equ           $-obuff                     ; causing DosExecPgm to fail

kbdin       dw          128,64 dup (0)              ; input and output buffers
kbdout      dw          128,64 dup (0)              ; for keyboard monitor

kbdpkt      db          128 dup (0)                 ; keyboard data packet
kpktlen dw              ?                           ; length of buffer/packet

pname       db          'SNAP.EXE',0                ; child process name
retcode dd              0                           ; child process info

vioinfo label           byte                        ; receives display mode
            dw          8                           ; length of structure
            db          0                           ; display mode type
            db          0                           ; colors
cols        dw          0                           ; number of columns
rows        dw          0                           ; number of rows

msg1        db          'SNAP utility installed!'
msg1_len equ            $-msg1

msg2        db          'Alt-F10 to capture screen into file SNAP.IMG.'
msg2_len equ            $-msg2

msg3        db          'Ctrl-F10 to shut down SNAP.'
msg3_len equ            $-msg3

msg4        db          'SNAP utility deactivated.'
msg4_len equ            $-msg4

msg5        db          'Error detected during SNAP installation:'
msg5_len equ            $-msg5

msg6        db          'Can''t create SNAP system semaphore.'
msg6_len equ            $-msg6

msg7        db          'Can''t start child copy of SNAP.'
msg7_len equ            $-msg7

msg8        db          'SNAP is already loaded.'
msg8_len equ            $-msg8
```

(continued)

Figure 18-9. *continued*

```
msg9      db        'Can''t open KBD$ monitor connection.'
msg9_len equ      $-msg9

msg10     db        'Can''t register as KBD$ monitor.'
msg10_len equ      $-msg10

msg11     db        'Can''t allocate thread stack.'
msg11_len equ      $-msg11

msg12     db        'Can''t create keyboard thread.'
msg12_len equ      $-msg12

msg13     db        'Can''t create snapshot thread.'
msg13_len equ      $-msg13

msg14     db        'Can''t create snapshot file.'
msg14_len equ      $-msg14

divider db        79 dup ('-'),cr,lf
divider_len equ $-divider


_DATA   ends

_TEXT   segment word public 'CODE'

        assume  cs:_TEXT,ds:DGROUP

main    proc    far                     ; entry point from OS/2

                                        ; get info segment selectors
        push    ds                      ; receives global info selector
        push    offset DGROUP:gseg
        push    ds                      ; receives local info selector
        push    offset DGROUP:lseg
        call    DosGetInfoSeg           ; transfer to OS/2

                                        ; build system semaphore
                                        ; and snapshot file names
        mov     es,gseg                 ; get foreground screen group
        mov     al,es:[0018h]
        aam                             ; convert to ASCII
        add     ax,'00'
        xchg    ah,al
```

(continued)

Figure 18-9. *continued*

```
        mov     word ptr fname1,ax      ; store into filename
        mov     word ptr sname1,ax      ; store into semaphore name

                                        ; does SNAPxx.LCK exist?
        push    ds                      ; receives semaphore handle
        push    offset DGROUP:shandle
        push    ds
        push    offset DGROUP:sname     ; semaphore name
        call    DosOpenSem              ; transfer to OS/2
        or      ax,ax                   ; was open successful?
        jz      main1                   ; jump, we're child SNAP

                                        ; we're the parent SNAP,
                                        ; create system semaphore
        push    1                       ; make it nonexclusive
        push    ds                      ; receives semaphore handle
        push    offset DGROUP:shandle
        push    ds                      ; system semaphore name
        push    offset DGROUP:sname
        call    DosCreateSem            ; transfer to OS/2
        jerr    error,msg6,msg6_len     ; jump if create failed

                                        ; set the semaphore...
        push    word ptr shandle+2      ; semaphore handle
        push    word ptr shandle
        call    DosSemSet               ; transfer to OS/2

                                        ; launch child SNAP...
        push    ds                      ; object name buffer
        push    offset DGROUP:obuff     ; receives failed dynlink
        push    obuff_len               ; length of buffer
        push    4                       ; child detached
        push    0                       ; NULL argument pointer
        push    0
        push    0                       ; NULL environment pointer
        push    0
        push    ds                      ; receives child info
        push    offset DGROUP:retcode
        push    ds                      ; pathname for child
        push    offset DGROUP:pname
        call    DosExecPgm              ; request launch of child
        jerr    error,msg7,msg7_len     ; jump if launch failed
```

(continued)

Figure 18-9. *continued*

```
                                              ; wait for child to load
        push    word ptr shandle+2            ; semaphore handle
        push    word ptr shandle
        push    -1                            ; timeout = indefinite
        push    -1
        call    DosSemWait                    ; transfer to OS/2

                                              ; close the semaphore...
        push    word ptr shandle+2            ; semaphore handle
        push    word ptr shandle
        call    DosCloseSem                   ; transfer to OS/2

        jmp     main3                         ; now exit

main1:                                        ; come here if child SNAP...
                                              ; check if already resident
        push    word ptr shandle+2            ; semaphore handle
        push    word ptr shandle
        push    0                             ; timeout = 0
        push    0
        call    DosSemWait                    ; transfer to OS/2
        or      ax,ax                         ; is semaphore clear?
        jnz     main2                         ; no, proceed

                                              ; yes, don't load again
        mov     dx,offset DGROUP:msg8         ; address of warning message
        mov     cx,msg8_len                   ; length of message
        jmp     error                         ; display message and exit

main2:                                        ; initialize semaphores...
        push    ds                            ; address of exit semaphore
        push    offset DGROUP:exitsem
        call    DosSemSet                     ; transfer to OS/2

        push    ds                            ; address of snapshot semaphore
        push    offset DGROUP:snapsem
        call    DosSemSet                     ; transfer to OS/2

                                              ; open monitor connection ...
        push    ds                            ; address of device name
        push    offset DGROUP:kname
        push    ds                            ; receives monitor handle
        push    offset DGROUP:khandle
        call    DosMonOpen                    ; transfer to OS/2
        jerr    error,msg9,msg9_len           ; jump if open failed
```

(continued)

Figure 18-9. *continued*

```
                                            ; register as keyboard monitor
        push    khandle                     ; handle from DosMonOpen
        push    ds                          ; monitor input buffer address
        push    offset DGROUP:kbdin
        push    ds                          ; monitor output buffer address
        push    offset DGROUP:kbdout
        push    1                           ; position = front of list
        mov     es,gseg                     ; foreground session number
        mov     al,byte ptr es:[0018h]      ; from global info segment
        xor     ah,ah
        push    ax
        call    DosMonReg                   ; transfer to OS/2
        jerr    error,msg10,msg10_len       ; jump if register failed

        push    stksize                     ; alloc. stack for WATCH thread
        push    ds                          ; variable to receive selector
        push    offset DGROUP:sel
        push    0                           ; not shareable
        call    DosAllocSeg                 ; transfer to OS/2
        jerr    error,msg11,msg11_len       ; jump, can't allocate stack

                                            ; create keyboard thread
        push    cs                          ; initial execution address
        push    offset _TEXT:watch
        push    ds                          ; receives thread ID
        push    offset DGROUP:watchID
        push    sel                         ; address of thread's stack
        push    stksize
        call    DosCreateThread             ; transfer to OS/2
        jerr    error,msg12,msg12_len       ; jump, can't create thread

                                            ; promote keyboard thread
        push    2                           ; scope = single thread
        push    3                           ; class = time critical
        push    0                           ; delta = 0
        push    watchID                     ; thread ID
        call    DosSetPrty                  ; transfer to OS/2

        push    stksize                     ; allocate stack for SNAP thread
        push    ds                          ; variable to receive selector
        push    offset DGROUP:sel
        push    0                           ; not shareable
        call    DosAllocSeg                 ; transfer to OS/2
        jerr    error,msg11,msg11_len       ; jump, can't allocate stack
```

(continued)

Figure 18-9. *continued*

```
                                        ; create snapshot thread
          push    cs                    ; initial execution address
          push    offset _TEXT:snap
          push    ds                    ; receives thread ID
          push    offset DGROUP:snapID
          push    sel                   ; address of thread's stack
          push    stksize
          call    DosCreateThread       ; transfer to OS/2
          jerr    error,msg13,msg13_len ; jump, can't create thread

          call    signon                ; announce installation

                                        ; tell parent we are running
          push    word ptr shandle+2    ; semaphore handle
          push    word ptr shandle
          call    DosSemClear           ; transfer to OS/2

                                        ; block on exit semaphore...
          push    ds                    ; semaphore handle
          push    offset DGROUP:exitsem
          push    -1                    ; timeout = indefinite
          push    -1
          call    DosSemWait            ; transfer to OS/2

          push    watchID               ; suspend keyboard thread
          call    DosSuspendThread      ; transfer to OS/2

          push    snapID                ; suspend snapshot thread
          call    DosSuspendThread      ; transfer to OS/2

                                        ; close monitor connection
          push    khandle               ; monitor handle
          call    DosMonClose           ; transfer to OS/2

                                        ; close system semaphore
          push    word ptr shandle+2    ; semaphore handle
          push    word ptr shandle
          call    DosCloseSem           ; transfer to OS/2

                                        ; close snapshot file
          push    fhandle               ; file handle
          call    DosClose              ; transfer to OS/2

          call    signoff               ; announce deinstallation
```

(continued)

Figure 18-9. *continued*

```
main3:  push    1               ; terminate all threads
        push    0               ; return success code
        call    DosExit         ; final exit to OS/2

main    endp

error   proc    near            ; fatal error encountered
                                ; DS:DX = message, CX = length

        test    khandle,-1      ; monitor active?
        jz      error1          ; no, jump

                                ; yes, shut it down
        push    khandle         ; monitor handle
        call    DosMonClose     ; transfer to OS/2

error1: mov     ax,word ptr shandle     ; system semaphore open?
        or      ax,word ptr shandle+2
        jz      error2          ; no, jump

                                ; clear semaphore, in case
                                ; we're the child SNAP
        push    word ptr shandle+2      ; semaphore handle
        push    word ptr shandle
        call    DosSemClear     ; transfer to OS/2

                                ; close the semaphore
        push    word ptr shandle+2      ; semaphore handle
        push    word ptr shandle
        call    DosCloseSem     ; transfer to OS/2

error2: mov     ax,1            ; get popup window
        call    popup

                                ; display title...
        push    ds              ; message address
        push    offset DGROUP:msg5
        push    msg5_len        ; message length
        push    10              ; Y
        push    (80-msg5_len)/2 ; X (center it)
        push    0               ; Vio handle
        call    VioWrtCharStr   ; transfer to OS/2

                                ; display error message...
        push    ds              ; message address
```

(continued)

Figure 18-9. *continued*

```
        push    dx
        push    cx                          ; message length
        push    12                          ; Y
        mov     ax,80                       ; X (center it)
        sub     ax,cx
        shr     ax,1
        push    ax
        push    0                           ; Vio handle
        call    VioWrtCharStr               ; transfer to OS/2

        push    0                           ; pause for 3 seconds
        push    3000
        call    DosSleep                    ; transfer to OS/2

        call    unpop                       ; release popup window

        push    1                           ; terminate all threads
        push    1                           ; return error code
        call    DosExit                     ; exit program

error   endp


watch   proc    far                         ; keyboard thread, monitors
                                            ; for snapshot or exit hot keys

        mov     kpktlen,kpktlen-kbdpkt      ; max buffer length for read

                                            ; get keyboard data packet...
        push    ds                          ; monitor input buffer address
        push    offset DGROUP:kbdin
        push    0                           ; wait until data available
        push    ds
        push    offset DGROUP:kbdpkt        ; receives keyboard data packet
        push    ds
        push    offset DGROUP:kpktlen       ; contains/receives length
        call    DosMonRead                  ; transfer to OS/2

        cmp     kbdpkt+2,0                  ; is this extended code?
        jnz     watch1                      ; no, pass it on

        cmp     kbdpkt+3,exitkey            ; is it exit hot key?
        jz      watch2                      ; jump if exit key

        cmp     kbdpkt+3,snapkey            ; is it snapshot hot key?
        jnz     watch1                      ; no, jump
```

(continued)

Figure 18-9. *continued*

```
            cmp     word ptr kbdpkt+12,0    ; is it break packet?
            jnz     watch                   ; yes, ignore it

                                            ; snapshot hot key detected
                                            ; clear snapshot semaphore...
            push    ds                      ; semaphore handle
            push    offset DGROUP:snapsem
            call    DosSemClear             ; transfer to OS/2
            jmp     watch                   ; discard this hot key

watch1:                                     ; not hot key, pass character
            push    ds                      ; monitor output buffer address
            push    offset DGROUP:kbdout
            push    ds                      ; keyboard data packet address
            push    offset DGROUP:kbdpkt
            push    kpktlen                 ; length of data packet
            call    DosMonWrite             ; transfer to OS/2

            jmp     watch                   ; get another packet

watch2:                                     ; exit hot key detected...
            cmp     word ptr kbdpkt+12,0    ; is it break packet?
            jnz     watch                   ; yes, ignore it

                                            ; clear exit semaphore...
            push    ds                      ; semaphore handle
            push    offset DGROUP:exitsem
            call    DosSemClear             ; transfer to OS/2

            jmp     watch                   ; let thread 1 shut down

watch       endp

snap        proc    far                     ; This thread blocks on the
                                            ; snapshot semaphore, then
                                            ; dumps the screen contents
                                            ; to the file SNAPxx.IMG.


                                            ; open/create snapshot file
            push    ds                      ; address of filename
            push    offset DGROUP:fname
            push    ds                      ; variable to receive file handle
            push    offset DGROUP:fhandle
            push    ds                      ; variable to receive action taken
            push    offset DGROUP:action
            push    0                       ; initial file size
```

(continued)

Figure 18-9. *continued*

```
        push    0
        push    0                       ; normal file attribute
        push    12h                     ; create or replace file
        push    21h                     ; write access, deny write
        push    0                       ; DWORD reserved
        push    0
        call    DosOpen                 ; transfer to OS/2
        jerr    error,msg14,msg14_len   ; jump if can't create

snap1:                                  ; write divider line
        push    fhandle                 ; file handle
        push    ds                      ; address of divider string
        push    offset DGROUP:divider
        push    divider_len             ; length of string
        push    ds                      ; receives bytes written
        push    offset DGROUP:wlen
        call    DosWrite                ; transfer to OS/2

                                        ; force disk update...
        push    fhandle                 ; file handle
        call    DosBufReset             ; transfer to OS/2

                                        ; wait on snapshot semaphore
        push    ds                      ; semaphore handle
        push    offset DGROUP:snapsem
        push    -1                      ; timeout = indefinite
        push    -1
        call    DosSemWait              ; transfer to OS/2

        mov     ax,3                    ; pop-up in transparent mode
        call    popup                   ; to read screen contents

                                        ; get screen dimensions...
        push    ds                      ; receives video mode info
        push    offset DGROUP:vioinfo
        push    0                       ; Vio handle
        call    VioGetMode              ; transfer to OS/2

        mov     bx,0                    ; BX := initial screen row

snap2:                                  ; read line from screen...
        mov     ax,cols                 ; width to read
        mov     slen,ax
        push    ds                      ; address of screen buffer
        push    offset DGROUP:scrbuf
        push    ds                      ; contains/receives length
```

(continued)

Figure 18-9. *continued*

```
        push    offset DGROUP:slen
        push    bx                      ; screen row
        push    0                       ; screen column
        push    0                       ; Vio handle
        call    VioReadCharStr          ; transfer to OS/2

        push    ds                      ; scan backwards from end
        pop     es                      ; of line to find last
        mov     cx,slen                 ; nonblank character
        mov     di,offset DGROUP:scrbuf
        add     di,slen
        dec     di
        mov     al,20h
        std
        repe scasb
        cld
        jz      snap3                   ; if Z = True, line was empty
        inc     cx                      ; otherwise correct the length
snap3:                                  ; write line to file...
        push    fhandle                 ; file handle
        push    ds                      ; address of data
        push    offset DGROUP:scrbuf
        push    cx                      ; clipped line length
        push    ds                      ; receives bytes written
        push    offset DGROUP:wlen
        call    DosWrite                ; transfer to OS/2

                                        ; write newline (CR-LF)
        push    fhandle                 ; file handle
        push    ds
        push    offset DGROUP:newline   ; address of newline
        push    nl_len                  ; length of newline
        push    ds                      ; receives bytes written
        push    offset DGROUP:wlen
        call    DosWrite                ; transfer to OS/2

        inc     bx                      ; bump screen row counter
        cmp     bx,rows                 ; whole screen done yet?
        jne     snap2                   ; no, write another

        push    440                     ; reward user with some
        push    200                     ; audible feedback
        call    DosBeep                 ; transfer to OS/2
```

(continued)

Figure 18-9. *continued*

```
          call     unpop                    ; release the screen

                                            ; done with screen capture,
                                            ; reset snapshot semaphore
          push     ds                       ; semaphore handle
          push     offset DGROUP:snapsem
          call     DosSemSet                ; transfer to OS/2

          jmp      snap1                    ; go wait on semaphore

snap      endp

signon    proc     near                     ; announce installation,
                                            ; display help message

          mov      ax,1                     ; put up popup window
          call     popup                    ; mode = wait, nontransparent

          push     ds                       ; message address
          push     offset DGROUP:msg1
          push     msg1_len                 ; message length
          push     10                       ; Y
          push     (80-msg1_len)/2          ; X (center it)
          push     0                        ; Vio handle
          call     VioWrtCharStr            ; transfer to OS/2

          push     ds                       ; message address
          push     offset DGROUP:msg2
          push     msg2_len                 ; message length
          push     13                       ; Y
          push     (80-msg2_len)/2          ; X (center it)
          push     0                        ; Vio handle
          call     VioWrtCharStr            ; transfer to OS/2

          push     ds                       ; message address
          push     offset DGROUP:msg3
          push     msg3_len                 ; message length
          push     15                       ; Y
          push     (80-msg3_len)/2          ; X (center it)
          push     0                        ; Vio handle
          call     VioWrtCharStr            ; transfer to OS/2

          push     0                        ; pause for 4 seconds
          push     4000                     ; so user can read message
          call     DosSleep                 ; transfer to OS/2
```

(continued)

Figure 18-9. *continued*

```
          call    unpop                       ; take down popup window
          ret                                 ; back to caller

signon endp

signoff proc   near                           ; announce deinstallation

          mov     ax,1                        ; put up popup window
          call    popup                       ; mode = wait, nontransparent

          push    ds                          ; message address
          push    offset DGROUP:msg4
          push    msg4_len                    ; message length
          push    12                          ; Y
          push    (80-msg4_len)/2             ; X (center it)
          push    0                           ; Vio handle
          call    VioWrtCharStr

          push    0                           ; pause for 2 seconds
          push    2000                        ; so user can read message
          call    DosSleep                    ; transfer to OS/2

          call    unpop                       ; take down popup window
          ret

signoff endp

popup  proc    near                           ; put up popup window
                                              ; AX = VioPopUp flags
                                              ; bit 0 = 0 no wait
                                              ;         1 wait for pop-up
                                              ; bit 1 = 0 nontransparent
                                              ;         1 transparent

          mov     pflags,ax                   ; set pop-up mode

          push    ds                          ; address of pop-up flags
          push    offset DGROUP:pflags
          push    0                           ; Vio handle
          call    VioPopUp                    ; transfer to OS/2
          ret                                 ; back to caller

popup  endp
```

(continued)

Figure 18-9. *continued*

```
unpop     proc     near                         ; take down popup window

          push     0                            ; Vio handle
          call     VioEndPopUp                  ; transfer to OS/2
          ret                                   ; back to caller

unpop     endp

_TEXT     ends

          end      main
```

```
/*
          SNAP.C

          A sample OS/2 device monitor that captures the current
          display into the file SNAPxx.IMG, where xx is the
          session number.  SNAP works in character mode only and
          and may not be used in a PM window.  The following keys
          are defined as defaults:

          Alt-F10   hot key to capture a screen
          Ctrl-F10  hot key to deinstall SNAP.EXE

          Compile with:  C> cl /F 2000 snap.c

          Usage is:  C> snap

          Copyright (C) 1988 Ray Duncan
*/

#include <stdio.h>
#include <string.h>

                                      /* hot key definitions */
#define SNAPKEY  0x71                 /* Alt-F10 to capture screen */
#define EXITKEY  0x67                 /* Ctrl-F10 to exit */

#define STKSIZE  2048                 /* stack size for threads */

#define WAIT     0                    /* parameters for DosMonRead */
#define NOWAIT   1                    /* and DosMonWrite */
```

(continued)

Figure 18-10. *SNAP.C, source code for SNAP.EXE sample device monitor.*

Figure 18-10. *continued*

```
#define API unsigned extern far pascal   /* API function prototypes */

API DosBeep(unsigned, unsigned);
API DosBufReset(unsigned);
API DosClose(unsigned);
API DosCloseSem(unsigned long far *);
API DosCreateThread(void (far *)(), unsigned far *, void far *);
API DosCreateSem(unsigned, unsigned long far *, char far *);
API DosExecPgm(char far *, int, int, char far *, char far *,
               int far *, char far *);
API DosExit(unsigned, unsigned);
API DosGetInfoSeg(unsigned far *, unsigned far *);
API DosMonClose(unsigned);
API DosMonOpen(char far *, unsigned far *);
API DosMonRead(void far *, unsigned, char far *, int far *);
API DosMonReg(unsigned, void far *, void far *, int, unsigned);
API DosMonWrite(void far *, char far *, int);
API DosOpen(char far *, unsigned far *, unsigned far *, unsigned long,
            unsigned, unsigned, unsigned, unsigned long);
API DosOpenSem(unsigned long far *, char far *);
API DosSemClear(unsigned long far *);
API DosSemSet(unsigned long far *);
API DosSemWait(unsigned long far *, unsigned long);
API DosSetPrty(int, int, int, int);
API DosSleep(unsigned long);
API DosSuspendThread(unsigned);
API DosWrite(unsigned, void far *, int, unsigned far *);
API VioEndPopUp(unsigned);
API VioGetMode(void far *, unsigned);
API VioPopUp(unsigned far *, unsigned);
API VioReadCharStr(char far *, int far *, int, int, unsigned);
API VioWrtCharStr(char far *, int, int, int, unsigned);

void signon(void);                       /* local function prototypes */
void signoff(void);
void popup(unsigned);
void unpop(void);
void far snap(void);
void far watch(void);
void errexit(char *);
```

(continued)

Figure 18-10. *continued*

```
                                        /* RAM semaphores */
unsigned long exitsem = 0;              /* exit hot key semaphore */
unsigned long snapsem = 0;              /* screen snapshot semaphore */

char sname[20];                         /* system semaphore name */
unsigned long shandle = 0;              /* system semaphore handle */

char fname[20];                         /* snapshot filename */
unsigned fhandle = 0;                   /* snapshot file handle */

char kname[] = "KBD$";                  /* keyboard device name */
unsigned khandle = 0;                   /* keyboard monitor handle */

struct _monbuf {                        /* monitor input and */
    int len;                            /* output buffers */
    char buf[128];
    } kbdin  = { sizeof(kbdin.buf)  } ,
     kbdout = { sizeof(kbdout.buf) } ;

struct _vioinfo {                       /* display mode info */
    int len;
    char type;
    char colors;
    int cols;
    int rows;
    } vioinfo;

char msg1[] = "SNAP utility installed!";
char msg2[] = "Alt-F10 to capture screen image into file SNAP.IMG,";
char msg3[] = "Ctrl-F10 to shut down SNAP.";
char msg4[] = "SNAP utility deactivated.";
char msg5[] = "Error detected during SNAP installation:";

main()
{
    char obuff[80];                     /* object name buffer */
    int retcode[2];                     /* receives child info */

    unsigned gseg, lseg;                /* receives selectors */
    char far *ginfo;                    /* global info segment pointer */

    unsigned snapID, watchID;           /* receives thread IDs */
    char snapstk[STKSIZE];              /* snapshot thread stack */
    char watchstk[STKSIZE];             /* keyboard thread stack */
```

(continued)

Figure 18-10. *continued*

```
    DosGetInfoSeg(&gseg, &lseg);          /* get info segment selectors */
    (long) ginfo = (long) gseg << 16;     /* make far pointer */


                                          /* build semaphore and filenames */
    sprintf(sname, "\\SEM\\SNAP%02d.LCK", ginfo[0x18]);
    sprintf(fname, "\\SNAP%02d.IMG",      ginfo[0x18]);

    if(DosOpenSem(&shandle, sname))       /* does \SEM\SNAPxx.LCK exist? */
    {

                                          /* no, we're parent SNAP */
                                          /* create system semaphore */
        if(DosCreateSem(1, &shandle, sname))
            errexit("Can't create SNAP system semaphore.");
        DosSemSet((unsigned long far *) shandle);


                                          /* start detached child SNAP */
        if(DosExecPgm(obuff, sizeof(obuff), 4, NULL, NULL, retcode, "snap.exe"))
            errexit("Can't start child copy of SNAP.");


                                          /* wait for child to load */
        DosSemWait((unsigned long far *) shandle, -1L);
        DosCloseSem((unsigned long far *) shandle);
    }
    else                                  /* if SNAPxx.LCK exists, */
    {                                     /* we're the child SNAP */


                                          /* abort if already resident */
        if(! DosSemWait((unsigned long far *) shandle, 0L))
            errexit("SNAP is already loaded.");

        DosSemSet(&exitsem);              /* initialize exit and */
        DosSemSet(&snapsem);              /* snapshot semaphores */

        if(DosMonOpen(kname, &khandle))   /* open monitor connection */
            errexit("Can't open KBD$ monitor connection.");


                                          /* register at head of chain */
        if(DosMonReg(khandle, &kbdin, &kbdout, 1, ginfo[0x18]))
            errexit("Can't register as KBD$ monitor.");


                                          /* create keyboard thread */
        if(DosCreateThread(watch, &watchID, watchstk+STKSIZE))
            errexit("Can't create keyboard thread.");

        DosSetPrty(2, 3, 0, watchID);     /* promote keyboard thread */
```

(continued)

Figure 18-10. *continued*

```
                                       /* create snapshot thread */
    if(DosCreateThread(snap, &snapID, snapstk+STKSIZE))
        errexit("Can't create snapshot thread.");

    signon();                          /* announce installation */

                                       /* tell parent we're running */
    DosSemClear((unsigned long far *) shandle);

    DosSemWait(&exitsem, -1L);         /* wait for exit hot key */

    DosSuspendThread(snapID);          /* suspend snapshot thread */
    DosSuspendThread(watchID);         /* suspend keyboard thread */
    DosMonClose(khandle);              /* close monitor connection */
                                       /* close system semaphore */
    DosCloseSem((unsigned long far *) shandle);
    DosClose(fhandle);                 /* close snapshot file */

    signoff();                         /* announce deinstallation */
    }

    DosExit(1, 0);                     /* final exit */
}


/*
    The 'watch' thread is responsible for monitoring the keyboard
    data stream.  It clears the 'snapsem' semaphore when the
    screen capture hot key is detected and clears the 'exitsem'
    semaphore when the deinstall hot key is detected.
*/
void far watch(void)
{
    char kbdpkt[128];                  /* monitor data packet */
    int kbdpktlen;                     /* data packet length */

    while(1)
    {
        kbdpktlen = sizeof(kbdpkt);    /* set buffer length */

                                       /* read monitor data */
        DosMonRead(&kbdin, WAIT, kbdpkt, &kbdpktlen);

                                       /* check for hot keys */
                                       /* ignore key breaks */
        if((kbdpkt[2] == 0) && (kbdpkt[3] == EXITKEY))
```

(continued)

Figure 18-10. *continued*

```
        {                                        /* exit hot key detected */
            if(kbdpkt[12] == 0) DosSemClear(&exitsem);
        }
        else if((kbdpkt[2] == 0) && (kbdpkt[3] == SNAPKEY))
        {                                        /* snapshot hot key detected */
            if(kbdpkt[12] == 0) DosSemClear(&snapsem);
        }                                        /* not hot key, pass it through */
        else DosMonWrite(&kbdout, kbdpkt, kbdpktlen);
    }
}


/*
    The 'snap' thread blocks on the 'snapsem' semaphore until it
    is cleared by the 'watch' thread, then captures the current
    screen contents into the snapshot file.
*/
void far snap(void)
{
    int i;                              /* scratch variable */
    unsigned action;                    /* receives DosOpen action */
    unsigned wlen;                      /* receives DosWrite length */
    char divider[81];                   /* snapshot divider line */
    char scrbuf[80];                    /* receives screen data */
    int slen;                           /* contains buffer size */

    memset(divider, '-', 79);           /* initialize divider line */
    divider[79] = 0x0d;
    divider[80] = 0x0a;

                                        /* create/replace snapshot file */
    if(DosOpen(fname, &fhandle, &action, 0L, 0, 0x12, 0x21, 0L))
        errexit("Can't create snapshot file.");

    while(1)
    {                                   /* write divider line */
        DosWrite(fhandle, divider, sizeof(divider), &wlen);
        DosBufReset(fhandle);           /* force file update */

        DosSemWait(&snapsem, -1L);      /* wait for hot key */

        popup(3);                       /* pop-up in transparent mode */
        vioinfo.len = sizeof(vioinfo);  /* get screen dimensions */
        VioGetMode(&vioinfo, 0);
```

(continued)

Figure 18-10. *continued*

```
        for(i = 0; i < vioinfo.rows; i++)
        {
            slen = vioinfo.cols;            /* read line from screen */
            VioReadCharStr(scrbuf, &slen, i, 0, 0);

                                            /* discard trailing spaces */
            while((slen > 0) && (scrbuf[slen-1] == 0x20)) slen--;

                                            /* write line to file */
            DosWrite(fhandle, scrbuf, slen, &wlen);
            DosWrite(fhandle, "\x0d\x0a", 2, &wlen);
        }

        DosBeep(440, 200);                  /* reward the user */
        unpop();                            /* release screen */
        DosSemSet(&snapsem);                /* reset snapshot semaphore */
    }
}


/*
    Display the installation and help messages in popup window.
*/
void signon(void)
{
    popup(1);                               /* acquire popup screen */
    VioWrtCharStr(msg1, sizeof(msg1), 10, ((80-sizeof(msg1))/2), 0);
    VioWrtCharStr(msg2, sizeof(msg2), 13, ((80-sizeof(msg2))/2), 0);
    VioWrtCharStr(msg3, sizeof(msg3), 15, ((80-sizeof(msg3))/2), 0);
    DosSleep(4000L);                        /* pause for 4 seconds */
    unpop();                                /* release popup screen */
}


/*
    Display exit message in popup window.
*/
void signoff(void)
{
    popup(1);                               /* acquire popup screen */
    VioWrtCharStr(msg4, sizeof(msg4), 12, ((80-sizeof(msg4))/2), 0);
    DosSleep(2000L);                        /* pause for 2 seconds */
    unpop();                                /* release popup screen */
}
```

(continued)

Figure 18-10. *continued*

```
/*
    Get popup screen, using wait/no-wait and
    transparent/nontransparent flags supplied by caller.
*/
void popup(unsigned pflags)
{
    VioPopUp(&pflags, 0);
}


/*
    Take down popup screen.
*/
void unpop(void)
{
    VioEndPopUp(0);
}


/*
    Common error exit routine.  Display error message on popup
    screen and terminate process.
*/
void errexit(char *errmsg)
{
    if(khandle != 0)                      /* close monitor handle */
        DosMonClose(khandle);             /* if monitor active */

    if(shandle != 0)                      /* clear and close the */
    {                                     /* SNAPxx.LCK semaphore */
        DosSemClear((unsigned long far *) shandle);
        DosCloseSem((unsigned long far *) shandle);
    }


    popup(1);                             /* get popup screen and */
                                          /* display error message */
    VioWrtCharStr(msg5, sizeof(msg5), 10, ((80-sizeof(msg5))/2), 0);
    VioWrtCharStr(errmsg, strlen(errmsg), 12, ((80-strlen(errmsg))/2), 0);
    DosSleep(3000L);                      /* let user read message */
    unpop();                              /* release popup screen */
    DosExit(1, 1);                        /* terminate, exitcode = 1 */
}
```

How SNAP Works

The SNAP program contains three threads of execution, which communicate using RAM semaphores (Figure 18-11).

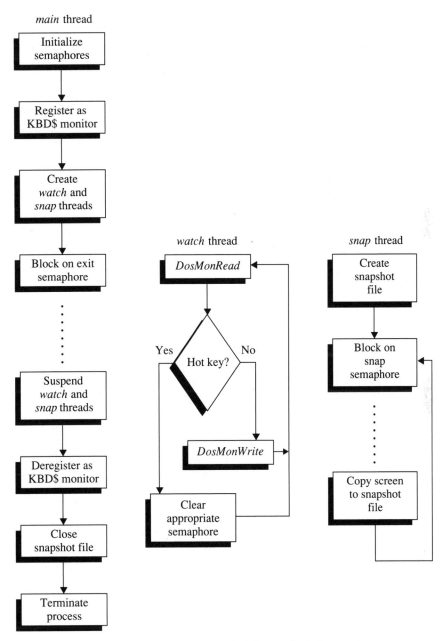

Figure 18-11. *General flow of control in the SNAP sample device monitor.*

The primary thread, called *main,* receives control from OS/2. It calls *DosGetInfoSeg* to get the selectors for the global and local information segments, extracts the screen group to be monitored from the global information segment, and registers itself as a keyboard monitor using *DosMonOpen* and *DosMonReg.* Next, it initializes two RAM semaphores that will be used for signaling: an exit semaphore and a screen snapshot semaphore. The *main* thread then activates two additional threads (*watch* and *snap*), displays the program's sign-on message, and blocks on the exit semaphore.

The *watch* thread simply executes successive calls to *DosMonRead* and *DosMonWrite* to pump the keyboard data through its buffers, monitoring the characters that pass for either of the two SNAP hot keys. Use of a dedicated thread for this purpose ensures that keyboard response time is not degraded. If *watch* detects the screen dump hot key (Alt-F10), it clears the snapshot semaphore to wake up the *snap* thread. If it sees the deinstall hot key (Ctrl-F10), it triggers the exit semaphore to wake up the *main* thread.

The *snap* thread creates the file SNAP*xx*.IMG and then blocks on the snapshot semaphore. Whenever the snapshot semaphore is cleared by the *watch* thread, the *snap* thread wakes up, copies the current screen display into SNAP*xx*.IMG, appends a divider line of hyphens, and forces an update of the file and its directory entry on disk. The *snap* thread then uses *DosBeep* to let the user know something happened, resets the snapshot semaphore, and goes back to sleep.

The *main* thread resumes execution only when the *watch* thread clears the exit semaphore. Upon reawakening it suspends the other two threads and then deregisters the process as a keyboard monitor. Finally, it closes the SNAP*xx*.IMG file, briefly displays a popup message that the program is removing itself from memory, and then terminates the process.

The initial portion of code for the *main* thread illustrates a useful OS/2 trick: placing a process in the background so that another command processor prompt is displayed, without requiring the user to start the program with the DETACH command. SNAP accomplishes this by emulating a UNIX/XENIX "fork" operation.

When the *main* thread first gets control, it tests to see whether a system semaphore with the name \SEM\SNAP*xx*.LCK exists. If not, it creates and sets the semaphore and then loads and executes another copy of SNAP with the *DosExecPgm* option 4 for "asynchronous execution, discard return code." The *main* thread waits for the new child process to clear the system semaphore (indicating that the process has been successfully loaded), and then it terminates.

If the *main* thread finds that the semaphore \SEM\SNAP*xx*.LCK already exists, it knows itself to be the child copy of SNAP. It clears the semaphore to notify the parent SNAP that it is running and then goes about its business of initializing its data structures and creating additional threads as already described. The child copy of SNAP is free to continue executing in the background; because it was spawned with option 4, CMD.EXE does not wait for it to terminate before issuing another prompt.

Building SNAP

To assemble the source file SNAP.ASM into the relocatable object module SNAP.OBJ, enter the following command:

```
[C:\] MASM SNAP.ASM;  <Enter>
```

To build the actual program SNAP.EXE, use the Linker to combine the file SNAP.OBJ, the module definition file SNAP.DEF (Figure 18-12), and the dynlink reference file OS2.LIB, as follows:

```
[C:\] LINK SNAP,,,OS2,SNAP  <Enter>
```

To compile the file SNAP.C into the executable file SNAP.EXE, type the following command:

```
[C:\] CL /F 2000  SNAP.C  <Enter>
```

The */F* switch allocates an extra-large stack so that stacks for the second and third threads can be allocated out of the main stack.

```
NAME SNAP NOTWINDOWCOMPAT
PROTMODE
STACKSIZE 4096
```

Figure 18-12. *SNAP.DEF, module definition file for SNAP.EXE device monitor.*

Using SNAP

You can load SNAP (when any protected mode screen group is selected) simply by entering its name:

```
[C:\] SNAP  <Enter>
```

A popup sign-on message appears briefly to let you know that SNAP is active and to remind you of the hot key assignments. That message is followed by a new prompt from the system's protected mode command interpreter (CMD.EXE).

While you are running other programs, SNAP remains resident, waiting to act upon one of two special keycodes. You can request a screen dump at any time by pressing Alt-F10. (A brief tone tells you that SNAP accomplished its task.) To remove SNAP from memory, press Ctrl-F10. You can alter the key assignments by editing the equates at the beginning of SNAP.ASM and reassembling the program.

SNAP is active only for the screen group in which it was loaded; it is not aware of keys that are entered when another screen group is brought to the foreground with the Task Manager. You can, however, load a copy of SNAP in each screen group in which you want to use it. The overhead of such additional copies is minuscule because OS/2 allows all the instantiations to share the same machine code segment. With some extra work, you could also modify SNAP so that a single copy registers itself as a device monitor for all the active screen groups in the system.

DYNAMIC LINK LIBRARIES

Dynamic link libraries (also called dynlink libraries or DLLs) are essentially subroutine packages that are bound to an application at load time or during execution, rather than at link time. But such a terse definition conveys little of the generality and power of this concept. The following list suggests some of the significant benefits of dynlink libraries:

- Code and read-only data in dynlink libraries is shared invisibly among all the processes (''clients'') that use the libraries, a provision which conserves physical memory and disk swap space.

- Code and data in dynlink libraries can be loaded on demand, so it does not occupy physical memory until it is needed.

- Dynlink library routines can be referenced symbolically (that is, by name), so a library and the applications that use it can be independently maintained and improved.

- Centralization of frequently used routines in dynlink libraries reduces the size of each application program file and conserves disk space.

- Dynlink libraries can contain IOPL segments that enable and disable interrupts and access I/O ports directly. I/O routines for devices that do not require interrupt handlers can be implemented in dynlink libraries rather than in true device drivers; the result, as evidenced by the *Vio* subsystem, is a much more flexible interface to applications than that provided by a true device driver.

Dynamic link libraries were pioneered and proven in real mode Windows, an environment that makes the most of a severely limited address space with a complex software emulation of virtual memory. But in OS/2, which can rely on hardware support for virtual memory and memory protection, dynlink libraries truly come into their own. Dynlink library segments reside in the global memory pool and can be freely moved, swapped, discarded, and reloaded on the basis of overall system activity.

In fact, OS/2's dynlink library support can be seen as a general-purpose overlay facility, fully integrated with the system's linker, loader, and virtual memory manager. Much of OS/2 itself, including most API entry points and the code for API functions that do not need to run at ring 0, is distributed in the form of dynlink libraries (see Chapter 2). This rather elegant merger of OS/2's services and its implementation keeps the system's fixed memory requirements to a minimum.

The routines in a dynlink library execute in user mode in the context of the client process. In other words, as far as the kernel's scheduler is concerned, a thread executing within a process is no different from a thread within a dynlink library bound to the process. No stack switching is involved; the library is viewed as an extension of the process. Consequently, the routines in a dynlink library have unrestricted access to the calling process's memory and its other resources, such as file, pipe, semaphore, and queue handles.

From the point of view of an application, however, every dynlink library (regardless of its origin) is indistinguishable from a component of the operating system: Each DLL routine accepts its parameters on the stack, is entered by a far call to a named entry point, and returns a status code in AX. Details as to the way a DLL routine does its work are invisible to the application; within the DLL, the routine might continue to execute in user mode, invoke an IOPL segment, request action by the kernel on behalf of the application, or use IPC mechanisms to request services from a server process on the same or another machine.

The system loader has yet another perspective. To the loader, every segmented executable file, whether it contains a DLL or an application, is simply another system resource called a *module.** The *module name* is contained in the file header and may or may not be the same as the name of the file. While a program is running or a dynlink library is in use, the segment and entry point tables from the EXE file header are kept resident so that the loader can easily locate discardable segments and LOADONCALL segments when they are needed.

If an additional copy of the same program is started, or if another process references the same library, the loader already has the necessary information in hand so that the system overhead for creating the new process or

---

* The term *module* as it is used in this chapter should not be confused with object modules, source code modules, or the like.

dynamic link is relatively small. The loader maintains a use count for each module. When all the instances of a program have terminated, or when all the clients of a dynlink library have released it or terminated, the module use count becomes zero, and the loader discards the module and associated tables and reclaims the memory.

This behavior of the loader has an interesting side effect. Any time that a program is running or that a dynlink library is in use, the file containing that module is held open by the loader with a sharing mode of deny-write; during this time, the file cannot be renamed, erased, or replaced. (This prohibition improves performance and reliability by eliminating multiple open/close operations and ensuring that a discardable segment cannot be modified between loads.) Because the operating system's base DLLs (such as DOSCALL1.DLL and VIOCALLS.DLL) are always in use by the Presentation Manager and CMD.EXE, you can't replace one of these DLLs on your bootable fixed disk unless you reboot the system from a self-contained floppy disk that does not use them.

Dynlink libraries differ in important ways from the two other kinds of libraries found in OS/2: object libraries and import libraries. Dynlink libraries are structured as segmented executable (new EXE) files with a special flag in the file header that prevents your running them directly from the command line; the routines in a DLL are suitable for immediate execution and are bound to an application (*dynamic linking*) at load time or run time.

In contrast, object libraries and import libraries are used at link time rather than at execution time and are stored in a special format understood only by the LINK, LIB, and IMPLIB utilities. The code in an object library requires further processing by the Linker before it can be executed, and it is permanently incorporated into a program or a DLL executable file (*static linking*). The records in import libraries do not usually contain executable code at all; they are merely stubs that represent individual DLL routines and signal the Linker to build the information necessary for dynamic linking into the EXE file header.

Dynamic Linking at Load Time

Dynamic linking at load time is easy to arrange. In fact, given that most OS/2 API entry points actually reside in dynlink libraries, you can appreciate that you have already been exposed to dynamic linking in every program in this book!

In a MASM program, the routines that are to be dynamically linked are simply declared as external with the *far* attribute, for example:

```
extrn DosWrite:far
```

In a C program, the routines are declared as external with the *far pascal* attributes (parameters pushed from left to right, and called routine clears the stack), for example:

```
extern unsigned far pascal DosWrite( ... );
```

If you include the API header files supplied with OS/2 development tools, these external declarations are made for you already.

When you link your program, you either specify the module and entry point names for the dynlinked routines with IMPORTS statements in the module definition (DEF) file, or you link the program with an import library that matches the dynlink library or libraries you are going to use at run time. (For example, OS2.LIB contains import records for the *Dos*, *Kbd*, *Mou*, and *Vio* API entry points.) The result of either method is the same: The Linker builds the names of the dynlink libraries and routines into tables in the EXE file header, along with pointers to each reference to the dynlink libraries in the executable code.

Imported dynlink library routines can also be specified in a module definition file by an *ordinal* rather than by name. An ordinal is merely the index to the position of the routine in the library's entry point table. Using ordinals speeds up dynamic linking and reduces the size of your application's EXE file (because the imported name table in the header will be smaller). But linking with ordinals has its disadvantages. You must be sure that you do not change the ordinals from one version of the library to another, or you must synchronize the library and all the applications that use it. Either way, you forfeit flexibility by using ordinals.

When your program is loaded for execution, the system loader inspects the file header's *module reference table* to determine which dynlink libraries the process uses. If these libraries are not already loaded, the loader invokes itself recursively to bring them into memory (along with any libraries *they* reference). The loader always assumes that a dynlink library has the extension DLL and that it can be found in one of the directories named in the LIBPATH directive in CONFIG.SYS. If any dynlink library cannot be located, or if memory is exhausted during the loading of libraries, the client program will not be loaded.

Some dynlink libraries have an initialization routine which must be called when they are loaded for the first time (*global initialization*) or each time they are bound to a new process (*instance initialization*). The type of initialization required, if any, is specified in the library's file header, as is the entry point of the initialization routine. The initialization routine might return an error code if it can't locate resources that the dynlink library will need later (such as a font file, a device, or additional memory), in which case loading of the client program is aborted.

When all necessary libraries are loaded and any necessary initialization of those libraries is complete, the loader inspects the segment tables for each module and creates an LDT selector for each program and dynlink library segment. All segments marked PRELOAD are brought into memory, and any necessary fixups are performed. (Segments marked LOADONCALL are not brought into memory and fixed up until they are referenced during program execution.)

Dynamic Linking at Run Time

Instead of letting the Linker and system loader do all the work of dynamic linking, you can elect to have your program create dynamic links to the libraries it needs (function by function) while it is executing. The API functions for runtime dynamic linking are summarized in Figure 19-1.

To establish dynamic links at run time, the program must first make the dynlink library's segments and entry points known to the system loader by calling *DosLoadModule*. This function requires the addresses of an ASCIIZ module name, a buffer, and a variable to receive a handle. The system loader looks in the directories named in the LIBPATH directive for a file with the specified module name and the extension DLL. If the library is found, its PRELOAD segments are brought into memory, any additional libraries that it references are also loaded, and a module handle is returned. If the library (or a library that it uses) is not found, *DosLoadModule* returns an

Function	Description
DosFreeModule	Releases linkage between process and dynlink library
DosGetModHandle	Returns handle for dynlink library if it is already loaded
DosGetModName	Retrieves fully qualified pathname of dynlink library
DosGetProcAddr	Obtains address of entry point within dynlink library
DosLoadModule	Loads dynlink library if not already loaded and returns handle for use with *DosGetProcAddr*

Figure 19-1. *Summary of OS/2 API calls used by applications to link to DLLs at run time.*

error code, and the name of the missing library is returned in the calling process's buffer.

Assuming that *DosLoadModule* is successful and a handle is obtained, the program must then obtain the entry points for each library function that it will use. To do so, it calls *DosGetProcAddr* with a module handle and the address of an ASCIIZ entry point name or an ASCIIZ or binary ordinal. *DosGetProcAddr* returns a selector and offset for the entry point in a variable. The program can then invoke the library routine by pushing the appropriate parameters onto the stack and performing an indirect far call through the variable.

After the program finishes using the dynlink library, it can release the library by calling *DosFreeModule* with the module handle. If no other process is using the library, it will be discarded and the memory it occupied will be reclaimed. After you call *DosFreeModule*, any entry points which were previously obtained for the library with *DosGetProcAddr* become invalid, and any attempt to use the library causes a GP fault. Figure 19-2 contains a skeleton example of runtime dynamic linking in a MASM program.

```
objbuf      db      64 dup (0)      ; receives failing module
                                    ; or entry point name

objbuf_len equ  $-objbuf

mname       db      'VIOCALLS',0    ; module name

mhandle dw      0                   ; receives module handle

ename       db      'VIOGETANSI',0  ; entry point name

eptr        dd      0               ; receives far pointer
                                    ; to entry point

            .
            .
            .

                                    ; attach to DLL...
            push    ds              ; receives failing dynlink
            push    offset DGROUP:objbuf
            push    objbuf_len      ; length of buffer
            push    ds              ; address of module name
            push    offset DGROUP:mname
```

(continued)

Figure 19-2. *Sample code sequence for runtime dynamic linking.*

Figure 19-2. *continued*

```
        push    ds                  ; receives module handle
        push    offset DGROUP:mhandle
        call    DosLoadModule       ; transfer to OS/2
        or      ax,ax               ; module found?
        jnz     error               ; jump if no such module

                                    ; get entry point...
        push    mhandle             ; module handle
        push    ds                  ; address of entry name
        push    offset DGROUP:ename
        push    ds                  ; receives entry pointer
        push    offset DGROUP:eptr
        call    DosGetProcAddr      ; transfer to OS/2
        or      ax,ax               ; entry point found?
        jnz     error               ; jump if no entry point


        .                           ; other processing here...
        .
        .

        call    eptr                ; indirect call to
                                    ; dynlink library routine


        .                           ; other processing here...
        .
        .

                                    ; module no longer needed,
                                    ; release it...
        push    mhandle             ; module handle
        call    DosFreeModule       ; transfer to OS/2
        or      ax,ax               ; should never fail
        jnz     error               ; but check anyway
        .
        .
        .
```

The two other API functions for dynamic linking at run time are rarely used. *DosGetModName* accepts a module handle (for a library or a process) and retrieves the fully qualified pathname for the module. *DosGetMod-Handle* accepts an ASCIIZ module name and returns a handle for the module if it is already loaded, or an error if it is not loaded; *DosGetModHandle* is strictly an existence test and does not increment the module's use count.

Designing New Dynlink Libraries

Designing and writing a new dynlink library is a straightforward process in either MASM or C. During the planning stage, you must address the following three design issues:

- The nature of the DLL interface to applications

- The type of DLL initialization (if any)

- The number and behavior of DLL data segments

You need to gauge carefully the range and complexity of the functions that the DLL will export to applications. If the functions are too few and too specific, the application programmer will be forced to write his or her own routines for special cases. On the other hand, if the routines are too numerous, the programmer will have difficulty remembering what is available. And if the routines are too primitive, the application programmer will not gain enough leverage by using the functions to make the effort worthwhile. The *Vio* subsystem that is supplied with OS/2 is an excellent example to imitate.

When you write a MASM dynlink library for use with MASM applications, the parameter passing between the application and the DLL can be register-based, stack-based, or a hybrid of the two. When you write a DLL in C, or one that is to be used with C applications, you have less freedom; the structure of the C language more or less forces you to use the same stack-based API as the "standard" OS/2 DLLs, for which the only open question is what each "function" will return as its "value." In either case, however, I strongly recommend that you follow the kernel API conventions — pass all parameters to the DLL on the stack, and return a status code in AX and any other information to the caller's variables. Symmetry with the rest of the system will reward you with fewer exceptions to remember and hence fewer bugs to fix.

An initialization routine in your DLL is optional. If you provide one, specify its entry point with an END statement in a MASM source file. A dynlink library written in C that requires initialization must, therefore, have at least one small module written in MASM, although the MASM routine which receives control at initialization time can call a C function to do the actual work.

If the DLL has an initialization routine, you must determine whether it will be called only when the library is first loaded (global initialization) or each time the library is attached by a client process (instance initialization). Global initialization is especially appropriate when a DLL controls a device; if the device is not available, the initialization routine returns an error. Instance initialization is useful when the DLL allocates private data structures or system resources on a per-client basis. In such cases, the initialization routine should also register a clean-up routine for each client with *DosExitList* so that the indicated routine will be notified when the client terminates and can clean up any resources or data that have been left hanging.

The question of the DLL's data segments goes hand in hand with global or instance initialization. Some DLLs need no data segments of their own — those that have no initialized data and no need to store any information across calls from the application, and that can use the stack for all their transient variables. Other DLLs, such as those controlling a single system resource such as a device, might need only a single data segment to store the state of the device and synchronize access to it by multiple processes.

The more common case, however, is the DLL which needs multiple unshared segments to store information across function calls on a per-client basis. Each time a new process attaches to the library, OS/2 loads a fresh copy of the DLL's data segments to map into the process's memory space. The system uses identical selectors in each process's LDT so that the same relocations in the DLL's shared code segments will serve for all. The selector magic inherent in OS/2's support for dynlink instance data is one of the most subtle but exquisite features of OS/2's design. During instance initialization, a DLL can also dynamically allocate memory that it can use on behalf of the client process.

Although the nature of the DLL's application interface is defined by its source code, the initialization type (global or instance) and behavior of each segment (preload or load-on-call, shared or unshared) is controlled by keywords in the module definition file. Figure 19-3 on the following page provides a summary of the definition file syntax for dynlink libraries (and for device drivers). Compare this summary with the similar figure in Chapter 3 on p. 33; some of the directives and defaults are different from those for applications. Appendix E provides a complete explanation of the syntax for module definition files.

LIBRARY [*modulename*] [**INITGLOBAL** ┆ INITINSTANCE]

Ignored if no initialization routine is present.

DESCRIPTION *'string'*

CODE [PRELOAD ┆ **LOADONCALL**] [EXECUTEONLY ┆ **EXECUTEREAD**]
[IOPL ┆ **NOIOPL**] [CONFORMING ┆ **NONCONFORMING**]

DATA [PRELOAD ┆ **LOADONCALL**] [READONLY ┆ **READWRITE**]
[NONE ┆ **SINGLE** ┆ MULTIPLE] [**SHARED** ┆ NONSHARED]
[IOPL ┆ **NOIOPL**]

SEGMENTS
name [CLASS ['*classname*']] [PRELOAD ┆ **LOADONCALL**]
[READONLY ┆ **READWRITE**] [EXECUTEONLY ┆ **EXECUTEREAD**]
[IOPL ┆ **NOIOPL**] [CONFORMING ┆ **NONCONFORMING**]
[**SHARED** ┆ NONSHARED]

Ignored for code segments and read-only data segments; these segments are always shared.

EXPORTS
exportname [= *internalname*] [@*ordinal*] [RESIDENTNAME] [*stackparams*]

Defines the number of stack cells passed to a procedure within an IOPL segment; when the routine is called, the hardware switches stacks and copies the specified number of words to the new stack.

IMPORTS
[*internalname* =] *modulename.entryname* ┆ *modulename.ordinal*

STUB *'filename.EXE'*

OLD *'filename.DLL'*

EXETYPE OS2

Figure 19-3. *Module definition file elements used for dynlink libraries and installable device drivers. Keywords must always be entered in uppercase letters. Defaults are in* **boldface** *and are not necessarily the same as those supplied for application programs.*

Writing DLLs in MASM

Figure 19-4 contains a code skeleton for a DLL written in MASM. Each procedure in the DLL should set up a stack frame so that it can access its parameters, save any registers that it is going to change, and reset the DS register to make its data segment addressable (if it has one). Procedures that serve as entry points must be declared *public* and *far* because they are entered by an intersegment call; procedures that are used only as subroutines within the DLL itself can be declared either *near* or *far*. To exit, a procedure should restore the caller's registers (except for AX) and then use RET with an offset to clear the parameters (if any) from the caller's stack.

```
DGROUP   group    _DATA

_DATA    segment word public 'DATA'
              .
              .
              .
_DATA    ends

_TEXT    segment word public 'CODE'

         assume   cs:_TEXT,ds:DGROUP

         public   MYFUNC

MYFUNC   proc     far               ; dynlink routine

         push     bp                ; set up stack frame
         mov      bp,sp

         push     ax                ; save affected registers
         push     bx
         push     cx
         push     dx
         push     si
         push     di
         push     ds

         mov      ax,DGROUP         ; make DLL's data
         mov      ds,ax             ; segment addressable
              .
              .
              .
```

Figure 19-4. *Skeleton for a DLL written in MASM.*   *(continued)*

Figure 19-4. *continued*

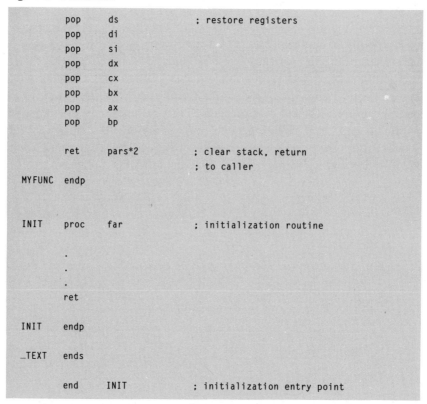

```
            pop     ds              ; restore registers
            pop     di
            pop     si
            pop     dx
            pop     cx
            pop     bx
            pop     ax
            pop     bp

            ret     pars*2          ; clear stack, return
                                    ; to caller
MYFUNC   endp


INIT     proc    far              ; initialization routine

            .
            .
            .
            ret

INIT     endp

_TEXT    ends

            end     INIT            ; initialization entry point
```

If an initialization routine is present, it is identified by the END directive and is also coded as a *far* procedure. Before calling the DLL initialization entry point, OS/2 sets up the registers as shown in Figure 19-5.

All other register values are undefined. If the module saves a copy of its own handle, it can pass the handle to client applications later, and they can use the handle to retrieve the library's fully qualified pathname with *DosGetModName*.

Register	Contents
CS:IP	Entry point defined in END directive
SS:SP	Current user stack
DS	Selector for DLL's DGROUP, if any; otherwise, selector for DGROUP of process attaching to DLL
AX	Module handle of the DLL

Figure 19-5. *Register contents at entry to a DLL initialization routine.*

The initialization routine exits with a far return, passing a status code in AX. Initialization routines depart from the conventions observed elsewhere in OS/2: They return zero to indicate an error and a nonzero value to indicate success. If the status returned is zero, the program that referenced the library is not loaded, and the name of the failing library is passed to that program's parent.

The module definition file for our skeleton DLL is shown in Figure 19-6. Real DLLs with many segments might have elaborate DEF files, but this one is quite simple. The key elements are the LIBRARY directive, which signals the Linker that entry point and stack declarations may be absent, and the EXPORTS statement, which designates the entry points for applications. Instance or global initialization and DGROUP for the DLL are controlled by optional parameters to the LIBRARY and DATA directives. Assign PRELOAD or LOADONCALL to each segment based on the likelihood that it will be used. In a simple DLL with only two segments (such as this skeleton example), both might as well be marked PRELOAD so that the time required to fetch them from disk will be hidden inside the overall load time of the application.

```
LIBRARY MYDLL INITGLOBAL
CODE PRELOAD
DATA PRELOAD MULTIPLE
EXPORTS
  MYFUNC
```

Figure 19-6. *Module definition file for the skeleton MASM dynlink library.*

A Complete Sample DLL

Figure 19-7 (on the following pages) and Figure 19-8 (on p. 476) contain the MASM source code and module definition file for a complete sample dynlink library called ASMHELP.DLL. The library exports two routines for use by MASM applications: *ARGC*, which counts the number of command line arguments, and *ARGV*, which returns the address and length of a specific command line argument.

```
        title    ASMHELP -- Sample MASM DLL
        page     55,132
        .286


;
; ASMHELP.ASM
;
; Source code for the MASM dynlink library ASMHELP.DLL.
;
; Assemble with  C> masm asmhelp.asm;
; Link with  C> link asmhelp,asmhelp.dll,,os2,asmhelp
;
; Exports two routines for use by MASM programs:
;
; ARGC  Returns count of command line arguments.
;       Treats blanks and tabs as whitespace.
;
;       Calling sequence:
;
;       push    seg argcnt       ; receives argument count
;       push    offset argcnt
;       call    ARGC
;
; ARGV  Returns address and length of specified
;       command line argument.  If called for
;       argument 0, returns address and length
;       of fully qualified pathname of program.
;
;       Calling sequence:
;
;       push    argno            ; argument number
;       push    seg argptr       ; receives argument address
;       push    offset argptr
;       push    seg arglen       ; receives argument length
;       push    offset arglen
;       call    ARGV
;
; Copyright (C) 1988 Ray Duncan
;

tab     equ     09h              ; ASCII tab
blank   equ     20h              ; ASCII space character
```

(continued)

Figure 19-7. *ASMHELP.ASM, the MASM source code for the dynlink library ASMHELP.DLL.*

Figure 19-7. *continued*

```
        extrn   DosGetEnv:far

DGROUP  group   _DATA


_DATA   segment word public 'DATA'

envseg  dw      ?               ; environment selector
cmdoffs dw      ?               ; command tail offset

_DATA   ends


_TEXT   segment word public 'CODE'

        assume  cs:_TEXT,ds:DGROUP

                                ; parameter for argc
argcnt  equ     [bp+6]          ; receives argument count

        public  argc
argc    proc    far             ; count command line arguments

        push    bp              ; make arguments addressable
        mov     bp,sp

        push    ds              ; save registers
        push    es
        push    bx
        push    cx

        mov     ax,seg DGROUP   ; point to instance data
        mov     ds,ax

        mov     es,envseg       ; set ES:BX = command line
        mov     bx,cmdoffs

        mov     ax,1            ; initialize argument count

argc0:  inc     bx              ; ignore useless first field
        cmp     byte ptr es:[bx],0
        jne     argc0

argc1:  mov     cx,-1           ; set flag = outside argument
```

(continued)

Figure 19-7. *continued*

```
argc2:  inc     bx                  ; point to next character

        cmp     byte ptr es:[bx],0
        je      argc3               ; exit if null byte

        cmp     byte ptr es:[bx],blank
        je      argc1               ; outside argument if ASCII blank

        cmp     byte ptr es:[bx],tab
        je      argc1               ; outside argument if ASCII tab

                                    ; otherwise not blank or tab,
        jcxz    argc2               ; jump if already inside argument

        inc     ax                  ; else found argument, count it
        not     cx                  ; set flag = inside argument
        jmp     argc2               ; and look at next character

argc3:                              ; store result into
                                    ; caller's variable...

        les     bx,argcnt           ; get address of variable
        mov     es:[bx],ax          ; store argument count

        pop     cx                  ; restore registers
        pop     bx
        pop     es
        pop     ds
        pop     bp

        xor     ax,ax               ; signal success

        ret     4                   ; return to caller
                                    ; and discard parameters
argc    endp


                                    ; parameters for argv...
argno   equ     [bp+14]             ; argument number
argptr  equ     [bp+10]             ; receives argument pointer
arglen  equ     [bp+6]              ; receives argument length
```

(continued)

Figure 19-7. *continued*

```
          public  argv
argv      proc    far             ; get address and length of
                                  ; command tail argument


          push    bp              ; make arguments addressable
          mov     bp,sp


          push    ds              ; save registers
          push    es
          push    bx
          push    cx
          push    di


          mov     ax,seg DGROUP   ; point to instance data
          mov     ds,ax


          mov     es,envseg       ; set ES:BX = command line
          mov     bx,cmdoffs


          mov     ax,argno        ; get argument number
          or      ax,ax           ; requesting argument 0?
          jz      argv8           ; yes, get program name


argv1:    inc     bx              ; scan off first field
          cmp     byte ptr es:[bx],0
          jne     argv1


          xor     ah,ah           ; initialize argument counter


argv2:    mov     cx,-1           ; set flag = outside argument


argv3:    inc     bx              ; point to next character


          cmp     byte ptr es:[bx],0
          je      argv7           ; exit if null byte


          cmp     byte ptr es:[bx],blank
          je      argv2           ; outside argument if ASCII blank


          cmp     byte ptr es:[bx],tab
          je      argv2           ; outside argument if ASCII tab


                                  ; if not blank or tab...
          jcxz    argv3           ; jump if inside argument
```

(continued)

Figure 19-7. *continued*

```
        inc    ah                      ; else count arguments found
        cmp    ah,al                   ; is this the one?
        je     argv4                   ; yes, go find its length

        not    cx                      ; no, set flag = inside argument
        jmp    argv3                   ; and look at next character

argv4:                                 ; found desired argument, now
                                       ; determine its length...
        mov    ax,bx                   ; save parameter starting address

argv5:  inc    bx                      ; point to next character

        cmp    byte ptr es:[bx],0
        je     argv6                   ; found end if null byte

        cmp    byte ptr es:[bx],blank
        je     argv6                   ; found end if ASCII blank

        cmp    byte ptr es:[bx],tab
        jne    argv5                   ; found end if ASCII tab

argv6:  xchg   bx,ax                   ; set ES:BX = argument address
        sub    ax,bx                   ; and AX = argument length
        jmp    argv10                  ; return to caller

argv7:  mov    ax,1                    ; set AX != 0 indicating
                                       ; error, argument not found
        jmp    argv11                  ; return to caller

argv8:                                 ; special handling for argv = 0
        xor    di,di                   ; find the program name by
        xor    al,al                   ; first skipping over all the
        mov    cx,-1                   ; environment variables...
        cld

argv9:  repne scasb                    ; scan for double null (can't use SCASW
        scasb                          ; because it might be odd address)
        jne    argv9                   ; loop if it was a single null

        mov    bx,di                   ; save program name address
        mov    cx,-1                   ; now find its length...
        repne scasb                    ; scan for another null byte
```

(continued)

Figure 19-7. *continued*

```
        not    cx                ; convert CX to length
        dec    cx
        mov    ax,cx             ; return length in AX

argv10:                          ; at this point AX = length,
                                 ; ES:BX points to argument

        lds    di,argptr         ; address of first variable
        mov    ds:[di],bx        ; store argument pointer
        mov    ds:[di+2],es

        lds    di,arglen         ; address of second variable
        mov    ds:[di],ax        ; store argument length

        xor    ax,ax             ; AX = 0 to signal success

argv11:                          ; common exit point

        pop    di                ; restore registers
        pop    cx
        pop    bx
        pop    es
        pop    ds
        pop    bp

        ret    10                ; return to caller
                                 ; and discard parameters
argv    endp


init    proc   far               ; DLL instance initialization

                                 ; get environment selector
                                 ; and offset of command tail
                                 ; for this process...

        push   seg DGROUP        ; receives environment selector
        push   offset DGROUP:envseg
        push   seg DGROUP        ; receives command tail offset
        push   offset DGROUP:cmdoffs
        call   DosGetEnv         ; transfer to OS/2
        or     ax,ax             ; call successful?
        jnz    init1             ; no, initialization error

        mov    ax,1              ; initialization OK,
        ret                      ; return AX = 1 for success
```

(continued)

Figure 19-7. *continued*

```
init1:  xor     ax,ax           ; initialization failed,
        ret                     ; return AX = 0 for error

init    endp

_TEXT   ends

        end     init            ; initialization entry point
```

```
LIBRARY ASMHELP INITINSTANCE
PROTMODE
CODE LOADONCALL
DATA LOADONCALL NONSHARED
EXPORTS
    ARGC
    ARGV
```

Figure 19-8. *ASMHELP.DEF, the module definition file for the dynlink library ASMHELP.DLL.*

The routines in ASMHELP.DLL are exactly analogous to the *argc* and *argv* available to C programs. Both are written according to the OS/2 API conventions. Parameters and the addresses of variables to receive results are passed on the stack. A status code is returned in AX (zero for no error), and any other information is placed in variables specified by the caller.

The routine *ARGC* always returns a value of 1 or greater—the name of the program itself is counted as a command line argument. The parameter for *ARGV* is zero-based; when it is zero, the routine extracts from the environment the fully qualified pathname from which the current process was loaded; for other values, it fetches the corresponding token from the command tail.

To create ASMHELP.DLL, type the following sequence of commands:

```
[C:\] MASM ASMHELP.ASM;  <Enter>
[C:\] LINK ASMHELP,ASMHELP.DLL,,OS2,ASMHELP  <Enter>
```

Then copy the file to one of the directories named in the LIBPATH directive in CONFIG.SYS so that the system loader can find it.

Figure 19-9 and Figure 19-10 (on p. 480) contain the source code and module definition file for SHOWARGS.EXE, a simple application that calls both routines in ASMHELP.DLL. To create SHOWARGS.EXE, type the following sequence of commands:

```
[C:\] MASM SHOWARGS.ASM;  <Enter>
[C:\] LINK SHOWARGS,,,OS2,SHOWARGS  <Enter>
```

The following is a sample SHOWARGS session:

```
[C:\] showargs foo bar  <Enter>

The command line contains 03 arguments
Argument 00 is:  C:\SOURCE\OS2\DLL\SHOWARGS.EXE
Argument 01 is:  foo
Argument 02 is:  bar
[C:\]
```

```
        title    SHOWARGS -- ASMHELP.DLL Demo
        page     55,132
        .286


;
; SHOWARGS.ASM
;
; Demonstrates parsing of command line by calls to ASMHELP.DLL.
;
; Assemble with:  C> masm showargs.asm;
; Link with:  C> link showargs,,,os2,showargs
;
; Usage is:  C> showargs [argument(s)]
;
; Copyright (C) 1988 Ray Duncan
;


stdin   equ    0              ; standard input handle
stdout  equ    1              ; standard output handle
stderr  equ    2              ; standard error handle


cr      equ    0dh            ; ASCII carriage return
lf      equ    0ah            ; ASCII linefeed
blank   equ    020h           ; ASCII blank
tab     equ    09h            ; ASCII tab
```

(continued)

Figure 19-9. *SHOWARGS.ASM, source code for sample program SHOWARGS.EXE, which uses the dynlink library ASMHELP.DLL.*

Figure 19-9. *continued*

```
                                 ; references to ASMHELP.DLL
         extrn    ARGC:far        ; returns argument count
         extrn    ARGV:far        ; returns pointer to argument

         extrn    DosWrite:far    ; references to OS/2
         extrn    DosExit:far
         extrn    DosGetEnv:far


DGROUP   group    _DATA


_DATA    segment word public 'DATA'


argno    dw       0              ; receives argument count
argptr   dw       0,0            ; receives argument pointer
arglen   dw       0              ; receives argument length


curarg   dw       0              ; current command line argument


wlen     dw       0              ; bytes actually written


msg1     db       cr,lf
         db       'The command line contains '
msg1a    db       'xx arguments'
msg1_len equ $-msg1


msg2     db       cr,lf
         db       'Argument '
msg2a    db       'xx is: '
msg2_len equ $-msg2


_DATA    ends



_TEXT    segment word public 'CODE'


         assume   cs:_TEXT,ds:DGROUP


main     proc     far            ; entry point from OS/2

                                 ; get number of command
                                 ; line arguments...

         push     ds             ; receives argument count
         push     offset DGROUP:argno
         call     argc           ; call ASMHELP.DLL
```

(continued)

Figure 19-9. *continued*

```
        mov     ax,argno        ; convert count to ASCII
        mov     bx,offset msg1a ; for output
        call    b2dec

                                ; now display number
                                ; of arguments...

        push    stdout          ; standard output handle
        push    ds              ; address of message
        push    offset DGROUP:msg1
        push    msg1_len        ; length of message
        push    ds              ; receives bytes written
        push    offset DGROUP:wlen
        call    DosWrite        ; transfer to OS/2

main1:                          ; display next argument...

        mov     ax,curarg       ; are we all done?
        cmp     ax,argno
        je      main2           ; yes, exit

        mov     bx,offset msg2a ; no, convert argument number
        call    b2dec

                                ; display argument number...
        push    stdout          ; standard output handle
        push    ds              ; address of message
        push    offset DGROUP:msg2
        push    msg2_len        ; length of message
        push    ds              ; receives bytes written
        push    offset DGROUP:wlen
        call    DosWrite        ; transfer to OS/2

                                ; get argument pointer...
        push    curarg          ; argument number
        push    ds              ; receives pointer
        push    offset DGROUP:argptr
        push    ds              ; receives length
        push    offset DGROUP:arglen
        call    argv            ; call ASMHELP.DLL

                                ; display the argument...
        push    stdout         *; standard output handle
        push    argptr+2        ; pointer to argument
        push    argptr
```

(continued)

Figure 19-9. *continued*

```
        push    arglen          ; length of argument
        push    ds              ; receives bytes written
        push    offset DGROUP:wlen
        call    DosWrite        ; transfer to OS/2

        inc     word ptr curarg ; go to next argument
        jmp     main1

main2:                          ; common exit point
        push    1               ; terminate all threads
        push    0               ; return code = zero
        call    DosExit         ; transfer to OS/2

main    endp


b2dec   proc    near            ; convert binary value 0-99
                                ; to two decimal ASCII
                                ; call with
                                ; AL = binary data
                                ; BX = address for 2 characters

        aam                     ; divide AL by 10, leaving
                                ; AH = quotient, AL = remainder
        add     ax,'00'         ; convert to ASCII
        mov     [bx],ah         ; store tens digit
        mov     [bx+1],al       ; store ones digit
        ret                     ; return to caller

b2dec   endp

_TEXT   ends

        end     main            ; defines entry point
```

```
NAME SHOWARGS
PROTMODE
STACKSIZE 4096
IMPORTS
    ASMHELP.ARGC
    ASMHELP.ARGV
```

Figure 19-10. *SHOWARGS.DEF, module definition file for SHOWARGS.EXE.*

Using Import Libraries

If your dynlink library contains many entry points, you can make life much easier for the programmers who use it by creating a matching import library. When an application that calls the dynlink library is being built, the Linker can use the import library to satisfy internal references to the dynlink library routines, thereby eliminating the need for IMPORTS statements in the application's module definition file.

Import libraries are built by the IMPLIB.EXE utility, which is supplied in the OS/2 Programmer's Toolkit. The parameters required by IMPLIB are the name of the import library to be built and the name of one or more module definition files containing EXPORTS statements for dynlink library entry points. The command line for IMPLIB takes the following form:

IMPLIB *libfile*.LIB *deffile*.DEF [*deffile*.DEF ...]

where the extensions LIB and DEF must be supplied as shown.

For example, to create an import library for ASMHELP.DLL, the command line would be the following:

```
[C:\] IMPLIB ASMHELP.LIB ASMHELP.DEF  <Enter>
```

Once ASMHELP.LIB is available, you can remove the IMPORT statements from SHOWARGS.DEF and link the utility using the import library instead:

```
[C:\] LINK SHOWARGS,,,OS2+ASMHELP,SHOWARGS  <Enter>
```

Writing DLLs in C

If you prefer to write your DLL in C, you need to use a few special tricks. First, each C function that will serve as an entry point from an application must be declared *far pascal*. Other functions, which are used only within the library, can use whichever style of parameter passing you prefer, although the *pascal* convention generates smaller, faster code. Pay close attention to every pointer because a dynlink routine is in some ways an extreme example of mixed-model C programming. Finally, include the following statement to prevent the C startup code from being dragged into the library by the Linker:

```
int _acrtused = 0;
```

When you compile your dynlink library, use the following switches:

Switch	Meaning
/c	Compile only (to allow you to link separately)
/Asnu	Small model; assume DS not equal to SS; save DS and reset it to point to the library's data segment at entry to each function
/Gs	Disable stack checking

In some cases, you may also need to use the /ND switch to name the data segment that is made addressable when a DLL function is entered.

The initialization routine, if any, must be written in MASM and assembled separately using the /Mx switch so that case is preserved in public and external names. The C-language body of the DLL must then be linked together with the MASM startup routine, OS2.LIB, and an appropriate module definition file.

Figure 19-11 on the following page contains the source code (CDLL.C) for a simple dynlink library, one that merely displays a message when its initialization routine and exported function are called. Figure 19-12 on p. 484 contains the MASM source code (CINIT.ASM) for the initialization entry point, and Figure 19-13 on p. 484 is the module definition file (CDLL.DEF).

```
/*
        CDLL.C

        C source code for the dynlink library CDLL.LIB.
        Requires the module CINIT.ASM.

        Compile with:  C> cl /c /Asnu /Gs cdll.c
        Assemble CINIT.ASM with:  C> masm /Mx cinit.asm;
        Link with:  C> link /NOI /NOD cdll+cinit,cdll.dll,,os2,cdll
        Create CDLL.LIB with:  C> implib cdll.lib cdll.def

        Copyright (C) 1988 Ray Duncan
/*

int _acrtused = 0;              /* don't link startup */
```

(continued)

Figure 19-11. *CDLL.C, source code for a simple dynlink library written in C. The function MYFUNC is exported for use by application programs; it displays a message and returns the sum of two numbers. The initialization function C_INIT is called when the DLL is first loaded from the entry point in CINIT.ASM (see Figure 19-12); in this example, it merely displays a message and returns a success code.*

Figure 19-11. *continued*

```
#define STDOUT 1                    /* standard output handle */

#define API unsigned extern far pascal

API DosWrite(unsigned, void far *, unsigned, unsigned far *);

static char funcmsg[] = "\nCDLL.MYFUNC is executing\n";
static char initmsg[] = "\nCDLL.C_INIT is executing\n";


/*
    MYFUNC is exported for use by application programs;
    it displays a message and returns the sum of 2 numbers.
*/

int far pascal MYFUNC(int a, int b)
{
    unsigned wlen;              /* receives length written */

                               /* display message that
                                   MYFUNC is executing */
    DosWrite(STDOUT,funcmsg,sizeof(funcmsg)-1,&wlen);

    return(a+b);               /* return function result */
}


/*
    C_INIT is called from the entry point in CINIT.ASM when
    a client process dynamically links to the library.
*/

int far pascal C_INIT(void)
{
    unsigned wlen;              /* receives length written */

                               /* display message that
                                   C_INIT is executing */
    DosWrite(STDOUT,initmsg,sizeof(initmsg)-1,&wlen);

    return(1);                 /* return success code */
}
```

```
        extrn   C_INIT:far

_TEXT   segment word public 'CODE'

        assume  cs:_TEXT

INIT    proc    far             ; initialization routine

        call    C_INIT          ; call C routine to
                                ; do the actual work

        ret                     ; back to caller with
                                ; AX = status code
                                ; ("value" from C_INIT)
INIT    endp

_TEXT   ends

        end     INIT
```

Figure 19-12. *CINIT.ASM, the MASM module containing the initialization entry point for CDLL.DLL (see Figure 19-11). The MASM routine INIT simply calls the C function C_INIT to do the actual work of initialization.*

```
LIBRARY CDLL INITINSTANCE
PROTMODE
CODE LOADONCALL
DATA LOADONCALL NONSHARED
EXPORTS
    MYFUNC
```

Figure 19-13. *CDLL.DEF, the module definition file for CDLL.DLL (see also Figures 19-11 and 19-12).*

To build the dynlink library CDLL.DLL, you would enter the following commands:

```
[C:\] CL /c /Asnu /Gs CDLL.C  <Enter>
[C:\] MASM /Mx CINIT.ASM;  <Enter>
[C:\] LINK /NOI /NOD CDLL+CINIT,CDLL.DLL,,OS2,CDLL  <Enter>
```

You can then create an import library for CDLL.DLL with the following command:

```
[C:\] IMPLIB CDLL.LIB CDLL.DEF  <Enter>
```

The entire process of building a dynlink library and an import library from MASM or C source code (or both) is diagrammed in Figure 19-14.

If you use C runtime library functions in your DLL, be sure to use the special reentrant libraries so that your DLL can be used safely by more than one thread or process at a time.

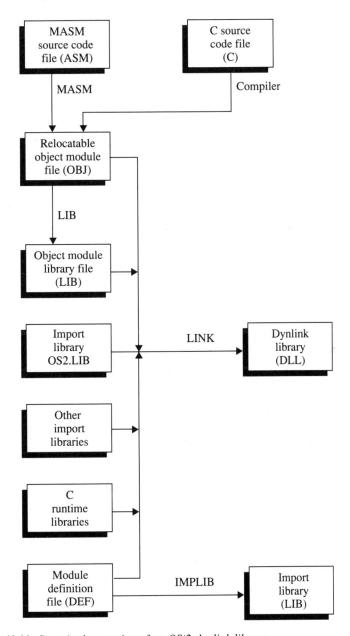

Figure 19-14. *Steps in the creation of an OS/2 dynlink library.*

OS/2 REFERENCE

PART ONE

KERNEL API

The entries in Part 1 of this reference section describe each of the kernel Application Program Interface (API) functions available in OS/2 versions 1.0 and 1.1. The API functions specific to the Presentation Manager are, of course, beyond the scope of this book. The *DosDevIOCtl* subfunctions are documented in Part 2 of this section, and the DevHlp (Device Driver Helper) functions, which cannot be called by application programs, are documented in Part 3.

Application programs invoke API functions by a far call to a named entry point. Parameters are passed on the stack; these may be values or pointers to variables (commonly structures). All kernel API functions return a status in register AX: zero if the function was successful, or a nonzero error code; the remaining registers are preserved. Other results are always returned in variables. A list of error codes is provided in Appendix A.

In this section, the calling sequence for each API function is described in a unified format that contains both the function's arguments and its results (aside from the status in AX). Parameters passed by value (such as WORD, DWORD) are always inputs to the function. Parameters passed by reference (such as PTR WORD) can be static data (such as a filename) or variables. In the latter case, the same storage locations can be used both to contain arguments and to receive results.

The following conventions are used to describe parameters passed by reference, in cases where the description would otherwise be ambiguous:

- "Contains" in the description indicates an input to the function. The program is responsible for placing the proper value in the variable before making the API function call.

- "Receives" indicates that the variable will receive a result; the program inspects the value after it returns from the function.

In nonambiguous cases (for example, a pointer to an ASCIIZ filename), the word "contains" or "receives" is not needed and is not used.

The term "pathname" refers to a directory or file specification that can include a drive, path (relative or complete), filename, and extension. A "fully qualified pathname" always includes a drive and a complete path from the root directory.

The following icons are used in this section:

[1.1]   API function added in OS/2 version 1.1; not available in version 1.0.

[IOPL]   Function that can be called from a ring 2 (IOPL) routine in OS/2 version 1.1, a so-called conforming function.

            Function that does nothing or is not allowed if the application is running in a Presentation Manager window.

[AVIO]   Advanced *Vio* function that is present to support the Presentation Manager and should not ordinarily be used by Kernel applications.

[FAPI]   Family API function that can be used in a bound (dual-mode) application program. Some FAPI functions are restricted when used in real mode; in such cases, the notes for the entry provide details.

Using the Kernel API Reference

Each OS/2 kernel API function is described in the following format:

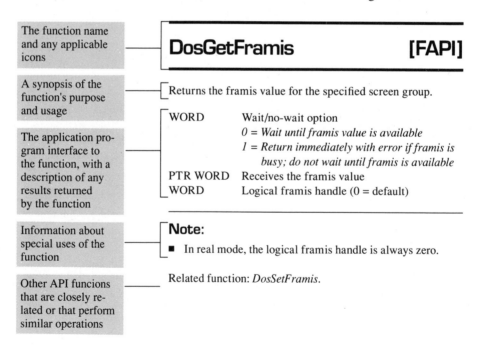

| The function name and any applicable icons | **DosGetFramis** | **[FAPI]** |

A synopsis of the function's purpose and usage — Returns the framis value for the specified screen group.

The application program interface to the function, with a description of any results returned by the function

WORD	Wait/no-wait option
	0 = Wait until framis value is available
	1 = Return immediately with error if framis is busy; do not wait until framis is available
PTR WORD	Receives the framis value
WORD	Logical framis handle (0 = default)

Information about special uses of the function

Note:

■ In real mode, the logical framis handle is always zero.

Other API funcions that are closely related or that perform similar operations — Related function: *DosSetFramis.*

In an assembly language program, you might code a call to this function as follows:

```
        extrn DosGetFramis:far
        .
        .
        .
framis  dw      0                       ; receives framis value
        .
        .
        .
        push    0                       ; wait if necessary
        push    ds                      ; receives framis value
        push    offset DGROUP:framis
        push    0                       ; logical framis handle
        call    DosGetFramis            ; transfer to OS/2
        or      ax,ax                   ; did function succeed?
        jnz     error                   ; jump if function failed
```

In a C program, you might code a call to this function as follows:

```
#define WAIT    0
#define NO_WAIT 1

extern unsigned far pascal
  DosGetFramis(unsigned, unsigned far *, unsigned);
        .
        .
        .
        unsigned framis, status;
        .
        .
        .
        status = DosGetFramis(WAIT, &framis, 0);
```

Kernel API Functions Listed Alphabetically

Function	Description
DosAllocHuge	Allocates huge memory block (> 64 KB)
DosAllocSeg	Allocates memory block (<= 64 KB)
DosAllocShrSeg	Allocates named shareable memory block
DosBeep	Generates tone
DosBufReset	Flushes file buffers, updates directory
DosCallback	Invokes ring 3 procedure on behalf of ring 2 (IOPL) code
DosCallNmPipe	Opens, writes, reads, and closes named pipe
DosCaseMap	Translates ASCII string in place
DosChDir	Selects current directory
DosChgFilePtr	Sets file pointer position
DosCLIAccess	Notifies intent to use CLI and STI
DosClose	Closes file, pipe, or device
DosCloseQueue	Closes queue (destroys if owner)
DosCloseSem	Closes system semaphore
DosConnectNmPipe	Waits for client to open pipe
DosCreateCSAlias	Obtains executable alias for data segment
DosCreateQueue	Creates named queue
DosCreateSem	Creates named system semaphore
DosCreateThread	Creates new execution thread in current process
DosCwait	Waits for termination of child process
DosDelete	Deletes file
DosDevConfig	Returns system hardware configuration
DosDevIOCtl	Device-specific commands and information
DosDisConnectNmPipe	Unilaterally closes named pipe
DosDupHandle	Duplicates or redirects handle
DosEnterCritSec	Suspends all other threads in process
DosErrClass	Returns information about error code
DosError	Disables or enables system critical error handler
DosExecPgm	Creates child process
DosExit	Terminates thread or process
DosExitCritSec	Reactivates other threads in same process
DosExitList	Registers routines to be executed at process termination
DosFileLocks	Locks or unlocks file region
DosFindClose	Releases directory search handle
DosFindFirst	Searches for first matching file
DosFindNext	Searches for additional matching files
DosFlagProcess	Sends event flag signal to another process
DosFreeModule	Releases handle for dynlink library
DosFreeSeg	Releases selector
DosFSRamSemClear	Releases fast-safe RAM semaphore
DosFSRamSemRequest	Obtains ownership of fast-safe RAM semaphore
DosGetCollate	Returns collating sequence table
DosGetCp	Returns current code page identifier
DosGetCtryInfo	Returns internationalization information

(continued)

Function	*Description*
DosGetDateTime	Returns current time, date, and day of week
DosGetDBCSEv	Returns table of double-byte character-set codes
DosGetEnv	Returns selector for process's environment
DosGetHugeShift	Returns incrementing value for huge memory block selectors
DosGetInfoSeg	Returns selectors for global and local read-only information segments
DosGetMachineMode	Returns flag indicating real or protected mode
DosGetMessage	Retrieves message from disk file
DosGetModHandle	Obtains handle for dynlink library
DosGetModName	Obtains filename of dynlink library
DosGetPID	Returns PID of current process and its parent
DosGetPPID	Returns PID of process's parent
DosGetProcAddr	Obtains entry point for dynlink library routine
DosGetPrty	Returns priority of thread
DosGetResource	Returns selector for read-only resource
DosGetSeg	Obtains selector for ''gettable'' memory segment
DosGetShrSeg	Obtains selector for existing named shareable segment
DosGetVersion	Returns OS/2 version number
DosGiveSeg	Obtains addressability for segment on behalf of another process
DosHoldSignal	Suspends signal processing for current process
DosInsMessage	Inserts variable text into body of message
DosKillProcess	Terminates another process
DosLoadModule	Loads dynlink library if it is not already loaded
DosLockSeg	Marks segment as not discardable
DosMakeNmPipe	Creates named pipe and returns handle
DosMakePipe	Creates anonymous pipe
DosMemAvail	Returns size of largest free block of physical memory
DosMkDir	Creates directory
DosMonClose	Terminates monitoring for character device
DosMonOpen	Returns handle for device monitoring
DosMonRead	Obtains monitor data packet
DosMonReg	Registers buffers for device monitor
DosMonWrite	Returns data packet to monitor chain
DosMove	Renames and/or moves file
DosMuxSemWait	Waits for one or more semaphores to become clear
DosNewSize	Changes size of file
DosOpen	Opens, replaces, or creates file, or opens device
DosOpenQueue	Opens existing named queue
DosOpenSem	Opens existing named system semaphore
DosPeekNmPipe	Reads named pipe without removing data from pipe
DosPeekQueue	Returns pointer to queue record without removing it from queue
DosPFSActivate	Selects printer code page and font
DosPFSCloseUser	Notifies font switcher that spool file is closed
DosPFSInit	Initializes printer code page and font switching
DosPFSQueryAct	Returns printer code page and font ID

(continued)

Function	Description
DosPFSVerifyFont	Checks existence of printer code page and font
DosPhysicalDisk	Returns information about partitionable fixed disks
DosPortAccess	Notifies intent to use range of I/O ports
DosPTrace	Allows controlled execution of another process
DosPurgeQueue	Discards all records in queue
DosPutMessage	Sends message to file, pipe, or device
DosQAppType	Returns application type (PM-aware, PM-compatible, etc.)
DosQCurDir	Returns current directory
DosQCurDisk	Returns current disk drive
DosQFHState	Returns file handle sharing and access characteristics
DosQFileInfo	Returns file size, attributes, and date and time stamps
DosQFileMode	Returns file attributes
DosQFSInfo	Returns file system information or volume label
DosQHandType	Returns handle type (file, pipe, or device)
DosQNmPHandState	Returns modes associated with named pipe handle
DosQNmPipeInfo	Returns characteristics of named pipe
DosQNmPipeSemState	Returns information for pipes associated with semaphore
DosQueryQueue	Returns number of records in queue
DosQSysInfo	Returns miscellaneous system information
DosQVerify	Returns state of read-after-write flag
DosR2StackRealloc	Increases size of stack used in ring 2 (IOPL) segment
DosRead	Reads data from file, pipe, or device
DosReadAsync	Asynchronous form of *DosRead*
DosReadQueue	Reads and removes record from queue
DosReallocHuge	Resizes huge memory block
DosReallocSeg	Resizes normal memory block
DosResumeThread	Reactivates thread in same process
DosRmDir	Deletes directory
DosScanEnv	Searches environment for string
DosSearchPath	Searches one or more directories for file
DosSelectDisk	Selects current disk drive
DosSelectSession	Switches session into foreground
DosSemClear	Unconditionally clears semaphore
DosSemRequest	Obtains ownership of semaphore
DosSemSet	Unconditionally sets semaphore
DosSemSetWait	Unconditionally sets semaphore and waits until it is cleared
DosSemWait	Waits until semaphore is cleared
DosSendSignal	Sends Ctrl-C or Ctrl-Break signal to another process
DosSetCp	Selects code page for process and session
DosSetDateTime	Sets current date and time
DosSetFHState	Sets file handle characteristics
DosSetFileInfo	Sets file time and date stamps
DosSetFileMode	Sets file attributes

(continued)

Function	Description
DosSetFSInfo	Adds or changes volume label
DosSetMaxFH	Sets maximum handles for current process
DosSetNmPHandState	Sets modes for named pipe handle
DosSetNmPipeSem	Associates system semaphore with named pipe
DosSetProcCp	Selects code page for process only
DosSetPrty	Sets priority of thread
DosSetSession	Sets session characteristics
DosSetSigHandler	Registers signal handler
DosSetVec	Registers handler for hardware exception
DosSetVerify	Sets system read-after-write flag
DosSizeSeg	Returns size of previously allocated segment
DosSleep	Suspends requesting thread for specified interval
DosStartSession	Creates new session and starts process within that session
DosStopSession	Terminates session
DosSubAlloc	Allocates memory from local heap
DosSubFree	Releases memory in local heap
DosSubSet	Initializes local heap
DosSuspendThread	Suspends execution of thread in same process
DosTimerAsync	Starts asynchronous one-shot timer
DosTimerStart	Starts asynchronous repeating timer
DosTimerStop	Stops timer
DosTransactNmPipe	Writes, then reads, named pipe
DosUnlockSeg	Marks segment as discardable
DosWaitNmPipe	Waits for availability of named pipe instance
DosWrite	Writes to file, pipe, or device
DosWriteAsync	Asynchronous form of *DosWrite*
DosWriteQueue	Writes record into queue
KbdCharIn	Returns keyboard character and scan code
KbdClose	Destroys logical keyboard
KbdDeRegister	Deregisters alternate keyboard subsystem
KbdFlushBuffer	Discards waiting keyboard characters
KbdFreeFocus	Releases bond between physical and logical keyboard
KbdGetCp	Returns keyboard code page identifier
KbdGetFocus	Binds logical to physical keyboard
KbdGetStatus	Returns logical keyboard status
KbdOpen	Creates logical keyboard
KbdPeek	Returns character-waiting status
KbdRegister	Registers alternate keyboard subsystem
KbdSetCp	Selects keyboard code page
KbdSetCustXT	Installs custom scan code translation table
KbdSetStatus	Sets logical keyboard characteristics
KbdStringIn	Reads buffered line from keyboard
KbdSynch	Serializes access to keyboard driver
KbdXlate	Translates scan code to ASCII character

(continued)

Function	*Description*
MouClose	Destroys logical mouse handle
MouDeRegister	Deregisters alternate mouse subsystem
MouDrawPtr	Displays mouse pointer
MouFlushQue	Discards waiting mouse events
MouGetDevStatus	Returns status of mouse driver
MouGetEventMask	Returns event mask for changes in mouse state
MouGetHotKey	Returns Task Manager mouse hot key if any
MouGetNumButtons	Returns number of supported mouse buttons
MouGetNumMickeys	Returns units of mouse movement per centimeter
MouGetNumQueEl	Returns number of waiting mouse events
MouGetPtrPos	Returns mouse pointer position
MouGetPtrShape	Returns mouse pointer shape and size
MouGetScaleFact	Returns scaling factors for mouse movement
MouInitReal	Initializes mouse driver for real mode screen group
MouOpen	Returns handle for mouse device
MouReadEventQue	Reads and removes mouse event packet from driver queue
MouRegister	Registers alternate mouse subsystem
MouRemovePtr	Defines exclusion area for mouse pointer
MouSetDevStatus	Sets mouse driver characteristics
MouSetEventMask	Sets event mask for changes in mouse state
MouSetHotKey	Sets mouse button combination for Task Manager hot key
MouSetPtrPos	Sets mouse pointer position
MouSetPtrShape	Sets mouse pointer shape and size
MouSetScaleFact	Sets scaling factors for mouse movement
MouSynch	Serializes access to mouse driver
VioAssociate	Associates *Vio* presentation space with device context
VioCreateLogFont	Creates logical font for use with *Vio* presentation space
VioCreatePS	Allocates *Vio* presentation space
VioDeleteSetId	Releases logical font identifier
VioDeRegister	Deregisters alternate video subsystem
VioDestroyPS	Destroys *Vio* presentation space
VioEndPopUp	Releases control of screen and keyboard by background process
VioGetAnsi	Returns code for ANSI support enabled/disabled
VioGetBuf	Returns address of logical video buffer
VioGetConfig	Returns hardware characteristics of video adapter
VioGetCp	Returns video code page identifier
VioGetCurPos	Returns cursor position
VioGetCurType	Returns cursor shape, size, and attribute
VioGetDeviceCellSize	Returns character cell height and width
VioGetFont	Returns address of font table
VioGetMode	Returns characteristics of current display mode
VioGetOrg	Returns screen origin for *Vio* presentation space

(continued)

Function	Description
VioGetPhysBuf	Returns selector for physical video display buffer
VioGetState	Returns palette registers, border color, intensity/blink toggle
VioModeUndo	Cancels *VioModeWait* call by another thread
VioModeWait	Blocks thread until video adapter state restore needed
VioPopUp	Asserts control of screen and keyboard by background process
VioPrtSc	Copies screen contents to printer
VioPrtScToggle	Enables or disables character echo to printer
VioQueryFonts	Returns list of available fonts for typeface
VioQuerySetIds	Returns list of loaded fonts
VioReadCellStr	Retrieves string of character-attribute pairs from display buffer
VioReadCharStr	Retrieves character string from display buffer
VioRegister	Registers alternate video subsystem
VioSavRedrawUndo	Cancels *VioSavRedrawWait* call by another thread
VioSavRedrawWait	Blocks thread until video buffer and adapter state restore needed
VioScrLock	Locks physical display for I/O
VioScrollDn	Scrolls display down
VioScrollLf	Scrolls display left
VioScrollRt	Scrolls display right
VioScrollUp	Scrolls display up
VioScrUnLock	Releases lock on physical display
VioSetAnsi	Enables or disables interpretation of ANSI escape sequences
VioSetCp	Selects video code page
VioSetCurPos	Sets cursor position
VioSetCurType	Sets cursor shape, size, and attribute
VioSetDeviceCellSize	Sets character cell height and width
VioSetFont	Downloads display font into adapter
VioSetMode	Selects display mode
VioSetOrg	Sets screen origin for *Vio* presentation space
VioSetState	Sets palette register values, border color, or intensity/blink toggle
VioShowBuf	Updates physical display from logical display buffer
VioShowPS	Updates display from *Vio* presentation space
VioWrtCellStr	Writes character-attribute pairs to display
VioWrtCharStr	Writes character string to display
VioWrtCharStrAtt	Writes character string with specified attribute to display
VioWrtNAttr	Changes attributes of one or more characters on display
VioWrtNCell	Initializes one or more display positions with character-attribute pair
VioWrtNChar	Initializes one or more display positions with character
VioWrtTTY	Writes character string to display in teletype mode

Dos API by Functional Group

Function	Description
File and Device Management	
DosBufReset	Flushes file buffers, updates directory
DosChgFilePtr	Sets file pointer position
DosClose	Closes file, pipe, or device
DosDelete	Deletes file
DosDupHandle	Duplicates or redirects handle
DosFileLock	Locks or unlocks file region
DosMove	Renames and/or moves file
DosNewSize	Changes size of file
DosOpen	Opens, replaces, or creates file, or opens device
DosQFHState	Returns file handle sharing and access characteristics
DosQFileInfo	Returns file size, attributes, and date and time stamps
DosQFileMode	Returns file attributes
DosQHandType	Returns handle type (file, pipe, or device)
DosRead	Reads data from file, pipe, or device
DosReadAsync	Asynchronous form of *DosRead*
DosSetFHState	Sets file handle characteristics
DosSetFileInfo	Sets file time and date stamps
DosSetFileMode	Sets file attributes
DosSetMaxFH	Sets maximum handles for current process
DosWrite	Writes to file, pipe, or device
DosWriteAsync	Asynchronous form of *DosWrite*
Disk and Directory Management	
DosChDir	Selects current directory
DosFindClose	Releases directory search handle
DosFindFirst	Searches for first matching file
DosFindNext	Searches for additional matching files
DosMkDir	Creates directory
DosPhysicalDisk	Returns information about partitionable fixed disks
DosQCurDir	Returns current directory
DosQCurDisk	Returns current disk drive
DosQFSInfo	Returns file system information or volume label
DosQVerify	Returns state of read-after-write flag
DosRmDir	Deletes directory
DosSearchPath	Searches one or more directories for file
DosSelectDisk	Selects current disk drive
DosSetFSInfo	Adds or changes volume label
DosSetVerify	Sets system read-after-write flag
Memory Management	
DosAllocHuge	Allocates huge memory block (> 64 KB)
DosAllocSeg	Allocates memory block (<= 64 KB)
DosAllocShrSeg	Allocates named shareable memory block

(continued)

Function	Description
Memory Management, *continued*	
DosCreateCSAlias	Obtains executable alias for data segment
DosFreeSeg	Releases selector
DosGetHugeShift	Returns incrementing value for huge memory block selectors
DosGetResource	Returns selector for read-only resource
DosGetSeg	Obtains selector for "gettable" memory segment
DosGetShrSeg	Obtains selector for existing named shareable segment
DosGiveSeg	Obtains addressability for segment on behalf of another process
DosLockSeg	Marks segment as not discardable
DosMemAvail	Returns size of largest free block of physical memory
DosR2StackRealloc	Increases size of stack used in IOPL segment
DosReallocHuge	Resizes huge memory block
DosReallocSeg	Resizes normal memory block
DosSizeSeg	Returns size of previously allocated segment
DosSubAlloc	Allocates memory from local heap
DosSubFree	Releases memory in local heap
DosSubSet	Initializes local heap
DosUnlockSeg	Marks segment as discardable
Thread Management	
DosCreateThread	Creates new execution thread in current process
DosEnterCritSec	Suspends all other threads in process
DosExit	Terminates thread
DosExitCritSec	Reactivates other threads in same process
DosGetPrty	Returns priority of thread
DosResumeThread	Reactivates thread in same process
DosSetPrty	Sets priority of thread
DosSuspendThread	Suspends execution of thread in same process
Process Management	
DosCwait	Waits for termination of child process
DosExecPgm	Creates child process
DosExit	Terminates process
DosExitList	Registers routines to be executed at process termination
DosGetPID	Returns PID of current process and its parent
DosGetPPID	Returns PID of process's parent
DosKillProcess	Terminates process
DosPTrace	Allows controlled execution for debugging of another process
Session Management	
DosSelectSession	Switches session into foreground
DosSetSession	Sets session characteristics
DosStartSession	Creates new session and starts process within that session
DosStopSession	Terminates session

(continued)

Function	Description
Semaphore Management	
DosCloseSem	Closes system semaphore
DosCreateSem	Creates named system semaphore
DosFSRamSemClear	Releases fast-safe RAM semaphore
DosFSRamSemRequest	Obtains ownership of fast-safe RAM semaphore
DosMuxSemWait	Waits for one or more semaphores to become clear
DosOpenSem	Opens existing named system semaphore
DosSemClear	Unconditionally clears semaphore
DosSemRequest	Obtains ownership of semaphore
DosSemSet	Unconditionally sets semaphore
DosSemSetWait	Unconditionally sets semaphore and waits until it is cleared
DosSemWait	Waits until semaphore is cleared
Pipe Management	
DosCallNmPipe	Opens, writes, reads, and closes named pipe
DosConnectNmPipe	Waits for client to open pipe
DosDisConnectNmPipe	Unilaterally closes named pipe
DosMakeNmPipe	Creates named pipe
DosMakePipe	Creates anonymous pipe
DosPeekNmPipe	Reads data from named pipe without removing it from pipe
DosQNmPHandState	Returns modes associated with named pipe handle
DosQNmPipeInfo	Returns characteristics of named pipe
DosQNmPipeSemState	Returns information for pipes associated with semaphore
DosSetNmPHandState	Sets modes for named pipe handle
DosSetNmPipeSem	Associates system semaphore with named pipe
DosTransactNmPipe	Writes, then reads, named pipe
DosWaitNmPipe	Waits for availability of named pipe instance
Queue Management	
DosCloseQueue	Closes queue (destroys if owner)
DosCreateQueue	Creates named queue
DosOpenQueue	Opens existing named queue
DosPeekQueue	Returns pointer to queue record without removing it from queue
DosPurgeQueue	Discards all records in queue
DosQueryQueue	Returns number of records in queue
DosReadQueue	Reads record and removes it from queue
DosWriteQueue	Writes record into queue
Signal Management	
DosFlagProcess	Sends event flag signal to another process
DosHoldSignal	Suspends signal processing for current process
DosSendSignal	Sends Ctrl-C or Ctrl-Break signal to another process
DosSetSigHandler	Registers signal handler

(continued)

Function	Description
Time, Date, and Timers	
DosGetDateTime	Returns current time, date, and day of week
DosSetDateTime	Sets current date and time
DosSleep	Suspends requesting thread for specified interval
DosTimerAsync	Starts asynchronous one-shot timer
DosTimerStart	Starts asynchronous repeating timer
DosTimerStop	Stops timer
Dynamic Linking	
DosFreeModule	Releases handle for dynlink library
DosGetModHandle	Obtains handle for dynlink library
DosGetModName	Obtains filename of dynlink library
DosGetProcAddr	Obtains entry point for dynlink library routine
DosLoadModule	Loads dynlink library if it is not already loaded
Device Monitors	
DosMonClose	Terminates monitoring for character device
DosMonOpen	Returns handle for device monitoring
DosMonRead	Obtains monitor data packet
DosMonReg	Registers buffers for device monitor
DosMonWrite	Returns data packet to monitor chain
Internationalization Support	
DosCaseMap	Translates ASCII string in place
DosGetCollate	Returns collating sequence table
DosGetCp	Returns current code page identifier
DosGetCtryInfo	Returns internationalization information
DosGetDBCSEv	Returns table of double-byte character set codes
DosPFSActivate	Selects printer code page and font
DosPFSCloseUser	Notifies font switcher that spool file is closed
DosPFSInit	Initializes printer code page and font switching
DosPFSQueryAct	Returns printer code page and font ID
DosPFSVerifyFont	Checks existence of printer code page and font
DosSetCp	Selects code page for process and session
DosSetProcCp	Selects code page for process only
Miscellaneous	
DosBeep	Generates tone
DosCallback	Calls ring 3 procedure on behalf of ring 2 (IOPL) procedure
DosCLIAccess	Notifies intent to use CLI and STI
DosDevConfig	Returns system hardware configuration
DosDevIOCtl	Device-specific commands and information
DosErrClass	Returns information about error code
DosError	Disables or enables system critical error handler
DosGetEnv	Returns selector for process's environment
DosGetInfoSeg	Returns selectors for global and local read-only information segments

(continued)

Function	Description
Micellaneous, *continued*	
DosGetMachineMode	Returns flag indicating real or protected mode
DosGetMessage	Retrieves message from disk file
DosGetVersion	Returns OS/2 version number
DosInsMessage	Inserts variable text into body of message
DosPortAccess	Notifies intent to use range of I/O ports
DosPutMessage	Sends message to file, pipe, or device
DosQAppType	Returns application type (PM-aware, PM-compatible, etc.)
DosQSysInfo	Returns miscellaneous system information
DosScanEnv	Searches environment for string
DosSetVec	Registers handler for hardware exception

Kernel API Functions

DosAllocHuge   [IOPL]   [FAPI]

Allocates a memory block of any size, limited only by the number of available selectors and the disk-swapping space, returning a base selector. The memory is movable and swappable. If the block is larger than one segment, it is addressed with logically contiguous selectors, and the increment between these selectors is calculated with the aid of *DosGetHugeShift*. A huge memory block is locked, unlocked, and freed as a unit by means of the base selector.

WORD	Number of complete 64 KB segments
WORD	Number of bytes in any partial last segment (0 = none)
PTR WORD	Receives base selector for huge memory block
WORD	Maximum number of 64 KB segments for subsequent *DosReallocHuge*
	(0 = block will not be expanded later)
WORD	Sharing option

Bit(s)	Significance (if set)
0	*Shareable with* DosGiveSeg
1	*Shareable with* DosGetSeg
2	*Discardable*
3–15	*Reserved (0)*

Notes:

■ A huge memory block may be shareable and/or discardable. If you use the discardable option, an implicit *DosLockSeg* is performed on the block when it is allocated. Huge memory blocks are discarded as a unit rather than on a segment-by-segment basis.

■ In real mode, the function rounds the requested size up to the next paragraph (multiple of 16 bytes) and returns a physical segment address. The sharing/discardable parameter must be zero, and the maximum number of segments parameter is ignored.

Related functions: *DosAllocSeg, DosFreeSeg, DosGetHugeShift, DosGetSeg, DosGiveSeg, DosLockSeg, DosReallocHuge, DosSizeSeg, DosUnlockSeg.*

DosAllocSeg   [IOPL] [FAPI]

Allocates a memory segment with a maximum size of 65,536 bytes (64 KB). The memory is movable and swappable.

WORD	Size of segment in bytes (0 = 65,536)
PTR WORD	Receives selector
WORD	Sharing option

Bit(s)	Significance (if set)
0	Shareable with DosGiveSeg
1	Shareable with DosGetSeg
2	Discardable
3–15	Reserved (0)

Notes:

- A segment may be shareable and/or discardable. If the discardable option is used, an implicit *DosLockSeg* is performed on the new block when it is allocated.

- In real mode, the function rounds the requested size up to the next paragraph (multiple of 16 bytes) and returns a physical segment address. The sharing/discardable parameter must be zero.

Related functions: *DosAllocHuge, DosAllocShrSeg, DosFreeSeg, DosGetSeg, DosGiveSeg, DosLockSeg, DosReallocSeg, DosSizeSeg, DosUnlockSeg.*

DosAllocShrSeg   [IOPL]

Allocates a named, shareable memory segment with a maximum size of 65,536 bytes (64 KB). The memory is swappable and movable. Any other process can obtain a selector for the same segment by calling *DosGetShrSeg.*

WORD	Size of segment in bytes (0 = 65,536)
PTR ASCIIZ	Segment name, in the form \SHAREMEM\name.ext
PTR WORD	Receives selector

Related functions: *DosAllocSeg, DosGetSeg, DosGetShrSeg, DosGiveSeg, DosSizeSeg.*

DosBeep   [IOPL] [FAPI]

Generates a tone of specified frequency and duration. The tone is synchronous; that is, the thread requesting *DosBeep* is suspended for the duration of the tone.

| WORD | Frequency in Hertz (Hz), in the range 37–32,767 |
| WORD | Duration in milliseconds (msec.) |

DosBufReset   [IOPL]   [FAPI]

Flushes OS/2's internal buffers associated with a handle. If the handle is associated with a file, any un-written data is physically written to disk, and the directory entry is updated.

WORD	File, pipe, or device handle (if handle = −1, all buffers for the process are written)

Notes:

- [1.1] If a file or named pipe is opened with the "write-through" option, OS/2 does not defer writes by internally buffering data written to that handle. However, the directory entry for the file is not updated until the process calls *DosClose* or *DosBufReset* or terminates.

- [1.1] If a client process is reading data from a named pipe, *DosBufReset* blocks until all the data is read.

Related functions: *DosClose, DosMakeNmPipe, DosOpen, DosWrite.*

DosCallback   [IOPL]   [1.1]

Calls a ring 3 function on behalf of code executing within a ring 2 (IOPL) segment.

DWORD	Address of ring 3 function

Note:

- You cannot use the ring 2 stack to pass parameters to the ring 3 routine. Pass all parameters in registers. For a complete list of conforming functions, see p. 304.

Related function: *DosR2StackRealloc.*

DosCallNmPipe   [1.1]

Opens a named pipe, writes a message to the pipe, reads a message from the pipe, and then closes it.

PTR ASCIIZ	Pipe name, in the form \PIPE*name.ext* for a local pipe or *machine*\PIPE*name.ext* for a remote pipe
PTR BUFFER	Contains data to be written to pipe
WORD	Length of data to be written to pipe
PTR BUFFER	Receives data from pipe
WORD	Length of buffer to receive data from pipe
PTR WORD	Receives actual length of data read from pipe
DWORD	Timeout interval in milliseconds (0 = use default timeout; −1 = wait indefinitely)

Notes:

- This function is used only by client processes.

- The pipe must be in message mode. If the buffer is too small for the message, the function fills the buffer and returns an error. To obtain the remaining data, you must make another call to *DosCallNmPipe*.

Related functions: *DosClose, DosMakeNmPipe, DosOpen, DosTransactNmPipe.*

DosCaseMap [FAPI]

Translates a string of ASCII characters in place, according to the specified country and code page, using a case-mapping table obtained from the file COUNTRY.SYS. In general, lowercase characters are mapped to uppercase, and accented or otherwise modified vowels are changed to their plain vowel equivalents.

| WORD | Length of string to case-map |
| PTR BUFFER | Country code data structure |

Offset	*Length*	*Description*
00H	*2*	*Country code (0 = default)*
02H	*2*	*Code page ID (0 = default)*

| PTR BUFFER | Contains character string to case-map |

Note:

- In real mode, the COUNTRY.SYS file is assumed to be in the root directory of the current drive.

Related functions: *DosGetCollate, DosGetCp, DosGetCtryInfo, DosGetDBCSEv, DosSetProcCp, DosSetCp.*

DosChDir [IOPL] [FAPI]

Selects the current directory for the current or specified drive. The current directory for each drive is maintained on a per-process basis and is inherited by child processes.

| PTR ASCIIZ | Directory pathname (may include a drive identifier) |
| DWORD | Reserved (0) |

Related functions: *DosQCurDir, DosQCurDisk, DosQSysInfo, DosSelectDisk.*

DosChgFilePtr [IOPL] [FAPI]

Sets the read/write pointer associated with a file handle. The file pointer determines the starting location for the next read or write operation and is automatically incremented by these operations. When a file is opened, the initial file pointer location is zero (start of file).

WORD	File handle
DWORD	Signed file pointer offset
WORD	Method
	0 *Relative to start of file*
	1 *Relative to current file pointer*
	2 *Relative to end of file*
PTR DWORD	Receives new absolute file pointer position

Note:

- You can find the size of a file by calling *DosChgFilePtr* with offset = 0 and method = 2 and then examining the returned file pointer, or by calling *DosQFileInfo*.

Related functions: *DosOpen, DosRead, DosReadAsync, DosWrite, DosWriteAsync*.

DosCLIAccess   [IOPL]   [FAPI]

Notifies the operating system that the process will disable and enable interrupts with the CLI and STI instructions. These instructions must be executed within an IOPL segment.

No parameters

Related function: *DosPortAccess*.

DosClose   [IOPL]   [FAPI]

Closes a handle for a file, pipe, or device, and releases the handle for reuse. If the handle was associated with a file, any unwritten data that is buffered within OS/2 is flushed to disk and the directory entry is updated if necessary.

WORD	Handle for file, pipe, or device

Note:

- [1.1] A call to *DosClose* for a named pipe in the "connected" state by either client or server puts the pipe into "closing" state. If the pipe is in any other state and the server closes it, the pipe is destroyed. To make a pipe in the "closing" state available again, the server must call *DosDisConnectNmPipe* followed by *DosConnectNmPipe*.

Related functions: *DosBufReset, DosDupHandle, DosMakeNmPipe, DosOpen*.

DosCloseQueue

Closes a queue. If the requesting process created the queue, the queue is destroyed.

WORD	Queue handle

Related functions: *DosCreateQueue, DosOpenQueue*.

DosCloseSem

Closes a system semaphore. If there are no other open handles for the semaphore in the system, the semaphore is destroyed.

DWORD   Semaphore handle

Related functions: *DosCreateSem, DosOpenSem*.

DosConnectNmPipe   [1.1]

Waits for a client process to open an instance of a named pipe.

WORD   Pipe handle

Notes:

■ This function is used only by server processes.

■ If the pipe is in blocking mode, *DosConnectNmPipe* waits if necessary for a client to open the pipe. If the pipe is in nonblocking mode, *DosConnectNmPipe* returns immediately with an error unless a client has already opened the pipe.

Related functions: *DosDisConnectNmPipe, DosMakeNmPipe, DosOpen*.

DosCreateCSAlias   [IOPL] [FAPI]

Returns an executable alias selector for a read-only or read/write data selector. Both the executable selector and the data selector refer to the same physical memory segment, but the executable selector can be loaded into the CS register whereas a data selector cannot.

WORD   Selector for data segment
PTR WORD   Receives executable selector

Notes:

■ The data selector must not refer to a shared or huge memory block.

■ In protected mode, the segment persists until both the data and executable selectors are released with *DosFreeSeg*. In real mode, the two selectors are identical and are physical segment addresses; consequently, the memory block is deallocated when either selector is passed to *DosFreeSeg*.

Related functions: *DosAllocSeg, DosFreeSeg*.

DosCreateQueue

Creates and opens a queue. The process that creates a queue is the queue owner and is the only process which can read records from the queue (although any process can write to a queue).

PTR WORD	Receives queue handle
WORD	Ordering method for queue records
	0 *First in, first out (FIFO)*
	1 *Last in, first out (LIFO)*
	2 *Priority (sender specifies priority 0–15)*
PTR ASCIIZ	Queue name, in the form \QUEUES*name.ext*

Related functions: *DosCloseQueue, DosOpenQueue*.

DosCreateSem   [IOPL]

Creates a named, global (system) semaphore. Other processes can subsequently obtain access to the semaphore with *DosOpenSem*.

WORD	Exclusive ownership option
	0 *Only owning process can modify semaphore*
	1 *Any process can modify semaphore*
PTR DWORD	Receives semaphore handle
PTR ASCIIZ	Semaphore name, in the form \SEM*name.ext*

Related functions: *DosCloseSem, DosOpenSem*.

DosCreateThread   [IOPL]

Creates an asynchronous thread of execution within the same process. The new thread is assigned the same priority as the thread which created it.

DWORD	Initial execution address for new thread
PTR WORD	Receives thread ID
DWORD	Initial stack base for new thread

Note:

■ The stack grows downward, so the supplied base address must be the address of the last byte plus one allocated for the stack.

Related functions: *DosEnterCritSec, DosExit, DosExitCritSec, DosGetPrty, DosResumeThread, DosSetPrty, DosSuspendThread*.

DosCwait [IOPL]

Waits for the termination of a child process and retrieves its termination type and exit code. The child process must have been started with *DosExecPgm* asynchronous option 2.

WORD	Child process subtree option
	0 *Wait for child process only*
	1 *Wait for child process and all of its descendants*
WORD	Wait option
	0 *Wait for child process to end*
	1 *Return immediately with an error if the child process is still running; do not wait for child process to end*
PTR DWORD	Receives termination information

Offset	Length	Description
00H	*2*	*Termination type*
		0 = normal termination (using DosExit)
		1 = critical error abort
		2 = execution fault (such as GP fault)
		3 = DosKillProcess signal
02H	*2*	*Child's exit code (from DosExit)*

PTR WORD	Receives PID of terminating process
WORD	PID of child process to wait for (0 = wait until any child process ends and return its PID)

Related functions: *DosExecPgm, DosExit, DosKillProcess.*

DosDelete [IOPL] . [FAPI]

Deletes a file by releasing its storage for reuse and removing its directory entry. You cannot delete read-only files or files that are currently opened by another process.

PTR ASCIIZ	Pathname of file to be deleted (cannot contain wildcards)
DWORD	Reserved (0)

Related functions: *DosQFileMode, DosRmDir, DosSetFileMode.*

DosDevConfig [IOPL] [FAPI]

Returns the machine model and configuration.

PTR BYTE	Receives device information
WORD	Type of information needed
	0 *Number of printers attached*
	1 *Number of serial ports*
	2 *Number of floppy disk drives*
	3 *Presence of math coprocessor (returns 0 = not present, 1 = present)*

(continued)

Type of information needed, *continued*

4   *PC submodel type*
5   *PC model type*
6   *Primary display adapter type (returns 0 = monochrome adapter,*
            1 = other)

WORD   Reserved (0)

Related function: *VioGetConfig*.

DosDevIOCtl   [IOPL]   [FAPI]

Returns device-specific information or allows a program to issue device-specific commands that are not supported by other API functions.

PTR BUFFER   Receives subfunction-specific data
PTR BUFFER   Contains subfunction-specific parameters
WORD   Function number
WORD   Category number
            1   *Serial port*
            2   *Reserved*
            3   *Pointer device (mouse)*
            4   *Keyboard*
            5   *Printer*
            6   *Light pen*
            7   *Mouse*
            8   *Logical disk*
            9   *Physical disk*
            10   *Character device monitor*
            11   *General device control*
            12–127   *Reserved for OS/2*
            128–255   *Available for user drivers and programs*
WORD   Device handle

Notes:

- The arguments and returned results for each *DosDevIOCtl* subfunction are documented in Part 2 of this reference section, which begins on p. 621.

- Category 7 functions use a handle obtained from *MouOpen*, and Category 9 functions use a handle supplied by *DosPhysicalDisk*. Handles for use with the remaining functions can be obtained from *DosOpen* or inherited from the parent process.

- In real mode, only a restricted set of category 1, 5, and 8 subfunctions are supported.

Related function: *DosOpen*.

DosDisConnectNmPipe [1.1]

Unilaterally breaks a named pipe connection between a server and a client; in so doing, denies a client process any further access to it. Any data waiting in the pipe is discarded.

WORD   Pipe handle

Notes:

- This function is used only by server processes.

- The client process should close the associated pipe handle even though it cannot use the pipe after the server has disconnected it.

Related functions: *DosClose, DosConnectNmPipe.*

DosDupHandle [IOPL] [FAPI]

Duplicates a handle and returns a new handle that refers to the same file, pipe, or device; alternatively, redirects an existing handle to refer to the same file, pipe, or device as another existing handle. If duplicate handles refer to a file, they have the same file pointer, and any sharing and access restrictions on the original handle are also duplicated.

WORD   Existing file, pipe, or device handle to be duplicated
PTR WORD   Contains handle to be redirected, or −1 to obtain a new handle; in the latter case, receives the new handle in the same location

Related functions: *DosChgFilePtr, DosClose, DosMakeNmPipe, DosMakePipe, DosRead, DosWrite.*

DosEnterCritSec [IOPL]

Disables execution of all other threads within the same process. You can reactivate the other threads with *DosExitCritSec.* Typically, this function is used to protect a thread's access to a variable which is also used by other threads.

No parameters

Notes:

- *DosEnterCritSec* calls can be nested, requiring an equivalent number of *DosExitCritSec* calls before the other threads are released.

- This function does not disable signal processing, which is still performed using the process's primary thread.

- Avoid making calls to other kernel API functions within a *DosEnterCritSec ... DosExitCritSec* sequence because some of these calls create additional threads on behalf of the process.

Related functions: *DosCreateThread, DosExitCritSec, DosResumeThread, DosSuspendThread.*

DosErrClass   [IOPL] [FAPI]

Returns an error class, recommended recovery action, and device type (locus) for an API error code.

WORD	Error code for analysis
PTR WORD	Receives error class

1	*Out of resources*
2	*Temporary situation*
3	*Authorization failed*
4	*Internal error in system software*
5	*Hardware failure*
6	*System software failure not fault of active process*
7	*Probable application error*
8	*File or item not found*
9	*File or item of invalid type or format*
10	*File or resource locked*
11	*Incorrect media or CRC error*
12	*Resource already exists or already committed, or action previously performed*
13	*Unclassified*
14	*Can't perform requested action*
15	*Timeout*

PTR WORD	Receives recommended recovery action
1	*Retry immediately*
2	*Delay and retry*
3	*Get corrected information from user*
4	*Terminate with cleanup*
5	*Terminate immediately without cleanup*
6	*Ignore error*
7	*Retry after user intervention to remove cause of error*

PTR WORD	Receives error locus
1	*Unknown*
2	*Block device*
3	*Network*
4	*Serial device*
5	*Memory*

Note:

■ Returned values might not be the same in real and protected mode.

Related function: *DosError*.

DosError   [IOPL] [FAPI]

Notifies the operating system that the process will handle unrecoverable critical (hardware-related) errors, or restores the handling of these errors to the operating system. Can also be used to disable notification pop-ups for CPU exceptions (faults), such as general protection faults or divide by zero, although the handling of such exceptions is not affected.

WORD	Critical error processing option	
	Bit(s)	**Significance**
	0	*0 = suspend system critical error processing; return errors to the requesting process*
		1 = resume system critical error processing
	1	*0 = enable exception (for example, divide by zero) notification popups*
		1 = disable exception pop-ups
	2–15	*Reserved (0)*

Notes:

- An exception terminates the process unless it has installed its own handler with *DosSetVec*. GP faults always terminate the process.

- You can disable critical error handling by the system for a particular file or device by setting the error mode bit with *DosOpen* or *DosSetFHandState*.

- In real mode, calling *DosError* with processing option = 0 causes the system's Int 24H (critical error) handler to return a "fail" code until you call *DosError* again with processing option = 1.

Related functions: *DosErrClass, DosOpen, DosSetFHandState, DosSetVec.*

DosExecPgm [IOPL] [FAPI]

Starts a child process within the same session. The child inherits the parent process's environment and file, pipe, and device handles unless the parent takes special action to prevent it. The parent can check the child process's status with *DosCwait* or terminate it with *DosKillProcess.*

PTR BUFFER	Object name buffer	
WORD	Length of object name buffer	
WORD	Child process execution mode	
	0	*Synchronous*
	1	*Asynchronous, no* DosCwait
	2	*Asynchronous, subsequent* DosCwait
	3	*Traceable (see* DosPTrace*)*
	4	*Asynchronous detached (orphan)*
	5	*Frozen*
PTR ASCIIZ	One or more ASCIIZ argument strings to be passed to child process; terminate entire set with an extra null byte (use null pointer if no argument strings)	
PTR ASCIIZ	One or more ASCIIZ environment strings to be passed to child process; terminate entire set with an extra null byte (use null pointer to pass copy of current process's environment)	
PTR DWORD	Receives child process information (*see Notes*)	
PTR ASCIIZ	Pathname of child process's executable file	

Notes:

- For synchronous child processes (execution mode 0), the returned information is as follows:

Offset	Length	Description
00H	2	Child termination type
		0 = *normal termination (using* DosExit*)*
		1 = *critical error abort*
		2 = *execution fault (such as GP fault)*
		3 = DosKillProcess *signal*
02H	2	Child exit code (from *DosExit*)

- For asynchronous child processes (execution modes 1 and 2), the returned information is as follows:

Offset	Length	Description
00H	2	Child process ID
02H	2	Nothing

- For child execution mode 2, the child process's termination type and exit code are collected with a subsequent call to *DosCwait*. Memory is consumed if *DosCwait* is not called; if the information is not needed, use child execution mode 1 instead.

- If the *DosExecPgm* call fails because of a missing dynlink module or entry point, the corresponding name is returned as an ASCIIZ string in the object name buffer.

- If the child program's pathname contains neither a drive nor a path element (i.e., no : or \ delimiters), the current directory and then each directory in the parent's PATH variable is searched for the executable file. The file's extension must be explicit.

- For compatibility with CMD.EXE, the argument strings should consist of the simple name of the program followed by the command tail, for example:

```
db      'MEP',0
db      ' MYFILE.DAT',0
db      0
```

- In real mode, child process execution modes 1 through 5 are not supported.

Related functions: *DosCwait, DosExit, DosKillProcess, DosPTrace, DosStartSession.*

DosExit   [IOPL] [FAPI]

Terminates a thread or process. When *DosExit* is used to terminate a process, the exit code can be collected by the parent process with *DosCwait*.

WORD	Action code	
	0	*Terminate current thread only*
	1	*Terminate process*
WORD	Exit (result) code	

Notes:

- If the action code is 0, but the requesting thread is the only thread or the last active thread in a process, the process is terminated. If termination routines have been registered with *DosExitList*, the primary thread is reactivated and used to execute each of them. All of the process's resources (memory, files, semaphores, etc.) are then freed.

- [1.0] Because the primary thread (thread 1) is used for signal handling, it should never be terminated unless the process is also terminated.

  [1.1] Termination of the primary thread always terminates the process, regardless of the value of the action code parameter.

- In real mode, threads are not supported, and this function always terminates the process.

Related functions: *DosCwait, DosExecPgm, DosExitList.*

DosExitCritSec [IOPL]

Enables execution of other threads within the same process; cancels a previous *DosEnterCritSec* call.

No parameters.

Note:

- If you nest calls to *DosEnterCritSec*, you must make an equivalent number of *DosExitCritSec* calls before the other threads are released.

Related functions: *DosCreateThread, DosEnterCritSec, DosResumeThread, DosSuspendThread.*

DosExitList [IOPL]

Maintains a list of procedures (sometimes called ExitList routines) that are called by the kernel when the current process terminates. These routines are executed before any resources still owned by the process (memory, files, semaphores, etc.) are freed by the kernel.

WORD	Request type	
	1	*Add ExitList routine*
	2	*Remove ExitList routine*
	3	*Processing complete (used by ExitList routines only)*
DWORD	Address of ExitList routine (ignored for request type 3)	

Notes:

- The ExitList routines are not guaranteed to execute in any particular order. Each ExitList routine uses the process's original stack, runs as the primary thread (thread 1), and must exit by calling *DosExitList* with request type 3.

- When an ExitList routine receives control, the reason for termination is on the stack at SS:SP + 4:

  0 = normal termination (using *DosExit*)
  1 = critical error abort
  2 = execution fault (such as GP fault)
  3 = *DosKillProcess* signal

  An ExitList routine cannot call *DosExecPgm* or *DosCreateThread.*

Related functions: *DosCreateThread, DosExecPgm, DosExit, DosKillProcess, DosSetSigHandler.*

DosFileLocks   [IOPL] [FAPI]

Locks and/or unlocks a file region. While a region is locked, other processes are not allowed to read or write the region. In this way, data integrity is maintained when multiple processes are using the same file. If a lock operation fails, some other process has already locked the same file region, and the current process should delay and try again, notify the user, or take some other appropriate recovery action.

WORD	File handle
PTR BUFFER	Contains description of region to be unlocked (*see Notes*)
PTR BUFFER	Contains description of region to be locked (*see Notes*)

Notes:

- The buffers that describe a file region are 8 bytes long:

Offset	*Length*	*Description*
00H	4	File offset
04H	4	Region length

  If you pass a null (zero) pointer for either buffer describing a file region, the corresponding action is omitted. Locking beyond the current end of file is not an error.

- The unlock range, if present, is processed before the lock range. Avoid locking regions that overlap.

- All access to a file by other processes can be blocked by opening the file with the deny-all sharing mode. In such cases, additional calls to *DosFileLocks* are not needed.

- When the process terminates, any remaining locks are released and the file is closed. Access to locked regions is not inherited by child processes.

Related functions: *DosExecPgm, DosOpen.*

DosFindClose   [IOPL] [FAPI]

Closes a directory search handle.

WORD	Directory search handle from *DosFindFirst*

Related functions: *DosFindFirst, DosFindNext.*

DosFindFirst   [IOPL] [FAPI]

Returns the first matching pathname, if any, and a directory search handle. If a match is found, information from the directory, such as the file's size, attributes, and time and date stamps, is returned; if no match is found, the function returns an error.

PTR ASCIIZ	Pathname to search for (may include wildcard characters)
PTR WORD	Contains −1 to allocate a new search handle, or 1 (a handle that is always available); in the former case, receives the new handle in the same location

WORD	Search attribute (bits may be combined)	
	Bit(s)	*Significance (if set)*
	0	*Read-only*
	1	*Hidden*
	2	*System*
	3	*Reserved (0)*
	4	*Directory*
	5	*Archive*
	6–15	*Reserved (0)*
PTR BUFFER	Receives search results (minimum length 36 bytes; *see Notes*)	
WORD	Length of buffer that receives search results	
PTR WORD	Contains maximum number of matches requested; receives the actual number of matches	
DWORD	Reserved (0)	

Notes:

- An attribute of 0 selects only normal files that match the pathname. When one or more attribute bits are set, the function returns all matching normal files as well as all matching files that have any of the same attributes.

- You can obtain multiple matches with one function call. The information for each matched file is packed into the result buffer in consecutive records with the following format:

Offset	*Length*	*Description*
00H	2	File date of creation
02H	2	File time of creation
04H	2	File date of last access
06H	2	File time of last access
08H	2	File date of last write
0AH	2	File time of last write
0CH	4	File size
10H	4	File allocation
14H	2	File attribute
16H	1	Length of filename (*n*)
17H+	*n+1*	ASCIIZ filename (does not include drive or path)

The date and time of file creation and last access are zero in FAT file systems. Note that the length of each record within the result buffer depends on the filename and is not a constant. The number of matches returned is the minimum of the number requested, the number which will fit into the result buffer, and the number which actually exist.

- The time fields are formatted as follows:

Bits	*Description*
0–4	2-second increments (0–29)
5–10	Minutes (0–59)
11–15	Hours (0–23)

- The date fields are formatted as follows:

Bits	Description
0–4	Day (1–31)
5–8	Month (1–12)
9–15	Year (relative to 1980)

- Directory search handles are not assigned from the same sequence as file, pipe, and device handles. Approximately 1000 search handles are available per process (memory permitting).

- In real mode, you can pass a directory handle of 1 or −1 on the first call to *DosFindFirst,* and a handle of 1 must always be used thereafter. In other words, only one search may be active at a time.

Related functions: *DosFindClose, DosFindNext, DosQFileInfo, DosSearchPath.*

DosFindNext   [IOPL]   [FAPI]

Finds the next match, if any, for an ambiguous pathname passed previously to *DosFindFirst.*

WORD	Directory search handle from previous *DosFindFirst*
PTR BUFFER	Receives search results (*see DosFindFirst*)
WORD	Length of buffer that receives search results
PTR WORD	Contains maximum number of matches requested; receives the actual number of matches

---

Notes:

- Use of this function presumes a previous *DosFindFirst* that returned at least one matching file. If there are no more matching files, an error is returned.

- In real mode, the directory handle must always be 1.

Related functions: *DosFindClose, DosFindFirst.*

DosFlagProcess   [IOPL]

Sends an event flag signal to another process or to a process and all its descendants. The destination process must be either the current process or a nondetached child process. The signal is ignored unless the receiving process has registered a handler for it with *DosSetSigHandler.*

WORD	PID of destination process	
WORD	Destination type	
	0	*Process and all its descendants*
	1	*Designated process only*
WORD	Event flag number	
	0	*Flag A*
	1	*Flag B*
	2	*Flag C*
WORD	Private data (passed to destination process, ignored by OS/2)	

Note:

- The destination process need not still be alive for its own descendants to receive the signal.

Related functions: *DosHoldSignal, DosSendSignal, DosSetSigHandler*.

DosFreeModule   [IOPL]

Closes a dynlink library handle. After all active handles for a library are released, the memory occupied by the library is released.

WORD   Dynlink library handle

Related functions: *DosGetModHandle, DosGetModName, DosGetProcAddr, DosLoadModule*.

DosFreeSeg   [IOPL] [FAPI]

Releases a selector for a memory block previously allocated with *DosAllocHuge, DosAllocSeg,* or *DosAllocShrSeg*. You can also use this function to release a selector obtained from *DosCreateCSAlias, DosGetSeg, VioGetPhysBuf,* etc., or to release a ''giveaway'' selector passed by another process. When all the selectors owned by all processes for a particular memory block have been freed, physical memory and swap file space are reclaimed.

WORD   Selector

Note:

- In protected mode, the data selector used as an argument to *DosCreateCSAlias* and the returned executable selector are distinct, and you can free either one without releasing the associated memory block. In real mode, the two segment addresses are the same, and freeing either one also releases the memory.

Related functions: *DosAllocHuge, DosAllocSeg, DosAllocShrSeg, DosCreateCSAlias*.

DosFSRamSemClear   [IOPL] [1.1]

Releases ownership of a fast-safe RAM semaphore.

PTR BUFFER   Control structure for fast-safe RAM semaphore, in the following format:

Offset	Length	Description
00H	2	*Contains length of structure (14 bytes in OS/2 version 1.1)*
02H	2	*Receives process ID of owner (0 = semaphore unowned)*
04H	2	*Receives thread ID of owner (0 = semaphore unowned)*
06H	2	*Receives semaphore reference count*
08H	2	*Field for use by semaphore owner*
0AH	4	*Storage for semaphore*

The requesting process should not modify shaded fields.

Related functions: *DosExitList, DosFSRamSemRequest, DosSemClear*.

DosFSRamSemRequest [IOPL] [1.1]

Obtains ownership of a fast-safe RAM semaphore or waits until the semaphore is available. The system saves information about the current semaphore owner for possible use by an ExitList cleanup routine. As a consequence, these semaphores are particularly appropriate for use by dynlink libraries with multiple client processes.

PTR BUFFER   Control structure for fast-safe RAM semaphore, in the following format:

Offset	Length	Description
00H	2	Contains length of structure (14 bytes in OS/2 1.1)
02H	2	Receives process ID of owner (0 = semaphore unowned)
04H	2	Receives thread ID of owner (0 = semaphore unowned)
06H	2	Receives semaphore reference count
08H	2	Field for use by semaphore owner
0AH	4	Storage for semaphore

The requesting process should not modify shaded fields.

DWORD   Timeout interval in milliseconds (0 = return immediately with an error if semaphore is owned; −1 = wait indefinitely) *

Notes:

- Nested calls to *DosFSRamSemRequest* are supported. The semaphore is not cleared, thereby releasing any blocked threads, until the number of calls to *DosFSRamSemClear* matches the number of requests.

- An ExitList procedure (registered with *DosExitList*) can call *DosFSRamSemRequest* for a fast-safe RAM semaphore that controls a resource. If the current owner of that semaphore was any thread in the same process, the *DosFSRamSemRequest* succeeds and the thread ID and reference count fields of the semaphore are forced to 1. The ExitList routine can then take any necessary measures to clean up the resource symbolized by the semaphore and call *DosFSRamSemClear* to release the semaphore.

Related functions: *DosExitList, DosFSRamSemClear, DosSemRequest.*

DosGetCollate [FAPI]

Obtains a character-collating table for the specified country and code page from the COUNTRY.SYS file. The collating table assigns sorting weights for each ASCII character; typically, uppercase and lowercase characters are given the same weight so that sorts will be case insensitive, and accented or otherwise modified vowels are given the same weight as their plain vowel equivalents.

WORD   Length of buffer to receive collating table
PTR BUFFER   Country code data structure

Offset	Length	Description
00H	2	Country code (0 = default)
02H	2	Code page ID (0 = default)

PTR BUFFER   Receives collating table (truncated if necessary to fit within buffer, or padded with zero bytes if buffer is larger than table)
PTR WORD   Receives actual length of collating table

Notes:

- The maximum table size is 256 bytes.

- In real mode, the COUNTRY.SYS file is assumed to be in the root directory of the current drive.

Related functions: *DosCaseMap, DosGetCp, DosGetCtryInfo, DosGetDBCSEv, DosSetCp, DosSetProcCp.*

DosGetCp [IOPL] [FAPI]

Obtains the current code page and a list of the other available ("prepared") code pages. The current code page is inherited from the parent process and can be changed with *DosSetCp* or *DosSetProcCp.*

WORD	Length of buffer to receive code page list		
PTR BUFFER	Receives code page list (truncated if necessary)		
	Offset	*Length*	*Description*
	00H	*2*	*Current code page ID*
	02H	*2*	*Alternate code page ID #1*
	04H	*2*	*Alternate code page ID #2*
	.	.	.
	.	.	.
	.	.	.
PTR WORD	Receives actual length of code page list		

Note:

- In real mode, the function returns no more than one current code page and one prepared code page.

Related functions: *DosCaseMap, DosGetCollate, DosGetCtryInfo, DosGetDBCSEv, DosSetCp, DosSetProcCp, KbdGetCp, VioGetCp.*

DosGetCtryInfo [FAPI]

Obtains country-dependent formatting information from the file COUNTRY.SYS.

WORD	Length of buffer to receive country information (38 bytes is sufficient in OS/2 versions 1.0 and 1.1)		
PTR BUFFER	Country code data structure		
	Offset	*Length*	*Description*
	00H	*2*	*Country code (0 = default)*
	02H	*2*	*Code page ID (0 = default)*
PTR BUFFER	Receives country information (truncated if necessary; *see Notes*)		
PTR WORD	Receives actual length of country information		

Notes:

- The format of the returned country information is as follows:

Offset	Length	Description
00H	2	Country code
02H	2	Code page ID
04H	2	Date format
		0 = mm/dd/yy
		1 = dd/mm/yy
		2 = yy/mm/dd
06H	5	ASCIIZ currency symbol
0BH	2	ASCIIZ thousands separator
0DH	2	ASCIIZ decimal separator
0FH	2	ASCIIZ date separator
11H	2	ASCIIZ time separator
13H	1	Bit field for currency format:

Bit(s)	*Significance*
0	*0 = currency symbol precedes value*
	1 = currency symbol follows value
1	*Spaces between currency symbol and value*
2	*0 = no effect*
	1 = ignore bits 0 and 1, currency symbol replaces decimal separator
3–7	*Reserved (0)*

Offset	Length	Description
14H	1	Number of decimal places in currency
15H	1	Time format

Bit(s)	*Significance*
0	*0 = 12-hour format with "a" or "p"*
	1 = 24-hour format
1–7	*Reserved (0)*

Offset	Length	Description
16H	4	Reserved (0)
1AH	2	ASCIIZ data list separator
1CH	10	Reserved (0)

- In real mode, the COUNTRY.SYS file is assumed to be in the root directory of the current drive. If an FAPI program is running under MS-DOS, some country information might be unavailable.

Related functions: *DosGetCp, DosSetCp, DosSetProcCp.*

DosGetDateTime   [IOPL]   [FAPI]

Obtains the current date, time, time zone, and day of the week.

PTR BUFFER   Receives date and time information in the following format:

Offset	Length	Description
00H	*1*	*Hour (0–23)*
01H	*1*	*Minute (0–59)*
02H	*1*	*Second (0–59)*

Offset	Length	Description
03H	*1*	*Hundredths of a second (0–99)*
04H	*1*	*Day (1–31)*
05H	*1*	*Month (1–12)*
06H	*2*	*Year (1980–2079)*
08H	*2*	*Time zone (minutes ± GMT, 300 = U.S. EST,*
		* −1 = undefined)*
0AH	*1*	*Day of the week (0 = Sunday, 1 = Monday, etc.)*

Related functions: *DosGetInfoSeg, DosSetDateTime.*

DosGetDBCSEv [FAPI]

Obtains a table of ranges for double-byte character set (DBCS) codes from the file COUNTRY.SYS.

WORD	Length of buffer to receive table (10 bytes is adequate in OS/2 versions 1.0 and 1.1)
PTR BUFFER	Country code data structure

Offset	Length	Description
00H	*2*	*Country code (0 = default)*
02H	*2*	*Code page ID (0 = default)*

PTR BUFFER	Receives DBCS code table (*see Notes*)

Notes:

- The DBCS table consists of 2-byte entries that define ranges for DBCS lead bytes. The table is terminated by a pair of zero bytes, unless it must be truncated to fit within the buffer. For example:

```
db      81h,9fh
db      0e0h,0fch
db      0,0
```

- In real mode, the COUNTRY.SYS file is assumed to be in the root directory of the current drive.

Related functions: *DosGetCp, DosGetCtryInfo, DosSetCp, DosSetProcCp.*

DosGetEnv [IOPL] [FAPI]

Returns the selector for the process's environment, and the offset to the argument strings (command line information) at the end of the environment.

PTR WORD	Receives selector for environment
PTR WORD	Receives offset of argument strings at end of environment

Note:

■ When a program is started by CMD.EXE, the argument strings consist of the ASCIIZ simple name of the program, followed by the ASCIIZ command tail, terminated by an additional null byte.

Related functions: *DosExecPgm, DosScanEnv, DosStartSession.*

DosGetHugeShift   [IOPL] [FAPI]

Returns a left shift count that is applied to the value 1 to obtain an incrementing value. The consecutive selectors for a huge memory block are calculated by applying this increment to the base selector returned by *DosAllocHuge*. You can also obtain the shift count from the global information segment.

PTR WORD   Receives shift count

Related functions: *DosAllocHuge, DosGetInfoSeg, DosReallocHuge.*

DosGetInfoSeg   [IOPL]

Returns selectors for the global and local (process-specific) read-only information segments.

PTR WORD   Receives selector for global information segment (*see Notes*)
PTR WORD   Receives selector for local information segment (*see Notes*)

Notes:

■ The global information segment has a fixed selector in the GDT and is read-only to user processes. Its format is as follows:

Offset	Length	Description
00H	4	Elapsed seconds from January 1, 1970
04H	4	Milliseconds since system was turned on or restarted
08H	1	Hour
09H	1	Minute
0AH	1	Second
0BH	1	Hundredths of a second
0CH	2	Time zone (minutes ± GMT, −1 if undefined)
0EH	2	Timer tick interval (units = 0.0001 seconds; value is 310 in OS/2 versions 1.0 and 1.1)
10H	1	Day (1–31)
11H	1	Month (1–12)
12H	2	Year (1980–2079)
14H	1	Day of week (0 = Sunday, 1 = Monday, etc.)
15H	1	OS/2 major version number
16H	1	OS/2 minor version number
17H	1	OS/2 revision letter, or zero
18H	1	Current foreground screen group
19H	1	Maximum number of screen groups
1AH	1	Shift count for huge segments

Offset	Length	Description
1BH	1	Protected mode–only indicator (0 = 3.x Box available, 1 = 3.x Box disabled)
1CH	2	PID of the last process to call *KbdCharIn* or *KbdGetFocus* in foreground screen group
1EH	1	Dynamic priority variation flag (0 = disabled, 1 = enabled)
1FH	1	Maximum wait (seconds)
20H	2	Minimum timeslice (msec.)
22H	2	Maximum timeslice (msec.)
24H	2	Boot drive (1 = A, 2 = B, etc.)
26H	32	System trace flags. Each bit corresponds to a trace major event code from 00H through 0FFH. If a bit is 1, tracing of the corresponding event is enabled.
46H	1	Maximum number of *Vio* windowable applications for Presentation Manager screen group (version 1.1)
47H	1	Maximum number of Presentation Manager applications in PM screen group (version 1.1)

- The local information segment has a fixed selector in every process's LDT and is read-only. Its format is as follows:

Offset	Length	Description
00H	2	Current process ID
02H	2	PID of parent
04H	2	Priority of current thread
06H	2	Current thread ID
08H	2	Screen group
0AH	2	Subscreen group
0CH	2	In-foreground flag (−1 if current process has keyboard focus)
0EH	1	Process type
		0 = full screen application
		1 = real mode process
		2 = Vio windowable application
		3 = Presentation Manager application
		4 = detached application
0FH	1	Reserved
10H	2	Environment selector (version 1.1)
12H	2	Command line offset within environment (version 1.1)
14H	2	Initial size of DGROUP (version 1.1)
16H	2	Initial size of process's default stack (version 1.1)
18H	2	Initial heap size (version 1.1)
1AH	2	Module handle (version 1.1)
1CH	2	DGROUP selector (version 1.1)

- [1.1] The last seven fields in the local information segment correspond to the values in registers AX, BX, CX, DX, SI, DI, and DS respectively at the initial entry to a process.

Related functions: *DosGetDateTime, DosGetEnv, DosGetHugeShift, DosGetPID, DosGetPPID, DosGetPrty, DosGetVersion, DosQAppType.*

DosGetMachineMode   [IOPL] [FAPI]

Returns a code for the current processor mode (real or protected). FAPI applications can use this information to adjust their use of dynlink calls when loaded in real mode.

PTR BYTE   Receives current machine mode
                    0   *Real mode*
                    1   *Protected mode*

Related functions: *DosDevConfig, DosGetInfoSeg, DosGetVersion, VioGetConfig.*

DosGetMessage   [FAPI]

Retrieves a message from the message segment in the program's EXE file or from a system message file, optionally inserting text into variable fields of the message body.

PTR BUFFER   Contains 0–9 far (DWORD) pointers to ASCIIZ strings that function inserts
                        into variable fields of message
WORD   Number of strings to insert (0–9)
PTR BUFFER   Receives message text from file, with strings inserted, truncated if necessary
WORD   Length in bytes of buffer to receive message text
WORD   Number of message in file
PTR ASCIIZ   Pathname of message file
PTR WORD   Receives actual length in bytes of message, including any variable text that was
                        inserted into message

Notes:

- The insertion points for variable strings are indicated by tokens in the form *%n*, such as *%1, %2*, etc.

- If the program has no message segment and the pathname of the message file does not contain : or \
  delimiters, the current directory, root directory, and any directories specified by DPATH (protected
  mode) or APPEND (real mode) are searched for the file.

Related functions: *DosInsMessage, DosPutMessage.*

DosGetModHandle   [IOPL]

Returns a module handle for a dynlink library if that library is already loaded. The use count for the module is not incremented.

PTR ASCIIZ   Module name of dynlink library
PTR WORD   Receives module handle

Note:

- The module name is specified in the DLL file header and is usually the same as the filename.

Related functions: *DosFreeModule, DosGetModName, DosGetProcAddr, DosLoadModule.*

DosGetModName   [IOPL]

Given a module handle for a dynlink library, returns the fully qualified pathname (drive, path, filename, and extension) for the corresponding DLL file. Can also be used to obtain the pathname for a process's EXE file, although this use is uncommon.

WORD	Module handle
WORD	Length in bytes of buffer to receive pathname
PTR BUFFER	Receives pathname

Note:

■ A dynlink library's handle is passed to its initialization routine in register AX. In contrast, a process's module handle is passed to it in register DI.

Related functions: *DosFreeModule, DosGetModHandle, DosGetProcAddr, DosLoadModule.*

DosGetPID   [IOPL]

Obtains the process ID of the current process, thread ID of the current thread, and the process ID of the process's parent.

PTR BUFFER   Receives information in the following form:

Offset	*Length*	*Description*
00H	*2*	*PID of current process*
02H	*2*	*Thread ID of current thread*
04H	*2*	*PID of parent process*

Related functions: *DosExecPgm, DosGetInfoSeg, DosGetPPID, DosStartSession.*

DosGetPPID   [IOPL] [1.1]

Obtains the process ID of the parent of any process.

WORD	PID of process of interest
PTR WORD	Receives PID of parent process

Related functions: *DosExecPgm, DosGetInfoSeg, DosGetPID, DosStartSession.*

DosGetProcAddr   [IOPL]

Obtains the selector and offset of the entry point for a dynlink library routine. A process can use *DosGetProcAddr* for selective dynamic linking at run time, rather than relying on the kernel's loader to establish all dynamic links at load time.

WORD	Module handle for dynlink library
PTR ASCIIZ	ASCIIZ name of library procedure
PTR DWORD	Receives selector and offset of entry point

Notes:

- Instead of the procedure name, the ASCIIZ string can contain the ordinal of the procedure with # as the first character, such as:

```
db      '#8',0
```

Alternatively, if the selector portion of the pointer to the name is zero, the offset portion is interpreted as the binary ordinal.

- Most *Dos* API functions cannot be dynamically linked by name at run time, and must be referenced by their ordinals. To obtain these ordinals, inspect the import library (either DOSCALLS.LIB or OS2.LIB). Note that the ordinals required by *DosGetProcAddr* are one-based, whereas the ordinals in import libraries are zero-based.

Related functions: *DosFreeModule, DosGetModHandle, DosGetModName, DosLoadModule.*

DosGetPrty   [IOPL]

Returns the priority of any thread within the current process or of the primary thread in another process.

WORD	Scope of inquiry		
	0		*Primary thread of specified process*
	2		*Thread within the current process*
PTR BUFFER	Receives priority information in a 2-byte structure:		

Offset	*Length*	*Description*
00H	*1*	*Priority level within class (0–31)*
01H	*1*	*Priority class*
		1 = idle-time
		2 = regular
		3 = time-critical

WORD	Process or thread ID (0 = current)

Note:

- [1.0] If the scope is 0 and the primary thread of the indicated process has terminated, an error is returned even if the process is still running.

Related functions: *DosCreateThread, DosSetPrty.*

DosGetResource   [IOPL]   [1.1]

Returns a selector for a resource. Resources are read-only data segments that contain icons, bitmaps, strings, or other data that are bundled into an EXE or DLL file with the resource compiler (RC.EXE).

WORD	Module handle
WORD	Resource type ID
WORD	Resource name ID
PTR WORD	Receives selector for resource

Notes:

- The module handle must be previously obtained with *DosLoadModule* or *DosGetModHandle*. If the module handle is zero, the resource is loaded from the current process's EXE file.

- The resource type and name identifiers are 16-bit values assigned to a resource when it is created. Although many resources can have the same type ID, the combination of the type ID and name ID for a particular resource must be unique.

Related functions: *DosGetModHandle, DosLoadModule*.

DosGetSeg   [IOPL]

Given a selector for a "gettable" segment, makes that segment addressable for the current process. The selector must be passed to the current process by the process that originally allocated it, using some form of interprocess communication.

WORD   Selector

Note:

- If the segment was originally allocated with the discardable option, the current process can unlock it for discard by calling *DosUnlockSeg*. Locking is an attribute of a memory segment and is not associated with the processes using the segment.

Related functions: *DosAllocHuge, DosAllocSeg, DosFreeSeg, DosGiveSeg*.

DosGetShrSeg   [IOPL]

Obtains a selector for a named, shareable memory segment. The segment must have been previously created with *DosAllocShrSeg*. When all of the selectors owned by all of the processes for a named segment have been released with *DosFreeSeg*, the segment is destroyed.

PTR ASCIIZ   Segment name, in the form \SHAREMEM*name.ext*
PTR WORD   Receives selector

Related functions: *DosAllocShrSeg, DosFreeSeg*.

DosGetVersion   [IOPL]   [FAPI]

Obtains the OS/2 version number.

PTR BUFFER   Receives version information in a 2-byte structure:

Offset	Length	Description
00H	1	Minor version number (00H for OS/2 version 1.0 and 0AH for OS/2 version 1.1)
01H	1	Major version number (0AH for OS/2 versions 1.0 and 1.1)

- The major version number is 10-based so that a bound Family application can distinguish between the OS/2 DOS compatibility box and an MS-DOS 1.x environment.

Related functions: *DosDevConfig, DosGetInfoSeg, DosGetMachineMode, VioGetConfig*.

DosGiveSeg   [IOPL]

Obtains a new selector, which can be used by another process, for a segment previously allocated with the "givable" option. The selector must be passed to the other process using some form of interprocess communication.

WORD	Selector, valid for the current process, for the segment to be shared
WORD	PID of process that will use new selector
PTR WORD	Receives new selector, which is valid for other process

---

Note:

- If the segment was originally allocated with the discardable option, the process receiving the giveaway selector can unlock it for discard by calling *DosUnlockSeg*. Locking is an attribute of a memory segment and is not associated with the processes using the segment.

Related functions: *DosAllocHuge, DosAllocSeg, DosFreeSeg, DosGetSeg*.

DosHoldSignal   [IOPL] [FAPI]

Enables or disables signal processing for the current process. SIGTERM signals are not affected. If you nest calls to *DosHoldSignal* to disable signal processing, you must make a corresponding number of enabling calls before signals are again received by the process.

WORD	Action code	
	0	*Enable signal processing*
	1	*Disable signal processing*

Notes:

- Signals which occur while signal processing is disabled are held until processing is reenabled.

- In real mode, only the signals SIGINTR (Ctrl-C) and SIGBREAK (Ctrl-Break) are recognized. (Both are treated as SIGINTR.)

Related functions: *DosFlagProcess, DosKillProcess, DosSendSignal, DosSetSigHandler*.

DosInsMessage [FAPI]

Inserts text into the variable fields of a message.

PTR BUFFER	Contains 0–9 far (DWORD) pointers to ASCIIZ strings that the function inserts into variable fields of message
WORD	Number of strings to insert (0–9)
PTR BUFFER	Contains message to be processed
WORD	Length of message to be processed
PTR BUFFER	Receives expanded message
WORD	Length of buffer to receive expanded message
PTR WORD	Receives actual length of expanded message

Note:

■ The insertion points for variable strings are indicated by tokens in the form %*n*, such as %1, %2, etc.

Related functions: *DosGetMessage, DosPutMessage, DosWrite*.

DosKillProcess [IOPL]

Terminates another process and (optionally) all its child processes by sending a SIGTERM signal. A process can protect itself against such signals with *DosSetSigHandler*.

WORD	Action code	
	0	*Designated process and all its descendants*
	1	*Designated process only*
WORD	PID of process to be terminated	

Related functions: *DosCwait, DosExit, DosSetSigHandler, DosStopSession*.

DosLoadModule [IOPL]

Loads a dynlink library, if it is not already loaded, and returns a module handle for the library. The handle may be used with *DosGetProcAddr* to obtain the addresses of procedures within the library.

PTR BUFFER	Object name buffer
WORD	Length of object name buffer
PTR ASCIIZ	Name of dynlink library
PTR WORD	Receives module handle

Notes:

■ Supply only the name of the library file, without a path or extension. The extension is always assumed to be DLL, and the location of the library is specified by the LIBPATH directive in the CONFIG.SYS file.

■ If the *DosLoadModule* call fails because of a missing dynlink module or entry point, the corresponding name is returned as an ASCIIZ string in the object name buffer.

Related functions: *DosFreeModule, DosGetModHandle, DosGetModName, DosGetProcAddr, DosGetResource*.

DosLockSeg   [IOPL]

Notifies the operating system that a segment should not be discarded, returning an error if the segment has already been discarded; reverses the effect of a previous *DosUnlockSeg* call. The segment is still swappable and movable while it is locked. Used only with segments that were allocated with the discardable option (bit 2). You can nest calls to *DosLockSeg* to a maximum of 255, at which point the segment becomes permanently locked.

WORD   Selector

Notes:

- If the segment has been discarded, the selector is still valid. You must reallocate the block with *DosReallocSeg* or *DosReallocHuge* (which also lock the segment) and then reload or regenerate the data in the segment.

- A segment may be locked or unlocked by any process that owns a selector for it. Locking is an attribute of a segment and not of the processes using the segment.

Related functions: *DosAllocHuge, DosAllocSeg, DosReallocHuge, DosReallocSeg, DosUnlockSeg.*

DosMakeNmPipe   [1.1]

Creates and opens a named pipe or a new instance of a named pipe, and returns a handle that you can use for subsequent access to the pipe. The process that creates a named pipe is the *server* and is the only process that can issue *DosConnectNmPipe* and *DosDisConnectNmPipe* calls.

PTR ASCIIZ   Pipe name, in the form \PIPE*name.ext* for a local pipe or
                             machine\PIPE*name.ext* for a remote pipe
PTR WORD   Receives pipe handle
WORD   Open mode for pipe

Bit(s)	*Significance*
0–2	Access mode
	000 = inbound (client to server)
	001 = outbound (server to client)
	010 = bidirectional
3–6	Reserved (0)
7	Inheritance
	0 = child process inherits pipe handle
	1 = child does not inherit handle
8–13	Reserved (0)
14	Write-through flag
	0 = writes to remote pipes can be buffered and deferred
	1 = writes to remote pipes must be synchronous with the request
15	Reserved (0)

WORD	Pipe characteristics	
	Bit(s)	*Significance*
	0–7	*Maximum instance count (255 = unlimited)*
	8	*Allowed read modes*
		0 = byte stream only
		1 = byte stream or message stream
		(bit 10 must also = 1)
	9	*Reserved (0)*
	10	*Write mode*
		0 = byte stream
		1 = message stream
	11–14	*Reserved (0)*
	15	*Blocking mode*
		0 = wait if necessary to complete read or write operation
		1 = return immediately with an error if read or write cannot be completed
WORD	Bytes to allocate for pipe's outbound data buffer (default = 1024)	
WORD	Bytes to allocate for pipe's inbound data buffer (default = 1024)	
DWORD	Default timeout interval in milliseconds for *DosWaitNmPipe* and *DosConnectNmPipe* (0 = 50 msec.)	

Notes:

- The maximum instance count is ignored after the first call to *DosMakeNmPipe* for a particular named pipe.

- After you create a named pipe, you can change its read mode and blocking mode with *DosSetNmPHandState*.

Related functions: *DosConnectNmPipe, DosMakePipe, DosOpen, DosQNmPHandState, DosSetNmPHandState, DosWaitNmPipe.*

DosMakePipe   [IOPL]

Creates an anonymous (unnamed) pipe and returns read and write handles for the pipe. Pipe handles are inherited by child processes and can be used to communicate with those processes. When all the read and write handles for a pipe have been closed, the pipe is destroyed.

PTR WORD	Receives read handle for pipe
PTR WORD	Receives write handle for pipe
WORD	Maximum pipe size (advisory only; 0 = default of 512 bytes; maximum size = 65,504 bytes)

Note:

- *DosRead* and *DosWrite* operate somewhat differently with pipes than they do with files or devices. If a pipe becomes full, *DosWrite* will block until enough data has been removed from the pipe so that the write can be completed; if a pipe is empty, *DosRead* will block until enough data is available.

Related functions: *DosClose, DosDupHandle, DosExecPgm, DosMakeNmPipe, DosRead, DosWrite.*

DosMemAvail [IOPL]

Returns the size of the largest block of free memory. If segment motion is not disabled, the total free memory is returned. The returned value is advisory only and is subject to change at any time as a result of activity by other processes. Calls to this function do not cause segment motion, swapping, or discarding.

PTR DWORD   Receives size of largest free block

DosMkDir [IOPL] [FAPI]

Creates a directory.

PTR ASCIIZ   Pathname of new directory (can include drive)
DWORD   Reserved (0)

Related functions: *DosChDir, DosQCurDir, DosQSysInfo, DosRmDir*.

DosMonClose

Releases a handle for a character device monitor; terminates all monitoring by the current process for the specified device.

WORD   Monitor handle from previous *DosMonOpen*

Related functions: *DosMonOpen, DosMonRead, DosMonReg, DosMonWrite*.

DosMonOpen

Returns a handle for a character device monitor, or an error if the driver for the device does not support monitors. To initiate monitoring, follow the *DosMonOpen* call with a call to *DosMonReg*.

PTR ASCIIZ   Name of character device
PTR WORD   Receives monitor handle

Note:

■ In OS/2 versions 1.0 and 1.1, the base character device drivers that support monitors are KBD$, PRN, and MOUSE$.

Related functions: *DosMonClose, DosMonRead, DosMonReg, DosMonWrite*.

DosMonRead

Reads a data packet from a character device monitor chain. The packet can be inspected, consumed, modified, or passed unchanged to *DosMonWrite*.

PTR BUFFER	Monitor input buffer specified in previous call to *DosMonReg*
WORD	Wait/no-wait flag
	0 *Wait until data is ready*
	1 *Return with error if no data is ready*
PTR BUFFER	Receives monitor data packet
PTR WORD	Contains length of buffer to receive packet; receives actual length of packet

Note:

- The thread responsible for *DosMonRead* and *DosMonWrite* calls should be promoted to time-critical priority with *DosSetPrty*. It should not call any other API functions that might block and thereby degrade the performance of the device being monitored.

Related functions: *DosMonClose, DosMonOpen, DosMonReg, DosMonWrite.*

DosMonReg

Registers input and output buffers for a character device monitor.

WORD	Monitor handle from previous call to *DosMonOpen*
PTR BUFFER	Monitor input buffer, with buffer length in the first word
PTR BUFFER	Monitor output buffer, with buffer length in the first word
WORD	Position requested in monitor chain
	0 *No preference*
	1 *Head of chain*
	2 *Tail of chain*
WORD	Monitor index (device-specific; use session number for keyboard and mouse monitors)

Notes:

- When multiple monitors request the head (or tail) position in the monitor chain, the first process becomes the actual head (or tail), the second process becomes second (or next-to-last), etc.

- A keyboard monitor that is started with the DETACH command (or the *DosExecPgm* option 4) can inspect the foreground screen group field of the global information segment to determine the session of its parent.

- The buffer size must be at least 20 bytes larger than the driver's monitor data packet. Although there is no general way to find the necessary buffer size at run time, 128 bytes is usually sufficient.

Related functions: *DosMonClose, DosMonOpen, DosMonRead, DosMonWrite.*

DosMonWrite

Writes a data packet into a character device monitor chain. The process can obtain this packet using a previous *DosMonRead* call, or the process can synthesize it and insert it into the monitor chain.

PTR BUFFER   Monitor output buffer specified in previous call to *DosMonReg*
PTR BUFFER   Contains monitor data packet to be passed to the next monitor in the chain
WORD   Length in bytes of data packet

Note:

- The thread responsible for *DosMonRead* and *DosMonWrite* calls should be promoted to time-critical priority with *DosSetPrty*. It should not call any other API functions that might block and thereby degrade the performance of the device being monitored.

Related functions: *DosMonClose, DosMonOpen, DosMonRead, DosMonReg*.

DosMove   [IOPL]   [FAPI]

Renames a file and/or moves it from one directory to another. You can also use this function to rename directories other than the root directory.

PTR ASCIIZ   Old pathname (no wildcard characters)
PTR ASCIIZ   New pathname (no wildcard characters)
DWORD   Reserved (0)

Notes:

- If a drive is included in the new pathname, it must match the drive specified in the old pathname or the current drive. An error is returned if any directory in the old or new pathnames does not exist.

- On FAT file systems in real mode, the filename and extension are truncated if necessary. In protected mode, if the filename or extension is too long, an error is returned.

Related function: *DosDelete*.

DosMuxSemWait   [IOPL]

Waits until at least one of a list of semaphores is cleared. Unlike the other semaphore wait functions, *DosMuxSemWait* is edge triggered; that is, the requesting thread will be unblocked even if the semaphore is set again before the thread can be dispatched.

PTR WORD   Receives list index (1–16) of semaphore that was cleared
PTR BUFFER   Contains a list of semaphores in the following format:

Offset	Length	Description
00H	2	Number of semaphores (1–16)
02H	2	Reserved (0)
04H	4	Semaphore handle #1

Offset	Length	Description
08H	2	Reserved (0)
0AH	4	Semaphore handle #2
.	.	.
.	.	.
.	.	.

DWORD   Timeout interval in milliseconds (0 = return immediately with an error if none of the semaphores is clear; −1 = wait indefinitely)

Related functions: *DosSemClear, DosSemSet, DosSemSetWait, DosSemWait.*

DosNewSize   [IOPL]   [FAPI]

Changes the size of a file. If the file is truncated, any data beyond the new end of file is lost; if the file is extended, the data beyond the previous end of file is undefined.

WORD   File handle
DWORD   New size of file in bytes

Note:

■ An error is returned if the file is read-only.

Related functions: *DosOpen, DosQFileInfo.*

DosOpen   [IOPL]   [FAPI]

Creates, opens, or replaces a file, returning a handle which can be used for subsequent access to the file. The initial file pointer position is zero (the start of file). You can also open character devices and existing named pipes by their logical names as though they were files.

PTR ASCIIZ   Pathname of file (no wildcard characters)
PTR WORD   Receives file handle
PTR WORD   Receives *DosOpen* action

Value	Meaning
1	*File existed and was opened*
2	*File did not exist and was created*
3	*File existed and was replaced*

DWORD   Initial file allocation in bytes (if file is being created or replaced)
WORD   File attribute (if file is being created)

Bit(s)	Significance (if set)
0	*Read-only*
1	*Hidden*
2	*System*
3–4	*Reserved (0)*
5	*Archive*
6–15	*Reserved (0)*

WORD	Open flag	
	Bits	**Significance**
	0–3	*Action to take if file exists*
		0000 = fail
		0001 = open
		0010 = replace
	4–7	*Action to take if file does not exist*
		0000 = fail
		0001 = create
	8–15	*Reserved (0)*
WORD	Open mode	
	Bit(s)	**Significance**
	0–2	*Access mode*
		000 = read-only
		001 = write-only
		010 = read/write
	3	*Reserved*
	4–6	*Sharing mode*
		001 = deny-read and deny-write (deny-all)
		010 = deny-write
		011 = deny-read
		100 = deny-none
	7	*Inheritance*
		0 = handle is inherited by child processes
		1 = handle is not inherited
	8–12	*Reserved (0)*
	13	*Error mode*
		0 = hardware errors are reported through the system critical error handler
		1 = hardware errors are returned to the process
	14	*Write-through flag*
		0 = writes can be buffered and deferred
		1 = writes must be synchronous with the request
	15	*DASD open flag (see Notes)*
		0 = open file or character device
		1 = open disk volume for direct access
DWORD	Reserved (0)	

Notes:

■ When a file is created or replaced with an initial allocation, the contents of the file are undefined. The system attempts to allocate contiguous disk storage for the initial allocation.

■ As an alternative to specifying a sharing mode of deny-write or deny-all, a program can use *DosFileLocks* to temporarily restrict access to specific regions of a file while it is updating them.

■ The handle for the file is inherited by child processes unless bit 7 of the open mode is set, and any sharing and access restrictions are also inherited. However, the inheritance and error mode bits associated with the handle, as well as any locks placed on file regions with *DosFileLocks*, are *not* inherited.

- You can use *DosSetFHandState* to change some handle characteristics controlled by the open mode parameter after the file is opened. Similarly, you can change a file's attribute after it is created with *DosSetFileMode*.

- On FAT file systems in real mode, the filename and extension are truncated if necessary. In protected mode, if the filename or extension is too long, an error is returned.

- A protected mode *DosOpen* request with the DASD open flag set (1) allows an entire volume to be treated as a single file. The ASCIIZ pathname must consist of a drive letter followed by a colon, and the open flag must be 01H (that is, open if exists, fail if doesn't exist). A handle is returned which can be used with *DosChgFilePtr*, *DosRead*, and *DosWrite* to access any sector of the volume. In real mode, if the DASD open bit is set, the device is not actually opened. Instead, a handle is returned that you must use with *DosDevIOCtl*.

- When a Family application is running under MS-DOS, the sharing and access mode parameters are ignored unless file sharing (SHARE.EXE) is loaded, and the write-through and error mode bits must always be cleared (0).

- [1.1] When an existing named pipe is opened, bits 3–13 and bit 15 of the open mode must be zero, and bits 0–2 have the following meanings:

      000 = inbound pipe (client to server)
      001 = outbound pipe (server to client)
      010 = bidirectional pipe

- [1.1] Named pipes are always opened by a client process in blocking and byte-stream mode. The mode can be changed with *DosSetNmPHandState*.

Related functions: *DosChgFilePtr*, *DosClose*, *DosDupHandle*, *DosExecPgm*, *DosMakeNmPipe*, *DosQFHandState*, *DosQFileInfo*, *DosQFileMode*, *DosQNmPHandState*, *DosSetFHandState*, *DosSetFileInfo*, *DosSetFileMode*, *DosSetNmPHandState*.

DosOpenQueue

Opens an existing queue and returns a handle, which can be used for subsequent access to the queue. A queue can be written by any process, but can be read only by the owner (creator) process.

PTR WORD	Receives PID of queue owner
PTR WORD	Receives queue handle
PTR ASCIIZ	Queue name, in the form \QUEUES*name.ext*

Note:

- The returned PID can be used with *DosGiveSeg* to make records written into the queue addressable by the queue owner.

Related functions: *DosCloseQueue*, *DosCreateQueue*.

DosOpenSem   [IOPL]

Opens an existing system (named) semaphore and returns a handle, which can be used for subsequent access to the semaphore. The semaphore must have been previously created with *DosCreateSem*. The semaphore persists until all the handles for it have been released with *DosCloseSem*.

| PTR DWORD | Receives semaphore handle |
| PTR ASCIIZ | Semaphore name, in the form \SEM*name.ext* |

Related functions: *DosCloseSem, DosCreateSem.*

DosPeekNmPipe [1.1]

Reads data from a named pipe without removing it from the pipe.

WORD	Pipe handle
PTR BUFFER	Receives data from pipe
WORD	Length of buffer to receive pipe data
PTR WORD	Receives actual length of data read from pipe
PTR BUFFER	Receives size information in the following format:

Offset	*Length*	*Description*
00H	*2*	*Bytes of data remaining in the pipe*
02H	*2*	*Bytes of data remaining in the inspected message*

PTR WORD	Pipe status
	1	*Disconnected*
	2	*Listening*
	3	*Connected*
	4	*Closing*

Note:

■ *DosPeekNmPipe* never blocks, regardless of the current blocking mode of the pipe.

Related functions: *DosCallNmPipe, DosRead, DosTransactNmPipe.*

DosPeekQueue

Retrieves the information associated with a queue record, without removing that record from the queue. Can be used by the queue owner to scan queue records so that they can be removed selectively (that is, not in their natural order) with *DosReadQueue*.

| WORD | Queue handle |
| PTR DWORD | Receives queue record identification data |

Offset	*Length*	*Description*
00H	*2*	*PID of queue writer*
02H	*2*	*Arbitrary data passed by queue writer*

PTR WORD	Receives length of queue record
PTR DWORD	Receives address of queue record
PTR WORD	Contains record selection flag

0 = return first queue record

1 = return next queue record

If nonzero, receives queue record identifier in the same location that can be used with a subsequent call to *DosReadQueue*

WORD	Wait/no-wait flag
	0 = wait if no queue record is available
	1 = return with error if queue is empty
PTR BYTE	Receives priority of queue record (0–15, not applicable if queue was not created with priority ordering)
DWORD	Handle of semaphore to be cleared when queue record becomes available, if wait/no-wait flag = 1; otherwise, a null pointer

Note:

- If multiple threads are calling *DosPeekQueue* or *DosReadQueue*, all must use the same RAM or system semaphore.

Related functions: *DosMuxSemWait, DosPurgeQueue, DosQueryQueue, DosReadQueue, DosSemSet, DosSemWait, DosWriteQueue.*

DosPFSActivate

Selects a code page and font for a specific process and printer. Intended for use by print spoolers and monitors; normal applications should use *DosDevIOCtl* for code page switching.

WORD	Handle for temporary spool file
PTR DWORD	Receives bytes written to spool file
PTR ASCIIZ	Logical name of printer device
WORD	Code page to make active
WORD	Font to make active
WORD	Process ID
DWORD	Reserved (0)

Note:

- If code page and font are both zero, the hardware default code page and font are used. If only the font ID is zero, any font can be used.

Related functions: *DosPFSCloseUser, DosPFSInit, DosPFSQueryAct, DosPFSVerifyFont.*

DosPFSCloseUser

Notifies the font switcher that a process has closed its spool file. The font switcher can then free any resources that were being used to track code page and font switching for the process. This function is intended for use by print spoolers and monitors and should not ordinarily be called by applications.

PTR ASCIIZ	Logical name of printer device
WORD	Process ID
DWORD	Reserved (0)

Related functions: *DosPFSActivate, DosPFSInit, DosPFSQueryAct, DosPFSVerifyFont.*

DosPFSInit

Initializes code page and font switching for a printer. This function is intended for use by print spoolers and monitors and should not ordinarily be called by applications.

PTR BUFFER   Hardware font definition list in the following format:

Offset	Length	Description
00H	2	Number of definitions in list
02H	2	Code page, definition #1
04H	2	Font ID, definition #1
06H	2	Code page, definition #2
08H	2	Font ID, definition #2
.	.	.
.	.	.

PTR ASCIIZ   Pathname of font file
PTR ASCIIZ   Printer type ID
PTR ASCIIZ   Logical name of printer device
WORD   Maximum number of spool instances for which code page and font switching are to be tracked (advisory only)
DWORD   Reserved (0)

Related functions: *DosPFSActivate, DosPFSCloseUser, DosPFSQueryAct, DosPFSVerifyFont.*

DosPFSQueryAct

Returns the active code page and font for a printer and process. This function is intended for use by print spoolers and monitors and should not ordinarily be called by applications.

PTR ASCIIZ   Logical name of printer device
PTR WORD   Receives code page
PTR WORD   Receives font ID
WORD   Process ID
DWORD   Reserved (0)

Related functions: *DosPFSActivate, DosPFSCloseUser, DosPFSInit, DosPFSVerifyFont.*

DosPFSVerifyFont

Indicates whether a code page and font are available for the specified printer. This function is intended for use by print spoolers and monitors and should not ordinarily be called by applications.

PTR ASCIIZ   Logical name of printer device
WORD   Code page to verify
WORD   Font ID to verify (ID = 0 indicates that any font within the specified code page is acceptable)
DWORD   Reserved (0)

Related functions: *DosPFSActivate, DosPFSCloseUser, DosPFSInit, DosPFSQueryAct.*

DosPhysicalDisk [IOPL]

Returns information about the number of partitionable fixed disks, or returns a handle that can be used to access a specific fixed disk with *DosDevIOCtl* calls.

WORD	Information request type
	1 *Obtain total number of partitionable disks*
	2 *Obtain handle for use with category 9*
	DosDevIOCtl *calls*
	3 *Release handle*
PTR BUFFER	Receives disk information (*see Notes*)
WORD	Length of buffer to receive disk information
PTR BUFFER	Contains user-supplied information (*see Notes*)
WORD	Length of user-supplied information

Notes:

■ The information returned by *DosPhysicalDisk* varies with the request type. It is formatted as follows:

Type	*Information*
1	Total number of partitionable disks in the system (2 bytes)
2	Handle for the specified partitionable disk (2 bytes)
3	None (pointer should be null)

■ The user-supplied information passed to *DosPhysicalDisk* also varies with the request type. It is formatted as follows:

Type	*Information*
1	None (pointer and length for user-supplied information should be null)
2	ASCIIZ string that specifies the partitionable disk. The string is always three characters long: a 1-based ASCII disk number, followed by a colon (:), terminated by a null byte.
3	Handle previously obtained with request type 2 (2 bytes)

Related functions: *DosDevIOCtl, DosQFSInfo*.

DosPortAccess [IOPL] [FAPI]

Requests or releases access to a continuous range of I/O ports. I/O ports can be read or written only within a ring 2 (IOPL) segment.

WORD	Reserved (0)
WORD	Request type
	0 *Obtain port access*
	1 *Release port access*
WORD	First port number
WORD	Last port number (may be same as first port number)

Notes:

- CLI/STI privilege is also granted by this function; a separate call to *DosCLIAccess* is not necessary.

- In OS/2 versions 1.0 and 1.1, this function call has no effect.

Related function: *DosCallback, DosCLIAccess, DosR2StackRealloc.*

DosPTrace   [IOPL]

Provides an interface for tracing and debugging of another protected mode process.

PTR BUFFER   Used for communication between the debugger, *DosPTrace* function, and the target process

Offset	Length	Description
00H	2	PID of process being debugged
02H	2	Thread ID of process being debugged
04H	2	Contains DosPTrace command code; receives DosPTrace result code
06H	2	Contains data for DosPTrace; receives DosPTrace error code or data
08H	2	Offset
0AH	2	Segment selector
0CH	2	Module handle
0EH	2	Register AX
10H	2	Register BX
12H	2	Register CX
14H	2	Register DX
16H	2	Register SI
18H	2	Register DI
1AH	2	Register BP
1CH	2	Register DS
1EH	2	Register ES
20H	2	Register IP
22H	2	Register CS
24H	2	CPU flags
26H	2	Register SP
28H	2	Register SS

Notes:

■ The *DosPTrace* commands are:

Value	Command
00H	Invalid command
01H	Return data from text (code) space
02H	Return data from data space
03H	Return register contents for specified thread
04H	Write data into text (code) space
05H	Write data into data space
06H	Set register contents for specified thread
07H	Run process (all threads)
08H	Terminate process
09H	Single-step process
0AH	Initialize *DosPTrace* buffer
0BH	Suspend specified thread
0CH	Resume specified thread
0DH	Convert segment number to selector
0EH	Return floating-point registers
0FH	Set floating-point registers
10H	Get module name

■ The *DosPTrace* codes returned at offset 04H of the structure are as follows:

Value	Significance
0	Success
−1	Error
−2	Signal
−3	Single step
−4	Breakpoint
−5	Parity error
−6	Process dying
−7	GP fault
−8	Library load
−9	Numeric coprocessor error

■ The *DosPTrace* values returned at offset 06H of the structure in the event of an error are as follows:

Value	Significance
1	Bad command
2	Process not found
3	Process not traceable

■ Call *DosExecPgm* with option 3 to load a process for debugging. The *DosPTrace* buffer is initialized with command code 0AH. Breakpoints are set by writing Int 03H opcodes into the child process's instruction space with command code 04H. The child process can then be executed with command codes 07H or 09H. The parent process regains control when the child process terminates, when it causes an exception (such as GP fault or divide by zero), or when a breakpoint is reached.

- For *DosPTrace* commands 0EH and 0FH, offsets 08H–0BH in the *DosPTrace* buffer contain a far pointer to a 94-byte area that contains or receives the floating-point registers.

Related function: *DosExecPgm*.

DosPurgeQueue

Discards all records from a queue. Only the queue's owner (creator) process can use this function.

WORD   Queue handle

Related functions: *DosPeekQueue, DosQueryQueue, DosReadQueue, DosWriteQueue*.

DosPutMessage   [FAPI]

Writes a message to a file, pipe, or device.

WORD   Handle for file, pipe, or device
WORD   Length of message
PTR BUFFER   Contains message to be written

Related functions: *DosGetMessage, DosInsMessage, DosWrite*.

DosQAppType   [IOPL]   [1.1]

Returns a code indicating the specified application's compatibility with the Presentation Manager and DOS compatibility mode.

PTR ASCIIZ   Pathname of application's executable file
PTR WORD   Receives application type

Bit(s)	Significance
0–2	*000 = application type unknown*
	001 = cannot run in a window
	010 = can run in a window (uses appropriate subset of Vio *calls)*
	011 = Presentation Manager application
3	*0 = not a bound (FAPI) application*
	1 = bound (FAPI) application
4	*0 = application program*
	1 = dynlink library (bits 0–3 = 0)
5	*0 = file is "new" (segmented) EXE format*
	1 = file is "old" EXE format (bits 0–4 = 0)
6–15	*Reserved*

Notes:

- The application type is specified at link time with the NAME directive in the module definition file or afterwards with the MARKEXE utility. If the type is *not* specified, this function returns "unknown," and the application is run full-screen by the Presentation Manager.

- If the application pathname contains a : or \ delimiter, the function searches only the specified drive and directory for the file. Otherwise, it searches all directories in the current process's PATH. You can supply any extension; however, if the extension is absent, it defaults to EXE.

- The application type of the current process can be obtained from the local information segment.

Related function: *DosGetInfoSeg.*

DosQCurDir [IOPL] [FAPI]

Returns the current directory for the specified drive. The current directory is maintained on a per-process basis and is inherited by child processes.

WORD	Drive number (0 = default, 1 = A, etc.)
PTR BUFFER	Receives ASCIIZ directory pathname
PTR WORD	Contains length of buffer to receive directory pathname; if buffer is too small, receives length of buffer needed (actual length of pathname is *not* returned in this variable)

Notes:

- The returned string does not include the drive identifier or a leading backslash.

- [1.1] The maximum path length for the system can be obtained with *DosQSysInfo.*

Related functions: *DosChDir, DosQCurDisk, DosQSysInfo, DosSelectDisk.*

DosQCurDisk [IOPL] [FAPI]

Returns a code for the current drive. The current drive is maintained on a per-process basis and is inherited by child processes.

PTR WORD	Receives current drive code (1 = A, 2 = B, etc.)
PTR DWORD	Receives logical drive bitmap (logical drives A–Z correspond to bits 0–25; a bit is set if the logical drive exists)

Related functions: *DosQCurDir, DosSelectDisk.*

DosQFHandState [IOPL] [FAPI]

Returns the sharing, access, inheritance, write-through, and error-handling characteristics associated with a file handle.

WORD	File handle	
PTR WORD	Receives handle state	
	Bit(s)	*Significance*
	0–2	*Access mode*
		0000 = read-only
		0001 = write-only
		0010 = read/write
	3	*Reserved*

Bit(s)	Significance
4–6	Sharing mode
	001 = deny-read/write (deny-all)
	010 = deny-write
	011 = deny-read
	100 = deny-none
7	Inheritance
	0 = handle is inherited by child processes
	1 = handle is not inherited
8–12	Reserved
13	Error mode
	0 = hardware errors are reported through the system critical error handler
	1 = hardware errors are returned to the process
14	Write-through flag
	0 = writes can be buffered and deferred
	1 = writes must be synchronous with the request
15	DASD open flag (see DosOpen)
	0 = handle represents file, pipe, or character device
	1 = handle represents disk volume for direct access

Note:

■ [1.1] If the handle refers to a named pipe, only bits 7 and 14 are significant.

Related functions: *DosOpen, DosQFileInfo, DosQFileMode, DosQNmPHandState, DosSetFHandState.*

DosQFileInfo   [IOPL]   [FAPI]

Given an active file handle, returns the date and time stamps, attributes, and size of the corresponding file.

WORD	File handle
WORD	Level of file information desired (always 1 for OS/2 versions 1.0 and 1.1)
PTR BUFFER	Receives file information, which has the following format for level 1:

Offset	Length	Description
00H	2	File date of creation
02H	2	File time of creation
04H	2	File date of last access
06H	2	File time of last access
08H	2	File date of last write
0AH	2	File time of last write
0CH	4	File size
10H	4	File allocation
14H	2	File attribute

WORD	Size of buffer to receive file information

Notes:

- For format of time, date, and attribute fields, see *DosFindFirst*. In FAT file systems, the date and time of creation and last access are always zero.

- In real mode, calls to this function will degrade the performance of *DosOpen*.

Related functions: *DosOpen, DosQFHandState, DosQFileMode, DosSetFileInfo.*

DosQFileMode   [IOPL]   [FAPI]

Returns the attributes of a file or directory.

| PTR ASCIIZ | Pathname of file |
| PTR WORD | Receives file attribute |

Bit(s)	Significance (if set)
0	Read-only
1	Hidden
2	System
3	Reserved (0)
4	Directory
5	Archive
6–15	Reserved (0)

| DWORD | Reserved (0) |

Related functions: *DosOpen, DosQFHandState, DosQFileInfo, DosSetFileMode.*

DosQFSInfo   [IOPL]   [FAPI]

Returns information about a logical volume, such as its name, available space, and allocation unit size.

WORD	Logical drive code (0 = current, 1 = A, 2 = B, etc.)
WORD	Level of file system information desired
	1 = get logical drive characteristics
	2 = get volume label
PTR BUFFER	Receives file system information (*see Notes*)
WORD	Size of buffer to receive file system information

Notes:

- Level 1 file system information has the following format:

Offset	Length	Description
00H	4	File system ID
04H	4	Sectors per allocation unit
08H	4	Total number of allocation units
0CH	4	Available allocation units
10H	2	Bytes per sector

- Level 2 file system information has the following format:

Offset	Length	Description
00H	2	Volume label date of creation
02H	2	Volume label time of creation
04H	1	Length *n* of ASCIIZ volume label (not including null byte)
05H	*n*+1	ASCIIZ volume label

- For date and time formats, see *DosFindFirst*.

Related functions: *DosDevIOCtl, DosPhysicalDisk, DosSetFSInfo*.

DosQHandType   [IOPL]

Returns a code indicating whether a handle is associated with a file, a pipe, or a device.

WORD   Handle for file, pipe, or device
PTR WORD   Receives handle information in a 2-byte structure

Offset	Length	Description
00H	*1*	*Handle type*
		0 = file
		1 = character device
		2 = pipe
01H	*1*	*Handle bits*

	Bit(s)	Significance
	0–6	*Reserved (0)*
	7	*0 = local device*
		1 = network device

PTR WORD   Receives attribute word from device driver header, if handle type = 1 (device)

Note:

- Programs can determine whether their standard input or standard output handles are redirected by calling *DosQHandType*. If the handle type is 1 (device), the program should then test bit 0 (for standard input) or 1 (for standard output) of the device driver attribute word. When no redirection is occurring, the program can obtain better performance by using *Kbd* and *Vio* calls instead of *DosRead* and *DosWrite*.

Related functions: *DosMakePipe, DosOpen, DosQFHandState, DosQFileInfo, DosQFileMode.*

DosQNmPHandState   [1.1]

Returns the maximum number of pipe instances, allowed read modes, current write mode, and blocking mode information associated with a named pipe handle.

WORD   Pipe handle

PTR WORD	Receives handle state	
	Bit(s)	*Significance*
	0–7	*Instances allowed (255 = unlimited)*
	8	*Allowed read modes*
		0 = byte stream only
		1 = byte stream or message stream
	9	*Reserved*
	10	*Write mode*
		0 = byte stream
		1 = message stream
	11–13	*Reserved (0)*
	14	*Server/client flag*
		0 = client
		1 = server
	15	*Blocking mode*
		0 = wait, if necessary, to complete read or write operation
		1 = return immediately with an error if read or write cannot be completed

Related functions: *DosMakeNmPipe, DosQFHandState, DosQHandType, DosSetNmPHandState.*

DosQNmPipeInfo [1.1]

Returns characteristics of the named pipe associated with a pipe handle.

WORD	Pipe handle		
WORD	Information level (always 1 in OS/2 version 1.1)		
PTR BUFFER	Receives pipe information		
	Offset	*Length*	*Description*
	00H	*2*	*Length of pipe buffer for outbound data*
	02H	*2*	*Length of pipe buffer for inbound data*
	04H	*1*	*Maximum number of pipe instances (0 = unlimited)*
	05H	*1*	*Current number of pipe instances*
	06H	*1*	*Length of pipe name (n)*
	07H+	*n+1*	*ASCIIZ pipe name*
PTR WORD	Length of buffer to receive pipe information		

Related functions: *DosMakeNmPipe, DosQNmPHandState.*

DosQNmPipeSemState [1.1]

Returns information about the named pipes associated with a particular system semaphore.

DWORD	Semaphore handle
PTR BUFFER	Receives information about each pipe associated with the semaphore, as a series of 6-byte entries (*see Note*)
WORD	Length of buffer to receive information

Note:

- The number of entries returned is the lesser of the number of pipes associated with the semaphore and the number of entries that can fit into the buffer. Each 6-byte entry takes the following form:

Offset	Length	Description
00H	1	Pipe status
		0 = end of information, remainder of buffer invalid
		1 = data available in pipe
		2 = free space available in pipe
		3 = pipe is closing
01H	1	Waiting flag
		1 = thread is waiting at other end of pipe
02H	2	Key associated with semaphore handle
04H	2	Bytes available to be read, or space available for writes (if pipe status = 1 or 2)

Related functions: *DosQNmPipeInfo, DosSetNmPipeSem.*

DosQSysInfo   [1.1]

Returns system information which does not change after the system is booted.

WORD	Information type
	0 = get maximum path length
PTR BUFFER	Receives system information
WORD	Length of buffer to receive information

Note:

- For information type 0, the receiving buffer need be only 2 bytes long. The drive identifier and leading backslash are included in the returned maximum length.

Related functions: *DosChDir, DosQCurDir.*

DosQueryQueue

Returns the number of records in a queue. Any process that has opened the queue can use this function; it is not restricted to the queue owner.

WORD	Queue handle
PTR WORD	Receives number of records in queue

Related functions: *DosPeekQueue, DosPurgeQueue, DosReadQueue, DosWriteQueue.*

DosQVerify   [IOPL] [FAPI]

Returns the current state of the system flag that controls read-after-write verification of disk transfers.

PTR WORD   Receives verify flag
                      0 = verify mode off
                      1 = verify mode on

Related function : *DosSetVerify*.

DosR2StackRealloc   [1.1]

Resizes the current thread's ring 2 stack.

WORD   New ring 2 stack size (bytes)

Note:

■ The new stack size cannot be smaller than the current ring 2 stack. The default stack size for execution within an IOPL segment is 512 bytes.

Related functions: *DosCallback, DosCLIAccess, DosPortAccess*.

DosRead   [IOPL] [FAPI]

Reads data from a file, pipe, or device into a buffer.

WORD   Handle for file, pipe, or device
PTR BUFFER   Receives data
WORD   Number of bytes requested
PTR WORD   Receives actual number of bytes read

Notes:

■ When reading from the keyboard in ASCII mode, the *DosRead* operation is terminated by character codes 0DH (^M) or 1AH (^Z). If the CPU is in real mode, the user's entry is limited to the number of characters specified minus one; subsequent characters are ignored and cause a beep. If the CPU is in protected mode, the user can continue to enter characters until the keyboard driver's buffer is full, but the number of characters returned to the program is limited to the number requested. If the keyboard handle is in binary mode, *DosRead* always waits until the requested number of characters are available.

■ When reading from a file, *DosRead* might return fewer bytes than requested if the end of file is reached; this is not an error condition.

■ When reading from an anonymous pipe, *DosRead* blocks if the pipe is empty until data is available.

- [1.1] When you are reading from a named pipe, the result of the operation depends on the blocking and read modes of the pipe. If the pipe is in byte-stream mode, *DosRead* blocks if the pipe is empty unless the pipe is also in nonblocking mode. In message mode, if the buffer is larger than the message, the actual length of the message is returned. If the buffer is too small for the message, the buffer is filled and an error is returned; the remaining data must be obtained with another call to *DosRead*.

Related functions: *DosCallNmPipe, DosChgFilePtr, DosMakeNmPipe, DosOpen, DosReadAsync, DosTransactNmPipe, DosWrite, DosWriteAsync.*

DosReadAsync   [IOPL]

Reads data from a file, pipe, or device into a buffer. The requesting thread continues to execute during the transfer, and a semaphore is cleared when the transfer is complete.

WORD	Handle for file, pipe, or device
DWORD	Handle of RAM semaphore to be cleared when transfer is complete
PTR WORD	Receives I/O error code (0 = no error)
PTR BUFFER	Receives data
WORD	Number of bytes requested
PTR WORD	Receives actual number of bytes read

Notes:

- See *DosRead* for special considerations applying to the keyboard, pipes, and files.

- The file pointer is updated before the *DosReadAsync* function returns, even though the data transfer has not been completed.

- The usual order of requests is *DosSemSet*, then *DosReadAsync*, followed by other processing and then *DosSemWait* or *DosMuxSemWait*.

Related functions: *DosChgFilePtr, DosMakeNmPipe, DosMuxSemWait, DosOpen, DosRead, DosSemSet, DosSemWait, DosWrite, DosWriteAsync.*

DosReadQueue

Reads and removes a record from a queue. Only the queue's owner (creator) process can call this function.

WORD	Queue handle		
PTR DWORD	Receives queue record identification data		
	Offset	*Length*	*Description*
	00H	*2*	*PID of queue writer*
	02H	*2*	*Arbitrary data passed by queue writer*
PTR WORD	Receives length of queue record		
PTR DWORD	Receives address of queue record		
WORD	Record identifier		
	0 = return first queue record		
	<>0 = return specific queue record		
	If nonzero, the identifier must have been obtained from a previous call to *DosPeekQueue*		

WORD	Wait/no-wait flag
	0 = wait if no queue record is available
	1 = return with error if queue is empty
PTR BYTE	Receives priority of queue record (0–15, with 15 = highest priority; not applicable if queue was not created with priority ordering)
DWORD	Handle of semaphore to be cleared when queue record becomes available, if wait/no-wait flag = 1; otherwise, null pointer

Note:

■ If multiple threads are calling *DosPeekQueue* or *DosReadQueue*, all must use the same RAM or system semaphore.

Related functions: *DosMuxSemWait, DosPeekQueue, DosPurgeQueue, DosQueryQueue, DosSemSet, DosSemWait, DosWriteQueue.*

DosReallocHuge   [IOPL] [FAPI]

Changes the size of a huge memory block previously allocated with *DosAllocHuge*. If the block is discardable, *DosReallocHuge* performs an implicit *DosLockSeg*. The givable, gettable, or discardable attributes of the block are not affected.

WORD	Number of complete 64 KB segments
WORD	Number of bytes in partial last segment (0 = none)
WORD	Base selector obtained from *DosAllocHuge*

Notes:

■ In protected mode, the function fails if the new size exceeds the maximum number of segments specified in the original *DosAllocHuge* call.

■ In real mode, the function rounds the requested size to the next paragraph (multiple of 16 bytes), and the maximum size specified in the original *DosAllocHuge* call is ignored.

Related functions: *DosAllocHuge, DosAllocSeg, DosFreeSeg, DosGetHugeShift, DosLockSeg, DosSizeSeg.*

DosReallocSeg   [IOPL] [FAPI]

Changes the size of a memory block previously allocated with *DosAllocSeg* or *DosAllocShrSeg*. If the block is discardable, *DosReallocSeg* performs an implicit *DosLockSeg*. The givable, gettable, or discardable attributes of the block are not affected.

WORD	New segment size in bytes (0 = 65,536)
WORD	Selector

Notes:

- Shared segments can be increased but not decreased in size.

- In real mode, the function rounds the requested size to the next paragraph (multiple of 16 bytes).

Related functions: *DosAllocSeg, DosFreeSeg, DosLockSeg, DosR2StackRealloc, DosReallocHuge, DosSizeSeg.*

DosResumeThread [IOPL]

Restarts a thread that was stopped with *DosSuspendThread.*

WORD   Thread ID

Related functions: *DosCreateThread, DosEnterCritSec, DosExitCritSec, DosSuspendThread.*

DosRmDir [IOPL] [FAPI]

Removes a directory. Cannot be used on the root directory, the current directory, or a directory which contains files.

PTR ASCIIZ   Pathname of directory
DWORD   Reserved (0)

Related functions: *DosDelete, DosMkDir, DosQSysInfo.*

DosScanEnv [IOPL]

Searches the current process's environment for a string in the form *name=value*; returns a pointer to *value*.

PTR ASCIIZ   Name of environment variable, must not include the = character
PTR DWORD   Receives address of ASCIIZ *value* string following the = character

Related functions: *DosGetEnv, DosSearchPath.*

DosSearchPath [IOPL]

Searches one or more directories for a file, returning the fully qualified pathname if it is found. You can specify the directories explicitly (separated by semicolons) or supply the name of an environment variable.

WORD   Function control flags
                           Bit(s)   *Significance*
                           0   *0 = search current directory only if it is explicitly named in path*
                                         1 = always search current directory before searching specified path

Bit(s)	Significance
1	0 = explicit path is supplied
	1 = name of environment variable is supplied; use the list of directories associated with that variable
2–15	Reserved

PTR ASCIIZ   Path to be searched (can contain multiple paths separated by semicolons) or name of an environment variable without a trailing = character

PTR ASCIIZ   Filename to be searched for (can contain wildcard characters)

PTR BUFFER   Receives fully qualified pathname (including an explicit drive and path from the root directory; wildcard characters in the filename or extension are not expanded)

WORD   Length of buffer to receive fully qualified pathname

Related functions: *DosFindFirst, DosGetEnv, DosScanEnv*.

DosSelectDisk   [IOPL] [FAPI]

Selects the current drive. The current drive is maintained on a per-process basis and is inherited by child processes.

WORD   Logical drive code (1 = A, 2 = B, etc.)

Related functions: *DosChDir, DosQCurDir, DosQCurDisk*.

DosSelectSession

Switches the current session or a child session into the foreground. You cannot use this function to select the descendant of a child session, or a child session which is not "related."

WORD   Session ID (0 = current session)

DWORD   Reserved (0)

Related functions: *DosSetSession, DosStartSession, DosStopSession*.

DosSemClear   [IOPL]

Unconditionally clears (releases) a semaphore.

DWORD   Semaphore handle

Note:

■ Ordinarily, a system semaphore which was created with the exclusive option can be cleared only by the process that owns it. However, at interrupt time, any thread can clear any semaphore.

Related functions: *DosFSRamSemClear, DosMuxSemWait, DosSemRequest, DosSemSetWait, DosSemWait*.

DosSemRequest [IOPL]

Obtains ownership of a semaphore. If the semaphore is already owned, the function waits until it is available. When used with system semaphores that were created with the exclusive option, *DosSemRequest* calls can be nested.

DWORD   Semaphore handle
DWORD   Timeout interval in milliseconds (0 = return immediately with an error if semaphore is owned; −1 = wait indefinitely)

Related functions: *DosFSRamSemRequest, DosSemClear.*

DosSemSet [IOPL]

Unconditionally sets a semaphore.

DWORD   Semaphore handle

Related functions: *DosMuxSemWait, DosSemClear, DosSemSetWait, DosSemWait.*

DosSemSetWait [IOPL]

Unconditionally sets a semaphore, then waits until it is cleared by another thread or process. This function is level-triggered; that is, if the semaphore is cleared and then set again before the waiting thread can be dispatched, the thread will continue to block.

DWORD   Semaphore handle
DWORD   Timeout interval in milliseconds (0 = return immediately with an error if semaphore is owned; −1 = wait indefinitely)

Related functions: *DosMuxSemWait, DosSemClear, DosSemSet, DosSemWait.*

DosSemWait [IOPL]

Waits until a semaphore is cleared. This function is level-triggered; that is, if the semaphore is cleared and then set again before the waiting thread can be dispatched, the thread will continue to block.

DWORD   Semaphore handle
DWORD   Timeout interval in milliseconds (0 = return immediately with an error if semaphore is owned; −1 = wait indefinitely)

Related functions: *DosMuxSemWait, DosSemClear, DosSemSet, DosSemSetWait.*

DosSendSignal [IOPL]

Sends a Ctrl-C or Ctrl-Break signal to the last process in a process subtree that has registered a handler for that signal.

WORD	PID of root process of a process subtree (must be a direct descendant of the current process)
WORD	Signal number
	1 = SIGINTR (Ctrl-C)
	4 = SIGBREAK (Ctrl-Break)

Note:

- The specified process need not still be alive if any of its descendants are alive to receive the signal.

Related functions: *DosFlagProcess, DosHoldSignal, DosSetSigHandler.*

DosSetCp [IOPL]

Selects a code page for the keyboard, display, and (if the spooler is loaded) the printer if it is opened subsequent to this function call. All processes in the current session use the new code page.

WORD	Code page identifier	
	000	*Default (none)*
	437	*USA*
	850	*Multilingual*
	860	*Portuguese*
	863	*French-Canadian*
	865	*Nordic*
WORD	Reserved (0)	

Related functions: *DosCaseMap, DosGetCollate, DosGetCp, DosGetCtryInfo, DosGetDBCSEv, DosSetProcCp, KbdSetCp, VioSetCp.*

DosSetDateTime [IOPL] [FAPI]

Sets the system date, time, and time zone.

PTR BUFFER	Receives date and time information in the following format:

Offset	*Length*	*Description*
00H	*1*	*Hour (0–23)*
01H	*1*	*Minute (0–59)*
02H	*1*	*Second (0–59)*
03H	*1*	*Hundredths of second (0–99)*

Offset	Length	Description
04H	1	Day (1–31)
05H	1	Month (1–12)
06H	2	Year (1980–2079)
08H	2	Time zone (minutes ± GMT, EST = 300, −1 = undefined)

Related functions: *DosGetDateTime, DosGetInfoSeg*.

DosSetFHandState   [IOPL]   [FAPI]

Sets the inheritance, write-through, and error-handling characteristics of a file, pipe, or device handle.

WORD   Handle
WORD   Handle state

Bit(s)	Significance
0–2	Reserved (must be 0)
3	Reserved (use value returned by DosQFHandState)
4–6	Reserved (must be 0)
7	Inheritance
	0 = handle inherited by child processes
	1 = handle is not inherited
8–12	Reserved (use value returned by DosQFHandState)
13	Error mode
	0 = hardware errors are reported through the system critical error handler
	1 = hardware errors are returned to the process
14	Write-through flag
	0 = writes may be buffered and deferred
	1 = writes must be synchronous with the request
15	Reserved (must be 0)

Notes:

- You cannot modify the sharing mode and access rights of a handle with this function because the new values might conflict with the values specified in previous calls to *DosOpen* by other processes.

- In real mode, the validity of the handle is not checked, and the write-through and error mode bits must always be cleared (0). If an FAPI program is running in an MS-DOS 2.x environment, you cannot set the inheritance bit.

- [1.1] If the handle refers to a named pipe, only bits 7 and 14 are significant.

Related functions: *DosNewSize, DosOpen, DosQFHandState, DosQNmPHandState, DosSetFileInfo, DosSetFileMode, DosSetNmPHandState*.

DosSetFileInfo   [IOPL] [FAPI]

Sets the time and date stamps in the directory entry for a file. The file must have been opened with write-only or read/write access rights.

WORD	File handle
WORD	File information level (always 1 in OS/2 versions 1.0 and 1.1)
PTR BUFFER	Contains file information, which has the following format for level 1:

Offset	Length	Description
00H	2	File date of creation
02H	2	File time of creation
04H	2	File date of last access
06H	2	File time of last access
08H	2	File date of last write
0AH	2	File time of last write

WORD	Length of file information buffer

Notes:

- Any date or time position that contains zero is ignored by this function. In FAT file systems, the creation and last access fields are not supported and should be zero.

- For format of time and date fields, see the notes for *DosFindFirst*.

Related functions: *DosNewSize, DosOpen, DosQFileInfo, DosSetFHandState, DosSetFileMode.*

DosSetFileMode   [IOPL] [FAPI]

Sets the attributes of a file or directory.

PTR ASCIIZ	Pathname of file
WORD	New attribute of file

Bit(s)	Significance (if set)
0	Read-only
1	Hidden
2	System
3–4	Reserved (0)
5	Archive
6–15	Reserved (0)

DWORD	Reserved (0)

Note:

- If the pathname refers to a directory, only the read-only and hidden attribute bits can be set.

Related functions: *DosNewSize, DosOpen, DosQFileMode, DosSetFHandState, DosSetFileInfo.*

DosSetFSInfo [IOPL] [FAPI]

Adds, modifies, or deletes a volume label.

WORD	Logical drive code (0 = default, 1 = A, 2 = B, etc.)
WORD	File system information level (always 2 in OS/2 versions 1.0 and 1.1)
PTR BUFFER	Contains file system information, which has the following format for level 2:

Offset	Length	Description
00H	1	Length n of ASCIIZ volume label (excluding null byte)
01H	n+1	ASCIIZ volume label

WORD	Length of buffer containing file system information

Related functions: *DosDevIOCtl, DosPhysicalDisk, DosQFSInfo.*

DosSetMaxFH [IOPL]

Sets the maximum number of active handles for files, pipes, and devices for the current process. Note that some handles are expended for the standard devices, dynlink libraries, and files, pipes, and device handles inherited from the parent process, even though the current process has explicitly opened none of these.

WORD	Number of file handles (default = 20, maximum = 255)

Related function: *DosOpen.*

DosSetNmPHandState [1.1]

Modifies the current read mode and blocking mode for a named pipe.

WORD	Pipe handle
WORD	Handle state

Bit(s)	Significance
0–7	Reserved (0)
8	Allowed read modes
	0 = byte stream only
	1 = byte stream or message stream
9–14	Reserved (0)
15	Blocking mode
	0 = wait, if necessary, to complete read or write operation
	1 = return immediately with an error if read or write cannot be completed

Note:

■ Bit 8 of the handle state cannot be set with this function unless the pipe was created with the "write message mode" bit set.

Related functions: *DosMakeNmPipe, DosQFHandState, DosQNmPHandState, DosSetFHandState.*

DosSetNmPipeSem [1.1]

Associates a system semaphore with a named pipe.

WORD	Pipe handle
DWORD	Semaphore handle
WORD	Semaphore key

Notes:

- The semaphore is cleared whenever the pipe has data available for reading or space available for writing.

- The key is returned by subsequent calls to *DosQNmPipeSemState*. It allows the process to determine which pipe is ready for I/O when several pipes are associated with the same semaphore.

- If a semaphore is already associated with the specified named pipe, it is replaced with the new semaphore.

Related functions: *DosCreateSem, DosMuxSemWait, DosOpenSem, DosQNmPipeSemState, DosSemWait.*

DosSetProcCp

Selects the process code page, code-page-related country-dependent information, and (if the spooler is loaded) the code page used by the printer for subsequent open operations. The keyboard and display code pages for the current process, and the code pages used by other processes, are not affected.

WORD	Code page identifier	
	000	*Default (none)*
	437	*USA*
	850	*Multilingual*
	860	*Portuguese*
	863	*French-Canadian*
	865	*Nordic*
WORD	Reserved (0)	

Related functions: *DosCaseMap, DosGetCollate, DosGetCp, DosGetCtryInfo, DosGetDBCSEv, DosSetCp, KbdSetCp, VioSetCp.*

DosSetPrty [IOPL]

Sets the priority of a single thread in the current process or of all threads within another process or an entire process subtree.

WORD	Scope of function	
	0	*All threads of another process*
	1	*All threads of another process and all of its descendants*
	2	*Single thread within the current process*

WORD	Priority class
	0 Current class unchanged
	1 Idle-time
	2 Regular
	3 Time-critical
WORD	Priority level (see Notes)
WORD	Process ID (scope = 0 or 1) or thread ID (scope = 2)

Notes:

- If the scope is 1, the specified process must be either the current process or a nondetached child process. The specified process need not still be alive for its descendants to be affected.

- When *DosSetPrty* is used on another process, only threads with default priority are affected; threads whose priority has been altered after the process was started are not affected.

- If the priority class is 1, 2, or 3, the priority level is the initial priority level (0–31) within the class. If the priority class is 0 (current class unchanged), the level parameter is an increment (−31 through 31) to be applied to the current level; the resulting level is clamped to the range 0–31.

Related functions: *DosCreateThread, DosGetPrty*.

DosSetSession

Determines whether a child session can be selected by the user, and/or whether the child session is made visible when the parent session is selected.

WORD	Session ID from previous *DosStartSession*		
PTR BUFFER	Session status data		
	Offset	*Length*	*Description*
	00H	2	*Length (always 6 in OS/2 versions 1.0 and 1.1)*
	02H	2	*Selectability indicator*
			0 = current setting unchanged
			1 = session is selectable
			2 = session is not selectable
	04H	2	*Binding indicator*
			0 = current setting unchanged
			1 = child session is bonded to parent; when either the parent or child session is selected, the child session is displayed
			2 = child session is not bonded to parent; parent session and child sessions can be selected and displayed independently

Note:

- *DosSetSession* can be used only to control a "related" session that was started by the current process.

Related functions: *DosSelectSession, DosStartSession, DosStopSession*.

DosSetSigHandler [IOPL] [FAPI]

Registers a handler for a signal, restores the default handler, causes the system to ignore the signal or return an error to the signaling process, or resets a signal during its handling so that another signal of the same type can be processed.

DWORD	Address of new signal handler
PTR DWORD	Receives address of previous signal handler (can use null pointer)
PTR WORD	Receives previous signal handler action (can use null pointer)
WORD	New signal handler action

0	*Install default system action*
1	*Ignore the signal*
2	*Register new handler for signal*
3	*Return an error to the signaling process*
4	*Reset the signal without affecting the disposition of the signal (used only by signal handler)*

WORD	Signal number of interest

1	*Ctrl-C (SIGINTR)*
2	*Broken pipe (SIGBROKENPIPE)*
3	*Program terminated (SIGTERM)*
4	*Ctrl-Break (SIGBREAK)*
5	*Event flag A*
6	*Event flag B*
7	*Event flag C*

Notes:

- A signal handler is given control under the primary thread of a process with the stack set up as follows:

SS:SP	32-bit return address for handler
SS:SP+4	Signal number
SS:SP+6	Private data from signaling process, if the signal number is 5, 6, or 7

- During its signal processing, the signal handler must reset the signal by calling *DosSetSigHandler* with action 4. The handler can retain control, resetting the stack and transferring to some other point in the application, or it can exit with a RET 4 instruction.

- In real mode, the Ctrl-C (SIGINTR) and Ctrl-Break (SIGBREAK) signals are treated as the same signal, and a handler can be installed only for SIGINTR.

- In OS/2 version 1.0, if thread 1 of a process terminates, the signal handlers revert to the default action. In version 1.1, if thread 1 terminates, the process is terminated.

Related functions: *DosFlagProcess, DosHoldSignal, DosSendSignal.*

DosSetVec   [IOPL] [FAPI]

Registers a handler for one of the following hardware exceptions: divide by zero, divide overflow, array bounds exceeded, invalid opcode, numeric coprocessor error, or numeric coprocessor not present. You cannot register handlers for general protection and stack faults; these exceptions are always handled by the operating system and terminate the process.

WORD	Exception type	
	0	*Divide by zero*
	4	*Overflow flag set and INTO executed*
	5	*Bounds exceeded*
	6	*Invalid opcode*
	7	*Numeric coprocessor not available*
	16	*Numeric coprocessor error*
DWORD	Address of exception handler	
PTR DWORD	Receives address of previous exception handler (cannot use null pointer)	

Notes:

- The handler is entered with flags and a far return address on the stack and with interrupts enabled. The handler can keep control (resetting its stack frame) and transfer to another point in the program, or it can return from the exception with an IRET.

- In real mode, you cannot register a handler for exception type 7 (numeric coprocessor not available) because it is not generated by 8086/88 machines.

Related functions: *DosError, DosSetSigHandler.*

DosSetVerify   [IOPL] [FAPI]

Turns on or turns off the system flag for read-after-write verification of disk transfers.

WORD	New value of verify flag	
	0	*Verify is disabled*
	1	*Verify is enabled*

Related function: *DosQVerify.*

DosSizeSeg   [IOPL] [1.1]

Returns the size of a memory segment in bytes.

WORD	Selector
PTR DWORD	Receives segment size

Notes:

- You must use the base selector returned by *DosAllocHuge* when you obtain the size of a huge segment.

- If a segment has been discarded, *DosSizeSeg* still returns the original allocation size for the segment.

Related functions: *DosAllocHuge, DosAllocSeg, DosAllocShrSeg, DosFreeSeg, DosReallocHuge, DosReallocSeg*.

DosSleep   [IOPL]   [FAPI]

Suspends execution for *at least* the requested interval. The actual interval can vary from the requested interval by one or more clock ticks depending on other activity in the system.

DWORD   Interval in milliseconds, rounded up by the system to the next multiple of a
                    clock tick interval (31 msec. in OS/2 versions 1.0 and 1.1)

Note:

- If the specified interval is zero, the thread simply yields the remainder of its current timeslice.

Related functions: *DosGetInfoSeg, DosTimerAsync, DosTimerStart*.

DosStartSession

Creates a new session (screen group) and starts a process within that session. In OS/2 version 1.1, this function can also be used to start a *Vio* or Presentation Manager application in a window.

PTR BUFFER   Contains session control data

Offset	Length	Description
00H	2	Structure length (always 24 bytes in OS/2 version 1.0; 24, 30, or 50 bytes in version 1.1)
02H	2	Related session flag
		0 = new session is independent
		1 = new session is related (child)
04H	2	Foreground/background flag
		0 = new session is in foreground
		1 = new session is in background
06H	2	Tracing option
		0 = process is not traceable
		1 = process is traceable
08H	4	Address of ASCIIZ program title
0CH	4	Address of ASCIIZ program pathname
10H	4	Address of ASCIIZ command tail
14H	4	Address of ASCIIZ queue name or null pointer

-------------------------------(End of 24-byte structure)-------------------------------

Offset	Length	Description
18H	*4*	*Address of environment block or null pointer*
1CH	*2*	*Inheritance option*
		0 = inherit Task Manager's default environment, current disk, and current directory
		1 = inherit parent's environment, handles, current disk, and current directory

----------------------------(End of 30-byte structure)----------------------------

1EH	*2*	*Program type*
		0 = use type from EXE file or Task Manager default
		1 = full screen
		2 = Vio application in window
		3 = Presentation Manager application
20H	*4*	*Address of ASCIIZ icon filename or null pointer*
24H	*4*	*Program handle for entry in install file (can be 0)*
28H	*2*	*Program control for initial state*
		0 = use installed state or Task Manager default
		1 = use size and position specified
		2 = minimized window
		3 = maximized window
		4 = invisible window
2AH	*2*	*Initial x coordinate, lower left corner of window*
2CH	*2*	*Initial y coordinate, lower left corner of window*
2EH	*2*	*Initial window width*
30H	*2*	*Initial window height*

----------------------------(End of 50-byte structure)----------------------------

PTR WORD   Receives session ID

PTR WORD   Receives PID

Notes:

- For independent sessions, the queue name parameter is ignored, and a session ID is not returned. You cannot specify an independent session as the target of a call to *DosSelectSession, DosSetSession,* or *DosStopSession.*

- A session ID is returned for related child sessions; it can be used with *DosSelectSession, DosSetSession,* and *DosStopSession.* If you specify a queue name, the Task Manager writes a record in the following form into the queue when the child session terminates:

Offset	Length	Description
00H	2	Session ID of terminating child session
02H	2	Exit code of process in child session

The queue can be read only by the process which requested the *DosStartSession.* After the queue message is received and processed, release its selector with *DosFreeSeg.*

- A child session is not equivalent to a child process started with *DosExecPgm*; the returned PID cannot be used with *DosCwait* or *DosSetPrty.*

- If the child session is in the foreground when its last process terminates, the parent session is brought to the foreground.

- [1.0] The environment of the initial process in the child session is empty; that is, it consists of a pair of zero bytes. In OS/2 version 1.1 the environment of the initial process is empty except for a copy of the parent's PATH.

- [1.1] If the 24-byte session control data structure is used, or if the 30- or 50-byte session control data structure is used and the inheritance option and environment block pointer are both zero, the new process's environment is determined by the PATH and SET directives in the CONFIG.SYS file, and the parent's handles, current disk, and current directory are not inherited.

- [1.1] If the 30- or 50-byte session control data structure is used, the inheritance option is 1, and the environment block pointer is zero, then the new process's environment is a copy of the parent's.

- [1.1] The initial window size and location parameters are expressed in graphics coordinates, and the origin, or $(x,y) = (0,0)$, is the lower left corner of the screen. These parameters are ignored if the program control parameter is not equal to 1.

Related functions: *DosCreateQueue, DosExecPgm, DosReadQueue, DosSelectSession, DosSetSession, DosStopSession*.

DosStopSession

Terminates a related child session that was created with *DosStartSession*. If the child session was in the foreground, the parent session is brought into the foreground.

WORD	Target session option
	0 Terminate only the specified session and its descendants
	1 Terminate all child sessions and their descendants
WORD	Session ID (ignored if target session option = 1)
DWORD	Reserved (0)

Related functions: *DosSelectSession, DosSetSession, DosStartSession*.

DosSubAlloc   [IOPL]   [FAPI]

Allocates a memory block from a heap that was previously initialized by *DosSubSet*.

WORD	Selector of segment containing heap
PTR WORD	Receives offset of allocated block
WORD	Size in bytes of requested block (rounded if necessary to next multiple of 4; maximum size is the size of the segment minus 8 bytes)

Related functions: *DosSubFree, DosSubSet*.

DosSubFree   [IOPL]   [FAPI]

Releases a memory block that was previously obtained with *DosSubAlloc*.

WORD	Selector of segment containing heap
WORD	Offset of block to free

WORD   Size in bytes of block to free (rounded if necessary to next multiple of 4)

Related functions: *DosSubAlloc, DosSubSet.*

DosSubSet   **[IOPL]   [FAPI]**

Initializes or resizes a heap.

WORD	Selector for segment that will contain heap
WORD	Action
	0 *Increase size of existing heap*
	1 *Initialize heap*
WORD	Total size in bytes of heap (minimum = 12 bytes; 0 = 65,536 bytes; rounded if necessary to next multiple of 4 bytes)

Related functions: *DosAllocSeg, DosReallocSeg, DosSubAlloc, DosSubFree.*

DosSuspendThread   **[IOPL]**

Suspends execution of another thread within the same process.

WORD   Thread ID

Related functions: *DosCreateThread, DosEnterCritSec, DosExitCritSec, DosResumeThread.*

DosTimerAsync   **[IOPL]**

Starts an asynchronous one-shot timer that clears a system semaphore after the specified interval. The function returns a handle that can be used to disable the timer with *DosTimerStop*. Set the semaphore before calling this function.

DWORD	Timer interval in milliseconds
DWORD	Handle for system semaphore
PTR WORD	Receives timer handle

Note:

- OS/2 rounds the specified interval to the next multiple of the system's timer tick interval, which is 31 msec. in OS/2 versions 1.0 and 1.1.

Related functions: *DosCreateSem, DosSemSet, DosSemWait, DosSleep, DosTimerStart, DosTimerStop.*

DosTimerStart   **[IOPL]**

Starts an asynchronous timer that periodically clears a system semaphore. The function returns a handle that can be used to disable the timer with *DosTimerStop*. Set the semaphore before calling this function, and set it again immediately each time it is cleared by the timer.

DWORD	Timer interval in milliseconds
DWORD	Handle for system semaphore
PTR WORD	Receives timer handle

Note:

- OS/2 rounds the specified interval up to the next multiple of the system's timer tick interval, which is 31 msec. in OS/2 versions 1.0 and 1.1.

Related functions: *DosCreateSem, DosSemSet, DosSemWait, DosSleep, DosTimerAsync, DosTimerStop.*

DosTimerStop [IOPL]

Stops a timer that was previously created with *DosTimerStart* or *DosTimerAsync.*

| WORD | Timer handle |

Related functions: *DosTimerAsync, DosTimerStart.*

DosTransactNmPipe [1.1]

Writes a message to a named pipe, and then reads a message from the same pipe.

WORD	Pipe handle
PTR BUFFER	Contains data to be written to pipe
WORD	Length of data to be written to pipe
PTR BUFFER	Receives data from pipe
WORD	Length of buffer to receive data from pipe
PTR WORD	Receives actual length of data read from pipe

Notes:

- This function fails if the pipe is not in message mode or contains any unread data.

- *DosTransactNmPipe* is not affected by a pipe's blocking mode; it does not return until a message is available. If the buffer is too small for the message, the buffer is filled and an error is returned. To obtain the remaining data, you must make another call to *DosTransactNmPipe.*

Related functions: *DosCallNmPipe, DosMakeNmPipe, DosRead, DosWrite.*

DosUnlockSeg [IOPL]

Notifies the operating system that it can discard a segment in low-memory situations; reverses the effect of a previous call to *DosLockSeg. DosLockSeg* and *DosUnlockSeg* calls may be nested. The segment must have been allocated by *DosAllocSeg* or *DosAllocHuge* with the "discardable" option.

| WORD | Selector |

Related functions: *DosAllocHuge, DosAllocSeg, DosLockSeg, DosReallocHuge, DosReallocSeg.*

DosWaitNmPipe [1.1]

Waits for an available instance of a named pipe. Call this function if *DosOpen* returns an error indicating that the pipe is busy (that is, all allowed instances of the pipe are in use). When *DosWaitNmPipe* succeeds, issue another *DosOpen* to obtain a named pipe handle.

PTR ASCIIZ   Pipe name, in the form \PIPE*name.ext* for a local pipe or
                    machine\PIPE*name.ext* for a remote pipe
DWORD   Timeout interval in milliseconds (0 = use pipe default timeout; −1 = wait
                    indefinitely)

Note:

■ This function is used only by client processes.

Related function: *DosOpen*.

DosWrite [IOPL] [FAPI]

Writes data from a buffer to a file, pipe, or device.

WORD   Handle for file, pipe, or device
PTR BUFFER   Contains data to be written
WORD   Requested number of bytes to be written
PTR WORD   Receives actual number of bytes written

Notes:

■ When writing to a file, *DosWrite* might transfer fewer bytes than requested if the disk containing the file becomes full; this is not an error condition.

■ When writing to an anonymous pipe that becomes full, *DosWrite* blocks until enough room is available in the pipe to hold the requested number of bytes.

■ [1.1] When writing to a named pipe in message mode or to a pipe in both byte-stream and blocking modes, *DosWrite* blocks until all the data can be written. When writing to a named pipe in byte-stream and nonblocking modes, *DosWrite* returns immediately, and the number of bytes written may be less than the number requested.

Related functions: *DosCallNmPipe, DosChgFilePtr, DosMakeNmPipe, DosRead, DosReadAsync, DosTransactNmPipe, DosWriteAsync.*

DosWriteAsync [IOPL]

Writes data from a buffer to a file, pipe, or device. The requesting thread continues to execute during the transfer, and a RAM semaphore is cleared when the transfer is complete.

WORD   Handle for file, pipe, or device
DWORD   Handle of RAM semaphore to be cleared when transfer is complete
PTR WORD   Receives I/O error code (0 = no error)

PTR BUFFER	Contains data to be written
WORD	Requested number of bytes to be written
PTR WORD	Receives actual number of bytes written

Notes:

- See *DosWrite* for special considerations applying to pipes and files.

- After you call *DosWriteAsync*, the data to be written should not be modified until the semaphore has been cleared.

- The file pointer is updated before the *DosWriteAsync* function returns, even though the data transfer has not been completed.

- The usual order of requests is *DosSemSet*, then *DosWriteAsync*, followed by other processing and then *DosSemWait* or *DosMuxSemWait*.

Related functions: *DosChgFilePtr, DosMakeNmPipe, DosMuxSemWait, DosRead, DosReadAsync, DosSemSet, DosSemWait, DosWrite.*

DosWriteQueue

Adds a record to a queue. Any process can write to a queue, but only the queue owner (creator) process can inspect or remove records in the queue.

WORD	Queue handle
WORD	Request identification data (passed to queue reader, but ignored by OS/2)
WORD	Length of queue record
DWORD	Address of queue record (valid selector must be obtained for the queue reader with *DosGiveSeg*, or the selector must be allocated as a ''gettable'' selector)
WORD	Queue record priority (*see Note*)

Note:

- The queue record priority can be in the range 0 through 15, and is only relevant if the queue was created with priority ordering. Priority 15 records are added to the head of the queue; priority 0 records are added to the tail. Records with the same priority are added to the queue in FIFO order.

Related functions: *DosPeekQueue, DosPurgeQueue, DosQueryQueue, DosReadQueue.*

KbdCharIn **[FAPI]**

Returns a character and scan code from the logical keyboard. The character is not echoed to the display.

PTR BUFFER	Receives character data		
	Offset	*Length*	*Description*
	00H	*1*	*ASCII character*
	01H	*1*	*Scan code*

Offset	Length	Description
02H	1	Status

Bit(s)	Significance (if set)
0	Shift status returned without character (valid only in binary mode when shift reporting is turned on)
1–4	Reserved (0)
5	On-the-spot conversion requested
6	Character ready
7	Interim character

Offset	Length	Description
03H	1	Reserved (0)
04H	2	Keyboard shift state

Bit	Significance (if set)
0	Right Shift key down
1	Left Shift key down
2	Either Ctrl key down
3	Either Alt key down
4	Scroll Lock on
5	Num Lock on
6	Caps Lock on
7	Insert on
8	Left Ctrl key down
9	Left Alt key down
10	Right Ctrl key down
11	Right Alt key down
12	Scroll Lock key down
13	Num Lock key down
14	Caps Lock key down
15	SysReq key down

Offset	Length	Description
06H	4	Time stamp (msec. since system was turned on or restarted)

WORD	Wait/no-wait flag
0	Wait for a character if none is ready
1	Do not wait for a character; return an error if no character is ready

| WORD | Keyboard handle (default = 0) |

Notes:

- Extended characters (such as function keys, cursor keys, and Alt-key combinations) are indicated by a 00H or an E0H in the ASCII character field. The key's identity is determined from the scan code.

- If the keyboard is in ASCII ("cooked") mode, some control keys (such as ^S) receive special handling. If binary ("raw") mode is turned on with *KbdSetStatus*, all control keys are passed through to the application; if shift reporting is also turned on, shift keys alone are also returned as keystrokes.

- To read double-byte character set (DBCS) codes, you must make two calls to *KbdCharIn*. The first character of a DBCS code is indicated by bit 7 = 1 in the status byte.

- In real mode, the keyboard handle is ignored.

Related functions: *DosRead, KbdPeek, KbdSetStatus, KbdStringIn.*

KbdClose

Destroys a logical keyboard that was created with *KbdOpen*. If the logical keyboard has the input focus, the focus is freed. Any characters waiting in the logical keyboard's input buffer are discarded.

WORD   Keyboard handle

Note:

- The default logical keyboard (0) cannot be closed.

Related functions: *KbdFlushBuffer, KbdFreeFocus, KbdOpen.*

KbdDeRegister

Restores the default keyboard input routines for the current screen group; deregisters any alternative keyboard API routines that were installed with *KbdRegister*.

No parameters

Related functions: *KbdRegister, MouDeRegister, VioDeRegister.*

KbdFlushBuffer   [FAPI]

Clears the keyboard input buffer and discards any waiting characters. The buffer is flushed only if the indicated keyboard has the input focus or is the default keyboard.

WORD   Keyboard handle (default = 0)

Note:

- In real mode, the keyboard handle is ignored.

Related functions: *KbdCharIn, KbdGetFocus, KbdStringIn.*

KbdFreeFocus

Removes the bond between the physical keyboard and the specified logical keyboard.

WORD   Keyboard handle

Note:

- The default keyboard handle (0) should not be used with this function.

Related functions: *KbdClose, KbdGetFocus, KbdOpen.*

KbdGetCp

Returns an identifier for the code page which is currently used by the keyboard subsystem to translate scan codes into ASCII characters.

DWORD	Reserved (0)
PTR WORD	Receives code page ID
WORD	Keyboard handle (default = 0)

Related functions: *DosGetCp, DosSetCp, KbdSetCp, VioGetCp, VioSetCp.*

KbdGetFocus

Binds the specified logical keyboard to the physical keyboard for subsequent input calls. Only one process and one logical keyboard can own the keyboard input focus at any given time; other processes calling *KbdGetFocus* will be blocked or receive an error status until the focus is available.

WORD	Wait/no-wait flag	
	0	*Wait until the keyboard is available*
	1	*Do not wait for the focus; return with an error if the keyboard is not available*
WORD	Keyboard handle	

Note:

■ The default keyboard handle (0) should not be used with this function.

Related functions: *KbdFreeFocus, KbdOpen.*

KbdGetStatus   [FAPI]

Obtains the current state of the keyboard, including the input mode, echo state, shift state, interim character flags, and the turnaround (logical end-of-line) character.

PTR BUFFER   Receives keyboard status in the following format:

Offset	Length	Description	
00H	*2*	*Size (10 in OS/2 versions 1.0 and 1.1)*	
02H	*2*	*Status*	
		Bit(s)	*Significance (if set)*
		0	*Echo is on*
		1	*Echo is off*
		2	*Binary ("raw") mode is on*
		3	*ASCII ("cooked") mode is on*
		4–6	*Reserved*
		7	*Turnaround character is 2 bytes*
		8	*Shift reporting is on*
		9–15	*Reserved*

Offset	Length	Description
04H	2	Turnaround character (if bit 7 of the status byte is 0, the upper byte of this field is undefined)
06H	2	Interim character flags

Bit(s)	Significance (if set)
0–4	Reserved
5	On-the-spot conversion requested
6	Reserved
7	Interim character
8–15	Reserved

Offset	Length	Description
08H	2	Keyboard shift state

Bit	Significance (if set)
0	Right Shift key down
1	Left Shift key down
2	Either Ctrl key down
3	Either Alt key down
4	Scroll Lock on
5	Num Lock on
6	Caps Lock on
7	Insert on
8	Left Ctrl key down
9	Left Alt key down
10	Right Ctrl key down
11	Right Alt key down
12	Scroll Lock key down
13	Num Lock key down
14	Caps Lock key down
15	SysReq key down

WORD   Keyboard handle (default = 0)

Notes:

- When the keyboard is in binary mode, and shift reporting is on, shift keys alone are also reported as keystrokes.

- In real mode, the keyboard handle is ignored, and the function does not support interim characters or the turnaround character.

Related function: *KbdSetStatus*.

KbdOpen

Creates a new logical keyboard and returns a handle, which can be used to bind the logical keyboard to the physical keyboard with *KbdGetFocus*. The new keyboard is initialized to use the system default code page.

PTR WORD   Receives keyboard handle

Related functions: *DosGetCp, DosSetCp, KbdClose, KbdFreeFocus, KbdGetCp, KbdGetFocus, KbdSetCp*.

KbdPeek   [FAPI]

Returns the next keyboard character and its scan code, if a character is waiting, without removing it from the keyboard input buffer. This allows a program to "look ahead" by one character.

PTR BUFFER   Receives character data

Offset	Length	Description
00H	1	ASCII character code
01H	1	Scan code
02H	1	Status

Bit(s)	Significance (if set)
0	Shift status returned without character
1–4	Reserved (0)
5	On-the-spot conversion requested
6	Character ready
7	Interim character

Offset	Length	Description
03H	1	Reserved (0)
04H	2	Shift state

Bit	Significance (if set)
0	Right Shift key down
1	Left Shift key down
2	Either Ctrl key down
3	Either Alt key down
4	Scroll Lock on
5	Num Lock on
6	Caps Lock on
7	Insert on
8	Left Ctrl key down
9	Left Alt key down
10	Right Ctrl key down
11	Right Alt key down
12	Scroll Lock key down
13	Num Lock key down
14	Caps Lock key down
15	SysReq key down

Offset	Length	Description
06H	4	Time stamp (msec. since the system was turned on or restarted)

WORD   Keyboard handle (default = 0)

Notes:

- If bit 6 of the status byte (offset 2 in the buffer) is 1, a character is ready and the remainder of the buffer is valid. If the same bit is 0, no character is waiting and the remaining data is undefined.

- Extended characters (such as cursor keys or Alt-key combinations) are indicated by a 00H or an E0H in the ASCII character field. The key is identified by examination of the scan code.

- If the keyboard is in ASCII ("cooked") mode, some control keys (such as ^S) receive special handling. If binary ("raw") mode is turned on with *KbdSetStatus*, all control keys are passed through to the application; if shift reporting is also turned on, shift keys alone are also returned as keystrokes.

- To read double-byte character set (DBCS) codes, make two calls to *KbdPeek*. The first character of a DBCS code is indicated by bit 7 = 1 in the status byte.

- In real mode, the function does not support interim characters and does not return the time stamp in the data structure. The status field can take the values 00H or 40H. The keyboard handle is ignored.

Related functions: *KbdCharIn, KbdSetStatus, KbdStringIn.*

KbdRegister

Registers a replacement routine to service one or more keyboard API functions for the current screen group. Functions which are not registered continue to be serviced by the Base Keyboard Subsystem (BKSCALLS.DLL).

PTR ASCIIZ	Pathname of dynlink library
PTR ASCIIZ	Name of library entry point
DWORD	Identifies the keyboard function(s) being registered

Bit(s)	*Function (if set)*
0	*KbdCharIn*
1	*KbdPeek*
2	*KbdFlushBuffer*
3	*KbdGetStatus*
4	*KbdSetStatus*
5	*KbdStringIn*
6	*KbdOpen*
7	*KbdClose*
8	*KbdGetFocus*
9	*KbdFreeFocus*
10	*KbdGetCp*
11	*KbdSetCp*
12	*KbdXlate*
13	*KbdSetCustXt*
14–31	*Reserved (0)*

Notes:

- A registered replacement for a keyboard subsystem receives control with the following items on the stack:
  - 32-bit KBDCALLS.DLL return address (top of stack)
  - 16-bit application program's DS register
  - 16-bit KBDCALLS.DLL internal return address
  - 16–bit function code

0	*KbdCharIn*
1	*KbdPeek*
2	*KbdFlushBuffer*
3	*KbdGetStatus*
4	*KbdSetStatus*
5	*KbdStringIn*
6	*KbdOpen*

16-bit function code, *continued*

7	*KbdClose*
8	*KbdGetFocus*
9	*KbdFreeFocus*
10	*KbdGetCp*
11	*KbdSetCp*
12	*KbdXlate*
13	*KbdSetCustXt*

□ 32-bit application return address

□ Function-specific parameters placed on stack by application program

The replacement routine must exit by a far return with the stack unchanged. The contents of AX are interpreted as follows:

AX <> –1	*Kbd* function performed, AX contains zero or error code; return to application
AX = –1	Replacement subsystem did nothing; invoke the appropriate base subsystem routine and return its status to the application

■ Replacement keyboard API routines can be registered by only one process per screen group at a time. *KbdRegister* calls by other processes fail until the default keyboard routines are restored with *KbdDeRegister*.

Related functions: *KbdDeRegister, KbdFlushBuffer, MouRegister, VioRegister*.

KbdSetCp

Selects the code page that is used to translate keyboard scan codes into ASCII characters for the current screen group.

WORD	Reserved (0)	
WORD	Code page ID	
	0000	*Default code page*
	0437	*USA*
	0850	*Multilingual*
	0860	*Portuguese*
	0863	*French-Canadian*
	0865	*Nordic*
WORD	Keyboard handle (default = 0)	

Related functions: *DosSetCp, KbdGetCp, KbdSetCustXt, VioSetCp*.

KbdSetCustXt

Installs a custom code page for the specified logical keyboard. The code page is used to translate scan codes to ASCII characters.

PTR BUFFER	Contains translate table
WORD	Keyboard handle (default = 0)

Note:

- The system uses the custom code page in its original location within the requesting process's memory space. The process must maintain the code page in place until another code page is selected with *KbdSetCp*, *DosSetCp*, or *KbdSetCustXt*.

Related functions: *DosSetCp*, *KbdSetCp*, *KbdXlate*, *VioSetCp*.

KbdSetStatus   [FAPI]

Sets the state of certain keyboard toggles and flags that affect the behavior of the keyboard input operations *KbdCharIn*, *KbdPeek*, and *KbdStringIn*.

PTR BUFFER   Contains keyboard status in the following form:

Offset	Length	Description
00H	2	Size (10 in OS/2 versions 1.0 and 1.1)
02H	2	Mask for changes to keyboard state

Bit(s)	Significance (if set)
0	Echo is on
1	Echo is off
2	Binary ("raw") mode is on
3	ASCII ("cooked") mode is on
4	Modify shift state
5	Modify interim character flag
6	Modify turnaround character
7	Turnaround character is two bytes (meaningful only if bit 6 = 1)
8	Turn on shift reporting
9–15	Reserved

Offset	Length	Description
04H	2	Turnaround character (if bit 7 of the mask word is 0, only the lower byte of this field is significant)
06H	2	Interim character flags

Bit(s)	Significance (if set)
0–4	Reserved (0)
5	On-the-spot conversion requested
6	Reserved (0)
7	Interim character
8–15	Reserved (0)

Offset	Length	Description
08H	2	Keyboard shift state

Bit(s)	Significance (if set)
0–3	Reserved
4	Scroll Lock on
5	Num Lock on
6	Caps Lock on
7	Insert on
8–15	Reserved

WORD   Keyboard handle (default = 0)

Notes:

- In normal use, *KbdGetStatus* should be called first to fill in the structure with valid information. The appropriate fields can then be changed and written back to the system with *KbdSetStatus*.

- If bits 0 and 1 of the keyboard mask are both cleared (0), the echo state of the keyboard is not altered. If bits 2 and 3 are both cleared (0), the binary/ASCII state of the keyboard is not altered. If bits 0 and 1 are both set or if bits 2 and 3 are both set, the *KbdSetStatus* call returns an error.

- In real mode, interim characters and the turnaround character are not supported. Binary mode with echo on is not supported. The keyboard handle is ignored.

Related functions: *KbdCharIn, KbdGetStatus, KbdPeek, KbdStringIn.*

KbdStringIn   [FAPI]

Reads a string of characters from the keyboard. If the keyboard is in ASCII ("cooked") mode, the usual editing keys are active.

PTR BUFFER	Receives keyboard input string		
PTR BUFFER	Keyboard buffer information in a 4-byte structure:		
	Offset	*Length*	*Description*
	00H	*2*	*Contains length of keyboard input buffer (maximum = 255)*
	02H	*2*	*Contains zero or length of data in buffer to be edited; receives actual length of input*
WORD	Wait/no-wait flag		
	0	*Wait for input* (see Notes)	
	1	*Do not wait for input*	
WORD	Keyboard handle (default = 0)		

Notes:

- If the second word of the keyboard information structure is nonzero, the data in the keyboard input buffer is used as a template for editing.

- During input in ASCII mode, if the wait/no-wait flag = 0, the function blocks until the Enter key is pressed or the buffer is full. Wait/no-wait flag = 1 is not supported in ASCII mode.

- When *KbdStringIn* is called in binary mode and the wait/no-wait flag = 0, the function blocks until the buffer is full. (The Enter key receives no special handling and is placed in the buffer like any other key.) If the wait/no-wait flag = 1, the function returns immediately with as many waiting characters as will fit into the buffer.

- In real mode, the keyboard handle is ignored.

Related functions: *DosRead, KbdCharIn, KbdGetStatus, KbdPeek, KbdSetStatus.*

KbdSynch

Serializes access to the keyboard device driver by multiple processes within a screen group. *KbdSynch* requests ownership of a system semaphore that is cleared each time a keyboard function completes.

WORD	Wait/no-wait flag	
	0	*Wait for the semaphore*
	1	*Do not wait for the semaphore*

Note:

- *KbdSynch* is intended for use by a keyboard subsystem and is not normally called by applications.

Related function: *DosDevIOCtl*.

KbdXlate

Translates a scan code and its shift states into an ASCII character code.

PTR BUFFER Contains a scan code in the second byte of a 16-byte keyboard translation record:

Offset	Length	Description	
00H	*1*	*ASCII character code*	
01H	*1*	*Scan code*	
02H	*1*	*Status*	
		Bit(s)	*Significance (if set)*
		0	*Shift status returned without character*
		1–4	*Reserved (0)*
		5	*On-the-spot conversion requested*
		6	*Character is ready*
		7	*Interim character*
03H	*1*	*Reserved (0)*	
04H	*2*	*Keyboard shift state*	
		Bit	*Significance (if set)*
		0	*Right Shift key down*
		1	*Left Shift key down*
		2	*Either Ctrl key down*
		3	*Either Alt key down*
		4	*Scroll Lock on*
		5	*Num Lock on*
		6	*Caps Lock on*
		7	*Insert on*
		8	*Left Ctrl key down*
		9	*Left Alt key down*
		10	*Right Ctrl key down*
		11	*Right Alt key down*
		12	*Scroll Lock key down*
		13	*Num Lock key down*
		14	*Caps Lock key down*
		15	*SysReq key down*

06H	4	*Time stamp (msec. since system was turned on or restarted)*
08H	2	*Keyboard device driver flags (see Notes)*
0AH	2	*Translation flags*

Bit(s)	Significance (if set)
0	*Translation complete*
1–15	*Reserved (0)*

0CH	2	*Translation shift state (initially set to 0; nonzero during a multibyte character translation; becomes 0 again when translation is completed)*
0EH	2	*Reserved (0)*

The calling process receives the translated ASCII character code in the first byte of the same structure.

WORD   Keyboard handle (default = 0)

Notes:

- A process might need to call *KbdXlate* several times to complete a character, so the translation shift state parameter should not be modified unless a ''fresh start'' to translation is desired. The function clears the translation shift state when the character translation is complete.

- Keyboard device driver flags (in bytes 8 and 9 of the translation record) are defined as follows:

Bit(s)	Significance
0–5	*Action code for driver (independent of scan code)*

00H	*No special action*
01H	*Keyboard acknowledge (ACK)*
02H	*Secondary key prefix*
03H	*Keyboard overrun*
04H	*Resend request from keyboard*
05H	*Reboot key combination*
06H	*Stand-alone dump request*
07H	*Shift key*
08H	*Pause request (usually Ctrl-Num Lock)*
09H	*Pseudo-pause request (usually Ctrl-S)*
0AH	*Wake-up request (any key after a pause or pseudo-pause request)*
0BH	*Invalid accent combination*
0CH–0FH	*Reserved*
10H	*Accent key, affects following key translation*
11H	*Break key (usually Ctrl-Break)*
12H	*Pseudo-break key (usually Ctrl-C)*
13H	*Print screen request*
14H	*Print echo request (usually Ctrl-PrtSc)*
15H	*Pseudo-print echo request (usually Ctrl-P)*
16H	*Print flush request (usually Ctrl-Alt-PrtSc)*
17H–3FH	*Reserved*

Bit(s)	Significance
6	*= 0 if key make (depression)*
	= 1 if key break (release)

Bit(s)	Significance
7	= 1 if prior key was secondary key prefix
8	= 1 if multimake (typematic repeated key)
9	= 1 if key was translated using the prior accent key
10–13	Reserved (0)
14–15	Used for communication between monitors

Related function: *KbdSetCustXt.*

MouClose

Closes the mouse device and releases the logical mouse handle. If no other processes in the current screen group have a mouse handle open, the function removes the mouse pointer from the screen.

WORD   Mouse handle

Related function: *MouOpen.*

MouDeRegister

Restores the default mouse input routines for the current screen group; deregisters an alternative mouse subsystem that was previously installed with *MouRegister.*

No parameters

Related functions: *KbdDeRegister, MouRegister, VioDeRegister.*

MouDrawPtr

Displays the mouse pointer on the screen. Any exclusion areas specified with a previous *MouRemovePtr* call are canceled.

WORD   Mouse handle

Related functions: *MouOpen, MouRemovePtr, MouSetDevStatus.*

MouFlushQue

Discards any waiting mouse events for the current screen group.

WORD   Mouse handle

Related functions: *MouGetNumQueEl, MouOpen, MouReadEventQue.*

MouGetDevStatus

Returns the status of the mouse driver.

PTR WORD	Receives mouse status	
	Bit(s)	*Significance (if set)*
	0	*Event queue is busy*
	1	*Blocking read is in progress*
	2	*Flush input queue in progress*
	3	*Pointer-draw routine disabled because of unsupported display mode*
	4–7	*Reserved (0)*
	8	*Pointer-draw routine disabled*
	9	*Mouse data is returned in relative mickeys rather than absolute screen coordinates*
	10–15	*Reserved (0)*
WORD	Mouse handle	

Note:

■ [1.1] If the application is running in a Presentation Manager window, the returned status is always zero.

Related functions: *MouGetNumMickeys, MouOpen, MouSetDevStatus.*

MouGetEventMask

Returns the mouse driver's event mask for the current screen group. The mask defines the types of mouse interrupts that will generate an event record in the mouse driver's input queue.

PTR WORD	Receives event mask	
	Bit(s)	*Significance (if set)*
	0	*Mouse movement, no buttons down*
	1	*Mouse movement, button 1 down*
	2	*Button 1 down*
	3	*Mouse movement, button 2 down*
	4	*Button 2 down*
	5	*Mouse movement, button 3 down*
	6	*Button 3 down*
	7–15	*Reserved (0)*
WORD	Mouse handle	

Note:

■ Button 1 is defined as the left mouse button.

Related functions: *MouOpen, MouReadEventQue, MouSetEventMask.*

MouGetHotKey

Returns a code indicating which mouse button or combination of mouse buttons is the system hot key.

PTR WORD	Receives hot key indicator	
	Bit(s)	*Significance (if set)*
	0	*No hot key defined (overrides bits 1–3)*
	1	*Button 1 is hot key*
	2	*Button 2 is hot key*
	3	*Button 3 is hot key*
	4–15	*Reserved (0)*
WORD	Mouse handle	

Notes:

- Button 1 is the left mouse button.

- If multiple bits (other than bit 0) are set, the hot key is interpreted as a simultaneous pressing of the specified buttons. For example, if bits 1 and 2 are set, simultaneous pressing of buttons 1 and 2 is interpreted as the hot key.

Related functions: *MouGetNumButtons, MouOpen, MouSetHotKey.*

MouGetNumButtons

Returns the number of buttons supported by the current screen group's mouse driver.

PTR WORD	Receives number of mouse buttons (1–3)
WORD	Mouse handle

Related functions: *MouGetHotKey, MouOpen.*

MouGetNumMickeys

Returns the number of mickeys (units of mouse movement) per centimeter for the current screen group.

PTR WORD	Receives number of mickeys per centimeter of mouse travel
WORD	Mouse handle

Related functions: *MouGetDevStatus, MouOpen, MouSetDevStatus.*

MouGetNumQueEl

Returns the number of mouse events for the current screen group that are waiting in the mouse driver's event queue.

PTR BUFFER	Receives mouse event queue information in the following format:		
	Offset	*Length*	*Description*
	00H	*2*	*Number of waiting mouse events*
	02H	*2*	*Maximum number of mouse events (queue size)*
WORD	Mouse handle		

Related functions: *MouFlushQue, MouOpen, MouReadEventQue.*

MouGetPtrPos

Returns the screen position of the mouse pointer, using text or pixel coordinates as appropriate for the current display mode. Coordinate (0,0) is the upper left corner of the screen.

PTR BUFFER	Receives mouse pointer position in the following format:		
	Offset	*Length*	*Description*
	00H	*2*	y *(row) coordinate*
	02H	*2*	x *(column) coordinate*
WORD	Mouse handle		

Note:

■ [1.1] If the application is running in a Presentation Manager window, the pointer position is always returned in text coordinates. If the application window does not have the input focus, the function returns an error.

Related functions: *MouOpen, MouReadEventQue, MouSetPtrPos.*

MouGetPtrShape

Retrieves the mouse pointer shape for the current screen group.

PTR BUFFER	Receives mouse pointer shape in the form of AND and XOR masks that are meaningful to the pointer-draw routine		
PTR BUFFER	Pointer definition data in the following format:		
	Offset	*Length*	*Description*
	00H	*2*	*Contains the length of the buffer to receive the pointer shape; receives the length in bytes of the data used to build a mouse pointer image for each bit plane in the current display mode*
	02H	*2*	*Receives columns in mouse pointer image*
	04H	*2*	*Receives rows in mouse pointer image*
	06H	*2*	*Receives column offset (from left) of the hot spot within the pointer image*
	08H	*2*	*Receives row offset (from top) of the hot spot within the pointer image*
WORD	Mouse handle		

Note:

- In text mode, the pointer width and height are always 1, and the row and column offsets of the hot spot are always 0.

Related functions: *MouOpen, MouSetPtrShape.*

MouGetScaleFact

Returns the scaling factors applied to mouse coordinates for the current screen group. The scaling factors define the number of mickeys (units of mouse movement) that are equivalent to eight pixels of screen movement.

PTR BUFFER   Receives scaling factors in the following format:

Offset	Length	Description
00H	2	y *(row) scaling factor (1–32,767; default = 8)*
02H	2	x *(column) scaling factor (1–32,767; default = 16)*

WORD   Mouse handle

Related functions: *MouGetNumMickeys, MouOpen, MouSetScaleFact.*

MouInitReal

Initializes the real mode mouse driver.

PTR ASCIIZ   Pathname of pointer-draw driver, or null pointer

Notes:

- The pointer-draw driver must have been previously loaded by a *DEVICE=* statement in the CONFIG.SYS file, or a null pointer can be supplied to use the system default pointer-draw driver.

- This function is intended for use only by the Session Manager and should not ordinarily be called by application programs.

Related function: *MouOpen.*

MouOpen

Opens the mouse device for the current screen group and returns a handle, which can be used for subsequent mouse operations. The mouse pointer is not visible until *MouDrawPtr* is called.

PTR ASCIIZ   Pathname of pointer-draw driver, or null pointer
PTR WORD   Receives mouse handle

Notes:

- The default mouse state after a *MouOpen* operation is as follows:
  - □ Row (y) scaling factor = 8 and column (x) scaling factor = 16 (see *MouSetScaleFact*)
  - □ All events reported (see *MouSetEventMask*)

- ◻ Mouse event queue empty (see *MouReadEventQue* and *MouGetNumQueEl*)
- ◻ All settable mouse device status bits = 0 (see *MouSetDevStatus*)
- ◻ Pointer at the center of the screen (see *MouSetPtrPos*)
- ◻ Default pointer shape (see *MouSetPtrShape*)
- ◻ Exclusion area defined as the entire screen (see *MouDrawPtr* and *MouRemovePtr*)

- ■ The pointer-draw driver must have been previously loaded by a *DEVICE=* statement in the CONFIG.SYS file, or a null pointer can be supplied to use the system default pointer-draw driver.

Related functions: *KbdOpen, MouClose, MouDrawPtr, MouSetPtrPos.*

MouReadEventQue

Returns the mouse event data packet that is at the head of the mouse driver's input queue for the current screen group (that is, the oldest waiting event). The application can control which types of events generate records in the event queue with *MouSetDevStatus*.

PTR BUFFER	Receives mouse event data		
	Offset	*Length*	*Description*
	00H	2	*Mouse event flags*

		Bit(s)	*Significance (if set)*
		0	*Mouse movement, no buttons down*
		1	*Mouse movement, button 1 down*
		2	*Button 1 down*
		3	*Mouse movement, button 2 down*
		4	*Button 2 down*
		5	*Mouse movement, button 3 down*
		6	*Button 3 down*
		7–15	*Reserved (0)*

	Offset	*Length*	*Description*
	02H	4	*Time stamp (msec. since system turned on or restarted)*
	06H	2	y *(row) coordinate*
	08H	2	x *(column) coordinate*
PTR WORD	Contains wait/no-wait flag		
	0		*Do not wait for mouse event; return all zeros for event data if no event is waiting*
	1		*Wait for mouse event if none is ready*
WORD	Mouse handle		

Notes:

- ■ When an application is running full screen, the coordinates are expressed in character positions or pixels depending on the current display mode. When it is running in a Presentation Manager window, character coordinates are always returned.

- ■ Button 1 is the left mouse button.

Related functions: *MouGetNumQueEl, MouGetPtrPos, MouOpen.*

MouRegister

Registers a replacement routine to service one or more mouse API functions for the current screen group. Functions which are not registered continue to be serviced by the Base Mouse Subsystem (BMSCALLS.DLL).

PTR ASCIIZ	Pathname of dynlink library
PTR ASCIIZ	Name of library entry point
DWORD	Identifies the mouse function(s) being registered

Bit(s)	Function (if set)
0	MouGetNumButtons
1	MouGetNumMickeys
2	MouGetDevStatus
3	MouGetNumQueEl
4	MouReadEventQue
5	MouGetScaleFact
6	MouGetEventMask
7	MouSetScaleFact
8	MouSetEventMask
9	MouGetHotKey
10	MouSetHotKey
11	MouOpen
12	MouClose
13	MouGetPtrShape
14	MouSetPtrShape
15	MouDrawPtr
16	MouRemovePtr
17	MouGetPtrPos
18	MouSetPtrPos
19	MouInitReal
20	MouSetDevStatus
21–31	Reserved (0)

Notes:

- A registered replacement for a mouse subsystem receives control with the following items on the stack:
  - □ 32-bit MOUCALLS.DLL return address (top of stack)
  - □ 16-bit application program's DS register
  - □ 16-bit MOUCALLS.DLL internal return address
  - □ 16-bit function code

0	MouGetNumButtons
1	MouGetNumMickeys
2	MouGetDevStatus
3	MouGetNumQueEl
4	MouReadEventQue
5	MouGetScaleFact
6	MouGetEventMask
7	MouSetScaleFact
8	MouSetEventMask

16-bit function code, *continued*

9	*MouGetHotKey*
10	*MouSetHotKey*
11	*MouOpen*
12	*MouClose*
13	*MouGetPtrShape*
14	*MouSetPtrShape*
15	*MouDrawPtr*
16	*MouRemovePtr*
17	*MouGetPtrPos*
18	*MouSetPtrPos*
19	*MouInitReal*
20	*MouSetDevStatus*

□ 32-bit application return address

□ Function-specific parameters placed on stack by application program

The replacement routine must exit by a far return with the stack unchanged. The contents of AX are interpreted as follows:

AX <> –1   *Mou* function performed, AX contains 0 or error code; return to application

AX = –1   Replacement subsystem did nothing; invoke the appropriate base subsystem routine and return its status to the application

■ Replacement mouse API routines can be registered by only one process per screen group at a time. *MouRegister* calls by other processes fail until the default mouse routines are restored with *MouDeRegister*.

Related functions: *KbdRegister, MouDeRegister, MouOpen, VioRegister.*

MouRemovePtr

Notifies the mouse driver not to draw the mouse pointer within the specified area. Such an exclusion area is cancelled with *MouDrawPtr* or replaced with another call to *MouRemovePtr*.

PTR BUFFER   Contains mouse pointer exclusion area definition in the following format:

Offset	Length	Description
00H	2	Upper left y *(row) coordinate*
02H	2	Upper left x *(column) coordinate*
04H	2	Lower right y *(row) coordinate*
06H	2	Lower right x *(column) coordinate*

WORD   Mouse handle

Notes:

■ After a *MouOpen* call, the initial exclusion area is the entire screen (that is, the mouse pointer is not visible).

■ Coordinates are expressed in character positions or pixels as appropriate for the current display mode.

Related functions: *MouDrawPtr, MouOpen, MouSetPtrShape.*

MouSetDevStatus

Configures the mouse driver for the current screen group.

PTR WORD   Contains mouse status flags

Bit(s)	*Significance (if set)*
0–7	*Reserved (0)*
8	*Do not call pointer-draw routine at mouse interrupt time*
9	*Return mouse movements in relative mickeys rather than absolute screen coordinates*
10–15	*Reserved (0)*

WORD   Mouse handle

Related functions: *MouGetDevStatus, MouGetNumMickeys, MouOpen.*

MouSetEventMask

Passes an event mask to the mouse driver for the current screen group. The mask defines the changes in mouse state that generate an event record in the driver's input queue.

PTR WORD   Contains event mask

Bit(s)	*Significance (if set)*
0	*Mouse movement, no buttons down*
1	*Mouse movement, button 1 down*
2	*Button 1 down*
3	*Mouse movement, button 2 down*
4	*Button 2 down*
5	*Mouse movement, button 3 down*
6	*Button 3 down*
7–15	*Reserved (0)*

WORD   Mouse handle

Note:

■ If a specific event is not enabled, it can still be reported in the event records generated by those events that *are* enabled.

Related functions: *MouGetEventMask, MouOpen.*

MouSetHotKey

Assigns a mouse button or combination of buttons as the system hot key.

PTR WORD   Contains hot key indicator

Bit(s)	*Significance (if set)*
0	*No hot key defined (overrides bits 1–3)*
1	*Button 1 is hot key*
2	*Button 2 is hot key*

Bit(s)	Significance (if set)
3	Button 3 is hot key
4–15	Reserved (0)

WORD — Mouse handle

Notes:

- Button 1 is the left mouse button.

- If multiple bits (other than bit 0) are set, the hot key is interpreted as a simultaneous pressing of the specified buttons. For example, if bits 1 and 2 are set, simultaneous pressing of buttons 1 and 2 is interpreted as the hot key.

- Only one process can set and reset the mouse hot key at a time. After a process has called *MouSetHotKey* with bit 0 of the hot key indicator = 0, requests from other processes fail until the same process has called *MouSetHotKey* with bit 0 of the hot key indicator = 1.

Related functions: *DosSystemService, MouGetHotKey, MouOpen.*

MouSetPtrPos

Repositions the mouse pointer. Supply the coordinates as a character or pixel position according to the current display mode. Position (0,0) is the upper left corner of the screen. The mouse pointer is not displayed if the new position lies within an exclusion area defined with *MouRemovePtr.*

PTR BUFFER — Contains mouse pointer position in the following format:

Offset	Length	Description
00H	2	y *(row) coordinate*
02H	2	x *(column) coordinate*

WORD — Mouse handle

Note:

- [1.1] If the application is running in a Presentation Manager window, always specify the position in text coordinates. If the application window does not have the input focus, the function returns an error.

Related functions: *MouDrawPtr, MouGetPtrPos, MouOpen, MouRemovePtr.*

MouSetPtrShape

Defines the mouse pointer's shape and size for the current screen group.

PTR BUFFER — Contains mouse pointer shape in the form of AND and XOR masks that are meaningful to the pointer-draw routine

PTR BUFFER — Pointer definition data in the following format:

Offset	Length	Description
00H	2	*On call, contains the length of the buffer to receive the pointer shape. Upon return, receives the total length, in bytes, of data used to build a mouse pointer image for each bit plane in the current display mode*

Offset	Length	Description
02H	2	Contains columns in mouse pointer image
04H	2	Contains rows in mouse pointer image
06H	2	Contains column offset (from left) of the hot spot within the pointer image
08H	2	Contains row offset (from top) of the hot spot within the pointer image

WORD   Mouse handle

Notes:

- For text display modes, specify the mouse pointer shape by a single word:

Bit(s)	Significance
0–7	Character
8–10	Foreground color
11	Intensity
12–14	Background color
15	Blinking

- In text mode, the pointer width and height are always 1, and the row and column offsets of the hot spot are always 0.

Related functions: *MouDrawPtr, MouGetPtrShape, MouOpen, MouRemovePtr.*

MouSetScaleFact

Assigns mouse scaling factors for the current screen group. The scaling factors define the number of mickeys (units of mouse movement) that constitute eight pixels of screen movement.

PTR BUFFER   Contains scaling factors in the following format:

Offset	Length	Description
00H	2	y (row) scaling factor (1–32,767; default = 8)
02H	2	x (column) scaling factor (1–32,767; default = 16)

WORD   Mouse handle

Related functions: *MouGetNumMickeys, MouGetScaleFact, MouOpen.*

MouSynch

Serializes access to the mouse device driver by multiple processes within a screen group. *MouSynch* requests ownership of a system semaphore that is cleared each time a mouse function completes.

WORD   Wait/no-wait flag

0	*Wait for the semaphore*
1	*Do not wait for the semaphore*

Related function: *DosDevIOCtl*.

VioAssociate [AVIO] [1.1]

Associates a *Vio* presentation space with a screen device context. The output from subsequent calls to *VioShowPS* and *VioShowBuf* is directed to the specified context.

DWORD	Device context handle
WORD	Presentation space handle

Notes:

- If the presentation space is currently associated with another device context, that link is broken. Similarly, if another presentation space is associated with the device context, that link is broken.

- If a NULL handle is supplied for the device context, the presentation space is disassociated from the device context.

Related functions: *VioCreatePS, VioShowBuf, VioShowPS*.

VioCreateLogFont [AVIO] [1.1]

Creates a logical font for use with a *Vio* presentation space. The system chooses the available physical font that most closely matches the specified attributes.

PTR BUFFER   Contains font attribute information

Offset	Length	Description	
00H	2	Length of structure (64 bytes in OS/2 version 1.1)	
02H	2	Font characteristics	
		Bit	Significance (if set)
		0	Italic
		1	Underline
		2	Reverse
		3	Outline (hollow)
		4	Strikeout
04H	4	Match number from VioQueryFonts (0 = use best match)	
08H	32	ASCIIZ typeface name	
28H	2	Font registry number	
2AH	2	Code page identifier	
2EH	4	Maximum baseline extent	
32H	4	Average character width	
36H	2	Width class	
38H	2	Weight class	

Offset	Length	Description		
3AH	2	Kerning/proportional spacing flags		
		Bit(s)	Significance (if set)	
		0	Reserved (0)	
		1	Nonproportional font	
		2	Kernable font (must be 0)	
		3–15	Reserved (0)	
3CH	2	Font quality		
		Bit(s)	Significance (if set)	
		0	Default (must be 1)	
		1	Draft (must be 0)	
		2	Proof (must be 0)	
		3–15	Reserved (0)	
3EH	2	Reserved (0)		

DWORD	Local identifier for the font (1–3)
PTR BUFFER	Eight character name for logical font
WORD	Presentation space handle

Note:

- If the entire attribute buffer is zero except for the code page, the default font for the specified code page is selected.

Related function: *VioQueryFonts*.

VioCreatePS   [AVIO] [1.1]

Creates a *Vio* presentation space of the specified dimensions and returns a handle.

PTR WORD	Receives presentation space handle
WORD	Height in character rows
WORD	Width in character columns
WORD	Presentation space format (0)
WORD	Number of attribute bytes (1 or 3)
WORD	Reserved (0)

Notes:

- The size of the presentation space (width * height * (number of attribute bytes + 1)) must not exceed 32 KB.

- If the number of attributes parameter is 1, then the total storage for each character position in the presentation space is two bytes, with the following format:

Offset	Length	Description
00H	1	Character code
01H	1	CGA text mode–compatible attribute

- If the number of attributes parameter is 3, then the total storage for each character position in the presentation space is four bytes, with the following format:

Offset	Length	Description
00H	1	Character code
01H	1	Foreground/background colors
02H	1	Underline, reverse, blink, font ID
03H	1	Spare (may be used by application)

Related functions: *VioAssociate, VioDestroyPS*.

VioDeleteSetID [AVIO] [1.1]

Releases an identifier that was previously assigned to a logical font with *VioCreateLogFont*.

DWORD   Logical font identifier (−1, 1, 2, or 3)
WORD   Presentation space handle

Note:

- If the logical font identifier is −1, the function releases all logical font identifiers.

Related functions: *VioCreateLogFont, VioCreatePS*.

VioDeRegister

Deactivates an alternative video subsystem that was previously registered for the current screen group. The default services provided by the Base Video Subsystem (BVSCALLS.DLL) for each *Vio* call are restored.

No parameters

Related functions: *KbdDeRegister, MouDeRegister, VioRegister*.

VioDestroyPS [AVIO] [1.1]

Destroys a *Vio* presentation space.

WORD   Presentation space handle

Related function: *VioCreatePS*.

VioEndPopUp

Ends a video display popup operation by a background process; releases control of the physical screen and keyboard previously obtained with *VioPopUp*.

WORD   Video handle (0 = default)

Related function: *VioPopUp*.

VioGetAnsi

Returns a flag indicating whether interpretation of ANSI escape sequences is enabled or disabled.

PTR WORD	Receives flag	
	0	*ANSI support is disabled*
	1	*ANSI support is enabled*
WORD	Video handle (0 = default)	

Related functions: *VioSetAnsi, VioWrtTTY.*

VioGetBuf [FAPI]

Returns a pointer to the logical video buffer (LVB). Because each screen group has its own distinct LVB, a process can manipulate the buffer directly at any time without interfering with those of other screen groups. The process requests update of the physical display from the LVB by calling *VioShowBuf.*

PTR DWORD	Receives pointer to logical video buffer
PTR WORD	Receives length in bytes of logical video buffer
WORD	Video handle (0 = default)

Note:

■ The dimensions of the LVB (columns and rows) for the current display mode can be obtained from *VioGetMode.*

Related functions: *VioGetMode, VioGetPhysBuf, VioShowBuf.*

VioGetConfig [FAPI]

Returns information about the video adapter and monitor.

WORD	Reserved (0)		
PTR BUFFER	Receives video configuration data in the following format:		
	Offset	*Length*	*Description*
	00H	*2*	*Length of structure (always 10 in OS/2 versions 1.0 and 1.1)*
	02H	*2*	*Adapter type*
			0 = Monochrome Adapter (MDA)
			1 = Color/Graphics Adapter (CGA)
			2 = Enhanced Graphics Adapter (EGA)
			3 = Video Graphics Array (VGA, PS/2)
			4–6 = reserved
			7 = 8514/A Display Adapter

Offset	Length	Description
04H	2	Display type
		0 = Monochrome Display
		1 = RGB Color Display
		2 = Enhanced Color Display
		3 = 8503 Analog Monochrome Display
		4 = 8512 or 8513 Analog Color Display
		5–8 = reserved
		9 = 8514 Analog Color Display
06H	4	Bytes of memory on video adapter

WORD   Video handle (0 = default)

Related functions: *DosDevConfig, VioGetState, VioGetMode.*

VioGetCp

Returns the identifier for the code page used by the video subsystem for the current screen group.

WORD   Reserved (0)
PTR WORD   Receives code page ID (0 = default ROM code page)
WORD   Video handle (0 = default)

Related functions: *DosGetCp, DosSetCp, KbdGetCp, VioSetCp.*

VioGetCurPos   [FAPI]

Returns the cursor position in text coordinates. Position (0,0) is the upper left corner of the display.

PTR WORD   Receives *y* (row) coordinate
PTR WORD   Receives *x* (column) coordinate
WORD   Video handle (0 = default)

Related functions: *VioGetCurType, VioSetCurPos.*

VioGetCurType   [FAPI]

Returns information about the cursor shape, size, and attribute.

PTR BUFFER   Receives cursor characteristics in the following format:

Offset	Length	Description
00H	2	Cursor start line
02H	2	Cursor end line
04H	2	Cursor width (0 = default; 1 = maximum valid value in text modes)
06H	2	Cursor attribute (0 = visible; −1 = hidden)

WORD   Video handle (0 = default)

Note:

- The valid values for the cursor starting and ending lines are determined by the character cell dimensions in the current display mode. You can calculate the size of the character cell from the information returned by *VioGetMode*.

Related functions: *VioGetCurPos, VioGetMode, VioSetCurType*.

VioGetDeviceCellSize   [AVIO]   [1.1]

Returns the character cell height and width in pels (pixels) for the specified presentation space.

PTR WORD	Receives pel rows per character cell
PTR WORD	Receives pel columns per character cell
WORD	Presentation space handle

Related functions: *VioCreatePS, VioSetDeviceCellSize*.

VioGetFont

Returns the specified or current font table. The font is a bitmap that defines the appearance of each character on the screen.

PTR BUFFER   Contains information about the type of font request, receives information about font characteristics.

Offset	Length	Description
00H	2	*Contains length (always 14 bytes in OS/2 versions 1.0 and 1.1)*
02H	2	*Contains request type* *0 = get current font* *1 = get ROM (default) font*
04H	2	*Contains width of character cell in pixels for desired font (text modes); receives width of character cell for font (graphics modes)*
06H	2	*Contains height of character cell in pixels for desired font (text modes); receives height of character cell for font (graphics modes)*
08H	4	*Contains address of buffer to receive font, or null pointer; in latter case, receives pointer to font*
0CH	2	*Contains length of buffer to receive font; receives actual length of font*

WORD   Video handle (0 = default)

Notes:

- See *VioSetFont* for a list of the available fonts on each type of display adapter.

- If a null pointer is supplied for the font buffer, OS/2 allocates memory to hold the font and returns a pointer to memory in the same location in the structure.

Related functions: *VioGetCp, VioSetFont*.

VioGetMode   [FAPI]

Returns the characteristics of the current display mode, including the screen dimensions, number of display-able colors, and display mode type (text or graphics).

PTR BUFFER   Contains length of structure in the first word; receives display mode information in the following format:

Offset	Length	Description
00H	2	Contains length (minimum 3, maximum 14 in OS/2 versions 1.0 and 1.1; lengths > 3 must be even)
02H	1	Display mode type

	Bit(s)	Significance
	0	0 = monochrome-compatible mode
		1 = other
	1	0 = text mode
		1 = graphics mode
	2	0 = enable color burst
		1 = disable color burst
	3–7	Reserved

Offset	Length	Description
03H	1	Displayable colors
		0 = monochrome-compatible mode
		1 = 2 colors
		2 = 4 colors
		4 = 16 colors
		8 = 256 colors
04H	2	Horizontal (x) resolution in text columns
06H	2	Vertical (y) resolution in text rows
08H	2	Horizontal (x) resolution in pixels
0AH	2	Vertical (y) resolution in pixels
0CH	2	Reserved (0)

WORD   Video handle (0 = default)

Note:

- On display adapters other than the CGA, the color burst bit is meaningless.

Related functions: *VioGetConfig, VioGetState, VioSetMode.*

VioGetOrg   [AVIO]   [1.1]

Returns the coordinates of the character which is currently displayed at the upper left corner of the presentation space's window.

PTR WORD   Receives row (y) coordinate
PTR WORD   Receives column (x) coordinate
WORD   Presentation space handle

Note:

- Coordinates returned are expressed in character columns and rows rather than in pels.

Related functions: *VioCreatePS, VioSetOrg*.

VioGetPhysBuf [FAPI]

Returns a selector or selectors which can be used to directly manipulate the video adapter's physical display buffer. This function, and the selectors it returns, can be used only while the process's screen group is in the foreground. Selectors are allocated from the process's LDT and should be released with *DosFreeSeg* when they are no longer needed.

PTR BUFFER — Contains physical address and length of video buffer; receives selector(s) for buffer in the following format:

Offset	Length	Description
00H	4	Contains starting address of video buffer, specified as a 32-bit physical (linear) address
04H	4	Contains length of video buffer
08H	n	Receives n/2 selectors that map to video buffer (one selector per 64 KB)

WORD — Video handle (0 = default)

Notes:

- The buffer addresses to be mapped must fall in the range A0000H through BFFFFH.

- The process should use *VioScrLock* to prevent session switching while it is altering the display buffer.

Related functions: *VioScrLock, VioScrUnLock*.

VioGetState

Returns current settings of the palette registers, the border (overscan) color, or the intensity/blink toggle.

PTR BUFFER — Contains request type; receives information about the video state (*see Notes*)
WORD — Video handle (0 = default)

Notes:

- The request block for the palette registers has the following format:

Offset	Length	Description
00H	2	Contains length of structure (maximum 38 in OS/2 versions 1.0 and 1.1)
02H	2	Contains 0 = get palette registers
04H	2	Contains number of first palette register to return (0–15)
06H	n	Receives contents of n/2 palette registers, 16 bits per register

- The request block for border (overscan) color has the following format:

Offset	Length	Description
00H	2	Contains length of structure (6 in OS/2 versions 1.0 and 1.1)
02H	2	Contains 1 = get border color
04H	2	Receives border color

- The request block for the intensity/blink toggle has the following format:

Offset	Length	Description
00H	2	Contains length of structure (6 in OS/2 versions 1.0 and 1.1)
02H	2	Contains 2 = get intensity/blink toggle
04H	2	Receives toggle value
		0 = blinking foreground colors are enabled
		1 = intensified background colors are enabled

Related functions: *VioGetConfig, VioGetMode, VioSetState.*

VioModeUndo

Cancels a *VioModeWait* call issued by another thread within the same process.

WORD	Ownership option for *VioModeWait*
	0 *Retain ownership*
	1 *Give up ownership*
WORD	Termination option (for thread currently blocked in *VioModeWait* call)
	0 *Return error code to thread*
	1 *Terminate thread*
WORD	Reserved (0)

Related function: *VioModeWait.*

VioModeWait

Notifies the application to restore the state of the video adapter after a *VioPopUp* by another process. The thread calling *VioModeWait* is blocked until the restore operation is needed. The thread must then write the appropriate values to the adapter and immediately reissue the *VioModeWait*.

WORD	Request type
	0 *Notify application to restore its video mode at the end of a video pop-up by another process*
	<> 0 *Reserved (not used in OS/2 version 1.0 or 1.1)*
PTR WORD	Receives code for the operation to be performed upon return from *VioModeWait*
	0 *Restore display mode*
	<> 0 *Reserved (not used in OS/2 version 1.0 or 1.1)*
WORD	Reserved (0)

Notes:

- File system and loader API functions should not be called by a *VioModeWait* thread; avoidance of such calls eliminates any chance of an attempted pop-up by the system's critical error handler.

- *VioModeWait* is used by applications which write directly to the control registers of the video adapter. Applications which only use *Vio* calls to set the video mode, palette registers, and so on need not use *VioModeWait*.

- OS/2 saves and restores the contents of the video display buffer across a pop-up.

- Graphics mode applications may need both a *VioModeWait* thread and a *VioSavRedrawWait* thread; the latter thread provides for saving and restoring both the state of the video adapter and the contents of the display buffer across switches between sessions.

Related functions: *VioModeUndo*, *VioSavRedrawUndo*, *VioSavRedrawWait*.

VioPopUp

Asserts control of the physical screen and keyboard, regardless of which session is currently in the foreground. After a successful *VioPopUp* call, the requesting process can use other *Vio* and *Kbd* calls to interact with the operator. During a pop-up, *Vio* calls by other processes are blocked and session switching is disabled.

PTR WORD	Contains option flags for pop-up	
	Bit(s)	*Significance*
	0	*0 = return immediately with error code if pop-up is not available*
		1 = wait until pop-up is available
	1	*0 = nontransparent mode; display is placed into 80-by-25 text mode, the screen is cleared, and the cursor is placed in the upper left corner*
		1 = transparent mode; if the display is in an 80-by-25 text mode, no mode change occurs, and the screen contents and cursor position are not disturbed
	2–15	*Reserved (0)*
WORD	Video handle (0 = default)	

Notes:

- Regardless of the mode (transparent or nontransparent), OS/2 always restores the contents of the screen at the time of the pop-up when the application issues *VioEndPopUp*.

- You cannot use the selector obtained from a previous *VioGetPhysBuf* call during a pop-up.

- You cannot use the following API calls during a pop-up:

DosExecPgm	*VioModeWait*	*VioRegister*	*VioScrUnLock*
VioDeRegister	*VioPopUp*	*VioSavRedrawUndo*	*VioSetAnsi*
VioGetBuf	*VioPrtSc*	*VioSavRedrawWait*	*VioSetMode*
VioGetPhysBuf	*VioPrtScToggle*	*VioScrLock*	*VioShowBuf*
VioModeUndo			

Related function: *VioEndPopUp*.

VioPrtSc

Copies the contents of the screen to the printer. The Base Video Subsystem (BVSCALLS.DLL) does not support this function in graphics modes; a process can install an alternate routine with *VioRegister. VioPrtSc* is intended for use by the Task Manager and should not be called by application programs.

WORD   Video handle (0 = default)

Related functions: *None*.

VioPrtScToggle

Enables or disables echoing of characters to the printer during processing of *DosWrite* (to standard output) or *VioWrtTTY* calls. *VioPrtScToggle* is intended for use by the Task Manager and should not be called by application programs.

WORD   Video handle (0 = default)

Related functions: *None*.

VioQueryFonts   [AVIO] [1.1]

Returns a list of the available fonts that match the specified typeface.

PTR DWORD   Contains the length of the buffer to receive the font metrics
PTR BUFFER   Receives one or more entries specifying the metrics of the matching fonts
                 (*see Notes*)
DWORD   Local font identifier (1–3)
PTR DWORD   Receives the number of matching fonts
PTR ASCIIZ   Typeface name of desired fonts
WORD   Presentation space handle

Notes:

- Unlike other kernel API functions, a nonzero value returned in AX does not necessarily indicate an error. The function returns the number of fonts not retrieved (because buffer space was insufficient), zero if all fonts were retrieved, or −1 if an error occurred.

- See *GpiQueryFontMetrics* in the Presentation Manager programmer's reference manual for the format of each font metrics entry.

Related functions: *VioCreateLogFont, VioCreatePS*.

VioQuerySetIds   [AVIO]   [1.1]

Returns a list of all loaded fonts.

PTR BUFFER	Receives local identifiers
PTR BUFFER	Receives 8-character font names
PTR BUFFER	Receives object types for the fonts
DWORD	Number of local font identifiers in use
WORD	Presentation space handle

Related functions: *VioCreateLogFont, VioCreatePS*.

VioReadCellStr   [FAPI]

Reads a series of character-attribute pairs (cells) from the logical video buffer (LVB), starting at the specified position.

PTR BUFFER	Receives character-attribute pairs from the logical screen
PTR WORD	Contains the length (in bytes) of the buffer to receive data from display; receives the actual number of bytes transferred to the buffer
WORD	Starting *y* (row) screen coordinate
WORD	Starting *x* (column) screen coordinate
WORD	Video handle (0 = default)

Notes:

- Each display position requires 2 bytes in the buffer. The character code is in the lower byte, and the character attribute is in the upper byte.

- Coordinate $(x,y)=(0,0)$ is the upper left corner of the display.

- Video attributes and colors are listed on p. 107.

Related functions: *VioReadCharStr, VioWrtCellStr*.

VioReadCharStr   [FAPI]

Reads a string of characters from the logical video buffer (LVB), starting at the specified position.

PTR BUFFER	Receives character string
PTR WORD	Contains the length in bytes of the buffer; receives the actual number of bytes transferred to the buffer
WORD	Starting *y* (row) screen coordinate
WORD	Starting *x* (column) screen coordinate
WORD	Video handle (0 = default)

Note:

- Coordinate $(x,y)=(0,0)$ is the upper left corner of the display.

Related functions: *VioReadCellStr, VioWrtCharStr*.

VioRegister

Registers replacement routine(s) to service one or more video API functions for the current screen group. Unregistered functions continue to be serviced by the Base Video Subsystem (BVSCALLS.DLL).

PTR ASCIIZ	Pathname of dynlink library
PTR ASCIIZ	Name of library entry point
DWORD	Identifies video function(s) being registered

Bit	Function Registered (if set)
0	VioGetCurPos
1	VioGetCurType
2	VioGetMode
3	VioGetBuf
4	VioGetPhysBuf
5	VioSetCurPos
6	VioSetCurType
7	VioSetMode
8	VioShowBuf
9	VioReadCharStr
10	VioReadCellStr
11	VioWrtNChar
12	VioWrtNAttr
13	VioWrtNCell
14	VioWrtTTY
15	VioWrtCharStr
16	VioWrtCharStrAtt
17	VioWrtCellStr
18	VioScrollUp
19	VioScrollDn
20	VioScrollLf
21	VioScrollRt
22	VioSetAnsi
23	VioGetAnsi
24	VioPrtSc
25	VioScrLock
26	VioScrUnLock
27	VioSavRedrawWait
28	VioSavRedrawUndo
29	VioPopUp
30	VioEndPopUp
31	VioPrtScToggle

DWORD	Identifies video function(s) being registered

Bit(s)	Function Registered (if set)
0	VioModeWait
1	VioModeUndo
2	VioGetFont
3	VioGetConfig
4	VioSetCp

Bit(s)	Function Registered (if set)
5	VioGetCp
6	VioSetFont
7	VioGetState
8	VioSetState
9–31	Reserved (0)

Notes:

■ A registered replacement for a video subsystem receives control with the following items on the stack:

□ 32-bit VIOCALLS.DLL return address (top of stack)

□ 16-bit application program's DS register

□ 16-bit VIOCALLS.DLL internal return address

□ 16-bit function code

0	VioGetPhysBuf
1	VioGetBuf
2	VioShowBuf
3	VioGetCurPos
4	VioGetCurType
5	VioGetMode
6	VioSetCurPos
7	VioSetCurType
8	VioSetMode
9	VioReadCharStr
10	VioReadCellStr
11	VioWrtNChar
12	VioWrtNAttr
13	VioWrtNCell
14	VioWrtCharStr
15	VioWrtCharStrAtt
16	VioWrtCellStr
17	VioWrtTTY
18	VioScrollUp
19	VioScrollDn
20	VioScrollLf
21	VioScrollRt
22	VioSetAnsi
23	VioGetAnsi
24	VioPrtSc
25	VioScrLock
26	VioScrUnLock
27	VioSavRedrawWait
28	VioSavRedrawUndo
29	VioPopUp
30	VioEndPopUp
31	VioPrtScToggle
32	VioModeWait
33	VioModeUndo
34	VioGetFont

16-bit function code, *continued*

35	*VioGetConfig*
36	*VioSetCp*
37	*VioGetCp*
38	*VioSetFont*
39	*VioGetState*
40	*VioSetState*

□ 32-bit application return address

□ Function-specific parameters placed on stack by application program

The replacement routine must exit by a far return with the stack unchanged. The contents of AX are interpreted as follows:

AX <> −1   *Vio* function performed, AX contains 0 or error code; return to application

AX = −1   Replacement subsystem did nothing; invoke the appropriate base subsystem routine and return its status to the application

■ Replacement video API routines can be registered by only one process per screen group at a time. *VioRegister* calls by other processes fail until the default video routines are restored with *VioDeRegister*.

Related functions: *KbdRegister, MouRegister, VioDeRegister*.

VioSavRedrawUndo

Cancels a *VioSavRedrawWait* call issued by another thread within the same process.

WORD	Ownership option for *VioSavRedrawWait*	
	0	*Retain ownership*
	1	*Give up ownership*
WORD	Termination option (for thread that is currently blocked in *VioSavRedrawWait* call)	
	0	*Return error code to thread*
	1	*Terminate thread*
WORD	Video handle (0 = default)	

Related functions: *VioModeUndo, VioModeWait, VioSavRedrawWait*.

VioSavRedrawWait

Notifies the application when the video buffer and adapter state need to be saved or restored, by blocking the requesting thread until the save or restore operation is required. Non–Presentation Manager applications which use graphics display modes must create a thread that calls *VioSavRedrawWait*, performs the appropriate save or restore upon return from the function, and then immediately reissues *VioSavRedrawWait*.

WORD	Save/redraw option	
	0	*Notify application for both save and redraw operations*
	1	*Notify application of redraw operations only*
PTR WORD	Receives notification type	
	0	*Save display and adapter state*
	1	*Restore display and adapter state*
WORD	Video handle (0 = default)	

Notes:

- Text mode applications do not need *VioSavRedrawWait* unless they write directly to the video adapter's registers; OS/2 always saves and restores the display buffer across session switches in text mode.

- Selectors obtained from a previous *VioGetPhysBuf* call can be used by the *VioSavRedrawWait* thread. However, do not call *VioScrLock* before accessing the display buffer.

- If an application begins execution in the background (for example, if it is invoked by the START command), the application might be notified to restore the screen before it has ever saved it.

Related functions: *VioModeUndo, VioModeWait, VioSavRedrawUndo.*

VioScrLock   [FAPI]

Locks access to the physical display for I/O. Used by a process to prevent screen switches while it manipulates the video adapter's physical display buffer or I/O ports.

WORD	Wait/no-wait flag	
	0	*Return immediately if screen is not available*
	1	*Wait until screen is available*
PTR BYTE	Receives status of lock operation	
	0	*Lock successful*
	1	*Lock not successful (process is in background, or a pop-up is in progress; relevant only if wait/no-wait flag = 0)*
WORD	Video handle (0 = default)	

Notes:

- If a session switch is requested, and a process which called *VioScrLock* does not release the screen with *VioScrUnLock* within a system-defined time limit, the session switch occurs anyway and the process is frozen until its session is restored to the foreground. The time limit is 30 seconds in OS/2 versions 1.0 and 1.1.

- In real mode, *VioScrLock* never returns an error.

Related functions: *VioGetPhysBuf, VioScrUnLock.*

VioScrollDn   [FAPI]
VioScrollLf
VioScrollRt
VioScrollUp

Scrolls all or part of the logical display down (*VioScrollDn*), left (*VioScrollLf*), right (*VioScrollRt*), or up (*VioScrollUp*) by one or more lines or columns, filling the new lines or columns with the specified character and attribute. The area to be scrolled is identified by the text coordinates of its upper left and lower right corners, with $(x,y)=(0,0)$ defined as the upper left corner of the display.

WORD	y (row) coordinate, upper left corner
WORD	x (column) coordinate, upper left corner
WORD	y (row) coordinate, lower right corner
WORD	x (column) coordinate, lower right corner
WORD	Number of lines or columns to scroll
PTR WORD	Contains character (lower byte) and attribute (upper byte) used to fill blanked lines or columns
WORD	Video handle (0 = default)

Notes:

■ If you call any of these functions with the upper left corner = (0,0), lower right corner = (−1,−1), and number of lines or columns to scroll = −1, the entire screen is filled with the specified character-attribute pair.

■ Video attributes and colors are listed on p. 107.

Related function: *VioWrtNCell*.

VioScrUnLock

Releases lock on the physical display; cancels the effect of a previous *VioScrLock* call. Used only by processes that access the video adapter's physical display buffer and I/O ports directly.

WORD	Video handle (0 = default)

Note:

■ In real mode, *VioScrUnLock* never returns an error.

Related function: *VioScrLock*.

VioSetAnsi

Enables or disables the interpretation of ANSI escape sequences for screen control and keyboard mapping.

WORD	On/off indicator	
	0	*Disable ANSI support*
	1	*Enable ANSI support (default condition)*
WORD	Video handle (0 = default)	

Related functions: *VioGetAnsi, VioWrtTTY*.

VioSetCp

Selects the code page used by the video subsystem for the current screen group. The code page defines the character set and should not be confused with the font (which defines the appearance of the characters on the screen).

WORD	Reserved (0)
WORD	Code page ID (0 = default ROM code page)
WORD	Video handle (0 = default)

Related functions: *DosSetCp, VioGetCp, VioSetFont.*

VioSetCurPos [FAPI]

Sets the cursor position in text coordinates. Position (0,0) is the upper left corner of the screen.

WORD	*y* (row) coordinate
WORD	*x* (column) coordinate
WORD	Video handle (0 = default)

Related functions: *VioGetCurPos, VioSetCurType.*

VioSetCurType [FAPI]

Sets the cursor size, shape, and attribute.

PTR BUFFER   Contains cursor characteristics in the following format:

Offset	*Length*	*Description*
00H	*2*	*Cursor start line*
02H	*2*	*Cursor end line*
04H	*2*	*Cursor width*
		0 = default
		1 = maximum legal value in text modes
06H	*2*	*Cursor attribute*
		0 = visible
		−1 = hidden

WORD   Video handle (0 = default)

Note:

■ The valid values for the cursor starting and ending lines are determined by the character cell dimensions in the current display mode. You can calculate the size of the character cell from the information returned by *VioGetMode.*

Related functions: *VioGetCurType, VioGetMode, VioSetCurPos.*

VioSetDeviceCellSize [AVIO] [1.1]

Sets the height and width of the character set in pels (pixels) for the specified presentation space.

WORD	Height in pels
WORD	Width in pels
WORD	Presentation space handle

Related functions: *VioCreatePS, VioQueryDeviceCellSize.*

VioSetFont

Downloads a display font into the video adapter (EGA, VGA, and PS/2 only). The font defines the appearance of each character on the screen and must be compatible with the current display mode.

PTR BUFFER   Contains information about the type of request and the address of the font table, as follows:

Offset	Length	Description
00H	2	Length (always 14 bytes in OS/2 versions 1.0 and 1.1)
02H	2	Request type
		0 = set current font
		<>0 = reserved
04H	2	Width of character cell in pixels
06H	2	Height of character cell in pixels
08H	4	Address of font table
0CH	2	Length in bytes of font table

WORD   Video handle (0 = default)

Notes:

- The current code page is reset. Subsequent *VioGetCp* calls return an error until *VioSetCp* or *DosSetCp* is called.

- Valid fonts for the various graphics display adapters are indicated in the following table:

Dimension	CGA	EGA	VGA
8-by-8	◆	◆	◆
8-by-14		◆	◆
8-by-16			◆
9-by-14		◆	◆
9-by-16			◆

Related functions: *DosSetCp, VioGetFont, VioSetCp.*

VioSetMode   [FAPI]

Selects the display mode for the current screen group. The cursor is initialized to its default type and position.

PTR BUFFER   Contains display mode information in the following format:

Offset	Length	Description
00H	2	Length (minimum 3, maximum 14 in OS/2 versions 1.0 and 1.1; if > 3 must be even)
02H	1	Display mode type

Bit	Significance
0	0 = monochrome-compatible mode
	1 = other
1	0 = text mode
	1 = graphics mode

Offset	Length	Description
	2	0 = enable color burst
		1 = disable color burst
	3–7	Reserved
03H	1	Displayable colors
		0 = monochrome-compatible mode
		1 = 2 colors
		2 = 4 colors
		4 = 16 colors
		8 = 256 colors
04H	2	Horizontal (x) resolution in text columns
06H	2	Vertical (y) resolution in text rows
08H	2	Horizontal (x) resolution in pixels
0AH	2	Vertical (y) resolution in pixels
0CH	2	Reserved (0)

WORD Video handle (0 = default)

Notes:

- Available text modes for the various adapters are the following:

Columns (x)	Rows (y)	MDA	CGA	EGA	VGA
40	25		◆	◆	◆
80	25	◆	◆	◆	◆
80	43			◆	◆
80	50				◆

- Available graphics modes for the various adapters are the following:

Columns (x)	Rows (y)	Colors	CGA	EGA	VGA
320	200	4	◆	◆	◆
320	200	16		◆	◆
320	200	256			◆
640	200	2	◆	◆	◆
640	200	16		◆	◆
640	350	2		◆	◆
640	350	4		◆	
640	350	16		◆	◆
640	480	2			◆
640	480	16			◆

- On display adapters other than the CGA, the color burst bit is ignored.

- [1.1] If the application is running in a Presentation Manager window, only text modes can be selected.

- In real mode, the screen is also cleared.

Related functions: *VioGetMode, VioSetState*.

VioSetOrg [AVIO] [1.1]

Sets the coordinates of the character to be displayed at the upper left corner of the presentation space's window.

WORD	Row (y) coordinate
WORD	Column (x) coordinate
WORD	Presentation space handle

Note:

■ Express the coordinates in character columns and rows rather than in pels.

Related functions: *VioCreatePS, VioGetOrg*.

VioSetState

Programs the palette registers, selects the border color, or sets the intensity/blink toggle for the current screen group.

PTR BUFFER	Contains video state information (*see Notes*)
WORD	Video handle (0 = default)

Notes:

■ The request block to set the palette registers has the following format:

Offset	Length	Description
00H	2	Contains length of structure (maximum 38 in OS/2 versions 1.0 and 1.1)
02H	2	Contains 0 = set palette registers
04H	2	Contains number of the first palette register to set (0–15)
06H	n	Contains color values for n/2 consecutive palette registers, 16 bits per register

■ The request block to set the border (overscan) color has the following format:

Offset	Length	Description
00H	2	Contains length of structure (6 in OS/2 versions 1.0 and 1.1)
02H	2	Contains 1 = set border color
04H	2	Contains border color

■ The request block to set the intensity/blink toggle has the following format:

Offset	Length	Description
00H	2	Contains length of structure (6 in OS/2 versions 1.0 and 1.1)
02H	2	Contains 2 = set intensity/blink toggle
04H	2	Contains toggle value
		0 = Enable blinking foreground colors
		1 = Enable intensified background colors

Related functions: *VioGetState, VioSetMode*.

VioShowBuf   [FAPI]

Updates the physical display buffer from the logical video buffer (LVB). Called by processes that use the pointer returned by *VioGetBuf* to manipulate the LVB directly. If the process's screen group is in the background, the *VioShowBuf* call is ignored.

WORD	Byte offset of changed area within LVB
WORD	Length of changed area in LVB
WORD	Video handle (0 = default)

Related function: *VioGetBuf*.

VioShowPS   [AVIO] [1.1]

Updates the display from a *Vio* presentation space.

WORD	Height of region
WORD	Width of region
WORD	Offset of region
WORD	Presentation space handle

Note:

- Express the height, width, and offset in character cells rather than in pels. The offset is relative to the first character in the presentation space and specifies the position of the upper left corner of the rectangle to be updated.

Related function: *VioCreatePS*.

VioWrtCellStr   [FAPI]

Writes a string of character-attribute pairs (cells) to the display, starting at the specified position. Position $(x,y)=(0,0)$ is the upper left corner of the display. The cursor position is not affected. Control codes, including ANSI escape sequences, are ignored and appear as their character-graphics equivalents.

PTR BUFFER	Contains character-attribute pairs
WORD	Length in bytes of data to display
WORD	Starting *y* (row) coordinate
WORD	Starting *x* (column) coordinate
WORD	Video handle (0 = default)

Notes:

- Each display position requires two bytes in the buffer. The character code is in the lower byte of a pair and the character attribute in the upper byte.

- Video attributes and colors are listed on p. 107.

Related functions: *VioReadCellStr, VioWrtCharStr, VioWrtCharStrAtt*.

VioWrtCharStr [FAPI]

Writes a character string to the display, starting at the specified position. Position $(x,y)=(0,0)$ is the upper left corner of the display. The cursor position is not affected. Control codes, including ANSI escape sequences, are ignored and appear on the display as their character-graphics equivalents.

PTR BUFFER	Contains character string
WORD	Number of characters
WORD	Starting y (row) coordinate
WORD	Starting x (column) coordinate
WORD	Video handle (0 = default)

Related functions: *VioReadCharStr, VioWrtCellStr, VioWrtCharStrAtt*.

VioWrtCharStrAtt [FAPI]

Writes a character string to the display, applying the specified attribute to each character, starting at the specified position. Position $(x,y)=(0,0)$ is the upper left corner of the display. The cursor position is not affected. Control codes, including ANSI escape sequences, are ignored and appear on the display as their character-graphics equivalents.

PTR BUFFER	Contains character string
WORD	Number of characters
WORD	Starting y (row) coordinate
WORD	Starting x (column) coordinate
PTR BYTE	Contains character attribute
WORD	Video handle (0 = default)

Note:

- Video attributes and colors are listed on p. 107.

Related functions: *VioWrtCellStr, VioWrtCharStr*.

VioWrtNAttr [FAPI]

Applies a character attribute to one or more characters on the display, starting at the specified position. Position $(x,y)=(0,0)$ is the upper left corner of the display. The cursor position is not affected.

PTR BYTE	Contains attribute
WORD	Replication count
WORD	Starting y (row) coordinate
WORD	Starting x (column) coordinate
WORD	Video handle (0 = default)

Note:

- Video attributes and colors are listed on p. 107.

Related functions: *VioWrtNCell, VioWrtNChar*.

VioWrtNCell [FAPI]

Writes one or more copies of the same character-attribute pair (cell) to the display, starting at the specified position. Position $(x,y)=(0,0)$ is the upper left corner of the display. The cursor position is not affected.

PTR WORD	Contains character in lower byte and attribute in upper byte
WORD	Replication count
WORD	Starting y (row) coordinate
WORD	Starting x (column) coordinate
WORD	Video handle (0 = default)

Note:

■ Video attributes and colors are listed on p. 107.

Related functions: *VioWrtNAttr, VioWrtNChar.*

VioWrtNChar [FAPI]

Writes one or more copies of the same character to the display, starting at the specified position. Position $(x,y)=(0,0)$ is the upper left corner of the display. The cursor position is not affected.

PTR BYTE	Contains character
WORD	Replication count
WORD	Starting y (row) coordinate
WORD	Starting x (column) coordinate
WORD	Video handle (0 = default)

Related functions: *VioWrtNAttr, VioWrtNCell.*

VioWrtTTY [FAPI]

Writes a character string to the display in "teletype mode," beginning at the current cursor position. Line wrapping and screen scrolling are provided, and the cursor position is updated. Backspace, carriage return, linefeed, and bell are detected and handled appropriately. Tabs are expanded to spaces using 8-column tab stops. If ANSI support is enabled (the default condition), ANSI escape sequences for screen control and keyboard remapping have their expected effects.

PTR BUFFER	Contains character string
WORD	Length of character string
WORD	Video handle (0 = default)

Related functions: *DosPutMessage, DosWrite, VioGetAnsi, VioSetAnsi, VioWrtCellStr, VioWrtCharStr, VioWrtCharStrAttr.*

DosDevIOCtl FUNCTIONS

The *DosDevIOCtl* functions are identified by category (for the associated device) and function number. The following table relates each category to the corresponding device and to the API function from which a device handle should be obtained.

Category	*Device*	*Handle From*
1	Serial port	*DosOpen*
2	Reserved for OS/2	
3	Pointer device	*DosOpen*
4	Keyboard	*DosOpen*
5	Printer	*DosOpen*
6	Light pen	
7	Mouse	*MouOpen*
8	Logical disk	*DosOpen*
9	Physical disk	*DosPhysicalDisk*
10	Character Device Monitor	*DosOpen*
11	General Device Control	*DosOpen*
12–127	Reserved for OS/2	
128–255	Reserved for user programs and drivers	

Category 1   Function 41H
Set Baud Rate   DosDevIOCtl

Parameter Buffer Format:

WORD   Baud rate (110, 150, 300, 600, 1200, 2400, 4800, 9600, or 19200)

Data Buffer Format:

None   Use null pointer

Category 1   Function 42H   DosDevIOCtl
Set Line Characteristics

Parameter Buffer Format:

BYTE   Data bits (5–8)
BYTE   Parity (0 = none; 1 = odd; 2 = even; 3 = mark; 4 = space)
BYTE   Stop bits (0 = 1; 1 = 1.5; 2 = 2)

Data Buffer Format:

None   Use null pointer

Category 1   Function 44H   DosDevIOCtl
Transmit Byte Immediate

Parameter Buffer Format:

BYTE   Character to be transmitted

Data Buffer Format:

None   Use null pointer

Category 1   Function 45H   DosDevIOCtl
Set Break Off

Parameter Buffer Format:

None   Use null pointer

Data Buffer Format:

WORD   COM error word (*see Category 1 Function 6DH, pp. 627–28*)

Category 1   Function 46H   DosDevIOCtl
Set Modem Control Signals

Parameter Buffer Format:

BYTE   Modem control signals ON mask
BYTE   Modem control signals OFF mask

ON Mask	OFF Mask	Meaning
01H	FFH	Set DTR
00H	FEH	Clear DTR
02H	FFH	Set RTS
00H	FDH	Clear RTS
03H	FFH	Set DTR and RTS
00H	FCH	Clear DTR and RTS

Data Buffer Format:

WORD   COM error word (*see Category 1 Function 6DH, pp. 627–28*)

Category 1   Function 47H
Stop Transmitting (as if XOFF received)

DosDevIOCtl

Parameter Buffer Format:

None   Use null pointer

Data Buffer Format:

None   Use null pointer

Category 1   Function 48H
Start Transmitting (as if XON received)

DosDevIOCtl

Parameter Buffer Format:

None   Use null pointer

Data Buffer Format:

None   Use null pointer

Category 1   Function 4BH
Set Break On

DosDevIOCtl

Parameter Buffer Format:

None   Use null pointer

Data Buffer Format:

WORD   COM error word (*see Category 1 Function 6DH, pp. 627–28*)

Category 1   Function 53H   DosDevIOCtl
Set Device Control Block (DCB)

Parameter Buffer Format:

WORD	Write timeout (in .01 seconds)
WORD	Read timeout (in .01 seconds)
BYTE	Flags byte 1

Bit	Significance (if set)
0	Enable DTR control mode
1	Enable input handshaking using DTR
2	Reserved (0)
3	Enable output handshaking using CTS
4	Enable output handshaking using DSR
5	Enable output handshaking using DCD
6	Enable input sensitivity using DSR
7	Reserved (0)

BYTE	Flags byte 2

Bit(s)	Significance (if set)
0	Enable XON/XOFF transmit flow control
1	Enable XON/XOFF receive flow control
2	Enable error replacement character
3	Enable null stripping
4	Enable break replacement character
5	Reserved (0)
6–7	RTS state
	00 = disable RTS control mode
	01 = enable RTS control mode
	10 = enable input handshaking using RTS
	11 = enable toggling on transmit mode

BYTE	Flags byte 3

Bit(s)	Significance (if set)
0	Enable write infinite timeout processing
1–2	Read timeout processing
	00 = invalid input
	01 = normal read timeout processing
	10 = wait for something, read timeout processing
	11 = no wait, read timeout processing
3–7	Reserved (0)

BYTE	Error replacement character
BYTE	Break replacement character
BYTE	XON character
BYTE	XOFF character

Data Buffer Format:

None	Use null pointer

Category 1   Function 61H   DosDevIOCtl
Get Baud Rate

Parameter Buffer Format:

None   *Use null pointer*

Data Buffer Format:

WORD   Baud rate

Category 1   Function 62H   DosDevIOCtl
Get Line Characteristics

Parameter Buffer Format:

None   *Use null pointer*

Data Buffer Format:

BYTE   Data bits (5–8)
BYTE   Parity (0 = none; 1 = odd; 2 = even; 3 = mark; 4 = space)
BYTE   Stop bits (0 = 1; 1 = 1.5; 2 = 2)
BYTE   Break status (0 = break not being transmitted; 1 = break being transmitted)

Category 1   Function 64H   DosDevIOCtl
Get COM Status

Parameter Buffer Format:

None   *Use null pointer*

Data Buffer Format:

BYTE   COM port status

Bit	*Significance (if set)*
0	*Transmit waiting for CTS to be turned on*
1	*Transmit waiting for DSR to be turned on*
2	*Transmit waiting for DCD to be turned on*
3	*Transmit waiting because XOFF received*
4	*Transmit waiting because XOFF transmitted*
5	*Transmit waiting because break being transmitted*
6	*Character waiting to transmit immediately*
7	*Receive waiting for DSR to be turned on*

Category 1   Function 65H
Get Transmit Data Status

DosDevIOCtl

Parameter Buffer Format:

None   *Use null pointer*

Data Buffer Format:

BYTE   Transmit data status

Bit(s)	*Significance (if set)*
0	*Write request packets in progress or queued*
1	*Data in driver transmit queue*
2	*Data currently being transmitted*
3	*Character waiting to be transmitted immediately*
4	*Waiting to transmit XON character*
5	*Waiting to transmit XOFF character*
6–7	*Reserved*

Category 1   Function 66H
Get Modem Output Control Signals

DosDevIOCtl

Parameter Buffer Format:

None   *Use null pointer*

Data Buffer Format:

BYTE   Modem output control signals

Bit(s)	*Significance (if set)*
0	*Data terminal ready (DTR)*
1	*Request to send (RTS)*
2–7	*Reserved*

Category 1   Function 67H
Get Modem Input Control Signals

DosDevIOCtl

Parameter Buffer Format:

None   *Use null pointer*

Data Buffer Format:

BYTE   Modem input control signals

Bit(s)	*Significance (if set)*
0–3	*Reserved*
4	*Clear to send (CTS)*
5	*Data set ready (DSR)*
6	*Ring indicator (RI)*
7	*Data carrier detect (DCD)*

Category 1   Function 68H   DosDevIOCtl
Get Number of Characters in Receive Queue

Parameter Buffer Format:

None   *Use null pointer*

Data Buffer Format:

WORD   Number of waiting characters
WORD   Size of receive queue

Category 1   Function 69H   DosDevIOCtl
Get Number of Characters in Transmit Queue

Parameter Buffer Format:

None   *Use null pointer*

Data Buffer Format:

WORD   Number of waiting characters
WORD   Size of transmit queue

Category 1   Function 6DH   DosDevIOCtl
Get COM Error Information

Parameter Buffer Format:

None   *Use null pointer*

Data Buffer Format:

WORD   COM error word

Bit(s)	Significance (if set)
0	Receive queue overrun
1	Receive hardware overrun
2	Parity error
3	Framing error
4–15	Reserved

Category 1   Function 72H   DosDevIOCtl
Get COM Event Information

Parameter Buffer Format:

None   *Use null pointer*

Data Buffer Format:

WORD   COM event information

Bit(s)	Significance (if set)
0	Character received and placed in queue
1	Reserved
2	Last character sent from transmit queue
3	Change in CTS state
4	Change in DSR state
5	Change in DCD state
6	Break detected
7	Parity, framing, or overrun error
8	Ring detected
9–15	Reserved

Category 1   Function 73H   DosDevIOCtl
Get Device Control Block (DCB)

Parameter Buffer Format:

None   *Use null pointer*

Data Buffer Format:

Same as parameter buffer format for Category 1 Function 53H (p. 624)

Category 3   Function 72H
Get Pointer-Draw Routine Address

DosDevIOCtl

Parameter Buffer Format:

None   *Use null pointer*

Data Buffer Format:

WORD   Return code
DWORD   Pointer-draw routine entry point
WORD   Pointer-draw routine data segment selector

Category 4   Function 50H
Set Code Page

DosDevIOCtl

Parameter Buffer Format:

DWORD   Contains pointer to keyboard code page

Data Buffer Format:

None   *Use null pointer*

Category 4   Function 51H
Set Input Mode

DosDevIOCtl

Parameter Buffer Format:

BYTE   Input mode; only bits 0 and 7 are significant:
                0xxxxxx0 = ASCII mode
                1xxxxxx0 = binary mode without shift reporting
                1xxxxxx1 = binary mode with shift reporting

Data Buffer Format:

None   *Use null pointer*

Category 4   Function 52H
Set Interim Character Flags

Parameter Buffer Format:

BYTE	Interim character flags	
	Bit(s)	*Significance (if set)*
	0–4	*Reserved (0)*
	5	*On-the-spot conversion requested*
	6	*Reserved (0)*
	7	*Interim character flag on*

Data Buffer Format:

None   *Use null pointer*

Category 4   Function 53H
Set Shift State

Parameter Buffer Format:

WORD	Shift state	
	Bit	*Significance (if set)*
	0	*Right Shift key down*
	1	*Left Shift key down*
	2	*Either Ctrl key down*
	3	*Either Alt key down*
	4	*Scroll Lock on*
	5	*Num Lock on*
	6	*Caps Lock on*
	7	*Insert on*
	8	*Left Ctrl key down*
	9	*Left Alt key down*
	10	*Right Ctrl key down*
	11	*Right Alt key down*
	12	*Scroll Lock key down*
	13	*Num Lock key down*
	14	*Caps Lock key down*
	15	*Sys Req key down*
BYTE	National language support (NLS) status (0 in USA)	

Data Buffer Format:

None   *Use null pointer*

Category 4   Function 54H
Set Typematic Rate and Delay

DosDevlOCtl

Parameter Buffer Format:

WORD   Delay in milliseconds
WORD   Repeat rate in characters per second

Data Buffer Format:

None   *Use null pointer*

Category 4   Function 55H
Notify Change of Foreground Session

DosDevlOCtl

Parameter Buffer Format:

WORD   Foreground session number
WORD   Switch/terminate flag
         0 = switching to specified session
         −1 = specified session is terminating

Data Buffer Format:

None   *Use null pointer*

Category 4   Function 56H
Set Task Manager Hot Key

DosDevlOCtl

Parameter Buffer Format:

WORD   Shift state

Bit(s)	*Significance (if set)*
0	*Right Shift key down*
1	*Left Shift key down*
2–7	*Reserved*
8	*Left Ctrl key down*
9	*Left Alt key down*
10	*Right Ctrl key down*
11	*Right Alt key down*
12	*Scroll Lock key down*
13	*Num Lock key down*
14	*Caps Lock key down*
15	*Sys Req key down*

BYTE   Scan code of hot key make (depression)
BYTE   Scan code of hot key break (release)
WORD   Hot key identifier (0–15)

Data Buffer Format:

None   *Use null pointer*

Category 4   Function 57H   DosDevIOCtl
Bind Logical Keyboard to Physical Keyboard

Parameter Buffer Format:

WORD   Keyboard handle

Data Buffer Format:

None   *Use null pointer*

Category 4   Function 58H   DosDevIOCtl
Set Code Page Identifier

Parameter Buffer Format:

DWORD   Pointer to code page
WORD   Code page ID
WORD   Reserved (must be 0)

Data Buffer Format:

None   *Use null pointer*

Category 4   Function 5CH   DosDevIOCtl
Set NLS and Custom Code Page

Parameter Buffer Format:

DWORD   Pointer to code page
WORD   Code page number
WORD   Code page to load
WORD   Hot key identifier

Data Buffer Format:

None   *Use null pointer*

Category 4   Function 5DH
Create Logical Keyboard

DosDevIOCtl

Parameter Buffer Format:

WORD   Handle to assign to new keyboard (0 = default keyboard)

Data Buffer Format:

None   Use null pointer

Category 4   Function 5EH
Destroy Logical Keyboard

DosDevIOCtl

Parameter Buffer Format:

WORD   Handle for keyboard (0 = default keyboard)

Data Buffer Format:

None   Use null pointer

Category 4   Function 71H
Get Input Mode

DosDevIOCtl

Parameter Buffer Format:

None   Use null pointer

Data Buffer Format:

BYTE   Input mode; only bits 0 and 7 are significant:
              0xxxxxx0 = ASCII mode
              1xxxxxx0 = binary mode without shift reporting
              1xxxxxx1 = binary mode with shift reporting

Category 4   Function 72H
Get Interim Character Flags

DosDevIOCtl

Parameter Buffer Format:

None   *Use null pointer*

Data Buffer Format:

BYTE   Interim character flags

Bit(s)	Significance (if set)
0–4	Reserved (0)
5	On-the-spot conversion requested
6	Reserved (0)
7	Interim character flag on

Category 4   Function 73H
Get Shift State

DosDevIOCtl

Parameter Buffer Format:

None   *Use null pointer*

Data Buffer Format:

WORD   Shift state

Bit	Significance (if set)
0	Right Shift key down
1	Left Shift key down
2	Either Ctrl key down
3	Either Alt key down
4	Scroll Lock on
5	Num Lock on
6	Caps Lock on
7	Insert on
8	Left Ctrl key down
9	Left Alt key down
10	Right Ctrl key down
11	Right Alt key down
12	Scroll Lock key down
13	Num Lock key down
14	Caps Lock key down
15	Sys Req key down

BYTE   National language support (NLS) status (0 in USA)

Category 4   Function 74H
Read Character Data Records

Parameter Buffer Format:

WORD   Transfer count

Bit(s)	Significance
0–14	Number of records requested
15	Wait/no-wait flag
	0 = wait if necessary for requested number of records
	1 = do not wait; transfer only records already waiting

Receives the actual number of character records in the same word

Data Buffer Format:

Receives 10 bytes per character as follows:

BYTE   ASCII character code

BYTE   Scan code

BYTE   Status

Bit(s)	Significance (if set)
0	Shift status returned without character (valid only in binary mode when shift reporting is turned on)
1–4	Reserved (0)
5	On-the-spot conversion requested
6	Character ready
7	Interim character

BYTE   Reserved (0)

WORD   Keyboard shift state

Bit	Significance (if set)
0	Right Shift key down
1	Left Shift key down
2	Either Ctrl key down
3	Either Alt key down
4	Scroll Lock on
5	Num Lock on
6	Caps Lock on
7	Insert on
8	Left Ctrl key down
9	Left Alt key down
10	Right Ctrl key down
11	Right Alt key down
12	Scroll Lock key down
13	Num Lock key down
14	Caps Lock key down
15	Sys Req key down

DWORD   Time stamp (msec. since system was turned on or restarted)

Category 4   Function 75H
Peek Character Data Record

DosDevIOCtl

Parameter Buffer Format:

WORD   Keyboard input status

Bit(s)	*Significance*
0	*0 = no character waiting*
	1 = at least 1 character waiting
1–14	*Reserved (0)*
15	*0 = ASCII ("cooked") mode*
	1 = binary ("raw") mode

Data Buffer Format:

Same as for Category 4 Function 74H (p. 635)

Category 4   Function 76H
Get Task Manager Hot Key

DosDevIOCtl

Parameter Buffer Format:

WORD   Contains 0 to obtain maximum number of hot keys supported by driver, 1 to obtain current number of hot keys; receives maximum or current number of hot keys in same location

Data Buffer Format:

If parameter buffer contains 1 on call, data buffer receives 6 bytes per hot key in the following format:

WORD   Shift state

Bit(s)	*Significance (if set)*
0	*Right Shift key down*
1	*Left Shift key down*
2–7	*Reserved*
8	*Left Ctrl key down*
9	*Left Alt key down*
10	*Right Ctrl key down*
11	*Right Alt key down*
12	*Scroll Lock key down*
13	*Num Lock key down*
14	*Caps Lock key down*
15	*Sys Req key down*

BYTE   Scan code of hot key make (depression)
BYTE   Scan code of hot key break (release)
WORD   Hot key identifier (0–15)

Category 4   Function 77H
Get Keyboard Type

DosDevIOCtl

Parameter Buffer Format:

None   *Use null pointer*

Data Buffer Format:

WORD	Keyboard type
	0 = PC/AT keyboard
	1 = Enhanced keyboard
DWORD	Reserved (0)

Category 4   Function 78H
Get Code Page ID

DosDevIOCtl

Parameter Buffer Format:

WORD	Current code page ID

Data Buffer Format:

None   *Use null pointer*

Category 4   Function 79H
Translate Scan Code to ASCII

DosDevIOCtl

Parameter Buffer Format:

WORD	Code page ID

Data Buffer Format:

10 BYTES	Character data record (see *KbdCharIn*)
WORD	Keyboard device driver flags (see *KbdXlate*)
WORD	Translate flags

Bit(s)	*Significance (if set)*
0	*Translation complete*
1–15	*Reserved*

WORD	Translate state word 1
WORD	Translate state word 2

Category 5   Function 42H
Set Frame Control

DosDevIOCtl

Parameter Buffer Format:

BYTE   Command information (should be 0)

Data Buffer Format:

BYTE   Characters per line (80 or 132)
BYTE   Lines per inch (6 or 8)

Category 5   Function 44H
Set Infinite Retry

DosDevIOCtl

Parameter Buffer Format:

BYTE   Command information (should be 0)

Data Buffer Format:

BYTE   Retry state
              0 = disable infinite retry
              1 = enable infinite retry

Category 5   Function 46H
Initialize Printer

DosDevIOCtl

Parameter Buffer Format:

BYTE   Command information (should be 0)

Data Buffer Format:

None   *Use null pointer*

Category 5   Function 48H
Activate Font

DosDevIOCtl

Parameter Buffer Format:

BYTE   Command information (should be 0)

Data Buffer Format:

WORD   Code page ID
WORD   Font ID

Category 5   Function 62H
Get Frame Control

DosDevIOCtl

Parameter Buffer Format:

BYTE   Command information (should be 0)

Data Buffer Format:

BYTE   Characters per line (80 or 132)
BYTE   Lines per inch (6 or 8)

Category 5   Function 64H
Return Infinite Retry Mode

DosDevIOCtl

Parameter Buffer Format:

BYTE   Command information (should be 0)

Data Buffer Format:

BYTE   Retry mode
              0 = infinite retry disabled
              1 = infinite retry enabled

Category 5   Function 66H
Return Printer Status

DosDevIOCtl

Parameter Buffer Format:

BYTE   Command information (should be 0)

Data Buffer Format:

BYTE   Printer status

Bit(s)	*Significance (if set)*
0	Timed out
1–2	Reserved
3	I/O error
4	Printer selected
5	Out of paper
6	Acknowledge
7	Printer not busy

Category 5   Function 69H
Query Active Font

DosDevIOCtl

Parameter Buffer Format:

BYTE   Command information (should be 0)

Data Buffer Format:

WORD   Current code page ID
WORD   Current font ID

Category 5   Function 6AH
Verify Code Page and Font

DosDevIOCtl

Parameter Buffer Format:

BYTE   Command information (should be 0)

Data Buffer Format:

WORD   Current code page ID
WORD   Current font ID

Category 7   Function 50H
Enable Pointer Drawing After Session Switch

DosDevIOCtl

Parameter Buffer Format:

None	*Use null pointer*

Data Buffer Format:

None	*Use null pointer*

Category 7   Function 51H
Notify of Display Mode Change

DosDevIOCtl

Parameter Buffer Format:

WORD   Length of structure (16 maximum)
BYTE   Display mode type

Bit(s)	*Significance*
0	*0 = monochrome compatible mode*
	1 = other
1	*0 = text mode*
	1 = graphics mode
2	*0 = color burst enabled*
	1 = color burst disabled
3–7	*Reserved (0)*

BYTE   Number of colors
            0 = monochrome compatible
            1 = 2 colors
            2 = 4 colors
            4 = 16 colors
            8 = 256 colors
WORD   Number of text columns
WORD   Number of text rows
WORD   Number of pixel columns
WORD   Number of pixel rows
2 BYTES   Reserved

Data Buffer Format:

None	*Use null pointer*

Category 7   Function 52H
Notify of Impending Session Switch

DosDevIOCtl

Parameter Buffer Format:

WORD	Session number	
WORD	Action	
	−1	*Specified session is terminating*
	>= 0	*Specified session is being selected*

Data Buffer Format:

None   *Use null pointer*

Category 7   Function 53H
Set Mouse Scaling Factors

DosDevIOCtl

Parameter Buffer Format:

WORD   Scaling factor for row (y) coordinates (0–32,767; default = 8)
WORD   Scaling factor for column (x) coordinates (0–32,767; default = 16)

Data Buffer Format:

None   *Use null pointer*

Category 7   Function 54H
Set Mouse Event Mask

DosDevIOCtl

Parameter Buffer Format:

WORD   Mouse event mask

Bit(s)	Significance (if set)
0	*Mouse movement, no buttons down*
1	*Mouse movement, button 1 down*
2	*Button 1 down*
3	*Mouse movement, button 2 down*
4	*Button 2 down*
5	*Mouse movement, button 3 down*
6	*Button 3 down*
7–15	*Reserved (0)*

Data Buffer Format:

None   *Use null pointer*

Category 7   Function 55H
Set Mouse Button for System Hot Key

DosDevIOCtl

Parameter Buffer Format:

WORD   Hot key identifier

Bit(s)	Significance (if set)
0	No hot key (overrides bits 1–3)
1	Button 1 is system hot key
2	Button 2 is system hot key
3	Button 3 is system hot key
4–15	Reserved (0)

Data Buffer Format:

None   *Use null pointer*

Category 7   Function 56H
Set Mouse Pointer Shape

DosDevIOCtl

Parameter Buffer Format:

WORD	Pointer image buffer length
WORD	Columns in pointer image
WORD	Rows in pointer image
WORD	Column offset (from left) of hot spot
WORD	Row offset (from top) of hot spot

Data Buffer Format:

BUFFER   Pointer image data (see *MouSetPtrShape*)

Category 7   Function 57H
Cancel Exclusion Area and Draw Mouse Pointer

DosDevIOCtl

Parameter Buffer Format:

None   *Use null pointer*

Data Buffer Format:

None   *Use null pointer*

Category 7   Function 58H
Set Exclusion Area for Mouse Pointer

DosDevIOCtl

Parameter Buffer Format:

WORD	Upper left *y* coordinate
WORD	Upper left *x* coordinate
WORD	Lower right *y* coordinate
WORD	Lower right *x* coordinate

Data Buffer Format:

None   *Use null pointer*

Category 7   Function 59H
Set Mouse Pointer Position

DosDevIOCtl

Parameter Buffer Format:

WORD	Row (*y*) coordinate
WORD	Column (*x*) coordinate

Data Buffer Format:

None   *Use null pointer*

Category 7   Function 5AH
Specify Address of Protected Mode Pointer-Draw Routine

DosDevIOCtl

Parameter Buffer Format:

DWORD	Pointer-draw routine's entry point
WORD	Reserved (0)
WORD	Pointer-draw routine's data segment selector

Data Buffer Format:

None   *Use null pointer*

Category 7   Function 5BH   DosDevIOCtl
Specify Address of Real Mode Pointer-Draw Routine

Parameter Buffer Format:

DWORD   Pointer-draw routine's entry point
WORD   Reserved (0)
WORD   Pointer-draw routine's data segment

Data Buffer Format:

None   *Use null pointer*

Category 7   Function 5CH   DosDevIOCtl
Set Mouse Driver Status

Parameter Buffer Format:

WORD   Mouse driver status

Bit(s)	Significance
0–7	*Reserved (0)*
8	*0 = pointer drawing enabled*
	1 = pointer drawing disabled
9	*0 = mouse data returned in screen coordinates*
	1 = mouse data returned in mickeys
10–15	*Reserved (0)*

Data Buffer Format:

None   *Use null pointer*

Category 7   Function 60H   DosDevIOCtl
Get Number of Mouse Buttons

Parameter Buffer Format:

None   *Use null pointer*

Data Buffer Format:

WORD   Number of mouse buttons (1–3)

Category 7   Function 61H
Get Number of Mickeys per Centimeter

DosDevIOCtl

Parameter Buffer Format:

None   *Use null pointer*

Data Buffer Format:

WORD   Mickeys per centimeter of mouse travel

Category 7   Function 62H
Get Mouse Driver Status

DosDevIOCtl

Parameter Buffer Format:

None   *Use null pointer*

Data Buffer Format:

WORD   Mouse driver status

Bit(s)	*Significance (if set)*
0	*Mouse event queue busy*
1	*Blocking read in progress*
2	*Flush event queue in progress*
3	*Pointer drawing disabled due to unsupported mode*
4–7	*Reserved (0)*
8	*Pointer drawing disabled*
9	*Mouse data returned in mickeys rather than in screen coordinates*
10–15	*Reserved (0)*

Category 7   Function 63H
Read Mouse Event Queue

DosDevIOCtl

Parameter Buffer Format:

WORD   Wait/no-wait flag
                0 = do not wait
                1 = wait until mouse event available

Data Buffer Format:

WORD	Mouse event flags	
	Bit(s)	*Significance (if set)*
	0	*Mouse movement, no buttons down*
	1	*Mouse movement, button 1 down*
	2	*Button 1 down*
	3	*Mouse movement, button 2 down*
	4	*Button 2 down*
	5	*Mouse movement, button 3 down*
	6	*Button 3 down*
	7–15	*Reserved (0)*

DWORD	Time stamp (msec. since system was turned on or restarted)
WORD	*y* (row) coordinate
WORD	*x* (column) coordinate

Category 7   Function 64H
Get Mouse Event Queue Status

DosDevIOCtl

Parameter Buffer Format:

None   *Use null pointer*

Data Buffer Format:

WORD	Number of events in queue
WORD	Size of event queue

Category 7   Function 65H
Get Mouse Driver Event Mask

DosDevIOCtl

Parameter Buffer Format:

None   *Use null pointer*

Data Buffer Format:

WORD	Mouse event mask	
	Bit(s)	*Significance (if set)*
	0	*Mouse movement, no buttons down*
	1	*Mouse movement, button 1 down*
	2	*Button 1 down*
	3	*Mouse movement, button 2 down*
	4	*Button 2 down*
	5	*Mouse movement, button 3 down*
	6	*Button 3 down*
	7–15	*Reserved (0)*

Category 7   Function 66H
Get Mouse Scaling Factors

DosDevIOCtl

Parameter Buffer Format:

None   *Use null pointer*

Data Buffer Format:

WORD   Scaling factor for row (*y*) coordinates (0–32,767; default = 8)
WORD   Scaling factor for column (*x*) coordinates (0–32,767; default = 16)

Category 7   Function 67H
Get Mouse Pointer Position

DosDevIOCtl

Parameter Buffer Format:

None   *Use null pointer*

Data Buffer Format:

WORD   Row (*y*) coordinate
WORD   Column (*x*) coordinate

Category 7   Function 68H
Get Mouse Pointer Shape

DosDevIOCtl

Parameter Buffer Format:

WORD   Pointer image buffer length
WORD   Columns in pointer image
WORD   Rows in pointer image
WORD   Column offset (from left) of hot spot
WORD   Row offset (from top) of hot spot

Data Buffer Format:

BUFFER   Pointer image data (see *MouSetPrtShape*)

Category 7   Function 69H
Get Mouse Button Used as System Hot Key

DosDevIOCtl

Parameter Buffer Format:

None   *Use null pointer*

Data Buffer Format:

WORD   Hot key identifier

Bit(s)	*Significance (if set)*
0	*No hot key (overrides bits 1–3)*
1	*Button 1 is system hot key*
2	*Button 2 is system hot key*
3	*Button 3 is system hot key*
4–15	*Reserved (0)*

Category 8   Function 00H
Lock Logical Drive

DosDevIOCtl

Parameter Buffer Format:

BYTE   Command information (should be 0)

Data Buffer Format:

None   *Use null pointer*

Category 8   Function 01H
Unlock Logical Drive

DosDevIOCtl

Parameter Buffer Format:

BYTE   Command information (should be 0)

Data Buffer Format:

None   *Use null pointer*

Category 8   Function 02H
Redetermine Media

Parameter Buffer Format:

BYTE   Command information (should be 0)

Data Buffer Format:

None   *Use null pointer*

Category 8   Function 03H
Set Logical Drive Map

Parameter Buffer Format:

BYTE   Command information (should be 0)

Data Buffer Format:

BYTE   Called with logical drive number (1 = A, 2 = B, etc.)

Category 8   Function 20H
Check if Block Device Removable

Parameter Buffer Format:

BYTE   Command information (should be 0)

Data Buffer Format:

BYTE   Status
              0 = removable
              1 = nonremovable

Category 8   Function 21H
Get Logical Drive Map

Parameter Buffer Format:

BYTE   Command information (should be 0)

Data Buffer Format:

BYTE   Receives currently mapped logical drive (1 = A, 2 = B, etc.), or zero if only one logical
              drive is mapped to the physical drive

Category 8   Function 43H
Set Device Parameters

DosDevIOCtl

Parameter Buffer Format:

BYTE   Command information

Bit(s)	Significance
0–1	00 = get BPB from medium
	01 = change default BPB for device
	10 = use specified BPB
2–7	Reserved (0)

Data Buffer Format:

31 BYTES	Extended BPB	
	WORD	Bytes per sector
	BYTE	Sectors per cluster
	WORD	Reserved sectors
	BYTE	Number of file allocation tables
	WORD	Number of root directory entries
	WORD	Total sectors
	BYTE	Medium descriptor
	WORD	Sectors per file allocation table
	WORD	Sectors per track
	WORD	Number of heads
	DWORD	Number of hidden sectors
	DWORD	Large total sectors
	6 BYTES	Reserved (0)

WORD   Number of cylinders

BYTE   Device type

    0 = 360 KB 5.25" floppy disk drive
    1 = 1.2 MB 5.25" floppy disk drive
    2 = 3.5" floppy disk drive
    3 = 8" single-density floppy disk drive
    4 = 8" double-density floppy disk drive
    5 = Fixed disk
    6 = Tape drive
    7 = Other

WORD   Device attributes

Bit(s)	Significance
0	0 = removable medium
	1 = nonremovable medium
1	0 = no change-line support
	1 = change-line supported
2–15	Reserved (0)

Category 8   Function 44H   DosDevIOCtl
Write Track

Parameter Buffer Format:

BYTE	Command information	
	Bit(s)	*Significance*
	0	*0 = track contains nonconsecutive sectors or does not start with 1*
		1 = track starts with 1 and contains only consecutive sectors
	1–7	*Reserved (0)*
WORD	Head	
WORD	Cylinder	
WORD	First sector	
WORD	Number of sectors	
DWORDS	Track layout field, with a DWORD for each sector; the first word is the sector number, and the second is the sector size in bytes	

Data Buffer Format:

BUFFER	Data to be written

Category 8   Function 45H   DosDevIOCtl
Format and Verify Track

Parameter Buffer Format:

BYTE	Command information	
	Bit(s)	*Significance*
	0	*0 = track contains nonconsecutive sectors or does not start with 1*
		1 = track starts with 1 and contains only consecutive sectors
	1–7	*Reserved (0)*
WORD	Head	
WORD	Cylinder	
WORD	Reserved (0)	
WORD	Number of sectors	
DWORDS	Track formatting table, with 4 bytes for each sector in the following order: cylinder, head, sector ID, and bytes per sector code (0 = 128 bytes, 1 = 256 bytes, 2 = 512 bytes, 3 = 1024 bytes)	

Data Buffer Format:

None	*Use null pointer*

Category 8   Function 63H
Get Device Parameters

DosDevIOCtl

Parameter Buffer Format:

BYTE   Command information

Bit(s)	*Significance*
0	*0 = Return recommended BPB for drive*
	1 = Return current BPB for drive
1–7	*Reserved (0)*

Data Buffer Format:

Same as data buffer format for Category 8 Function 43H (p. 651)

Category 8   Function 64H
Read Track

DosDevIOCtl

Parameter Buffer Format:

BYTE   Command information

Bit(s)	*Significance*
0	*0 = track contains nonconsecutive sectors or does not start with 1*
	1 = track starts with 1 and contains only consecutive sectors
1–7	*Reserved (0)*

WORD	Head
WORD	Cylinder
WORD	First sector
WORD	Number of sectors
DWORDS	Track layout field, with a DWORD for each sector; the first word is the sector number, and the second is the sector size in bytes

Data Buffer Format:

BUFFER   Receives data from disk

Category 8   Function 65H
Verify Track

DosDevIOCtl

Parameter Buffer Format:

Same as parameter buffer format for the preceding function, Category 8 Function 64H

Data Buffer Format:

None   *Use null pointer*

Category 9   Function OOH
Lock Physical Drive

DosDevIOCtl

Parameter Buffer Format:

BYTE   Command information (should be 0)

Data Buffer Format:

None   Use null pointer

Category 9   Function 01H
Unlock Physical Drive

DosDevIOCtl

Parameter Buffer Format:

BYTE   Command information (should be 0)

Data Buffer Format:

None   Use null pointer

Category 9   Function 44H
Write Physical Track

DosDevIOCtl

Parameter Buffer Format:

Same as parameter buffer format for Category 8 Function 44H (p. 652)

Data Buffer Format:

BUFFER   Data to be written

Category 9   Function 63H
Get Physical Device Parameters

DosDevIOCtl

Parameter Buffer Format:

BYTE   Command information (should be 0)

Data Buffer Format:

WORD	Reserved (0)
WORD	Number of cylinders
WORD	Number of heads
WORD	Sectors per track
8 BYTES	Reserved (0)

Category 9   Function 64H
Read Physical Track

Parameter Buffer Format:

Same as parameter buffer format for Category 8 Function 64H (p. 653)

Data Buffer Format:

BUFFER   Receives data from disk

Category 9   Function 65H
Verify Physical Track

Parameter Buffer Format:

Same as parameter buffer format for Category 8 Function 64H (p. 653)

Data Buffer Format:

None   *Use null pointer*

Category 10   Function 40H
Register Monitor

Parameter Buffer Format:

BYTE   Command information (should be 0)

Data Buffer Format:

WORD	Placement
	0 = No preference
	1 = Head of chain
	2 = Tail of chain
WORD	Monitor index (driver-dependent, usually screen group)
DWORD	Address of monitor input buffer
WORD	Offset of monitor output buffer

Category 11   Function 01H
Flush Input Buffer

DosDevIOCtl

Parameter Buffer Format:

BYTE   Command information (should be 0)

Data Buffer Format:

None   *Use null pointer*

Category 11   Function 02H
Flush Output Buffer

DosDevIOCtl

Parameter Buffer Format:

BYTE   Command information (should be 0)

Data Buffer Format:

None   *Use null pointer*

Category 11   Function 60H
Query Monitor Support

DosDevIOCtl

Parameter Buffer Format:

BYTE   Command information (should be 0)

Data Buffer Format:

None   *Use null pointer*

DevHlp FUNCTIONS

The entries in this section describe each of the kernel Device Helper (DevHlp) functions available in OS/2 versions 1.0 and 1.1. These functions help OS/2 device drivers manage memory, CPU execution mode, request queues, ring buffers for character device I/O, monitors, and interrupts.

The icons in the entry headers indicate the circumstances in which a particular DevHlp function can be used; they have the following meanings:

[K]	Function can be called when driver is in kernel mode; that is, when its strategy routine is called with a command code other than 0.
[Int]	Function can be called while the driver is servicing a hardware interrupt.
[U]	Function can be called in user mode; that is, it can be called while the driver is servicing a software interrupt by a real mode process.
[Init]	Function can be called during a driver's initialization; that is, it can be called when the driver's strategy routine is called with command code 0.
[1.1]	Function not available prior to OS/2 version 1.1.

Device drivers invoke DevHlp functions by a far call to a common entry point. The entry point is passed to the driver by the kernel in an *Initialize* request packet when the driver is loaded. Unlike the OS/2 API used by applications, the DevHlp interface is register based. A particular DevHlp function is selected by the value in DL; other registers are used to pass function-specific values or addresses.

A typical DevHlp call takes the following form:

```
dhptr    dd      ?               ; DevHlp entry point from
                                 ; Initialize request packet

          .
          .
          .

         mov     dl,function     ; selects DevHlp function

          .                      ; load other registers
          .                      ; with function-specific
          .                      ; parameters

         call    [dhptr]         ; indirect far call to
                                 ; DevHlp entry point
```

Results, if any, from a DevHlp function are usually returned in CPU flags and registers. Most functions clear the Carry flag to signal success and set the Carry flag to signal an error.

DevHlp Functions Listed Alphabetically

Function Name	Hex	Dec	Description
ABIOSCall	36H	54	Invokes an ABIOS service
ABIOSCommonEntry	37H	55	Invokes an ABIOS common entry point
AllocGDTSelector	2DH	45	Allocates one or more GDT selectors
AllocPhys	18H	24	Allocates a fixed block of memory
AllocReqPacket	0DH	13	Allocates a block of memory large enough to contain the largest defined request packet
AttachDD	2AH	42	Returns IDC entry point to a specified driver
Block	04H	04	Suspends the requesting thread
DeRegister	21H	33	Removes monitor from a monitor chain
DevDone	01H	01	Signals completion of a request packet
EOI	31H	49	Issues an End-Of-Interrupt to the 8259 PIC
FreeLIDEntry	35H	53	Releases the logical ID for a device
FreePhys	19H	25	Releases memory allocated by a previous call to *AllocPhys*
FreeReqPacket	0EH	14	Releases memory previously allocated by a call to *AllocReqPacket*
GetDOSVar	24H	36	Returns a bimodal pointer to a kernel variable
GetLIDEntry	34H	52	Obtains a logical ID for a device
Lock	13H	19	Locks a memory segment
MonFlush	23H	35	Removes all data from a monitor chain

(continued)

Function Name	Hex	Dec	Description
MonitorCreate	1FH	31	Creates an empty monitor chain or destroys a monitor chain
MonWrite	22H	34	Writes a data record into the monitor chain
PhysToGDTSelector	2EH	46	Maps a 32-bit physical address to a GDT selector
PhysToUVirt	17H	23	Converts a 32-bit physical address to a user virtual address
PhysToVirt	15H	21	Converts a 32-bit physical address to a virtual address
ProtToReal	30H	48	Switches the processor from protected mode into real mode
PullParticular	0BH	11	Removes the specified request packet from the driver's request packet queue
PullReqPacket	0AH	10	Removes the next waiting request packet from the driver's request packet queue
PushReqPacket	09H	09	Adds a request packet to the driver's request packet queue
QueueFlush	10H	16	Discards all data in the queue
QueueInit	0FH	15	Initializes a character queue
QueueRead	12H	18	Returns and removes the oldest waiting character from a character queue
QueueWrite	11H	17	Adds a character to a character queue
RealToProt	2FH	47	Switches the processor from real mode to protected mode
Register	20H	32	Adds a device monitor to a device monitor chain
RegisterStackUsage	38H	56	Indicates expected stack usage of device driver to interrupt manager
ResetTimer	1EH	30	Removes a timer handler for the device driver
ROMCritSection	26H	38	Protects a driver's handler from preemption
Run	05H	05	Releases blocked threads
SchedClockAddr	00H	00	Gets kernel's clock tick entry point
SemClear	07H	07	Clears a RAM or system semaphore
SemHandle	08H	08	Returns a system semaphore handle that can be used at task time or interrupt time
SemRequest	06H	06	Claims a system or RAM semaphore
SendEvent	25H	37	Notifies kernel that a key requiring special processing has been detected
SetIRQ	1BH	27	Captures the hardware interrupt vector for the specified IRQ level
SetROMVector	1AH	26	Replaces a real mode software interrupt handler with the driver's handler
SetTimer	1DH	29	Adds a timer handler to the list of the system's timer handlers
SortReqPacket	0CH	12	Inserts a read or write request packet into a request packet queue

(continued)

Function Name	Hex	Dec	Description
TCYield	03H	03	Yields the CPU so that time-critical threads can execute
TickCount	33H	51	Adds a timer handler to the system's list of timer handlers
Unlock	14H	20	Unlocks a memory segment
UnPhysToVirt	32H	50	Notifies the kernel that virtual addresses are no longer needed
UnSetIRQ	1CH	28	Releases ownership of a hardware interrupt
VerifyAccess	27H	39	Verifies a process's right of access to memory
VirtToPhys	16H	22	Converts a virtual address to a 32-bit physical address
Yield	02H	02	Yields the CPU so that threads with the same or higher priority can execute

DevHlp Functions Listed Numerically

Hex	Dec	Function Name	Description
00H	00	*SchedClockAddr*	Gets kernel's clock tick entry point
01H	01	*DevDone*	Signals completion of a request packet
02H	02	*Yield*	Yields the CPU so that threads with the same or higher priority can execute
03H	03	*TCYield*	Yields the CPU so that time-critical threads can execute
04H	04	*Block*	Suspends the requesting thread
05H	05	*Run*	Releases blocked threads
06H	06	*SemRequest*	Claims a system or RAM semaphore
07H	07	*SemClear*	Clears a RAM or system semaphore
08H	08	*SemHandle*	Returns a system semaphore handle that can be used at task time or interrupt time
09H	09	*PushReqPacket*	Adds a request packet to the driver's request packet queue
0AH	10	*PullReqPacket*	Removes the next waiting request packet from the driver's request packet queue
0BH	11	*PullParticular*	Removes the specified request packet from the driver's request packet queue
0CH	12	*SortReqPacket*	Inserts a read or write request packet into a request packet queue
0DH	13	*AllocReqPacket*	Allocates a block of memory large enough to contain the largest defined request packet
0EH	14	*FreeReqPacket*	Releases memory previously allocated by a call to *AllocReqPacket*
0FH	15	*QueueInit*	Initializes a character queue
10H	16	*QueueFlush*	Discards all data in the queue
11H	17	*QueueWrite*	Adds a character to a character queue
12H	18	*QueueRead*	Returns and removes the oldest waiting character from a character queue

(continued)

Hex	Dec	Function Name	Description
13H	19	*Lock*	Locks a memory segment
14H	20	*Unlock*	Unlocks a memory segment
15H	21	*PhysToVirt*	Converts a 32-bit physical address to a virtual address
16H	22	*VirtToPhys*	Converts a virtual address to a 32-bit physical address
17H	23	*PhysToUVirt*	Converts a 32-bit physical address to a user virtual address
18H	24	*AllocPhys*	Allocates a fixed block of memory
19H	25	*FreePhys*	Releases memory allocated by a previous call to *AllocPhys*
1AH	26	*SetROMVector*	Replaces a real mode software interrupt handler with the driver's handler
1BH	27	*SetIRQ*	Captures the hardware interrupt vector for the specified IRQ level
1CH	28	*UnSetIRQ*	Releases ownership of a hardware interrupt
1DH	29	*SetTimer*	Adds a timer handler to the list of the system's timer handlers
1EH	30	*ResetTimer*	Removes a timer handler for the device driver
1FH	31	*MonitorCreate*	Creates an empty monitor chain or destroys a monitor chain
20H	32	*Register*	Adds a device monitor to a device monitor chain
21H	33	*DeRegister*	Removes monitor from a monitor chain
22H	34	*MonWrite*	Writes a data record into the monitor chain
23H	35	*MonFlush*	Removes all data from a monitor chain
24H	36	*GetDOSVar*	Returns a bimodal pointer to a kernel variable
25H	37	*SendEvent*	Notifies kernel that a key requiring special processing has been detected
26H	38	*ROMCritSection*	Protects a driver's handler from preemption
27H	39	*VerifyAccess*	Verifies a process's right of access to memory
2AH	42	*AttachDD*	Returns IDC entry point to a specified driver
2DH	45	*AllocGDTSelector*	Allocates one or more GDT selectors
2EH	46	*PhysToGDTSelector*	Maps a 32-bit physical address to a GDT selector
2FH	47	*RealToProt*	Switches the processor from real mode to protected mode
30H	48	*ProtToReal*	Switches the processor from protected mode into real mode
31H	49	*EOI*	Issues an End-Of-Interrupt to the 8259 PIC
32H	50	*UnPhysToVirt*	Notifies the kernel that virtual addresses are no longer needed
33H	51	*TickCount*	Adds a timer handler to the system's list of timer handlers
34H	52	*GetLIDEntry*	Obtains a logical ID for a device
35H	53	*FreeLIDEntry*	Releases the logical ID for a device
36H	54	*ABIOSCall*	Invokes an ABIOS service
37H	55	*ABIOSCommonEntry*	Invokes an ABIOS common entry point
38H	56	*RegisterStackUsage*	Indicates expected stack usage of device driver to interrupt manager

ABIOSCall

Invokes an ABIOS service on behalf of the requesting driver.

Call with:

AX	Logical ID
DH	Subfunction
	0 = start
	1 = interrupt
	2 = timeout
DL	36H
DS:SI	Address of ABIOS request block

Returns:

If function successful

Carry flag	Clear

If function unsuccessful

Carry flag	Set
AX	Error code

Notes:

- The ABIOS request block must be located in the driver's data segment.

- If the driver is in user mode, it should protect the execution of the ABIOS routine from interruption by first calling the DevHlp *ROMCritSection*.

Related functions: *ABIOSCommonEntry, FreeLIDEntry, GetLIDEntry, ROMCritSection.*

ABIOSCommonEntry

[K]   [Int]   [U]   [Init]

Invokes an ABIOS common entry point on behalf of the requesting driver.

Call with:

DH	Subfunction
	0 = start
	1 = interrupt
	2 = timeout
DL	37H
DS:SI	Address of ABIOS request block

Returns:

If function successful

Carry flag	Clear

If function unsuccessful

Carry flag	Set
AX	Error code

Notes:

■ The ABIOS request block must be located in the driver's data segment.

■ If the driver is in user mode, it should protect the execution of the ABIOS routine from interruption by first calling the DevHlp *ROMCritSection*.

Related functions: *ABIOSCall, FreeLIDEntry, GetLIDEntry, ROMCritSection*.

AllocGDTSelector

[Init]

Allocates one or more GDT selectors for use by the device driver.

Call with:

CX	Number of selectors requested
DL	2DH
ES:DI	Address of array to receive selectors

Returns:

If function successful

Carry flag   Clear

If function unsuccessful

Carry flag   Set
AX   Error code

Notes:

- The allocated selectors can be used at task time or at interrupt time.

- The DevHlp *PhysToGDTSelector* maps a particular physical memory address onto one of the allocated GDT selectors. The addressability remains valid until *PhysToGDTSelector* is called again with the same selector.

Related functions: *PhysToGDTSelector, PhysToUVirt.*

AllocPhys   [K]   [Init]

Allocates a fixed block of memory.

Call with:

AX:BX	Size in bytes
DH	Block position
	0 = above 1 MB
	1 = below 1 MB
DL	18H

Returns:

If function successful

Carry flag   Clear
AX:BX   32-bit physical address

If function unsuccessful

Carry flag   Set
AX   Error code

Notes:

- The DevHlp *UnLock* has no effect on memory allocated by this function.

- Avoid allocation of fixed memory below the 1 MB boundary; such allocations reduce the amount of memory available for real mode applications.

Related functions: *AllocReqPacket, FreePhys.*

AllocReqPacket   [K]

Allocates a block of memory large enough to contain the largest defined request packet and returns a bimodal pointer to the block.

Call with:

DH	Wait/no-wait option
	0 = wait for available request packet
	1 = do not wait for request packet
DL	0DH

Returns:

If function successful

Carry flag	Clear
ES:BX	Address of request packet

If function unsuccessful

Carry flag	Set

Notes:

- The memory blocks allocated with this function are a scarce system resource. Release these blocks as quickly as possible with the DevHlp *FreeReqPacket*.

- The state of the interrupt flag is not preserved.

Related functions: *AllocPhys, FreeReqPacket*.

AttachDD   [K] [Init] [1.1]

Returns the address of the inter–device driver communication (IDC) entry point for the specified driver.

Call with:

DL	2AH
DS:BX	Address of device name
DS:DI	Address of buffer to receive entry point information (*see Notes*)

Returns:

If function successful

Carry flag	Clear

and buffer filled as described below

If function unsuccessful

Carry flag	Set

Notes:

- The device name must be 8 bytes long and must exactly match the name field in the header of the driver which is being attached. Because the name fields of block device driver headers are not necessarily unique, this function is ordinarily used only to attach to character device drivers.

- The supplied buffer must be at least 12 bytes long and is filled by the system as follows:

Offset	Length	Description
00H	2	Real mode offset of IDC entry point
02H	2	Real mode segment of IDC entry point
04H	2	Real mode data segment for specified driver
06H	2	Protected mode offset of IDC entry point
08H	2	Protected mode selector of IDC entry point
0AH	2	Protected mode data selector for specified driver

- When a driver wants to call another driver, it must first check the current CPU mode and verify that a nonzero IDC entry point address was returned by *AttachDD* for that mode. It must then set the DS register appropriately on behalf of the destination driver and enter the driver via a far call.

Block   [K] [U]

Suspends the requesting thread. The thread is awakened when the specified timeout interval elapses or when another thread calls the DevHlp *Run* with the same event ID.

Call with:

AX:BX	Event ID
DI:CX	Timeout interval in milliseconds (−1 = wait indefinitely)
DH	Interruptible flag
	0 = interruptible
	1 = noninterruptible
DL	04H

Returns:

If event wakeup

Carry flag	Clear

If timeout wakeup

Carry flag	Set
Zero flag	Set
AL	00H

If unusual wakeup

Carry flag	Set
Zero flag	Clear
AL	<> 00H

Notes:

- Always call *Block* with DH = 0 unless the sleep will be for less than 1 second.

- Disable interrupts before calling *Block*; in this way, you avoid deadlocks or race conditions with the thread which will call *Run*. When the thread resumes execution, interrupts are already enabled.

- The event ID is an arbitrary 32-bit value. Take care to use a value that is not likely to be duplicated by other drivers because *Run* awakens *all* threads that have called *Block* with the same event ID.

Related functions: *DevDone, Run, SemRequest.*

DeRegister [K]

Removes all monitors associated with the specified process from a monitor chain.

Call with:

AX	Monitor chain handle (from *MonitorCreate*)
BX	Process ID
DL	21H

Returns:

If function successful

Carry flag	Clear
AX	Number of monitors remaining in chain

If function unsuccessful

Carry flag	Set
AX	Error code

Note:

- Call this function only in protected mode.

Related functions: *MonitorCreate, Register.*

DevDone [K] [Int]

Sets the Done bit in the status word of a request packet and then unblocks any threads waiting in the kernel for the completion of the request.

Call with:

DL	01H
ES:BX	Address of request packet

Returns:

Nothing

Notes:

- The driver should store any necessary information, such as error flags, in the request packet before calling *DevDone*.

- Do *not* call *DevDone* with the address of a request packet that was allocated with *AllocReqPacket*.

- If a request is completed by the strategy routine at task time, the driver need not call *DevDone* — it can set the Done bit in the request packet status word and return.

Related functions: *Block, EOI, Run.*

EOI   [Int]   [Init]

Issues an End-Of-Interrupt (EOI) to the 8259 programmable interrupt controller(s) as appropriate for the interrupt level.

Call with:

AL	IRQ number (00H–0FH)
DL	31H

Returns:

Nothing

Notes:

- If the specified interrupt level is for the slave 8259, then an EOI is issued to both the master and slave 8259.

- The state of the interrupt flag is not changed. To minimize the danger of excessive nested interrupts, make the DevHlp *EOI* call as late as possible in interrupt processing, disable interrupts immediately before the call, and leave them disabled until the IRET.

Related functions: *SetIRQ, UnSetIRQ.*

FreeLIDEntry   [K]   [Init]

Releases the logical ID (LID) for a device.

Call with:

AX	LID
DL	35H
DS	Driver's data segment

Returns:

If function successful

Carry flag	Clear

If function unsuccessful

Carry flag	Set
AX	Error code

Note:

■ A driver which is deinstalling should release any LID it obtained previously during its initialization.

Related functions: *ABIOSCall, ABIOSCommonEntry, GetLIDEntry.*

FreePhys [K] [Init]

Releases memory allocated by a previous call to the DevHlp *AllocPhys.*

Call with:

AX:BX	32-bit physical address
DL	19H

Returns:

If function successful

Carry flag	Clear

If function unsuccessful

Carry flag	Set

Note:

■ A driver which is deinstalling should release any memory it allocated during its initialization.

Related functions: *AllocPhys, FreeReqPacket.*

FreeReqPacket [K]

Releases memory previously allocated by a call to the DevHlp *AllocReqPacket.*

Call with:

DL	0EH
ES:BX	Address of request packet

Returns:

Nothing

Note:

■ The state of the interrupt flag is not preserved.

Related functions: *AllocReqPacket, FreePhys.*

GetDOSVar

[K]   [Init]

Returns a bimodal pointer to a kernel variable.

Call with:

AL	Variable of interest
	1 = global information segment (T, I)
	2 = local information segment (T)
	3 = reserved
	4 = stand-alone dump facility (T, I)
	5 = system reboot (T, I)
	6 = MSATS facility (T, I)
	7 = system yield flag (T)
	8 = system time-critical yield flag (T)
	9 = reserved
	10 = reserved
	11 = real mode code page ID (T)
DL	24H

T = address valid at task time
I = address valid at interrupt time

Returns:

If function successful

Carry flag	Clear
AX:BX	Address of variable (*see Note*)

If function unsuccessful

Carry flag	Set

Note:

The value placed in AL determines the nature of the variable returned by this function, as follows:

Value in AL	Description of Variable
1	WORD containing the selector for the global information segment
2 or 11	DWORD containing the full 32-bit virtual address of the corresponding structure
4, 5, or 6	DWORD containing the address of a kernel entry point
7 or 8	BYTE that is nonzero if a thread with the same or higher priority (AL = 7) or time-critical priority (AL = 8) is ready to execute.

Related functions: *Register, TCYield, Yield.*

GetLIDEntry [U] [K] [Init]

Obtains a logical ID (LID) for a device.

Call with:

AL	Device ID
BL	LID specifier
	0 = return first unclaimed LID
	<>0 = return relative LID
DH	LID type
	0 = unshared LID
	1 = shareable LID (DMA, POS)
DL	34H
DS	Driver's data segment

Returns:

If function successful

Carry flag	Clear
AX	LID

If function unsuccessful

Carry flag	Set
AX	Error code

Related functions: *ABIOSCall, ABIOSCommonEntry, FreeLIDEntry.*

Lock [K] [Init]

Locks a memory segment so that it will not be swapped or moved during an I/O operation.

Call with:

AX	Selector/segment
BH	Duration
	0 = short-term (2 seconds or less)
	1 = long-term
BL	Wait/no-wait flag
	0 = wait until segment available and locked
	1 = do not wait if segment unavailable
DL	13H

Returns:

If function successful

Carry flag	Clear
AX:BX	Lock handle

If function unsuccessful

Carry flag	Set
AX	Undefined
BX	Undefined

Notes:

- Addresses received by the driver in read or write request packets need not be locked before use.

- The driver should verify the requesting process's access to the segment by calling the DevHlp *VerifyAccess* before calling *Lock*, and it should not yield the CPU between the two calls.

- If a long-term lock is requested, the kernel can move the segment to the region reserved for fixed memory allocations before returning.

Related functions: *UnLock, VerifyAccess, VirtToPhys.*

MonFlush   [K]

Removes all data from a monitor chain. A special flush record is sent through the chain to notify all monitors to discard any data in their internal buffers.

Call with:

AX	Monitor chain handle (from *MonitorCreate*)
DL	23H

Returns:

If function successful

Carry flag	Clear
AX	0000H

If function unsuccessful

Carry flag	Set
AX	Error code

Notes:

- Subsequent *MonWrite* calls fail (or block) until the flush record emerges from the monitor chain.

- This function can be called only in protected mode.

- The state of the interrupt flag is not preserved.

Related functions: *DeRegister, MonitorCreate, MonWrite, Register.*

MonitorCreate   [K]   [Init]

Creates an empty monitor chain or destroys a monitor chain.

Call with:

AX	0 (to create new monitor chain)
	Monitor chain handle (to destroy monitor chain)
DL	1FH
ES:SI	Address of monitor chain buffer
DS:DI	Address of notification routine

Returns:

If function successful

Carry flag	Clear
AX	Monitor chain handle (if called with AX = 0)

If function unsuccessful

Carry flag	Set
AX	Error code

Notes:

- This function can be called only in protected mode.

- The first word of the monitor chain buffer must contain the buffer length in bytes.

- The driver places data into the monitor chain by calling the DevHlp *MonWrite*. When data emerges from the monitor chain, the kernel's monitor dispatcher places the data in the driver's monitor chain buffer and calls the notification routine previously registered with *MonitorCreate*.

- The notification routine is entered in protected mode with the following:

ES:SI	Address of monitor chain buffer
DS	Selector for driver's data segment

  The length of the data record is placed in the first word of the monitor chain buffer.

Related functions: *DeRegister, MonFlush, MonWrite, Register.*

MonWrite [K] [Int] [U]

Writes a data record into the monitor chain so that it can pass to the processes registered as device monitors.

Call with:

AX	Monitor chain handle (from *MonitorCreate*)
CX	Length of data record (bytes)
DH	Wait/no-wait flag
	0 = wait for write complete
	1 = do not wait for write complete
DL	22H
DS:SI	Address of data record (must be in driver data segment)

Returns:

If function successful

Carry flag   Clear
AX   0000H

If function unsuccessful

Carry flag   Set
AX   Error code

Notes:

- The wait/no-wait flag must be 1 for calls to *MonWrite* at interrupt time.

- The data record must not be larger than the size of the driver's monitor chain buffer minus 2 bytes.

- A *MonFlush* in progress can cause the *MonWrite* to fail with a not-enough-memory error code.

- The state of the interrupt flag is not preserved.

Related functions: *DeRegister, MonitorCreate, MonFlush, Register.*

PhysToGDTSelector   [K]   [Int]   [U]   [Init]

Maps a 32-bit physical address to a GDT selector. The selector must have been previously obtained during driver initialization with *AllocGDTSelector*.

Call with:

AX:BX   32-bit physical address
CX   Length in bytes (0 = 65,536)
DL   2EH
SI   Selector

Returns:

If function successful

Carry flag   Clear

If function unsuccessful

Carry flag   Set
AX   Error code

Notes:

- The addressability of the GDT selector remains unchanged until the next call to *PhysToGDTSelector* with the same selector.

- The selector is for private use by the driver only and cannot be used in DevHlp calls or passed to a process.

- If the driver is in real mode, it can call the DevHlp *RealToProt* to switch the CPU into protected mode in order to use the GDT selector. The driver must then restore the CPU mode by calling *ProtToReal*.

Related functions: *AllocGDTSelector, PhysToUVirt, PhysToVirt, ProtToReal, RealToProt, VirtToPhys.*

PhysToUVirt [K] [Init]

Converts a 32-bit physical address to a virtual address. In protected mode, a selector is allocated from the current LDT and must then be freed by a call to *PhysToUVirt*. In real mode, the physical address is converted to a segment-offset pair if it is below the 1 MB boundary.

Call with:

AX:BX	32-bit physical address
CX	Length in bytes (0 = 65,536)
DH	Request type
	0 = get executable selector
	1 = get read/write data selector
	2 = release selector
DL	17H

Returns:

If function successful

Carry flag	Clear
ES:BX	Virtual address (if called with DH = 0 or 1)

If function unsuccessful

Carry flag	Set
AX	Error code

Notes:

- *PhysToUVirt* allows a driver to make a fixed memory area (such as a video adapter refresh buffer or the driver's data segment) addressable for a process. The selector obtained from *PhysToUVirt* is typically passed to the process in a *Generic IOCtl* data buffer.

- For request type 2, the selector to be freed is placed in register AX, and the contents of registers BX and CX are ignored.

- Do not use the virtual address returned by this function in system calls.

Related functions: *PhysToGDTSelector, PhysToVirt, VirtToPhys.*

PhysToVirt [K] [Int] [Init]

Converts a 32-bit physical address to a virtual address. If the function is called in real mode, the results depend on the physical address, current CPU mode, and hardware configuration.

Call with:

AX:BX	32-bit physical address
CX	Length in bytes (0 = 65,536)
DH	Destination for result
	0 = leave result in DS:SI
	1 = leave result in ES:DI
DL	15H

Returns:

If function successful

Carry flag	Clear
Zero flag	Mode switch indicator
	Flag clear if no CPU mode switch
	Flag set if CPU mode has changed
DS:SI	Virtual address (if called with DH = 0)
ES:DI	Virtual address (if called with DH = 1)

If function unsuccessful

Carry flag	Set
AX	Error code

Notes:

- The returned virtual address does not remain valid if the driver blocks, yields, or is interrupted. Do not call DevHlp services other than *PhysToVirt* while the virtual address is needed.

- On PC/AT-compatible machines, if the CPU is in real mode and the physical address is above 1 MB, no mode switch is performed; instead, the destination segment register is loaded with a special value that provides addressability to the memory, and the function returns with interrupt disabled and the Zero flag clear. The addressability will be lost if the segment register is reloaded.

- On PS/2-compatible machines, if the CPU is in real mode and the physical address is above 1 MB, the CPU is switched to protected mode, and the function returns with the Zero flag set.

- If the destination for the virtual address is DS:SI, and no mode switch occurs, ES is preserved. If the CPU is switched to protected mode, and ES points to the driver's data segment, the segment address is replaced with the corresponding selector; otherwise, ES is set to zero.

- If the destination for the virtual address is ES:DI, and no mode switch occurs, DS is preserved. If the CPU is switched to protected mode, and DS points to the driver's data segment, the segment address is replaced with the corresponding selector; otherwise, DS is set to zero.

- If the Z flag indicates that a mode switch has occurred, the driver must recalculate virtual addresses previously obtained with this function. The driver should therefore first convert the address most likely to cause a mode switch.

- The driver must call *UnPhysToVirt* before it issues a call to DevHlp *EOI* or returns to the kernel to release the virtual address or addresses. Only one call to *UnPhysToVirt* is needed, regardless of the number of preceding *PhysToVirt* calls. *UnPhysToVirt* will also restore the previous CPU mode if necessary.

Related functions: *PhysToGDTSelector, PhysToUVirt, UnPhysToVirt, VirtToPhys.*

ProtToReal [K] [Int]

Switches the processor from protected mode into real mode.

Call with:

DL   30H
DS   Driver's data segment

Returns:

If function successful

Carry flag   Clear

If function unsuccessful (mode was not changed)

Carry flag   Set

Notes:

- If the CPU mode is changed, the contents of the CS, DS, and SS registers are reset appropriately.

- The contents of ES are not preserved.

- The CPU mode at entry to the driver must always be restored before the driver returns.

- The driver can use the SMSW instruction to obtain the machine status word and determine the current mode. The PE bit (0) is set if the processor is in protected mode.

Related functions: *PhysToGDTSelector, RealToProt.*

PullParticular [K] [Int]

Removes the specified request packet from the driver's request packet queue.

Call with:

DL   0BH
DS:SI   Address of request queue head
ES:BX   Address of request packet

Returns:

If function successful

Carry flag   Clear

If function unsuccessful

Carry flag   Set

Related functions: *PullReqPacket, PushReqPacket, SortReqPacket.*

PullReqPacket   [K]   [Int]

Removes the next waiting request packet from the driver's request packet queue and returns a pointer to the packet.

Call with:

DL	0AH
DS:SI	Address of request queue head

Returns:

If function successful

Carry flag	Clear
ES:BX	Address of request packet

If function unsuccessful

Carry flag	Set

Related functions: *PullParticular, PushReqPacket, SortReqPacket.*

PushReqPacket   [K]

Adds a request packet to the driver's request packet queue.

Call with:

DL	09H
DS:SI	Address of request queue head
ES:BX	Address of request packet

Returns:

Nothing

Note:

■ The request queue head is a DWORD which you should initialize to zero before the first call to *SortReqPacket* or *PushReqPacket.*

Related functions: *AllocReqPacket, PullParticular, PullReqPacket, SortReqPacket.*

QueueFlush   [K]   [Int]   [U]

Resets the pointers for the specified character queue, discarding any data in the queue.

Call with:

DL   10H
DS:BX   Address of character queue structure

Returns:

Nothing

Related functions: *QueueInit, QueueRead, QueueWrite.*

QueueInit   [K]   [Int]   [U]   [Init]

Initializes a character queue for subsequent use by *QueueRead*, *QueueWrite*, and *QueueFlush*. Character queues are first in, first out and are implemented as simple ring buffers.

Call with:

DL   0FH
DS:BX   Address of character queue structure

Returns:

Nothing

Note:

■ A character queue has the following structure:

Offset	*Length*	*Description*
00H	2	Size of queue buffer (*n*)
02H	2	Buffer out index
04H	2	Number of characters in queue
06H	*n*	Buffer for character queue

Before calling *QueueInit*, the driver must initialize the first word in the structure with the length of the buffer area.

Related functions: *QueueFlush, QueueRead, QueueWrite.*

QueueRead   [K]   [Int]   [U]

Returns and removes the oldest waiting character from a character queue. If the queue is empty, the function returns an error.

Call with:

DL   12H
DS:BX   Address of character queue structure

Returns:

If function successful

Carry flag   Clear
AL   Character

If function unsuccessful (queue is empty)

Carry flag   Set

Related functions: *QueueFlush, QueueInit, QueueWrite.*

QueueWrite   [K]   [Int]   [U]

Adds a character to a character queue. If the queue is full, the function returns an error.

Call with:

AL   Character
DL   11H
DS:BX   Address of character queue structure

Returns:

If function successful

Carry flag   Clear

If function unsuccessful (queue is full)

Carry flag   Set

Related functions: *QueueFlush, QueueInit, QueueRead.*

RealToProt   [K]   [Int]

Switches the processor from real mode to protected mode.

Call with:

DL   2FH
DS   Driver's data segment

Returns:

If function successful

Carry flag   Clear

If function unsuccessful (mode was not changed)

Carry flag   Set

Notes:

- If the CPU mode is changed, the contents of the CS, DS, and SS registers are reset appropriately.

- The contents of ES are not preserved.

- The CPU mode at entry to the driver must always be restored before the driver returns.

- The driver can use the SMSW instruction to obtain the machine status word and determine the current mode. The PE bit (0) is clear if the processor is in real mode.

Related functions: *PhysToGDTSelector, ProtToReal.*

Register   [K]

Adds a device monitor to a monitor chain.

Call with:

AX	Monitor handle (from *MonitorCreate*)
CX	Process ID of device monitor
DH	Placement flag
	0 = no preference
	1 = head of monitor chain
	2 = tail of monitor chain
DL	20H
ES:SI	Address of process's monitor input buffer
ES:DI	Address of process's monitor output buffer

Returns:

If function successful

Carry flag	Clear

If function unsuccessful

Carry flag	Set
AX	Error code

Notes:

- This function can be called only in protected mode.

- When a process calls *DosMonReg*, the kernel passes the addresses of the monitor input and output buffers and the placement flag to the driver in a *DosDevIOCtl* Category 10 Function 40H request packet. The driver must obtain the PID of the process from the local information segment.

- A single process can register more than one monitor. The first word of the monitor input and output buffers must contain the length of the buffer (including the length word itself). The buffers must be at least 20 bytes longer than the size of the driver's monitor data packet.

Related functions: *DeRegister, GetDOSVar, MonFlush, MonitorCreate, MonWrite.*

RegisterStackUsage [Init] [1.1]

Notifies the kernel's interrupt dispatcher of the driver's interrupt-time stack requirements.

Call with:

DL   38H
DS:BX   Address of stack information structure (*see Notes*)

Returns:

If function successful

Carry flag   Clear

If function unsuccessful

Carry flag   Set

Notes:

- The supplied structure must be 14 bytes long and formatted as follows:

Offset	Length	Description
00H	2	Contains the value 14 (the total length of the structure in bytes)
02H	2	Interrupt flags

		Bit(s)	Significance
		0	0 = *driver's interrupt handler does not enable interrupts*
			1 = *driver's interrupt handler enables interrupts*
		1–15	*Reserved*

Offset	Length	Description
04H	2	IRQ level used by driver
06H	2	Bytes of stack needed by driver's interrupt handler while interrupts are disabled
08H	2	Bytes of stack needed by driver's interrupt handler while interrupts are enabled
0AH	2	Bytes of stack needed by driver's interrupt handler after call to DevHlp EOI
0CH	2	Maximum number of levels of nested interrupts expected by driver

- If the specified number of nested interrupts is exceeded, the kernel's interrupt dispatcher disables that IRQ level until the system is restarted.

- A driver that handles multiple interrupt levels must make a separate call to *RegisterStackUsage* for each IRQ level.

- This function can be called only during driver initialization. If the function returns an error, the driver is expected to release any memory and IRQ levels it has allocated and abort its installation.

ResetTimer   [K] [Int] [Init]

Notifies the kernel that the driver's timer handler should no longer be called on timer tick interrupts.

Call with:

DL	1EH
CS:AX	Address of timer handler
DS	Driver's data segment

Returns:

If function successful

Carry flag   Clear

If function unsuccessful

Carry flag   Set

Related functions: *SetTimer, TickCount*.

ROMCritSection   [U]

Protects a driver's handler for real mode software interrupts from preemption by disabling session switching.

Call with:

AL	Critical section flag
	0 = exit critical section
	<>0 = enter critical section
DL	26H

Returns:

Nothing

Related functions: *ABIOSCall, ABIOSCommonEntry, SetROMVector*.

Run   [K] [Int] [U]

Awakens all previously blocked threads that have the specified event identifier.

Call with:

AX:BX	Event ID
DL	05H

Returns:

If no threads awakened

Zero flag	Set
AX	0000H

If one or more threads awakened

Zero flag	Clear
AX	Number of threads awakened

Related functions: *Block, DevDone, SemClear.*

SchedClockAddr   [K] [Init]

Returns a bimodal pointer to the kernel's clock tick entry point. *SchedClockAddr* is called by the real time clock device driver during its initialization. The driver's clock tick interrupt handler calls the address returned by *SchedClockAddr* to distribute clock ticks throughout the system.

Call with:

DL	00H
DS:AX	Address of DWORD variable

Returns:

Bimodal pointer to kernel entry point placed in variable.

Note:

- The driver must call the kernel clock tick entry point twice for each clock tick interrupt: once prior to calling the DevHlp *EOI*, and once afterwards. The parameters for the call are the following:

AL	Milliseconds since last call
DH	*EOI* indicator
	0 = prior to EOI
	1 = after EOI

Related functions: *EOI, SetIRQ.*

SemClear   [K] [Int] [U]

Clears (releases) a RAM or system semaphore. Any threads that were blocking on the semaphore become eligible for execution.

Call with:

AX:BX	Semaphore handle
DL	07H

Returns:

If function successful

Carry flag   Clear

If function unsuccessful

Carry flag   Set
AX   Error code

Notes:

- RAM semaphores that will be used at interrupt time must be located in the driver's data segment or in locked storage.

- System semaphores can be created or opened only by a process. The process passes the semaphore handle to the driver in a *DosDevIOCtl* parameter buffer, and the driver then calls the DevHlp *SemHandle* to convert the handle to a value that it can use at task time or at interrupt time. A device driver cannot access system semaphores in user mode.

Related functions: *SemHandle, SemRequest.*

SemHandle   [K]   [Int]

Converts a system semaphore handle obtained by a process into a handle that the driver can use at task time or interrupt time, or releases a handle previously obtained with this function.

Call with:

AX:BX   Semaphore handle
DH   Action
                0 = releasing handle
                1 = obtaining handle
DL   08H

Returns:

If function successful

Carry flag   Clear
AX:BX   New handle for semaphore

If function unsuccessful

Carry flag   Set
AX   Error code

Notes:

- If *SemHandle* is called with the handle of a RAM semaphore, it returns the same handle.

- The state of the interrupt flag is not preserved.

Related functions: *SemClear, SemRequest.*

SemRequest   [K] [U]

Claims a system or RAM semaphore. If the semaphore is already owned, the requesting thread is blocked until the semaphore becomes available or a timeout occurs.

Call with:

AX:BX	Semaphore handle
DI:CX	Timeout in milliseconds
	0 = do not wait if semaphore already owned
	−1 = wait indefinitely
DL	06H

Returns:

If function successful

Carry flag	Clear

If function unsuccessful

Carry flag	Set
AX	Error code

Notes:

- RAM semaphores that will be used at interrupt time must be located in the driver's data segment or in locked storage.

- System semaphores can only be created or opened by a process. The process passes the semaphore handle to the driver in a *DosDevIOCtl* parameter buffer, and the driver then calls the DevHlp to convert the handle to a value that it can use at task time or at interrupt time. System semaphores may not be accessed by a device driver in user mode.

- The state of the interrupt flag is not preserved.

Related functions: *SemClear, SemHandle.*

SendEvent   [K] [Int]

Called by the keyboard device driver to indicate the occurrence of an event of interest to the Task Manager or signal handlers.

Call with:

AH	Event type
	0 = Reserved
	1 = Ctrl-Break
	2 = Ctrl-C
	3 = Ctrl-NumLock
	4 = Ctrl-PrtSc

Event type, *continued*
5 = Shift-PrtSc
6 = Session-switch hot key

BX   Parameter (*see Note*)
DL   25H

Returns:

If function successful

Carry flag   Clear

If function unsuccessful (signal not sent)

Carry flag   Set

Note:

■ The parameters corresponding to the possible event types are as follows:

Event	Argument
0	Reserved (0)
1	Reserved (0)
2	Reserved (0)
3	Foreground session number
4	Reserved (0)
5	Reserved (0)
6	Hot key ID (*see DosDevIOCtl Category 4 Function 56H*)

SetIRQ   [K]   [Init]

Captures the hardware interrupt vector for the specified IRQ level.

Call with:

BX   IRQ number (00H–0FH)
DH   Sharing flag
            0 = interrupt not shareable
            1 = interrupt shareable
DL   1BH
DS   Driver's data segment
CS:AX   Address of interrupt handler

Returns:

If function successful

Carry flag   Clear

If function unsuccessful

Carry flag   Set

Note:

- The SetIRQ call fails if the IRQ level is already owned by another driver that specified it not shareable, is owned by a real mode interrupt handler, or is the IRQ used to cascade the slave 8259 interrupt controller (IRQ 2).

Related functions: *EOI, UnSetIRQ.*

SetROMVector   [K]   [Init]

Replaces a real mode software interrupt handler with the driver's handler, returning the address of the previous handler.

Call with:

BX	Interrupt number (00H–FFH)
DL	1AH
CS:AX	Address of interrupt handler
CS:SI	Address of WORD variable to receive real mode DS

Returns:

If function successful

Carry flag	Clear
AX:DX	Real mode pointer to previous handler

Real mode DS for driver placed in variable.

If function unsuccessful

Carry flag	Set

Notes:

- Interrupt numbers 08H–0FH, 50H–57H, and 70H–77H, which are reserved for hardware interrupts, cannot be used with this function.

- The driver's interrupt handler receives control in user mode, and the contents of all registers except for CS:IP are unpredictable. The driver must load the DS register with the value returned by the *SetROMVector* call so that it can address its own data segment.

Related functions: *ROMCritSection, SetIRQ.*

SetTimer   [K]   [Init]

Adds a timer handler to the system's list of timer handlers to be called on each timer tick.

Call with:

DL	1DH
DS	Driver's data segment
CS:AX	Address of timer handler

Returns:

If function successful

Carry flag   Clear

If function unsuccessful

Carry flag   Set

Notes:

- You can register a maximum of 32 driver timer handlers.

- A driver timer handler is entered with a far call, exits with a far return, and must preserve all registers.

Related functions: *ResetTimer, TickCount.*

SortReqPacket   [K]

Inserts a read or write request packet into a request packet queue, sorting the packets in order of starting sector number.

Call with:

DL	0CH
DS:SI	Address of request queue head
ES:BX	Address of request packet

Returns:

Nothing

Note:

- The request queue head is a DWORD, which should be initialized to zero before the first call to *SortReqPacket* or *PushReqPacket.*

Related functions: *AllocReqPacket, PullParticular, PullReqPacket, PushReqPacket.*

TCYield   [K]

Yields the CPU so that any eligible threads with time-critical priority can execute.

Call with:

DL	03H

Returns:

Nothing

Notes:

- *TCYield* is a subset of the DevHlp *Yield*; if *Yield* is called, an additional call to *TCYield* is unnecessary.

- The driver can check the system's time-critical yield flag to determine whether a call to *TCYield* is necessary. Make this check at maximum intervals of 3 milliseconds. The address of the flag is obtained with *GetDOSVar*.

- The state of the interrupt flag is not preserved.

Related functions: *Block, GetDOSVar, Run, Yield*.

TickCount   [K] [Int] [U] [Init]

Adds a timer handler to the system's list of timer handlers. The handler is called at the specified interval of 1 or more clock ticks. *TickCount* can also be called to change the interval for a handler previously registered with *TickCount* or *SetTimer*.

Call with:

BX	Tick count between calls (0 = 65,536 ticks)
DL	33H
CS:AX	Address of timer handler
DS	Driver's data segment

Returns:

If function successful

Carry flag   Clear

If function unsuccessful

Carry flag   Set

Notes:

- You can register a maximum of 32 driver timer handlers.

- A driver timer handler is entered with a far call, exits with a far return, and must preserve all registers.

- The driver cannot call this function in user mode or interrupt mode to register a new handler.

Related functions: *ResetTimer, SetTimer*.

Unlock   [K] [Init]

Unlocks a memory segment that was previously marked nonmovable and nonswappable by a call to the DevHlp *Lock*.

Call with:

AX:BX	Lock handle (from *Lock*)
DL	14H

Returns:

If function successful

Carry flag   Clear

If function unsuccessful

Carry flag   Set

Note:

■ This function cannot be used on memory allocated with the DevHlp *AllocPhys*; such memory is permanently fixed.

Related functions: *Lock, VirtToPhys*.

UnPhysToVirt   [K]   [Int]   [Init]

Notifies the kernel that the virtual addresses obtained with previous *PhysToVirt* calls are no longer needed. If *PhysToVirt* changed the CPU mode, the original mode is restored.

Call with:

DL	32H

Returns:

If no mode change

Zero flag   Clear

If mode was changed

Zero flag   Set

Note:

■ If a mode switch occurs, the CS and SS segment registers are reset appropriately. The DS and ES registers are initialized to point to the driver's data segment, regardless of their previous contents.

Related function: *PhysToVirt*.

UnSetIRQ   [K]   [Int]   [Init]

Releases ownership of a hardware interrupt.

Call with:

BX	IRQ number (00H–0FH)
DL	1CH
DS	Driver's data segment

Returns:

If function successful

Carry flag	Clear

If function unsuccessful

Carry flag	Set

Related functions: *EOI, SetIRQ.*

VerifyAccess · [K]

Verifies a process's right of access to a range of memory addresses.

Call with:

AX:DI	Address of memory
CX	Length in bytes (0 = 65,536)
DH	Type of access
	0 = read access
	1 = read/write access
DL	27H

Returns:

If function successful (access verified)

Carry flag	Clear

If function unsuccessful (access not allowed)

Carry flag	Set

Notes:

- A driver must verify addresses received from a process in a *DosDevIOCtl* call or by some other means prior to locking or accessing those addresses. Addresses passed to the driver in a read or write request packet have been previously locked and verified by the kernel and need not be verified by the driver.

- In real mode, a success flag is always returned.

Related functions: *Lock, Unlock, VirtToPhys.*

VirtToPhys [K] [Init]

Converts a virtual address (segment:offset or selector:offset) to a 32-bit physical address.

Call with:

DL	16H
DS:SI	Virtual address

Returns:

If function successful

Carry flag	Clear
AX:BX	32-bit physical address

If function unsuccessful

Carry flag	Set

Note:

■ The virtual address should be locked before calling *VirtToPhys* unless the segment is known to be locked already.

Related functions: *Lock, PhysToUVirt, PhysToVirt, UnLock.*

Yield [K]

Yields the CPU so that any eligible threads with the same or a higher priority can execute.

Call with:

DL	02H

Returns:

Nothing

Notes:

■ The driver can check the system's yield flag to determine whether a call to *Yield* is necessary. Make this check at maximum intervals of 3 milliseconds. The address of the flag is obtained with *GetDOSVar*.

■ The state of the interrupt flag is not preserved.

Related functions: *Block, GetDOSVar, Run, TCYield.*

APPENDIXES

OS/2 ERROR CODES

Decimal	Hex	Meaning
0	0000H	No error
1	0001H	Invalid function number
2	0002H	File not found
3	0003H	Path not found
4	0004H	Out of handles
5	0005H	Access denied
6	0006H	Invalid handle
7	0007H	Memory control blocks destroyed
8	0008H	Insufficient memory
9	0009H	Invalid memory block address
10	000AH	Invalid environment
11	000BH	Invalid format
12	000CH	Invalid access code
13	000DH	Invalid data
14	000EH	Unknown unit
15	000FH	Invalid disk drive
16	0010H	Cannot remove current directory
17	0011H	Not same device
18	0012H	No more files
19	0013H	Disk write-protected
20	0014H	Unknown unit
21	0015H	Drive not ready
22	0016H	Unknown command
23	0017H	Data error (CRC)
24	0018H	Bad request structure length
25	0019H	Seek error
26	001AH	Unknown type of medium

(continued)

Decimal	Hex	Meaning
27	001BH	Sector not found
28	001CH	Printer out of paper
29	001DH	Write fault
30	001EH	Read fault
31	001FH	General failure
32	0020H	Sharing violation
33	0021H	Lock violation
34	0022H	Invalid disk change
35	0023H	FCB unavailable
36	0024H	Sharing buffer exceeded
37–49	0025H–0031H	Reserved
50	0032H	Unsupported network request
51	0033H	Remote machine not listening
52	0034H	Duplicate name on network
53	0035H	Network name not found
54	0036H	Network busy
55	0037H	Device no longer exists on network
56	0038H	NetBIOS command limit exceeded
57	0039H	Error in network adapter hardware
58	003AH	Incorrect response from network
59	003BH	Unexpected network error
60	003CH	Remote adapter incompatible
61	003DH	Print queue full
62	003EH	Insufficient memory for print file
63	003FH	Print file canceled
64	0040H	Network name deleted
65	0041H	Network access denied
66	0042H	Incorrect network device type
67	0043H	Network name not found
68	0044H	Network name limit exceeded
69	0045H	NetBIOS session limit exceeded
70	0046H	File sharing temporarily paused
71	0047H	Network request not accepted
72	0048H	Print or disk redirection paused
73–79	0049H–004FH	Reserved
80	0050H	File already exists
81	0051H	Reserved
82	0052H	Cannot make directory
83	0053H	Fail on Int 24H (critical error)
84	0054H	Too many redirections
85	0055H	Duplicate redirection
86	0056H	Invalid password
87	0057H	Invalid parameter
88	0058H	Network device fault

(continued)

OS/2 Error Codes. *continued*

Decimal	Hex	Meaning
89	0059H	No process slots available
90	005AH	System error
91	005BH	Timer service table overflow
92	005CH	Timer service table duplicate
93	005DH	No items to work on
94	005EH	Reserved
95	005FH	Interrupted system call
96–99	0060H–0063H	Reserved
100	0064H	Open semaphore limit exceeded
101	0065H	Exclusive semaphore already owned
102	0066H	*DosCloseSem* found semaphore set
103	0067H	Too many exclusive semaphore requests
104	0068H	Operation invalid at interrupt time
105	0069H	Semaphore owner terminated
106	006AH	Semaphore limit exceeded
107	006BH	Insert drive B disk into drive A
108	006CH	Drive locked by another process
109	006DH	Write on pipe with no reader
110	006EH	Open/create failed due to explicit fail command
111	006FH	Buffer too small
112	0070H	Disk is full
113	0071H	No more search handles
114	0072H	Invalid target handle for *DosDupHandle*
115	0073H	Bad user virtual address
116	0074H	Error on display write or keyboard read
117	0075H	Invalid *DosDevIOCtl* category
118	0076H	Invalid value for verify flag
119	0077H	Driver does not support *DosDevIOCtl*
120	0078H	Invalid function called
121	0079H	Timed out waiting for semaphore
122	007AH	Insufficient data in buffer
123	007BH	Invalid character or bad filename
124	007CH	Unimplemented information level
125	007DH	No volume label found
126	007EH	Invalid module handle
127	007FH	Procedure not found in module
128	0080H	No child processes found
129	0081H	Child processes still running
130	0082H	Invalid handle operation for direct disk access
131	0083H	Cannot seek to negative offset
132	0084H	Cannot seek on pipe or device
133	0085H	Drive has previously joined drives

(continued)

Decimal	Hex	Meaning
134	0086H	Drive is already joined
135	0087H	Drive is already substituted
136	0088H	Drive is not joined
137	0089H	Drive is not substituted
138	008AH	Cannot join to joined drive
139	008BH	Cannot substitute to substituted drive
140	008CH	Cannot join to substituted drive
141	008DH	Cannot substitute to joined drive
142	008EH	Drive is busy
143	008FH	Cannot join or substitute drive to directory on same drive
144	0090H	Must be subdirectory of root
145	0091H	Joined directory must be empty
146	0092H	Path is already used in substitute
147	0093H	Path is already used in join
148	0094H	Path is being used by another process
149	0095H	Cannot join or substitute drive having directory that is target of previous substitute
150	0096H	System trace error
151	0097H	*DosMuxSemWait* errors
152	0098H	System limit on *DosMuxSemWait* calls exceeded
153	0099H	Invalid list format
154	009AH	Volume label too big
155	009BH	Cannot create another TCB
156	009CH	Signal refused
157	009DH	Segment is discarded
158	009EH	Segment was not locked
159	009FH	Bad thread ID address
160	00A0H	Bad environment pointer
161	00A1H	Bad pathname for *DosExecPgm*
162	00A2H	Signal already pending
163	00A3H	Unknown medium
164	00A4H	No more threads available
165	00A5H	Monitors not supported
166–179	00A6H–00B3H	Reserved
180	00B4H	Invalid segment number
181	00B5H	Invalid call gate
182	00B6H	Invalid ordinal
183	00B7H	Shared segment or system semaphore already exists
184	00B8H	No child process running
185	00B9H	Child process is still alive
186	00BAH	Invalid flag number
187	00BBH	Semaphore does not exist
188	00BCH	Invalid starting code segment

(continued)

Decimal	Hex	Meaning
189	00BDH	Invalid stack segment
190	00BEH	Invalid module type
191	00BFH	Wrong EXE file header
192	00C0H	Invalid EXE file, LINK errors
193	00C1H	Invalid EXE format
194	00C2H	Iterated data exceeds 64 KB
195	00C3H	Invalid minimum allocation size
196	00C4H	Invalid dynamic link from ring 2 segment
197	00C5H	IOPL not enabled in CONFIG.SYS
198	00C6H	Invalid segment descriptor privilege level
199	00C7H	Automatic data segment exceeds 64 KB
200	00C8H	Ring 2 segment must be movable
201	00C9H	Relocation chain exceeds segment limit
202	00CAH	Infinite loop in relocation chain
203	00CBH	Environment variable not found
204	00CCH	Not current country
205	00CDH	No process with handler to receive signal
206	00CEH	Filename or extension too long
207	00CFH	Ring 2 stack in use
208	00D0H	Meta expansion too long
209	00D1H	Invalid signal number
210	00D2H	Inactive thread
211	00D3H	File system information not available
212	00D4H	Locked error
213	00D5H	Bad dynamic link
214	00D6H	Too many modules
215	00D7H	Nesting not allowed
216	00D8H	Cannot shrink ring 2 stack
217–229	00D9H–00E5H	Reserved
230	00E6H	Nonexistent pipe or invalid operation
231	00E7H	Specified pipe is busy
232	00E8H	No data on nonblocking pipe read
233	00E9H	Pipe disconnected by server
234	00EAH	Additional data is available
235–239	00EBH–00EFH	Reserved
240	00F0H	Network session was canceled
241–261	00F1H–0105H	Reserved
262	0106H	Stack too large
263–302	0107H–012EH	Reserved
303	012FH	Invalid process ID
304	0130H	Invalid priority level increment or decrement
305	0131H	Not a descendant process
306	0132H	Requestor not Task Manager
307	0133H	Invalid priority class
308	0134H	Invalid scope

(continued)

Decimal	Hex	Meaning
309	0135H	Invalid thread ID
310	0136H	Cannot shrink *DosSubSet* segment
311	0137H	Out of memory (*DosSubAlloc*)
312	0138H	Invalid block specified (*DosSubFree*)
313	0139H	Bad size parameter (*DosSubAlloc* or *DosSubFree*)
314	013AH	Bad flag parameter (*DosSubSet*)
315	013BH	Invalid segment selector
316	013CH	Message too long for buffer
317	013DH	Message ID number not found
318	013EH	Unable to access message file
319	013FH	Invalid message file format
320	0140H	Invalid insertion variable count
321	0141H	Unable to perform function
322	0142H	Unable to wake up
323	0143H	Invalid system semaphore handle
324	0144H	No timers available
325	0145H	Reserved
326	0146H	Invalid timer handle
327	0147H	Date or time invalid
328	0148H	Internal system error
329	0149H	Current queue name does not exist
330	014AH	Current process is not queue owner
331	014BH	Current process owns queue
332	014CH	Duplicate queue name
333	014DH	Queue record does not exist
334	014EH	Inadequate queue memory
335	014FH	Invalid queue name
336	0150H	Invalid queue priority parameter
337	0151H	Invalid queue handle
338	0152H	Queue link not found
339	0153H	Queue memory error
340	0154H	Previous queue record was at end of queue
341	0155H	Process does not have access to queues
342	0156H	Queue is empty
343	0157H	Queue name does not exist
344	0158H	Queues not initialized
345	0159H	Unable to access queues
346	015AH	Unable to add new queue
347	015BH	Unable to initialize queues
348	015CH	Reserved
349	015DH	Invalid *Vio* function replaced
350	015EH	Invalid pointer to parameter
351–354	015FH–0162H	Reserved

(continued)

Decimal	Hex	Meaning
355	0163H	Unsupported screen mode
356	0164H	Invalid cursor width value
357	0165H	Reserved
358	0166H	Invalid row value
359	0167H	Invalid column value
360–365	0168H–016DH	Reserved
366	016EH	Invalid wait flag setting
367	016FH	Screen not previously locked
368	0170H	Reserved
369	0171H	Invalid session ID
370	0172H	No sessions available
371	0173H	Session not found
372	0174H	Title cannot be changed
373	0175H	Invalid parameter (*Kbd*)
374	0176H	Reserved
375	0177H	Invalid wait parameter
376	0178H	Invalid length for keyboard
377	0179H	Invalid echo mode mask
378	017AH	Invalid input mode mask
379	017BH	Invalid monitor parameters
380	017CH	Invalid device name string
381	017DH	Invalid device handle
382	017EH	Buffer too small
383	017FH	Buffer empty
384	0180H	Data record too large
385	0181H	Reserved
386	0182H	Mouse handle invalid or closed
387–388	0183H–0184H	Reserved
389	0185H	Invalid display mode parameters
390	0186H	Reserved
391	0187H	Invalid entry point
392	0188H	Invalid function mask
393	0189H	Reserved
394	018AH	Pointer drawn
395	018BH	Invalid frequency for *DosBeep*
396	018CH	Cannot find COUNTRY.SYS file
397	018DH	Cannot open COUNTRY.SYS file
398	018EH	Country code not found
399	018FH	Information truncated to fit buffer
400	0190H	Selected type does not exist
401	0191H	Selected type not in file
402	0192H	*Vio* function for Task Manager only
403	0193H	Invalid string length (*Vio*)
404	0194H	*VioDeRegister* not allowed
405	0195H	Popup screen not allocated

(continued)

Decimal	Hex	Meaning
406	0196H	Pop-up already on screen
407	0197H	*Kbd* function for Task Manager only
408	0198H	Invalid ASCIIZ string length (*Kbd*)
409	0199H	Invalid function replacement mask
410	019AH	*KbdRegister* not allowed
411	019BH	*KbdDeRegister* not allowed
412	019CH	*Mou* function for Task Manager only
413	019DH	Invalid ASCIIZ string length (*Mou*)
414	019EH	Invalid replacement mask
415	019FH	*MouRegister* not allowed
416	01A0H	*MouDeRegister* not allowed
417	01A1H	Invalid action specified
418	01A2H	INIT called more than once
419	01A3H	Screen group number not found
420	01A4H	Caller is not shell
421	01A5H	Invalid parameters (*Vio*)
422	01A6H	Save/restore already owned
423	01A7H	Thread unblocked by *VioModeUndo* or *VioSavRedrawUndo*
424	01A8H	Reserved
425	01A9H	Caller not Task Manager
426	01AAH	*VioRegister* not allowed
427	01ABH	No *VioModeWait* thread exists
428	01ACH	No *VioSavRedrawWait* thread exists
429	01ADH	Function invalid in background
430	01AEH	Function not allowed during pop-up
431	01AFH	Caller is not the base shell
432	01B0H	Invalid status requested
433	01B1H	No-wait parameter out of bounds
434	01B2H	Cannot lock screen
435	01B3H	Invalid wait parameter
436	01B4H	Invalid *Vio* handle
437	01B5H	Reserved
438	01B6H	Invalid length for *Vio* function
439	01B7H	Invalid *Kbd* handle
440	01B8H	Out of *Kbd* handles
441	01B9H	Cannot create logical keyboard
442	01BAH	Code page load failed
443	01BBH	Invalid code page ID
444	01BCH	No code page support
445	01BDH	Keyboard focus required
446	01BEH	Caller already has focus
447	01BFH	Keyboard subsystem is busy
448	01C0H	Invalid code page

(continued)

Decimal	Hex	Meaning
449	01C1H	Cannot get keyboard focus
450	01C2H	Session is not selectable
451	01C3H	Parent/child session not in foreground
452	01C4H	Not parent of specified child
453	01C5H	Invalid session start mode
454	01C6H	Invalid session start option
455	01C7H	Invalid session bonding option
456	01C8H	Invalid session select option
457	01C9H	Session started in background
458	01CAH	Invalid session stop option
459	01CBH	Reserved parameters not 0
460	01CCH	Session parent process already exists
461	01CDH	Invalid data length
462	01CEH	Parent session not bound
463	01CFH	Retry request block allocation
464	01D0H	Unavailable for detached process (*Kbd*)
465	01D1H	Unavailable for detached process (*Vio*)
466	01D2H	Unavailable for detached process (*Mou*)
467	01D3H	No font available to support mode
468	01D4H	User font active
469	01D5H	Invalid code page specified
470	01D6H	System displays do not support code page
471	01D7H	Current display does not support code page
472	01D8H	Invalid code page
473	01D9H	Code page list is too small
474	01DAH	Code page not moved
475	01DBH	Mode switch initialization error
476	01DCH	Code page not found
477	01DDH	Internal error
478	01DEH	Invalid session start trace indicator
479	01DFH	*Vio* internal resource error
480	01E0H	*Vio* shell initialization error
481	01E1H	No Task Manager hard errors
482	01E2H	*DosSetCp* unable to set display or keyboard code page
483	01E3H	Error during *Vio* pop-up
484	01E4H	Critical section overflow
485	01E5H	Critical section underflow
486	01E6H	Reserved parameter is not 0
487	01E7H	Bad physical address
488	01E8H	No selectors requested
489	01E9H	Not enough GDT selectors available
490	01EAH	Not a GDT selector
491	01EBH	Invalid program type
492	01ECH	Invalid program control

(continued)

OS/2 Error Codes. *continued*

Decimal	Hex	Meaning
493	01EDH	Invalid program inheritance option
494	01EEH	*Vio* function not allowed in PM window
495	01EFH	Function not supported in non-PM screen group
496	01F0H	*Vio* shield already owned
497	01F1H	*Vio* handles exhausted
498	01F2H	*Vio* error occurred, details sent to error log
499	01F3H	Invalid display context
500	01F4H	*Kbd* input not available
501	01F5H	*Mou* input not available
502	01F6H	Invalid mouse handle
503	01F7H	Invalid debugging parameters
504	01F8H	*Kbd* function not allowed in PM window
505	01F9H	*Mou* function not allowed in PM window
506	01FAH	Invalid icon file

ASCII AND IBM EXTENDED CHARACTER SETS

Char	Number Dec	Hex	Control		Char	Number Dec	Hex	Control	
	0	00H	NUL	(Null)	←	27	1BH	ESC	(Escape)
☺	1	01H	SOH	(Start of heading)	∟	28	1CH	FS	(File separator)
☻	2	02H	STX	(Start of text)	↔	29	1DH	GS	(Group separator)
♥	3	03H	ETX	(End of text)	▲	30	1EH	RS	(Record separator)
♦	4	04H	EOT	(End of transmission)	▼	31	1FH	US	(Unit separator)
♣	5	05H	ENQ	(Enquiry)	<space>	32	20H		
♠	6	06H	ACK	(Acknowledge)	!	33	21H		
•	7	07H	BEL	(Bell)	"	34	22H		
◘	8	08H	BS	(Backspace)	#	35	23H		
○	9	09H	HT	(Horizontal tab)	$	36	24H		
◙	10	0AH	LF	(Linefeed)	%	37	25H		
♂	11	0BH	VT	(Vertical tab)	&	38	26H		
♀	12	0CH	FF	(Formfeed)	'	39	27H		
♪	13	0DH	CR	(Carriage return)	(	40	28H		
♫	14	0EH	SO	(Shift out)	)	41	29H		
☼	15	0FH	SI	(Shift in)	*	42	2AH		
►	16	10H	DLE	(Data link escape)	+	43	2BH		
◄	17	11H	DC1	(Device control 1)	,	44	2CH		
↕	18	12H	DC2	(Device control 2)	–	45	2DH		
‼	19	13H	DC3	(Device control 3)	.	46	2EH		
¶	20	14H	DC4	(Device control 4)	/	47	2FH		
§	21	15H	NAK	(Negative acknowledge)	0	48	30H		
▬	22	16H	SYN	(Synchronous idle)	1	49	31H		
↨	23	17H	ETB	(End transmission block)	2	50	32H		
					3	51	33H		
↑	24	18H	CAN	(Cancel)	4	52	34H		
↓	25	19H	EM	(End of medium)	5	53	35H		
→	26	1AH	SUB	(Substitute)	6	54	36H		

(continued)

Char	Dec	Hex		Char	Dec	Hex	Control		Char	Dec	Hex
7	55	37H		g	103	67H			ù	151	97H
8	56	38H		h	104	68H			ÿ	151	98H
9	57	39H		i	105	69H			Ö	152	99H
:	58	3AH		j	106	6AH			Ü	154	9AH
;	59	3BH		k	107	6BH			¢	155	9BH
<	60	3CH		l	108	6CH			£	156	9CH
=	61	3DH		m	109	6DH			¥	157	9DH
>	62	3EH		n	110	6EH			₧	158	9EH
?	63	3FH		o	111	6FH			ƒ	159	9FH
@	64	40H		p	112	70H			á	160	A0H
A	65	41H		q	113	71H			í	161	A1H
B	66	42H		r	114	72H			ó	162	A2H
C	67	43H		s	115	73H			ú	163	A3H
D	68	44H		t	116	74H			ñ	164	A4H
E	69	45H		u	117	75H			Ñ	165	A5H
F	70	46H		v	118	76H			ª	166	A6H
G	71	47H		w	119	77H			º	167	A7H
H	72	48H		x	120	78H			¿	168	A8H
I	73	49H		y	121	79H			⌐	169	A9H
J	74	4AH		z	122	7AH			¬	170	AAH
K	75	4BH		{	123	7BH			½	171	ABH
L	76	4CH		¦	124	7CH			¼	172	ACH
M	77	4DH		}	125	7DH			¡	173	ADH
N	78	4EH		~	126	7EH			«	174	AEH
O	79	4FH		Δ	127	7FH	DEL (Delete)		»	175	AFH
P	80	50H		Ç	128	80H			░	176	B0H
Q	81	51H		ü	129	81H			▒	177	B1H
R	82	52H		é	130	82H			▓	178	B2H
S	83	53H		â	131	83H			│	179	B3H
T	84	54H		ä	132	84H			┤	180	B4H
U	85	55H		à	133	85H			╡	181	B5H
V	86	56H		å	134	86H			╢	182	B6H
W	87	57H		ç	135	87H			╖	183	B7H
X	88	58H		ê	136	88H			╕	184	B8H
Y	89	59H		ë	137	89H			╣	185	B9H
Z	90	5AH		è	138	8AH			║	186	BAH
[	91	5BH		ï	139	8BH			╗	187	BBH
\	92	5CH		î	140	8CH			╝	188	BCH
]	93	5DH		ì	141	8DH			╜	189	BDH
^	94	5EH		Ä	142	8EH			╛	190	BEH
—	95	5FH		Å	143	8FH			┐	191	BFH
`	96	60H		É	144	90H			└	192	C0H
a	97	61H		æ	145	91H			┴	193	C1H
b	98	62H		Æ	146	92H			┬	194	C2H
c	99	63H		ô	147	93H			├	195	C3H
d	100	64H		ö	148	94H			─	196	C4H
e	101	65H		ò	149	95H			┼	197	C5H
f	102	66H		û	150	96H			╞	198	C6H

(continued)

Char	Number Dec	Hex	Char	Number Dec	Hex	Char	Number Dec	Hex
╟	199	C7H	┌	218	DAH	φ	237	EDH
╚	200	C8H	█	219	DBH	∈	238	EEH
╔	201	C9H	▄	220	DCH	∩	239	EFH
╩	202	CAH	▌	221	DDH	≡	240	F0H
╦	203	CBH	▐	222	DEH	±	241	F1H
╠	204	CCH	▀	223	DFH	≥	242	F2H
═	205	CDH	α	224	E0H	≤	243	F3H
╬	206	CEH	β	225	E1H	⌠	244	F4H
╧	207	CFH	Γ	226	E2H	⌡	245	F5H
╨	208	D0H	π	227	E3H	÷	246	F6H
╤	209	D1H	Σ	228	E4H	≈	247	F7H
╥	210	D2H	σ	229	E5H	°	248	F8H
╙	211	D3H	μ	230	E6H	•	249	F9H
╘	212	D4H	τ	231	E7H	·	250	FAH
╒	213	D5H	Φ	232	E8H	√	251	FBH
╓	214	D6H	Θ	233	E9H	η	252	FCH
╫	215	D7H	Ω	234	EAH	²	253	FDH
╪	216	D8H	δ	235	EBH	■	254	FEH
┘	217	D9H	∞	236	ECH		255	FFH

RESOURCES

Periodicals

"Environments," biweekly column by Charles Petzold. *PC Magazine*. Ziff Davis Publishing, New York, N.Y.

Microsoft Systems Journal. Microsoft Corp., Redmond, Wash.

Assembly Language

Assembly Language Primer for the IBM PC and XT. Robert Lafore. New York: New American Library, 1984. ISBN 0-452-25711-5.

8086/8088/80286 Assembly Language. Leo Scanlon. New York: Brady Communications Co., 1988. ISBN 0-13-246919-7.

C Language

Microsoft C Programming for the IBM. Robert Lafore. Indianapolis, Ind.: Howard K. Sams & Co., 1987. ISBN 0-672-22515-8.

Proficient C. Augie Hansen. Redmond, Wash.: Microsoft Press, 1987. ISBN 1-55615-007-5.

The C Programming Language, 2d ed. Brian Kernighan and Dennis Ritchie. Englewood Cliffs, N.J.: Prentice-Hall Inc., 1988. ISBN 0-13-110362-8.

C: A Reference Manual, 2d ed. Samuel Harbison and Guy Steele. Englewood Cliffs, N.J.: Prentice-Hall Inc., 1987. ISBN 0-13-109802-0.

Microsoft OS/2

Inside OS/2. Gordon Letwin. Redmond, Wash.: Microsoft Press, 1988. ISBN 1-55615-117-9.

Programming the OS/2 Presentation Manager. Charles Petzold. Redmond, Wash.: Microsoft Press, 1989. ISBN 1-55615-170-5.

IBM Operating System/2 Technical Reference. IBM Corp. IBM Technical Directory, P.O. Box 2009, Racine, Wis. 53404. Part no. 6280201.

Operating System Fundamentals

Operating Systems: Design and Implementation. Andrew S. Tanenbaum. Englewood Cliffs, N.J.: Prentice-Hall Inc., 1987. ISBN 0-13-637406-9.

An Introduction to General Systems Thinking. Gerald Weinberg. New York: John Wiley and Sons, 1975. ISBN 0-471-92563-2.

Operating System Concepts. James Peterson and Abraham Silberschatz. Reading, Mass.: Addison-Wesley Publishing Co., 1983. ISBN 0-201-06097-3.

Intel 80286 and 80386

Inside the 80286. Edmund Strauss. New York: Brady Publishing (Prentice-Hall Inc.), 1986. ISBN 0-89303-582-3.

The 80386 Book. Ross P. Nelson. Redmond, Wash.: Microsoft Press, 1988. ISBN 1-55615-138-1.

Dr. Dobb's Toolbook of 80286/80386 Programming. Edited by Philip Robinson. Redwood City, Calif.: M&T Publishing Inc., 1988. ISBN 0-934375-42-9.

iAPX 286 Programmer's Reference Manual. Intel Corp. Literature Dept., 3065 Bowers Ave., Santa Clara, Calif. 95051. Order no. 210498.

iAPX 286 Operating Systems Writer's Guide. Intel Corp. Literature Dept., 3065 Bowers Ave., Santa Clara, Calif. 95051. Order no. 121960.

80386 Programmer's Reference Manual. Intel Corp. Literature Dept., 3065 Bowers Ave., Santa Clara, Calif. 95051. Order no. 230985.

80386 System Software Writer's Guide. Intel Corp. Literature Dept., 3065 Bowers Ave., Santa Clara, Calif. 95051. Order no. 231499.

80387 Programmer's Reference Manual. Intel Corp. Literature Dept., 3065 Bowers Ave., Santa Clara, Calif. 95051. Order no. 231917.

PC, PC/AT, and PS/2 Architecture

The IBM Personal Computer from the Inside Out, rev. ed. Murray Sargent and Richard L. Shoemaker. Reading, Mass.: Addison-Wesley Publishing Co., 1986. ISBN 0-201-06918-0.

Programmer's Guide to PC and PS/2 Video Systems. Richard Wilton. Redmond, Wash.: Microsoft Press, 1987. ISBN 1-55615-103-9.

Personal Computer AT Technical Reference. IBM Corp. IBM Technical Directory, P.O. Box 2009, Racine, Wis. 53404. Part no. 6280070.

Options and Adapters Technical Reference. IBM Corp. IBM Technical Directory, P.O. Box 2009, Racine, Wis. 53404. Part no. 6322509.

Personal System/2 Model 50/60/70/80 Technical Reference. IBM Corp. IBM Technical Directory, P.O. Box 2009, Racine, Wis. 53404. Part no. 68X2330.

BIOS and ABIOS Interface Technical Reference. IBM Corp. IBM Technical Directory, P.O. Box 2009, Racine, Wis. 53404. Part no. 68X2341.

OS/2 LOAD
MODULE FORMAT

OS/2 programs, dynlink libraries, and device drivers reside on the disk in load modules called segmented executable files, or "new EXE" files. The new EXE file format, which is also used by Microsoft Windows, is a superset of the "old EXE" format used by MS-DOS.

Components of a Segmented Executable File

A segmented EXE file is composed of many distinct but interrelated elements, as shown in Figure D-1 on the following page. A hex dump of a simple OS/2 program (the PORTS.EXE file from Chapter 14) is shown in Figure D-2, beginning on p. 717, with the various elements of the file marked. You can use the Microsoft utility program EXEHDR.EXE to display much of the information described in this section for any specific OS/2 program, library, or driver.

Throughout the remainder of this appendix, the term *counted string* is used to refer to a string that consists of a length byte followed by the ASCII characters of the actual string. The value of the length byte does not include the length byte itself, and the string is not terminated by a null byte.

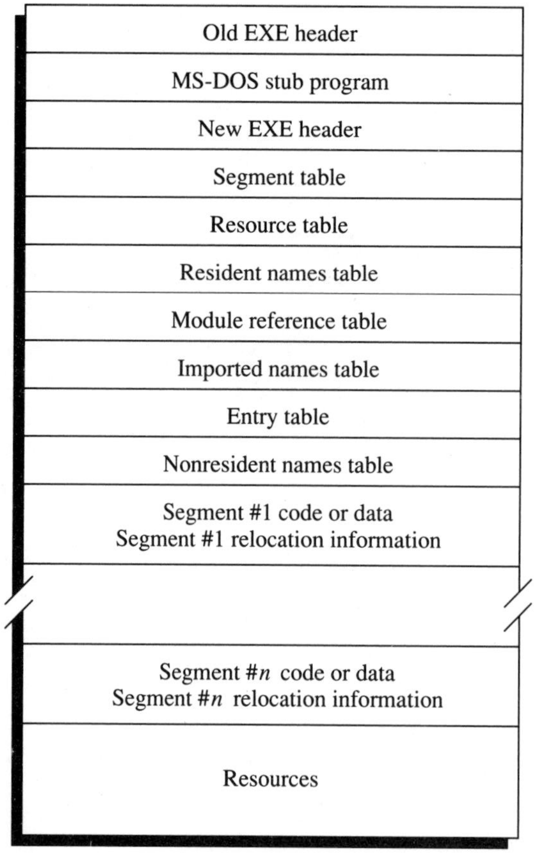

Figure D-1. *Block diagram of a file containing an OS/2 program, dynlink library, or device driver.*

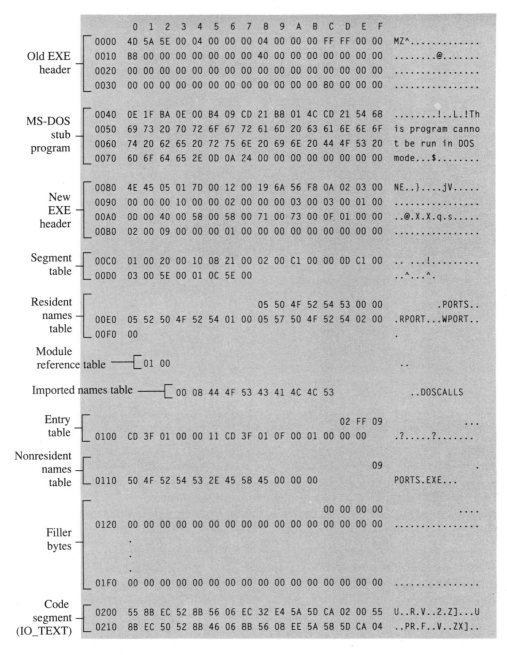

```
                0 1 2 3 4 5 6 7 8 9 A B C D E F
            0000  4D 5A 5E 00 04 00 00 00 04 00 00 00 FF FF 00 00   MZ^.............
Old EXE     0010  B8 00 00 00 00 00 00 00 40 00 00 00 00 00 00 00   ........@.......
header      0020  00 00 00 00 00 00 00 00 00 00 00 00 00 00 00 00   ................
            0030  00 00 00 00 00 00 00 00 00 00 00 00 80 00 00 00   ................

            0040  0E 1F BA 0E 00 B4 09 CD 21 B8 01 4C CD 21 54 68   ........!..L.!Th
MS-DOS      0050  69 73 20 70 72 6F 67 72 61 6D 20 63 61 6E 6E 6F   is program canno
stub        0060  74 20 62 65 20 72 75 6E 20 69 6E 20 44 4F 53 20   t be run in DOS
program     0070  6D 6F 64 65 2E 0D 0A 24 00 00 00 00 00 00 00 00   mode...$........

            0080  4E 45 05 01 7D 00 12 00 19 6A 56 F8 0A 02 03 00   NE..}....jV.....
New         0090  00 00 00 10 00 00 02 00 00 00 03 00 03 00 01 00   ................
EXE         00A0  0D 00 40 00 58 00 58 00 71 00 73 00 0F 01 00 00   ..@.X.X.q.s.....
header      00B0  02 00 09 00 00 00 01 00 00 00 00 00 00 00 00 00   ................

Segment     00C0  01 00 20 00 10 08 21 00 02 00 C1 00 00 0D C1 00   .. ...!.........
table       00D0  03 00 5E 00 01 0C 5E 00                           ..^...^.

Resident                              05 50 4F 52 54 53 00 00           .PORTS..
names       00E0  05 52 50 4F 52 54 01 00 05 57 50 4F 52 54 02 00   .RPORT...WPORT..
table       00F0  00                                               .

Module
reference table  ──[ 01 00                                         ..

Imported names table  ──[ 00 08 44 4F 53 43 41 4C 4C 53            ..DOSCALLS

Entry                                       02 FF 09                    ...
table       0100  CD 3F 01 00 00 11 CD 3F 01 0F 00 01 00 00 00     .?.....?.......

Nonresident                                          09
names                                                             09
table       0110  50 4F 52 54 53 2E 45 58 45 00 00 00             PORTS.EXE...

                                            00 00 00 00                 ....
Filler      0120  00 00 00 00 00 00 00 00 00 00 00 00 00 00 00 00   ................
bytes              .
                   .
                   .
            01F0  00 00 00 00 00 00 00 00 00 00 00 00 00 00 00 00   ................

Code        0200  55 8B EC 52 8B 56 06 EC 32 E4 5A 5D CA 02 00 55   U..R.V..2.Z]...U
segment     0210  8B EC 50 52 8B 46 06 8B 56 08 EE 5A 58 5D CA 04   ..PR.F..V..ZX]..
(IO_TEXT)
```

(continued)

Figure D-2. *Simple segmented executable file (the PORTS.EXE program from Chapter 14). Note that this program has no resource table nor any resources at the end of the file.*

Figure D-2. *continued*

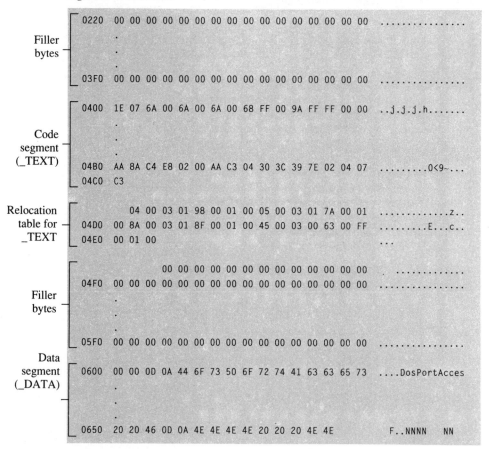

Old EXE Header

The format of the "old EXE" header is shown in Figure D-3. The most important parts of this header are the familiar MS-DOS signature ("MZ") for a relocatable executable file, the value 0040H at offset 0018H, which is the offset of the MS-DOS stub program and which also signals the existence of a "new EXE" header, and the 32-bit offset to the "new EXE" header at offset 003CH.

00H	Signature byte 1 'M'
01H	Signature byte 2 'Z'
02H	Length of file header and program image MOD 512
04H	Length of file header and program image in 512-byte pages
06H	Number of relocation table items for MS-DOS stub program
08H	Size of old EXE header in paragraphs
0AH	Minimum paragraphs of extra memory needed for execution of MS-DOS stub program
0CH	Maximum paragraphs of extra memory needed for execution of MS-DOS stub program
0EH	Segment displacement of stub program stack
10H	Contents of SP register at stub program entry
12H	Checksum
14H	Contents of IP register at stub program entry
16H	Segment displacement of stub program code
18H	File offset of first stub program relocation item (0040H indicates segmented file present)
1AH	Overlay number (0)
1CH	Reserved
24H	OEM identifier
26H	OEM information
28H	Reserved
3CH	File offset of new EXE header
40H	

Figure D-3. *Old EXE header at the beginning of an OS/2 executable file.*

MS-DOS Stub Program

The MS-DOS stub program, which is executed if the EXE file is loaded in real mode under MS-DOS or in DOS compatibility mode under OS/2, always begins at offset 0040H in the file. If you do not explicitly specify a stub program in the DEF file when you link the OS/2 program, the Linker inserts a program that displays an error message and terminates.

The stub program has its own relocation table and can be of any size. The entry point, stack size, and the locations of the relocation table, code, and data for the stub program are specified in the old EXE header.

When a program is "bound" for use as a Family application, the BIND utility replaces the original stub program with a "real mode loader" and an additional routine for each OS/2 API function that the program uses. When the bound program is run, the real mode loader gains control, performs all necessary relocations, and patches each API function call to point to a routine that translates the parameters on the stack into the appropriate parameters in registers and executes a software interrupt.

New EXE Header

The new EXE header is much more complicated than the old EXE header. The fields of the new EXE header are shown in Figure D-4. Some header fields are set by DEF file directives and describe the characteristics and behavior of a program or library, as well as the initial size of the stack and local heap. The remaining fields specify the locations and sizes of other file elements such as the resident and nonresident names tables and the segment table. (The actual code and data segments are described in the segment table rather than in the new EXE header.)

A critical field in the new EXE header is the file alignment unit size at offset 32H. This size is expressed as a power of 2; for example, the value 9 represents a file unit size of 512 bytes. Each component of an executable file (except for resources) begins at an offset within the file that is a multiple of the alignment unit size, and many of the tables within the file express locations and sizes in multiples of this unit.

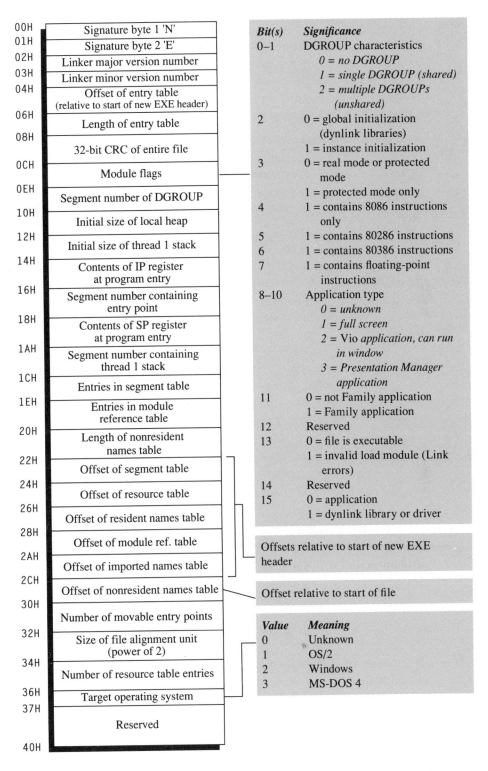

Figure D-4. *New EXE header, which follows the MS-DOS compatible stub program in an OS/2 executable file.*

Segment Table

The segment table describes the size, location within the file, and characteristics of each of the program's code and data segments. This table is read into memory by the OS/2 loader; it remains resident as long as the program or library is in use so that the loader can quickly locate discardable or load-on-demand code and data segments within the file.

Each entry in the table is 8 bytes long and has the following format:

Offset	Length	Description	
00H	2	Offset of beginning of segment within file (expressed as multiple of file unit size)	
02H	2	Length of segment (0 = 65,536 bytes)	
04H	2	Segment flags	
		Bit(s)	*Significance*
		0–2	*Segment type*
			0 = code
			1 = data
		3	*0 = noniterated data*
			1 = iterated data
		4	*0 = fixed*
			1 = movable
		5	*0 = impure or nonshareable*
			1 = pure or shareable
		6	*0 = load-on-call*
			1 = preload
		7	*0 = execute/read if code, read/write if data*
			1 = execute-only if code, read-only if data
		8	*0 = no relocation table*
			1 = relocation table present
		9	*0 = nonconforming*
			1 = conforming
		10–11	*Privilege level*
		12	*0 = nondiscardable*
			1 = discardable
		13	*0 = 16-bit code segment*
			1 = 32-bit code segment
		14	*0 = normal segment*
			1 = huge segment
		15	*Reserved*
06H	2	Minimum allocation size for segment (0 = 65,536 bytes)	

When other tables refer to segments, they use a one-based number that corresponds to an entry in the segment table.

Resource Table

The resource table is used in Presentation Manager applications to specify the size, location, and type of resources at the end of the file. The table starts with a 16-bit resource shift count: a power of 2 which defines the resource unit size. (Resources can use a different unit size than the one specified in the new EXE header for all other elements of the file.)

The resource shift count is followed by two or more resource type headers, each header followed by resource entries that define the location, size, and characteristics of the associated resources. The end of the main portion of the resource table is indicated by a resource type header with a zero byte in the resource type position.

Resource type headers have the following format:

Offset	Length	Description
00H	2	Resource type identifier (if bit 15 = 1) or offset to type string (if bit 15 = 0)
02H	2	Number of resources for this type
04H	4	Reserved

Each resource entry is formatted as follows:

Offset	Length	Description	
00H	2	Offset of resource within file (as multiple of resource unit size)	
02H	2	Length of resource (as multiple of resource unit size)	
04H	2	Resource flags	
		Bit(s)	*Significance*
		0–3	*Reserved*
		4	*0 = fixed*
			1 = movable
		5	*0 = impure or nonshareable*
			1 = pure or shareable
		6	*0 = load-on-call*
			1 = preload
		7–11	*Reserved*
		12–15	*Discard priority*
06H	2	Resource number (if bit 15 = 1) or offset to name string if bit 15 = 0)	
08H	4	Reserved	

When resources and their types are identified with names rather than numbers, the names are stored as a series of counted strings at the end of the resource table (after the zero byte indicating that there are no more resource type headers). The offsets to a name or type string in a resource type header or resource entry are relative to the beginning of the resource table itself. The end of the block of strings is indicated by a single zero byte.

Resident Names Table

The resident names table lists all the entry points in the program or dynlink library (defined with EXPORTS statements in the DEF file) that were not assigned ordinal numbers. Each entry in the table is a counted string followed by a one-based index to the entry table. The end of the resident names table is indicated by an entry consisting of a single zero byte.

The first entry in the resident names table is the module name and has an entry table index of zero.

Module Reference Table

The module reference table consists of a series of word-size (16-bit) entries. Each entry is the offset of a module name in the imported names table. The number of entries in the module reference table — that is, the total number of modules from which functions are imported — is found at offset 1EH in the new EXE header.

Imported Names Table

Each entry in the imported names table is a counted string that names an imported function or a module that contains imported functions. Imported functions are dynamically linked at load time.

The offset of the beginning of each module name is given by the corresponding word in the module reference table. The offsets of function names are found within relocation records.

Entry Table

The entry table defines the segment, offset, and type of each entry point within the EXE file. The entry points are bundled together by segment, the number of bundles in the entry table varying from one bundle to many.

Each bundle begins with two bytes. The first byte contains the number of entry point records in the bundle; the second byte contains FFH if the segment is movable or the segment number if the segment is fixed.

When a bundle describes a movable segment (the usual case in an OS/2 application), the remainder of the bundle is one or more 6-byte entries in the following format:

Offset	Length	Description
00H	1	Entry point flags
		Bit(s) *Significance*
		0 *0 = entry point not exported*
		1 = entry point exported
		1 *0 = entry point uses instance data*
		1 = entry point uses single data
		2 *Reserved*
		3–7 *Number of stack parameter words*
01H	2	Int 3FH instruction (CDH 3FH)
03H	1	Segment number of entry point
04H	2	Offset of entry point within segment

The entries in bundles for fixed segments are 3 bytes long and have the following format:

Offset	Length	Description
00H	1	Entry point flags (*See above*)
01H	2	Offset of entry point within segment

When the loader must locate an entry point by its ordinal number, it first scans all the bundles in the entry table until it finds one with the appropriate segment number. It then multiplies the ordinal number by the appropriate size (3 or 6) and uses the result as an index into the bundle.

Nonresident Names Table

The nonresident names table lists all the entry points in the program or dynlink library (defined with EXPORTS statements in the DEF file) that were assigned explicit ordinal numbers. Each entry in the table is a counted string followed by a one-based index to the entry table. The end of the table is indicated by an entry consisting of a single zero byte.

The first entry in the nonresident names table is either the description string specified in the DEF file or the filename if the DEF file contains no description string; the first entry has an entry table index of zero.

Code and Data Segments

The beginning of each code segment and data segment is aligned within the file as specified by the field at offset 32H in the new EXE header. A segment may be iterated data or noniterated data, as indicated by the field at offset 04H in the corresponding entry in the segment table.

Iterated segments take the following form:

Offset	Length	Description
00H	2	Number of iterations
02H	2	Bytes per iteration (*n*)
04H	*n*	Actual data for each iteration

The size of a noniterated segment is specified by the field at offset 02H in the corresponding segment table entry. If the segment table indicates that a segment has relocation information, the segment's code or data is followed immediately by a 16-bit value for the number of relocation items and then by one or more 8-byte entries for each relocation item. The format for this 8-byte entry depends on the type of relocation item it represents — the three types found in normal applications are internal references, imported ordinals, and imported names.

The format for an internal reference relocation entry, that is, a reference to another segment in the same executable file, has the following form:

Offset	Length	Description
00H	1	Type of relocation
		0 = 8-bit offset
		2 = 16-bit segment
		3 = 32-bit far pointer
		5 = 16-bit offset
		11 = 48-bit far pointer
		13 = 32-bit offset
01H	1	0 or 4 (indicates internal reference)
02H	2	Offset of relocation item within segment
04H	1	FFH if movable segment or number of fixed segment
05H	1	Reserved (0)
06H	2	Ordinal of entry point if segment movable, otherwise offset of entry point within its segment

The format for an imported ordinal relocation entry, that is, a reference to an entry point in another module which is being imported by ordinal number, has the following form:

Offset	Length	Description
00H	1	Type of relocation (*See above*)
01H	1	1 or 5 (indicates imported ordinal)
02H	2	Offset of relocation item within segment
04H	2	One-based index to module reference table
06H	2	Function ordinal number

The format for an imported name relocation entry, that is, a reference to an entry point in another module which is being imported by name, has the following form:

Offset	Length	Description
00H	1	Type of relocation (*See above*)
01H	1	2 or 6 (indicates imported name)
02H	2	Offset of relocation item within segment
04H	2	One-based index to module reference table
06H	2	Offset to name of imported function in imported names table

If bit 2 of the byte at offset 01H in a relocation entry is set, the address or value of the external reference is to be added to the contents of the address in the target segment. Otherwise, the address in the target segment contains the offset of the next location in the target segment that requires the same relocation; in other words, all the locations that should be replaced with the same address or value are chained together. The end of the chain is indicated by a −1.

Resources

Resources are static data blocks such as icons, cursors, menus, and bitmaps that are bound into the executable file for a Presentation Manager application with the Resource Compiler (RC.EXE). Each resource has a name and a type, which can be represented either as a binary 16-bit value or as an ASCII string. The combination of the name and type is unique for each resource in a particular executable file.

A Kernel application can (but seldom does) contain resources. It can load and obtain a selector for a specific resource with the API function *DosGetResource*.

The NEWEXE.H Header File

The C header file NEWEXE.H (Figure D-5 on the following pages) defines the load module and is the ultimate recourse when you need information about the format. Using the *#include* directive, you can include this header in C programs that must access EXE or DLL files.

```
/*
 *      NEWEXE.H (C) Copyright Microsoft Corp 1984-1987
 *
 *      Data structure definitions for the OS/2 & Windows
 *      executable file format.
 */

#define EMAGIC       0x5A4D            /* Old magic number */
#define ENEWEXE      sizeof(struct exe_hdr)
                                       /* Value of E_LFARLC for new .EXEs */
#define ENEWHDR      0x003C            /* Offset in old hdr. of ptr. to new */
#define ERESWDS      0x0010            /* No. of reserved words (OLD) */
#define ERES1WDS     0x0004            /* No. of reserved words in e_res */
#define ERES2WDS     0x000A            /* No. of reserved words in e_res2 */
#define ECP          0x0004            /* Offset in struct of E_CP */
#define ECBLP        0x0002            /* Offset in struct of E_CBLP */
#define EMINALLOC    0x000A            /* Offset in struct of E_MINALLOC */

struct exe_hdr                         /* DOS 1, 2, 3 .EXE header */
  {
    unsigned short    e_magic;         /* Magic number */
    unsigned short    e_cblp;          /* Bytes on last page of file */
    unsigned short    e_cp;            /* Pages in file */
    unsigned short    e_crlc;          /* Relocations */
    unsigned short    e_cparhdr;       /* Size of header in paragraphs */
    unsigned short    e_minalloc;      /* Minimum extra paragraphs needed */
    unsigned short    e_maxalloc;      /* Maximum extra paragraphs needed */
    unsigned short    e_ss;            /* Initial (relative) SS value */
    unsigned short    e_sp;            /* Initial SP value */
    unsigned short    e_csum;          /* Checksum */
    unsigned short    e_ip;            /* Initial IP value */
    unsigned short    e_cs;            /* Initial (relative) CS value */
    unsigned short    e_lfarlc;        /* File address of relocation table */
    unsigned short    e_ovno;          /* Overlay number */
    unsigned short    e_res[ERES1WDS];/* Reserved words */
    unsigned short    e_oemid;         /* OEM identifier (for e_oeminfo) */
    unsigned short    e_oeminfo;       /* OEM information; e_oemid specific */
    unsigned short    e_res2[ERES2WDS];/* Reserved words */
    long              e_lfanew;        /* File address of new exe header */
  };

#define E_MAGIC(x)     (x).e_magic
#define E_CBLP(x)      (x).e_cblp
#define E_CP(x)        (x).e_cp
#define E_CRLC(x)      (x).e_crlc
```

(continued)

Figure D-5. *The NEWEXE.H C header file, which defines the structure of the tables in OS/2 load modules.*

```
#define E_CPARHDR(x)      (x).e_cparhdr
#define E_MINALLOC(x)     (x).e_minalloc
#define E_MAXALLOC(x)     (x).e_maxalloc
#define E_SS(x)           (x).e_ss
#define E_SP(x)           (x).e_sp
#define E_CSUM(x)         (x).e_csum
#define E_IP(x)           (x).e_ip
#define E_CS(x)           (x).e_cs
#define E_LFARLC(x)       (x).e_lfarlc
#define E_OVNO(x)         (x).e_ovno
#define E_RES(x)          (x).e_res
#define E_OEMID(x)        (x).e_oemid
#define E_OEMINFO(x)      (x).e_oeminfo
#define E_RES2(x)         (x).e_res2
#define E_LFANEW(x)       (x).e_lfanew


#define NEMAGIC           0x454E          /* New magic number */
#define NERESBYTES        9               /* Nine bytes reserved (now) */
#define NECRC             8               /* Offset into new header of NE_CRC */


struct new_exe                            /* New .EXE header */
  {
    unsigned short        ne_magic;       /* Magic number NE_MAGIC */
    unsigned char         ne_ver;         /* Version number */
    unsigned char         ne_rev;         /* Revision number */
    unsigned short        ne_enttab;      /* Offset of Entry Table */
    unsigned short        ne_cbenttab;    /* Number of bytes in Entry Table */
    long                  ne_crc;         /* Checksum of whole file */
    unsigned short        ne_flags;       /* Flag word */
    unsigned short        ne_autodata;    /* Automatic data segment number */
    unsigned short        ne_heap;        /* Initial heap allocation */
    unsigned short        ne_stack;       /* Initial stack allocation */
    long                  ne_csip;        /* Initial CS:IP setting */
    long                  ne_sssp;        /* Initial SS:SP setting */
    unsigned short        ne_cseg;        /* Count of file segments */
    unsigned short        ne_cmod;        /* Entries in Module Reference Table */
    unsigned short        ne_cbnrestab;   /* Size of non-resident name table */
    unsigned short        ne_segtab;      /* Offset of Segment Table */
    unsigned short        ne_rsrctab;     /* Offset of Resource Table */
    unsigned short        ne_restab;      /* Offset of resident name table */
    unsigned short        ne_modtab;      /* Offset of Module Reference Table */
    unsigned short        ne_imptab;      /* Offset of Imported Names Table */
    long                  ne_nrestab;     /* Offset of Non-resident Names Table */
    unsigned short        ne_cmovent;     /* Count of movable entries */
    unsigned short        ne_align;       /* Segment alignment shift count */
    unsigned short        ne_cres;        /* Count of resource entries */
```

(continued)

```
    unsigned char        ne_exetyp;        /* Target operating system */
    char                 ne_res[NERESBYTES];
                                            /* Pad structure to 64 bytes */
  };

#define NE_MAGIC(x)       (x).ne_magic
#define NE_VER(x)         (x).ne_ver
#define NE_REV(x)         (x).ne_rev
#define NE_ENTTAB(x)      (x).ne_enttab
#define NE_CBENTTAB(x)    (x).ne_cbenttab
#define NE_CRC(x)         (x).ne_crc
#define NE_FLAGS(x)       (x).ne_flags
#define NE_AUTODATA(x)    (x).ne_autodata
#define NE_HEAP(x)        (x).ne_heap
#define NE_STACK(x)       (x).ne_stack
#define NE_CSIP(x)        (x).ne_csip
#define NE_SSSP(x)        (x).ne_sssp
#define NE_CSEG(x)        (x).ne_cseg
#define NE_CMOD(x)        (x).ne_cmod
#define NE_CBNRESTAB(x)   (x).ne_cbnrestab
#define NE_SEGTAB(x)      (x).ne_segtab
#define NE_RSRCTAB(x)     (x).ne_rsrctab
#define NE_RESTAB(x)      (x).ne_restab
#define NE_MODTAB(x)      (x).ne_modtab
#define NE_IMPTAB(x)      (x).ne_imptab
#define NE_NRESTAB(x)     (x).ne_nrestab
#define NE_CMOVENT(x)     (x).ne_cmovent
#define NE_ALIGN(x)       (x).ne_align
#define NE_CRES(x)        (x).ne_cres
#define NE_RES(x)         (x).ne_res
#define NE_EXETYP(x)      (x).ne_exetyp

#define NE_USAGE(x)       (WORD)*((WORD *)(x)+1)
#define NE_PNEXTEXE(x)    (WORD)(x).ne_cbenttab
#define NE_ONEWEXE(x)     (WORD)(x).ne_crc
#define NE_PFILEINFO(x)   (WORD)((DWORD)(x).ne_crc >> 16)


/*
 * Target operating systems
 */

#define NE_UNKNOWN        0x0                /* Unknown (any "new-format" OS) */
#define NE_OS2            0x1                /* Microsoft/IBM OS/2 (default) */
#define NE_WINDOWS        0x2                /* Microsoft Windows */
#define NE_DOS4           0x3                /* Microsoft MS-DOS 4.x */
```

(continued)

Figure D-5. *continued*

```
/*
 *  Format of NE_FLAGS(x):
 *
 *   p                                        Not-a-process
 *    x                                       Unused
 *     e                                      Errors in image
 *      x                                     Unused
 *       b                                    Bound as family app
 *        ttt                                 Application type
 *           f                                Floating-point instructions
 *            3                               386 instructions
 *             2                              286 instructions
 *              0                             8086 instructions
 *               P                            Protected mode only
 *                p                           Per-process library initialization
 *                 i                          Instance data
 *                  s                         Solo data
 */
#define NENOTP          0x8000              /* Not a process */
#define NEIERR          0x2000              /* Errors in image */
#define NEBOUND         0x0800              /* Bound as family app */
#define NEAPPTYP        0x0700              /* Application type mask */
#define NENOTWINCOMPAT  0x0100              /* Not compatible with P.M. Windowing */
#define NEWINCOMPAT     0x0200              /* Compatible with P.M. Windowing */
#define NEWINAPI        0x0300              /* Uses P.M. Windowing API */
#define NEFLTP          0x0080              /* Floating-point instructions */
#define NEI386          0x0040              /* 386 instructions */
#define NEI286          0x0020              /* 286 instructions */
#define NEI086          0x0010              /* 8086 instructions */
#define NEPROT          0x0008              /* Runs in protected mode only */
#define NEPPLI          0x0004              /* Per-Process Library Initialization */
#define NEINST          0x0002              /* Instance data */
#define NESOLO          0x0001              /* Solo data */


struct new_seg                             /* New .EXE segment table entry */
  {
    unsigned short    ns_sector;           /* File sector of start of segment */
    unsigned short    ns_cbseg;            /* Number of bytes in file */
    unsigned short    ns_flags;            /* Attribute flags */
    unsigned short    ns_minalloc;         /* Minimum allocation in bytes */
  };
```

(continued)

```
#define NS_SECTOR(x)    (x).ns_sector
#define NS_CBSEG(x)     (x).ns_cbseg
#define NS_FLAGS(x)     (x).ns_flags
#define NS_MINALLOC(x)  (x).ns_minalloc


/*
 *
 *   x                          Unused
 *    h                         Huge segment
 *     c                        32-bit code segment
 *      d                       Discardable segment
 *       DD                     I/O privilege level (286 DPL bits)
 *         c                    Conforming segment
 *          r                   Segment has relocations
 *           e                  Execute/read only
 *            p                 Preload segment
 *             P                Pure segment
 *              m               Movable segment
 *               i              Iterated segment
 *                 ttt          Segment type
 */
#define NSTYPE          0x0007          /* Segment type mask */
#define NSCODE          0x0000          /* Code segment */
#define NSDATA          0x0001          /* Data segment */
#define NSITER          0x0008          /* Iterated segment flag */
#define NSMOVE          0x0010          /* Movable segment flag */
#define NSSHARED        0x0020          /* Shared segment flag */
#define NSPRELOAD       0x0040          /* Preload segment flag */
#define NSEXRD          0x0080          /* Execute-only (code segment), or
                                         *  read-only (data segment)
                                         */
#define NSRELOC         0x0100          /* Segment has relocations */
#define NSCONFORM       0x0200          /* Conforming segment */
#define NSDPL           0x0C00          /* I/O privilege level (286 DPL bits) */
#define SHIFTDPL        10              /* Left shift count for SEGDPL field */
#define NSDISCARD       0x1000          /* Segment is discardable */
#define NS32BIT         0x2000          /* 32-bit code segment */
#define NSHUGE          0x4000          /* Huge memory segment, length of
                                         * segment and minimum allocation
                                         * size are in segment sector units
                                         */
#define NSPURE          NSSHARED        /* For compatibility */

#define NSALIGN 9       /* Segment data aligned on 512 byte boundaries */

#define NSLOADED        0x0004     /* ns_sector field contains memory addr */
```

(continued)

```
struct new_segdata                       /* Segment data */
  {
    union
      {
        struct
          {
            unsigned short     ns_niter;      /* number of iterations */
            unsigned short     ns_nbytes;     /* number of bytes */
            char               ns_iterdata;   /* iterated data bytes */
          } ns_iter;
        struct
          {
            char               ns_data;       /* data bytes */
          } ns_noniter;
      } ns_union;
  };


struct new_rlcinfo                       /* Relocation info */
  {
    unsigned short      nr_nreloc;      /* number of relocation items that */
  };                                    /* follow */

struct new_rlc                           /* Relocation item */
  {
    char                nr_stype;       /* Source type */
    char                nr_flags;       /* Flag byte */
    unsigned short      nr_soff;        /* Source offset */
    union
      {
        struct
          {
            char        nr_segno;       /* Target segment number */
            char        nr_res;         /* Reserved */
            unsigned short nr_entry;    /* Target Entry Table offset */
          }             nr_intref;      /* Internal reference */
        struct
          {
            unsigned short nr_mod;      /* Index into Module Reference Table */
            unsigned short nr_proc;     /* Procedure ordinal or name offset */
          }             nr_import;      /* Import */
        struct
          {
            unsigned short nr_ostype;   /* OSFIXUP type */
            unsigned short nr_osres;    /* reserved */
          }             nr_osfix;       /* Operating system fixup */
      }                 nr_union;       /* Union */
  };
```

(continued)

```
#define NR_STYPE(x)    (x).nr_stype
#define NR_FLAGS(x)    (x).nr_flags
#define NR_SOFF(x)     (x).nr_soff
#define NR_SEGNO(x)    (x).nr_union.nr_intref.nr_segno
#define NR_RES(x)      (x).nr_union.nr_intref.nr_res
#define NR_ENTRY(x)    (x).nr_union.nr_intref.nr_entry
#define NR_MOD(x)      (x).nr_union.nr_import.nr_mod
#define NR_PROC(x)     (x).nr_union.nr_import.nr_proc
#define NR_OSTYPE(x)   (x).nr_union.nr_osfix.nr_ostype
#define NR_OSRES(x)    (x).nr_union.nr_osfix.nr_osres


/*
 *  Format of NR_STYPE(x):
 *
 *  xxxxx                      Unused
 *       sss                   Source type
 */
#define NRSTYP      0x0f        /* Source type mask */
#define NRSBYT      0x00        /* lo byte */
#define NRSSEG      0x02        /* 16-bit segment */
#define NRSPTR      0x03        /* 32-bit pointer */
#define NRSOFF      0x05        /* 16-bit offset */
#define NRSPTR48    0x0B        /* 48-bit pointer */
#define NRSOFF32    0x0D        /* 32-bit offset */


/*
 *  Format of NR_FLAGS(x):
 *
 *  xxxxx                      Unused
 *       a                     Additive fixup
 *        rr                   Reference type
 */
#define NRADD       0x04        /* Additive fixup */
#define NRRTYP      0x03        /* Reference type mask */
#define NRRINT      0x00        /* Internal reference */
#define NRRORD      0x01        /* Import by ordinal */
#define NRRNAM      0x02        /* Import by name */
#define NRROSF      0x03        /* Operating system fixup */


/* Resource type or name string */
struct rsrc_string
    {
    char rs_len;               /* number of bytes in string */
    char rs_string[ 1 ];       /* text of string */
    };
```

(continued)

```
#define RS_LEN( x )      (x).rs_len
#define RS_STRING( x )  (x).rs_string

/* Resource type information block */
struct rsrc_typeinfo
    {
    unsigned short rt_id;
    unsigned short rt_nres;
    long rt_proc;
    };


#define RT_ID( x )     (x).rt_id
#define RT_NRES( x )  (x).rt_nres
#define RT_PROC( x )  (x).rt_proc


/* Resource name information block */
struct rsrc_nameinfo
    {
    /* The following two fields must be shifted left by the value of  */
    /* the rs_align field to compute their actual value. This allows */
    /* resources to be larger than 64k, but they do not need to be   */
    /* aligned on 512 byte boundaries, the way segments are.         */
    unsigned short rn_offset;    /* file offset to resource data */
    unsigned short rn_length;    /* length of resource data */
    unsigned short rn_flags;     /* resource flags */
    unsigned short rn_id;        /* resource name id */
    unsigned short rn_handle;    /* If loaded, then global handle */
    unsigned short rn_usage;     /* Initially zero. Number of times */
                                 /* the handle for this resource has */
                                 /* been given out */

    };


#define RN_OFFSET( x ) (x).rn_offset
#define RN_LENGTH( x ) (x).rn_length
#define RN_FLAGS( x )  (x).rn_flags
#define RN_ID( x )     (x).rn_id
#define RN_HANDLE( x ) (x).rn_handle
#define RN_USAGE( x )  (x).rn_usage

#define RSORDID        0x8000       /* if high bit of ID set then integer id */
                                    /* otherwise ID is offset of string from
                                           the beginning of the resource table */
```

(continued)

```
                                    /* Ideally these are the same as the */
                                    /* corresponding segment flags */
#define RNMOVE       0x0010         /* Moveable resource */
#define RNPURE       0x0020         /* Pure (read-only) resource */
#define RNPRELOAD    0x0040         /* Preloaded resource */
#define RNDISCARD    0xF000         /* Discard priority level for resource */

/* Resource table */
struct new_rsrc
    {
    unsigned short rs_align;    /* alignment shift count for resources */
    struct rsrc_typeinfo rs_typeinfo;
    };

#define RS_ALIGN( x ) (x).rs_align
```

MODULE DEFINITION FILE SYNTAX

Module definition (DEF) files are simple ASCII text files that are interpreted by the Linker during the construction of an application program, dynlink library, or device driver. The directives in DEF files cause information to be built into the executable file's header, which is later interpreted by the system when the program, library, or driver is loaded.

Enter all DEF file directives and keywords in uppercase letters. File, segment, group, and procedure names can be lowercase or uppercase. Lines beginning with a semicolon (;) are treated as comments. The directives documented in this appendix are listed in the following table, Figure E-1.

Directive	Description
CODE	Assigns characteristics to code segments
DATA	Assigns characteristics to data segments
DESCRIPTION	Embeds text in executable file
EXETYPE	Specifies host operating system
EXPORTS	Names functions exported for dynamic linking by other programs
HEAPSIZE	Specifies initial size of local heap (C programs only)
IMPORTS	Names functions that will be dynamically linked at load time
LIBRARY	Builds dynlink library or device driver
NAME	Builds application program
OLD	Specifies ordinal compatibility with previous version of dynlink library
PROTMODE	Flags file as executable in protected mode only
REALMODE	Allows file to be executed in real mode
SEGMENTS	Assigns characteristics to selected segments
STACKSIZE	Specifies size of stack used by primary thread
STUB	Embeds MS-DOS–compatible program in new executable file

Figure E-1. *DEF file directives documented in this appendix.*

Each directive is explained in a separate entry with its options and key-words. The entries are in alphabetic order and do not reflect the usual order of directives in an actual DEF file. Default keywords are shown in **boldface**. Directives, options, and keywords that are relevant only to real mode Microsoft Windows applications or Windows dynlink libraries are omitted.

For summaries of DEF file syntax, see p. 33 (for applications) and p. 466 (for dynlink libraries).

CODE

Declares the characteristics of all segments whose classnames are 'CODE' or end with 'CODE'.

Syntax: CODE [*load*] [*execute*] [*privilege*] [*conforming*]

load specifies when the segment is to be brought into memory:

PRELOAD	Loaded when the process is started
LOADONCALL	Not loaded until it is first accessed

execute controls whether the segment can be read as well as executed:

EXECUTEONLY	Can be executed but not read
EXECUTEREAD	Can be executed and read

privilege specifies whether the segment has I/O privilege (runs at ring 2) and can use the instructions IN, INS, OUT, OUTS, CLI, and STI:

IOPL	Has I/O privilege
NOIOPL	Does not have I/O privilege

conforming determines whether the segment can be called from ring 2 and ring 3 or only from ring 3:

CONFORMING	Can be called from either ring 2 or ring 3 and executes at the caller's privilege level
NONCONFORMING	Can be called only from ring 3 and executes at its natural privilege level

Note:

- If the CODE directive is absent, the default attributes for all segments whose classnames are 'CODE' or end with 'CODE' are LOADONCALL EXECUTEREAD NOIOPL NONCONFORMING.

Related directives: DATA, SEGMENTS.

DATA

Declares the characteristics of all segments whose classnames are not 'CODE' or do not end with 'CODE'.

Syntax: DATA [*load*] [*readwrite*] [*instance*] [*shared*] [*privilege*]

load specifies when the segment is to be brought into memory:

PRELOAD	Loaded when the process is started
LOADONCALL	Not loaded until it is first accessed

readwrite controls whether the segment can be written as well as read:

READONLY	Can be read but not written
READWRITE	Can be read and written

instance describes the automatic data segment (DGROUP):

NONE	No DGROUP present (dynlink libraries only)
SINGLE	Single copy of DGROUP shared by all instances of the program or library (default for dynlink libraries)
MULTIPLE	Separate copy of DGROUP created for each instance of the program or library (default for applications)

shared specifies whether the segment can be shared among all instances of the program:

SHARED	One copy of the segment shared among all instances of a program (default for dynlink libraries)
NONSHARED	Separate copy of the segment created for each instance of the program (default for applications)

privilege specifies whether access to the data segment is limited to code running at ring 2:

IOPL	Can be accessed only by code running in ring 2
NOIOPL	Can be accessed by ring 2 or ring 3 code

Notes:

- The *shared* option is ignored if the segment is READONLY; READONLY segments are always SHARED.

- If a *shared* keyword is present but an *instance* keyword is not, the Linker overrides the default for the absent keyword to make it consistent with the other. For example, DATA SINGLE forces SHARED, and DATA MULTIPLE forces NONSHARED. Similarly, DATA SHARED forces SINGLE, and DATA NONSHARED forces MULTIPLE. If conflicting keywords are present, the Linker issues a warning.

- If the DATA directive is absent, the default attributes of all segments not covered by the CODE directive are LOADONCALL READWRITE MULTIPLE NONSHARED NOIOPL for applications and LOADONCALL READWRITE SINGLE SHARED NOIOPL for dynlink libraries.

Related directives: CODE, SEGMENTS.

DESCRIPTION

Allows source control or copyright information to be embedded in the executable file.

Syntax: DESCRIPTION *'string'*

Note:

■ The *string* must be enclosed in single quotation marks and can be a maximum of 128 bytes. It is not available to the program itself and does not occupy space in the program's code or data segments.

Related directives: *None*.

EXETYPE

Specifies the operating system with which the application or dynlink library will be used.

Syntax: EXETYPE *system*

        system specifies the host operating system:

OS2	Microsoft OS/2 version 1.0 or later
WINDOWS	Microsoft Windows
DOS4	Multitasking MS-DOS (currently sold only by European OEMs, not the same as the USA MS-DOS/PC-DOS version 4)

Note:

■ If the EXETYPE directive is absent, **OS2** is assumed.

Related directives: REALMODE, PROTMODE.

EXPORTS

Makes functions available for dynamic linking by other programs or dynlink libraries, and/or signals the OS/2 loader to set up call gates for routines within an IOPL segment.

Syntax: EXPORTS
        statement
        statement
        .
        .
        .

        where each *statement* takes the following form:

        entryname [=*internalname*] [@*ordinal* [RESIDENTNAME]] [*stackparams*]

        entryname is the name by which the function can be imported (with the IMPORTS directive) by other programs or dynlink libraries, and/or (in the case of functions being exported from an IOPL segment) the name by which the function is called from ring 3 segments.

internalname is the exported function's actual name within the source code.

ordinal is an integer number assigned to the function to allow faster dynamic linking.

RESIDENTNAME causes the system loader to keep the exported function's name resident in memory at all times while the module is in use.

stackparams declares the number of stack words that are passed to the routine by the caller (relevant for exported IOPL routines only).

Notes:

- If *entryname* and *internalname* are the same, *=internalname* can be omitted.

- To minimize synchronization problems between the source code for dynlink libraries and client processes, use ordinal numbers only to refer to functions in modules that are very stable.

- The *stackparams* information is built into the call gate created at load time for functions exported from an IOPL segment. The hardware automatically copies the function's arguments from the ring 3 stack to the ring 2 stack.

Related directive: IMPORTS.

HEAPSIZE

Defines the initial size of a C application's local heap.

Syntax: HEAPSIZE *bytes*

Notes:

- The *bytes* parameter is assumed to be a decimal number. You can specify hex and octal numbers using C notation.

- The local heap is located in DGROUP along with the near data and default stack, and memory can be allocated from the heap with *malloc()* and related functions. Regardless of the heap's initial size, it is expanded at run time whenever necessary until DGROUP has reached its maximum size of 65,536 bytes.

- If HEAPSIZE is absent, the default initial heap size is **0** bytes.

Related directive: STACKSIZE.

IMPORTS

Identifies functions to be imported from other modules (typically dynlink libraries). When functions are imported, the addresses in the function calls are bound at load time rather than at link time.

Syntax: IMPORTS
            statement
            statement
            ⋮

where each *statement* takes the following form:

[*internalname=*] *module.entryname* ¦ *module.ordinal*

module is the filename and module name (which must be the same) of the dynlink library that contains the imported function.

internalname is the unique ASCII name by which the program being linked refers to the function to be imported.

entryname is the name by which the function was exported when the dynlink library was linked.

ordinal is an integer number that identifies the imported function.

Notes:

- When *internalname* and *entryname* are the same (as they are in most cases), *internalname=* can be omitted.

- When an *ordinal* is used, it must correspond with the ordinal specified in the dynlink library's EXPORTS directive for the same function. Use of ordinals speeds up the loadtime dynlink process but introduces additional dependence between client process and dynlink libraries that complicates the maintenance of both.

- When an import library (such as OS2.LIB) is used in linking, IMPORTS directives are not needed for those functions that have import reference records in the library.

Related directive: EXPORTS.

LIBRARY

Specifies that a dynlink library or device driver is being built.

Syntax: LIBRARY [*modulename*] [*initialization*]

modulename identifies the module when importing or exporting functions.

initialization is relevant only for dynlink libraries:

INITGLOBAL   initialization entry point is only called when the dynlink library is first loaded.

INITINSTANCE   initialization entry point is called when dynlink library is first loaded and each time a new application dynamically links to the library.

Notes:

- The *modulename* should ordinarily be the same as the name of the executable file. If *modulename* is absent, the filename (without the extension) is used by default.

- The NAME and LIBRARY directives cannot occur together in the same DEF file. If LIBRARY is present, it must precede all other directives. If both NAME and LIBRARY are absent, NAME is assumed.

Related directive: NAME.

NAME

Indicates that an application program is being built.

Syntax: NAME [*modulename*] [*apptype*]

modulename identifies the module to the system loader when multiple instances of the same program are running simultaneously.

apptype declares the program's compatibility with the Presentation Manager:

WINDOWAPI   Application is written to Presentation Manager conventions.

WINDOWCOMPAT   Application uses subset of *Vio*, *Mou*, and *Kbd* calls and can run in a Presentation Manager window.

NOTWINDOWCOMPAT   Application uses *Vio*, *Mou*, or *Kbd* calls that are not allowed in a Presentation Manager window, or accesses the video hardware directly, and must be run in its own screen group.

Notes:

- The *modulename* should ordinarily be the same as the name of the executable file. If *modulename* is absent, the filename (without the extension) is used by default.

- The *apptype* corresponds to the codes returned by the API function *DosQAppType*. There is no default for *apptype*; if it is absent, *DosQAppType* returns "unknown" and the application is run full-screen.

- The NAME and LIBRARY directives cannot occur together in the same DEF file. If NAME is present, it must precede all other directives. If both NAME and LIBRARY are absent, NAME is assumed.

Related directive: LIBRARY.

OLD

Used when building a dynlink library to preserve the association between ordinals and entry points in a previous version of the library.

Syntax: OLD '*filename*.DLL'

Notes:

- The *filename* is the name of an existing dynlink library; it must be enclosed in single quotes, and the extension must be explicit. If *filename* is not found in the current directory, the Linker searches each directory named in the *PATH* environment variable.

- When the OLD directive is used, exported functions in the new library that match exported names in the old library are assigned the same ordinal numbers, unless *either* of the following is true:

  □ The function name in the old library has no associated ordinal.

  □ You use EXPORTS to assign explicitly an ordinal number to the function in the the new library's DEF file.

Related directives: EXPORTS, IMPORTS.

PROTMODE

Indicates that the application can be executed only in protected mode.

Syntax: PROTMODE

Note:

■ If both PROTMODE and REALMODE directives are absent, the system loader assumes that the module can be run in either real mode or protected mode.

Related directives: EXETYPE, REALMODE.

REALMODE

Indicates that the application can be executed in real mode under MS-DOS or in the DOS compatibility environment under OS/2.

Syntax: REALMODE

Note:

■ If both PROTMODE and REALMODE directives are absent, the system loader assumes that the module can be run in either real mode or protected mode.

Related directives: EXETYPE, PROTMODE.

SEGMENTS

Overrides default segment characteristics or those assigned with CODE and DATA directives on a segment-by-segment basis. Can also be used to control segment order.

Syntax: SEGMENTS
            statement
            statement

            .
            .
            .

        where each *statement* takes the following form:

        segname [CLASS ['*classname*']] [*attribute*]

        segname is the segment name assigned with the SEGMENT mnemonic (MASM programs),
            by the compiler according to the memory model (C programs), or by the programmer with
            /NT or /ND switches.

CLASS assigns a class name to the segment so that the Linker will group it with other segments with the same class name.

attribute can be any combination of the following alternative keywords:
PRELOAD ¦ LOADONCALL
READONLY ¦ READWRITE
EXECUTEONLY ¦ EXECUTEREAD
IOPL ¦ NOIOPL
CONFORMING ¦ NONCONFORMING
SHARED ¦ NONSHARED

Notes:

- The *segname* may be optionally enclosed in single quote marks; it *must* be quoted if *segname* is CODE or DATA to differentiate it from the CODE and DATA directives.

- Typical class names are 'CODE', 'DATA', and 'FAR_DATA'. If CLASS is absent, or if CLASS is present but *classname* is absent, a class name of 'CODE' is assumed.

- See the entries for the CODE and DATA directives for the meanings of each *attribute* keyword.

- If no *attribute* keywords are present, the segment is assigned default attributes depending on its class. If at least one attribute is supplied, the default CODE or DATA attributes are not used, and any attribute that is not explicit is taken from the following list:
  LOADONCALL
  EXECUTEREAD (if class CODE)
  READWRITE (if class DATA)
  NONSHARED
  NONCONFORMING (if class CODE)
  NOIOPL

Related directives: CODE, DATA.

STACKSIZE

Defines the size of the application's default stack, that is, the stack that is used by the application's primary thread when it is first entered from OS/2.

Syntax: STACKSIZE *bytes*

Notes:

- The *bytes* parameter is assumed to be a decimal number. You can specify hex and octal numbers using C notation.

- If the STACKSIZE directive is present, it overrides any stack segment declared in the application source code or with the Linker /STACK switch.

Related directive: HEAPSIZE.

STUB

Specifies an MS-DOS–compatible program that is embedded into the new EXE or DLL file. The stub program receives control if the program being linked is executed under MS-DOS or in the DOS compatibility environment under OS/2.

Syntax: STUB '*filename*.EXE'

Notes:

- The *filename* must be enclosed in single quotation marks, and the extension must be explicit. If *filename* is not found in the current directory, the Linker searches the directories listed in the *PATH* environment variable.

- If the STUB directive is absent, the Linker automatically inserts an MS-DOS–compatible program that displays the message *This program cannot be run in DOS mode* and terminates.

Related directives: *None*.

GLOSSARY

3.x Box

See DOS compatibility environment.

alias

A selector (and associated descriptor) that refers to the same physical memory as another selector and descriptor, but with different access rights or characteristics.

allocation unit

See cluster.

anonymous pipe

A high performance, first-in-first-out mechanism for interprocess communications. Anonymous pipes can be used only by closely related processes.

Application Program Interface (API)

The calling convention by which OS/2 makes its services available to application programs.

ASCII mode

The default mode for keyboard input. In ASCII mode (also known as cooked mode), some keys and key sequences (such as the Enter key, Ctrl-S, Ctrl-P, Ctrl-Q, and Ctrl-Z) are intercepted and receive special treatment by the operating system.

ASCIIZ

A character string that is terminated by a zero byte.

asynchronous access

File access in which the operating system returns control to the requesting process immediately and notifies the process by some other means when the read or write is complete.

background process

A process associated with a screen group that is not currently being displayed.

base device drivers

The device drivers for the keyboard, display, disk, printer, and clock that are always loaded during system initialization.

binary mode

A mode that can be selected by programs for keyboard input. In binary mode (also known as raw mode), all characters are passed through to the application, and the editing keys are not active.

BIOS parameter block (BPB)

A structure that describes the characteristics of a logical disk volume. A copy of the BPB for a specific volume is always found in that volume's boot sector and can be used to calculate the locations of the FAT, root directory, and file storage areas.

block

To prevent a thread from executing until a resource becomes available, an event occurs, or a timeout elapses.

block device

A peripheral device (such as a disk drive) that transfers data in chunks of fixed size rather than one byte at a time.

boot sector

Logical sector zero of a disk volume, which contains information about the volume's characteristics and a short bootstrap program.

BPB

See BIOS parameter block.

call gate

A special LDT or GDT descriptor that represents a procedure entry point rather than a memory segment. Call gates provide controlled transitions from higher-numbered rings (lower privilege levels) to lower-numbered rings (higher privilege levels).

captive thread

A thread that is created within a dynlink library on behalf of an application (but without its knowledge) and that executes only within the library; also, a thread that is used to call an API function and that is not allowed to return from the function call until a specific event occurs.

character device

A peripheral device that transfers data one byte at a time, such as the keyboard or serial port.

child process

A process created by another process (called its parent process).

cluster

The unit of allocation of file storage on a logical disk volume; each file consists of one or more clusters. The number of sectors in a cluster is always a power of 2.

code page

A table that maps hardware-specific codes (such as keyboard scan codes) to character codes.

command subtree

A process and all its descendants.

compatibility box

See DOS compatibility environment.

context switch

The act of suspending the execution of a thread, saving its context, and giving control of the CPU to another thread (which might or might not belong to the same process).

cooked mode

See ASCII mode.

counted string

A string that is represented by a byte containing the length of the string (not including the length byte itself), followed by the characters of the string.

critical error

See hard error.

critical section

A sequence of code that manipulates a resource (such as a data structure) in a nonreentrant manner.

daemon process

A process that performs a utility function without interaction with the user, for example, the OS/2 swapper process.

descriptor table

A table that maps selectors to physical segments of memory. *See also* global descriptor table; local descriptor table.

device driver

A program that transforms I/O requests from the OS/2 kernel into commands to the hardware.

device monitor

A process that registers itself with the OS/2 kernel and with a device driver to track or modify the raw data stream of that driver.

disk bootstrap

A small program in the boot sector which brings the initial portions of the operating system into memory for execution.

DLL

See dynamic link library.

DOS compatibility environment

A special OS/2 screen group that emulates an MS-DOS environment and can be used to run one real mode application at a time alongside one or more protected mode applications.

dynamic link

A reference within a program to an external procedure or value that is resolved at load time or run time.

dynamic link library

A subroutine package that is bound to an application at load time or during execution, rather than at link time.

dynamic link subsystem

A module that manages a resource and makes the capabilities of the resource available to the rest of the system by exporting function names that can be dynamically linked.

dynlink

    See dynamic link.

encapsulation

    The principle of hiding the internal implementation of a program, function, or service so that its clients can tell what it does but not how it accomplishes its task.

environment strings

    A block of ASCIIZ strings that are associated with each process and inherited from the parent process.

ExitList

    A list of procedures, registered by the process, that are called by OS/2 when the process terminates for any reason.

Family API

    The subset of OS/2 API functions that have direct counterparts in the functions supported by MS-DOS version 2.0 or later and in the services of the IBM PC ROM BIOS.

Family application

    A program that has been processed by the BIND utility so that it can run in either protected mode or real mode. A Family application must not contain any machine instructions specific to the 80286 or 80386 and can call only those OS/2 services that are members of the Family API.

fast-safe RAM semaphore

    A semaphore designed to meet the needs of dynlink libraries. It combines the speed of RAM semaphores and the advantages of system semaphores—"counting" and cross-process usability. *See also* RAM semaphore; system semaphore.

FAT

    See file allocation table.

file allocation table (FAT)

    A table in the control area of a logical disk volume that defines the current usage for each cluster in that volume's file storage area.

file handle

    A value returned by OS/2 when a file is opened or created; used in subsequent function calls to represent the file.

file locking

The restricting of access to a file by other processes.

file pointer

A value, maintained internally by OS/2 for each file handle, which determines the starting point for the next read or write operation associated with that handle.

file system

The component of the operating system that manages files and directories and translates file function calls by an application into requests to the disk driver for transfers of logical sectors; also, the interdependent tables and directories on a disk that define the location of each file and directory on that disk.

file system name space

All the possible name constructions that have the format of valid filenames.

forced event

An event or action that is forced upon a thread or a process from an external source; for example, a Ctrl-C or Ctrl-Break signal.

foreground process

A process that is executing in the currently visible screen group and can therefore interact with the user.

GDT

See global descriptor table.

general protection (GP) fault

An error that occurs when a program executes an instruction that is not allowed at its privilege level, uses an invalid memory address, or accesses a valid address in an invalid manner. When a GP fault occurs, OS/2 receives control and terminates the process.

giveaway shared memory

A memory block for which the allocating process can obtain a selector that can be passed to and used by another process.

global data segment

A data segment that is shared among all instances of a dynlink library; that is, only one copy of the segment exists, regardless of the number of client processes that are bound to the library. *See also* instance data segment.

global descriptor table (GDT)
> The descriptor table that defines the memory segments owned by the operating system and its drivers.

global heap
> The RAM which can be dynamically allocated for use by OS/2 subsystems and processes. The global heap is administered by the OS/2 memory manager.

global initialization
> Execution of a dynlink library's initialization routine only when the library is initially loaded. *See also* instance initialization.

GP fault
> *See* general protection fault.

graphical user interface
> A term commonly used for a user interface that runs in graphics mode and relies on pointing devices, dialog boxes, menus, and graphical objects such as icons, buttons, and scroll bars to interact with the user. OS/2's graphical user interface is a component of the Presentation Manager.

handle
> A binary value that represents a system resource, such as a file, pipe, semaphore, or queue.

hard error
> An error that arises from a hardware error, resource conflict, or program bug that a process cannot be expected to recover from or that requires user intervention.

hot key
> The keystroke or key sequence that activates a background process (usually a monitor) or the Task Manager.

huge segments
> Memory blocks consisting of two or more physical segments that are assigned logically consecutive selectors.

import libraries
> Special object module libraries that contain reference records for the entry points in dynlink libraries.

installable device drivers

Device drivers, such as the mouse driver, that are loaded during system initialization as the result of a DEVICE directive in the CONFIG.SYS file.

instance data segment

A memory segment that holds data specific to each instance of a dynlink library; that is, a separate copy of the segment is created for each client process that dynamically links to the library. *See also* global data segment.

instance initialization

Execution of a dynlink library's initialization routine each time a new client process dynamically links to the library. *See also* global initialization.

interactive process

A program that requires (or can require) interaction with the user and that calls (or can call) *Kbd, Mou,* or *Vio* functions. *See also* daemon process.

interleaving

The mapping of consecutive physical disk sector addresses onto noncontiguous physical sectors to improve performance.

interprocess communication (IPC)

The exchange of information between two or more processes via semaphores, pipes, queues, shared memory, or signals. Threads within the same process can also use IPC methods to communicate.

I/O privilege level (IOPL)

A privilege level that allows the instructions CLI, STI, IN, INS, OUT, and OUTS to be executed without causing a GP fault.

IPC

See interprocess communication.

kernel

The part of OS/2 that executes at the highest privilege level (ring 0) and contains the scheduler, file system, memory manager, and other vital services.

Kernel application

A program that executes only in protected mode and uses the OS/2 kernel API for keyboard, screen, and mouse I/O.

LDT

See local descriptor table.

loadtime dynamic linking

> The establishment of a link between a process and a dynamic link library when the process is first loaded into memory. The occurrence of this linkage at load time is controlled by information in the program file header.

local descriptor table (LDT)

> A table that exists for each active process and that defines the memory which is owned or shared by that process.

logical device

> A symbolic name for a physical device, such as the name COM1 for the first serial port.

logical drive

> A file system, represented by a letter and a colon (such as A:), containing a boot sector, root directory, file allocation table, and zero to many sub-directories and files. A single physical drive can be represented as several logical drives.

memory manager

> The component of OS/2 that is responsible for dynamic allocation of memory from the global heap. *See also* physical memory manager; virtual memory manager.

memory overcommit

> The allocation of more memory to a process than physically exists.

memory protection

> The ability of the hardware to detect any attempt by an application program to access memory that does not belong to it or for which it has an insufficient privilege level.

module definition file

> A file that describes the segment characteristics of an OS/2 application program or dynlink library. The DEF file is processed by the Linker during the creation of an executable file.

monitor dispatcher

> A component of the OS/2 kernel that arbitrates among device monitor applications, the kernel, and a device driver and moves data from the driver through the buffers of one or more device monitors and back to the driver.

multitasking

The sharing of CPU time among two or more tasks so that they appear to be running simultaneously.

named pipe

A first-in-first-out interprocess communication mechanism that is similar to anonymous pipes but is not restricted to use by closely related processes.

object name buffer

The buffer that receives the name of a dynlink library or entry point.

parent process

A process that creates another process (called a child process).

physical memory

The RAM (random access memory) physically installed in the machine.

physical memory manager

The component of OS/2 that is responsible for allocating physical memory and managing descriptor tables.

PID

See process ID.

pipe

See anonymous pipe; named pipe.

preemptive multitasking

The ability of the operating system to divide CPU time among two or more tasks without their cooperation; sometimes called time-slicing.

Presentation Manager

The graphical user interface for OS/2. *See also* graphical user interface.

primary thread

The thread that begins execution of a process and is used to field signals directed to that process.

priority

The numeric value assigned to each active thread in the system. Threads with a higher priority are assigned the CPU in preference to those with a lower priority.

privilege level

One of four levels (or rings) at which code executes in protected mode. The privilege level determines which machine instructions can be executed and which memory segments can be accessed.

process

The executing instance of a program file. A process can own memory, files, pipes, semaphores, and other system resources and can contain more than one thread of execution.

process ID (PID)

A number that OS/2 assigns to a process when the process is created. Each active process has a different PID.

process subtree

See command subtree.

protected mode

The operating mode of the 80286 microprocessor that supports memory protection, virtual memory, and privilege levels.

queue

An ordered list of data segments or records (called queue elements).

RAM semaphore

A semaphore that is referenced by its address; such semaphores are fast but have limited functionality. *See also* fast-safe RAM semaphore; system semaphore.

random access

The reading and writing of nonsequential records.

raw mode

See binary mode.

real mode

The operating mode of the 80286 microprocessor that emulates the operation of an Intel 8086/88 processor. Memory protection, virtual memory, and privilege levels are not supported in real mode.

record locking

The restricting of access to a region of a file by other processes.

ring

    See privilege level.

runtime dynamic linking

    The establishment of a link between a process and a dynamic link library after the process has begun execution. The process provides OS/2 with a module name and an entry point name, and the operating system returns an entry point address.

scheduler

    The part of OS/2 that decides which thread to run and how long to run it before assigning the CPU to another thread; also, the part of OS/2 that determines the priority value for each thread.

screen group

    One or more processes that share (generally in a serial fashion) a single logical screen, keyboard, and mouse; also called a session.

search handle

    A binary value associated with a search context. OS/2 returns such a handle when a search for a particular set of files or directories is initiated.

sector

    A unit of storage on a disk; usually 512 bytes.

segment

    A contiguous block of memory that is represented by a selector.

segment swapping

    The transfer of segments between physical memory and a disk file by the virtual memory manager.

selector

    A value that can be loaded into a segment register in protected mode and that indexes an entry in a descriptor table.

semaphore

    An interprocess communication mechanism that has only two states and that is commonly used to signal between threads or processes or to represent ownership of a resource.

sequential access

    The reading or writing of consecutive data in a file.

session

　　See screen group.

SFT

　　See system file table.

shared memory

　　A memory segment that can be accessed by more than one process.

signaling

　　The use of semaphores to indicate that an event has occurred or that an action should be taken.

signal

　　An interprocess communication mechanism that is analogous to a hardware interrupt.

stack frame

　　The portion of a thread's stack that contains the parameters and local variables for a particular procedure.

static linking

　　The resolution of external references during the creation of an executable file. *See also* dynamic link.

subsystem

　　See dynamic link subsystem.

swapping

　　See segment swapping.

synchronous access

　　File access during which the thread requesting the read or write operation is suspended until the transfer is complete. *See also* asynchronous access.

system file table (SFT)

　　An internal OS/2 table that contains an entry for every file or device that any given process in the system is using.

system semaphore

　　A semaphore that is referred to by name and whose storage is managed by OS/2; more powerful than a RAM semaphore but somewhat slower. *See also* fast-safe RAM semaphore; RAM semaphore.

task

> *See* process.

Task Manager

> The Presentation Manager program that lists all currently running programs and allows the user to switch among them. Roughly equivalent to the Session Manager in OS/2 version 1.0.

thread

> A point of execution within a process; each thread is associated with a priority, register contents, and a state (blocked, ready to execute, or executing). A process always contains one or more threads.

thread ID

> A number that identifies a particular thread within a process.

timer tick

> A hardware interrupt that allows the operating system to regain control at predetermined intervals.

timeslice

> The amount of execution time that the scheduler will give a thread before reassigning the CPU to another thread of equal priority.

time-slicing

> *See* preemptive multitasking.

turnaround character

> Logical end-of-line character, usually the Enter key.

virtual memory

> The memory space allocated to and used by a process, which may be larger than available physical memory.

virtual memory manager

> The component of OS/2 that is responsible for moving memory segments between physical memory and the disk swap file to provide the illusion of a larger memory space.

write-through

> The immediate transfer of data from RAM to disk at the time of a process's write request, as opposed to the deferral of the actual write operation by buffering the data within OS/2.

Index

Special Characters

61, 67
* 63
*– 64
+ 58, *61*, 63
–+ 64
. 199
.. 199
: 132, 165
; 58, 64
< 330
> 330
>> 330
@ 58, 64
\ 172, 189
¦ 330
2> 330
2>> 330
.286 directive 44, 69
3.x box 10

A

ABIOS. *See* ROM ABIOS (advanced basic
    I/O system)
ABIOSCall (DevHlp function) *389*, 662
ABIOSCommonEntry (DevHlp function)
    389, 663
AllocGDTSelector (DevHlp function) *386*,
    392, 663–64
AllocPhys (DevHlp function) 361, *386*,
    391–92, 664
AllocReqPacket (DevHlp function) *388*,
    394–95, 665
all-points-addressable (graphics) mode,
    video 95, 96
all-points-addressable (APA) output
    devices 5
alphanumeric (text) mode, video 95
anonymous pipes 280–83
APA. *See* all-points-addressable
    (graphics) mode
API. *See* Application Program Interface
    (API) functions
API.LIB file 65–66
application program(s) 27–47
    data flow between character device and
        419

application program(s), *continued*
    data flow between character device
        and, when device monitor is
        registered *421*
    entry conditions 37–39
    example creation of, using
        programming tools 67, *68*, 69–70
    execution of, and Application Program
        Interface 39–41
    files 34–35
    loading 35–37
    module definition files 32
        syntax summary *33*
    place in system layering 11, *12, 13*
    privilege levels 6–7, *13*
    processing typical I/O requests from
        397–99
    process termination 42
    sample HELLO file 42–47
    source structure 28–31
    types of, and complexity levels 27–28
    using IOPL segments in 305–6
    writing 49 (*see also* programming
        tools)
Application Program Interface (API)
        functions 5. *See also* Family API
        (FAPI)
    available during device driver
        initialization *362*
    device monitor *420*
    direct disk access 202
    Dos functions listed by functional
        group *498–502*
    file management *132*
    IOPL segments 303, *304*, 305
    Kbd (keyboard) 75, 79
    listed alphabetically *492–97*
    manipulation of drives, directories, and
        volume labels *167*
    memory management *210*
    Mou mouse *86–87, 88*
    multitasking management 231, *232*
    to obtain information on environment,
        system state, and capabilities *40*
    pipe management *284*
    process execution and 39–41
    queue management *289*
    quick reference 490–91

escape sequences, ANSI 98
    positioning cursor with *101*
    selecting reverse video attribute with
        99–100
event flags 295, 296
EXEC function 232
EXECSORT program 340–46
    EXECSORT.ASM source code *341–45*
    EXECSORT.DEF module definition
        file *346*
EXETYPE directive in DEF files *737,*
    740
executable (EXE) program files 34–35.
        See also application program(s);
        segmented executable file,
        components of
ExitList procedures 279, 280
EXPORTS directive in DEF files 32, 306,
        315, 481, *737,* 740–41
extended character set 707–9
extended keys 74
external commands 18
extrn directive 44

F

Family API (FAPI) 39
family applications 27
far attribute 30, 41, 44, 45, 460, 481
far pointers 5
fast-safe RAM semaphores 274, 276
    use of 279–80
FAT. *See* file allocation table
file allocation table (FAT) *192,* 195–97
    compatibility with future versions of
        OS/2 131
    dump of first block of *196*
file management 131–63. *See also*
        directories; disk(s); disk drives;
        volume(s)
    API functions for *132, 498*
    creating, opening, and closing files
        133–39
    file and record locking 145–46
    file finder utility 175–90
    forcing disk updates 145
    handles and filenames 132–33
    reading and writing files 139–44
    renaming and deleting files 146
    sample programs DUMP.ASM and
        DUMP.C for displaying file
        contents 147–63
File Manager (Presentation Manager) 19

filename(s) 38
    extensions *50–51,* 133
    handles and 132–33
    hex and ASCII dump containing *39*
file pointer 140
files area, disk *192,* 199–200
filters 329–46
    building 331–39
    keyboard input with *DosRead* 78
    operation of 331
    system support for 329–30
    using, as child processes 339–46
FIND.C filter program *338–39*
FIND filter 329, 337
fixed disk partitions 201, *202*
Flush Input Buffers command code *358,*
        368–69
Flush Output Buffers command code *358,*
        368–69
FORMAT program 197
free() function 224
FreeLIDEntry (DevHlp function) 374,
        389, 669–69
FreePhys (DevHlp function) 374, *386,*
        391, 669
FreeReqPacket (DevHlp function) *388,*
        394–95, 669–70

G

GDT. *See* global descriptor table
Generic IOCtl command code *359,* 371–
        72, 428
GetDOSVar (DevHlp function) *389,* 390–
        91, 396, 670
Get Fixed Disk Map command code *359,*
        375–76
GetLIDEntry (DevHlp function) *389,* 671
Get Logical Drive Map command code
        359, 373
global descriptor table (GDT) 22, 212
global heap 209
global information segment, setting date
        and time with 319–21
global initialization 461, 465
global memory 214–16
glossary 747–60
graphical user interface. *See* Presentation
        Manager
graphics (all-points-addressable) mode 95,
        96
group directive 30, 44

H

handles
    filenames and 132–33
    pipe *vs* file 282
    using anonymous pipes to redirect
        child process's 281, *282–83*
hardware management, with DevHlp
    functions *386*, 391
header, device driver 351, *352*
    attribute word 352, *353*
    source code for block and character *354*
header, EXE files 34
    new 720, *721*
    old 718, *719*
HEAPSIZE directive in DEF files 32,
    737, 741
HELLO program (HELLO.EXE)
    example using programming tools
        67–70
    HELLO.ASM source file 42, *43–44,*
        45–46, 52
    HELLO.DEF module definition file
        46, 47
    HELLO.MAP map file produced by
        Linker *57*
    HELLO.OBJ object file 52, 57
    HELLO.REF ASCII text file *61–62*
high level language (HLL) naming
    conventions 30, *31*
huge memory blocks 217–20

I

IBM extended character set 708–9
identification field, disk boot sector 195
IDT. *See* interrupt descriptor table
idle-time thread category 237–38
IMPLIB utility 32, 49, 481
imported names table 724
import libraries 32
    vs dynlink libraries 459
    using with dynlink libraries 481
IMPORTS .DEF file directive 32, *737*,
    741–42
Init (Initialization) command code *358*,
    359–62
    API calls used during operation of *362*
    BIOS parameter block (BPB) 360, *361*
    request packet format *360*
init mode, device driver 350, 351
input mode 74
input/output (I/O) 397–99. *See also* device
    driver(s); IOPL (I/O privilege);
    keyboard input; mouse, input;

input/output (I/O), *continued. See also*
    parallel ports; printer; redirectable
    I/O; request packets, I/O; serial
    ports; video display
Input Status command code *358*, 368
installable file systems 10
instance initialization 461, 465
Intel 80286 microprocessor 3, 210–13
Intel 80386 microprocessor 3
inter-driver communication (IDC) points
    348
internal commands 18
internationalization, API functions
    supporting *501*
interprocess communication (IPC) 8–9,
    271–99
    anonymous pipes 280–83
    named pipes 283–86
    queues 288–94
    semaphores 272–80
    shared memory 286–88
    signals 295–99
interrupt descriptor table (IDT) 22
interrupt mode, device driver 350
interrupt routine, device driver
    adding interrupt handling 401–2
    basic task of 357–58
    custom drivers 399–400
interrupt time (asynchronous), device
    driver 351
interrupt vectors 391
IOPL (I/O privilege) 301–16
    API functions and 303, *304*, 305
    description of 302, *303*
    in dynlink libraries 457
    sample application PORTS 307–16
    using in OS/2 applications 305–6
IPC. *See* interprocess communication

K

KBD$ device driver 84, *85*
    device monitor for 420, *425*
KBD01.SYS file 23, 84
Kbd API functions, keyboard input with
    74, *75*, 76–77
KBDCALLS.DLL 16, 84, *85*
KbdCharIn (API function) 573–74
    keyboard input with 74–75, *76*
KbdClose (API function) *75*, 575
KbdDeRegister (API function) *75*, 85, 575
KbdFlushBuffer (API function) *75*, 575
KbdFreeFocus (API function) *75*, 84, 575
KbdGetCp (API function) *75*, 576

MouSetHotKey (API function) *87*, 593–94
MouSetPtrPos (API function) *86*, 594
MouSetPtrShape (API function) *86*,
    594–95
MouSetScaleFact (API function) *87*, 595
MouSynch (API function) *87*, 595–96
MS-DOS operating system 3, *4*
    compatibility with OS/2 10
    device drivers under 347, 348
MS-DOS stub program 720
MSG.DLL 16
multitasking 7–8, 227–69. *See also*
        interprocess communication (IPC)
    API functions for 231–43
        managing processes 232–36
        managing sessions 240–42
        managing threads 237–39
    configuring OS/2 multitasker 242–43
    device drivers and 348
    file and record locking 145–46
    in OS/2 228–31
    sample command processor TINYCMD
        243–54
    sample multithreaded application
        DUMBTERM 254–69
multithreading
    DUMBTERM application
        demonstrating 254–69
    source code for demonstration of
        238–39

N

NAME directive in DEF files 32, *737*,
    743
named pipes 283–86
    API functions for *284*
    state transitions for *285*
near attribute 30, 45
NEWEXE.H header file 727, *728–36*
NLS.DLL 17
Nondestructive Read command code *358*,
    367
nonresident names table, 725

O

object module libraries 32, 34, 62. *See
        also* import libraries; Library
        Manager (LIB) utility
    description of 34
    vs dynlink libraries 459
OLD directive in DEF files *737*, 743
ordinals, specifying dynlink libraries with
    460

OS2KRNL 21–22, *23*
OS2LDR 21, *22*
OS2.LIB 65, 69
OS/2 operating system 3
    bypassing, and directly accessing
        adapter I/O ports 301–2
    compatibility with MS-DOS 10
    kernel applications (*see* application
        program(s))
    key features 4–10
    loading, initialization 20–26
    multitasking in 228–31 (*see also*
        multitasking)
    programming tools (*see* programming
        tools)
    structure 12–20 (*see also* command
        processor; device driver(s) (.SYS);
        dynamic link libraries (DLL);
        kernel; Presentation Manager)
    system layers 11, *12, 13*
    unique features of device drivers under
        347–49
Output Status command code *358*, 368

P

page directive 44
paragraph address 6
parallel ports 119
parent directory 199
parent process 232–34, 271
parent sessions 240–42
Partitionable Fixed Disk command code
    359, 374–75
partitions, fixed disk 201, *202*
pascal keyword 41, 460, 481
path 165
pathnames 132–33, 146, 172
    child process 233
    of processes in child sessions 240
Physical Memory Manager (PMM) 22
physical video buffer 94
PhysToGDTSelector (DevHlp function)
    387, 392, 674–75
PhysToUVirt (DevHlp function) *385, 387*,
    392, 675
PhysToVirt (DevHlp function) *385, 387*,
    392, 393, 418, 675–76
pipes 8, 271
    anonymous 280–83
    API functions for managing *284, 500*
    named 283–86
pointer, driver for 91
POINTER$ driver 91, 92

Ray Duncan

Ray Duncan received a B.A. in chemistry at the University of California, Riverside, and an M.D. at the University of California, Los Angeles; he specialized in pediatrics and neonatology at the Cedars-Sinai Medical Center in Los Angeles. Duncan has been involved with microcomputers since the Altair days and has written many articles for personal computer magazines, including *Dr. Dobb's Journal, Programmer's Journal,* and *BYTE;* he is currently a contributing editor to *PC Magazine.* In addition, Duncan is the founder of Laboratory Microsystems Incorporated, a software house specializing in FORTH interpreters and compilers. Duncan is the general editor of THE MS-DOS ENCYCLOPEDIA and is the author of ADVANCED MS-DOS PROGRAMMING.

The manuscript for this book was prepared and submitted to Microsoft Press in electronic form. Text files were processed and formatted using Microsoft Word.

Cover design by Tom Draper
Interior text design by Darcie S. Furlan
Illustrations by Becky Geisler-Johnson
Principal typography by Ruth Pettis and Jean Trenary

Text composition by Microsoft Press in Times Roman with display in Eurostile Demi, using the Magna composition system and the Linotronic 300 laser imagesetter.

Hardcore Computer Books

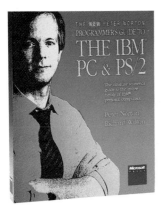

THE *NEW* PETER NORTON PROGRAMMER'S GUIDE TO THE IBM PC® & PS/2®

Peter Norton and Richard Wilton

A must-have classic on mastering the inner workings of IBM microcomputers—now completely updated to include the PS/2 line. Sharpen your programming skills and learn to create simple, clean, portable programs with this successful combination of astute programming advice, proven techniques, and solid technical data. Covers the microprocessors; ROM BIOS basics and ROM BIOS services; video, disk and keyboard basics; DOS basics, interrupts, and functions (through version 4); device drivers and video programming; and programming in C, QuickBasic, and TurboPascal. Accept no substitutes; this is the book to have.

$22.95   [Book Code 86-96635]

INSIDE OS/2

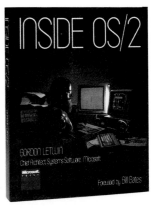

Gordon Letwin

"The best way to understand the overall philosophy of OS/2 will be to read this book."   **Bill Gates**

Here—from Microsoft's Chief Architect of Systems Software—is an exciting technical examination of the philosophy, key development issues, programming implications, and a look at the role of OS/2 in the office of the future. Letwin provides the first in-depth look at each of OS/2's design elements. This is a valuable and revealing programmer-to-programmer discussion of the graphical user interface, multitasking, memory management, protection, encapsulation, interprocess communication, and direct device access. You can't get a more inside view.

$19.95   [Book Code 86-96288]

ADVANCED OS/2 PROGRAMMING

Ray Duncan

Authoritative information, expert advice, and great assembly-language code make this comprehensive overview of the features and structure of OS/2 indispensable to any serious OS/2 programmer. Duncan addresses a range of significant OS/2 issues: programming the user interface; mass storage; memory management; multitasking; interprocess communications; customizing filters, device drivers, and monitors; and using OS/2 dynamic link libraries. A valuable reference section includes detailed information on each of the more than 250 system service calls in version 1.1 of the OS/2 kernel.

$24.95   [Book Code 86-96106]   [Available 12/20/88]

PROGRAMMING WINDOWS

Charles Petzold

Your fastest route to successful application programming with Windows. Full of indispensable reference data, tested programming advice, and page after page of creative sample programs and utilities. Topics include getting the most out of the keyboard, mouse, and timer; working with icons, cursors, bitmaps, and strings; exploiting Windows' memory management; creating menus; taking advantage of child window controls; incorporating keyboard accelerators; using dynamic link libraries; and mastering the Graphics Device Interface (GDI). A thorough, up-to-date, and authoritative look at Windows' rich graphical environment.

$24.95, softcover   [Book Code 86-96049]
$34.95, hardcover   [Book Code 86-96130]

Available wherever books and software are sold. Or order directly from Microsoft Press.

Solid Technical Information. Expert Advice.

ADVANCED MS-DOS® PROGRAMMING, 2nd ed.
Ray Duncan

The preeminent source of MS-DOS information for assembly-language and C programmers—now completely updated with new data and programming advice covering: ROM BIOS for the IBM PC, PC/AT, PS/2, and related peripherals; MS-DOS through version 4; version 4 of the LIM EMS; and OS/2 compatibility considerations. Duncan addresses key topics, including character devices, mass storage, memory allocation and management, and process management. In addition, there is a healthy assortment of updated assembly-language and C listings that range from code fragments to complete utilities. And the reference section, detailing each MS-DOS function and interrupt, is virtually a book within a book.
$24.95   [Book Code 86-96668]

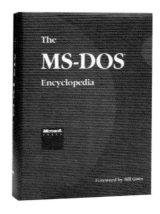

THE MS-DOS® ENCYCLOPEDIA

The ultimate reference for insight, data, and advice to make your MS-DOS programs reliable, robust, and efficient. 1600 pages packed with version-specific data. Annotations of more than 100 system function calls, 90 user commands, and a host of key programming utilities. Hundreds of hands-on examples, thousands of lines of code, and handy indexes. Plus articles on debugging, writing filters, installable device drivers, TSRs, Windows, memory management, the future of MS-DOS, and much more. Researched and written by a team of MS-DOS experts—many involved in the creation and development of MS-DOS. Covers MS-DOS through version 3.2, with a special section on version 3.3.
$134.95   [Book Code 86-96122]

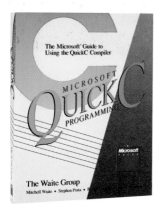

MICROSOFT® QUICKC® PROGRAMMING
The Waite Group

Your springboard to the core of Microsoft QuickC. This book is loaded with practical information and advice on every element of QuickC, along with hundreds of specially constructed listings. Included are the tools to help you master QuickC's built-in libraries; manage file input and output; work with strings, arrays, pointers, structures, and unions; use the graphics modes; develop and link large C programs; and debug your source code.
$19.95   [Book Code 86-96114]

MICROSOFT® QUICKBASIC, 2nd ed.
Douglas Hergert

"No matter what your level of programming experience, you'll find this book irreplaceable when you start to program in QuickBASIC."
Online Today

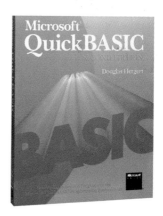

This new edition of MICROSOFT QUICKBASIC—completely updated for version 4 —is a great introduction to all the development tools, features, and user-interface enhancements in Microsoft QuickBASIC. And there's more—six specially designed, full-length programs including a database manager, an information-gathering and data-analysis program, and a chart program that reenforce solid structured programming techniques.
$19.95   [Book Code 86-96387]

Available wherever books and software are sold. Or order directly from Microsoft Press.